# PRACTICAL MACHINE LEARNING FOR DATA ANALYSIS USING PYTHON

# PRACTICAL MACHINE LEARNING FOR DATA ANALYSIS USING PYTHON

ABDULHAMIT SUBASI

*Professor of Information Systems at Effat University, Jeddah, Saudi Arabia*

Academic Press is an imprint of Elsevier
125 London Wall, London EC2Y 5AS, United Kingdom
525 B Street, Suite 1650, San Diego, CA 92101, United States
50 Hampshire Street, 5th Floor, Cambridge, MA 02139, United States
The Boulevard, Langford Lane, Kidlington, Oxford OX5 1GB, United Kingdom



**Notices**

Knowledge and best practice in this field are constantly changing. As new research and experience broaden our understanding, changes in research methods, professional practices, or medical treatment may become necessary.

Practitioners and researchers must always rely on their own experience and knowledge in evaluating and using any information, methods, compounds, or experiments described herein. In using such information or methods they should be mindful of their own safety and the safety of others, including parties for whom they have a professional responsibility.

To the fullest extent of the law, neither the Publisher nor the authors, contributors, or editors, assume any liability for any injury and/or damage to persons or property as a matter of products liability, negligence or otherwise, or from any use or operation of any methods, products, instructions, or ideas contained in the material herein.

**Library of Congress Cataloging-in-Publication Data**
A catalog record for this book is available from the Library of Congress

**British Library Cataloguing-in-Publication Data**
A catalogue record for this book is available from the British Library

ISBN: 978-0-12-821379-7

For information on all Academic Press publications
visit our website at https://www.elsevier.com/books-and-journals

*Publisher:* Mara Conner
*Editorial Project Manager:* Rafael G. Trombaco
*Production Project Manager:* Paul Prasad Chandramohan
*Designer:* Christian Bilbow

Typeset by Thomson Digital

*A huge thank to my parents for always expecting me*
*to do my best, and telling me I could accomplish anything,*
*no matter what it was.*

*To my wife, Rahime, for her patience and support.*

*To my wonderful children,*
*Seyma Nur, Tuba Nur and Muhammed Enes.*
*You are always in my heart and the joys in my life.*

*To those who read this book,*
*and appreciate the work that goes into it, thank you.*
*If you have any feedback, please let me know.*

**Abdulhamit Subasi**

# Contents

## 3. Machine learning techniques 91



## 4. Classification examples for healthcare 203



## 5. Other classification examples 323

# Preface

Rapid developments in machine learning solutions and adoption across various sectors of industry enable the learning of complex models of real-world problems from observed (training) data through systemic solutions in different fields. Significant time and effort are required to create effective machine learning models and achieve reliable outcomes. The main project concepts can be grasped by building robust data pipelines and analyzing and visualizing data using feature extraction, selection, and modeling. Therefore, the extensive need for a reliable machine learning solution involves a development framework that not only is suitable for immersive machine learning modeling but also succeeds in preprocessing, visualization, system integration, and robust support for runtime deployment and maintenance setting. Python is an innovative programming language with multipurpose features, simple implementation and integration, an active developer community, and an ever-increasing machine learning ecosystem, contributing to the expanding adoption of machine learning.

Intelligent structures and data-driven enterprises are becoming a reality, and the developments in techniques and technologies are enabling this to happen. With data being of utmost importance, the market for machine learning and data science practitioners has never been larger than it is now. In fact, the world is facing a shortage of data scientists and machine learning experts. Arguably the most demanding job in the 21st century involves developing some significant expertise in this domain.

Machine learning techniques are computing algorithms, including artificial neural networks, k-nearest neighbor, support vector machines, decision tree algorithms, and deep learning. Machine learning applications are currently of great interest in economics, security, healthcare, biomedicine, and biomedical engineering. This book describes how to use machine learning techniques to analyze the data in these fields.

The author of this book has a great deal of practical experience in the implementation of real-world problems utilizing Python and its machine learning ecosystem. *Practical Machine Learning for Data Analysis Using Python* aims to improve the skill levels of readers and qualify them to create practical machine learning solutions. Moreover, this book is a problem solver's guide for building intelligent real-world systems. It offers a systematic framework that includes principles, procedures, practical examples, and code. The book also contributes to the critical skills needed by its readers to understand and solve various machine learning problems.

This book is an excellent reference for readers developing machine learning techniques by using real-world case studies in the Python machine learning environment. It focuses on building a foundation of machine learning knowledge to solve different case studies from different fields in the real world, including biomedical signal analysis, healthcare, security, economy, and finance. In addition, it focuses on a broad variety of models for machine learning, including regression, classification, clustering, and forecasting.

This book consists of seven chapters. Chapter 1 gives an introduction to data analysis using machine learning techniques. Chapter 2 provides an overview of data preprocessing such as feature extraction, transformation, feature selection, and dimension reduction. Chapter 3 offers an overview of machine learning techniques such as naïve Bayes, k-nearest neighbor, artificial neural networks, support vector machines, decision tree, random forest, bagging, boosting, stacking, voting, deep neural network, recurrent neural network, and convolutional neural networks, for forecasting, prediction, and classification. Chapter 4 presents classification examples for healthcare. It includes electrocardiogram (ECG), electroencephalogram (EEG), and electromyogram (EMG) signal-processing techniques commonly used in the analysis and recognition of biomedical signals. In addition, it presents several medical data classifications, such as human activity recognition, microarray gene expression data classification for cancer detection, breast cancer detection, diabetes detection, and heart disease detection. Chapter 5 considers several applications, including intrusion detection, phishing website detection, spam e-mail detection, credit scoring, credit card fraud detection, handwritten digit recognition, image classification, and text classification. Chapter 6 provides regression examples, such as stock market analysis, economic variable forecasting, electrical load forecasting, wind speed forecasting, tourism demand forecasting, and house prices prediction. Chapter 7 includes several examples related to unsupervised learning (clustering).

The main intent of this book is to help a wide range of readers to solve their own real-world problems, including IT professionals, analysts, developers, data scientists, and engineers. Furthermore, this book is intended to be a useful textbook for postgraduate and research students working in the areas of data science and machine learning. It also formulates a basis for researchers who are interested in applying machine learning methods to data analysis. In addition, this book will help a broad readership, including researchers, professionals, academics, and graduate students from a wide range of disciplines, who are beginning to look for applications in biomedical signal analysis, healthcare data analysis, financial and economic data forecasting, computer security, and more.

Executing the code examples provided in this book requires Python 3.x or higher versions to be installed on macOS, Linux, or Microsoft Windows. The examples throughout the book frequently utilize the essential libraries of Python, such as SciPy, NumPy, Scikit-learn, matplotlib, pandas, OpenCV, Tensorflow, and Keras, for scientific computing.

# Acknowledgments

First of all, I would like to thank my publisher Elsevier and its team of dedicated professionals who have made this book-writing journey very simple and effortless, as well as all those who have worked in the background to make this book a success.

I would like to thank Sara Pianavilla and Rafael Trombaco for their great support. Also, I would like to thank Paul Prasad Chandramohan for being patient in getting everything necessary to complete this book.

Abdulhamit Subasi

CHAPTER

# 1

# Introduction

## 1.1 What is machine learning?

With improved computation power and storage of computers, our era became the "age of information" or the "age of data." Additionally we must analyze *big data* and create intelligent systems by utilizing the concepts and techniques from *artificial intelligence, data science, data mining*, and *machine learning*. Of course, most of us have learned these terms and realize that *"data is the new oil."* The most important task that organizations and businesses have employed in the last decade to utilize their data and understand and employ this information is for making better informed decisions. In fact, with big developments in technology, a successful environment has been created around fields such as machine learning, artificial intelligence, and deep learning. Researchers, engineers, and data scientists have created frameworks, tools, techniques, algorithms, and methodologies to achieve intelligent systems and models that can automate tasks, detect anomalies, perform complex analyses, and predict events (Sarkar, Bali, & Sharma, 2018).

Machine learning is defined as computational techniques utilizing the experience to enhance performance or to achieve precise predictions. The *experience* denotes the previous information available to the learner that is naturally received from the electronic data recorded and made available for investigation. This data might be in the shape of digitized human-labeled training sets or other kinds of information collected by interacting with the ecosystem. In all situations, the data size and quality are critical for the accomplishment of the predictions made by the predictor. Machine learning is composed of creating competent and precise prediction *algorithms*. As in other fields of computer science, crucial measures of the quality of these methods are their space and time complexity. Nevertheless, in machine learning, the concept of *sample complexity is needed* to assess the sample size necessary for the algorithm to learn a group of notions. Usually, theoretical learning guarantees a method based on the complication of the model classes studied and the amount of training endured. As the performance of a learning technique is based on the data and features employed, machine learning is characteristically associated with statistics and data analysis. Typically, learning algorithms are data-driven techniques merging important concepts in computer science with concepts from probability, statistics, and optimization. Furthermore, these kinds of applications relate to broad categories

**Practical Machine Learning for Data Analysis Using Python. http://dx.doi.org/10.1016/B978-0-12-821379-7.00001-1**

of learning problems. The main types of learning problems are classification, regression, ranking, clustering, and dimension reduction (Mohri, Rostamizadeh, & Talwalkar, 2018).

In *classification*, a category is assigned to every item. The number of categories can be small or large depending on the type of problem. In *regression*, a real value is predicted for every item. Stock value prediction or variations of economic variable prediction are regression problems. In regression problems, the penalty for an incorrect prediction is based on the value of the difference between the predicted and true values, whereas in the classification problem, there is characteristically no concept of closeness among different categories. In *ranking*, items are ordered according to certain measures. In *clustering*, items are partitioned into homogeneous regions. Clustering is generally employed to analyze big data sets. For instance, in case of social network analysis, clustering algorithms are used to identify "communities" inside large groups of people. *Manifold learning*, or *dimensionality reduction*, is used to transform an initial representation of items into a lower-dimensional representation while keeping some properties of the initial representation. The aims of machine learning are to achieve precise predictions for unseen data and design robust and effective algorithms to yield these predictions, even for big-scale problems (Mohri et al., 2018).

Machine learning employs right features to create accurate models, which accomplish the right tasks. Actually, *features* define the relevant objects in our domain. A *task* is an abstract representation of a problem to be solved related to those domain objects. The general form of this is classifying them into two or more classes. Most of these tasks can be characterized as mapping from data points to outputs. This mapping or *model* is itself formed as the output of a machine learning method by utilizing training data (Flach, 2012). We will discuss tasks and problems, which can be solved by utilizing machine learning. No matter what type of machine learning models encountered, they are designed to solve only a small number of tasks and utilize only a few numbers of features.

Most of the time, the knowledge or insight we are trying to extract from raw data will not be understandable by looking at the data. Machine learning converts data into information. Machine learning sits at the intersection of statistics, engineering, and computer science and is frequently seen in other fields. It can be used in a variety of fields, such as finance, economy, politics, geosciences, and medicine. It is a tool to solve different problems. Any field that requires understanding and working with data can benefit from machine learning methods. There are many problems in which the solution is not deterministic. Hence, we need statistics for these problems (Harrington, 2012).

This book presents an example-based approach to cover different practices, concepts, and problems related to Machine Learning. The main idea is to give readers enough knowledge on how we can solve the Machine Learning problems, and how we can use the main building blocks of Machine Learning in data analysis. This will enable the reader to learn about how Machine Learning can be utilized to analyze data.

### 1.1.1 Why is machine learning needed?

Human beings are the most intelligent creatures in this world. They can define, create, asses, and solve complex problems. The human brain is still not explored completely, and therefore artificial intelligence has still not beaten human intelligence in various ways. In view of what you have studied so far, although the conventional programming model is rather good and domain expertise and human intelligence are absolutely vital components in making data-driven decisions, machine learning is needed to produce precise and quicker decisions. The machine learning technique considers data and anticipated outputs or results, if any, and utilizes the computer to create the program, which can be identified as a model. This model can then be employed in the future to make required decisions and produce anticipated outputs from new data. The machine attempts to employ input data and anticipated outputs to learn characteristic patterns from the data, which can eventually help create a model similar to a computer program that may help in making data-driven decisions in the future (classify or predict) for novel input data points by utilizing the learned information from past experience. This will be clear when we consider a real-world problem, such as handling infrastructure for a decision support company. In order to solve a problem with machine learning, we should implement the following steps.

- Utilize device data and logs to obtain sufficient historical data in a certain data warehouse.
- Determine key data attributes, which might be beneficial for creating a model.
- Monitor and record device attributes and their behavior for long time intervals, which contain normal device behavior and anomalous device behavior or outliers.
- Use these input and output pairs with any particular machine learning method to create a model that learns characteristic design patterns and detects consistent output.
- Rearrange this model by utilizing unseen values of device attributes to predict if a specific device is working normally or of it may produce a prospective output. Hence when a machine learning model is developed, it can be organized easily to create an intelligent framework around it such that devices cannot only be monitored reactively but potential problems can be proactively detected and even fixed before any issue appears.

In fact, the workflow debated earlier with the series of stages required for creating a machine learning model is considerably more complicated than how it has been depicted. However, this is just to highlight and help you think more theoretically rather than technically in the case of machine learning processes and also show that you need to change your thinking from the conventional ways toward a more data-driven manner. The magnificence of machine learning is that it is never domain constrained and you can employ algorithms to eliminate obstacles covering several areas, industries, and businesses. Similarly, it is not necessary to employ output data points to construct a model; occasionally input data is adequate for unsupervised learning (Sarkar et al., 2018).

### 1.1.2 Making data-driven decisions

Extracting crucial insights or information from the data is the main goal of companies and business organizations investing deeply in a good workforce like artificial intelligence and machine learning. The concept of data-driven decisions is not novel and has been used for decades in the field of statistics, management information systems, and operations research to improve effectiveness of decisions. Obviously, it is easier to talk than to implement since we can clearly utilize data to make any perceptive decisions. Additional imperative characteristics of this problem is that generally we utilize the power of intuition or reasoning to make decisions based on what we have experienced in the past. Our brain is a powerful element that helps us recognize people in images, understand what our colleagues or friends are saying, decide whether to accept or refuse a business transaction, and so on. Our brain does most of the thinking for us. This is precisely why it is hard for machines to learn and solve problems such as computing tax rebates or loan interests. Remedies to these problems are to utilize different approaches such as data-driven machine learning techniques to improve the decisions. Although data-driven decision making is of vital meaning, it also needs to be implemented at scale and with efficiency. The main idea of utilizing artificial intelligence or machine learning techniques is to automate tasks or procedures by learning specific patterns from the data (Sarkar et al., 2018).

Nowadays, the majority of the workforce in developed countries is moving from manual labor to *knowledge work*. Events are much more uncertain at the moment; "minimize risk" job assignments, such as "maximize profits" and "find the best marketing strategy," are all too common. The knowledge accessible from the World Wide Web creates the work of knowledgeable employees even tougher. Producing wisdom from all the data with our job in mind turns out to be a more crucial talent. With so many economic activities reliant on information, we cannot afford to be lost in the data. Machine learning helps to analyze all the data and extract valuable information (Harrington, 2012).

### 1.1.3 Definitions and key terminology

It is common practice to calculate something and sort out the significant portions later. The items that should be assessed are called features or attributes and form an instance (Harrington, 2012). One of the crucial steps in machine learning is the feature extraction. Accordingly, the data to be processed, composed of several points, and characteristic and informative features can be extracted by employing different feature extraction techniques. These informative and characteristic parameters describe the behavior of the data, which may specify a precise achievement. Highlighting informative and characteristic features can describe data in better ways. These features can be extracted employing diverse feature extraction algorithms, which are another step in data analysis to make simpler the succeeding stage for classification (Graimann, Allison, & Pfurtscheller, 2009). It is crucial to deal with a smaller number of samples that express suitable features of the data to accomplish better performance. Features are generally collected into a feature vector by transforming data into a related feature vector known as feature extraction. Characteristic features of data are examined by a data classification structure, and based on those distinctive features, the class of the data is decided (Subasi, 2019a).

The extracted features of the problem are not enough to completely explain the nature of data for many cases. Particularly, while describing the problem, employing a suboptimal or redundant feature set creates this kind of problem. Instead of seeking better features, it is better to assume that there is a nonlinear relation between input and output of the given system. For instance, an automatic diagnostic system for disease detection that uses biosignal wave forms employs the processed data as input. The aim is to study the relationship between the information that is given to the system and associated with disease. After training, when we give new data to the system, it will identify the correct disease. These kinds of tasks can be accomplished by machine learning techniques easily (Begg, Lai, & Palaniswami, 2008; Subasi, 2019b).

There are several computational intelligence techniques, such as supervised learning, unsupervised learning, reinforcement learning, and deep learning. Among these learning paradigms, the most studied one is the supervised learning technique that is based on function estimation. A set of examples is given to the supervised learning formulas by an external supervisor with the class label. The system identifies the hidden relationship between the sample set and desired output. After this training phase, it is easy to predict the output for unknown examples. Reinforcement learning, stochastic learning, and risk minimization are some paradigms in supervised learning (Begg et al., 2008; Subasi, 2019b).

*Classification* is one of the duties in machine learning. For instance, we want to differentiate epileptic EEG signals from a normal EEG signal. We must use the EEG equipment and then hire a neurologist (EEG expert) to analyze the EEG signal taken from a subject. This might be expensive and cumbersome, and the expert neurologist can only be in one place at a time. We can automate this process by attaching the EEG equipment to a computer to identify the epileptic patient. How do we then decide if a subject has epilepsy or not? This task is termed as ***classification,*** and there are numerous machine learning techniques that are good at classification. The class in this example is the epileptic or normal. If we decided on a machine learning technique to utilize for classification, the next step is to train the algorithm or allow it to learn. In order to train the algorithm, it must be fed quality data known as a ***training set***. A training set is the set of ***training examples*** that is used to train the machine learning algorithms. Each training instance has numerous features and one ***target variable (class)***. The target variable is utilized to predict with the machine learning technique. In classification the target variable takes on a nominal value, and in the task of regression its value can be continuous. The target variable (class) is known in the training set. The machine learns by discovering some relationship between the features and the target variable. The target variable is the types or classes, so it can be reduced to take nominal values. In the classification problem the target variables (*classes*) are assumed to be a finite number of classes. To test machine learning algorithms, usually a part of the training set of data (separate dataset), called a ***test set,*** is utilized. Firstly, the training example is given as input to the program during the machine learning process. Then, the test set is given as an input to the program. The target variable for each instance from the test set is not given to the program, and the program finds to which class each instance belongs. The target variable or class that the training sample belongs to is then compared to the predicted value, and the performance of the algorithm is evaluated (Harrington, 2012).

A canonical problem of epileptic seizure detection will be presented as a running example to demonstrate some elementary definitions and to define the employment and assessment of machine learning techniques in practice. Epileptic seizure detection involves the issue of learning to automatically classify EEG signals as either normal or epileptic.

*Examples*: Items or instances of data employed for learning or assessment. In our epilepsy problem, these examples are related to the recording of EEG signals employed for training and testing.

*Features*: The set of attributes, generally represented as a vector, that are related to an example. In the case of EEG signals, some related features can include the mean value, standard deviation, mean power, skewness and kurtosis of the signal, and so on.

*Labels*: Values or categories given to examples. In classification problems, examples are given to specific categories, for instance, the normal and epileptic categories in a binary classification problem. In regression, items are assigned real-valued labels.

*Training sample*: Examples utilized to train a learning algorithm. In the EEG problem, the training sample is composed of a set of EEG signals along with their related labels. The training sample differs for diverse learning scenarios.

*Validation sample*: Examples employed to adjust the parameters of a learning method when dealing with labeled data. Learning methods naturally have one or more tunable parameters, and the validation sample is utilized to choose suitable values for these model parameters.

*Test sample*: Examples employed to assess the performance of a learning technique. The test sample is a part of the training and validation set and is not available in the learning stage. In the epilepsy problem, the test sample is composed of a recording of EEG signals for which the learning algorithm should predict labels based on features. These predictions are then compared with the labels of the test sample to evaluate the performance of the algorithm.

*Loss function*: A function that calculates the difference, or loss, between the predicted label and the true label.

Now the learning stages of the epilepsy problem are defined. We can begin with a given group of labeled instances. First the data is randomly partitioned into a training set, a validation set, and a test set. The size of each of these sets is based on a different consideration. For instance, the amount of signal kept for validation is based on the number of adjustable parameters of the algorithm. Moreover, once the labeled set is comparatively small, the amount of training data is generally selected to be larger than that of the test set, as the learning performance is directly based on the training sample. Then, relevant features of the examples should be extracted. This is a crucial step in the design of machine learning solutions. Valuable and informative features can successfully guide the learning algorithm, whereas deprived or uninformative ones can be deceptive. Even though the selection of the features is crucial, it is left to the user. This selection reflects the user's *prior knowledge* about the learning task, which in practice can have a dramatic effect on the performance of learners. Now, the selected features are used to train the learning algorithm by fixing diverse values of its adjustable parameters. For each value of these parameters, the algorithm chooses a different model out of the model set. Among them the model achieving the best performance on the validation set is chosen. In the final stage, utilizing the chosen model, the labels of the examples can be predicted in the test set. The performance of the classifier is assessed by utilizing the loss function related to the problem to compare the predicted and true labels. Hence, the performance of an algorithm is of course assessed based on its test error on the test set. A learning algorithm can be *consistent*; that is, it achieves perfect performance on the examples of the training set but has a poor performance on the test set. This happens for consistent learners defined by very complex decision surfaces, which tend to memorize a comparatively small training set instead of seeking to generalize well. This highlights the key difference between memorization and generalization, which is the essential property required for a precise learning algorithm (Mohri et al., 2018)

### 1.1.4 Key tasks of machine learning

Epileptic seizure detection is a binary classification problem that might be the most common problem in machine learning. One apparent variation is to consider classification tasks with more than two classes. For example, it might be asked to separate different types of EEG signals. This can be done as a combination of two binary classification problems: the first problem is to separate them as normal or abnormal, and the second problem is, among abnormal EEG signals, to differentiate them as an epileptic or other disease. But, some potentially valuable information can get lost in this way, because some abnormal EEGs might seem to be epileptic rather than another type of disease. Because of this, it is helpful to view *multi-class classification* as a machine learning problem in its own right.

Main task in classification is to predict which class a sample of data falls into. ***Regression,*** which is another task in machine learning, is the prediction of a numeric value. Regression and classification are examples of ***supervised learning***. This kind of problem is identified as supervised because we are telling the algorithm what to predict. ***Unsupervised learning*** is the opposite of supervised learning in which there is no label or target value for the data. A task in which similar items are grouped together is known as ***clustering***. Moreover, we need to find statistical values that define the data in unsupervised learning. This is defined as *density estimation*. Another task of unsupervised learning is to reduce the data from several features to a small number in a way that it can be properly visualized in two or three dimensions (Harrington, 2012). ***Association rules*** are a type of pattern that are popular in marketing applications, and the result of such patterns can be frequently found on online shopping web sites (Flach, 2012).

### 1.1.5 Machine learning techniques

Machine learning has numerous algorithms, techniques, and methods that can be utilized to create models to solve real-world problems employing data. Naturally, the same machine learning approaches can be categorized in different ways under many umbrellas (Sarkar et al., 2018). Some of the main fields of machine learning methods are as follows:

1. Methods based on the amount of human supervision in the learning process.
   a. Supervised learning
   b. Unsupervised learning
   c. Semisupervised learning
   d. Reinforcement learning
2. Methods based on the ability to learn from incremental data samples.
   a. Batch learning
   b. Online learning
3. Methods based on their approach to generalization from data samples.
   a. Instance-based learning
   b. Model-based learning

## 1.2 Machine learning framework

The best way to solve a real-world machine learning or analytics problem is to use a machine learning framework, starting from collecting the data to transforming it into valuable information or knowledge employing machine learning techniques. A machine learning framework is mainly composed of elements associated with data retrieval and extraction, preparation, modeling, evaluation, and deployment (Harrington, 2012; Sarkar et al., 2018).

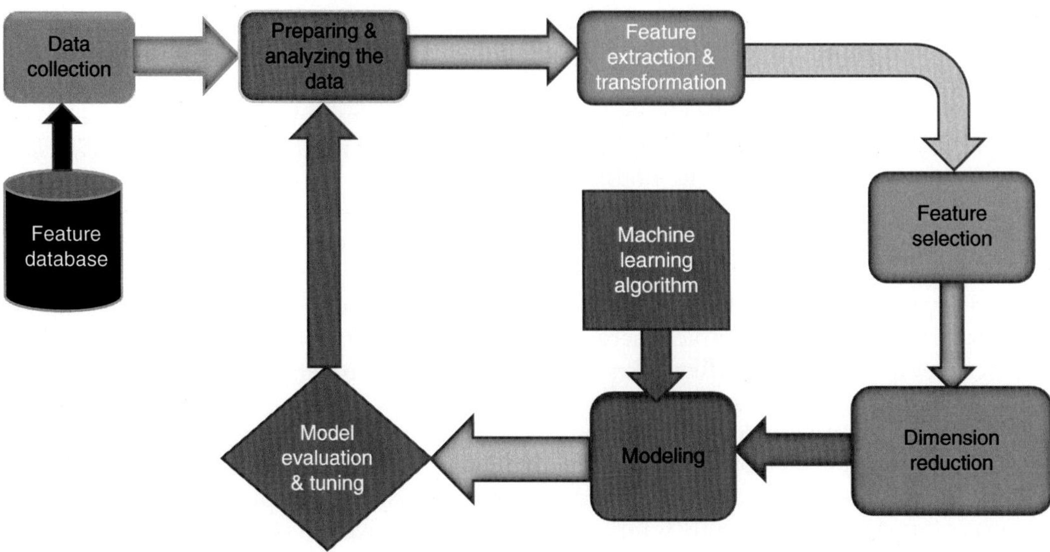


FIGURE 1.1 A typical machine learning framework.

Fig. 1.1 presents an overview of a typical machine learning framework with the main stages highlighted in their blocks.

To understand and develop an application utilizing machine learning framework, the procedures in the following sections must be used.

## 1.2.1 Data collection

This task is undertaken to extract, record, and collect the required data needed for analysis. Generally, this includes utilization of the historical data warehouses, data marts, data lakes, and so on. An evaluation is carried out based on the data available in the organization and if additional data is needed. You should collect the samples by scraping a website and extracting data, or you can get information from an RSS feed or an API. This data can be taken from the web (i.e., open data sources) or it can be taken from other channels, such as surveys, purchases, experiments, and simulations. You might have a device collect wind speed measurements and send them to you, or blood glucose levels, or anything you can measure. The number of choices is endless. To save some time and effort, you can use publicly available data. This stage includes data collection, extraction, and acquisition from several data sources (Harrington, 2012; Sarkar et al., 2018).

## 1.2.2 Data description

Data description includes an initial analysis of the data to comprehend more about the data, its source, attributes, volume, and relationships. The following aspects are critical to create a suitable data description (Sarkar et al., 2018).

- Data sources (SQL, NoSQL, Big Data), record of origin (ROO), record of reference (ROR)

- Data volume (size, number of records, total databases, tables)
- Data attributes and their description (variables, data types)
- Relationship and mapping schemes (understand attribute representations)
- Basic descriptive statistics (mean, median, variance)
- Focus on which attributes are important for the business

### 1.2.3 Exploratory data analysis

Exploratory data analysis is one of the first main analysis steps in the lifecycle. The aim is to explore and understand the data in detail. Descriptive statistics, charts, plots, and visualizations can be utilized to look at the various data attributes and find relations and correlations. Once data is collected, you need to make sure it is in a useable format. Some algorithms require features in a specific format; some algorithms can deal with target variables and features like strings, integers, etc. In this stage, data is preprocessed, cleaned, and manipulated as needed. Data preprocessing, cleaning, wrangling, and performing initial exploratory data analysis is carried out in this stage as well. The following aspects are some of the main tasks in this step (Harrington, 2012; Sarkar et al., 2018).

- Explore, describe, and visualize data attributes.
- Choose data and attribute subsets, which seem the most crucial for the problem.
- Make widespread assessments to find relationships and associations and test hypotheses.
- Note missing data points, if any.

### 1.2.4 Data quality analysis

Data quality analysis is the final step in the data understanding stage in which the quality of data is analyzed in the datasets and potential shortcomings, errors, and issues are determined. These need to be resolved before analyzing the data further or starting modeling efforts. Data analysis can be as simple as looking at the data that has been parsed in a text editor to make sure the previous stage is really working. The data can be checked to determine if any pattern is obvious or if a few data points are massively different from the rest of the data. Plotting data in different dimensions might help. The focus on data quality analysis includes the following (Harrington, 2012; Sarkar et al., 2018).

- Missing values
- Inconsistent values
- Wrong information due to data errors (manual/automated)
- Wrong metadata information

### 1.2.5 Data preparation

Data preparation is another step that takes place after getting enough knowledge of the problem and related dataset. Data preparation is mostly a set of tasks to clean, wrangle, and prepare the data before running machine learning techniques and creating models. An imperative point to remember is that data preparation generally is the most time-consuming stage in the data mining lifecycle. But this phase must be carried out very carefully, because poor data may lead to poor models and inadequate performance results (Sarkar et al., 2018).

### 1.2.6 Data integration

The process of data integration is principally needed once there are multiple datasets that need to be integrated or merged. This can be achieved in two ways. Appending different datasets by combining them is naturally carried out for datasets having the same attributes. Merging different datasets together that have dissimilar attributes or columns is accomplished by employing common fields like keys (Sarkar et al., 2018).

### 1.2.7 Data wrangling

The process of data wrangling includes data processing, normalization, cleaning, and formatting. Data in its raw form is hardly utilized by machine learning techniques to build models. Therefore, the data should be processed based on its form, cleaned of underlying errors and inconsistencies, and formatted into more useable formats for machine learning algorithms. The following aspects are the major tasks related to data wrangling (Sarkar et al., 2018).

- Managing missing values (remove rows, impute missing values)
- Managing data inconsistencies (delete rows, attributes, fix inconsistencies)
- Correcting inappropriate metadata and annotations
- Managing unclear attribute values
- Arranging and formatting data into necessary formats (CSV, JSON, relational)

### 1.2.8 Feature scaling and feature extraction

In this stage important features or attributes are extracted from the raw data or new features are created from existing features. Data features frequently should be scaled or normalized to avoid producing biases with machine learning algorithms. Moreover, it is often necessary to choose a subset of all existing features based on feature quality and importance. This procedure is called feature selection. Feature extraction is producing new attributes or variables from existing attributes based on certain logic, rules, or hypothesis (Sarkar et al., 2018).

### 1.2.9 Feature selection and dimension reduction

Feature selection is fundamentally choosing a subset of features or attributes from the dataset based on parameters like attribute quality, importance, conventions, significance, and restrictions. Occasionally even machine learning techniques are utilized to select significant attributes based on the data (Sarkar et al., 2018). Dimension reduction is a process to reduce the dimension of the original feature vector, while keeping the most distinctive information and removing the remaining unrelated information, for the purpose of decreasing the computational time in a classifier (Phinyomark et al., 2013). Most of the feature extraction approaches produce redundant features. In fact, to enhance the performance of a classifier and accomplish a minimum classification error, some types of feature reduction approaches that yield a new set of features should be used. Numerous techniques are used for dimension reduction and feature selection to accomplish a better classification accuracy (Wołczowski and Zdunek, 2017)

### 1.2.10 Modeling

In modeling, the data features are usually fed to a machine learning algorithm to create the model. The machine learning algorithm must be fed with good clean data from the previous stages to extract valuable information or knowledge. Naturally the machine learning algorithm should be optimized with the intention of reducing errors and generalizing the representations learned from the data. This knowledge is readily useable by a machine for the next stage. The model is formed in this stage. There is no training stage in case of unsupervised learning, because there is no target value. Modeling is one of the main stages in the process in which most of the analysis takes place utilizing clean, formatted data and its attributes to create models for solving problems. This is an iterative process, as presented in Fig. 1.1, along with model evaluation and all the preceding stages leading to modeling. The basic idea is to create multiple models iteratively while trying to get the best model that satisfies the performance criteria data (Sarkar et al., 2018).

### 1.2.11 Selecting modeling techniques

In this phase, a list of appropriate data mining and machine learning techniques, frameworks, tools, and algorithms are picked up. Techniques, which are proven to be robust and suitable in solving the problem, are typically chosen based on inputs and insights from data analysts and data scientists. These are principally determined by the current existing data, data mining targets, business targets, algorithm constraints, and limitations (Sarkar et al., 2018).

### 1.2.12 Model building

The procedure of model building is also identified as training the model utilizing the data and features from the existing dataset. A combination of data (features) and machine learning techniques together achieve a model that tries to generalize on the training data and give essential results in the form of insights and/or predictions. Usually several algorithms are employed to realize multiple modeling approaches on the same dataset and solve the same problem to create the best model, which realizes outputs closer to the performance criteria. Key issue is to keep track of the models produced, the model parameters being utilized, and their outcomes (Sarkar et al., 2018).

### 1.2.13 Model assessment and tuning

In this phase, the information learned in the previous stage is utilized. Every model is evaluated based on different metrics, such as model accuracy, precision, recall, F-measure, and mean absolute error. The model parameters must also be tuned based on techniques, such as grid search and cross-validation, to achieve a model that provides the best results. Tuned models are also matched with the data mining targets to determine if the desired results as well as desired performance will be achieved. Model tuning is also called hyperparameter optimization in the machine learning domain. The performance of the created model is evaluated by using several metrics to see how well it does. Models have several parameters that must be tuned in a process called hyperparameter optimization to create models with optimal results. In the case of supervised learning, known metrics are used to evaluate the model. In unsupervised learning, other metrics are utilized to evaluate the success of the model (Harrington, 2012; Sarkar et al., 2018).

The final models from the modeling phase satisfy the performance criteria with respect to data mining objectives and have the desired performance results, such as accuracy, regarding the model evaluation metrics. The evaluation phase includes a detailed evaluation and review of the final models and the results that are taken from them. When the models that have achieved the desirable and relevant results are created, a comprehensive evaluation of the model is performed based on the following constraints (Sarkar et al., 2018).

- Model performance, as defined with success criteria
- Reproducible and reliable results from models
- Robustness, scalability, and ease of implementation
- Potential extensibility of the model
- Satisfactory model assessment results
- Ranking final models depending on the quality of results and their importance based on orientation with business goals
- Any assumptions or limitations, which are overturned by the models
- Cost of implementation of the whole machine learning framework, from data extraction and processing to modeling and predictions

### 1.2.14 Implementation and examining the created model

Created models are implemented and frequently examined based on their prediction results. Deploying the chosen models to construction and becoming confident about the transition from training to construction is continuous. A suitable plan for implementation is formed based on necessary assets, servers, hardware, software, and so on. Models are validated, saved, and installed on systems and servers. Moreover, a plan is created for frequent monitoring and maintenance of models to regularly assess their performance, check their validity, and replace or update models once needed (Sarkar et al., 2018).

### 1.2.15 Supervised machine learning framework

The supervised machine learning techniques works with supervised, labeled data to train models and then predict outcomes for unseen test data samples. Some processes, such as feature scaling, extraction, and selection, must remain constant in the way that the same features are utilized for training the model and the same features are extracted from unseen test data samples to test the model in the prediction phase. Fig. 1.2 shows a classical supervised machine learning framework. As can be seen in the figure, the two stages of model train-

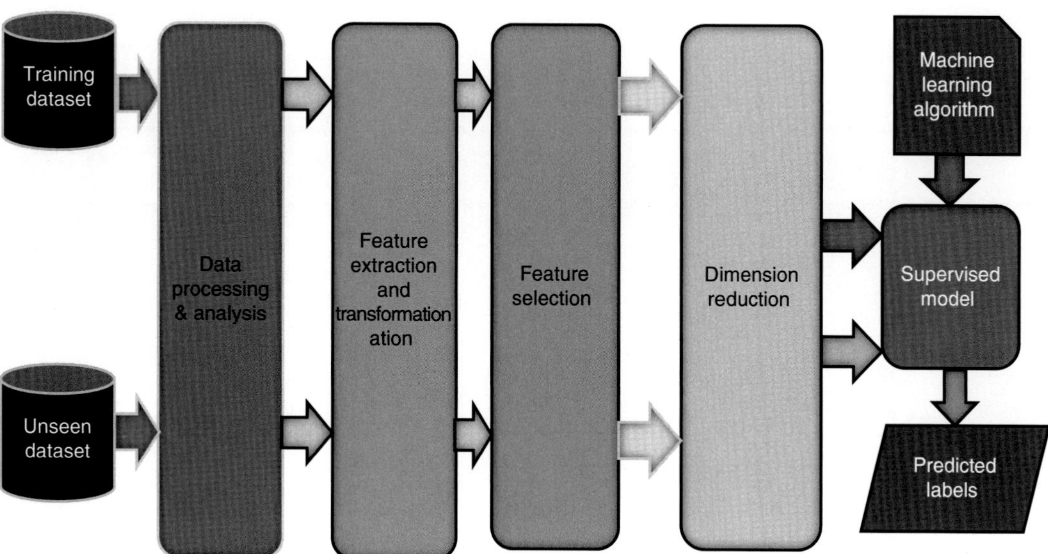


FIGURE 1.2 Supervised machine learning framework.

ing and prediction are highlighted. Moreover, as mentioned earlier, the same stages of data processing, feature scaling, extraction, selection, and dimension reduction are utilized for both data employed in training the model and new data samples for which the model predicts outcomes. This is a crucial point, which we should remember whenever any supervised model is being built. Also, as seen in the figure, the model is a combination of a supervised machine learning technique with training data features and related labels. In the prediction (testing) phase, the created model will take features from new unseen data samples and yield predicted labels (Sarkar et al., 2018).

### 1.2.16 Unsupervised machine learning framework

In unsupervised machine learning, patterns, associations, relationships, and clusters are extracted from the data. The procedures regarding the feature scaling, extraction, selection, and dimension reduction are the same as supervised learning, but there is no concept of prelabeled data in this case. Therefore, the unsupervised machine learning framework can be a bit more different than the supervised framework. Fig. 1.3 shows a classical unsupervised machine learning framework. As is seen in Fig. 1.3, labeled data is not employed for training the unsupervised model. In unsupervised machine learning, the training data without labels goes through the same data preparation stage as in the supervised learning framework, and the unsupervised model is built with an unsupervised machine learning technique with the same features used in training. In the prediction phase, features from new (unseen) data samples are extracted and pass through the model, which gives related results according to the type of machine learning task to be performed, such as clustering, pattern detection, association rules, or dimensionality reduction (Sarkar et al., 2018).

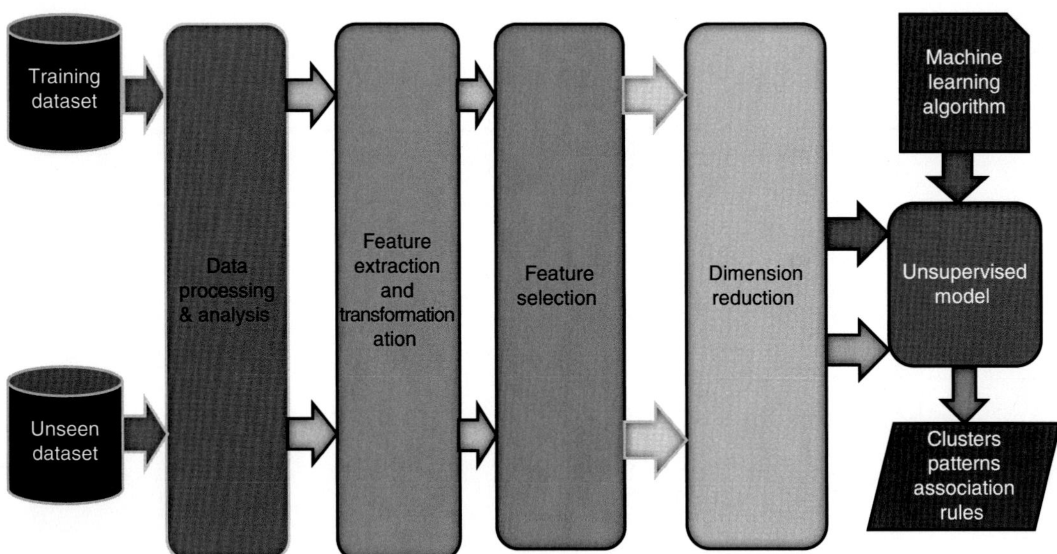


FIGURE 1.3 Unsupervised machine learning framework.

## 1.3 Performance evaluation

Model evaluation is the process of choosing the most suitable among the different models, with their types, features, and tuning parameters. This is determined in the predictive performance assessment whereby the most accurate models are chosen. The predicted model utilizes different performance measures for quality assessment along with determining target estimate reliability. Various performance measures can be employed based on the intended application of the expected model. The most crucial aspect of a model's quality is its generalization properties. The procedure for model evaluation comprises several steps for estimating the accuracy of a model in generalizing subsets of a domain with out-of-sample data. However, it has no significant use since the sorting of the training data is not the primary purpose of classification models. The true performance of the chosen model is defined by its expected yields on the whole domain. They aid in reliably estimating the unknown values of the adopted performance measures on the entire domain that contains previously unseen instances (Cichosz, 2014). Learning model performance evaluation is used to obtain a reliable assessment of the model's predictive performance, that is, the target approximation's quality that the model represents. Various performances can be utilized depending on the intended application of the model under consideration. The generalization properties are essential for the quality of this model, because its creation is usually based on the training data set, typically a small subset of the entire domain. Therefore, according to Cichosz (2014), it is important to differentiate between the particular dataset value (dataset performance), training set value (training performance), and its true performance or expected performance in the full domain.

A crucial issue that should be kept in mind with all these machine learning problems is that they do not have a "correct" answer. This is different from several other issues in computer science with which you are familiar. In some situations, the features utilized to define the data only give a sign of what their class might be but do not comprise enough "signal" to predict the class perfectly. For these reasons, performance evaluation of learning algorithms is crucial, and we must have some idea about learning level of an algorithm to accomplish on new data in terms of prediction performance. Suppose we want to discover how well our newly trained model performs. One task we can perform is to count the number of correctly classified EEG signals, both epileptic and normal, and divide that by the total number of examples to obtain a proportion, which is called the *accuracy* of the classifier. However, this does not indicate whether overfitting is occurring (Flach, 2012).

A better idea might be to use only some portion of the data for training and the remaining as a ***test set***. If overfitting arises, the test set performance will be substantially lower than the training set performance. Nevertheless, even if we choose the test instances randomly from the data, and the test instances are noisy, most of the test instances will be similar to the training instances. In practice this train–test split is therefore repeated in a process called *cross-validation*, where the data is randomly divided into ten parts of equal size and nine parts are used for training and one part for testing. We repeat this ten times using each part once for testing. At the end, we calculate the average test set performance. Cross-validation can also be useful to other supervised learning problems, but unsupervised learning methods typically need to be evaluated differently (Flach, 2012).

To evaluate performance of the machine learning techniques in regression (forecasting), the statistical quality measures, including root mean-squared error (RMSE), mean-absolute error (MAE), relative absolute error (RAE), root relative squared error (RRSE), and correlation coefficient (R) (Table 1.1) should be employed instead of accuracy, F-measure, receiver operating characteristic (ROC) area, and Kappa statistic. In the regression, instead of determining if predicted value is right or wrong, we should consider how close or how far off the predicted values are versus the observed values. These measures are defined by assuming the numeric predictions for the n test cases and the actual (observed) values ($a_i$) and the predicted (estimated) ones ($P_i$) for the test case i as follows:

**TABLE 1.1** Prediction performance metrics for regression.

| | |
|---|---|
| Mean-absolute error (MAE) | $\text{MAE} = \frac{\lvert p_1 - a_1\rvert + \ldots + \lvert p_n - a_n\rvert}{n}$ |
| Root mean-squared error (RMSE) | $\text{RMSE} = \sqrt{\frac{(p_1 - a_1)^2 + \ldots + (p_n - a_n)^2}{n}}$ |
| Relative absolute error (RAE) | $\text{RAE} = \frac{\sum_{i=1}^{n}\lvert p_i - a_i\rvert}{\sum_{i=1}^{n}\lvert a_i - \bar{a}\rvert}$ |
| Root relative squared error (RRSE) | $\text{RRSE} = \sqrt{\frac{\sum_{i=1}^{n}(p_i - a_i)^2}{\sum_{i=1}^{n}(a_i - \bar{a})^2}}$ |
| Correlation coefficient (R) | $R = \frac{S_{PA}}{S_P S_A}$ |

$$\bar{a}=\frac{1}{n}\sum_{i=1}^{n}a_i,\quad \bar{p}=\frac{1}{n}\sum_{i=1}^{n}p_i,$$
$$S_A=\frac{1}{n-1}\sum_{i=1}^{n}(a_i-\bar{a})^2,\quad S_P=\frac{1}{n-1}\sum_{i=1}^{n}(p_i-\bar{p})^2,\quad S_{PA}=\frac{1}{n-1}\sum_{i=1}^{n}(p_i-\bar{p})(a_i-\bar{a}) \tag{1.1}$$

A model's dataset performance is obtained when the selected performance measures of a dataset are calculated, taking into account the true class labels. The dataset performance characterizes the degree of resemblance with the dataset's target concept. On the other hand, the training performance is established by evaluating the model on the training set that is used to come up with the model. This model dataset performance is useful for better comprehension of the model; however, it is not of key interest because the classification of the training data is not the purpose or aim of classification models. Finally, the model's expected performance represents the true performance of the whole domain. The model's true performance means that it can correctly classify arbitrary new instances from the domain under consideration. The performance would always remain unknown but can be approximated using dataset performance since the true or expected performance is generally not available for the domain. The appropriate procedures of evaluation are required to assess the true performance, which mostly contains previously unseen instances (that is, to estimate the values of the unknown adopted performance on the entire domain) (Cichosz, 2014).

The *no free lunch theorem* states that no learning algorithm can beat another once assessed over all possible classification problems, and accordingly the performance of any learning algorithm, over the set of all possible learning problems, is no better than random guessing. The way to eliminate the curse of the no free lunch theorem is to explore more about this distribution and utilize this knowledge in our choice of learning algorithm (Flach, 2012).

### 1.3.1 Confusion matrix

The performance of classifier models can be summarized by means of a *confusion matrix*. This matrix provides an important insight into the model's capability to predict particular classes, as well as its generalization properties. Nevertheless, the confusion matrix does not always give an anticipated ability to compare and rank various models based on their functionalities or performance and to select the best among several candidate models. The confusion matrix can provide multiple measures of performance, but only those applicable to two-class models. These models can be represented by using the set C = {0,1}, where 0 can be shown as the negative class and 1 as the positive class. In the same manner, an individual can refer to an instance, x, as a positive instance given c(x) = 1 and a negative one when c(x) = 0. It is only required when there is some asymmetry between classes. To apply the same performance measures on models with two or more categories, it would take extra effort. The convention used in the confusion matrix is that the positive or negative refers to the class values predicted by the model, and the true or false relates to the accuracy of the predicted model (Cichosz, 2014). A 2 x 2 confusion matrix is shown in Fig. 1.4.

In this matrix, every row refers to actual classes as recorded in the test set, and each column to classes as predicted by the classifier. A wide range of performance indicators can be calculated from a confusion matrix. The simplest of these is *accuracy*, which is the proportion of correctly classified test instances.

| | PREDICTED CLASS | | |
|---|---|---|---|
| ACTUAL CLASS | | Class=Yes | Class=No |
| | Class=Yes | (TP) | (FN) |
| | Class=No | (FP) | (TN) |

**FIGURE 1.4** Representation of confusion matrix.

- The error in misclassification is represented as the ratio of instances incorrectly classified to all the instances:

$$\text{Misclassification Error} = \frac{FP + FN}{\text{TP} + \text{TN} + \text{FP} + \text{FN}} \tag{1.2}$$

- To calculate the accuracy of the model, the proportion of correct classification to all instances that are used, can be represented by the formula:

$$Accuracy = \frac{\text{TP} + \text{TN}}{\text{TP} + \text{TN} + \text{FP} + \text{FN}} \tag{1.3}$$

- The true positive rate (TPR) or sensitivity is calculated using the ratio of instances classified correctly as positive to all the positive instances, represented by the formula:

$$TPR = \frac{TP}{TP + FN} \tag{1.4}$$

- The false positive rate (FPR) or specificity is given using the ratio of instances classified incorrectly as positive to all the negative instances, and the formula is:

$$FPR = \frac{TN}{\text{TN} + \text{FP}} \tag{1.5}$$

- The precision of the model is the ratio of instances classified correctly as positive to all the instances positively classified:

$$Precision = \frac{\text{TP}}{\text{TP} + \text{FP}} \tag{1.6}$$

- Finally, the recall is the ratio between the instances classified correctly to the instances that are not sorted correctly:

$$Recall = \frac{\text{TP}}{\text{TP} + \text{FN}} \tag{1.7}$$

### 1.3.2 F-measure analysis

One way is to calculate the harmonic mean of precision and recall, which in the information retrieval literature is known as the *F-measure* (Flach, 2012). This is a statistical analysis that measures the accuracy of the test using the weighted harmonic mean of both the recall and precision. According to Sokolova, Japkowicz, and Szpakowicz (Sokolova, Japkowicz, & Szpakowicz, 2006), the F-measure is a composite measure that uses assistance algorithms with an advanced sensitivity and encounters simulations with higher specificity. The F-score attains the best value, that is, perfect precision as well as recall, represented by the value 1. The lowest recall and precision means the worst F-score and would be represented by the value 0. The more realistic measure provided by the F-score can be achieved by using both recall and precision in the test performance. The technique is usually used in the retrieval of information for document classification and classification inquiry performance. However, the F-measures do not take into consideration the true negatives. Measures such as the Cohen's kappa and Matthews correlation coefficient may be preferable when evaluating the binary classifier performance. The F-score is widely used in the processing of natural language in literature, for instance, word segmentation and entity recognition evaluation.

$$F-Measure = \frac{Precision{*}Recall}{Precision + Recall} \tag{1.8}$$

### 1.3.3 ROC analysis

A receiver operating characteristic (ROC) curve is taken from a coverage curve by normalizing the axes to [0, 1]. But generally, coverage curves can be rectangular whereas ROC curves always occupy the unit square. Moreover, while in a coverage plot the area under the coverage curve gives the absolute number of correctly ranked pairs; in an ROC plot the area under the ROC curve (AUC) is the ranking accuracy (Flach, 2012). One tool that enhances the classifier performance assessment/evaluation in multiple points of operation, comparison, and selection is the ROC analysis. ROC was the methodology used for detecting radar signals during World War II and turned out to be profitable for the classifier evaluation. It uses the Cartesian coordinate system with the y-axis representing the TPR (true positive rate) and the x-axis representing the RPR (false positive rate). The two axes make the ROC's plane as the single point on the plane that can visualize the fundamental tradeoff between the true positive and false positive, representing the discrete classifier performance. Similarly, a single point of operation in a scoring classifier set is also established as a point on the ROC plane. The TPR of 1 and the FPR of 0, that is, (0,1), shows the perfect operating point, where all instances are correctly classified. The (1,0) is a point with the TPR of 0 and the FPR of 1, which is the worst operating point, having all instances classified incorrectly. The point correlation factor of (0,0) represents a classifier that will often predict a 0 class yielding neither positives nor negatives. The (1,1) point on the plane represents the classifier that would always generate or predict class 1. To obtain the ROC analysis curve, all the possible operating points of the scoring classifiers on the plane are joined with the line segments. Therefore, visuals display the performance of the classifier independent on the obtained cutoff values. The curve shows the entire range of various operating points, which have subsequent varying levels of the tradeoff of the TPRs and FPRs in a single plot. The scoring classifier performance that relies only on its scoring function element can be indicated graphically using the ROC curve. The scoring expression captures the knowledge regarding the relationship between attributes and class values. It is significant to find all possible operating points of a classifier score to produce the ROC curve, based on the generated ratings for the whole dataset domain (Cichosz, 2014).

### 1.3.4 Kappa statistic

The kappa statistic takes the expected model into consideration by subtracting it from predictor's successes. It represents the results as a part of the total for a perfect predictor model. Its measure of performance is more robust than the simple calculation of percent agreement, because it considers the agreement possibility is occurring by chance. The agreement level between the predicted and observed dataset classification, as well as agreement correction that arises by chance, is done using the Kappa statistic. It does not consider the costs, similar to the plain success rate (Hall, Witten, & Frank, 2011).

$$k = \frac{p_o - p_e}{1 - p_e} = 1 - \frac{1 - p_o}{1 - p_e} \tag{1.9}$$

Where $P_0$ is observed agreement and defined as

$$P_0 = \frac{TP + TN}{TP + TN + FP + FN} \tag{1.10}$$

and $P_e$ measures the probability of random agreement (Yang & Zhou, 2015). Overall random agreement probability is the probability that they agreed on either Yes or No, that is,

$$P_e = P_{YES} + P_{NO} \tag{1.11}$$

where

$$P_{YES} = \frac{TP + FP}{TP + TN + FP + FN} * \frac{TP + FN}{TP + TN + FP + FN} \tag{1.12}$$

$$P_{NO} = \frac{FN + TN}{TP + TN + FP + FN} * \frac{FP + TN}{TP + TN + FP + FN} \tag{1.13}$$

For evaluators in complete agreement, $k = 1$. Otherwise, no agreement in evaluators other than the chance expectation, that is, $p_e$, k = 1. The kappa value can be negative, which means that there is no actual agreement or there is worse than a random agreement between the two raters.

### 1.3.5 What is measured

Performance measures are sometimes called *evaluation measures*. But, the measurements need not be scalars; an ROC curve is also counted as a measurement in this context. The suitability of any of these depends on how performance is defined related to the question of *experimental objective*. It is crucial not to confuse performance measures and experimental objectives. There is often a difference between the two. For example, in machine learning the situation is generally more tangible, and our experimental objective (accuracy) is something we can measure on unseen data. But there might be several unknown factors for which we should account. For instance, the model may need to operate in diverse *operating contexts* with different class distributions. Although assessing accuracy in future contexts is our experimental objective, the fact that we are anticipating the widest possible range of class distributions means that the evaluation measure we must utilize in our test data is not accuracy but average recall. The example reveals that if we select accuracy as the evaluation measure, we are making an implicit hypothesis in which the class distribution of the test set is representative of the operating context of the model to be deployed. Hence, it is good practice to record adequate information to be able to replicate the contingency table if required. Enough set of measurements can be true positive rate, true negative rate, false positive rate, false negative rate, the class distribution, and the size of the test set. Precision and recall is generally reported in the information retrieval literature. *The combination of precision and recall, which is the F-measure, is insensitive to the number of true negatives.* This is not a deficit of the F-measure; quite the contrary, it is beneficial in domains where negatives abound, and it might be easy to achieve high accuracy by always predicting negative. Hence, if you choose F-measure as an evaluation measure, an implicit claim that true negatives are not relevant for your operating context is achievable. Another evaluation measure is the *predicted positive rate*, which is the number of positive predictions in proportion to the number of instances. Although the predicted positive rate does not tell us much about the classification performance of the classifier, it gives us what the classifier estimates to be the class distribution. In some cases, AUC might be a good evaluation measure since it is linearly related to the expected accuracy (Flach, 2012).

### 1.3.6 How they are measured

The evaluation measures discussed so far are calculated from a confusion matrix. The issues are (1) which data to base our measurements on, and (2) how to evaluate the predictable uncertainty related to each measurement. How do we get $k$ independent estimates of *accuracy*? In practice, the quantity of labeled data available is generally too small to set aside a validation sample since it would leave an inadequate quantity of training data. Instead, a widely adopted method known as *k-fold cross-validation* is utilized to develop the labeled data both for *model selection* and for training. If we have sufficient data, we can sample $k$ independent test sets of size $n$ and evaluate *accuracy* on each of them. If we are assessing a learning algorithm rather than a given model, we should keep training data that needs to be apart from the test data. If we do not have much data, the *cross-validation (CV)* procedure is generally applied. In CV the data is randomly partitioned into $k$ parts or "folds"; use one-fold for testing, train a model on the remaining $k - 1$ folds, and assess it on the test fold. This procedure is repeated $k$ times until each fold has been employed for testing once. Cross-validation is conventionally applied with $k = 10$, although this is somewhat arbitrary. Alternatively, we can set $k = n$ and train on all but one test instance, repeated $n$ times; this is known as *leave-one-out* cross-validation. If the learning algorithm is sensitive to the class distribution, *stratified cross-validation* should be applied to achieve roughly the same class distribution in each fold (Flach, 2012).

The special case of $k$-fold cross-validation, where $k = m$, is leave-one-out cross-validation, because at each iteration exactly one instance is left out of the training sample. The average leave-one-out error is an almost unbiased estimate of the average error of an algorithm and can be employed to obtain simple agreements for the algorithms. Generally, the leave-one-out error is very expensive to calculate, because it needs training $k$ times on samples of size $m - 1$, but for some algorithms it admits a very effective calculation. Moreover, $k$-fold cross-validation is typically utilized for performance evaluation in model selection. In that case, the full labeled sample is split into $k$ random folds without any difference between training and test samples for a fixed parameter setting. The performance reported in the $k$-fold cross-validation on the full sample as well as the standard deviation of the errors is measured on each fold (Mohri et al., 2018).

### 1.3.7 How to interpret estimates

Once we have estimates of a related evaluation measure for the models or learning techniques, we can use them to choose the best one. The main problem is how to deal with the intrinsic ambiguity in these estimates. Confidence intervals and significance tests are the key concepts to be discussed. Note that *confidence intervals are statements about estimates rather than statements about the true value of the evaluation measure*. The *p-value* is used for significance testing. The idea of *significance testing* can be extended to learning algorithms evaluated in cross-validation. For a pair of algorithms, we estimate the difference in accuracy on each fold. The $p$-value is estimated using the normal distribution, and the null hypothesis is rejected if the $p$-value is below significance level. Sometimes uncertainty in the process produces a bell-shaped sampling distribution, similar to the normal distribution but slightly more heavy-tailed. This distribution is called the *t-distribution*. The extent to which the t-distribution is more heavy-tailed than the normal distribution is regulated by the number of *degrees of freedom*. The whole procedure is known as the *paired t-test* (Flach, 2012).

### 1.3.8 *k*-Fold cross-validation in scikit-learn

In most practical applications, the available examples are divided into three sets. The first set is employed for training the model and the second is employed as a validation set for model selection. After the best model is selected, the performance of the output predictor is tested on the third set (test set) (Shalev-Shwartz & Ben-David, 2014).

The validation procedure defined so far assumes there are a lot of data, and we can sample a new validation set. But in some cases, the amount of data is not sufficient, and we do not want to "waste" data on validation. The $k$-fold cross-validation method is considered to yield an accurate estimate of the true error without wasting too much data. In $k$-fold cross validation the original training set is divided into $k$ subsets (folds) of size $m/k$. For each fold, the model is trained on the combination of the other folds, and then the error of its output is calculated employing the fold. Finally, the average of all these errors is the estimate of the true error. The special case $k = m$, where $m$ is the number of examples, is called *leave-one-out* (LOO). $k$-Fold cross-validation is often used for model selection (or parameter tuning), and once the best parameter is chosen, the algorithm is retrained using this parameter on the entire training set (Shalev-Shwartz & Ben-David, 2014). A pseudocode of $k$-fold cross-validation for model selection is given in the following.

```
from sklearn.model_selection import cross_val_score
from sklearn.datasets import load_iris
from sklearn.discriminant_analysis import LinearDiscriminantAnalysis
iris = load_iris()
clf = LinearDiscriminantAnalysis(solver = "svd", store_covariance = True)
scores = cross_val_score(clf, iris.data, iris.target, cv = 5)
scores.mean()
```

### 1.3.9 How to choose the right algorithm

To choose the right algorithm among the different algorithms, we must consider the goal. If you are trying to forecast or predict a target value, then you need to investigate supervised learning. If not, then unsupervised learning is the best solution. If the supervised learning is chosen, what is the target value? If it is a discrete value, then classification must be utilized; if the target values are a continuous number of values, then regression must be used. In chapter 3, supervised learning techniques, such as classification and regression and clustering, will be explained. The second thing you should consider is your data. Are the features nominal or continuous? Are there missing values in the features? Are there outliers in the data? All of these features about your data can help you narrow the algorithm selection process. Moreover, there is no single answer to what the best algorithm is or what will give you the best results. You should try several algorithms and check their performance. There are other machine learning tools, which can be utilized to enhance the performance of a machine learning technique (Harrington, 2012).

## 1.4 The Python machine learning environment

Now we can discuss the programming language to implement machine learning algorithms. A programming language must be understandable by a wide range of people. Moreover, the programming language should have libraries written for a number of tasks. A programming language with an active developer community is needed. Python is the best choice for these reasons, and it is a great language for machine learning for a large number of reasons. First, Python has clear syntax. The clear syntax of Python has earned it the name *executable pseudo-code*. The default installation of Python already includes high-level data types, such as lists, tuples, dictionaries, sets, and queues. You can program in any way you are familiar with, such as object-oriented, procedural, and functional. With Python it is easy to process and manipulate text that makes it perfect for processing nonnumeric data. A large number of people and organizations use Python, so there is ample development and documentation. Python is popular and many examples are available, which makes learning fast. Moreover, the popularity means that there are lots of modules available for many applications. Python is popular in the scientific and financial communities as well. A number of scientific libraries, such as

SciPy and NumPy, allow you to do vector and matrix operations. Furthermore, the scientific libraries SciPy and NumPy are compiled using lower-level languages like C, which make computations much faster. The scientific tools in Python work well with a plotting tool called Matplotlib, which can plot 2D and 3D and can handle most types of plots commonly used in the scientific world. A new module for Python, called Pylab, seeks to combine NumPy, SciPy, and Matplotlib into one environment and installation (Harrington, 2012).

Python is an interpreted language, which means the source code of a Python program is converted into *bytecode* that is then executed by the Python virtual machine. Python is different from major compiled languages, such as C and C + +, as Python code is not required to be *built* and *linked* like code for these languages. This distinction makes for two important points:

- **Python code is fast to develop**: As the code is not needed to be compiled and built, Python code can be readily changed and executed. This makes for a fast development cycle.
- **Python code is not as fast in execution**: Since the code is not directly compiled and executed and an additional layer of the Python virtual machine is responsible for execution, Python code runs a little slow as compared to conventional languages like C, C + +, etc.

Strengths

Python has steadily risen in the charts of widely used programming languages and, according to several surveys and research, it is the fifth most important language in the world. Recently several surveys depicted Python to be the most popular language for machine learning and data science! We will compile a brief list of advantages that Python offers that will likely explain its popularity.

**Easy to learn**: Python is a relatively easy-to-learn language. Its syntax is simple for a beginner to learn and understand. When compared with languages like C or Java, there is minimal boilerplate code required in executing a Python program.

**Supports multiple programming paradigms**: Python is a multiparadigm, multipurpose programming language. It supports object-oriented programming, structured programming, functional programming, and even aspect-oriented programming. This versatility allows it to be used by a multitude of programmers.

**Extensible**: Extensibility of Python is one of its most important characteristics. Python has a huge number of modules easily available that can be readily installed and used. These modules cover every aspect of programming from data access to implementation of popular algorithms. This easy-to-extend feature ensures that a Python developer is more productive, as a large array of problems can be solved by available libraries.

**Active open-source community**: Python is open source and supported by a large developer community. This makes it robust and adaptive. The bugs encountered are easily fixed by the Python community. Being open source, developers can tinker with the Python source code if necessary.

## 1.4.1 Pitfalls

Although Python is a very popular programming language, it comes with its own share of pitfalls. One of the most important limitations it suffers is in terms of execution speed. Being an interpreted language, it is slow when compared to compiled languages. This limitation can be a bit restrictive in scenarios where extremely high performance code is required. This is a major area of improvement for future implementations of Python, and every subsequent Python version addresses it. Although we have to admit it can never be as fast as a compiled language, we are convinced that it makes up for this deficiency by being super-efficient and effective in other departments.

You can install Python and the necessary libraries individually using a prepackaged Python distribution that comes with necessary libraries (i.e., Anaconda). Anaconda is a packaged compilation of Python along with a whole suite of libraries, including core libraries that are widely used in data science. The main advantage of this distribution is that we do not need an elaborate setup and it works well on all flavors of operating systems and platforms, especially Windows. The Anaconda distribution comes with a wonderful IDE, Spyder (Scientific Python Development Environment), as well as other useful utilities like Jupyter Notebooks, the IPython console, and the excellent package management tool Conda (Sarkar et al., 2018).

### 1.4.2 Drawbacks

The only real drawback of Python is that it is not as fast as Java or C. You can, however, call C-compiled programs from Python. This gives you the best of both worlds and allows you to incrementally develop a program. If the program is built in a modular fashion, you can first get it up and running in Python and then, to improve speed, start building portions of the code in C. The Boost C + + library makes this easy to do. Other tools, such as Cython and PyPy, allow you write typed versions of Python with performance gains over regular Python. If an idea for a program or application is flawed, then it will be flawed at low speed as well as high speed. If an idea is a bad idea, writing code can make it fast or scale (Harrington, 2012).

### 1.4.3 The NumPy library

NumPy is the backbone of machine learning in Python. It is one of the most important libraries in Python for numerical computations. It adds support to core Python for multidimensional arrays (and matrices) and fast vectorized operations on these arrays. It is employed in almost all machine learning and scientific computing libraries. The extent of popularity of NumPy is verified by the fact that major OS distributions, like Linux and MacOS, bundle NumPy as a default package instead of considering it as an add-on package (Sarkar et al., 2018).

### 1.4.4 Pandas

Pandas is a vital Python library for data manipulation, wrangling, and analysis. It functions as an intuitive and easy-to-use set of tools for execution operations on any kind of data. Pandas allows you to work with both cross-sectional data and time series–based data. DataFrame is the most important and useful data structure that is employed for almost all types of data representation and manipulation in Pandas. Unlike NumPy arrays, a DataFrame can contain heterogeneous data. Naturally, tabular data are characterized by means of DataFrames, which are analogous to Excel sheets or SQL tables. This is really beneficial in representing raw datasets as well as processed feature sets in machine learning and data science. All the operations can be performed along the axes, rows, and columns in a DataFrame (Sarkar et al., 2018).

## 1.5 Summary

Models form the fundamental concept in machine learning since they comprise what is being learned from the data in order to solve a given task. There is a significant range of machine learning models that can be chosen. One motivation for this is the ubiquity of the tasks that machine learning aims to solve: classification, regression, clustering, and association discovery, to name but a few. Examples of each of these tasks can be found in virtually every branch of science and engineering. Mathematicians, engineers, psychologists, computer scientists, and many others have discovered—and sometimes rediscovered—ways to solve these tasks. They have all brought their specific background to bear, and accordingly the principles creating these models are all different. This diversity is a good thing because it supports machine learning as a powerful and exciting discipline (Flach, 2012).

Machine learning is a technique utilizing valuable and informative features that create the right models to produce the right tasks. These tasks include binary and multiclass classification, regression, clustering, and descriptive modeling. Models for the first few of these tasks are learned in a supervised fashion that need labeled training datasets. If you want to know how good the model is, you also need labeled test datasets separate from the training datasets to assess your model on the dataset on which it was trained. A test dataset is required to expose any overfitting that occurs. **Unsupervised learning**, on the other hand, works with unlabeled datasets and, therefore, there are no test datasets as such. For example, to assess a specific partition of dataset into clusters, one can estimate the average distance from the cluster center. Other forms of unsupervised learning include learning associations and categorizing hidden variables, such as film genres. Predictive models whose outputs include the target variable and descriptive models that describe interesting structures in the dataset can be distinguished. Generally, predictive models are learned in a supervised manner whereas descriptive models are produced by unsupervised learning techniques (Flach, 2012).

Because this book is a practical machine learning book, we will focus on specific use cases, problems, and real-world case studies in subsequent chapters. It is crucial to realize formal descriptions, notions, and foundations related to learning algorithms, data management, model construction, assessment, and arrangement. Therefore, we try to cover all these features, including problems relevant to data mining and machine learning workflows, so that you gain a foundational framework that can be utilized and you can tackle any of the real-world problems we present in subsequent chapters. Moreover, we cover several interdisciplinary areas related to machine learning. This book mainly examines practical or applied machine learning for data analysis, so the focus of the chapters is the application of machine learning algorithms to solve real-world problems. Therefore, basic level of proficiency in Python and machine learning would be helpful. But, since this book considers different levels of expertise for numerous readers, chapters 2 and 3 explain the key aspects of machine learning and constructing machine learning pipelines. We will also discuss the usage of Python for building machine learning systems and the main tools and frameworks naturally utilized to solve machine learning problems. There will be lots of code snippets, examples, and multiple case studies. We utilize Python 3 and present all our examples with related code files for a more interactive experience. You can try all the examples yourself as you go through the book and adopt them in solving your own real-world problems.

The role of features in machine learning has been discussed. There is no model without features, and occasionally a single feature is sufficient to create a model. Data does not always exist with ready-made features, and generally we must construct or transform features. Because of this, machine learning is generally known as an iterative process in which we have extracted or selected the right features after we have created the model, and if the model does not achieve good performance we need to analyze its performance to realize in what ways the features must be enhanced. Hence in the next chapter we talk about preprocessing, which includes dimension reduction, feature extraction, feature selection, and feature transformation. In chapter 3, several machine learning techniques are explained. Classification examples for healthcare are given in chapter 4 and other classification examples are given in chapter 5. Regression (forecasting) examples are presented in chapter 6, and chapter 7 is dedicated to unsupervised learning (clustering) examples.

## References

Begg, R., Lai, D. T., & Palaniswami, M. (2008). *Computational intelligence in biomedical engineering*. Boca Raton, FL: CRC Press.

Cichosz, P. (2014). *Data mining algorithms: Explained using R*. West Sussex, UK: John Wiley & Sons.

Flach, P. (2012). *Machine learning: The art and science of algorithms that make sense of data*. Cambridge, UK: Cambridge University Press.

Graimann, B., Allison, B., & Pfurtscheller, G. (2009). Brain–computer interfaces: A gentle introduction. In *Brain-Computer Interfaces* (pp. 1–27). Berlin, Heidelberg: Springer.

Hall, M., Witten, I., & Frank, E. (2011). *Data mining: Practical machine learning tools and techniques*. Burlington, MA: Morgan Kaufmann.

Harrington, P. (2012). *Machine learning in action*. Shelter Island, NY: Manning Publications Co.

Mohri, M., Rostamizadeh, A., & Talwalkar, A. (2018). *Foundations of machine learning*. Cambridge, MA: MIT press.

Phinyomark, A., Quaine, F., Charbonnier, S., Serviere, C., Tarpin-Bernard, F., & Laurillau, Y. (2013). EMG feature evaluation for improving myoelectric pattern recognition robustness. *Expert Systems with Applications*, *40*(12), 4832–4840.

Sarkar, D., Bali, R., & Sharma, T. (2018). Practical Machine Learning with Python. A Problem-Solvers Guide To Building Real-World Intelligent Systems, Springer Science+Business Media, New York.

Shalev-Shwartz, S., & Ben-David, S. (2014). *Understanding machine learning: From theory to algorithms*. New York, NY: Cambridge University press.

Sokolova, M., Japkowicz, N., & Szpakowicz, S. (2006). Beyond accuracy, F-score and ROC: a family of discriminant measures for performance evaluation. 1015-1021. Springer.

Subasi, A. (2019a). Electroencephalogram-controlled assistive devices. In K. Pal, H. -B. Kraatz, A. Khasnobish, S. Bag, I. Banerjee, & U. Kuruganti (Eds.), *Bioelectronics and medical devices* (pp. 261–284). https://doi.org/10.1016/B978-0-08-102420-1.00016-9.

Subasi, A. (2019b). Practical Guide for Biomedical Signals Analysis Using Machine Learning Techniques, A MATLAB Based Approach (1st Edition). United Kingdom: Academic Press.

Wołczowski, A., & Zdunek, R. (2017). Electromyography and mechanomyographysignal recognition: experimental analysis using multi-wayarray decomposition methods. *Biocybernetics and Biomedical Engineering*, *37*(1), 103–113 https://doi.org/10.1016/j.bbe.2016.09.004.

Yang, Z., & Zhou, M. (2015). Kappa statistic for clustered physician–patients polytomous data. *Computational Statistics & Data Analysis*, *87*, 1–17.

CHAPTER

# 2

# Data preprocessing

## 2.1 Introduction

In machine learning, whether the algorithm is classification or regression, data are used as inputs and fed to the learner for decision-making. Ideally, there is no need for feature extraction or selection as a separate process; the classifier (or regressor) must use any features, removing the irrelevant ones. But there are many reasons why we are concerned with reducing dimensionality as an independent preprocessing step:

- In most learning algorithms the complexity is based on the number of input dimensions, as well as on the size of the data sample, and for reduced memory and computation, we are interested in reducing the dimensionality of the problem. Dimension reduction also reduces the complexity of the learning algorithm during testing.
- If an input is not informative, we can save the cost by extracting it.
- Simple models are more robust on small datasets. Simple models have less variance; that is, they diverge less reliant on specific samples, including outliers, noise, etc.
- If data can be represented with fewer features, we can gain a better idea of the process that motivates the data, and this allocates knowledge extraction.
- If data can be described by fewer dimensions without loss of information, it can be plotted and analyzed visually for structure and outliers.

The complexity of any learner depends on the quantity of inputs. This affects both space and time complexity and the required number of training examples to train such a learner (Alpaydin, 2014). In this chapter, we discuss feature selection methods, which choose a subset of informative features while pruning the rest, and feature extraction methods, which form fewer new features from the original inputs and dimension reduction techniques.

In situations where the data have a huge number of features, it is always necessary to decrease its dimension or to find a lower-dimensional depiction conserving some of its properties. The crucial arguments for dimensionality reduction (or manifold learning) techniques are:

**Computational:** to compress the original data as a preprocessing step to speed up succeeding operations on the data.

**Visualization:** to visualize the data for tentative analysis by mapping the input data into two- or three-dimensional spaces.

**Practical Machine Learning for Data Analysis Using Python. http://dx.doi.org/10.1016/B978-0-12-821379-7.00002-3**

**Feature extraction:** to confidently produce a smaller and more efficient, informative, or valuable set of features.

The benefits of **dimensionality reduction** are generally represented via simulated data, such as the Swiss roll dataset. Dimensionality reduction can be represented as follows.

Consider a sample $S = (x_1, \ldots, x_m)$, a feature mapping $\Phi: X \to R_N$, and the data matrix $X \in R_N \times m$ defined as $(\Phi(x_1), \ldots, \Phi(x_m))$. The $i^{th}$ data point is represented by $x_i = \Phi(x_i)$, or the $i_{th}$ column of X, which is an N-dimensional vector. Dimensionality reduction methods generally aim to find, for k & N, a k-dimensional representation of the data, $Y \in Rk \times m$, that is in some way faithful to the original representation X. In this chapter we will discuss several methods that address this problem. We first present the most generally employed dimensionality reduction technique known as principal component analysis (PCA).We then introduce a kernelized version of PCA (KPCA) and show the connection between KPCA and manifold learning algorithms (Mohri, Rostamizadeh, & Talwalkar, 2018; Subasi, 2019).

This chapter explains different feature extraction methods and dimension reduction techniques for data analysis by giving diverse examples in Python. Furthermore, in this chapter, principal component analysis (PCA), independent component analysis (ICA), linear discriminant analysis (LDA), entropy, and statistical values are introduced as dimension reduction techniques. The aim of this chapter is to assist researchers in choosing an appropriate preprocessing technique for data analysis. Therefore, the fundamental preprocessing methods that are utilized for the classification of data are discussed in this chapter. Toward the end of each section, appropriate Python functions with various data applications will be demonstrated with an example. Most of the examples are taken from Python–scikit-learn library (https://scikit-learn.org/stable/) and then adapted.

## 2.2 Feature extraction and transformation

There are a lot of possibilities in machine learning when playing with the features. In signal processing and text classification in general, the biomedical signals or documents do not come with built-in features; rather, they must be constructed by the developer of the machine learning algorithm. This feature construction (or extraction) procedure is critical for the accomplishment of a machine learning algorithm. Extracting informative and valuable features in a biomedical signal analysis is a wisely engineered depiction that manages to amplify the "signal" and attenuate the "noise" related to classification tasks. Nevertheless, it is easy to comprehend problems in which this would be the wrong thing to do, for example, if we aim to train a classifier to differentiate between normal and abnormal biomedical signals. It is most natural to construct a model in terms of the given features. But we are allowed to modify the features as we see fit, or even to produce new features. For example, real-valued features generally comprise redundant features that can be eliminated by discretization. One attractive and multidimensional characteristic of features is that they may cooperate in several ways. Occasionally such interaction can be exploited, sometimes it can be ignored, and sometimes it creates a challenge. There are additional ways where features can be correlated (Flach, 2012).

### 2.2.1 Types of features

Consider two features, one describing a person's age and the other their house number. Both features map into the integers, but the way we utilize those features can be rather different. Calculating the average age of a group of people is meaningful, but an average house number is perhaps not beneficial! These, in turn, depend on whether the feature values are represented on a meaningful *scale*. In spite of appearances, house numbers are not actually integers but ***ordinals***. They can be employed to determine that number 10's neighbors are number 8 and number 12, but we cannot assume that the distance between 8 and 10 is the same as the distance between 10 and 12. Because of the lack of a linear scale, it is not meaningful to add or subtract house numbers, which prevents operations such as averaging (Flach, 2012).

### 2.2.2 Statistical features

Numerous statistical features can be extracted from each subsample data point, as they are the main distinguishing values to describe the distribution of the data. The features are the minimum, maximum, mean, median, mode, standard deviation, variance, first quartile, third quartile, and interquartile range (IQR) of the data vector (Subasi, 2019). The varieties of calculations on features are generally stated as statistics or aggregates. Three main types are ***shape statistics***, ***statistics of dispersion***, and ***statistics of central tendency***. Each of these can be represented either as a tangible property of a given sample (sample statistics) or a hypothetical property of an unknown population. The statistical values—namely, mean, standard deviation, skewness, and kurtosis—are generally utilized to reduce the dimension of data. The first and second-order statistics are critical in data analysis. On the other hand, second-order statistics are not enough for many time series data. Hence, higher-order statistics should also be used for a better description of the data. Although the first and second-order statistics designate mean and variance, the higher-order statistics designate higher-order moments (Mendel, 1991). If X(n) is a random process, the moments of X(n) can be represented as the coefficients in Taylor series expansion of the moment producing function (Kutlu & Kuntalp, 2012; Subasi, 2019).

$$m_2(i) = E\left[X(n), X(n+i)\right] \tag{2.1}$$

$$\phi_x(w) = E\left[\exp(jwx)\right] \tag{2.2}$$

If discrete time series has zero mean, then the moments are defined as:

$$m_3(i,j) = E\left[X(n), X(n+i)\cdot X(n+j)\right] \tag{2.3}$$

$$m_4(i,j,k) = E\left[X(n), X(n+i)\cdot X(n+j)\cdot X(n+k)\right] \tag{2.4}$$

where E[•] is the expected value of the random process X(•) (Kutlu & Kuntalp, 2012).

Higher-order statistics (HOS) denote the cumulants with orders of three and higher-order-computed numbers, which are linear combinations of lower-order moments and lower-order cumulants. The moments and cumulants are calculated and then employed as features under the assumption that the time series samples are random variables taken from an unknown distribution, P(x). The moment about zero, $\mu_n(0)$ (raw moment), of a continuous distribution, P(x), is mathematically represented in the following equation:

$$\mu_n(0) = \int x^n P(x) \tag{2.5}$$

In the case of time series, discrete distribution of P(x) describes the moment as given in Eq. (2.6)

$$\mu_n(0) = \sum x^n P(x) \tag{2.6}$$

Moments can be taken about a point, a, in which case Eq. (2.1) is calculated as shown in Eq. (2.7)

$$\mu_n(a) = \sum (x-a)^n P(x) \tag{2.7}$$

The first moment, $\mu_1$, characterizes the mean; the second moment, $\mu_2$, characterizes the variance; and the third moment, $\mu_3$, the skewness of the distribution that computes the asymmetry degree. The fourth-order moment is kurtosis, measuring the distribution peakedness. Central moments are moments taken from the distribution mean. The cumulants, $k_n$, of a distribution are taken from the probability density function, $P(x)$. The higher-order cumulants are revealed to be linear combinations of the moments (Begg, Lai, & Palaniswami, 2008; Subasi, 2019). Supposing raw moments, the first four cumulants can be characterized evidently as given in Eq. (2.8)

$$\begin{aligned} k_1 &= \mu_1 \\ k_2 &= \mu_2 - \mu_1^2 \\ k_3 &= 2\mu_1^3 - 3\mu_1\mu_2 + \mu_3 \\ k_4 &= -6\mu_1^4 + 12\mu_1^2\mu_2 - 3\mu_2^2 - 4\mu_1\mu_3 + \mu_4 \end{aligned} \tag{2.8}$$

The most significant statistics of central tendency are the *mean*,

$$\mu = \frac{1}{M}\sum_{j=1}^{M} |y_j| \tag{2.9}$$

the *median*, and the *mode* (Flach, 2012).

The second type of calculation on features are statistics of dispersion (spread), which are the average squared deviation from the mean (*variance*), and its square root (*standard deviation*).

$$\sigma = \sqrt{\frac{1}{M}\sum_{j=1}^{M} (y_j - \mu)^2} \tag{2.10}$$

Variance and standard deviation mainly measure the same thing, but the latter has the benefit that it is represented on the same scale as the feature itself. A simpler dispersion statistic is the *range*, which is the difference between maximum and minimum value. Other statistics of dispersion are the *percentiles*. The $p$-th percentile is the value such that $p$ percent of the instances fall below it. If we have 100 instances, the 80th percentile is the value of the 81st instance in a list of increasing values. If $p$ is a multiple of 25, the percentiles are also called *quartiles*. Percentiles and quartiles are special cases of *quantiles*. Once we have quantiles, we can measure dispersion as the distance between different quantiles. For instance, the *interquartile range* is the difference between the third and first quartile (i.e., the 75th and 25th percentile).

The skew and "peakedness" of a distribution are measured by skewness and kurtosis, which are the third and fourth *central moment* of the sample. Obviously, the first central moment is the average deviation from the mean, and the second central moment is the average squared deviation from the mean, called the variance. The third central moment $m_3$ might be negative or positive. *Skewness* is defined as

$$\varphi = \sqrt{\frac{1}{M}\sum_{j=1}^{M}\frac{(y_j-\mu)^3}{\sigma^3}}, \tag{2.11}$$

where $\sigma$ is the sample's standard deviation. A positive value of skewness indicates the right-skewed distribution whereas negative skewness indicates the left-skewed case. *Kurtosis* is defined as

$$\phi = \sqrt{\frac{1}{M}\sum_{j=1}^{M}\frac{(y_j-\mu)^4}{\sigma^4}} \tag{2.12}$$

Positive excess kurtosis indicates that the distribution is more sharply peaked than the normal distribution (Flach, 2012).

Meanwhile, several feature extraction methods yield a feature vector that is too big to be used as an input to a classifier. By using first, second, third, and fourth-order cumulants, the reduced feature sets can be calculated. The capability of transforming a set of coefficients into a reduced feature set designates one of the critical steps in any learning task, as this reduced feature set characterizes the behavior of the time series data in a better way (Subasi, 2019).

**Example 2.1**

The following Python code is used to calculate the statistical values, such as mean, median, standard deviation, skewness, and kurtosis of a vector. Note that this example is adapted from Python–scikit-learn.

```
# descriptive statistics
import scipy as sp
import scipy.stats as stats
import numpy as np
from matplotlib import pyplot as plt
```

```
from sklearn.datasets.samples_generator import make_blobs
#Create a dataset
X, y = make_blobs(n_samples = 300, centers = 4, cluster_std = 0.60, random_
state = 0)
plt.scatter(X[:,0], X[:,1])

X_mean = sp.mean(X[:,1])
print('Mean = ',X_mean)

X_mean = np.mean(X[:,1])
print('Mean = ',X_mean)

X_SD = sp.std(X[:,1])
print('SD = ',X_SD)
X_SD = np.std(X[:,1])
print('SD = ',X_SD)

X_median = sp.median(X[:,1])
print('Median = ',X_median)
X_median = np.median(X[:,1])
print('Median = ',X_median)

X_skewness = stats.skew(X[:,1])
print('Skewness = ',X_skewness)

X_kurtosis = stats.kurtosis(X[:,1])
print('Kurtosis = ',X_kurtosis)
```

### 2.2.3 Structured features

It is generally implicitly supposed that an instance is a vector of feature values. This states that there is no other information existing about an instance apart from the information extracted by its feature values. Defining an instance with its vector of feature values is called an *abstraction*, which is the result of filtering out redundant information. Defining an e-mail as a vector of word frequencies is an example of an abstraction. But occasionally it is essential to circumvent such abstractions and keep more information about an instance that can be taken by a finite vector of feature values. For instance, an e-mail can be represented as a long string, or as a sequence of words and punctuation marks, or as a tree that captures the HTML mark-up, and so on. Features that work on such structured instance spaces are called *structured features*. The significant characteristic of structured features is that they involve *local variables* that denote objects other than the instance itself. Nevertheless, it is possible to employ other forms of *aggregation* over local variables. Structured features can be built either prior to learning a model or simultaneously with it. The first scenario is often called *propositionalisation* because the features can be seen as a translation from first-order logic to propositional logic without local variables. The main challenge with propositionalisation approaches is how to deal with combinatorial explosion of the number of potential features (Flach, 2012).

### 2.2.4 Feature transformations

The objective of *feature transformations* is to improve the effectiveness of a feature by eliminating, changing, or adding information. The best-known feature transformations are those that turn a feature of one type into another of the next type down this list. Nevertheless, there are also transformations that change the scale of quantitative features or add a scale (or order) to ordinal, categorical, and Boolean features. The simplest feature transformations are entirely deductive in the sense that they achieve a well-defined result that does not need to make any choices. *Binarization* transforms a categorical feature into a set of Boolean features, one for each value of the categorical feature. This loses information since the values of a single categorical feature are mutually exclusive but are sometimes required if a model cannot handle more than two feature values. *Unordering* trivially turns an ordinal feature into a categorical one by removing the ordering of the feature values. This is generally needed, as most learning models cannot handle ordinal features directly. An interesting alternative is to add a scale to the feature by means of calibration (Flach, 2012).

The ***sklearn.preprocessing*** package provides several custom utility functions and transformer classes to transform raw feature vectors into a representation that is more appropriate for the downstream estimators. Usually, learning algorithms benefit from standardization of the dataset. If there are some outliers in the set, scalers, robust transformers, and normalizers are more appropriate.

### 2.2.5 Thresholding and discretization

*Thresholding* converts an ordinal or a quantitative feature into a Boolean feature by finding a feature value to divide. Such thresholds can be chosen in a supervised or unsupervised way. Unsupervised thresholding characteristically includes the computing of some statistic over the data, while supervised thresholding requires sorting the data on the feature value and passing through this ordering to optimize a specific objective function, such as information gain. If thresholding can be generalized to numerous thresholds, one of the mostly utilized nondeductive feature transformations is reached. In *discretization* a quantitative feature is converted into an ordinal feature. Every ordinal value is denoted as a *bin* and related to an interval of the original quantitative feature (Flach, 2012).

### 2.2.6 Data manipulation

There are two main approaches to transforming dissimilar features into the same scale: **standardization** and **normalization**. These terms are generally employed rather loosely in diverse areas, and their meanings should be derived from the context. Generally, normalization denotes the rescaling of features to a range of [0, 1] that is a special case of min-max scaling. To normalize the data, the min-max scaling can simply be applied to every feature column (Raschka, 2015).

**Example 2.2**

The following Python code is used to represent the min-max scaling process, which is realized in scikit-learn. Note that this example is adapted from Python–scikit-learn. An alternative standardization is scaling features to lie between a given minimum and maximum value, often between 0 and 1, or so that the maximum absolute value of each feature is scaled to unit size. This can be achieved using MinMaxScaler or MaxAbsScaler, respectively. The motivation to use this scaling includes robustness to very small standard deviations of features and preserving zero entries in sparse data. Here is an example to scale a toy data matrix to the [0, 1] range.

```
from sklearn import preprocessing
import numpy as np
X_train = np.array([[ 1., -1., 2.],
                    [ 2., 0., 0.],
                    [ 0., 1., -1.]])
print('Original Matrix:\n',X_train)
min_max_scaler = preprocessing.MinMaxScaler()
X_train_minmax = min_max_scaler.fit_transform(X_train)
print('Scaled Matrix:\n',X_train_minmax)
```

### 2.2.7 Standardization

**Standardization** of datasets is a **well-known requirement for a variety of machine learning algorithms** implemented in scikit-learn. They may not achieve a good performance if the individual features do not more or less look like standard normally distributed data, which is Gaussian with **zero mean and unit variance**. In practice the shape of the distribution is generally ignored and the data are just transformed to center by removing the mean value of each feature, and then scaled by dividing nonconstant features by their standard deviation. The preprocessing module further presents a utility class StandardScaler that utilizes the Transformer API to evaluate the mean and standard deviation on a training set in a way that the same transformation can be later utilized on the testing set (scikit-learn, n.d.).

**Example 2.3**

The following Python code is used to represent the simple scaling process, which is realized in scikit-learn. Note that this example is adapted from Python–scikit-learn. The function scale provides a quick and easy way to perform this operation on a single array-like dataset:

```
from sklearn import preprocessing
import numpy as np
X_train = np.array([[ 1., -1., 2.],
                    [ 2., 0., 0.],
                    [ 0., 1., -1.]])
X_scaled = preprocessing.scale(X_train)
```

```
X_scaled
#%%
#Scaled data has zero mean and unit variance:

X_scaled.mean(axis = 0)
#%%
X_scaled.std(axis = 0)
```

Normalization utilizing the min-max scaling is a generally employed method that is suitable once the values in a bounded interval are needed. Standardization can be more practical for several machine learning techniques since various linear models initialize the weights to 0 or small random values close to 0. By means of standardization, the feature columns are centered at mean 0 with standard deviation 1 in a way that the feature columns produce a normal distribution. Moreover, standardization keeps valuable information about the outliers and makes the algorithm less sensitive to them in contrast to min-max scaling that scales the data to a limited range of values. Like MinMaxScaler, standardization is also implemented as a class StandardScaler in scikit-learn. It is also imperative to highlight that the StandardScaler can fit only when on the training data and to utilize those parameters to transform the test set or any new data point (Raschka, 2015).

### Example 2.4

The following Python code is used to represent the scaling process, which is realized in scikit-learn. The preprocessing module further provides a utility class StandardScaler that implements the Transformer API to compute the mean and standard deviation on a training set so as to be able to later reapply the same transformation on the testing set. This class is hence suitable for use in the early steps of a sklearn.pipeline.Pipeline. Note that this example is adapted from Python–scikit-learn. StandardScaler can be used as follows:

```
from sklearn import preprocessing
import numpy as np
X_train = np.array([[ 2., -2., 5.],
                    [ 4., 0., 0.],
                    [ 0., 2., -4.]])
print('Original Matrix:\n',X_train)
scaler = preprocessing.StandardScaler().fit(X_train)
scaler
print('Scalar Mean:',scaler.mean_)
print('Scalar:',scaler.scale_)
X_train_scaled = scaler.transform(X_train)
print('Scaled Matrix:\n',X_train_scaled)
```

Using the preceding code, we loaded the StandardScaler class from the preprocessing module and initialized a new StandardScaler object. Using the fit method, StandardScaler estimated the parameters μ (sample mean) and σ (standard deviation) for each feature dimension from the training data. By calling the transform method, we then standardized the training data using those estimated parameters μ and σ. Note that we used the same scaling parameters to standardize the test set so that both the values in the training and test dataset are comparable to each other (Raschka, 2015). Scikit-learn also implements a large variety of different performance metrics that are available via the metrics module.

## Example 2.5

The following Python code is used to represent the scaling process, which is realized in scikit-learn. The StandardScaler is suitable for use in the early steps of a sklearn.pipeline.Pipeline. In this example we create the dataset using the sklearn.datasets.samples_generator. Note that this example is adapted from Python–scikit-learn. StandardScaler can be used as follows:

```
from matplotlib import pyplot as plt
from sklearn.datasets.samples_generator import make_blobs
from sklearn import preprocessing
import numpy as np
#Create a dataset
X, y = make_blobs(n_samples = 100, centers = 4, cluster_std = 0.60, random_
state = 0)
plt.scatter(X[:,0], X[:,1])

print('Original Matrix:\n',X)
scaler = preprocessing.StandardScaler().fit(X)
scaler

print('Scalar Mean:',scaler.mean_)
print('Scalar:',scaler.scale_)
X_scaled = scaler.transform(X)
print('Scaled Matrix:\n',X_scaled)
```

Another transformation is the nonlinear transformation. Two categories of transformations are available: quantile transforms and power transforms. Both quantile and power transforms are based on monotonic transformations of the features and thus preserve the rank of the values along each feature. QuantileTransformer and quantile_transform provide a nonparametric transformation to map the data to a uniform distribution with values between 0 and 1.

### Example 2.6

The following Python code is used to represent the QuantileTransformer process, which is realized in scikit-learn. In this example we employ the Iris dataset that exists in sklearn.datasets, and the scatter plot is also drawn in two dimensions. Note that this example is adapted from Python–scikit-learn. QuantileTransformer can be used as follows:

```
import numpy as np
import matplotlib.pyplot as plt
from sklearn.datasets import load_iris
from sklearn import preprocessing

iris = load_iris()
X, y = iris.data, iris.target

X = iris.data[:, :2] # we only take the first two features.
y = iris.target

plt.figure(2, figsize = (8, 6))
plt.clf()

#%%
#Transform data
quantile_transformer = preprocessing.QuantileTransformer(random_state = 0)
X_trans = quantile_transformer.fit_transform(X)
np.percentile(X[:, 0], [0, 25, 50, 75, 100])

np.percentile(X_trans[:, 0], [0, 25, 50, 75, 100])
#%%
# Plot the original data points
plt.scatter(X[:, 0], X[:, 1], c = y, cmap = plt.cm.Set1,
                 edgecolor = 'k')
plt.xlabel('Sepal length')
plt.ylabel('Sepal width')
plt.title('Original data points')
plt.xticks(())
plt.yticks(())

#%%
# Plot the transformed data points
plt.scatter(X_trans[:, 0], X[:, 1], c = y, cmap = plt.cm.Set1,
                 edgecolor = 'k')
plt.xlabel('Sepal length')
plt.ylabel('Sepal width')
plt.title('Transformed data points')
plt.xticks(())
plt.yticks(())
```

## Example 2.7

This example is the modification of the Example 2.6 where we use the QuantileTransformer again. In this example, scatter plot is drawn in three dimensions.

```
import numpy as np
import matplotlib.pyplot as plt
from sklearn.datasets import load_iris
from mpl_toolkits.mplot3d import Axes3D
from sklearn.model_selection import train_test_split
from sklearn import preprocessing

iris = load_iris()
X, y = iris.data, iris.target

X = iris.data[:, :3] # we only take the first two features.
y = iris.target

plt.figure(3, figsize = (8, 6))
plt.clf()

#%%
#Transform data
quantile_transformer = preprocessing.QuantileTransformer(random_state = 0)
X_trans = quantile_transformer.fit_transform(X)

np.percentile(X[:, 0], [0, 25, 50, 75, 100])
np.percentile(X_trans[:, 0], [0, 25, 50, 75, 100])

#%%
# Plot the original data points
fig = plt.figure(1, figsize = (8, 6))
ax = Axes3D(fig, elev = -150, azim = 110)
ax.scatter(X[:, 0], X[:, 1], X[:, 2], c = y,
                cmap = plt.cm.Set1, edgecolor = 'k', s = 40)
ax.set_title('Original data points')
ax.set_xlabel('Sepal length')
ax.w_xaxis.set_ticklabels([])
ax.set_ylabel('Sepal width')
ax.w_yaxis.set_ticklabels([])
ax.set_zlabel('Sepal height')
ax.w_zaxis.set_ticklabels([])

plt.show()
#%%
# Plot the transformed data points

fig = plt.figure(1, figsize = (8, 6))
ax = Axes3D(fig, elev = -150, azim = 110)
ax.scatter(X_trans[:, 0], X_trans[:, 1], X_trans[:, 2], c = y,
                cmap = plt.cm.Set1, edgecolor = 'k', s = 40)
```

```
ax.set_title('Transformed data points')
ax.set_xlabel('Sepal length')
ax.w_xaxis.set_ticklabels([])
ax.set_ylabel('Sepal width')
ax.w_yaxis.set_ticklabels([])
ax.set_zlabel('Sepal height')
ax.w_zaxis.set_ticklabels([])

plt.show()
```

### 2.2.8 Normalization and calibration

Thresholding and discretization are feature transformations that eliminate the measure of a quantitative feature. If adapting the scale of a quantitative feature is done in an unsupervised manner, it is generally termed *normalization*, while calibration utilizes the supervised approaches. *Feature normalization* is mostly needed to eliminate the effect of several quantitative features measured on different scales. If the features are normally distributed, it can be converted into *z-scores* by centering on the mean and dividing by the standard deviation. *Feature calibration* is known as a supervised feature transformation adding a meaningful measure carrying class information to arbitrary features (Flach, 2012).

#### Example 2.8

The following Python code is used to represent the normalization process, which is realized in scikit-learn. In this example we utilize the Iris dataset, which exists in sklearn.datasets, and 3-D scatter plot is also drawn before and after normalization using ***preprocessing.normalize***. Note that this example is adapted from Python–scikit-learn. Normalization is a process of scaling individual samples to have unit norm. This process can be useful if you plan to use a quadratic form such as the dot-product or any other kernel to quantify the similarity of any pair of samples. The function normalize provides a quick and easy way to perform this operation on several datasets, either using the l1 or l2 norms.

```
import numpy as np
import matplotlib.pyplot as plt
from sklearn.datasets import load_iris
from mpl_toolkits.mplot3d import Axes3D
from sklearn.model_selection import train_test_split
from sklearn import preprocessing

iris = load_iris()
X, y = iris.data, iris.target

X = iris.data[:, :3] # we only take the first two features.
y = iris.target

plt.figure(3, figsize = (8, 6))
plt.clf()

#%%
# Plot the original data points
```

```
# Plot the original data points
fig = plt.figure(1, figsize = (8, 6))
ax = Axes3D(fig, elev = -150, azim = 110)
ax.scatter(X[:, 0], X[:, 1], X[:, 2], c = y,
                cmap = plt.cm.Set1, edgecolor = 'k', s = 40)
ax.set_title('Original data points')
ax.set_xlabel('Sepal length')
ax.w_xaxis.set_ticklabels([])
ax.set_ylabel('Sepal width')
ax.w_yaxis.set_ticklabels([])
ax.set_zlabel('Sepal height')
ax.w_zaxis.set_ticklabels([])

plt.show()
#%%
X_normalized = preprocessing.normalize(X, norm = 'l2')
# Plot the normalized data points
fig = plt.figure(1, figsize = (8, 6))
ax = Axes3D(fig, elev = -150, azim = 110)
ax.scatter(X_normalized[:, 0], X_normalized[:, 1], X_normalized[:, 2],
c = y,
                cmap = plt.cm.Set1, edgecolor = 'k', s = 40)
ax.set_title('Transformed data points')
ax.set_xlabel('Sepal length')
ax.w_xaxis.set_ticklabels([])
ax.set_ylabel('Sepal width')
ax.w_yaxis.set_ticklabels([])
ax.set_zlabel('Sepal height')
ax.w_zaxis.set_ticklabels([])
plt.show()
```

### 2.2.9 Incomplete features

Missing feature values at training time produces problems. First, a missing feature value might be correlated with the target variable. These features must be designated as "missing" value since a tree model can split on it, but this would not be the case for a linear model. *Imputation* is a process of filling in the missing values. This process can be implemented by utilizing the per-class means, medians, or modes over the observed values of the feature. A more complicated way is to find the feature correlation by creating a predictive model for each incomplete feature and employ that model to "predict" the missing value (Flach, 2012).

For a variety of reasons, numerous real-world datasets include missing values, generally encoded as blanks, NaNs, or other placeholders. Such datasets, however, are incompatible with scikit-learn estimators that assume that all values in an array are numerical and that all have and hold meaning. A simple approach to employ incomplete datasets is to discard entire rows and/or columns containing missing values. Nevertheless, this comes at the price of losing data that might be important (even though incomplete). A better strategy is to impute the missing values, that is, to infer them from the known part of the data. The MissingIndicator transformer is helpful to transform a dataset into related binary matrix demonstrating the existence of missing values in the dataset. This transformation is beneficial in combination with imputation. Once utilizing imputation, keeping the information about which values had been missing can be informative. NaN is generally employed as the placeholder for missing values. But it enforces the data type to be float. The parameter missing_values allows for identifying other placeholders, such as integer. In the following example, -1 will be used as missing values (scikit-learn, n.d.).

### Example 2.9

The following Python code is used to represent the *imputation*, a process of filling in the missing values in scikit-learn. In this example we utilize the Iris dataset, which exists in sklearn.datasets, and the 3-D scatter plot is also drawn before and after imputation using SimpleImputer, MissingIndicator. Note that this example is adapted from Python–scikit-learn.

```
import numpy as np
from sklearn.datasets import load_iris
from sklearn.impute import SimpleImputer, MissingIndicator
from sklearn.model_selection import train_test_split
from sklearn.pipeline import FeatureUnion, make_pipeline
from sklearn.tree import DecisionTreeClassifier
X, y = load_iris(return_X_y = True)
mask = np.random.randint(0, 2, size = X.shape).astype(np.bool)
X[mask] = np.nan
X_train, X_test, y_train, _ = train_test_split(X, y, test_size = 100,random_state = 0)

#%%
"""Now a FeatureUnion is created. All features will be imputed utilizing SimpleImputer,
in order to enable classifiers to work with this data. Moreover, it adds the
indicator variables from MissingIndicator."''
transformer = FeatureUnion(
                transformer_list = [
                ('features', SimpleImputer(strategy = 'mean')),
                ('indicators', MissingIndicator())])
transformer = transformer.fit(X_train, y_train)
results = transformer.transform(X_test)
results.shape

#%%%
"""Of course, the transformer cannot be utilized to make any predictions.
this should be wrapped in a Pipeline with a classifier (e.g., a DecisionTreeClassifier)
```

```
to be able to make predictions."""'
clf = make_pipeline(transformer, DecisionTreeClassifier())
clf = clf.fit(X_train, y_train)
results = clf.predict(X_test)
results.shape
```

### 2.2.10 Feature extraction methods

Feature extraction deals with the problem of finding the most informative, distinctive, and reduced set of features, to improve the success of data storage and processing. Important feature vectors remain the most common and suitable signal representation for the classification problems. Numerous scientists in diverse areas, who are interested in data modelling and classification are combining their effort to enhance the problem of feature extraction. The current advances in both data analysis and machine learning fields made it possible to create a recognition system, which can achieve tasks that could not be accomplished in the past. Feature extraction lies at the center of these advancements with applications in data analysis (Guyon, Gunn, Nikravesh, & Zadeh, 2006; Subasi, 2019).

In *feature extraction*, we are concerned about finding a new set of $k$ dimensions, which are combinations of the original $d$ dimensions. The widely known and most commonly utilized feature extraction methods are *principal component analysis* and *linear discriminant analysis*, unsupervised and supervised learning techniques. Principal component analysis is considerably similar to two other unsupervised linear methods, *factor analysis* and *multidimensional scaling*. When we have not one but two sets of observed variables, *canonical correlation analysis* can be utilized to find the joint features, which explain the dependency between the two (Alpaydin, 2014).

Conventional classifiers do not contain a process to deal with class boundaries. Therefore, if the input variables (number of features) are big as compared to the number of training data, class boundaries may not overlap. In such situations, the generalization ability of the classifier may not be sufficient. Hence, to improve the generalization ability, usually a small set of features from the original input variables are formed by feature extraction, dimension reduction, or feature selection. The most efficient characteristic in creating a model with high generalization capability is to utilize informative and distinctive sets of features. Nevertheless, as there is no effective way of finding an original set of features for a certain classification problem, it is essential to find a set of original features by trial and error. If the number of features is so big and every feature has an insignificant effect on the classification, it is more appropriate to transform the set of features into a reduced set of features. In data analysis, raw data are transformed into a set of features by means of a linear transformation. If every feature in the original set of features has an effect on the classification, the set is reduced by feature extraction, feature selection, or dimension reduction. By feature selection or dimension reduction, ineffective or redundant features are removed in a way that the higher generalization performance and faster classification by the initial set of features can be accomplished (Abe, 2010; Subasi, 2019).

For efficient classification, an accurate feature extraction technique is needed to extract informative and distinctive sets of features from the original dataset. In essence, if the extracted features do not exactly represent the data used and are not relevant, a classification algorithm using such features may have problems describing the classes of the features (Siuly et al.Siuly, Li, & Zhang, 2016). Accordingly, the classification performance can be poor. One of the critical steps in the classification of biomedical signals is the feature extraction. Hence, the biomedical signals, composed of several data points, and informative and distinctive features can be extracted by employing different feature extraction methods. These informative and distinctive parameters describe the behavior of the biomedical signals, which may designate a specific action or activity. The signal patterns utilized in biomedical signal analysis can be characterized by frequencies and amplitudes. These features can be extracted utilizing diverse feature extraction algorithms, which are another crucial step in signal processing to simplify the succeeding stage for classification (Graimann, Allison, & Pfurtscheller, 2009). As all waveforms have limited duration and frequency, efficient decomposition of the biomedical signals is required for the integration of time, frequency, and space dimensions. Biomedical signals can be decomposed using time-frequency (TF) methods that can detect changes in both time and frequency (Kevric & Subasi, 2017; Sanei, 2013; Subasi, 2019).

It is important to deal with smaller data that describe appropriate features of the signals to achieve a better performance. Features are typically collected into a feature vector by transforming signals into a related feature vector known as feature extraction. Distinguishing features of a signal are analyzed by a signal classification framework, and depending on those distinguishing features, class of the signal is decided (Siuly et al., 2016). The feature extraction techniques can be categorized into four groups: parametric methods, nonparametric methods, eigenvector methods, and time-frequency methods. The model-based or parametric methods produce a signal model with known functional form and then estimate the parameters in the produced model. The autoregressive (AR) model, moving average (MA) model, autoregressive-moving average (ARMA) model, and Lyapunov exponents are popular parametric methods. The AR model is suitable to represent spectra with narrow peaks (Kay, 1993; Kay & Marple, 1981; Proakis & Manolakiss; Stoica & Moses, 1997). The nonparametric methods are based on the descriptions of power spectral density (PSD) to deliver spectral estimates. Two well-known, nonparametric methods are the periodogram and the correlogram; these provide a practically high resolution for adequately long data lengths, but they have poor spectral estimation since their variance is high and does not decrease with increasing data length. Eigenvector methods are used to estimate the frequencies and powers of signals from noise-corrupted measurements. These methods are produced by eigen decomposition of the correlation matrix of the noise-corrupted signal. The eigenvector methods, such as the Pisarenko, minimum-norm, and multiple signal classification (MUSIC) are the best fitting to signals, which are supposed to be composed of several sinusoids suppressed with noise (Proakis & Manolakis, 2007; Stoica & Moses, 1997). The time-frequency methods are broadly used in biomedical signal processing and analysis. Time–frequency methods, such as short-time Fourier transform (STFT), wavelet transform (WT), discrete wavelet transform (DWT), stationary wavelet transform (SWT), and wavelet packet decomposition (WPD) decompose signals in both time and frequency domain (Siuly et al., 2016). Short time Fourier transform (STFT), Wigner-Ville distribution, Cohen class kernel functions, wavelet transform (WT), discrete wavelet transform (DWT), stationary wavelet transform (SWT), wavelet packet decomposition (WPD), dual tree complex wavelet transform (DT-CWT), tunable Q wavelet transform (TQWT), empirical wavelet transform (EWT), empirical mode decomposition

(EMD), ensemble EMD (EEMD), variational mode decomposition (VMD), and complete EEMD (CEEMD) are widely known time-frequency methods (Subasi, 2019).

The purpose of the feature extraction is to extract features from the original signal to achieve reliable classification. Feature extraction is the most critical step of the biomedical signal classification, as the classification performance may be degraded if the features are not extracted in a suitable way. The feature extraction step must reduce the original data to a lower dimension that contains most of the valuable information included in the original vector. Therefore, it is crucial to find the key features that describe the whole dataset, based on the nature of that dataset. Diverse statistical features can be extracted from each subsample data point since they are the most characteristic values to define the distribution of the biomedical signals. The features can be the minimum, maximum, mean, median, mode, standard deviation, variance, first quartile, third quartile, and interquartile range (IQR) of the biomedical signals (Siuly et al., 2016; Subasi, 2019).

In recent decades, several feature extraction algorithms have been broadly employed in data analysis. The performance of a classifier is reliant on the nature of the data to be classified. There is no single classifier that operates best on all given problems. Several real-world tests have been applied to compare classifier performance and to recognize the characteristics of data that determine the performance of the classifier. The total classification accuracy and confusion matrix are widely known methods to evaluate the performance of a classification system. Recently, receiver operating characteristic (ROC) curves have been employed to assess the trade-off between true- and false-positive rates of a given classification algorithm (Siuly et al., 2016; Subasi, 2019).

### 2.2.11 Feature extraction using wavelet transform

Each transform provides additional information, which normally reveals a new understanding about the original waveform. Several time-frequency methods do not fully solve the time-frequency problem. The wavelet transform characterizes one more way of describing the time-frequency characteristics of a waveform. But the waveform can be split into scale segments rather than time sections (Semmlow, 2004). Wavelets consist of two parameters of which one is for scaling in time and another for sliding in time. A wavelet is an oscillating function with energy concentrated in time for enhanced representation of transient signals. The bandpass filter characteristic is just one of several mathematical properties a wavelet function must have. Wavelet analysis tries to achieve satisfactory localization in both time and frequency. Sliding and scaling, two new degrees of freedom, allow the analysis of the fine structures and global waveforms in signals. A multiresolution analysis characterizes the important idea of analyzing signals at different scales with a growing level of resolution (Sörnmo & Laguna, 2005). Comprehensive descriptions of wavelet analysis using mathematics can be found in several good books, which also include the topic of filter banks (Basseville & Nikiforov, 1993; Gustafsson, 2000).

#### *2.2.11.1 The continuous wavelet transform (CWT)*

A family of wavelets $\psi_{s,\tau}(t)$ is characterized by sliding and scaling the mother wavelet $\psi(t)$ with the continuous-valued parameters $\tau$ and $s$,

$$\psi_{s,\tau}(t) = \frac{1}{\sqrt{s}}\psi\left(\frac{t-\tau}{s}\right) \tag{2.13}$$

where the factor $1/\sqrt{s}$ makes sure that all scaled functions contain the same energy. The wavelet expands for $s > 1$ and contracts for $0 < s < 1$.

The probing function $\psi_{s,\tau}(t)$ always has an oscillatory form. For $s = 1$ and $\tau = 0$, it takes on its natural form, called the mother wavelet $\psi_{1,0}(t) \equiv \psi(t)$, together with several of its family members created by contraction and dilation. If a wavelet is contracted to a smaller time scale, that makes it more localized in time and less localized in frequency because the resultant bandpass frequency response has increased bandwidth and has moved to higher frequencies. The continuous wavelet transform (CWT) $\omega(s,\tau)$ of a continuous-time signal $x(t)$ is identified by comparing the signal $x(t)$ to the probing function $\psi_{s,\tau}(t)$:

$$\omega(s,\tau) = \int_{-\infty}^{+\infty} x(t)\psi_{s,\tau}(t)\,dt \tag{2.14}$$

creating two-dimensional mapping onto the time-scale domain. As the last equation represents the convolution between the signal $x(t)$ and a filter with impulse response $\psi(-t/s)/\sqrt{s}$, the CWT can be viewed as a linear filter. As the CWT decomposes the waveform into coefficients of two variables $s$ and $\tau$, we need to perform a double integration to reconstruct the original waveform from the wavelet coefficients (Bodenstein, Schneider, & Malsburg, 1985):

$$x(t) = \frac{1}{C_\psi}\int_{-\infty}^{\infty}\int_{0}^{\infty}\omega(s,\tau)\psi_{s,\tau}(t)\frac{d\tau ds}{s^2}, \tag{2.15}$$

$$\text{where } C_\psi = \int_{0}^{\infty}\frac{|\Psi(f)|^2}{|f|}df < \infty, \tag{2.16}$$

and $\Psi(f)$ represents the Fourier transform of $\psi(t)$. The simplest wavelet is the Haar wavelet, a member of the Walsh basis functions. Another popular wavelet is the Mexican hat wavelet, defined by the equation:

$$\psi(t) = \left(1-2t^2\right)e^{-t^2} \tag{2.17}$$

The Morlet wavelet, named after a pioneer of wavelet analysis, is given by the equation:

$$\psi(t) = e^{-t^2}\cos\left(\pi\sqrt{\frac{2}{\ln 2}}t\right) \tag{2.18}$$

A wide variety of wavelets have been suggested, each one possessing some feature particularly suitable for certain applications. Wavelets provide a trade-off between time and frequency localization. However, they do not occur at an exact time or frequency. More precisely, they are not exactly contained in either time or frequency but rather well contained in both. These ranges are also associated with the time and frequency resolution of the CWT. The shorter wavelet time range delivers an improved capability to isolate local time events but at the cost of frequency resolution, because the wavelet only responds to high-frequency components. On the other hand, the CWT delivers enhanced frequency resolution for the longer wavelet length. This integrated compromise between time and frequency resolution makes CWT appropriate for analyzing signals that contain fast-changing (high-frequency) components covered by slowly changing (low frequency) ones (Semmlow, 2004; Subasi, 2019).

**Example 2.10**

The following Python code is used to extract the ECG signal features utilizing continuous wavelet transform (CWT).

```
#==========================================================================
# Continuous wavelet transform
# =========================================================================
import numpy as np
import matplotlib.pyplot as plt
import pywt
import pywt.data

ecg = pywt.data.ecg()
plt.plot(ecg)
plt.xlabel("Samples")
plt.ylabel("ECG in mV")
plt.show()

#Continuous wavelet transform.
from scipy import signal
import matplotlib.pyplot as plt
widths = np.arange(1, 31)
cwtmatr = signal.cwt(ecg, signal.ricker, widths)
plt.imshow(cwtmatr, extent = [-1, 1, 31, 1], cmap = 'PRGn', aspect = 'auto',
                     vmax = abs(cwtmatr).max(), vmin = -abs(cwtmatr).max())
plt.show()
```

#### *2.2.11.2 The discrete wavelet transform (DWT)*

The only major problem of CWT is its infinite redundancy, as it generates countless coefficients than are really needed to precisely describe the original signal. This redundancy becomes expensive only if we need to reconstruct the original signal, because all coefficients will be utilized making the calculation struggle rather unnecessary. The discrete wavelet transform (DWT) generally produces the coefficient frugality by limiting the variation in scale and sliding to powers of 2; thus, it is sometimes termed as the dyadic wavelet transform, having the same abbreviation (DWT). Nevertheless, we can still precisely form the original signal from the discrete coefficients of the dyadic wavelet transform (Bodenstein et al., 1985). If the chosen wavelet belongs to an orthogonal family, the DWT even represents a nonredundant bilateral transform (Semmlow, 2004).

Dyadic sampling of the two wavelet parameters is defined as,

$$s = 2^{-j}, \tau = k2^{-j}, \tag{2.19}$$

where $j$ and $k$ are both integers. Therefore, the discretized probing function becomes:

$$\psi_{j,k}(t) = 2^{j/2}\psi(2jt - k) \tag{2.20}$$

Inserting Eq. (2.20) into Eq. (2.14), we get the discrete wavelet transform (DWT):

$$\omega_{j,k} = \int_{-\infty}^{\infty} x(t)\psi_{j,k}(t)\,dt \tag{2.21}$$

The original signal is recovered by the inverse DWT, or the wavelet series expansion

$$x(t) = \sum_{j=-\infty}^{\infty}\sum_{k=-\infty}^{\infty} \omega_{j,k}\psi_{j,k}(t) \tag{2.22}$$

where $\psi_{j,k}(t)$ is a set of orthonormal basis functions. The wavelet series expansion characterizes the sum over two indices, $j$ and $k$, that are related to scaling and sliding of the basis functions $\psi_{j,k}(t)$.

Here, we present a new concept known as the scaling function that simplifies the application and calculation of the DWT. The calculation of the finest resolution is done at first, followed by the calculation of the coarser resolutions by means of a smoothed form of the original waveform rather than the original waveform itself. This smoothed form is obtained employing the scaling function, which is sometimes called the smoothing function (Semmlow, 2004; Subasi, 2019).

## Example 2.11

The following Python code is used to extract the ECG signal features utilizing discrete wavelet transform (DWT) with 6-level decomposition. It prints and then plots the approximate and detailed coefficients.

```
# =====================================================================
# =====================================================================
# Discrete wavelet transform
# =====================================================================
#
# Created on Sat Sep 14 23:20:26 2019
#
# @author: asubasi
# =====================================================================
print(__doc__)

import numpy as np
import matplotlib.pyplot as plt
```

```
from scipy import signal
from scipy.misc import electrocardiogram

ecg = electrocardiogram()
fs = 360
time = np.arange(ecg.size) / fs
plt.plot(time, ecg)
plt.xlabel("time in s")
plt.ylabel("ECG in mV")
plt.xlim(9, 10.2)
plt.ylim(-1, 1.5)
plt.show()
#%%

import numpy as np
import matplotlib.pyplot as plt

import pywt
import pywt.data

ecg = pywt.data.ecg()
mode = pywt.Modes.sp1DWT = 1
#db1 = pywt.Wavelet('db1')
waveletname = 'db1'
#waveletname = 'sym5'
coeff = pywt.wavedec(ecg, waveletname, level = 6)
cA6,cD6,cD5,cD4, cD3, cD2, cD1 = coeff

print('cA1\n',cD1)
print('cA2\n',cD2)
print('cA3\n',cD3)
print('cA4\n',cD4)
print('cA5\n',cD5)
print('cD5\n',cD6)
print('cD5\n',cA6)
fig, ax = plt.subplots(figsize = (6,1))
ax.set_title("Original ECG Signal: ")
ax.plot(ecg)
plt.show()

#%%
fig, axarr = plt.subplots(nrows = 7, ncols = 1, figsize = (9,9))
axarr[0].plot(cD1, 'r')
axarr[0].set_ylabel("cD1", fontsize = 14, rotation = 90)

axarr[1].plot(cD2, 'r')
axarr[1].set_ylabel("cD2", fontsize = 14, rotation = 90)
axarr[2].plot(cD3, 'r')
axarr[2].set_ylabel("cD3", fontsize = 14, rotation = 90)
```

```
axarr[3].plot(cD4, 'r')
axarr[3].set_ylabel("cD4", fontsize = 14, rotation = 90)

axarr[4].plot(cD5, 'r')
axarr[4].set_ylabel("cD5", fontsize = 14, rotation = 90)

axarr[5].plot(cD6, 'r')
axarr[5].set_ylabel("cD6", fontsize = 14, rotation = 90)

axarr[6].plot(cA6, 'r')
axarr[6].set_ylabel("cA6", fontsize = 14, rotation = 90)

axarr[1].set_yticklabels([])
axarr[0].set_title("Coefficients", fontsize = 14)
plt.tight_layout()
plt.show()
```

#### *2.2.11.3 The stationary wavelet transform (SWT)*

The stationary wavelet transform (SWT) calculates all the decimated discrete wavelet transforms (DWTs) for a given signal at one time. More specifically, for level 1, the SWT is accomplished by convolving the signal with the suitable filters as in the DWT but without using down-sampling. Then the detail and approximation coefficients at level 1 will be the same as the signal length. The general step j convolves the approximation coefficients at level j −1, with suitable filters without down-sampling, to yield the detail and approximation coefficients at level j (Zhang et al., 2015).

DWT is a decomposition of the signal x(t) that can be considered as a successive band-pass filtering and down-sampling; $x(t) = x_0(t)$ is decomposed into two parts: $y_1(t)$ presents the high frequent parts of $x_0(t)$ and $x_1(t)$ presents the low frequent parts. The DWT is computationally faster and can be realized by consecutive filter banks. Unfortunately, the DWT is not shift-invariant once employed with discrete time series x(t). If the input time series x(t) is shifted, the resulting coefficients may become totally different. The stationary wavelet transform (Nason & Silverman, 1995) has no such issues. Mainly, the SWT is DWT, but the down-sampling step is replaced by an up-sampling (Sudakov et al., 2017; Subasi, 2019).

### Example 2.12

The following Python code is used to extract the ECG signal features utilizing stationary wavelet transform (SWT) with 5-level decomposition. It prints and then plots the approximate and detailed coefficients.

```
# ===================================================================
# Stationary wavelet transform
# ===================================================================
"""
Created on Sat Sep 14 23:20:26 2019
@author: asubasi
"""
print(__doc__)
```

```
import numpy as np
import matplotlib.pyplot as plt
from scipy import signal
from scipy.misc import electrocardiogram

ecg = electrocardiogram()
fs = 360
time = np.arange(ecg.size) / fs
plt.plot(time, ecg)
plt.xlabel("time in s")
plt.ylabel("ECG in mV")
plt.xlim(9, 10.2)
plt.ylim(-1, 1.5)
plt.show()
#%%

import pywt
import matplotlib.pyplot as plt
import numpy as np

#db1 = pywt.Wavelet('db1')
waveletname = 'db1'
#waveletname = 'sym5'
coeffs = pywt.swt(ecg, waveletname, level = 5)
print('cA1\n',coeffs[0][0])
print('cA2\n',coeffs[1][0])
print('cA3\n',coeffs[2][0])
print('cA4\n',coeffs[3][0])
print('cA5\n',coeffs[4][0])

print('cD5\n',coeffs[4][1])
print('cD4\n',coeffs[3][1])
print('cD3\n',coeffs[2][1])
print('cD2\n',coeffs[1][1])
print('cD1\n',coeffs[0][1])

fig, ax = plt.subplots(figsize = (6,1))
ax.set_title("Original ECG Signal: ")
ax.plot(ecg)
plt.show()

#%%
fig, axarr = plt.subplots(nrows = 5, ncols = 2, figsize = (6,6))

axarr[0, 0].plot(coeffs[0][0], 'r')
axarr[0, 1].plot(coeffs[0][1], 'g')
axarr[0, 0].set_ylabel("Level {}".format(1), fontsize = 14, rotation = 90)
axarr[1, 0].plot(coeffs[1][0], 'r')
axarr[1, 1].plot(coeffs[1][1], 'g')
```

```
axarr[1, 0].set_ylabel("Level {}".format(2), fontsize=14, rotation=90)

axarr[2, 0].plot(coeffs[2][0], 'r')
axarr[2, 1].plot(coeffs[2][1], 'g')
axarr[2, 0].set_ylabel("Level {}".format(3), fontsize=14, rotation=90)

axarr[3, 0].plot(coeffs[3][0], 'r')
axarr[3, 1].plot(coeffs[3][1], 'g')
axarr[3, 0].set_ylabel("Level {}".format(4), fontsize=14, rotation=90)

axarr[4, 0].plot(coeffs[4][0], 'r')
axarr[4, 1].plot(coeffs[4][1], 'g')
axarr[4, 0].set_ylabel("Level {}".format(5), fontsize=14, rotation=90)

axarr[1, 0].set_yticklabels([])
axarr[0, 0].set_title("Approximation coefficients", fontsize=14)
axarr[0, 1].set_title("Detail coefficients", fontsize=14)
axarr[0, 1].set_yticklabels([])
plt.tight_layout()
plt.show()
```

#### 2.2.11.4 The wavelet packet decomposition (WPD)

The wavelet transform achieves better time resolution of a signal by decomposing it into a set of basic functions. The wavelet packet decomposition (WPD) is identified as the extension of the DWT, in which the low frequency components—namely, approximations—are decomposed. On the other hand, WPD uses both the approximations (low frequency components) and the details (high-frequency components) (Daubechies, 1990; Learned & Willsky, 1995; Unser & Aldroubi, 1996). DWT and WPD differ from each other since WPD splits both the low and high-frequency components into their sublevels. Consequently, WPD produces an enhanced frequency resolution for a decomposed signal. WPD is considered as a continuous time wavelet transform, which is established at various frequencies at each scale or level. The wavelet packet decomposition is helpful to combine different levels of decomposition for building the original signal (Kutlu & Kuntalp, 2012). The decomposition of WPD is realized in two steps. In the first step, the filter/down-sampling cascade is modified. In the WPD structure at each level of the cascade both branches (approximation and detailed coefficients) are further filtered and down-sampled. In the second step, the tree is modified such that the most appropriate decomposition of a given signal is chosen, applying an entropy-based criterion. This procedure is known as pruning of a decomposition tree (Blinowska & Zygierewicz, 2011; Subasi, 2019).

**Example 2.13**

The following Python code is used to extract the ECG signal features utilizing wavelet packed decomposition (WPD) with 5-level decomposition. Then it plots the approximate and detailed coefficients.

```
#================================================================
# Wavelet packed decomposition (WPD)
#================================================================
```

```
"""
Created on Sat Sep 14 23:20:26 2019
@author: asubasi
"""'

print(__doc__)

import numpy as np
import matplotlib.pyplot as plt

from scipy import signal
from scipy.misc import electrocardiogram

ecg = electrocardiogram()
fs = 360
time = np.arange(ecg.size) / fs
plt.plot(time, ecg)
plt.xlabel("time in s")
plt.ylabel("ECG in mV")
plt.xlim(9, 10.2)
plt.ylim(-1, 1.5)
plt.show()
#%%
import pywt
import matplotlib.pyplot as plt
import numpy as np

#waveletname = 'db1'
waveletname = pywt.Wavelet('db1')
fig, ax = plt.subplots(figsize = (6,1))
ax.set_title("Original ECG Signal: ")
ax.plot(ecg)
plt.show()

fig, axarr = plt.subplots(nrows = 5, ncols = 2, figsize = (6,6))
wp= pywt.WaveletPacket(ecg, waveletname, mode = 'symmetric', maxlevel = 6)
axarr[0, 0].plot(wp['a'].data, 'r')
axarr[0, 1].plot(wp['d'].data, 'g')
axarr[0, 0].set_ylabel("Level {}".format(1), fontsize = 14, rotation = 90)

axarr[1, 0].plot(wp['aa'].data, 'r')
axarr[1, 1].plot(wp['dd'].data, 'g')
axarr[1, 0].set_ylabel("Level {}".format(2), fontsize = 14, rotation = 90)

axarr[2, 0].plot(wp['aaa'].data, 'r')
axarr[2, 1].plot(wp['ddd'].data, 'g')
axarr[2, 0].set_ylabel("Level {}".format(3), fontsize = 14, rotation = 90)
```

```
axarr[3, 0].plot(wp['aaaa'].data, 'r')
axarr[3, 1].plot(wp['dddd'].data, 'g')
axarr[3, 0].set_ylabel("Level {}".format(4), fontsize=14, rotation=90)

axarr[4, 0].plot(wp['aaaaa'].data, 'r')
axarr[4, 1].plot(wp['ddddd'].data, 'g')
axarr[4, 0].set_ylabel("Level {}".format(5), fontsize=14, rotation=90)

axarr[1, 0].set_yticklabels([])
axarr[0, 0].set_title("Approximation coefficients", fontsize=14)
axarr[0, 1].set_title("Detail coefficients", fontsize=14)
axarr[0, 1].set_yticklabels([])
plt.tight_layout()
plt.show()
```

## 2.3 Dimension reduction

Dimension reduction is a process to reduce the dimension of the original feature vector, while keeping the most distinctive information and removing the remaining unrelated information, for decreasing the computational time in a classifier (Phinyomark et al., 2013). Most of the feature extraction approaches produce redundant features. Actually, to enhance the performance of a classifier and accomplish a minimum classification error, some types of feature selection/reduction approaches, which yield a new set of features, should be used. Numerous techniques are used for dimension reduction and feature selection to accomplish a better classification accuracy (Wołczowski & Zdunek, 2017). In feature selection and dimension reduction, the minimum subset of features must be chosen from the original set of features that realizes the maximum generalization ability. To realize this, the generalization ability of a subset of features must be estimated during the process of feature selection (Abe, 2010; Subasi, 2019).

The dimension of data may be needed to analyze the data to accomplish more accurate results. A small number of parameters are used to reduce the dimension of the data in different ways. Moreover, the features or dimensions must be minimized for realizing better classification accuracy. For example, the wavelet-based time frequency approaches generate wavelet coefficients to describe the distribution of a signal energy in both time and frequency domains, and they describe the biomedical signals with a set of wavelet coefficients. As the wavelet-based feature extraction tools yield the feature vector that has too big of a size to be employed as an input to a classifier, a dimension reduction technique should be utilized to extract a smaller number of features from the wavelet coefficients. Recently various dimension reduction methods, such as Lyapunov exponents, low or higher-order statistics, and entropies, have been employed for dimension reduction. Approximate entropy, which is a measure of complexity, can be applied to a noisy dataset and is superior to spectral entropy, Kolmogorov–Sinai entropy, and fractal dimension. Sample entropy presents less dependence on data length. Fuzzy entropy is another measure for complexity and originated from the fuzzy set theory. Another way of reducing dimension is to employ first, second, third, and fourth-order statistics of the sub-bands; the reduced feature set is calculated from the sub-bands of the time-frequency decomposition (Subasi, 2019).

Dimension reduction is another alternative to feature selection; for instance, principal component analysis (PCA) is used efficiently in various studies. Like feature selection it yields a low-dimensional representation, which helps to create lower capacity predictors to improve generalization. But unlike feature selection it may keep information from all the original input variables. In essence, these methods are purely unsupervised, and they may remove low variance variations that are highly predictive of the target label or keep some with high variance but are irrelevant for the classification task at hand. It is possible to combine dimension reduction with a feature extraction algorithm to be utilized on the reduced dimensions in order to select those most appropriate for classification or vice versa (Bengio et al., 2006; Subasi, 2019).

Generally, a subset of the original feature set can achieve better classification accuracy than if all the features were used. The reason is that the existence of redundant features with reduced discriminative power may confuse the classifier. Thus the feature selection is of ultimate significance in producing a more accurate model. There are numerous existing methods for feature selection of an optimal set of features to describe the problem (Begg et al., 2008; Subasi, 2019).

Feature extraction transforms the data in the high-dimensional space to a lower dimensional space. The data transformation may be linear, as in principal component analysis (PCA), but many nonlinear dimension reduction techniques also exist. Dimension reduction can be done by linear discriminant analysis, principal component analysis, independent component analysis, etc. These approaches will be defined to make our understanding clear about dimension reduction. For two-dimensional non-Gaussian data set, PCA extracts component with maximal variance and ICA extracts component with maximal independence. ICA considers signal elements as random variables with Gaussian distribution and minimized second-order statistics. Clearly, for any non-Gaussian distribution, largest variances would not correspond to PCA basis vectors. ICA minimizes both second-order and higher-order dependencies in the input data and attempts to find the basis for which the data (when projected onto them) are statistically independent. LDA finds the vectors in the underlying space that best discriminate among classes (Delac et al., 2005; Subasi, 2019).

Dimension reduction is a method for taking data from a high-dimensional space and mapping it into a new space that has considerably less dimension. This procedure is directly relevant to the idea of compression. There are many reasons to reduce the dimension of the data. First, high-dimensional data require computational challenges. Furthermore, in some circumstances high dimensionality may lead to poor generalization abilities of the learning algorithm. Finally, dimension reduction can be employed for interpretability of the data, for finding meaningful structure of the data, and for illustration purposes. In this chapter, popular dimension reduction techniques are described. In these techniques, the reduction is accomplished by using a linear transformation to the original data (Shalev-Shwartz & Ben-David, 2014).

Large datasets, as well as data containing many features, produce computational problems in the training of predictive models. Methods for reducing the *data dimension* of a dataset, such as $K$-means clustering, reduces the *feature dimension*, or number features, of a dataset. A conventional approach for dimension reduction, principal component analysis (PCA), often utilized for general data analysis is a comparatively poor tool for reducing the feature dimension of predictive modeling data. However, PCA shows a fundamental mathematical archetype, the *matrix factorization*, which offers a valuable way of organizing our thinking about a wide collection of significant learning models (Watt, Borhani, & Katsaggelos, 2016).

Once we start extracting features or attributes from raw data samples, sometimes feature space contains huge numbers of features. This causes various challenges, including analyzing and visualizing data with thousands or millions of features that make the feature space very complex, causing problems related to training models, memory, and space constraints. This is known as the "curse of dimensionality." Unsupervised techniques can also be utilized in these circumstances in which we reduce the number of features or attributes for each data sample. These techniques decrease the number of feature variables by extracting or selecting a set of principal or representative features. There are numerous popular algorithms available for dimensionality reduction, such as principal component analysis (PCA), nearest neighbors, and discriminant analysis (Sarkar, Bali, & Sharma, 2018).

### 2.3.1 Feature construction and selection

New features can be constructed from different original features. A new feature can be built from two Boolean or categorical features by producing their Cartesian product. When the new features have been produced it is easy to choose an appropriate subset of them before learning. This will speed up learning and prevent overfitting. There are many methods for feature selection. The *filter* method scores features utilizing a specific metric, and then the top-scoring features are chosen. Several metrics can be employed for feature scoring, such as information gain, the $\chi 2$ statistic, and the correlation coefficient. The main disadvantage of a simple filter method is not to take into account a redundancy between features. Moreover, feature filters do not distinguish dependencies among features since they are uniquely dependent on marginal distributions (Flach, 2012).

*Feature selection* is concerned with finding $k$ of the $d$ dimensions, which give us the most informative features, and we discard the other $(d - k)$ dimensions. In *subset selection*, we are concerned about finding the best subset of the set of features. The best subset includes the least number of dimensions, which contribute to accuracy the most. The remaining, unimportant dimensions will be discarded. A suitable error function can be utilized in both classification and regression problems. There are two main approaches. *Forward selection* starts with no variables and adds them one by one, at each step adding the one that decreases the error the most until any further additions do not decrease the error. *Backward selection* starts with all variables and removes them one by one, at each step removing the one that decreases the error the most until any further removal increases the error significantly. In both cases, checking the error has to be done on a validation set apart from the training set since the general accuracy will be tested. Usually lower training error is achieved with more features, but not necessarily lower validation error. To decrease complexity, we may decide to remove a feature if its elimination produces only a minor increase in error. Subset selection is supervised in that outputs are employed by the classifier or regressor to evaluate the error, but it can be utilized with any classification or regression method (Alpaydin, 2014).

### 2.3.2 Univariate feature selection

Univariate feature selection performs feature selection by selecting the best features based on univariate statistical tests. It is a preprocessing step to an estimator. Scikit-learn implements feature selection routines as objects that implement the transform method.

- **SelectKBest** removes all but the k highest-scoring features.
- **SelectPercentile** removes all but a user-specified, highest-scoring percentage of features.
- These use common univariate statistical tests for each feature: false positive rate **SelectFpr**, false discovery rate **SelectFdr**, or family wise error **SelectFwe**.
- **GenericUnivariateSelect** allows univariate feature selection with a configurable strategy. This allows selection of the best univariate selection strategy with hyper-parameter search estimator.

These objects take as input a scoring function that returns univariate scores and p-values (or only scores for **SelectKBest** and **SelectPercentile**):

- For regression: f_regression, mutual_info_regression
- For classification: chi2, f_classif, mutual_info_classif

The methods based on F-test estimate the degree of linear dependency between two random variables. On the other hand, mutual information methods can capture any kind of statistical dependency, but being nonparametric, they require more samples for accurate estimation (scikit-learn, n.d.).

#### Example 2.14

The following Python code is used to represent the feature selection process, which is realized in scikit-learn. In this example we utilize the Iris dataset, which exists in sklearn.datasets and select features using sklearn.feature_selection.SelectKBest. The number of features are determined by k value, and there are two in this example. Note that this example is adapted from Python–scikit-learn.

```
# ==========================================================================
# Univariate feature selection
# ==========================================================================
"""
Created on Sat Sep 14 23:20:26 2019
@author: asubasi
"""


from sklearn.datasets import load_iris
from sklearn.feature_selection import SelectKBest
from sklearn.feature_selection import chi2
iris = load_iris()
X, y = iris.data, iris.target
print(X)
```

```
X.shape

#%%
X_new = SelectKBest(chi2, k = 2).fit_transform(X, y)
print(X_new)
X_new.shape
```

**Example 2.15**

The following Python code is showing univariate feature selection process, which is realized in scikit-learn. In this example we utilize the Breast Cancer dataset, which exists in sklearn.datasets, and select features using sklearn.feature_selection.SelectPercentile and sklearn.feature_selection.f_classif. Note that this example is adapted from Python–scikit-learn. Noisy (noninformative) features are added to the Breast Cancer data and univariate feature selection is utilized. For every feature, the p-values for the univariate feature selection and the corresponding weights of an SVM are plotted. The univariate feature selection chooses the informative features, and these have larger SVM weights. Among the total sets of features, only the first four features are important and informative, and they have the highest score with univariate feature selection. The SVM assigns a bigger weight to one of these features but also chooses many of the noninformative features. Utilizing univariate feature selection before the SVM raises the SVM weight attributed to the important and informative features accordingly improves the performance.

```
# ==================================================================
# Univariate feature selection
# ==================================================================
"""
Created on Fri Oct 4 00:16:28 2019
@author: asubasi
"""

print(__doc__)

import numpy as np
import matplotlib.pyplot as plt

from sklearn import datasets, svm
from sklearn.feature_selection import SelectPercentile, f_classif
# ######################################################################
#######
# Import some data to play with

# The Breast Cancer dataset
Breast_Cancer = datasets.load_breast_cancer()
# Some noisy data not correlated
E = np.random.uniform(0, 0.1, size = (len(Breast_Cancer.data), 20))
```

```
# Add the noisy data to the informative features
X = np.hstack((Breast_Cancer.data, E))
y = Breast_Cancer.target
plt.figure(1)
plt.clf()
X_indices = np.arange(X.shape[-1])
# ######################################################################
#######
# Univariate feature selection with F-test for feature scoring
# We use the default selection function: the 10% most significant features
selector = SelectPercentile(f_classif, percentile = 10)
selector.fit(X, y)
scores = -np.log10(selector.pvalues_)
scores /= scores.max()
plt.bar(X_indices - .45, scores, width = .2,
  label = r'Univariate score ($-Log(p_{value})$)', color = 'darkorange',
  edgecolor = 'black')
# ######################################################################
#######
# Compare to the weights of an SVM
clf = svm.SVC(kernel = 'linear')
clf.fit(X, y)

svm_weights = (clf.coef_ ** 2).sum(axis = 0)
svm_weights /= svm_weights.max()

plt.bar(X_indices - .25, svm_weights, width = .2, label = 'SVM weight',
                 color = 'navy', edgecolor = 'black')

clf_selected = svm.SVC(kernel = 'linear')
clf_selected.fit(selector.transform(X), y)

svm_weights_selected = (clf_selected.coef_ ** 2).sum(axis = 0)
svm_weights_selected /= svm_weights_selected.max()

plt.bar(X_indices[selector.get_support()] - .05, svm_weights_selected,
  width = .2, label = 'SVM weights after selection', color = 'c',
  edgecolor = 'black')

plt.title("Comparing feature selection")
plt.xlabel('Feature number')
plt.yticks(())
plt.axis('tight')
plt.legend(loc = 'upper right')
plt.show()
```

## Example 2.16

The following Python code is showing univariate feature selection process, which is realized in scikit-learn. In this example we utilize the breast cancer dataset, which exists in sklearn.datasets. We show how to perform univariate feature selection before running SVC (support vector classifier) to enhance the model performance. It is seen from the figure that our model achieves best performance when all of the features are utilized. Note that this example is adapted from Python–scikit-learn.

```
#=========================================================================
# SVM-Anova: SVM with univariate feature selection
#=========================================================================
"""
Created on Fri Oct 4 14:24:39 2019
@author: asubasi
"""
print(__doc__)
import numpy as np
import matplotlib.pyplot as plt
from sklearn.feature_selection import SelectPercentile, chi2
from sklearn.model_selection import cross_val_score
from sklearn.pipeline import Pipeline
from sklearn.preprocessing import StandardScaler
from sklearn.svm import SVC
from sklearn import datasets
# #######################################################################
#######
# Import some data to play with

Breast_Cancer = datasets.load_breast_cancer()
X = Breast_Cancer.data
y = Breast_Cancer.target

# #######################################################################
#######
# Create a feature-selection transform, a scaler and an instance of SVM
that we
# combine together to have an full-blown estimator
clf = Pipeline([('anova', SelectPercentile(chi2)),
                ('scaler', StandardScaler()),
               ('svc', SVC(gamma = "auto"))])
# #######################################################################
#######
# Plot the cross-validation score as a function of percentile of features
score_means = list()
score_stds = list()
percentiles = (1, 3, 6, 10, 15, 20, 30, 40, 60, 80, 100)
```

```
for percentile in percentiles:
  clf.set_params(anova__percentile = percentile)
  this_scores = cross_val_score(clf, X, y, cv = 5)
  score_means.append(this_scores.mean())
  score_stds.append(this_scores.std())

plt.errorbar(percentiles, score_means, np.array(score_stds))
plt.title(
    'Performance of the SVM-Anova varying the percentile of features
selected')
plt.xticks(np.linspace(0, 100, 11, endpoint = True))
plt.xlabel('Percentile')
plt.ylabel('Accuracy Score')
plt.axis('tight')
plt.show()
```

### 2.3.3 Recursive feature elimination

For a machine learning model, which designates weights to features (e.g., the coefficients of a linear model), recursive feature elimination (RFE) is utilized to select features by recursively considering smaller and smaller sets of features. At first the machine learning model is trained on the initial set of features, and the significance of each feature is taken either through a coef_ attribute or through a feature_importances_ attribute. Then, the least informative

**Example 2.17**

The following Python code is used to represent the recursive feature elimination with cross-validation process, which is realized in scikit-learn. In this example we utilize the Breast Cancer dataset, which exists in sklearn.datasets and select features using sklearn.feature_selection.RFECV, and we use a recursive feature elimination with automatic tuning of the number of features selected with cross-validation. RFECV performs RFE in a cross-validation loop to find the optimal number of features. Note that this example is adapted from Python–scikit-learn.

```
# ======================================================================
# Recursive feature elimination with cross-validation
# ======================================================================
"""
Created on Thu Oct 3 23:42:44 2019
```

```
@author: asubasi
"""
print(__doc__)
import matplotlib.pyplot as plt
from sklearn.svm import SVC
from sklearn.model_selection import StratifiedKFold
from sklearn.feature_selection import RFECV
from sklearn.datasets import load_breast_cancer
Breast_Cancer = load_breast_cancer()

X = Breast_Cancer.data
y = Breast_Cancer.target

# Create the RFE object and compute a cross-validated score.
svc = SVC(kernel = "linear")
# The "accuracy" scoring is proportional to the number of correct
# classifications
rfecv = RFECV(estimator = svc, step = 1, cv = StratifiedKFold(2),
        scoring = 'accuracy')
rfecv.fit(X, y)

print("Optimal number of features : %d" % rfecv.n_features_)
# Plot number of features VS. cross-validation scores
plt.figure()
plt.xlabel("Number of features selected")
plt.ylabel("Cross validation score (nb of correct classifications)")
plt.plot(range(1, len(rfecv.grid_scores_) + 1), rfecv.grid_scores_)
plt.show()
```

features are removed from the current set of features. This process is recursively repeated on the pruned set until the optimum number of features are selected (scikit-learn, n.d.).

### 2.3.4 Feature selection from a model

SelectFromModel is a meta-transformer, which can be utilized along with any model that has a coef_ or feature_importances_ attribute after fitting. The features are considered insignificant and deleted if the related coef_ or feature_importances_ values are below the required threshold parameter. Apart from identifying the threshold numerically, there are built-in heuristics for finding a threshold using a string argument. Available heuristics are "mean," "median," and float multiples like "0.1*mean" (scikit-learn, n.d.).

**Example 2.18**

The following Python code is used to represent the feature selection from a model process, which is realized in scikit-learn. In this example we utilize the breast cancer dataset, which exists in sklearn.datasets and select features using sklearn.feature_selection.SelectFromModel. Note that this example is adapted from Python–scikit-learn.

```
# ==================================================================
# Feature selection from a model
# ==================================================================
from sklearn.ensemble import ExtraTreesClassifier
from sklearn.feature_selection import SelectFromModel
from sklearn import datasets
Breast_Cancer = datasets.load_breast_cancer()
X = Breast_Cancer.data
y = Breast_Cancer.target
X.shape
#%%
clf = ExtraTreesClassifier(n_estimators = 50)
clf = clf.fit(X, y)
clf.feature_importances_
model = SelectFromModel(clf, prefit = True)
X_new = model.transform(X)
X_new.shape
```

## 2.3.5 Principle component analysis (PCA)

*Principal component analysis* (*PCA*) is an algebraic feature-building method in which new features are constructed as linear combinations of the given features. The first principal component is specified by the direction of maximum variance in the data; the second principal component is the direction of maximum variance orthogonal to the first component, and so on (Flach, 2012). PCA is an unsupervised technique in that does not utilize the output information, and the criterion is to maximize the variance. The principal component $w_1$ computes the sample after projection on to $w_1$ so that the difference between the sample points becomes most apparent (Alpaydin, 2014). PCA is a subdivision of statistics known as multivariate analysis. As the name implies, multivariate analysis deals with the analysis of multiple variables or measurements. Multivariate data can be denoted in M-dimensional space, where each spatial dimension contains one signal. Generally, multivariate analysis aims to produce results that consider the relationship between the multiple variables, as well as within the variables, and uses tools that work on all the data. The key issue of multivariate analysis is to find transformations of the multivariate data, which produces a smaller dataset. For example, it may include related information in a multidimensional variable, which can be characterized by using less dimensions (i.e., variables), and the reduced set of variables may be more meaningful than the original dataset. Transformations, which reduce the dimension of a multivariable dataset, convert one set of variables into a new set to yield new variables, which are relatively small as compared to the original data. Since the values of these variables are relatively small, they may not comprise much beneficial information to the overall dataset and, hence, can be removed. With a suitable transformation, a big number of variables that contribute only marginally to the total information can be removed. The data transformation used to accomplish a new set of variables is a linear function, as linear transformations are simpler to estimate. As a linear transformation, this procedure can be represented as a rotation and perhaps scaling of the original dataset in M-dimensional space. In PCA, the objective is to transform the dataset to produce a new set of variables (principal components) that are uncorrelated. The aim is to reduce the dimension of the data, not necessarily to produce more meaningful variables. PCA can reduce the number of variables in a dataset without loss of information and find new variables with better meaning. It transforms a set of correlated variables into a new set of uncorrelated variables. If the variables in a dataset are already uncorrelated, PCA is impractical. Furthermore, the principal components are orthogonal and are well-organized in terms of the variability they describe (Semmlow, 2004; Subasi, 2019).

In big datasets with lots of features, it may be more appropriate to find a smaller and more compact feature representation using a feature transformation. One technique is to utilize PCA that employs a projection to the features to yield a reduced representation. Assume that the training set contains $n$ training examples, that is, $X=\{x_1, x_2, ..., x_j\}$, then the algorithm produces principal components $P_k$ that are linear combinations of the original features $\boldsymbol{X}$ (Begg et al., 2008). This can be written as

$$\boldsymbol{Pk} = \boldsymbol{a}_{k1}\boldsymbol{x}_1 + \boldsymbol{a}_{k2}\boldsymbol{x}_2 + ... + \boldsymbol{a}_n\boldsymbol{x}_{kn}. \tag{2.23}$$

where $\sum_i a_{ki}^2 = 1$.

The principal component vectors are formed in a way that are orthogonal to each other and, for this reason, have the highest variance (principal components). Usually, the training data are first normalized to zero mean and unit variance before employing the PCA algorithm (Begg et al., 2008; Subasi, 2019).

Dimension reduction usually transforms a high-dimensional space to a lower-dimensional space with minimum information loss. The process is known as feature extraction. The PCA is a well-known feature extraction method and allows the elimination of the second-order correlation between given random processes. The PCA linearly transforms a high-dimensional input vector into a lower-dimensional one whose components are uncorrelated by computing the eigenvectors of the covariance matrix of the input signal. The PCA normally utilizes the optimization of some information criterion, such as the maximization of the variance of the projected signal or the minimization of the reconstruction error. The goal of the PCA is to extract m orthonormal directions $\mathbf{w}_i \in \mathrm{R}^n$, $i=1, 2, ..., \mathrm{M}$, in the input space that interpret for the minimum variance of the signal. Subsequently, an input vector $\mathrm{x} \in \mathrm{R}^n$ is transformed into a lower M-dimensional space without losing vital intrinsic information. The vector x can be represented by being projected onto the M-dimensional subspace spanned by $\mathbf{w}_i$ using the inner products $\mathbf{x}^T\mathbf{w}_i$. This produces the dimension reduction (Du & Swamy, 2006; Subasi, 2019).

PCA is a method to decompose a multichannel signal into components that are linearly independent, that is, temporally and spatially uncorrelated. The samples from all channels are treated at a given time interval as a point in the space of dimension equal to the number of channels. The original time series can be enhanced as a linear combination of these components to produce a reduction in data dimension by neglecting the smallest variance. PCA can be realized by means of the singular value decomposition (SVD) algorithm (Blinowska & Zygierewicz, 2011). At this step, the PCA is employed to reduce the dimensionality of the dataset and to yield less numbers of uncorrelated variables that are used as features for better classification of data. Generally, the recorded multichannel signals are huge in number, comprehending a large amount of redundant information, and are highly correlated. The PCA is beneficial to transforming a number of correlated variables into a smaller number of uncorrelated variables, termed principal components. The principal components describe the most informative data carried by the original signals to deliver the discriminative information about those signals. Hence, the PCA features work better in different signal classification (Siuly et al., 2016; Subasi, 2019). Feature selection is a practical and universal scheme for reducing the dimension of the feature space once working on predictive modeling problems. Principal component analysis (PCA) is a common dimension reduction technique and works by transforming the data into an appropriate lower-dimensional feature subspace (Watt et al., 2016).

PCA is one of scikit-learn's transformer classes, in which the model using the training data is fitted before both the training data and the test data are transformed utilizing the same model parameters.

### Example 2.19

The following Python code is used to represent the dimension reduction using PCA, which is realized in scikit-learn. In this example we utilize the Iris dataset, which exists in sklearn.datasets, and reduce dimension using sklearn.decomposition.PCA. PCA is utilized to decompose a multivariate dataset in a set of successive orthogonal components, which represent a maximum amount of the variance. In scikit-learn, PCA is implemented as a decomposition object, which is sklearn.decomposition.PCA, and can be employed on new data to project it on these components. PCA centers but does not scale the input data for each feature before utilizing the SVD. The optional parameter whiten = True makes it possible to project the data onto the singular space while scaling each component to unit variance. This is generally helpful if the models downstream make strong assumptions on the isotropy of the signal. Below is an example of the Iris dataset, which is comprised of four features projected on the two dimensions that explain the most variance. Note that this example is adapted from Python–scikit-learn.

```
#=====================================================================
# Principal component analysis (PCA)
#=====================================================================
import matplotlib.pyplot as plt
from sklearn import datasets
from sklearn.decomposition import PCA

iris = datasets.load_iris()
X = iris.data
y = iris.target
target_names = iris.target_names
```

```
pca = PCA(n_components = 2)
X_r = pca.fit(X).transform(X)
# Percentage of variance explained for each components
print('explained variance ratio (first two components): %s'
                   % str(pca.explained_variance_ratio_))
#%%
# ========================================================================
# 2D presentation
# ========================================================================
# Plot the original data points
plt.figure(2, figsize = (6, 5))
plt.clf()
plt.scatter(X[:, 0], X[:, 1], c = y, cmap = plt.cm.Set1,
  edgecolor = 'k')
plt.xlabel('Sepal length')
plt.ylabel('Sepal width')
plt.title('Original data points')
plt.xticks(())
plt.yticks(())

#%%
plt.figure()
colors = ['navy', 'turquoise', 'darkorange']
lw = 2

for color, i, target_name in zip(colors, [0, 1, 2], target_names):
  plt.scatter(X_r[y == i, 0], X_r[y == i, 1], color = color, alpha = .8,
lw = lw,
                 label = target_name)
plt.legend(loc = 'best', shadow = False, scatterpoints = 1)
plt.title('PCA of IRIS dataset')
Below is an example of the iris dataset, which is projected on the 3
dimensions that explain most variance.
#%%
# ========================================================================
# #3D presentation
# ========================================================================
import numpy as np
import matplotlib.pyplot as plt
from sklearn.decomposition import PCA
from sklearn.datasets import load_iris
from mpl_toolkits.mplot3d import Axes3D
from sklearn import preprocessing
```

```
iris = load_iris()
X, y = iris.data, iris.target


X = iris.data
y = iris.target


plt.figure(3, figsize = (8, 6))
plt.clf()


#%%
# Plot the original data points
fig = plt.figure(1, figsize = (6, 5))
ax = Axes3D(fig, elev = -150, azim = 110)
ax.scatter(X[:, 0], X[:, 1], X[:, 2], c = y,
     cmap = plt.cm.Set1, edgecolor = 'k', s = 40)
ax.set_title('Original data points')
ax.set_xlabel('Sepal length')
ax.w_xaxis.set_ticklabels([])
ax.set_ylabel('Sepal width')
ax.w_yaxis.set_ticklabels([])
ax.set_zlabel('Sepal height')
ax.w_zaxis.set_ticklabels([])
plt.show()
#%%
#Transform data
pca = PCA(n_components = 3)
X_PCA = pca.fit(X).transform(X)
# Plot the PCA transformed data points
fig = plt.figure(1, figsize = (6, 5))
ax = Axes3D(fig, elev = -150, azim = 110)
ax.scatter(X_PCA[:, 0], X_PCA[:, 1], X_PCA[:, 2], c = y,
   cmap = plt.cm.Set1, edgecolor = 'k', s = 40)
ax.set_title('PCA of IRIS dataset')
ax.set_xlabel('PCA1')
ax.w_xaxis.set_ticklabels([])
ax.set_ylabel('PCA2')
ax.w_yaxis.set_ticklabels([])
ax.set_zlabel('PCA3')
ax.w_zaxis.set_ticklabels([])
plt.show()
```

### 2.3.6 Incremental PCA

Incremental principal component analysis (IPCA) is naturally employed as an alternative to PCA once the dataset to be decomposed is too large to fit in memory. IPCA constructs a low-rank approximation for the input data utilizing an amount of memory that is independent of the number of input data samples. It is still dependent on the input data features, but changing the batch size allows for control of memory usage. The example given below helps as a visual check that IPCA can find a similar projection of the data to PCA while only processing a few samples at a time (scikit-learn, n.d.)

**Example 2.20**

The following Python code is used to represent the dimension reduction using incremental PCA, which is realized in scikit-learn. In this example we utilize the Breast Cancer dataset, which exists in sklearn.datasets, and reduce dimension using sklearn.decomposition.IncrementalPCA. Incremental PCA is utilized to decompose a multivariate dataset in a set of successive orthogonal components, which represent a maximum amount of the variance. In scikit-learn, PCA is implemented as a decomposition object, which is sklearn.decomposition.IncrementalPCA and can be employed on new data to project it onto these components. Note that this example is adapted from Python–scikit-learn.

```
# ======================================================================
# Incremental PCA with breast cancer dataset
# ======================================================================
import numpy as np
from sklearn.model_selection import train_test_split
from sklearn.decomposition import PCA, IncrementalPCA
from sklearn import datasets
# #######################################################################
#######
# Import some data to play with

Breast_Cancer = datasets.load_breast_cancer()
X = Breast_Cancer.data
y = Breast_Cancer.target

n_components = 2
ipca = IncrementalPCA(n_components = n_components, batch_size = 10)
X_ipca = ipca.fit_transform(X)

pca = PCA(n_components = n_components)
X_pca = pca.fit_transform(X)

colors = ['navy', 'turquoise', 'darkorange']

for X_transformed, title in [(X_ipca, "Incremental PCA"), (X_pca, "PCA")]:
    plt.figure(figsize = (8, 8))
```

```
        for color, i, target_name in zip(colors, [0, 1, 2],
Breast_Cancer.target_names):
       plt.scatter(X_transformed[y == i, 0], X_transformed[y ==
i, 1],
       color = color, lw = 2, label = target_name)
        if "Incremental" in title:
       err = np.abs(np.abs(X_pca) - np.abs(X_ipca)).mean()
       plt.title(title + " of iris dataset\nMean absolute un-
signed error "
        "%.6f" % err)
        else:
       plt.title(title + " of iris dataset")
       plt.legend(loc = "best", shadow = False, scatterpoints = 1)
        plt.axis([-1000, 2000, -500, 500])
plt.show()
```

### 2.3.7 Kernel principal component analysis

Most of the machine learning algorithms can make assumptions about the linear separability of the input data. Nevertheless, if we are dealing with nonlinear problems that can be encountered rather frequently in real-world applications, linear transformation techniques for dimensionality reduction, such as PCA and LDA, may not be the best choice. In this case, a kernelized version of PCA, or kernel PCA, can be more suitable. Using kernel PCA, the data that is not linearly separable can be transformed onto a new, lower-dimensional subspace, which is appropriate for linear classifiers (Raschka, 2015). Scikit-learn has implementation of the kernel PCA class in the sklearn.decomposition submodule. The usage is similar to the standard PCA class, and the kernel can be specified via the kernel parameter.

#### Example 2.21

The following Python code is used to represent the dimension reduction using incremental PCA, which is realized in scikit-learn. In this example we utilize the Iris dataset, which exists in sklearn.datasets, and reduce dimension using sklearn.decomposition.KernelPCA. Kernel PCA is utilized when the data is not linearly separable. The linearly inseparable data can be transformed onto a new, lower-dimensional subspace, which is appropriate for linear classifiers. In scikit-learn, PCA is implemented as a decomposition object, which is sklearn.decomposition.IncrementalPCA, and can be employed on new data to project it on these components. Note that this example is adapted from Python–scikit-learn.

```
# ==================================================================
# Kernel PCA example
# ==================================================================
import matplotlib.pyplot as plt
from sklearn import datasets
from sklearn.decomposition import PCA, KernelPCA
```

```
iris = datasets.load_iris()
X = iris.data
y = iris.target
target_names = iris.target_names

pca = PCA(n_components = 2)
X_pca = pca.fit(X).transform(X)

kpca = KernelPCA(kernel = "rbf", fit_inverse_transform = True, gamma = 10)
X_kpca = kpca.fit_transform(X)

# Percentage of variance explained for each components
print('explained variance ratio (first two components): %s'
  % str(pca.explained_variance_ratio_))
#%%
# Plot the original data points
plt.figure(2, figsize = (8, 6))
plt.clf()

plt.scatter(X[:, 0], X[:, 1], c = y, cmap = plt.cm.Set1,
  edgecolor = 'k')
plt.xlabel('Sepal length')
plt.ylabel('Sepal width')
plt.title('Original data points')
plt.xticks(())
plt.yticks(())

#%%
#Plot PCA applied Iris Data
plt.figure()
colors = ['navy', 'turquoise', 'darkorange']
lw = 2
for color, i, target_name in zip(colors, [0, 1, 2], target_names):
  plt.scatter(X_pca[y == i, 0], X_pca[y == i, 1], color = color, alpha = .8,
lw = lw,
  label = target_name)
plt.legend(loc = 'best', shadow = False, scatterpoints = 1)
plt.title('PCA of IRIS dataset')
#%%
#Plot Kernel PCA applied Iris Data
plt.figure()
for color, i, target_name in zip(colors, [0, 1, 2], target_names):
  plt.scatter(X_kpca[y == i, 0], X_kpca[y == i, 1], alpha = .8, color = color,
    label = target_name)
plt.legend(loc = 'best', shadow = False, scatterpoints = 1)
plt.title('KPCA of IRIS dataset')
plt.show()
```

## 2.3.8 Neighborhood components analysis

Principal component analysis (PCA) is used to identify the combination of principal components, which interpret the most variance in the data. Neighborhood components analysis (NCA) tries to find a feature space such that a stochastic nearest neighbor algorithm will give the best accuracy. Like LDA, it is a supervised method. NCA applies a clustering of the data, which is visually meaningful in spite of the large reduction in dimension. NCA can be utilized to accomplish supervised dimensionality reduction. The input data are projected onto a linear subspace composed of the directions that minimize the NCA objective. The anticipated dimensionality can be set employing the parameter n_components (scikit-learn, n.d.).

### Example 2.22

This example compares different (linear) dimensionality reduction methods applied on the Iris dataset, which exists in sklearn. datasets. The dataset contains 50 samples of each class. Moreover this example compares the dimensionality reduction with PCA (sklearn.decomposition.PCA), sparse PCA (sklearn.decomposi-tion.SparsePCA), and NCA (NeighborhoodComponentsAnalysis) applied on the Iris dataset. PCA is utilized for these data to identify the combination of attributes (principal components, or direc¬tions in the feature space), which comprise the most variance in the data. Here the different samples are plotted on the first two principal components. Sparse PCA is another method, which employs the lasso (elastic net) to produce modified principal components with sparse loadings. NCA tries to find a feature space such that a stochastic nearest neighbor algorithm will give the best accuracy. It is a supervised technique and requires a clustering of the data, which is visually meaningful de¬spite the large reduction in dimension. Note that this example is adapted from Python–scikit-learn. (scikit-learn, n.d.).

```
# ======================================================================
# Dimensionality reduction with PCA, sparse PCA, and NCA
# ======================================================================
import numpy as np
import matplotlib.pyplot as plt
from sklearn import datasets
from sklearn.model_selection import train_test_split
from sklearn.decomposition import PCA
from sklearn.discriminant_analysis import LinearDiscriminantAnalysis
from sklearn.neighbors import (KNeighborsClassifier,
                    NeighborhoodComponentsAnalysis)
from sklearn.pipeline import make_pipeline
from sklearn.preprocessing import StandardScaler
from sklearn.decomposition import SparsePCA

n_neighbors = 3
random_state = 0
```

```
# Load Iris dataset
iris = datasets.load_iris()
X = iris.data
y = iris.target
target_names = iris.target_names
# Split into train/test
X_train, X_test, y_train, y_test = \
    train_test_split(X, y, test_size = 0.5, stratify = y,
            random_state = random_state)

dim = len(X[0])
n_classes = len(np.unique(y))

# Reduce dimension to 2 with PCA
pca = make_pipeline(StandardScaler(),
                PCA(n_components = 2, random_state = random_state))

# Reduce dimension to 2 with Sparce PCA
spca = make_pipeline(StandardScaler(),SparsePCA(n_components = 2,
            normalize_components = True, random_state = 0))
# Reduce dimension to 2 with NeighborhoodComponentAnalysis
nca = make_pipeline(StandardScaler(),
             NeighborhoodComponentsAnalysis(n_components = 2,
                random_state = random_state))

# Use a nearest neighbor classifier to evaluate the methods
knn = KNeighborsClassifier(n_neighbors = n_neighbors)

# Make a list of the methods to be compared
dim_reduction_methods = [('PCA', pca), ('Sparce PCA', spca), ('NCA', nca)]

# plt.figure()
for i, (name, model) in enumerate(dim_reduction_methods):
    plt.figure()
  # plt.subplot(1, 3, i + 1, aspect = 1)

    # Fit the method's model
    model.fit(X_train, y_train)

    # Fit a nearest neighbor classifier on the embedded training set
  knn.fit(model.transform(X_train), y_train)

    # Compute the nearest neighbor accuracy on the embedded test set
  acc_knn = knn.score(model.transform(X_test), y_test)

  # Embed the data set in 2 dimensions using the fitted model
  X_embedded = model.transform(X)
```

```
    # Plot the projected points and show the evaluation score
  plt.scatter(X_embedded[:, 0], X_embedded[:, 1], c=y, s=30, cmap='Set1')
    plt.title("{}, KNN (k={})\nTest accuracy={:.2f}".format(name,
  n_neighbors,
acc_knn))
plt.show()
```

### 2.3.9 Independent component analysis

Independent component analysis (ICA) is a statistical modeling technique as an extension of the PCA. The ICA was originally introduced for blind source separation (BSS) and then modified for dimension reduction and feature extraction. The ICA can be used for BSS, dimension reduction, feature extraction, and signal detection. While the undercomplete ICA can be used for feature extraction, the overcomplete ICA can be used for dimension reduction based on multiscale and redundant basis sets (Du & Swamy, 2006). The idea of ICA is to decompose the signals into their fundamental independent components. The joint source signals are assumed independent from each other, and this notion plays a crucial role in denoising and separating the signals (Sanei & Chambers, 2013; Subasi, 2019).

ICA is a statistical signal processing method that decomposes a multichannel signal into components that are statistically independent. The objective of the ICA is to estimate

$$y - W^T X \tag{2.24}$$

such that the components of y must be statistically independent. The higher-order statistics of the original signals are needed to estimate the signal, rather than the second-order moment or covariance of the samples as used in the PCA. The Cramer–Rao bound is utilized to estimate the source signals in the ICA based on the assumption that all independent components have finite variance (Du & Swamy, 2006). To find the independent components in the light of the central limit theorem, components of least Gaussian distributions should be found. To realize this method, the heuristic, which assumes that the needed independent components should have identical distributions, must be followed (Hyvärinen & Oja, 2000; Subasi, 2019). Independent component analysis is implemented in scikit-learn using the **Fast ICA** algorithm. Since the ICA model does not contain a noise term, for the model to be accurate, whitening can be useful. This can be achieved internally utilizing the whiten argument or manually using one of the PCA variants. It is naturally employed to separate mixed signals (*blind source separation*) (scikit-learn, n.d.)

**Example 2.23**

The following Python code illustrates visually in the feature space a comparison by results utilizing two different component analysis methods, namely PCA and ICA. Representing ICA in the feature space provides the view of "geometric ICA." ICA is an algorithm that finds directions in the feature space related to the projections with high non-Gaussianity. These directions need not be orthogonal in the original feature space, but they are orthogonal in the denoised feature space, where all directions are related to the same variance. PCA, on the other hand, finds orthogonal directions in the raw feature space that are related to directions looking for maximum variance. In this example, independent sources are simulated utilizing a highly non-Gaussian process, with a low number of degrees of freedom (top left figure). They are combined to produce observations (top right figure). In this raw observation space, directions described by PCA are shown by green vectors. The signal is shown in the PCA space, after whitening by the variance related to the PCA vectors (lower left). ICA is responsible for finding a rotation in this space to determine the directions of the largest non-Gaussianity (lower right). Note that this example is taken from Python–scikit-learn.

```
# ==========================================================================
# FastICA on 2D point clouds
# ==========================================================================
# Authors: Alexandre Gramfort, Gael Varoquaux
# License: BSD 3 clause
import numpy as np
import matplotlib.pyplot as plt
from sklearn.decomposition import PCA, FastICA
# ########################################################################
#######
# Generate sample data
rng = np.random.RandomState(42)
S = rng.standard_t(1.5, size = (20000, 2))
S[:, 0] *= 2.

# Mix data
A = np.array([[1, 1], [0, 2]]) # Mixing matrix

X = np.dot(S, A.T) # Generate observations

pca = PCA()
S_pca_ = pca.fit(X).transform(X)

ica = FastICA(random_state = rng)
S_ica_ = ica.fit(X).transform(X) # Estimate the sources

S_ica_ /= S_ica_.std(axis = 0)
# ########################################################################
#######
# Plot results
def plot_samples(S, axis_list = None):
  plt.scatter(S[:, 0], S[:, 1], s = 2, marker = 'o', zorder = 10,
      color = 'steelblue', alpha = 0.5)
       if axis_list is not None:
      colors = ['green', 'red']
       for color, axis in zip(colors, axis_list):
```

```
        axis /= axis.std()
            x_axis, y_axis = axis
            # Trick to get legend to work
            plt.plot(0.1 * x_axis, 0.1 * y_axis, linewidth=2, color=color)
            plt.quiver(0, 0, x_axis, y_axis, zorder=11, width=0.01, scale=6,
            color=color)
            plt.hlines(0, -3, 3)
            plt.vlines(0, -3, 3)
            plt.xlim(-3, 3)
            plt.ylim(-3, 3)
            plt.xlabel('x')
            plt.ylabel('y')
plt.figure()
plt.subplot(2, 2, 1)
plot_samples(S / S.std())
plt.title('True Independent Sources')

axis_list = [pca.components_.T, ica.mixing_]
plt.subplot(2, 2, 2)
plot samples(X / np.std(X), axis_list = axis_list)
legend = plt.legend(['PCA', 'ICA'], loc = 'upper right')
legend.set_zorder(100)

plt.title('Observations')

plt.subplot(2, 2, 3)
plot_samples(S_pca_ / np.std(S_pca_, axis = 0))
plt.title('PCA recovered signals')

plt.subplot(2, 2, 4)
plot_samples(S_ica_ / np.std(S_ica_))
plt.title('ICA recovered signals')

plt.subplots_adjust(0.09, 0.04, 0.94, 0.94, 0.26, 0.36)
plt.show()
```

ICA is utilized to estimate sources given noisy measurements. Imagine three instruments playing instantaneously and three microphones recording the mixed signals. ICA is employed to recover the sources, that is, what is played by each instrument. Notably, PCA fails at recovering our instruments because the relevant signals reflect non-Gaussian processes (scikit-learn, n.d.)

### Example 2.24

**Blind source separation using FastICA:** The following Python code is used to represent dimension reduction using ICA, which is realized in scikit-learn. ICA is employed to evaluate sources given noisy measurements. Imagine three instruments playing simultaneously and three microphones recording the mixed signals. ICA is employed to recover the sources, that is, what is played by each instrument. Notably, PCA fails at recovering our instruments as the associated signals reflect non-Gaussian processes. In this example we utilize the combination of three different signals with an additive noise component and utilize sklearn.decomposition.FastICA to separate sources. In scikit-learn, fast ICA is implemented as a decomposition object, which is sklearn.decomposition. FastICA and can be employed to separate signal sources. Note that this example is adapted from Python–scikit-learn.

```
# ======================================================================
# Blind source separation using FastICA
# ======================================================================
import numpy as np
import matplotlib.pyplot as plt
from scipy import signal
from sklearn.decomposition import FastICA, PCA
# ######################################################################
#######
# Generate sample data
np.random.seed(0)
n_samples = 2000
time = np.linspace(0, 8, n_samples)

s1 = np.sin(2 * time) # Signal 1 : sinusoidal signal
s2 = np.sign(np.sin(3 * time)) # Signal 2 : square signal
s3 = signal.sawtooth(2 * np.pi * time) # Signal 3: saw tooth signal

S = np.c_[s1, s2, s3]
S += 0.2 * np.random.normal(size = S.shape) # Add noise

S /= S.std(axis = 0) # Standardize data
# Mix data
A = np.array([[1, 1, 1], [0.5, 2, 1.0], [1.5, 1.0, 2.0]]) # Mixing matrix
X = np.dot(S, A.T) # Generate observations

# Compute ICA
ica = FastICA(n_components = 3)
S_ = ica.fit_transform(X) # Reconstruct signals
A_ = ica.mixing_ # Get estimated mixing matrix

# We can 'prove' that the ICA model applies by reverting the unmixing.
assert np.allclose(X, np.dot(S_, A_.T) + ica.mean_)
```

```
# For comparison, compute PCA
pca = PCA(n_components = 3)
H = pca.fit_transform(X) # Reconstruct signals based on orthogonal compo-
nents

# ######################################################################
#######

# Plot results
plt.figure(2, figsize = (8, 6))
models = [X, S, S_, H]
names = ['Observations (mixed signal)',
      'True Sources',
      'ICA recovered signals',
      'PCA recovered signals']
colors = ['red', 'steelblue', 'orange']
#colors = ['navy', 'turquoise', 'darkorange']
for ii, (model, name) in enumerate(zip(models, names), 1):
      plt.subplot(4, 1, ii)
      plt.title(name)
      for sig, color in zip(model.T, colors):
      plt.plot(sig, color = color)
plt.subplots_adjust(0.09, 0.04, 0.94, 0.94, 0.26, 0.46)
plt.show()
```

### 2.3.10 Linear discriminant analysis (LDA)

*Linear discriminant analysis* (LDA) is a supervised technique for dimensionality reduction in classification problems.

PCA is extensively employed for feature extraction. As a modification of PCA, kernel PCA has been taking extensive acceptance. As the PCA does not utilize class information, the first principal component is not effectively important for class separation. On the other hand, LDA looks for the axis that maximally splits training data projected on this axis into two classes. Applications of LDA are limited to cases in which each class consists of one cluster, and they are not closely overlapped. By proper selection of kernels and their parameter values, kernel discriminant analysis (KDA) eliminates the limitation of LDA. It can be extended to multi-class problems as well. KDA is utilized as criteria for feature selection and kernel selection as well as feature extraction (Abe, 2010; Subasi, 2019).

Among dimension reduction methods, LDA is well-known and extensively used. LDA aims to maximize the ratio of the between-class scatter and total data scatter in projected space, and the label of each data is needed. Nevertheless, in real applications, the labeled data are rare and unlabeled data are in large quantity, so LDA is difficult to apply under such cases (Subasi, 2019; Wang, Lu, Gu, Du, & Yang, 2016).

## Example 2.25

The following Python code uses LDA for dimension reduction. Below is an example of the iris dataset that consists of four features projected on the two dimensions, which explain most variance. The Iris dataset includes three types of Iris flowers (Setosa, Versicolour, and Virginica) with four attributes: sepal length, sepal width, petal length, and petal width. LDA finds attributes that constitute the most variance "between classes." LDA, in contrast to PCA, is a particularly supervised method using known class labels. In this example we utilize the sklearn.discriminant_analysis.LinearDiscriminantAnalysis to reduce the dimension. In scikit-learn, LDA is implemented as a discriminant_analysis object, which is sklearn.discriminant_analysis.LinearDiscriminantAnalysis and can be employed to reduce the dimension. Note that this example is adapted from Python–scikit-learn.

```
# ==========================================================================
# LDA 2D projection of Iris dataset
# ==========================================================================
import matplotlib.pyplot as plt
from sklearn import datasets
from sklearn.discriminant_analysis import LinearDiscriminantAnalysis

iris = datasets.load_iris()
X = iris.data
y = iris.target
target_names = iris.target_names

lda = LinearDiscriminantAnalysis(n_components = 2)
X_r2 = lda.fit(X, y).transform(X)

# Percentage of variance explained for each components
print('explained variance ratio (first two components): %s'
    % str(lda.explained_variance_ratio_))
#%%
# ==========================================================================
# 2D presentation
# ==========================================================================
# Plot the original Iris data points
plt.figure(2, figsize = (6, 5))
colors = ['turquoise', 'blue', 'red']
for color, i, target_name in zip(colors, [0, 1, 2], target_names):
  plt.scatter(X[y == i, 0], X[y == i, 1], alpha = .8, color = color,
        label = target_name)
plt.legend(loc = 'best', shadow = False, scatterpoints = 1)
plt.title('Original IRIS dataset')
plt.xlabel('Sepal length')
plt.ylabel('Sepal width')
```

```
plt.show()
#%%
#LDA applied Iris Data
plt.figure(2, figsize = (6, 5))
colors = ['turquoise', 'blue', 'red']
for color, i, target_name in zip(colors, [0, 1, 2], target_names):
    plt.scatter(X_r2[y == i, 0], X_r2[y == i, 1], alpha = .8, color = color,
    label = target_name)
plt.legend(loc = 'best', shadow = False, scatterpoints = 1)
plt.title('LDA applied IRIS dataset')
plt.show()
```

### 2.3.11 Entropy

Entropy is a degree of uncertainty. The level of chaos in the data can be calculated using entropy of the system. Higher entropy indicates higher uncertainty and a more chaotic system. Entropy is given as

$$x(n) \int_{\min(x)}^{\max(x)} P_x \log\left(\frac{1}{p_x}\right) dx \tag{2.25}$$

where $p_x$ is the probability density function (PDF) of signal x(n). Generally, the distribution can be a joint PDF once the data channels are jointly treated. Even though this measure is employed for a single-channel signal, it can be easily extended to multichannel or even multidimensional signals. Therefore, normally, the distribution can be a joint PDF once the multichannel signals are jointly treated. On the other hand, the PDF can be replaced by a conditional PDF in places in which the incidence of an event is subject to another event. In this context, the entropy is termed as conditional entropy. Entropy is very susceptible to noise. Noise increases the uncertainty and noisy signals have higher entropy, even if the original signal is well-ordered. Entropy is utilized in the computation of many other beneficial parameters, such as mutual information, negentropy, non-Gaussianity, and Kulback–Leibler divergence. These variables are comprehensively used in the estimation of the degree of nonlinearity of the systems and correspondence of signals (Sanei, 2013).

**Example 2.26**

The following Python code uses entropy and relative entropy for dimension reduction. We will utilize a sample dataset, which is produced randomly and contains four different centers. In this example we utilize the scipy.special.entr to find the entropy of a given vector. In scipy, ***entr*** is implemented as a special object, which is scipy.special.entr and can be employed to calculate the entropy. Similarly, elementwise function scipy.special.rel_entr is utilized for computing the relative entropy.

```
# =====================================================================
# Entropy dimension reduction
# =====================================================================
from matplotlib import pyplot as plt
from sklearn.datasets.samples_generator import make_blobs
from scipy import special

#Create a dataset
X, y = make_blobs(n_samples = 300, centers = 4, cluster_std = 0.60, random_
state = 0)

#%%
# Plot the original data points
plt.figure(2, figsize = (6, 5))
plt.clf()
plt.scatter(X[:, 0], X[:, 1], c = y, cmap = plt.cm.Set1,
        edgecolor = 'k')
plt.xlabel('X')
plt.ylabel('Y')
plt.title('Original data points')
plt.xticks(())
plt.yticks(())

#%%
#Calculate the Entropy of a vector
X_entropy = special.entr(X[:,1])
print('Entropy = ',X_entropy)

#Elementwise function for computing relative entropy
#special.rel_entr(x, y)
X_rel_entr = special.rel_entr(X[:,0], X[:,1])
print('Relative Entropy = ',X_rel_entr)
```

## 2.4 Clustering for feature extraction and dimension reduction

$K$-means clustering reduces the data dimension by finding appropriate representatives or *centroids* for clusters, or groups, of data points. All elements of every cluster are then characterized by their cluster's corresponding centroid. Thus the problem of clustering is partitioning data into clusters with similar characteristics, and with $K$-means especially this characteristic is geometric closeness in the feature space. When this is represented clearly, it can be employed to create a learning problem for an accurate recovery of cluster centroids, dropping the impractical notion. Denoting by **c***k* the centroid of the *k*th cluster and *Sk* the set of indices of the subset of those *P* data points, denoted **x**1 .. . $\mathbf{x}_P$, belonging to this cluster, the points in the *k*th cluster must lie close to its centroid, which might be written mathematically as for all *k* = 1 .. . *K*. These needed relations can be represented more appropriately by first stacking the centroids column-wise into the *centroid matrix*.

$$C = c_1\, c_2 \cdots c_K \tag{2.26}$$

Then designating by **e***k* the *k*th standard basis vector (that is a $K \times 1$ vector with a 1 in the *k*th slot and zeros elsewhere), we may represent $\mathbf{C}_{ek}$ = **c***k*, and hence the relations in Eq. (2.26) may be represented for each *k* as

$$C_{ek} \approx xp \text{ for all } p \in Sk. \tag{2.27}$$

Next, to write these equations even more appropriately we stack the data column-wise into the *data matrix* **X** =$\mathbf{x}_1\ \mathbf{x}_2\ \cdots \mathbf{x}_P$ and produce a $K \times P$ *assignment matrix* **W**. The *p*th column of this matrix, represented as **w***p*, is the standard basis vector related to the cluster to which the *p*th point belongs, that is, **w***p* = **e***k* if $p \in Sk$. With this **w***p* notation we can represent each equation in Eq. (2.27) as **Cw***p* ≈ **x***p* for all $p \in Sk$, or using matrix notation all *K* such relations simultaneously as

$$CW \approx X. \tag{2.28}$$

We can forget the assumption that we know the locations of cluster centroids as well as which points are assigned to them, that is, an accurate depiction of the centroid matrix **C** and assignment matrix **W**. We want to *learn* the correct values for these two matrices. In particular, we know that the ideal **C** and **W** fulfill the compact relationships depicted in Eq. (2.28), that is, that **CW** ≈ **X** or, in other words, that **CW** − **X**2*F* is small while **W** is composed of appropriately selected standard basis vectors associated with the data points to their respective centroids. Note that the aim is nonconvex, and since we cannot minimize over both **C** and **W** at the same time, it is solved via *alternating minimization*, that is, by alternately minimizing the objective function over one of the variables (**C** or **W**) while keeping the other variable fixed (Watt et al., 2016).

## Example 2.27

The following Python code presents K-means clustering. We will utilize the Iris dataset, which includes three types (classes) of Iris flowers (Setosa, Versicolour, and Virginica) with four attributes: sepal length, sepal width, petal length, and petal width. In this example we utilize the sklearn. cluster.KMeans to find the clusters of the Iris dataset. In scikit-learn, K-means is implemented as a cluster object, which is sklearn.cluster.KMeans, and employed to find the clusters. Note that this example is adapted from Python–scikit-learn.

```
# ===========================================================================
# K-means clustering
# ===========================================================================
from sklearn.datasets import load_iris
from sklearn.cluster import KMeans
from sklearn.svm import SVC
import numpy as np
iris = load_iris()
X = iris['data']
y = iris['target']
""''
sklearn.cluster.KMeans(n_clusters = 8,  init = 'k-means + +',  n_init = 10,
max_iter = 300, tol = 0.0001,
precompute_distances = 'auto', verbose = 0, random_state = None, copy_x = True,
n_jobs = None,
algorithm = 'auto')
""''

kmeans = KMeans(n_clusters = 3)
kmeans.fit(X)
y_kmeans = kmeans.predict(X)
plt.scatter(X[:, 0], X[:, 1], c = y_kmeans, s = 50, cmap = 'viridis')
centers = kmeans.cluster_centers_
plt.scatter(centers[:, 0], centers[:, 1], c = 'black', s = 200, alpha = 0.5);
#%%
from sklearn.metrics import pairwise_distances_argmin
def find_clusters(X, n_clusters, rseed = 2):
    # 1. Randomly choose clusters
     rng = np.random.RandomState(rseed)
    i = rng.permutation(X.shape[0])[:n_clusters]
     centers = X[i]

     while True:
       # 2a. Assign labels based on closest center
      labels = pairwise_distances_argmin(X, centers)

     # 2b. Find new centers from means of points
      new_centers = np.array([X[labels == i].mean(0)
                   for i in range(n_clusters)])

    # 2c. Check for convergence
      if np.all(centers == new_centers):
          break
      centers = new_centers
```

```
                    return centers, labels
centers, labels = find_clusters(X, 3)
plt.scatter(X[:, 0], X[:, 1], c = labels,
        s = 50, cmap = 'viridis');

#%%
centers, labels = find_clusters(X, 3, rseed = 0)
plt.scatter(X[:, 0], X[:, 1], c = labels,
          s = 50, cmap = 'viridis');

#%%
labels = KMeans(3, random_state = 0).fit_predict(X)
plt.scatter(X[:, 0], X[:, 1], c = labels,
        s = 50, cmap = 'viridis');
```

## Example 2.28

The following Python code presents Gaussian mixture model for clustering. We will utilize the Breast Cancer dataset, which includes two types (classes) of data (Malign and Benign) with 30 attributes. In this example we utilize the sklearn.mixture.GaussianMixture to find the clusters of the Iris dataset. In scikit-learn, K-means is implemented as a cluster object, which is sklearn.mixture. GaussianMixture and employed to find the clusters. Note that this example is adapted from Python–scikit-learn.

```
# ===========================================================================
# Gaussian mixture model for clustering
# ===========================================================================
import numpy as np
from matplotlib import pyplot as plt
from sklearn import datasets
# ###########################################################################
#######
# Import some data to play with
Breast_Cancer = datasets.load_breast_cancer()
X = Breast_Cancer.data
y = Breast_Cancer.target

from sklearn.mixture import GaussianMixture
gmm = GaussianMixture(n_components = 2).fit(X)
proba = gmm.predict_proba(X)
y_gmm = gmm.predict(X)

plt.scatter(X[:, 0], X[:, 1], c = y_gmm, s = 50, cmap = 'viridis')
centers = gmm.cluster_centers_
plt.scatter(centers[:, 0], centers[:, 1], c = 'black', s = 200, alpha = 0.5);
#%%
from sklearn.metrics import pairwise_distances_argmin
```

```
def find_clusters(X, n_clusters, rseed=2):
    # 1. Randomly choose clusters
    rng = np.random.RandomState(rseed)
    i = rng.permutation(X.shape[0])[:n_clusters]
    centers = X[i]

    while True:
        # 2a. Assign labels based on closest center
        labels = pairwise_distances_argmin(X, centers)
        # 2b. Find new centers from means of points
        new_centers = np.array([X[labels == i].mean(0)
                        for i in range(n_clusters)])

        # 2c. Check for convergence
        if np.all(centers == new_centers):
            break
        centers = new_centers

    return centers, labels

centers, labels = find_clusters(X, 2)
plt.scatter(X[:, 0], X[:, 1], c = labels,
                s = 50, cmap = 'viridis');
#%%
centers, labels = find_clusters(X, 2, rseed = 0)
plt.scatter(X[:, 0], X[:, 1], c = labels,
                s = 50, cmap = 'viridis');
```

## Example 2.29

The following Python code presents the usage of K-means clustering as a feature extractor. We will utilize the Iris dataset, which includes three types (classes) of Iris flowers (Setosa, Versicolour, and Virginica) with four attributes: sepal length, sepal width, petal length, and petal width. In this example we utilize the sklearn.cluster.KMeans to extract the features of the Iris dataset. In scikit-learn, K-means is implemented as a cluster object, which is sklearn.cluster.KMeans and employed to extract the features. Note that this example is adapted from Python–scikit-learn.

```
# ==================================================================
# K-means as a feature extractor
# ==================================================================
from sklearn.model_selection import train_test_split
from sklearn.datasets import load_iris
from sklearn.cluster import KMeans
from sklearn.svm import SVC
import numpy as np
iris = load_iris()
X = iris['data']
y = iris['target']
```

```
#%%
#Classify the original Iris data
Xtrain, Xtest, ytrain, ytest = train_test_split(X, y, test_size = 0.3, ran-
dom_state = 0)
svm = SVC().fit(Xtrain,ytrain)
ypred = svm.predict(Xtest)

#%%
from sklearn import metrics
print('Accuracy:', np.round(metrics.accuracy_score(ytest,ypred),4))
print('Precision:', np.round(metrics.precision_score(ytest,
                 ypred,average = 'weighted'),4))
print('Recall:', np.round(metrics.recall_score(ytest,ypred,
                 average = 'weighted'),4))
print('F1 Score:', np.round(metrics.f1_score(ytest,ypred,
                 average = 'weighted'),4))
#print('AUC:', np.round(metrics.roc_auc_score(ytest, ypred)))
print('Cohen  Kappa  Score:',  np.round(metrics.cohen_kappa_score(ytest,
ypred)))
print('Matthews  Corrcoef:',  np.round(metrics.matthews_corrcoef(ytest,
ypred)))
print('\t\tClassification Report:\n', metrics.classification_report(ypred,
ytest))
#%%
from sklearn.metrics import confusion_matrix
from io import BytesIO #neded for ploting
import seaborn as sns; sns.set()
import matplotlib.pyplot as plt

mat = confusion_matrix(ytest, ypred)
sns.heatmap(mat.T, square = True, annot = True, fmt = 'd', cbar = False)
plt.xlabel('true label')
plt.ylabel('predicted label');

plt.savefig("Confusion.jpg")
# Save SVG in a fake file object.
f = BytesIO()
plt.savefig(f, format = "svg")

#%%
#Extract Features using K-Means and Then Classify
kmeans = KMeans(n_clusters = 10).fit(X)
distances = np.column_stack([np.sum((X - center)**2, axis = 1)**0.5 for
center in kmeans.cluster_centers_])
```

```
Xtrain, Xtest, ytrain, ytest = train_test_split(distances, y, test_
size = 0.3, random_state = 0)
svm = SVC().fit(Xtrain,ytrain)
ypred = svm.predict(Xtest)

#%%
from sklearn import metrics
print('Accuracy:', np.round(metrics.accuracy_score(ytest,ypred),4))
print('Precision:', np.round(metrics.precision_score(ytest,
                 ypred,average = 'weighted'),4))
print('Recall:', np.round(metrics.recall_score(ytest,ypred,
                 average = 'weighted'),4))
print('F1 Score:', np.round(metrics.f1_score(ytest,ypred,
                 average = 'weighted'),4))
#print('AUC:', np.round(metrics.roc_auc_score(ytest, ypred)))
print('Cohen Kappa Score:', np.round(metrics.cohen_kappa_score(ytest,
ypred)))
print('Matthews Corrcoef:', np.round(metrics.matthews_corrcoef(ytest,
ypred)))
print('\t\tClassification Report:\n', metrics.classification_report(ypred,
ytest))
#%%
from sklearn.metrics import confusion_matrix
from io import BytesIO #neded for plot
import seaborn as sns; sns.set()
import matplotlib.pyplot as plt

mat = confusion_matrix(ytest, ypred)
sns.heatmap(mat.T, square = True, annot = True, fmt = 'd', cbar = False)
plt.xlabel('true label')
plt.ylabel('predicted label');

plt.savefig("Confusion.jpg")
# Save SVG in a fake file object.
f = BytesIO()
plt.savefig(f, format = "svg")
```

## Example 2.30

The following Python code presents the usage of Gaussian mixture model as a feature extractor. We will utilize the Breast Cancer dataset, which includes two types (classes) of data (Malign and Benign) with 30 attributes. In this example we utilize the sklearn.mixture.GaussianMixture to extract the features of the Breast Cancer dataset. In scikit-learn, GaussianMixture is implemented as a mixture object, which is sklearn.mixture.GaussianMixture and employed to extract the features. Note that this example is adapted from Python–scikit-learn.

```
# ===========================================================================
# Gaussian mixture model as a feature extractor
# ===========================================================================
from sklearn.model_selection import train_test_split
from sklearn.cluster import KMeans
from sklearn.svm import SVC
import numpy as np
from sklearn import datasets

# ##########################################################################
#######
# Import Breast Cancer data to play with
Breast_Cancer = datasets.load_breast_cancer()
X = Breast_Cancer.data
y = Breast_Cancer.target

#%%
# Classify the original Breast Cancer Dataset
Xtrain, Xtest, ytrain, ytest = train_test_split(X, y, test_size = 0.3, ran-
dom_state = 0)
svm = SVC().fit(Xtrain,ytrain)
ypred = svm.predict(Xtest)

#%%
from sklearn import metrics
print('Accuracy:', np.round(metrics.accuracy_score(ytest,ypred),4))
print('Precision:', np.round(metrics.precision_score(ytest,
                 ypred,average = 'weighted'),4))
print('Recall:', np.round(metrics.recall_score(ytest,ypred,
                 average = 'weighted'),4))
print('F1 Score:', np.round(metrics.f1_score(ytest,ypred,
                 average = 'weighted'),4))
#print('AUC:', np.round(metrics.roc_auc_score(ytest, ypred)))
print('Cohen  Kappa  Score:',  np.round(metrics.cohen_kappa_score(ytest,
ypred)))
print('Matthews  Corrcoef:',  np.round(metrics.matthews_corrcoef(ytest,
ypred)))
print('\t\tClassification Report:\n', metrics.classification_report(ypred,
ytest))
#%%
from sklearn.metrics import confusion_matrix
from io import BytesIO #neded for plot
import seaborn as sns; sns.set()
import matplotlib.pyplot as plt

mat = confusion_matrix(ytest, ypred)
sns.heatmap(mat.T, square = True, annot = True, fmt = 'd', cbar = False)
```

```
plt.xlabel('true label')
plt.ylabel('predicted label');
plt.savefig("Confusion.jpg")
# Save SVG in a fake file object.
f = BytesIO()
plt.savefig(f, format = "svg")

#%%
# Extract Features Using Gaussian Mixture Model and then Classify
from sklearn.mixture import GaussianMixture
gmm = GaussianMixture(n_components = 15).fit(X)
proba = gmm.predict_proba(X)
Xtrain, Xtest, ytrain, ytest = train_test_split(proba, y, test_size = 0.3,
random_state = 0)
svm = SVC().fit(Xtrain,ytrain)
ypred = svm.predict(Xtest)

#%%
from sklearn import metrics
print('Accuracy:', np.round(metrics.accuracy_score(ytest,ypred),4))
print('Precision:', np.round(metrics.precision_score(ytest,
                 ypred,average = 'weighted'),4))
print('Recall:', np.round(metrics.recall_score(ytest,ypred,
                 average = 'weighted'),4))
print('F1 Score:', np.round(metrics.f1_score(ytest,ypred,
                 average = 'weighted'),4))
#print('AUC:', np.round(metrics.roc_auc_score(ytest, ypred)))
print('Cohen  Kappa  Score:',  np.round(metrics.cohen_kappa_score(ytest,
ypred)))
print('Matthews  Corrcoef:',  np.round(metrics.matthews_corrcoef(ytest,
ypred)))
print('\t\tClassification Report:\n', metrics.classification_report(ypred,
ytest))

#%%
from sklearn.metrics import confusion_matrix
from io import BytesIO #neded for plot
import seaborn as sns; sns.set()
import matplotlib.pyplot as plt

mat = confusion_matrix(ytest, ypred)
sns.heatmap(mat.T, square = True, annot = True, fmt = 'd', cbar = False)
plt.xlabel('true label')
plt.ylabel('predicted label');
plt.savefig("Confusion.jpg")
# Save SVG in a fake file object.
f = BytesIO()
plt.savefig(f, format = "svg")
```

## References


Abe, S. (2010). Feature selection and extraction. In Support Vector Machines for Pattern Classification (pp. 331-341). Springer, London, UK.

Alpaydin, E. (2014). *Introduction to machine learning*. Cambridge, MA, London, England: MIT press.

Basseville, M., & Nikiforov, I.V. (1993). Detection of abrupt changes: Theory and application (Vol. 104). Prentice Hall Englewood Cliffs.

Begg, R., Lai, D. T., & Palaniswami, M. (2008). *Computational intelligence in biomedical engineering*. Boca Raton, FL: CRC Press.

Bengio, Y., Delalleau, O., Roux, N., Paiement, J.-F., Vincent, P., & Ouimet, M. (2006). Feature Extraction: Foundations and Applications, chapter Spectral Dimensionality Reduction (pp. 519–550). Springer, Berlin, Heidelberg.

Blinowska, K. J., & Zygierewicz, J. (2011). *Practical biomedical signal analysis using MATLAB®*. Boca Raton, FL: CRC Press.

Bodenstein, G., Schneider, W., & Malsburg, C. (1985). Computerized EEG pattern classification by adaptive segmentation and probability-density-function classification. Description of the method. *Computers in Biology and Medicine*, *15*(5), 297–313.

Daubechies, I. (1990). The wavelet transform, time-frequency localization and signal analysis. *IEEE Transactions on Information Theory*, *36*(5), 961–1005.

Delac, K., Grgic, M., & Grgic, S. (2005). A comparative study of PCA, ICA, and LDA. 99-106.

Du, K. -L., & Swamy, M. (2006). Principal component analysis networks. In *Neural Networks in a Softcomputing Framework* (pp. 295–351). London, UK: Springer.

Flach, P. (2012). *Machine learning: The art and science of algorithms that make sense of data*. Cambridge, UK: Cambridge University Press.

Graimann, B., Allison, B., & Pfurtscheller, G. (2009). Brain–computer interfaces: A gentle introduction. In *Brain-Computer Interfaces* (pp. 1–27). Berlin, Heidelberg: Springer.

Gustafsson, F., & Gustafsson, F. (2000). Adaptive filtering and change detection (Vol. 1). Wiley, New York.

Guyon, I., Gunn, S., Nikravesh, M., & Zadeh, L. (2006). Feature Extraction: Foundations and Applications (Studies in Fuzziness and Soft Computing) Springer. Secaucus, NJ, USA.

Hyvärinen, A., & Oja, E. (2000). Independent component analysis: Algorithms and applications. *Neural Networks*, *13*(4–5), 411–430.

Kay, S. M. (1993). *Fundamentals of statistical signal processing, vol. I: estimation theory*. NJ: Prentice Hall Upper Saddle River.

Kay, S. M., & Marple, S. L. (1981). Spectrum analysis—A modern perspective. *Proceedings of the IEEE*, *69*(11), 1380–1419.

Kevric, J., & Subasi, A. (2017). Comparison of signal decomposition methods in classification of EEG signals for motor-imagery BCI system. *Biomedical Signal Processing and Control*, *31*, 398–406.

Kutlu, Y., & Kuntalp, D. (2012). Feature extraction for ECG heartbeats using higher order statistics of WPD coefficients. *Computer Methods and Programs in Biomedicine*, *105*(3), 257–267.

Learned, R. E., & Willsky, A. S. (1995). A wavelet packet approach to transient signal classification. *Applied and Computational Harmonic Analysis*, *2*(3), 265–278.

Mendel, J. M. (1991). Tutorial on higher-order statistics (spectra) in signal processing and system theory: Theoretical results and some applications. *Proceedings of the IEEE*, *79*(3), 278–305.

Mohri, M., Rostamizadeh, A., & Talwalkar, A. (2018). *Foundations of machine learning*. Cambridge, MA: MIT press.

Nason, G.P., & Silverman, B.W. (1995). The stationary wavelet transform and some statistical applications. In Wavelets and statistics (pp. 281-299). Springer, New York, NY.

Phinyomark, A., Quaine, F., Charbonnier, S., Serviere, C., Tarpin-Bernard, F., & Laurillau, Y. (2013). EMG feature evaluation for improving myoelectric pattern recognition robustness. *Expert Systems with Applications*, *40*(12), 4832–4840.

Proakis, John G., & Manolakis, Dimitris G. (2007). *Digital signal processing: Principles, algorithms and applications*. Englewood Cliffs: Pearson Prentice Hall.

Raschka, S. (2015). *Python machine learning*. Birmingham, UK: Packt Publishing Ltd.

Sanei, S. (2013). *Adaptive processing of brain signals*. West Sussex, UK: John Wiley & Sons.

Sanei, S., & Chambers, J. A. (2013). *EEG signal processing*. West Sussex, UK: John Wiley & Sons.

Sarkar, D., Bali, R., & Sharma, T. (2018). Practical machine learning with Python. A problem-solvers guide to building real-world intelligent systems. Apress, Berkeley, CA.

Scikit-learn: Machine learning in Python—Scikit-learn 0.21.3 documentation. (n.d.). Retrieved September 25, 2019, from https://scikit-learn.org/stable/index.html.

Semmlow, J. (2004). Biosignal and biomedical image processing: MATLAB-based applications. 2004. Marcel Decker. Inc., New York, NY.

Shalev-Shwartz, S., & Ben-David, S. (2014). *Understanding machine learning: From theory to algorithms*. New York, NY: Cambridge University Press.

Siuly, S., Li, Y., & Zhang, Y. (2016). *EEG signal analysis and classification*. Cham, Switzerland: Springer International Publishing.

Sörnmo, L., & Laguna, P. (2005). *Bioelectrical signal processing in cardiac and neurological applications (Vol. 8)*. London, UK: Academic Press.

Stoica, P., & Moses, R. L. (1997). *Introduction to spectral analysis (Vol. 1)*. NJ: Prentice Hall Upper Saddle River.

Subasi, A. (2019). In *Practical guide for biomedical signals analysis using machine learning techniques, a MATLAB based approach* (1st ed.). London, UK: Academic Press, Elsevier Inc.

Sudakov, O., Kriukova, G., Natarov, R., Gaidar, V., Maximyuk, O., Radchenko, S., & Isaev, D. (2017). Distributed system for sampling and analysis of electroencephalograms. *IEEE*, *1*, 306–310.

Unser, M., & Aldroubi, A. (1996). A review of wavelets in biomedical applications. *Proceedings of the IEEE*, *84*(4), 626–638.

Wang, S., Lu, J., Gu, X., Du, H., & Yang, J. (2016). Semi-supervised linear discriminant analysis for dimension reduction and classification. *Pattern Recognition*, *57*, 179–189.

Watt, J., Borhani, R., & Katsaggelos, A. K. (2016). *Machine learning refined: Foundations, algorithms and applications*. Cambridge, UK: Cambridge University Press.

Wołczowski, A., & Zdunek, R. (2017). Electromyography and mechanomyography signal recognition: Experimental analysis using multi-way array decomposition methods. *Biocybernetics and Biomedical Engineering*, *37*(1), 103–113 https://doi.org/10.1016/j.bbe.2016.09.004.

Zhang, Y., Dong, Z., Liu, A., Wang, S., Ji, G., Zhang, Z., & Yang, J. (2015). Magnetic resonance brain image classification via stationary wavelet transform and generalized eigenvalue proximal support vector machine. *Journal of Medical Imaging and Health Informatics*, *5*(7), 1395–1403.

CHAPTER

# 3

# Machine learning techniques

## 3.1 Introduction

A machine learning model is defined using certain parameters to produce a computer program by optimizing the parameters of the model using training data or past experience. Machine learning uses statistical analysis to generate models, as the key goal is to make inferences from the training sample. In some cases, the training algorithm's efficiency may be as critical as the accuracy of its classification. Machine learning techniques are used in various areas as a decision support system (Alpaydin, 2014).

Learning is an interdisciplinary phenomenon that covers many elements of mathematics, statistics, computer science, economics, physics, psychology, and neuroscience. Remarkably, all human activities are not related to intelligence, so there are some places where a machine can behave or respond better. There are some intelligent tasks that humans do not really perform and machines can accomplish better than humans. Nonetheless, because the structural behaviors and decision-making render it important to understand the system response and components for efficient decision-making, classical machine learning models in complex systems may not achieve the required intelligent response. There is a systemic understanding of every behavior, action, or decision. In contrast, from a systematic point of view, each activity can result from some other event or series of events. Those relationships are complicated and hard to comprehend. Two learning characteristics involve learning for predictable behavior in the environment and learning for unpredictable behavior in the system. It is necessary to look at learning concepts and models from the viewpoint of new expectations, because systems and machines are expected to behave intelligently even in a nonpredictive scenarios. These expectations make it essential to learn continuously and from several sources of information. The essential part is the interpretation and adaptation of data for these systems and their efficient application (Kulkarni, 2012).

There are different types of learning techniques utilized for different purposes. Clustering methods can be used to separate and divide samples or objects into a number of classes; the user can only identify and feed the number of clusters into the clustering algorithm. Classification is similar to clustering except that a set of previously labeled data is used to train the classifier. Thus somehow the test data are categorized using the similarity of a category of labeled data. In practice the goal is to find and identify a boundary between two or more classes based on their measured features. There is always an ambiguity about which

Practical Machine Learning for Data Analysis Using Python. http://dx.doi.org/10.1016/B978-0-12-821379-7.00003-5

features are used and how those features are extracted and enhanced in clustering and classification. Over the last decades, many classification algorithms have been suggested. Linear discriminant analysis (LDA), naive Bayes (NB), k-nearest neighbors (k-NN), artificial neural networks (ANNs), support vector machines (SVMs), and decision tree algorithms are the most popular machine learning algorithms. Moreover there are many clustering algorithms, such as k-means, fuzzy c-means, dbscan, and optics, as well (Sanei, 2013; Subasi, 2019).

## 3.2 What is machine learning?

Machine learning is the study of computer algorithms to help formulate accurate predictions and reactions in certain circumstances, or to act intelligently. Generally, machine learning is about learning to create better circumstances in the future based on what was learned in the past. Machines learn from existing information, knowledge, and experience; hence, machine learning is the development of programs that allow us to analyze data from different sources by selecting relevant data and utilizing those data to predict the behavior of the system in similar or different scenarios. Machine learning also classifies objects and activities to support decisions for new input scenarios. The motivation for machine learning is that additional intelligence and learning is needed to address uncertain situations (Kulkarni, 2012).

### 3.2.1 Understanding machine learning

Machine learning became popular in the 1990s once researchers began making it a prominent subfield of artificial intelligence (AI) because algorithms that borrow ideas from probability, statistics, and AI are more successful than fixed, rule-based models that require manual effort. Moreover, machine learning is a multidisciplinary field that has progressively evolved over time and is still evolving. Obviously, it evolved quickly since the 1990s with the discovery of support vector machines, random forests, long short-term memory networks (LSTMs), and the progress of frameworks in both machine and deep learning that include scikit-learn, PyTorch, TensorFlow, and Theano. The rise of intelligent systems, including IBM Watson, DeepFace, and AlphaGo, began recently (Sarkar, Bali, & Sharma, 2018).

### 3.2.2 What makes machines learn?

There are many real-world problems that individuals, companies, and organizations are working to address for their benefit. It is beneficial to train machines under many conditions, and some of them are as follows:

- There is a lack of enough human expertise in a domain.
- Scenarios and behavior are continuously changing.
- People have adequate expertise in a domain, but it is difficult to properly explain or transfer this skill into computational tasks, such as speech recognition, translation, scene recognition, cognitive tasks, and so on.
- Addressing domain-specific issues on a massive scale comprising data with too many dynamic requirements and restrictions.

Such situations are simple examples for which learning machines are more efficient at saving energy, time, and resources than trying to set up intelligent frameworks that can be constrained in efficiency, coverage, scope, and wisdom. With the existence of large volumes of historical data, the machine learning model can be utilized to accomplish tasks by making machines gain sufficient experience in analyzing data patterns over a period of time and then using this experience to solve problems by means of limited, labor-intensive intervention in the future. The main idea remains to solve problems for which machine learning methods can be conceptually easy to define (Sarkar et al., 2018).

The typical machine learning tasks can be described as follows:

- **Classification or categorization**: This characteristically includes a list of tasks or problems for which the machine should use data points or samples and allocate a specific category or class to every sample.
- **Regression**: These kinds of tasks typically include carrying out a prediction in a way that a real numerical value will be the output instead of a class or category for an input data point.
- **Anomaly detection**: This activity includes transferring event logs, transaction reports, and other data points in such a manner as to detect abnormal and anomalous patterns/ events that differ from normal behavior.
- **Structured annotation**: This generally includes doing some analysis on input data points and adding structured metadata as annotations to the original data that describe extra information and relations between the data elements.
- **Translation**: Automated machine translation functions are, of course, the hallmark of machine learning, allowing examples of input data belonging to a particular language to be translated into another language.
- **Clustering or grouping**: Clusters or groups are generally formed from input data samples utilizing machine learning by checking characteristic latent patterns, similarities, and relationships between the input data points themselves. Generally there is a lack of prelabeled or preannotated data for these tasks; hence they form a part of unsupervised machine learning (Sarkar et al., 2018).

### 3.2.3 Machine learning is a multidisciplinary field

Machine learning is generally considered to be a subfield of artificial intelligence, and even a subfield of computer science in some perspectives. Machine learning contains ideas that have been inherited over a period of time and adapted from several disciplines, rendering it a real multidisciplinary and interdisciplinary field. A crucial point to remember is that this is not a comprehensive list of fields or domains but rather a reflection of the key machine learning subject areas. The major fields or domains related to machine learning include the following:

- computer science
- mathematics
- statistics
- artificial intelligence
- data mining

- deep learning
- data science
- natural language processing

*Data science* is an extensive interdisciplinary field spanning all the other fields that are subfields within it. The idea behind data science is using methodologies, algorithms, and techniques to extract information from data and domain knowledge. Concepts of *data mining* and pattern recognition techniques, such as *knowledge discovery of databases* (KDD), developed after relational databases became prominent. These fields concentrate more on the capability and method of extracting information from big datasets. Machine learning derives concepts, which are more related to the analysis phase. *Artificial intelligence* (AI) is a superset involving machine learning as one of its focused areas. The fundamental concept of AI is to develop an intelligence as revealed by machines based on their awareness of their environment and input parameters/attributes and their response to performing anticipated tasks based on expectations. Machine learning generally deals with algorithms and techniques that can be utilized to recognize data, construct representations, and accomplish tasks such as predictions. Another major subfield of AI associated with machine learning is *natural language processing* (NLP), which derives mainly from computer science and computational linguistics. Currently, *text analytics* is a prominent area among data scientists for processing, extracting, and understanding natural human language. *Deep learning* is a subfield of machine learning that deals with methods associated with representative learning to improve data by gaining experience. It employs a hierarchical and layered structure to represent the given input attributes and its current surroundings, utilizing a nested, layered hierarchy of concept representations. Hence machine learning can be utilized to solve real-world problems. This provides us with a decent overview of the broad landscape of the multidisciplinary field of machine learning (Sarkar et al., 2018).

### 3.2.4 Machine learning problem

The problems that require intelligence are contained in the group of machine learning problems. Characteristic problems are face recognition, character recognition, spam filtering, speech recognition, document classification, fraud detection, anomaly detection, stock market forecasting, weather forecasting, and occupancy forecasting. Remarkably, many complex issues that involve decision-making can also be considered problems designed for machine learning. These problems include, for instance, learning from experiences and observations and looking for solutions in both known and unknown search spaces. They comprise the classification of objects and mapping them to decisions and solutions. The classification of any types of objects or events is a machine learning problem (Kulkarni, 2012). Machine learning is extensively utilized in real-world problems that may be impossible to solve by traditional approaches (Sarkar et al., 2018). The real-world applications of machine learning can be classified as follows:

- healthcare data analysis
- anomaly detection
- fraud detection and prevention
- product recommendations in online shopping platforms

- sentiment and emotion analysis
- weather forecasting
- stock market forecasting
- content recommendation
- market basket analysis
- customer segmentation
- speech recognition
- churn prediction
- click-through predictions
- failure/defect detection and prevention
- object and scene recognition in images and video
- e-mail spam filtering

### 3.2.5 Goals of learning

The key objective of machine learning is to produce learning algorithms with practical value. The goals of machine learning are defined as development and improvement of computer algorithms and models to meet decision-making needs in real-world situations. Remarkably, from washing machines and microwave ovens to the automated landing of aircraft, machine learning plays a crucial role in all modern applications and appliances. The era of machine learning has introduced techniques from simple data analysis and pattern recognition to fuzzy logic and inferencing. Since machine learning is data driven and data sources are minimal, and the recognition of useful data is difficult most of the time, the sources provide large piles of data, including significant relationships and correlations between them. Machine learning can extract these relationships, which is an area of data mining applications. The aim of machine learning is to enable the building of intelligent systems that can be employed in solving real-life problems. The complexity of algorithms, the amount and quality of information, the computational power of the computing engine, and the effectiveness and reliability of the system architecture determine the quantity of intelligence. The quantity of intelligence is produced through algorithm development, learning, and evolution (Kulkarni, 2012).

### 3.2.6 Challenges in machine learning

Machine learning is a quickly developing and exciting scientific area with a lot of opportunity and prospect. But it comes with its own set of challenges because of the complicated nature of machine learning algorithms, their dependency on data, and their not being one of the more classical computing models. The following points include some of the main problems of machine learning.

- Problems with data quality lead to problems with data processing and extraction of features.
- Data acquisition, processing, and retrieval are procedures that are very tedious and time-consuming.
- There is a lack of high-quality and sufficient training data in many scenarios.

- Feature extraction, particularly hand-crafting features, is one of the most difficult tasks in machine learning. Recently, deep learning seems to have gained some value in this area.
- Expressing business obstacles evidently, with well-defined objectives and aims, can be problematic.
- Overfitting and underfitting models may lead to poor quality of the model learning configurations and relationships from the training data, leading to detrimental performance.
- The curse of dimensionality can be a real challenge, that is, too many features.
- It is not easy to implement complex models in the real world.

This is not a comprehensive list of challenges faced by machine learning currently, but it is certainly a list of the top issues faced by data scientists and analysts in machine learning projects or tasks, in particular (Sarkar et al., 2018).

## 3.3 Python libraries

Python is a programming language employed across both academia and enterprises to create and utilize machine learning algorithms. We will explain different machine learning techniques, such as *TensorFlow* where we can create neural network–based models on datasets. Moreover, we will explain how to utilize *Keras*, which is a high-level interface to create deep learning models easily and has a concise API, capable of running on top of TensorFlow. In addition, there are many excellent frameworks for deep learning, such as Theano, PyTorch, MXNet, Caffe, and Lasagne (Sarkar et al., 2018).

### 3.3.1 Scikit-learn

Scikit-learn (https://scikit-learn.org/stable/) is one of Python's most popular and crucial machine learning and data science applications for Python (Pedregosa et al., 2011). This applies to a wide range of machine learning algorithms that include key areas of machine learning, such as classification, regression, and clustering. The library incorporated all the standard machine learning algorithms, such as support vector machines, logistic regression, random forests, K-means clustering, and hierarchical clustering, perhaps the cornerstone for practical machine learning. Scikit-learn is mainly implemented with Python, but for achieving better performance some of the core code is implemented in Cython. It also utilizes wrappers around popular implementations of learning algorithms, such as support vector machine and logistic regression. Scikit-learn will be used broadly in subsequent chapters, so the intent here is to become familiar with the structure of the library and its core components (Sarkar et al., 2018). Scikit-learn library is constructed on a rather small and modest list of core API ideas and design patterns. The core APIs of scikit-learn are as follows:

**Dataset representation**: The data representation of most machine learning tasks is relatively similar to one another. In general, a data point collection will be represented by a data point vector stacking; each row in the data characterizes a vector for a particular observation of the data point, called a dataset. A data point vector includes multiple independent variables (or features) and one or more dependent variables.

**Estimators**: The estimator interface is one of the scikit-learn library's most crucial elements. The estimator interface is used by all machine learning algorithms in the package. The learning phase is conducted in a two-step development. The first step is the initialization of the estimator object, which includes choosing the suitable class object for the algorithm and providing the hyperparameters or parameters. The second step is utilizing the fit function to the data provided. The fit function can learn the machine learning algorithm's performance parameters and describe them as the object's general attributes for simple final model examination. The fit function data are normally given as an input-output pair. In addition to the machine learning algorithms, many methods of data transformation are also introduced using the estimator APIs, such as feature scaling and Principal Component Analysis (PCA). It makes it possible to view transformation processes in an appropriate way for simple data transformation and simple mechanisms.

**Predictors**: Using a trained estimator for unknown data the predictor interface is applied to generate predictions, forecasts, etc. For instance, the predictor interface will provide predicted classes for the unknown test set in the case of a supervised learning problem. The predictor interface also includes support for providing measured performance values. A predictor design requirement is for creating a score function that will provide the sample output with a scalar value that will measure the model's performance. In the future, these values will be used to adjust machine learning models.

**Transformers**: It is very common in machine learning to transform input data before creating a model. Many data transformations are modest, for example, replacing missing data with a constant by using a log transformation, whereas some data transformations are similar to learning algorithms like PCA. Many estimator objects can make the transformer interface simplify the transformation process. This interface helps us conduct a nontrivial transformation on the input data and provide the result to our actual learning algorithm. Since the transformer object maintains the estimator employed for transformation, it is very straightforward to use the same transformation to unknown test data utilizing transformation function (Sarkar et al., 2018).

### Example 3.1

The following Python code is used to represent regression by using the scikit-learn library APIs. In this example we utilize the Boston house prices dataset, which exists in sklearn.datasets. Note that this example is adapted from Python–scikit-learn. This example uses the Boston house prices dataset to illustrate a two-dimensional plot of this regression technique. This dataset contains 506 instances, and there are 13 numeric/categorical attributes and one target. The attribute information is as follows:

CRIM per capita crime rate by town
ZN proportion of residential land zoned for lots over 25,000 sq ft
INDUS proportion of nonretail business acres per town
CHAS Charles River dummy variable (=1 if tract bounds river; 0 otherwise)
NOX nitric oxides concentration (parts per 10 million)
RM average number of rooms per dwelling
AGE proportion of owner-occupied units built prior to 1940
DIS weighted distances to five Boston employment centers

RAD index of accessibility to radial highways
TAX full-value property-tax rate per $10,000
PTRATIO pupil-teacher ratio by town
B 1000(Bk - 0.63)^2 where Bk is the proportion of blacks by town
LSTAT % lower status of the population
MEDV median value of owner-occupied homes in $1000s
This dataset is a copy of *University of California* (UCI) machine learning housing dataset. You can access the web page at https://archive.ics.uci.edu/ml/machine-learning-databases/housing/.

```
# Code source: Jaques Grobler
# License: BSD 3 clause

# ========================================================================
# Linear regression example using scikit-learn API
# ========================================================================
import matplotlib.pyplot as plt
import numpy as np
from sklearn import datasets, linear_model
from sklearn.metrics import mean_squared_error, r2_score
from sklearn.metrics import mean_absolute_error
from sklearn.model_selection import train_test_split

# Load the Boston House prices dataset
boston = datasets.load_boston()
X = boston.data
y = boston.target

Xtrain, Xtest, ytrain, ytest = train_test_split(X, y, test_size = 0.5,
random_state = 0)
# Create linear regression object
regr = linear_model.LinearRegression()
# Train the model using the training sets
regr.fit(Xtrain, ytrain)
# Make predictions using the testing set
ypred = regr.predict(Xtest)

# The coefficients
print('Coefficients: \n', regr.coef_)
#Intercept
print('Intercept: \n', regr.intercept_ )
# The mean absolute error
print("MAE = %5.3f" % mean_absolute_error(ytest, ypred))
# Explained variance score: 1 is perfect prediction
print("R^2 = %0.5f" % r2_score(ytest, ypred))
```

```
# The mean squared error
print("MSE = %5.3f" % mean_squared_error(ytest, ypred))

# Plot outputs
fig, ax = plt.subplots()
ax.scatter(ytest, ypred, edgecolors = (0, 0, 0))
ax.plot([y.min(), y.max()], [y.min(), y.max()], 'k--', lw = 4)
ax.set_xlabel('Measured')
ax.set_ylabel('Predicted')
plt.show()
```

### 3.3.2 TensorFlow

TensorFlow is an open source machine learning library implemented by Google. TensorFlow was built on Google's internal system to drive its development and research processes. TensorFlow can be viewed as an initiative by Google to provide an update to Theano by providing easy-to-use frameworks for deep learning, neural networks, and machine learning with a strong emphasis on rapid prototyping and modeling. This introduces definitions where symbolic mathematical expressions can be converted into conceptual diagrams. Such graphs are then compiled and efficiently implemented into lower-level code. TensorFlow also automatically allows use of Central Processing Units (CPUs) and Graphical Processing Units (GPUs). In addition, TensorFlow works much better on a tensor processing unit (TPU), which was designed by Google. In addition to having a Python API, TensorFlow is also exposed by APIs to languages such as C + +, Haskell, Java, and Go. TensorFlow supports higher-level services that make the machine learning process simple based on model creation as well as the implementation across various processes for development and model serving. Similarly, TensorFlow aimed to make applications easy to understand and provide comprehensive documentation. It is possible to install the TensorFlow library using pip or conda install feature. Remember that you will also need upgraded dask and pandas libraries on your framework for effective implementation of TensorFlow (Sarkar et al., 2018). At https://www.tensorflow.org/ you can always find the documentation for TensorFlow, which provides several samples for more details. We will provide some basic examples here regarding deep learning with TensorFlow.

### 3.3.3 Keras

Keras is Python's high-level deep learning platform that can operate on top of TensorFlow. The most important advantage of using Keras, created by Francois Chollet, is the time saved by its easy-to-use but efficient high-level APIs, allowing quick prototyping for a concept. Keras helps us use TensorFlow's principles in a much more straightforward and user-friendly way without writing unnecessary boilerplate software to create deep learning models. The principal reason for success of Keras is its ease of elasticity and flexibility. In addition to providing easy access to specialized libraries, Keras assures that we can still utilize the benefits provided by the TensorFlow package. Using the common pip or conda install command,

Keras can be installed easily. We must presume that we have TensorFlow installed because it needs to be used as a backend for the creation of the Keras model (Sarkar et al., 2018).

### 3.3.4 Building a model with Keras

The Keras model construction process is a three-step process. The first step is to define the model's structure. This is achieved by selecting the base model we would like to use, either a sequential model or a functional model. By adding layers to the model, we will further expand the model once we have defined a base model for our problem. We will start with the input layer to which we will feed our input data's feature vectors. The layers to be added to the model will be dictated by the requirements of the model. Keras provides a bunch of layers that can be added to the system (hidden layers, fully connected, Convolutional Neural Network (CNN), Long short-term memory (LSTM), Recurrent neural network (RNN), etc.), and we will describe most of them while running through our deep learning model. We need to stack these layers together in a complex way in order to achieve our ultimate prototype model and insert the final output layer. The next phase in the machine learning cycle is to compile the framework model that we defined in the first stage. In addition to the model architecture, the learning process must define the following additional three significant parameters (Sarkar et al., 2018):

- **Optimizer**: A training process's simplest explanation is the optimization of a loss function. Once we created the model and loss function, we must decide the optimizer to define the specific method or algorithm for optimization, which can be used to train the model and decrease the loss or error. This could be a string identifier for the optimizers already implemented, a function or an object we could implement for the optimizer class.
- **Loss function**: A loss function, also defined as an objective function, must define the target of minimizing loss/error that will exploit our model to achieve the best output over several epochs. For some preimplemented loss functions like cross-entropy loss for classification or mean squared error for regression, it may again be a string identifier, or it may be a custom loss function that can be created.
- **Performance metrics**: A metric is a representation of learning process that can be quantified. We can identify a performance measure that we want to monitor while generating a model—for example, accuracy for a classification method—which will teach us about the training process's success. It helps to assess the performance of the model.

The last step in the process of model building is to implement the compiled method to start the process of training. To figure out the required parameters and weights of our model during the training process, this will execute the lower level compiled code (Sarkar et al., 2018).

### 3.3.5 The natural language tool kit

Human languages vary from the languages of computer programming. These are not designed to be translated as are programming languages into a limited set of mathematical operations. Natural languages are what people use to communicate. Written with a programming language, a computer program asks a machine precisely what to do. But there are no natural language compilers or interpreters. Natural language processing is an area of research concerning the processing of natural languages in computer science and artificial intelligence (AI). In particular, this process includes translating natural language into information (numbers) that can be used by a machine to learn about the world. And sometimes this environment is used to produce natural language text that represents that understanding. If the computer program you are creating understands natural language, it can operate on or even respond to these statements. But these actions and reactions are not precisely defined, giving you, the natural language pipeline designer, more flexibility (Hapke, Lane, & Howard, 2019).

A natural language processing system is often referred to as a pipeline, as it typically involves several processing phases in which natural language streams from one end and the processed data flows out the other. Eventually you will have the power to write code that does exciting, unpredictable things like having a dialogue that can make computers look a little more human. It may appear like magic; all advanced technology does at first. But we're drawing the curtain away so you can play inside, and you'll soon discover all the tools and equipment you need to give yourself the magic tricks. It is not natural for machines to have the ability to process anything natural. It is kind of like constructing a building with architectural drawings that can do something useful. If computers can interpret languages that are not programmed for machines to learn, it seems impossible (Hapke et al., 2019).

Python has been designed to be a practical language from scratch. It also reveals many of its own language production tools. Both of these characteristics make it a logical choice for learning the processing of natural language. It is a great language in an enterprise environment to create stable output pipelines for NLP algorithms, with many contributors to a common codebase. They even use Python, whenever possible, instead of the "universal language" of arithmetic and computational symbols (Hapke et al., 2019).

Natural languages cannot be translated directly into an exact collection of mathematical operations, but they contain information and guidance that can be derived. These pieces of information or instructions can be processed, indexed, checked, and acted upon instantly. One of those acts in response to a statement could produce a sequence of words. This is the "dialog engine or chatbot role you are going to build." Natural languages have an additional challenge of decoding, which is even more difficult to solve. Natural language speakers and writers assume that the person doing the copying (listening and reading) is a human being, not a computer (Hapke et al., 2019).

This mind hypothesis about the human language interpreter turned out to be a strong assumption. It enables us to say a lot with few words when we presume that the processor has access to knowledge of the world throughout a period. This degree of compression for computers is still out of control. There is no simple "theory of mind" in an NLP pipeline to which you can refer. Nevertheless, strategies to help machines create ontologies of common sense knowledge, or knowledge bases, help to understand statements based on this information (Hapke et al., 2019).

A search engine could produce more meaningful results by indexing web sites and document archives in a way that takes the context of natural language text into consideration. Autocomplete uses NLP to complete the thought and is widespread to mobile phone keyboards and search engines. Most word processors, browser plugins, or text editors have spelling correctors, grammar checkers, composers of concordance, or coaches of style using NLP. Many dialog engines (chatbots) utilize natural language search to find an answer to the message from their conversation partner. In addition to writing brief responses in chatbots or virtual assistants, NLP pipelines that produce (compose) text can also be utilized to compile much longer text passages. The Associated Press utilizes NLP as "robot journalists" to compose entire articles on financial news or reports on sporting events. Bots can write weather forecasts that look like weather in your hometown, since human meteorologists use NLP-functional word processors to draft scripts. And in the cat and mouse game between spam filters and spam producers for text, the spam filters have maintained their advantage but may be losing in other contexts such as social networks. And these "puppet masters," with the wealth and incentive to manipulate popular opinion, appear to be foreign governments and large corporations (Hapke et al., 2019).

Chatbots produced approximately 20% of the messages about the 2016 U.S. presidential election. Such bots reflect the views of their owners and programmers. More than just short social network posts can be created by NLP systems. On Amazon and elsewhere, NLP can be used to compose long film or product reviews. Most reviewers are producing autonomous NLP pipelines that have never set foot in a movie theater or purchased the product being reviewed. On Slack, IRC, and even customer service websites chatbots have to interact with ambiguous commands and queries. And chatbots equipped with voice recognition and production systems can even manage long conversations with an unspecified aim or "objective function," such as booking at a local restaurant. To companies that need something more than a phone tree but don't want to pay people to help their customers, NLP programs can answer phones. According to computational resource limitations, early NLP frameworks had to utilize the computational power of their human brains to model and implement complex logical rules to obtain information from a string of natural language. This is an NLP approach based on patterns. The patterns, like our regular expression, need not be simply character series variations. Furthermore, NLP frequently includes patterns of sequences of words or parts of speech or other "higher-level" patterns (Hapke et al., 2019).

Python's most powerful library to deal with text content may be the Natural Language Tool Kit (NLTK). NLTK and its significant modules are presented in this section, with a brief description of its main modules. Similar to other standard libraries there is a significant difference in the NLTK collection. In particular, we don't need to access any auxiliary data in the case of other libraries. But to access the full potential of the NLTK library we need some auxiliary data, mainly various corpora. Various functions and modules in the library use this information (Sarkar et al., 2018).

A process of collecting the documents of interest in a single dataset is the starting point of any text analytics process. This dataset is essential for processing and evaluating the next steps. Such document collection is generally referred to as a corpus. Different versions of the corpus are called corpora. The NLTK module nltk.corpus provides the necessary functions that can be utilized in a variety of formats to read corpus data. It promotes business training from the NLTK package-bundled datasets as well (Sarkar et al., 2018).

Tokenization is one of the key steps of preprocessing and standardization of language. Every text file has several elements, such as sentences, phrases, and terms, that make up the document. The tokenization method can be used to break the file into smaller components. This tokenization can be used in sentences, terms, clauses, etc. Using sentence tokenization and word tokenization is the most popular way of tokenizing any text. The nltk.tokenize module of the NLTK library offers features that enable any textual data to be easily tokenized (Sarkar et al., 2018).

A text file is constructed on the basis of different grammatical rules and structures. The grammar is based on the text document's language. The tagging method would involve getting a text corpus, tokenizing the text, and assigning details such as tags to each word in the corpora metadata. The module nltk.tag contains various algorithms that can be used for tagging and other related activities (Sarkar et al., 2018).

A word may have various forms depending on what portion of the speech it describes. The stemming method is used to convert all of a word's different forms into the base form, known as the root step. Lemmatization is similar to stemming, but the basic form is known as the root word and it is always a word that is correct in terms of semantics and lexicography. This conversion is crucial, because many times the core word contains more information about the document that these different forms can dilute. The NLTK nltk.stem framework contains various methods that can be used to stem and lemmatize a corpus (Sarkar et al., 2018).

Chunking is another process similar to parsing and tokenization, but the key difference is that we will target phrases found in the text instead of attempting to parse every word. We may tag phrases with additional parts of speech information by using the chunking procedure, which is crucial to understanding the document's structure. The NLTK module nltk.chunk is made up of the required techniques that can be used by our corpora to implement the chunking procedure (Sarkar et al., 2018).

Sentiment analysis is one the most popular techniques on text data. Processing of sentiment is the procedure of taking a text document and attempting to determine the opinion and polarity presented by the document. Polarity in a text file reference may indicate that the information reflects the emotion, for example, positive, negative, or neutral. Using different algorithms and at different levels of text segmentation, the sentiment analysis on textual data can be accomplished. The nltk.sentiment module is the application that can be used on text documents to perform various sentiment analyses (Sarkar et al., 2018).

Classification of text documents may include learning from several text documents (corpus) the sentiment, topic, theme, class, etc., and then using the trained model to label unknown documents in the future. The major difference from ordinary structured data is that we will use unstructured text in the context of feature representations. Clustering means bringing different documents together according to some measure of similarity, such as semantic similarity. Usually, the modules nltk.classify and nltk.cluster are used to execute these operations once we do the required engineering and extraction functionality. There are many other text analytics frameworks, such as pattern, genism, textblob, and spacy (Sarkar et al., 2018).

## 3.4 Learning scenarios

Common scenarios of machine learning vary in the categories of training data available to the learner, the sequence and algorithm of processing training data, and the test data utilized to assess the learning algorithm.

***Supervised learning***: The learner uses a series of labeled samples as training data and predicts all unseen instances. This is the most common scenario correlated with problems of classification regression and ranking. Examples of supervised learning are anomaly detection, face recognition, signal and image classification, weather forecasting, and stock market forecasting.

***Unsupervised learning***: The learner solely receives unlabeled training data and predicts all unseen instances. Since there is usually no labeled instance in that environment, quantitative assessment of a learner's performance can be challenging. Clustering and reduction of dimensionality are forms of unsupervised learning problems.

***Semisupervised learning***: The learner receives a training sample composed of both labeled and unlabeled instances and predicts all unseen instances. Semisupervised learning are typical situations in which it is easy to access unlabeled data, but labels are costly to obtain. Various types of applications-related problems, like classification regression and ranking processes, can be presented as semisupervised learning instances. The idea is that distribution of unlabeled instances can help the learner achieve better performance than in the supervised setting. The focus of modern empirical and practical machine learning study is the analysis of the circumstances under which this can really be achieved.

***Transductive inference***: As in the semisupervised case, together with a set of unlabeled test points the learner receives a labeled learning sample. The aim of transductive inference, however, is to predict labels for these specific test points only. Transductive inference seems to be an easier task and is in accordance with the situation used in a number of modern applications. Nonetheless, the assumptions under which a better performance can be obtained in this environment, as in the semisupervised system, are research questions that have not been properly addressed.

***Online learning***: This interactive method contains multiple rounds, as opposed to previous situations, and training and testing steps are intermixed. The learner gets an unlabeled learning point at each stage, makes a prediction, receives the true label, and causes a loss. The goal in the online setting is to mitigate cumulative loss throughout all rounds. Unlike the previous settings mentioned, online learning does not allow any distributional assumption. Moreover, in this case, instances and their labels may be selected adversarially.

***Reinforcement learning***: The learner continually engages with the environment to collect information, influencing the environment in some situations and obtaining an immediate reward for each activity. The learner's goal is to optimize his reward with the environment over a series of acts and iterations. Nonetheless, the environment does not provide long-term incentive feedback, and the learner faces the problem of discovery and manipulation, as it must make a selection between exploring unseen activities to find out information or leveraging the already collected information.

***Active learning***: The learner receives training samples adaptively and interactively, usually by querying an oracle to ask for labels on new instances. The goal of active learning is to produce a performance that is equivalent to the standard supervised learning case, but with less examples labeled. Active learning is generally employed in systems in which the labels are expensive to acquire, such as applications in computational biology. Many other methods and somewhat more demanding learning scenarios can be found (Mohri, Rostamizadeh, & Talwalkar, 2018).

## 3.5 Supervised learning algorithms

Supervised learning algorithms include learning algorithms that use training data and associated labels during the model training process with each data sample. The key objective is to learn from the input data samples' corresponding output mapping or relationship.

This trained model can then be utilized later to predict output for any new set of input data instance that was previously unseen during the process of model training. Such approaches are defined as supervised, as the model learns from data samples, whereas in the training phase the required performance labels/responses are already known in advance. Supervised learning basically attempts to model the relationship between the inputs and their corresponding outputs from the training data so that we can predict output responses to new data inputs based on the previously learned knowledge of the relationships and mapping between the inputs and their target outputs. Supervised training approaches consist of two major classes, classification and regression, based on the type of machine learning problems to be solved (Sarkar et al., 2018).

### 3.5.1 Classification

Classification-based tasks are a subfield of supervised machine learning in which the key goal is to predict output labels or reactions that are categorical in nature of input data related to what the model has learned during the training phase. Therefore, each output response belongs to a specific discrete category or class. Popular classification algorithms are logistic regression (LR), linear discriminant analysis (LDA), artificial neural networks (ANN), support vector machines (SVM), k-nearest neighbors (k-NN), naive Bayes (NB), decision trees (DT), ensembles like random forests and gradient boosting, and deep learning techniques (Sarkar et al., 2018).

A wide range of diverse problems can be solved by machine learning techniques. In a classification task, it is necessary to learn a proper classifier from training data. Classification is just one range of possible tasks in which a model can learn. Others are regression and clustering. For each of these tasks we will explain how problems are solved with machine learning techniques, what kind of information is needed, how performance of the models is evaluated, and how we can choose the best model. The objects of interest in machine learning are generally referred to as *instances*. The set of all possible instances is called the *instance space*. To accomplish the task under consideration a *model* needs to be created. In order to create such a model, a *training set* with *labeled instances* (sometimes called *examples)* is utilized. Part of the labeled data is generally set aside, where it is called a *test set*, for testing or assessing a classifier. The basic type of input space arises once instances are designated by a fixed number of *features* (attributes) (Flach, 2012).

A credit is an allowance of money to be paid back with interest, usually in installments, loaned by a financial institution, such as a bank. It is crucial that the bank can forecast in advance the risk associated with a loan, which is the possibility that the customer may default and not pay back the entire amount. This is both to ensure the bank makes a profit and also not to burden a customer with a loan beyond their financial capacity. The bank measures the risk in credit scoring given the amount of credit and the customer information. The aim of this information from specific applications is to infer a general rule that codes the relationship between the attributes of a customer and the risk involved. That is, to calculate the risk for a new application, the machine learning program applies a template to the past data and then chooses to accept or refuse it accordingly (Alpaydin, 2014).

There are several machine learning applications in *data science*. One of them is *optical character recognition*, which involves recognizing character codes from images. People have diverse handwriting styles; characters may be typically written large or small, with a pencil or pen, and there might be several images related to the same character. There are machine learning algorithms that learn sequences and model different variations. In the case of *face recognition*, the input is an image, the classes are people to be recognized, and the learning algorithm has to learn to relate face images to the identities. This problem is harder than optical character recognition since there are several classes, the input image is larger, and a face is three-dimensional and differences in pose and lighting cause noteworthy variations. Moreover, there might be occlusion of certain inputs; for instance, glasses may hide the eyes and eyebrows and a beard may hide the chin. In *medical diagnosis*, the inputs are the related information about the patient and the classes are the illnesses. The inputs contain, for instance, the patient's age, gender, past medical history, current symptoms, blood tests, EEG, EMG, ECG signals, MRI, or PET, images. Some tests cannot be applied to the patient, and thus these inputs might be missing. In the case of a medical diagnosis, a wrong decision may result in inappropriate or lack of treatment, and it is preferable for the classifier to reject and defer a decision to a human expert in cases of doubt. The data is sound signals for *speech recognition*, and the classes are spoken words. The interaction to be learned in this case is from an acoustic signal to a language term. Because of variations in gender, age, or accent, several people pronounce the same word in different ways, which makes this task rather difficult. The best way to create a language model is to learn it from a large amount of data. The applications of machine learning to *natural language processing* are continually expanding. *Spam filtering* is one in which spam generators on one side and filters on the other side keep generating more and more clever ways to outwit each other. Document analysis is another exciting example, such as analyzing posts or blogs on social networking sites to extract "trending" topics or to determine what to advertise. *Biometrics* is the authentication or recognition of people by utilizing their physiological or behavioral characteristics and needs an integration of inputs from diverse modalities. Physiological characteristics might be images of the fingerprint, face, palm, and iris; behavioral characteristics might be dynamics of signature, gait, voice, and keystroke. Machine learning can be utilized to recognize different modalities to obtain an overall accept/reject decision (Alpaydin, 2014).

### 3.5.2 Forecasting, prediction, and regression

***Regression*** is a machine learning task in which the main aim is the estimation of value. Regression techniques are based on sets of input data and output responses that are continuous numerical values, unlike classification, in which they have distinct classes or categories. Regression models utilize input data features or attributes and their accompanying numerical output values to learn basic relations and associations between inputs and their corresponding outputs. One of the most common real-world examples of regression is stock market forecasting. A ***simple regression*** model can be built to forecast stock prices based on data related to the previous stock market values. Simple linear regression models attempt to model data relationships with one feature or descriptive variable x and a single response variable y with the goal of predicting y. ***Lasso regression*** is a special regression type that performs normal regression and generalizes the model well through regularization and selection of features or variables. Lasso is the least complete operator of shrinkage and choice. ***Ridge regression*** is another special regression type that performs normal regression and generalizes the model by regularizing to prevent the model overfitting. Generalized linear models are basic implementations that can be used to model data that forecasts various types of output responses (Sarkar et al., 2018).

### 3.5.3 Linear models

In machine learning, *linear models* are of particular relevance since they are simple. Linear models are *parametric*, which means that they have a fixed form with a small number of numeric parameters that can be learned from data. Since linear models are stable, small variations in the training data have only limited impact on the learned model. Linear models are less likely to overfit the training data than some other models since they have comparatively few parameters. The reverse of this sometimes results in *underfitting*. Moreover, linear models have low variance but high bias. Such models are generally desirable once you have limited data and need to avoid overfitting. Linear models exist for all predictive tasks, including classification, probability estimation, and regression (Flach, 2012).

A simple linear regression model assumes that the regression function E(Y | X) is linear in the inputs $X_1, \ldots, X_p$. Linear models were developed primarily in the precomputer era of statistics, but there are still good reasons to study and use them even in today's computer age. These are simple and mostly include a summary of how the inputs influence the output. We can sometimes outperform fancy nonlinear models for predictive purposes, especially in cases with small training instances, poor signal-to-noise ratio, or sparse data. Finally, linear approaches can be extended to input transformations, and this extends their scope considerably. Such generalizations are sometimes referred to as forms of basic function (Hastie, Tibshirani, Friedman, & Franklin, 2005).

#### Example 3.2

The following Python code is used to represent linear regression by using the scikit-learn library APIs. In this example we utilize the diabetes dataset, which exists in sklearn.datasets. The dataset contains 10 baseline variables—age, sex, body mass index, average blood pressure, and six blood serum measurements—taken from 442 diabetes patients, as well as the response of interest, a quantitative measure of disease progression 1 year after baseline. Hence there are 442 instances with the 10 attributes.

Column 11 is a quantitative measure of disease progression 1 year after baseline. Each of these 10 attributes were mean-centered and scaled by standard deviation times n_samples (i.e., the sum of squares of each column totals 1). The original data can be downloaded from: https://www4.stat.ncsu.edu/~boos/var.select/diabetes.html'.

This example utilizes all the features of the diabetes dataset to illustrate a two-dimensional plot of this regression technique. The straight line seen in the plot demonstrates how linear regression tries to draw a straight line, which minimizes the residual sum of squares between the observed responses in the dataset, and the responses predicted by the linear approximation. The correlation coefficient $R^2$, mean absolute error (MAE), and mean squared error (MSE) are also calculated. Note that this example is adapted from Python–scikit-learn.

```
# Code source: Jaques Grobler
# License: BSD 3 clause
# ==========================================================================
# Linear regression example
# ==========================================================================
import matplotlib.pyplot as plt
import numpy as np
from sklearn import datasets, linear_model
from sklearn.metrics import mean_squared_error, r2_score
from sklearn.metrics import mean_absolute_error
from sklearn.model_selection import train_test_split

# Load the diabetes dataset
diabetes = datasets.load_diabetes()
diabetes_X = diabetes.data
y = diabetes.target
Xtrain, Xtest, ytrain, ytest = train_test_split(X, y, test_size = 0.5, ran-
dom_state = 0)

# Create linear regression object
regr = linear_model.LinearRegression()
# Train the model using the training sets
regr.fit(Xtrain, ytrain)
# Make predictions using the testing set
ypred = regr.predict(Xtest)

# The coefficients
print('Coefficients: \n', regr.coef_)
#Intercept
print('Intercept: \n', regr.intercept_ )
# Explained variance score: 1 is perfect prediction
print("R^2 = %0.5f" % r2_score(ytest, ypred))
# The mean absolute error
print("MAE = %5.3f" % mean_absolute_error(ytest, ypred))
# The mean squared error
print("MSE = %5.3f" % mean_squared_error(ytest, ypred))

# Plot outputs
fig, ax = plt.subplots()
ax.scatter(ytest, ypred, edgecolors = (0, 0, 0))
ax.plot([y.min(), y.max()], [y.min(), y.max()], 'k--', lw = 4)
ax.set_xlabel('Measured')
ax.set_ylabel('Predicted')
plt.show()
```

### Example 3.3

The following Python code is used to represent ridge regression by using the scikit-learn library APIs. In this example we utilize the diabetes dataset, which exists in sklearn.datasets and is described in the previous example. This example utilizes all the features of the diabetes dataset to illustrate a two-dimensional plot of this regression technique. The straight line seen in the plot demonstrates how linear regression tries to draw a straight line, which minimizes the residual sum of squares between the observed responses in the dataset, and the responses predicted by the linear approximation. The correlation coefficient $R^2$, MAE, and MSE are also calculated. Note that this example is adapted from Python–scikit-learn.

```
# ======================================================================
# Ridge regression example
# ======================================================================
import matplotlib.pyplot as plt
from sklearn import datasets, linear_model
from sklearn.metrics import mean_squared_error, r2_score
from sklearn.metrics import mean_absolute_error
from sklearn.model_selection import train_test_split

# Load the diabetes dataset
diabetes = datasets.load_diabetes()
diabetes_X = diabetes.data
y = diabetes.target
Xtrain, Xtest, ytrain, ytest = train_test_split(X, y, test_size = 0.5, ran-
dom_state = 0)

# Create linear regression object
regr = linear_model.Ridge(alpha = .5)
# Train the model using the training sets
regr.fit(Xtrain, ytrain)
# Make predictions using the testing set
ypred = regr.predict(Xtest)

# The coefficients
print('Coefficients: \n', regr.coef_)
#Intercept
print('Intercept: \n', regr.intercept_ )
# Explained variance score: 1 is perfect prediction
print("R^2 = %0.5f" % r2_score(ytest, ypred))
# The mean absolute error
print("MAE = %5.3f" % mean_absolute_error(ytest, ypred))
# The mean squared error
print("MSE = %5.3f" % mean_squared_error(ytest, ypred))
```

```
# Plot outputs
fig, ax = plt.subplots()
ax.scatter(ytest, ypred, edgecolors = (0, 0, 0))
ax.plot([y.min(), y.max()], [y.min(), y.max()], 'k--', lw = 4)
ax.set_xlabel('Measured')
ax.set_ylabel('Predicted')
plt.show()
```

## Example 3.4

The following Python code is used to represent lasso regression by using the scikit-learn library APIs. In this example we utilize the Boston house prices dataset, which exists in sklearn.datasets. This example utilizes all the features of the Boston house prices dataset. The straight line seen in the plot demonstrates how linear regression tries to draw a straight line, which minimizes the residual sum of squares between the observed responses in the dataset, and the responses predicted by the linear approximation. The correlation coefficient $R^2$, MAE, and MSE are also calculated. Note that this example is adapted from Python–scikit-learn.

```
# ===========================================================================
# Lasso regression example
# ===========================================================================
import matplotlib.pyplot as plt
import numpy as np
from sklearn import datasets, linear_model
from sklearn.metrics import mean_squared_error, r2_score
from sklearn.metrics import mean_absolute_error
from sklearn.model_selection import train_test_split
# Load the Boston House prices dataset
boston = datasets.load_boston()
X = boston.data
y = boston.target
Xtrain, Xtest, ytrain, ytest = train_test_split(X, y, test_size = 0.5, ran-
dom_state = 0)

# Create linear regression object
regr = linear_model.Lasso(alpha = 0.1)
# Train the model using the training sets
regr.fit(Xtrain, ytrain)

# Make predictions using the testing set
ypred = regr.predict(Xtest)

# The coefficients
print('Coefficients: \n', regr.coef_)
```

```
#Intercept
print('Intercept: \n', regr.intercept_ )
# Explained variance score: 1 is perfect prediction
print("R^2 = %0.5f" % r2_score(ytest, ypred))
# The mean absolute error
print("MAE = %5.3f" % mean_absolute_error(ytest, ypred))
# The mean squared error
print("MSE = %5.3f" % mean_squared_error(ytest, ypred))
# Plot outputs
fig, ax = plt.subplots()
ax.scatter(ytest, ypred, edgecolors = (0, 0, 0))
ax.plot([y.min(), y.max()], [y.min(), y.max()], 'k--', lw = 4)
ax.set_xlabel('Measured')
ax.set_ylabel('Predicted')
plt.show()
```

## Example 3.5

The following Python code is used to represent the transformation of target in regression by using the scikit-learn library APIs. In this example we utilize the Boston house prices dataset, which exists in sklearn.datasets. This example utilizes the transformed features of the Boston house prices dataset using ***TransformedTargetRegressor***. TransformedTargetRegressor transforms the targets y before fitting a regression model. The predictions are mapped back to the original space via an inverse transform. The regressor, which is utilized for prediction, and the transformer, which is applied to the target variable can be taken as an argument. The straight line seen in the plot demonstrates how linear regression tries to draw a straight line, which minimizes the residual sum of squares between the observed responses in the dataset, and the responses predicted by the linear approximation. The correlation coefficient $R^2$, MAE, and MSE are also calculated. It can be seen from the example that the target transformation improved the performance of the regression model. Note that this example is adapted from Python–scikit-learn.

```
# ======================================================================
#Transforming target in regression
# ======================================================================
from sklearn.compose import TransformedTargetRegressor
from sklearn.preprocessing import QuantileTransformer
from sklearn.linear_model import LinearRegression
from sklearn.model_selection import train_test_split
from sklearn.metrics import mean_squared_error, r2_score
from sklearn.metrics import mean_absolute_error
from sklearn.datasets import load_boston
```

```
# Load the Boston house prices dataset
boston = load_boston()
X = boston.data
y = boston.target
X_train, X_test, y_train, y_test = train_test_split(X, y, random_state = 0)

# =========================================================================
# Prediction without transformation
# =========================================================================

# Create linear regression object
regr = LinearRegression()
# Train the model using the training sets
regr.fit(X_train, y_train)
# Make predictions using the testing set
y_pred = regr.predict(X_test)

print('R^2 score without Transformation: {0:.2f}'.format(regr.score(X_
test, y_test)))
# Explained variance score: 1 is perfect prediction
print("R^2 = %0.5f" % r2_score(y_test, y_pred))
# The mean absolute error
print("MAE = %5.3f" % mean_absolute_error(y_test, y_pred))
# The mean squared error
print("MSE = %5.3f" % mean_squared_error(y_test, y_pred))

# Plot outputs
fig, ax = plt.subplots()
ax.scatter(y_test, y_pred, edgecolors = (0, 0, 0))
ax.plot([y.min(), y.max()], [y.min(), y.max()], 'k--', lw = 4)
ax.set_xlabel('Measured')
ax.set_ylabel('Predicted')
plt.title('Without Transformation')
plt.show()

# =========================================================================
# Prediction with transformation
# =========================================================================
transformer = QuantileTransformer(output_distribution = 'normal')
regressor = LinearRegression()
regr = TransformedTargetRegressor(regressor = regressor,
              transformer = transformer)
```

```
X_train, X_test, y_train, y_test = train_test_split(X, y, random_state = 0)
regr.fit(X_train, y_train)
y_pred = regr.predict(X_test)

print('R^2 score with Transformation: {0:.2f}'.format(regr.score(X_test,
y_test)))
# Explained variance score: 1 is perfect prediction
print("R^2 = %0.5f" % r2_score(y_test, y_pred))
# The mean absolute error
print("MAE = %5.3f" % mean_absolute_error(y_test, y_pred))
# The mean squared error
print("MSE = %5.3f" % mean_squared_error(y_test, y_pred))

# Plot outputs
fig, ax = plt.subplots()
ax.scatter(y_test, y_pred, edgecolors = (0, 0, 0))
ax.plot([y.min(), y.max()], [y.min(), y.max()], 'k--', lw = 4)
ax.set_xlabel('Measured')
ax.set_ylabel('Predicted')
plt.title('With Transformation')
plt.show()
```

## Example 3.6

The following Python code compares Bayesian ridge regression with ordinary least squares (OLS) by using the scikit-learn library APIs. In this example we utilize the Boston house prices dataset, which exists in sklearn.datasets. The plot shows the true house prices and estimated house prices by using Bayesian ridge regression and ordinary least squares (OLS). The correlation coefficient $R^2$, MAE, and MSE are also calculated. Note that this example is adapted from Python–scikit-learn.

```
 # Bayesian ridge regression

# ========================================================================
print(__doc__)
import matplotlib.pyplot as plt
from scipy import stats
from sklearn.model_selection import train_test_split
from sklearn.metrics import mean_squared_error, r2_score
from sklearn.metrics import mean_absolute_error
from sklearn.datasets import load_boston
from sklearn.linear_model import BayesianRidge, LinearRegression

# Load the Boston house prices dataset
boston = load_boston()
```

```
X = boston.data
y = boston.target
X_train, X_test, y_train, y_test = train_test_split(X, y, random_
state = 0)

# #############################################################################
# Fit the Bayesian ridge regression and an OLS for comparison
regr = BayesianRidge(compute_score = True)
regr.fit(X_train, y_train)
y_pred_bayesian = regr.predict(X_test)
ols = LinearRegression()
ols.fit(X_train, y_train)
y_pred_linear = ols.predict(X_test)

# #############################################################################
# Plot true house prices, estimated house prices
lw = 2
plt.figure(figsize = (6, 5))
plt.title("Real and Predicted House Prices")
plt.plot(y_pred_bayesian, color = 'lightgreen', linewidth = lw,
label = "Bayesian Ridge estimate")
plt.plot(y_test, color = 'gold', linewidth = lw, label = "Ground truth")
plt.plot(y_pred_linear, color = 'navy', linestyle = '--', label = "OLS esti-
mate")
plt.xlabel("Houses")
plt.ylabel("House Prices")
plt.legend(loc = "best", prop = dict(size = 12))
```

## Example 3.7

The following Python code utilizes Ridge linear classifier by using the scikit-learn library APIs. In this example we utilize the Iris dataset, which exists in sklearn.datasets. The Iris dataset contains 150 (50 in each of three classes) instances with 4 numeric predictive attributes and the class. The attributes are sepal length, sepal width, petal length, and petal width, all in cm. The classes are Iris-Setosa, Iris-Versicolour, and Iris-Virginica. The Iris dataset is classified by using Ridge linear classifier. The classification accuracy, precision, recall, F1 score, Cohen kappa score, and Matthews correlation coefficient are calculated. The classification report and confusion matrix are also given. Note that this example is adapted from Python–scikit-learn.

```
# =============================================================================
# Ridge classifier example
# =============================================================================
import numpy as np
```

```
from sklearn.datasets import load_iris
from sklearn.model_selection import train_test_split
from sklearn.linear_model import RidgeClassifier

iris = load_iris()
X, y = iris.data, iris.target
Xtrain, Xtest, ytrain, ytest = train_test_split(X, y, test_size = 0.3, ran-
dom_state = 0)

clf = RidgeClassifier(tol = 1e-2, solver = "sag")
clf.fit(Xtrain,ytrain)
ypred = clf.predict(Xtest)

from sklearn import metrics
print('Accuracy:', np.round(metrics.accuracy_score(ytest,ypred),4))
print('Precision:', np.round(metrics.precision_score(ytest,
          ypred,average = 'weighted'),4))
print('Recall:', np.round(metrics.recall_score(ytest,ypred,
          average = 'weighted'),4))
print('F1 Score:', np.round(metrics.f1_score(ytest,ypred,
          average = 'weighted'),4))
print('Cohen  Kappa  Score:',  np.round(metrics.cohen_kappa_score(ytest,
ypred),4))
print('Matthews  Corrcoef:',  np.round(metrics.matthews_corrcoef(ytest,
ypred),4))
print('\t\tClassification Report:\n', metrics.classification_report(ypred,
ytest))

from sklearn.metrics import confusion_matrix
from io import BytesIO #neded for plot
import seaborn as sns; sns.set()
import matplotlib.pyplot as plt

mat = confusion_matrix(ytest, ypred)
sns.heatmap(mat.T, square = True, annot = True, fmt = 'd', cbar = False)
plt.xlabel('true label')
plt.ylabel('predicted label');

plt.savefig("Confusion.jpg")
# Save SVG in a fake file object.
f = BytesIO()
plt.savefig(f, format = "svg")
```

### 3.5.4 The perceptron

If there is a linear decision boundary dividing the classes, the labeled data is termed *linearly separable*. The least-squares classifier can find a dividing decision boundary if any exists, but it is not guaranteed. A linear classifier, which can accomplish exact separation on linearly separable data, is the *perceptron*, initially proposed as a simple neural network. The perceptron repeats over the training set, updating the weight vector each time it comes across an incorrectly classified example (Flach, 2012).

The perceptron was first proposed by F. Rosenblatt (Rosenblatt, 1958). It can be employed to classify patterns. A perceptron is a feed-forward neuron in which the data flow is unidirectional from input to output. In the input layer, each input data item in the elements is multiplied by a constant weight factor $w_{ij}$ and passes through the neurons of the succeeding layer. Each neuron of the input layer can propagate its output to either only one or to several neurons of the intermediate layer. Every element of the intermediate layer adds its inputs to a net value that will be multiplied with a variable weight and propagated to the neurons of the output layer. Every neuron of the output layer is linked to all elements of the intermediate layer. Depending on their weighted input net, these elements deliver either the value 0 or the value 1. During the learning process of perceptrons, the anticipated output $z_i$ for every neuron in the output layer is known. Hence, it can be continuously compared with the calculated output $o_i$ (Veit, 2012).

**Example 3.8**

The following Python code utilizes the perceptron classifier by applying the scikit-learn library APIs. In this example we utilize the optical recognition of handwritten digits dataset, which exists in sklearn.datasets. The optical recognition of handwritten digits dataset contains 5620 instances with 64 numeric (8 x 8 image of integer pixels in the range 0...16) predictive attributes and the class. This is a copy of the test set of the UCI machine learning handwritten digits datasets (https://archive.ics.uci.edu/ml/datasets/Optical+Recognition+of+Handwritten+Digits).

The dataset is composed of images of handwritten digits: 10 classes in which each class refers to a digit. The handwritten digits dataset is divided into training and test set and then classified by using perceptron classifier. The classification accuracy, precision, recall, F1 score, Cohen kappa score, and Matthews correlation coefficient are calculated. The classification report and confusion matrix are also given. Note that this example is adapted from Python–scikit-learn.

```
#=====================================================================
# Perceptron example
#=====================================================================
import numpy as np
from sklearn.datasets import load_digits
from sklearn.linear_model import Perceptron
from sklearn.model_selection import train_test_split

X, y = load_digits(return_X_y = True)
```

```
Xtrain, Xtest, ytrain, ytest = train_test_split(X, y, test_size = 0.3, ran-
dom_state = 0)

#Create the Model
clf = Perceptron(tol = 1e-3, random_state = 0)
#Train the Model with Training dataset
clf.fit(Xtrain,ytrain)
#Predict the Model with Test dataset
ypred = clf.predict(Xtest)
print("Score:",clf.score(Xtest, ytest))

#Evaluate the Model and Print Performance Metrics
from sklearn import metrics
print('Accuracy:', np.round(metrics.accuracy_score(ytest,ypred),4))
print('Precision:', np.round(metrics.precision_score(ytest,
          ypred,average = 'weighted'),4))
print('Recall:', np.round(metrics.recall_score(ytest,ypred,
          average = 'weighted'),4))
print('F1 Score:', np.round(metrics.f1_score(ytest,ypred,
          average = 'weighted'),4))
print('Cohen Kappa Score:', np.round(metrics.cohen_kappa_score(ytest,
ypred),4))
print('Matthews Corrcoef:', np.round(metrics.matthews_corrcoef(ytest,
ypred),4))
print('\t\tClassification Report:\n', metrics.classification_report(ypred,
ytest))
from sklearn.metrics import confusion_matrix
print("Confusion Matrix:\n",confusion_matrix(ytest, ypred))

#Plot Confusion Matrix
from sklearn.metrics import confusion_matrix
from io import BytesIO #neded for plot
import seaborn as sns; sns.set()
import matplotlib.pyplot as plt

mat = confusion_matrix(ytest, ypred)
sns.heatmap(mat.T, square = True, annot = True, fmt = 'd', cbar = False)
plt.xlabel('true label')
plt.ylabel('predicted label');

plt.savefig("Confusion.jpg")
# Save SVG in a fake file object.
f = BytesIO()
plt.savefig(f, format = "svg")
```

### 3.5.5 Logistic regression

Logistic regression, despite its name, is a classification model rather than regression model. Logistic regression is a simple and more efficient method for binary and linear classification problems. It is a classification model, which is very easy to realize and achieves very good performance with linearly separable classes. It is an extensively employed algorithm for classification in industry. The logistic regression model, like the Adaline and perceptron, is a statistical method for binary classification that can be generalized to multiclass classification. Scikit-learn has a highly optimized version of logistic regression implementation, which supports multiclass classification task (Raschka, 2015).

#### Example 3.9

The following Python code employs the logistic regression classifier by using the scikit-learn library APIs. In this example we utilize the optical recognition of handwritten digits dataset, which exists in sklearn.datasets. The handwritten digits dataset is divided into training and test set and then classified by using the logistic regression classifier. The classification accuracy, precision, recall, F1 score, Cohen kappa score, and Matthews correlation coefficient are calculated. The classification report and confusion matrix are also given. Note that this example is adapted from Python–scikit-learn.

```
# ===================================================================
# Classification with logistic regression
# ===================================================================
print(__doc__)

# Authors: Alexandre Gramfort <alexandre.gramfort@inria.fr>
#          Mathieu Blondel <mathieu@mblondel.org>
#          Andreas Mueller <amueller@ais.uni-bonn.de>
# License: BSD 3 clause

import numpy as np
import matplotlib.pyplot as plt
from sklearn.model_selection import train_test_split
from sklearn.linear_model import LogisticRegression
from sklearn import datasets
from sklearn.preprocessing import StandardScaler

digits = datasets.load_digits()
X, y = digits.data, digits.target
Xtrain, Xtest, ytrain, ytest = train_test_split(X, y, test_size = 0.3, ran-
dom_state = 0)
clf = LogisticRegression(C = 50, multi_class = 'multinomial',
penalty = 'l1', solver = 'saga', tol = 0.1)
```

```
clf.fit(Xtrain, ytrain)
ypred = clf.predict(Xtest)

#Print performance metrics
from sklearn import metrics
print('Accuracy:', np.round(metrics.accuracy_score(ytest,ypred),4))
print('Precision:', np.round(metrics.precision_score(ytest,
          ypred,average = 'weighted'),4))
print('Recall:', np.round(metrics.recall_score(ytest,ypred,
          average = 'weighted'),4))
print('F1 Score:', np.round(metrics.f1_score(ytest,ypred,
          average = 'weighted'),4))
print('Cohen  Kappa  Score:',  np.round(metrics.cohen_kappa_score(ytest,
ypred),4))
print('Matthews  Corrcoef:',  np.round(metrics.matthews_corrcoef(ytest,
ypred),4))
print('\t\tClassification Report:\n', metrics.classification_report(ypred,
ytest))

from sklearn.metrics import confusion_matrix
from io import BytesIO #neded for plot
import seaborn as sns; sns.set()
import matplotlib.pyplot as plt

mat = confusion_matrix(ytest, ypred)
sns.heatmap(mat.T, square = True, annot = True, fmt = 'd', cbar = False)
plt.xlabel('true label')
plt.ylabel('predicted label');

plt.savefig("Confusion.jpg")
# Save SVG in a fake file object.
f = BytesIO()
plt.savefig(f, format = "svg")
```

## Example 3.10

The following Python code utilizes the logistic regression classifier by using the Scikit-learn library APIs. In this example we utilize the Iris dataset, which exists in sklearn.datasets. The Iris dataset is classified with the logistic regression classifier by using 10-fold cross-validation. The classification accuracy, precision, recall, F1 score, Cohen kappa score, and Matthews correlation coefficient are calculated. Note that this example is adapted from Python–scikit-learn.

```
# ===========================================================================
# Logistic regression example with cross-validation
# ===========================================================================
from sklearn.linear_model import LogisticRegressionCV
from sklearn.model_selection import cross_val_score
from sklearn.datasets import load_iris
import warnings

#To prevent warnings
warnings.filterwarnings("ignore")

iris = load_iris()
X, y = iris.data, iris.target

CV = 10 #10-fold cross validation
model = LogisticRegressionCV(cv = CV, random_state = 0, multi_
class = 'multinomial').fit(X, y)

#Evaluate Model Using 10-Fold Cross Validation and Print Performance
Metrics
Acc_scores = cross_val_score(model, X, y, cv = CV)
print("Accuracy: %0.3f (+/- %0.3f)" % (Acc_scores.mean(), Acc_scores.
std() * 2))
f1_scores = cross_val_score(model, X, y, cv = CV,scoring = 'f1_macro')
print("F1 score: %0.3f (+/- %0.3f)" % (f1_scores.mean(), f1_scores.std()
* 2))
Precision_scores = cross_val_score(model, X, y,
cv = CV,scoring = 'precision_macro')
print("Precision score: %0.3f (+/- %0.3f)" % (Precision_scores.mean(),
Precision_scores.std() * 2))
Recall_scores = cross_val_score(model, X, y, cv = CV,scoring = 'recall_
macro')
print("Recall score: %0.3f (+/- %0.3f)" % (Recall_scores.mean(), Recall_
scores.std() * 2))
from sklearn.metrics import cohen_kappa_score, make_scorer
kappa_scorer = make_scorer(cohen_kappa_score)
Kappa_scores = cross_val_score(model, X, y, cv = CV,scoring = kappa_scorer)
print("Kappa score: %0.3f (+/- %0.3f)" % (Kappa_scores.mean(), Kappa_
scores.std() * 2))
```

### 3.5.6 Linear discriminant analysis

LDA is a classifier used to find a linear combination of features, which separates two or more classes of data. The succeeding combination can be used as a linear classifier. In LDA, the classes are expected to be normally distributed. Like PCA, LDA can be utilized for both dimension reduction and classification. In a two-class dataset, the a priori probabilities for class 1 and class 2 are $p_1$ and $p_2$; the class means and overall mean are $\mu_1$, $\mu_2$, and $\mu$; and the class variances are $cov_1$ and $cov_2$ respectively.

$$\mu = p_1 \times \mu_1 + p_2 \times \mu_2 \tag{3.1}$$

Then, within-class and between-class scatters are used to represent the needed criteria for class separability. The scatter measures for a multiclass situation are calculated as:

$$S_w = \sum_{j=1}^{C} p_j x cov_j \tag{3.2}$$

where C refers to the number of classes and

$$cov_j = (x_j - \mu_j)(x_j - \mu_j)^T \tag{3.3}$$

The between-class scatter is calculated as:

$$S_b = \frac{1}{C} \sum_{j=1}^{C} (\mu_j - \mu)(\mu_j - \mu)^T \tag{3.4}$$

Then, the aim is to find a discriminant plane to maximize the ratio of between-class to within-class scatters (variances):

$$J_{LDA} = \frac{wS_b w^T}{wS_w w^T} \tag{3.5}$$

In practical cases, the class covariances and means are not known, but they can be calculated from the training set. Either the maximum likelihood estimate or the maximum a posteriori estimate can be used instead of the exact value in the above equations (Sanei, 2013; Subasi, 2019).

## Example 3.11

The following Python code utilizes the logistic regression classifier by using the scikit-learn library APIs. In this example we utilize the MNIST handwritten digits dataset, which is available at http://yann.lecun.com/exdb/mnist/.

The training set includes 60,000 examples, and a test set includes 10,000 examples. This dataset is a subset of a larger set available from NIST. The digits were normalized in size and centered in a fixed-size image. The original black-and-white (bilevel) images from NIST were normalized in size to fit in a 20 x 20 pixel box while preserving their aspect ratio. The resulting images contain gray levels as a result of the anti-aliasing technique utilized by the normalization algorithm. The images were centered in a 28 x 28 image by computing the center of mass of the pixels and translating the image so as to position this point at the center of the 28 x 28 field. The MNIST handwritten digits dataset is divided into training and test set and then classified by using the LDA classifier. The classification accuracy, precision, recall, F1 score, Cohen kappa score and Matthews correlation coefficient are calculated. The classification report and confusion matrix are also given. Note that this example is adapted from Python–scikit-learn.

```
# ===================================================================
# LDA example with training and test set
# ===================================================================
import numpy as np
import time
from sklearn.discriminant_analysis import LinearDiscriminantAnalysis
from sklearn.model_selection import train_test_split
from sklearn.datasets import fetch_openml

# Turn down for faster convergence
train_samples = 5000

# Load data from https://www.openml.org/d/554
X, y = fetch_openml('mnist_784', version = 1, return_X_y = True)
Xtrain, Xtest, ytrain, ytest = train_test_split(X, y, test_size = 0.3, ran-
dom_state = 0)

#lda = LinearDiscriminantAnalysis(solver = "svd", store_covariance = True)
#clf = LinearDiscriminantAnalysis(solver = 'lsqr', shrinkage = 'auto')
clf = LinearDiscriminantAnalysis(solver = 'lsqr', shrinkage = None)
clf.fit(Xtrain,ytrain)
ypred = clf.predict(Xtest)

from sklearn import metrics
print('Accuracy:', np.round(metrics.accuracy_score(ytest,ypred),4))
print('Precision:', np.round(metrics.precision_score(ytest,
          ypred,average = 'weighted'),4))
print('Recall:', np.round(metrics.recall_score(ytest,ypred,
          average = 'weighted'),4))
print('F1 Score:', np.round(metrics.f1_score(ytest,ypred,
          average = 'weighted'),4))
print('Cohen Kappa Score:', np.round(metrics.cohen_kappa_score(ytest,
ypred),4))
print('Matthews Corrcoef:', np.round(metrics.matthews_corrcoef(ytest,
ypred),4))
print('\t\tClassification Report:\n', metrics.classification_report(ypred,
ytest))
from sklearn.metrics import confusion_matrix
print("Confusion Matrix:\n", confusion_matrix(ytest, ypred))
```

## Example 3.12

The following Python code utilizes the LDA classifier by using the scikit-learn library APIs. In this example we utilize the Iris dataset, which exists in sklearn.datasets. The Iris dataset is classified with LDA classifier by using 10-fold cross-validation. The classification accuracy, precision, recall, F1 score, Cohen kappa score, and Matthews correlation coefficient are calculated. Note that this example is adapted from Python–scikit-learn.

```
#=====================================================================
# LDA example with cross-validation
#=====================================================================
from sklearn.discriminant_analysis import LinearDiscriminantAnalysis
from sklearn.model_selection import cross_val_score
from sklearn.datasets import load_iris
from sklearn.metrics import cohen_kappa_score, make_scorer
iris = load_iris()
X, y = iris.data, iris.target

# fit model no training data
#lda = LinearDiscriminantAnalysis(solver = "svd", store_covariance = True)
#model = LinearDiscriminantAnalysis(solver = 'lsqr', shrinkage = 'auto')
model = LinearDiscriminantAnalysis(solver = 'lsqr', shrinkage = None)

CV = 10 #10-Fold Cross Validation
#Evaluate Model Using 10-Fold Cross Validation and Print Performance
Metrics
Acc_scores = cross_val_score(model, X, y, cv = CV)
print("Accuracy: %0.3f (+/- %0.3f)" % (Acc_scores.mean(), Acc_scores.
std() * 2))
f1_scores = cross_val_score(model, X, y, cv = CV,scoring = 'f1_macro')
print("F1 score: %0.3f (+/- %0.3f)" % (f1_scores.mean(), f1_scores.std()
* 2))
Precision_scores = cross_val_score(model, X, y,
cv = CV,scoring = 'precision_macro')
print("Precision score: %0.3f (+/- %0.3f)" % (Precision_scores.mean(),
Precision_scores.std() * 2))
Recall_scores = cross_val_score(model, X, y, cv = CV,scoring = 'recall_
macro')
print("Recall score: %0.3f (+/- %0.3f)" % (Recall_scores.mean(), Recall_
scores.std() * 2))
kappa_scorer = make_scorer(cohen_kappa_score)
Kappa_scores = cross_val_score(model, X, y, cv = CV,scoring = kappa_scorer)
print("Kappa score: %0.3f (+/- %0.3f)" % (Kappa_scores.mean(), Kappa_
scores.std() * 2))
```

### 3.5.7 Artificial neural networks

An artificial neural network (ANN) is a model that is inspired by the human brain and the way it functions. The nodes and their interconnections are like the neurons in our brain. There is a big difference between the ANN and a human brain. The brain has many neurons as processing units, operating in parallel, whereas the computer has only a restricted number of processors. Moreover, the neurons are simpler and slower in speed as compared to the computer processors. The computational power on a larger scale is another difference between the brain and the computer systems. Neurons consist of networks or synapses that work in a parallel manner. The processor in a computer system is active, whereas the memory of the system is passive. However, in the brain, the memory and the processing unit are distributed together as the processing takes place through the neurons, whereas the memory is positioned in the synapses (Alpaydin, 2014). A standard ANN has an input layer, an output layer, and, between input and output, at least one hidden layer. ANN always has several layers of nodes, definite link patterns and layer connections, connection weights, and node (neuron) activation functions that map weighted inputs to outputs. Throughout the training process, the weights are changed. The backpropagation algorithm is a technique to train ANNs, and it has the following two key stages: propagation and weight update.

*Propagation*

1. To generate the output values from the output layer, the input data sample vectors are propagated forward through the neural network.
2. Compare the produced output vector with the actual (desired) output vector for that input data vector.
3. Calculate the error at the output units.
4. Backpropagate error values to each node (neuron).

*Weight update*

1. Calculate the weight gradients by multiplying the output error and input activation.
2. Utilize the learning rate to calculate the percentage of the gradient from the original weight by subtraction and then update the node weight. With many iterations (epochs), these two stages are repeated several times until we have reliable results. Backpropagation is usually employed in conjunction with optimization algorithms such as stochastic gradient descent. A multilayer perceptron (MLP) is a fully connected feed-forward artificial neural network with at least three layers (input, output, and at least one hidden layer). Backpropagation can be employed to train MLPs and even deep neural networks (multilayered MLPs) (Sarkar et al., 2018).

#### Example 3.13

The following Python code utilizes MLP classifier by using the scikit-learn library APIs. In this example we utilize the Iris dataset, which exists in sklearn.datasets. The Iris dataset is divided into training and test set and then classified by using MLP classifier. The classification accuracy, precision, recall, F1 score, Cohen kappa score, and Matthews correlation coefficient are calculated. The classification report and confusion matrix are also given. Note that this example is adapted from Python–scikit-learn.

```
# ======================================================================
# MLP example with training and test set
# ======================================================================
import numpy as np
from sklearn.datasets import load_iris
from sklearn.model_selection import train_test_split
from sklearn.neural_network import MLPClassifier

#Load Iris Dataset
iris = load_iris()
X, y = iris.data, iris.target
#Create Train and Test set
Xtrain, Xtest, ytrain, ytest = train_test_split(X, y, test_size = 0.3, ran-
dom_state = 0)

#Create the Model
mlp = MLPClassifier(hidden_layer_sizes = (100, ), learning_rate_init = 0.001,
alpha = 1, momentum = 0.9,max_iter = 1000)
#Train the Model with Training dataset
mlp.fit(Xtrain,ytrain)
#Test the Model with Testing dataset
ypred = mlp.predict(Xtest)

from sklearn import metrics
print('Accuracy:', np.round(metrics.accuracy_score(ytest,ypred),4))
print('Precision:', np.round(metrics.precision_score(ytest,
          ypred,average = 'weighted'),4))
print('Recall:', np.round(metrics.recall_score(ytest,ypred,
          average = 'weighted'),4))
print('F1 Score:', np.round(metrics.f1_score(ytest,ypred,
          average = 'weighted'),4))
print('Cohen  Kappa  Score:',  np.round(metrics.cohen_kappa_score(ytest,
ypred)))
print('Matthews  Corrcoef:',  np.round(metrics.matthews_corrcoef(ytest,
ypred)))
print('\t\tClassification Report:\n', metrics.classification_report(ypred,
ytest))

from sklearn.metrics import confusion_matrix
from io import BytesIO #neded for plot
import seaborn as sns; sns.set()
import matplotlib.pyplot as plt

mat = confusion_matrix(ytest, ypred)
sns.heatmap(mat.T, square = True, annot = True, fmt = 'd', cbar = False)
```

```
plt.xlabel('true label')
plt.ylabel('predicted label');

plt.savefig("Confusion.jpg")
# Save SVG in a fake file object.
f = BytesIO()
plt.savefig(f, format = "svg")
```

## Example 3.14

The following Python code utilizes MLP classifier by using the scikit-learn library APIs. In this example we utilize the Iris dataset, which exists in sklearn.datasets. The Iris dataset is classified with MLP classifier by using 10-fold cross-validation. The classification accuracy, precision, recall, F1 score, Cohen kappa score, and Matthews correlation coefficient are calculated. Note that this example is adapted from Python–scikit-learn.

```
# ======================================================================
# MLP example with cross-validation
# ======================================================================
import numpy as np
from sklearn.datasets import load_iris
from sklearn.neural_network import MLPClassifier
from sklearn.model_selection import cross_val_score
from sklearn.metrics import cohen_kappa_score, make_scorer

#Load Iris Dataset
iris = load_iris()
X, y = iris.data, iris.target
#Create the Model
model = MLPClassifier(hidden_layer_sizes = (100, ), learning_rate_
init = 0.001,
        alpha = 1, momentum = 0.9,max_iter = 1000)

CV = 10 #10-Fold Cross Validation
#Evaluate Model Using 10-Fold Cross Validation and Print Performance
Metrics
Acc_scores = cross_val_score(model, X, y, cv = CV)
print("Accuracy: %0.3f (+/- %0.3f)" % (Acc_scores.mean(), Acc_scores.
std() * 2))
f1_scores = cross_val_score(model, X, y, cv = CV,scoring = 'f1_macro')
print("F1 score: %0.3f (+/- %0.3f)" % (f1_scores.mean(), f1_scores.std()
* 2))
Precision_scores = cross_val_score(model, X, y,
cv = CV,scoring = 'precision_macro')
```

```
print("Precision score: %0.3f (+/- %0.3f)" % (Precision_scores.mean(),
Precision_scores.std() * 2))
Recall_scores = cross_val_score(model, X, y, cv = CV,scoring = 'recall_
macro')
print("Recall score: %0.3f (+/- %0.3f)" % (Recall_scores.mean(), Recall_
scores.std() * 2))
kappa_scorer = make_scorer(cohen_kappa_score)
Kappa_scores = cross_val_score(model, X, y, cv = CV,scoring = kappa_scorer)
print("Kappa score: %0.3f (+/- %0.3f)" % (Kappa_scores.mean(), Kappa_
scores.std() * 2))
```

## Example 3.15

The following Python code is used to represent the MLP regression by using the scikit-learn library APIs. In this example we utilize the California housing dataset that includes data drawn from the 1990 U.S. census. All the block groups reporting zero entries for the independent and dependent variables are excluded. The final data includes 20,640 observations on 9 attributes. The dataset may also be downloaded from StatLib mirrors. This example utilizes all the features of the California housing dataset. The straight line seen in the plot demonstrates how MLP regression tries to draw a straight line, which minimizes the residual sum of squares between the observed responses in the dataset, and the responses predicted by the MLP approximation. The correlation coefficient $R^2$, MAE, and MSE are also calculated. Note that this example is adapted from Python–scikit-learn.

```
# =======================================================================
# MLP regression example with California housing dataset
# =======================================================================
import matplotlib.pyplot as plt
import numpy as np
from sklearn.neural_network import MLPRegressor
from sklearn.datasets.california_housing import fetch_california_housing
from sklearn.metrics import mean_squared_error, r2_score
from sklearn.metrics import mean_absolute_error
from sklearn.model_selection import train_test_split

# Load the California Housing dataset
cal_housing = fetch_california_housing()
X, y = cal_housing.data, cal_housing.target
names = cal_housing.feature_names
Xtrain, Xtest, ytrain, ytest = train_test_split(X, y, test_size = 0.1,
random_state = 0)

# Create MLP regression object
print("Training MLPRegressor...")
```

```
regr = MLPRegressor(activation = 'logistic')
# Train the model using the training sets
regr.fit(Xtrain, ytrain)
# Make predictions using the testing set
ypred = regr.predict(Xtest)
# Explained variance score: 1 is perfect prediction
print("R^2 = %0.5f" % r2_score(ytest, ypred))
# The mean absolute error
print("MAE = %5.3f" % mean_absolute_error(ytest, ypred))
# The mean squared error
print("MSE = %5.3f" % mean_squared_error(ytest, ypred))
# Plot outputs
fig, ax = plt.subplots()
ax.scatter(ytest, ypred, edgecolors = (0, 0, 0))
ax.plot([y.min(), y.max()], [y.min(), y.max()], 'k--', lw = 4)
ax.set_xlabel('Measured')
ax.set_ylabel('Predicted')
plt.show()
```

### 3.5.8 k-Nearest neighbors

When provided with a big training dataset, the k-nearest neighbors method appears to be labor intensive, as it has been mostly utilized in pattern recognition. Learning by analogy is the method on which the nearest neighbors are based. To detail this, it actually means that learning by analogy is used for classifying the nearest neighbors, and it is done by making a comparison of closely related training tuple and the given test tuple. Hence "n" attributes are used for the recognition of the training tuples where, in the n-dimensional space, every tuple relates to a separate point. In case of an unidentified tuple, the role of the k-nearest neighbors classifier becomes to explore the pattern space for all closely located k training tuples, and they are called the k-nearest neighbors. The distance metric is used to define the level of closeness, like Euclidean distance. For any k-nearest neighbors, the most basic class is linked with the unidentified tuple. When k becomes equal to one, it means that the tuple that is unidentified is linked with the class of the closest training tuple in pattern space. Usually, the value of k is larger when the number of training tuples is large (Han, Pei, & Kamber, 2011). The number of main elements is three in this method, which includes a set of labeled objects or records, a distance metric to identify the distance that exists between objects, and the k value to discern the nearest neighbors. When classification needs to be determined for an unlabeled object, the distance between the labeled object and the object itself needs to be computed, and thereby the identification of the k-nearest neighbors is attained. Therefore the nearest neighbors' class labels are employed in order to identify the object's class label (Wu et al., 2008).

Unless the training set includes identical instances from different classes, the classes can be separated perfectly on the training set, as the set memorized all training examples. Moreover, by choosing the right examples any decision boundary can be more or less represented. Hence, the k-nearest neighbors classifier has low bias but also high variance. This results in a risk of overfitting if the training data is limited, noisy, or unrepresentative. Actually, high-dimensional instance spaces can be challenging for the *curse of dimensionality*. High-dimensional spaces tend to be extremely sparse, where each point is far away from virtually every other point, and hence pairwise distances tend to be uninformative. But even if you eliminate the curse of dimensionality, it is not a simple matter of counting the number of features, since there are many reasons why the effective dimensionality of the instance space might be much smaller than the number of features. For example, some of the features may be irrelevant and drown out the relevant features' signal in the distance calculations. In such a case it would be better, before creating a distance-based model, to reduce dimensionality by using *feature selection*. On the other hand, the data may live on a *manifold* of lower dimension than the instance space that permits other dimensionality-reduction techniques, such as *principal component analysis*. Obviously, only output targets (or exemplars) can be kept in the exemplar database, but if we can find a way of combining these, we can eliminate this restriction by applying the k-nearest neighbors method. The k-nearest neighbors classifier takes a vote between the $k \geq 1$ nearest exemplars of the instance to be classified and predicts the majority class. If $k$-nearest neighbors is used for regression problems, the apparent way to combine the predictions from the $k$ neighbors is by taking the mean value that is also distance-weighted (Flach, 2012).

### Example 3.16

The following Python code utilizes k-NN classifier by using the scikit-learn library APIs. In this example we utilize the MNIST handwritten digits dataset (details are explained previously). The MNIST handwritten digits dataset is divided into training and test set and then classified by using k-NN classifier. The classification accuracy, precision, recall, F1 score, Cohen kappa score, and Matthews correlation coefficient are calculated. The classification report and confusion matrix are also given. Note that this example is adapted from Python–scikit-learn.

```
# ===============================================================
# k-NN example with training and test set
# ===============================================================
import time
import numpy as np
from sklearn.datasets import fetch_openml
from sklearn.model_selection import train_test_split
from sklearn.preprocessing import StandardScaler
from sklearn.utils import check_random_state
from sklearn.neighbors import KNeighborsClassifier

print(__doc__)

# Turn down for faster convergence
train_samples = 5000
```

```
# Load data from https://www.openml.org/d/554
X, y = fetch_openml('mnist_784', version = 1, return_X_y = True)

random_state = check_random_state(0)
permutation = random_state.permutation(X.shape[0])
X = X[permutation]
y = y[permutation]
X = X.reshape((X.shape[0], -1))
Xtrain, Xtest, ytrain, ytest = train_test_split(X, y, train_size = train_
samples, test_size = 10000)
#Transform data using standart scaler
scaler = StandardScaler()
Xtrain = scaler.fit_transform(Xtrain)
Xtest = scaler.transform(Xtest)

#Create the Model
clf = KNeighborsClassifier(n_neighbors = 5)
#Train the model with Training Dataset
clf.fit(Xtrain,ytrain)
#Test the model with Testset
ypred = clf.predict(Xtest)

#Evaluate the Model and Print Performance Metrics
from sklearn import metrics
print('Accuracy:', np.round(metrics.accuracy_score(ytest,ypred),4))
print('Precision:', np.round(metrics.precision_score(ytest,
           ypred,average = 'weighted'),4))
print('Recall:', np.round(metrics.recall_score(ytest,ypred,
           average = 'weighted'),4))
print('F1 Score:', np.round(metrics.f1_score(ytest,ypred,
           average = 'weighted'),4))
print('Cohen  Kappa  Score:',  np.round(metrics.cohen_kappa_score(ytest,
ypred),4))
print('Matthews  Corrcoef:',  np.round(metrics.matthews_corrcoef(ytest,
ypred),4))
print('\t\tClassification Report:\n', metrics.classification_report(ypred,
ytest))
from sklearn.metrics import confusion_matrix
print("Confusion Matrix:\n",confusion_matrix(ytest, ypred))

#Plot Confusion Matrix
from sklearn.metrics import confusion_matrix
from io import BytesIO #neded for plot
```

```
import seaborn as sns; sns.set()
import matplotlib.pyplot as plt

mat = confusion_matrix(ytest, ypred)
sns.heatmap(mat.T, square = True, annot = True, fmt = 'd', cbar = False)
plt.xlabel('true label')
plt.ylabel('predicted label');

plt.savefig("Confusion.jpg")
# Save SVG in a fake file object.
f = BytesIO()
plt.savefig(f, format = "svg")
```

## Example 3.17

The following Python code utilizes k-NN classifier by using the scikit-learn library APIs. In this example we utilize the Iris dataset, which exists in sklearn.datasets. The Iris dataset is classified with k-NN classifier by using 10-fold cross-validation. The classification accuracy, precision, recall, F1 score, Cohen kappa score, and Matthews correlation coefficient are calculated. Note that this example is adapted from Python–scikit-learn.

```
# ============================================================================
# k-NN example with cross-validation
# ============================================================================
from sklearn.neighbors import KNeighborsClassifier
from sklearn.model_selection import cross_val_score
from sklearn.datasets import load_iris
iris = load_iris()
X, y = iris.data, iris.target

#Create a Model
model = KNeighborsClassifier(n_neighbors = 5)

CV = 10 #10-Fold Cross Validation
#Evaluate Model Using 10-Fold Cross Validation and Print Performance
Metrics
Acc_scores = cross_val_score(model, X, y, cv = CV)
print("Accuracy: %0.3f (+/- %0.3f)" % (Acc_scores.mean(), Acc_scores.
std() * 2))
f1_scores = cross_val_score(model, X, y, cv = CV,scoring = 'f1_macro')
print("F1 score: %0.3f (+/- %0.3f)" % (f1_scores.mean(), f1_scores.std()
* 2))
```

```
Precision_scores = cross_val_score(model, X, y, cv = CV,scoring = 'preci-
sion_macro')
print("Precision score: %0.3f (+/- %0.3f)" % (Precision_scores.mean(),
Precision_scores.std() * 2))
Recall_scores = cross_val_score(model, X, y, cv = CV,scoring = 'recall_
macro')
print("Recall score: %0.3f (+/- %0.3f)" % (Recall_scores.mean(), Recall_
scores.std() * 2))
from sklearn.metrics import cohen_kappa_score, make_scorer
kappa_scorer = make_scorer(cohen_kappa_score)
Kappa_scores = cross_val_score(model, X, y, cv = CV,scoring = kappa_scorer)
print("Kappa score: %0.3f (+/- %0.3f)" % (Kappa_scores.mean(), Kappa_
scores.std() * 2))
```

## Example 3.18

The following Python code is used to represent the k-NN regression by using the scikit-learn library APIs. In this example we utilize the California housing dataset explained previously. The straight line seen in the plot demonstrates how k-NN regression tries to draw a straight line, which minimizes the residual sum of squares between the observed responses in the dataset, and the responses predicted by the k-NN approximation. The correlation coefficient $R^2$, MAE, and MSE are also calculated. Note that this example is adapted from Python–scikit-learn.

```
# =====================================================================
# k-NN regression example with California housing dataset
# =====================================================================
import matplotlib.pyplot as plt
import numpy as np
from sklearn.neighbors import KNeighborsRegressor
from sklearn.datasets.california_housing import fetch_california_housing
from sklearn.metrics import mean_squared_error, r2_score
from sklearn.metrics import mean_absolute_error
from sklearn.model_selection import train_test_split

# Load the California Housing dataset
cal_housing = fetch_california_housing()
X, y = cal_housing.data, cal_housing.target
names = cal_housing.feature_names
Xtrain, Xtest, ytrain, ytest = train_test_split(X, y, test_size = 0.1,
random_state = 0)

# Create a Regression object
print("Training Regressor...")
```

```
regr = KNeighborsRegressor(n_neighbors = 2)
# Train the model using the training sets
regr.fit(Xtrain, ytrain)
# Make predictions using the testing set
ypred = regr.predict(Xtest)

# Explained variance score: 1 is perfect prediction
print("R^2 = %0.5f" % r2_score(ytest, ypred))
# The mean absolute error
print("MAE = %5.3f" % mean_absolute_error(ytest, ypred))
# The mean squared error
print("MSE = %5.3f" % mean_squared_error(ytest, ypred))

# Plot outputs
fig, ax = plt.subplots()
ax.scatter(ytest, ypred, edgecolors = (0, 0, 0))
ax.plot([y.min(), y.max()], [y.min(), y.max()], 'k--', lw = 4)
ax.set_xlabel('Measured')
ax.set_ylabel('Predicted')
plt.show()
```

### 3.5.9 Support vector machines

Support vector machines (SVMs) are one of the main machine-learning algorithms that are not only accurate but also highly robust. The objective of SVMs is to locate the most suitable function of classification to separate the classes in the training data when undertaking the two-class learning task. In case of the linearly separable dataset, the role of the linear function of classification is to make the comparison of the separating hyperplane that goes through the center of the two classes, separating the two. Because there are a number of linear hyperplanes, the role of the SVM broadens to ensure that the margin, which is the most suitable function for the purpose, is employed by increasing the margin to the maximum between the classes. Instinctively, the definition of margin is the space between the classes. In mathematical terms, this margin is the shortest possible space between the hyperplane point and the closely located data points. Having this geometric definition is very important to augment the margin; despite the fact that there are a vast number of hyperplanes, no more than two can be utilized by the SVM. Determining the most extreme margin of hyperplanes that make the best use of generalization is the motivation that drives investigating SVMs. It permits the most appropriate classification performance on training data, as well as perfectly classifies future data (Wu et al., 2008). It can also be employed for generalization of the highly distributed data. As compared to the other classification methods like Bayes and ANN, it indicates an improved accuracy in classification. The training process relies on the sequential technique of minimization, and classification accuracy is found to be better in SVM, as it gives improved generalization capacity (Ray, Mohanty, & Panigrahi, 2019).

## Example 3.19

The following Python code utilizes SVM classifier through the Scikit-learn library APIs. In this example we utilize the optical recognition of handwritten digits dataset, which exists in sklearn. datasets. The optical recognition of handwritten digits dataset is divided into training and test set and then classified by using SVM classifier. The classification accuracy, precision, recall, F1 score, Cohen kappa score, and Matthews correlation coefficient are calculated. The classification report and confusion matrix are also given. Note that this example is adapted from Python–scikit-learn.

```
# =====================================================================
# SVM example with training and test set
# =====================================================================
import numpy as np
from sklearn.model_selection import train_test_split
from sklearn.preprocessing import StandardScaler
from sklearn.utils import check_random_state
from sklearn import svm
from sklearn.datasets import load_digits

#Load dataset and split to training and testing set
X, y = load_digits(return_X_y = True)
Xtrain, Xtest, ytrain, ytest = train_test_split(X, y, test_size = 0.3, ran-
dom_state = 0)

#Transfrom the data using Standard Scaler
scaler = StandardScaler()
Xtrain = scaler.fit_transform(Xtrain)
Xtest = scaler.transform(Xtest)

C = 10.0 # SVM regularization parameter
#Create the Model
clf =svm.SVC(kernel = 'linear', C = C)
#Train the model with Training Dataset
clf.fit(Xtrain,ytrain)
#Test the model with Testset
ypred = clf.predict(Xtest)

#Evaluate the Model and Print Performance Metrics
from sklearn import metrics
print('Accuracy:', np.round(metrics.accuracy_score(ytest,ypred),4))
print('Precision:', np.round(metrics.precision_score(ytest,
            ypred,average = 'weighted'),4))
print('Recall:', np.round(metrics.recall_score(ytest,ypred,
            average = 'weighted'),4))
```

```
print('F1 Score:', np.round(metrics.f1_score(ytest,ypred,
           average = 'weighted'),4))
print('Cohen Kappa Score:', np.round(metrics.cohen_kappa_score(ytest,
ypred),4))
print('Matthews Corrcoef:', np.round(metrics.matthews_corrcoef(ytest,
ypred),4))
print('\t\tClassification Report:\n', metrics.classification_report(ypred,
ytest))
from sklearn.metrics import confusion_matrix
print("Confusion Matrix:\n",confusion_matrix(ytest, ypred))

#Plot Confusion Matrix
from sklearn.metrics import confusion_matrix
from io import BytesIO #neded for plot
import seaborn as sns; sns.set()
import matplotlib.pyplot as plt

mat = confusion_matrix(ytest, ypred)
sns.heatmap(mat.T, square = True, annot = True, fmt = 'd', cbar = False)
plt.xlabel('true label')
plt.ylabel('predicted label');

plt.savefig("Confusion.jpg")
# Save SVG in a fake file object.
f = BytesIO()
plt.savefig(f, format = "svg")
```

## Example 3.20

The following Python code utilizes SVM classifier through the Scikit-learn library APIs. In this example we utilize the Iris dataset, which exists in sklearn.datasets. The Iris dataset is classified with SVM classifier by using 10-fold cross-validation. The classification accuracy, precision, recall, F1 score, Cohen kappa score, and Matthews correlation coefficient are calculated. Note that this example is adapted from Python–scikit-learn.

```
# ======================================================================
# SVM example with cross-validation
# ======================================================================
from sklearn import svm
from sklearn.model_selection import cross_val_score
from sklearn.datasets import load_iris
iris = load_iris()
X, y = iris.data, iris.target
```

```
C = 50.0 # SVM regularization parameter
# fit model no training data
model = svm.SVC(kernel = 'linear', C = C)

CV = 10 #10-Fold Cross Validation
#Evaluate Model Using 10-Fold Cross Validation and Print Performance
Metrics
Acc_scores = cross_val_score(model, X, y, cv = CV)
print("Accuracy: %0.3f (+/- %0.3f)" % (Acc_scores.mean(), Acc_scores.
std() * 2))
f1_scores = cross_val_score(model, X, y, cv = CV,scoring = 'f1_macro')
print("F1 score: %0.3f (+/- %0.3f)" % (f1_scores.mean(), f1_scores.std()
* 2))
Precision_scores = cross_val_score(model, X, y,
cv = CV,scoring = 'precision_macro')
print("Precision score: %0.3f (+/- %0.3f)" % (Precision_scores.mean(),
Precision_scores.std() * 2))
Recall_scores = cross_val_score(model, X, y, cv = CV,scoring = 'recall_
macro')
print("Recall score: %0.3f (+/- %0.3f)" % (Recall_scores.mean(),
Recall_scores.std() * 2))
from sklearn.metrics import cohen_kappa_score, make_scorer
kappa_scorer = make_scorer(cohen_kappa_score)
Kappa_scores = cross_val_score(model, X, y, cv = CV,scoring = kappa_scorer)
print("Kappa score: %0.3f (+/- %0.3f)" % (Kappa_scores.mean(), Kappa_
scores.std() * 2))
```

## Example 3.21

The following Python code is used to represent the transformation of target in regression by using SVR from the scikit-learn library. In this example we utilize the Boston house prices dataset, which exists in sklearn.datasets. This example employs the transformed features of the Boston house price dataset using ***TransformedTargetRegressor.*** TransformedTargetRegressor transforms the targets y before fitting a regression model. The predictions are mapped back to the original space via an inverse transform. It takes as an argument the regressor, which is utilized for prediction, and the transformer, which is applied to the target variable. The straight line seen in the plot demonstrates how SVR regression tries to draw a straight line, which minimizes the residual sum of squares between the observed responses in the dataset, and the responses predicted by the SVR approximation. The correlation coefficient $R^2$, MAE, and MSE are also calculated. The example shows that the target transformation improved the performance of the SVR regression model. Note that this example is adapted from Python–scikit-learn.

```
# ====================================================================
# SVR regression example with Boston house prices dataset
# ====================================================================
```

```
# ==========================================================================
#Transforming target in regression
# ==========================================================================
from sklearn.compose import TransformedTargetRegressor
from sklearn.preprocessing import QuantileTransformer
from sklearn.svm import SVR
from sklearn.model_selection import train_test_split
from sklearn.metrics import mean_squared_error, r2_score
from sklearn.metrics import mean_absolute_error
from sklearn.datasets import load_boston

# Load the Boston House prices dataset
boston = load_boston()
X = boston.data
y = boston.target
X_train, X_test, y_train, y_test = train_test_split(X, y, random_
state = 0)

# ==========================================================================
# Prediction without Transformation
# ==========================================================================

#Create Regression object
regr = SVR(gamma = 'scale', C = 200.0, epsilon = 0.2)
# Train the model using the training sets
regr.fit(X_train, y_train)
# Make predictions using the testing set
y_pred = regr.predict(X_test)

print('R^2 score without Transformation: {0:.2f}'.format(regr.score(X_
test, y_test)))
# Explained variance score: 1 is perfect prediction
print("R^2 = %0.5f" % r2_score(y_test, y_pred))
# The mean absolute error
print("MAE = %5.3f" % mean_absolute_error(y_test, y_pred))
# The mean squared error
print("MSE = %5.3f" % mean_squared_error(y_test, y_pred))

# Plot outputs
fig, ax = plt.subplots()
ax.scatter(y_test, y_pred, edgecolors = (0, 0, 0))
ax.plot([y.min(), y.max()], [y.min(), y.max()], 'k--', lw = 4)
ax.set_xlabel('Measured')
ax.set_ylabel('Predicted')
```

```
plt.title('Without Transformation')
plt.show()

# =====================================================================
# Prediction with Transformation
# =====================================================================
transformer = QuantileTransformer(output_distribution = 'normal')
regressor = SVR(gamma = 'scale', C = 200.0, epsilon = 0.2)
regr = TransformedTargetRegressor(regressor = regressor,
             transformer = transformer)
X_train, X_test, y_train, y_test = train_test_split(X, y, random_state = 0)
regr.fit(X_train, y_train)
y_pred = regr.predict(X_test)

print('R^2 score with Transformation: {0:.2f}'.format(regr.score(X_test,
y_test)))
# Explained variance score: 1 is perfect prediction
print("R^2 = %0.5f" % r2_score(y_test, y_pred))
# The mean absolute error
print("MAE = %5.3f" % mean_absolute_error(y_test, y_pred))
# The mean squared error
print("MSE = %5.3f" % mean_squared_error(y_test, y_pred))

# Plot outputs
fig, ax = plt.subplots()
ax.scatter(y_test, y_pred, edgecolors = (0, 0, 0))
ax.plot([y.min(), y.max()], [y.min(), y.max()], 'k--', lw = 4)
ax.set_xlabel('Measured')
ax.set_ylabel('Predicted')
plt.title('With Transformation')
plt.show()
```

### 3.5.10 Decision tree classifiers

A decision tree is a dividing-and-conquering recursive data structure. It is a powerful non-parametric approach that can be used for classification as well as regression. In parametric estimation, a model is represented over the entire input space and trained with full training data from its parameters. It is then easy to use the same template and set of parameters for any test input. In nonparametric estimation, the input space is divided into local regions, described by a distance measure like the Euclidean norm, and the associated local model created from the training data in that region is used for each source. A decision tree is a hierarchical supervised learning model in which a smaller number of stages define the local region in a series of sequential splits. A decision tree is made up of internal decision nodes and terminal leaves. Each decision node uses a test function that labels the branches with discrete scores. A test is used at every node with an input, and one of the branches is chosen depending on the result. This process starts at the root and is conducted recursively before reaching a leaf node. A decision tree is a nonparametric model in the sense that no parametric structure is presumed for category densities and the tree assembly is not a static a priori, but the tree expands by inserting leaves and branches during the learning process depending on the nature of the problem inherent in the data. In the case of classification, each leaf node has an output label that is the class code, and it is a numerical value in regression. A leaf node identifies a localized region in the input space where instances in this region have the same classification labels or numerical outputs that are very similar in regression. The region boundaries are well-specified by the discriminants that can be coded on the path from the root to the leaf node in the inner nodes. The hierarchical allocation of decision results in the region containing an input being easily found. Moreover, the decision tree is easy to interpret and can be converted into an easily understandable set of IF-THEN rules. Decision trees are therefore widely accepted and preferred to more accurate but less interpretable approaches (Alpaydin, 2014; Subasi, 2019).

The decision tree learning models are ambitious and, beginning from the root with the complete training information, the best split must be checked in each phase. It divides the training data into two or more, depending on whether the selected feature is discrete or numerical. We then continue to divide recursively with the relevant subset until there is no longer any need to split, at which stage a leaf node is generated and labeled. In the case of a decision tree for classification, namely a classification tree, impurity measures are utilized for the goodness of a split. A split is valid after dividing for all branches if all branch-selecting instances belong to the same category. Entropy is a potential way of measuring impurity (Quinlan and Ross, 1986). Nevertheless, entropy is not the only feasible measure. Therefore, for all attributes, binary and numeric, the impurity should be calculated, and the impurity that has minimum entropy chosen. Then the development of the tree proceeds recursively and parallel to all branches that are not pure, until all are pure. This is the basis of the CART (classification and regression tree) algorithm (Breiman, Friedman, Olshen, & Stone, 1984), ID3 algorithm (Quinlan and Ross, 1986), and its extension C4.5 (Alpaydin, 2014; Quinlan, 1993; Subasi, 2019).

Usually, the node is not more divided if the number of training instances reaching the node is less than a certain percentage of the training set; to stop building a tree earlier than this is called tree prepruning. Another approach to have simplified trees is by postpruning, which works better than prepruning in reality. In the postpruning cycle, the tree grows completely until all the leaves are pure, without any training error. Subsequently, subtrees, which result in overfitting, have to be identified and pruned. The pruning set must be put aside from the initial labeled set that is not used during training. Every subtree must be substituted by a leaf node labeled with the training instances specified by the subtree. If the leaf node does not yield worse than the subtree on the pruning set, the subtree should also be pruned and the leaf node must be retained, as the additional complexity of the subtree is not sufficient; otherwise, the subtree should be preserved. If prepruning is compared to postpruning, prepruning is quicker, but postpruning generally results in a more accurate tree (Alpaydin, 2014; Subasi, 2019).

Tree models are one of the most common machine learning models. Because of their recursive "divide-and-conquer" existence, trees are descriptive and easy to understand, and of particular interest to computer scientists. Tree models are not limited to classification but can be used to solve almost any problem of machine learning, including ranking and estimation of probability, regression, and clustering. It is possible to define the tree structure common to all these models (Flach, 2012).

## Example 3.22

The following Python code utilizes DT classifier by employing the scikit-learn library APIs. In this example we utilize the MNIST handwritten digits dataset (for which details are explained previously). The MNIST handwritten digits dataset is divided into training and test set and then classified by using DT classifier. The classification accuracy, precision, recall, F1 score, Cohen kappa score, and Matthews correlation coefficient are calculated. The classification report and confusion matrix are also given. Note that this example is adapted from Python–scikit-learn.

```
# ==================================================================
# Decision tree example with training and testset
# ==================================================================
import time
import numpy as np
from sklearn.datasets import fetch_openml
from sklearn.model_selection import train_test_split
from sklearn.preprocessing import StandardScaler
from sklearn.utils import check_random_state
from sklearn import tree
print(__doc__)

# Turn down for faster convergence
train_samples = 5000

# Load data from https://www.openml.org/d/554
X, y = fetch_openml('mnist_784', version = 1, return_X_y = True)

random_state = check_random_state(0)
permutation = random_state.permutation(X.shape[0])
X = X[permutation]
y = y[permutation]
X = X.reshape((X.shape[0], -1))

Xtrain, Xtest, ytrain, ytest = train_test_split(
X, y, train_size = train_samples, test_size = 10000)
```

```
scaler = StandardScaler()
Xtrain = scaler.fit_transform(Xtrain)
Xtest = scaler.transform(Xtest)

#Create the Model
clf = tree.DecisionTreeClassifier()
#Train the Model with Training dataset
clf.fit(Xtrain,ytrain)
#Test the Model with Testing dataset
ypred = clf.predict(Xtest)

#Evaluate the Model and Print Performance Metrics
from sklearn import metrics
print('Accuracy:', np.round(metrics.accuracy_score(ytest,ypred),4))
print('Precision:', np.round(metrics.precision_score(ytest,
          ypred,average = 'weighted'),4))
print('Recall:', np.round(metrics.recall_score(ytest,ypred,
          average = 'weighted'),4))
print('F1 Score:', np.round(metrics.f1_score(ytest,ypred,
          average = 'weighted'),4))
print('Cohen  Kappa  Score:',  np.round(metrics.cohen_kappa_score(ytest,
ypred),4))
print('Matthews  Corrcoef:',  np.round(metrics.matthews_corrcoef(ytest,
ypred),4))
print('\t\tClassification Report:\n', metrics.classification_report(ypred,
ytest))

from sklearn.metrics import confusion_matrix
print("Confusion Matrix:\n",confusion_matrix(ytest, ypred))
from sklearn.metrics import confusion_matrix
from io import BytesIO #neded for plot
import seaborn as sns; sns.set()
import matplotlib.pyplot as plt

mat = confusion_matrix(ytest, ypred)
sns.heatmap(mat.T, square = True, annot = True, fmt = 'd', cbar = False)
plt.xlabel('true label')
plt.ylabel('predicted label');

plt.savefig("Confusion.jpg")
# Save SVG in a fake file object.
f = BytesIO()
plt.savefig(f, format = "svg")
```

## Example 3.23

The following Python code utilizes DT classifier by employing the scikit-learn library APIs. In this example we utilize the Iris dataset, which exists in sklearn.datasets. The Iris dataset is classified with DT classifier by using 10-fold cross-validation. The classification accuracy, precision, recall, F1 score, Cohen kappa score, and Matthews correlation coefficient are calculated. Note that this example is adapted from Python–scikit-learn.

```
# ==========================================================================
# Decision tree example with cross-validation
# ==========================================================================


from sklearn import tree
from sklearn.model_selection import cross_val_score
from sklearn.datasets import load_iris
iris = load_iris()
X, y = iris.data, iris.target


# fit model no training data
model = tree.DecisionTreeClassifier()


CV = 10 #10-Fold Cross Validation
#Evaluate Model Using 10-Fold Cross-Validation and Print Performance
Metrics
Acc_scores = cross_val_score(model, X, y, cv = CV)
print("Accuracy: %0.3f (+/- %0.3f)" % (Acc_scores.mean(), Acc_scores.
std() * 2))
f1_scores = cross_val_score(model, X, y, cv = CV,scoring = 'f1_macro')
print("F1 score: %0.3f (+/- %0.3f)" % (f1_scores.mean(), f1_scores.std()
* 2))
Precision_scores = cross_val_score(model, X, y,
cv = CV,scoring = 'precision_macro')
print("Precision score: %0.3f (+/- %0.3f)" % (Precision_scores.mean(),
Precision_scores.std() * 2))
Recall_scores = cross_val_score(model, X, y,
cv = CV,scoring = 'recall_macro')
print("Recall score: %0.3f (+/- %0.3f)" % (Recall_scores.mean(), Recall_
scores.std() * 2))
from sklearn.metrics import cohen_kappa_score, make_scorer
kappa_scorer = make_scorer(cohen_kappa_score)
Kappa_scores = cross_val_score(model, X, y, cv = CV,scoring = kappa_scorer)
print("Kappa score: %0.3f (+/- %0.3f)" % (Kappa_scores.mean(), Kappa_
scores.std() * 2))
```

### Example 3.24

The following Python code is used to represent the transformation of target in regression by employing DT regressor from the scikit-learn library. In this example we utilize the Boston house prices dataset, which exists in sklearn.datasets. This example employs the transformed features of the Boston house prices dataset using ***TransformedTargetRegressor.*** TransformedTargetRegressor transforms the targets y before fitting a regression model. The predictions are mapped back to the original space via an inverse transform. It takes as an argument the regressor, which is utilized for prediction, and the transformer, which is applied to the target variable. The straight line seen in the plot demonstrates how DT regression tries to draw a straight line, which minimizes the residual sum of squares between the observed responses in the dataset, and the responses predicted by the DT regressor. The correlation coefficient $R^2$, MAE, and MSE are also calculated. It is shown in the example that the target transformation improved the performance of the DT regression model. Note that this example is adapted from Python–scikit-learn.

```
# ======================================================================
# Decision tree regression example with Boston house prices dataset
# ======================================================================
# ======================================================================
#Transforming target in regression
# ======================================================================
from sklearn.compose import TransformedTargetRegressor
from sklearn.preprocessing import QuantileTransformer
from sklearn.tree import DecisionTreeRegressor
from sklearn.model_selection import train_test_split
from sklearn.metrics import mean_squared_error, r2_score
from sklearn.metrics import mean_absolute_error
from sklearn.datasets import load_boston

# Load the Boston house prices dataset
boston = load_boston()
X = boston.data
y = boston.target
X_train, X_test, y_train, y_test = train_test_split(X, y, random_
state = 0)

# ======================================================================
# Prediction without Transformation
# ======================================================================

#Create Regression object
regr = DecisionTreeRegressor(random_state = 0)
# Train the model using the training sets
```

```
regr.fit(X_train, y_train)
# Make predictions using the testing set
y_pred = regr.predict(X_test)

print('R^2 score without Transformation: {0:.2f}'.format(regr.score(X_
test, y_test)))
# Explained variance score: 1 is perfect prediction
print("R^2 = %0.5f" % r2_score(y_test, y_pred))
# The mean absolute error
print("MAE = %5.3f" % mean_absolute_error(y_test, y_pred))
# The mean squared error
print("MSE = %5.3f" % mean_squared_error(y_test, y_pred))
# Plot outputs
fig, ax = plt.subplots()
ax.scatter(y_test, y_pred, edgecolors = (0, 0, 0))
ax.plot([y.min(), y.max()], [y.min(), y.max()], 'k--', lw = 4)
ax.set_xlabel('Measured')
ax.set_ylabel('Predicted')
plt.title('Without Transformation')
plt.show()

# ==============================================================
# Prediction with Transformation
# ==============================================================
transformer = QuantileTransformer(output_distribution = 'normal')
regressor = DecisionTreeRegressor(random_state = 0)
regr = TransformedTargetRegressor(regressor = regressor,
               transformer = transformer)
X_train, X_test, y_train, y_test = train_test_split(X, y, random_state = 0)
regr.fit(X_train, y_train)
y_pred = regr.predict(X_test)

print('R^2 score with Transformation: {0:.2f}'.format(regr.score(X_test,
y_test)))
# Explained variance score: 1 is perfect prediction
print("R^2 = %0.5f" % r2_score(y_test, y_pred))
# The mean absolute error
print("MAE = %5.3f" % mean_absolute_error(y_test, y_pred))
# The mean squared error
print("MSE = %5.3f" % mean_squared_error(y_test, y_pred))

# Plot outputs
fig, ax = plt.subplots()
```

```
ax.scatter(y_test, y_pred, edgecolors=(0, 0, 0))
ax.plot([y.min(), y.max()], [y.min(), y.max()], 'k--', lw=4)
ax.set_xlabel('Measured')
ax.set_ylabel('Predicted')
plt.title('With Transformation')
plt.show()
```

### 3.5.11 Naive Bayes

Another important classification technique is the naive Bayes technique. Firstly, an earlier step of variable selection takes place where variables that are highly correlated are eliminated because of increased similarity in their mechanism of classes' separation. This means independence can approximate the relationships between the variables. Secondly, assuming the interactions to be zero leads toward an implicit regularization step, so the model variance is reduced, leading to classifications that are more accurate. Thirdly, in some scenarios, when there is a correlation between the variables, the overlapping takes place between the optimal decision surface and independent assumption so that the assumption has no effect on performance. Fourthly, the decision surface that the naive Bayes model produces has a complex nonlinear shape even though the surface is considered linear. For many reasons, this technique appears to be feasible. It is exceptionally easy to construct, because it does not require any difficult schemes for iterative parameter estimation. Users who are not skilled in making classifications can also understand its classification logic. Lastly, it may not be the best possible classifier for some applications; however, it can do quite well under particular circumstances (Wu et al., 2008).

#### Example 3.25

The following Python code utilizes naïve Bayes classifier by employing the scikit-learn library APIs. In this example we utilize the MNIST handwritten digits dataset (for which details are explained previously). The MNIST handwritten digits dataset is divided into training and test set and then classified by using the naive Bayes classifier. The classification accuracy, precision, recall, F1 score, Cohen kappa score, and Matthews correlation coefficient are calculated. The classification report and confusion matrix are also given. Note that this example is adapted from Python–scikit-learn.

```
#=========================================================================
# Naive Bayes example with training and testset
#=========================================================================
import time
import numpy as np
from sklearn.datasets import fetch_openml
# Import train_test_split function
```

```
from sklearn.model_selection import train_test_split
from sklearn.preprocessing import StandardScaler
from sklearn.utils import check_random_state
#Import Gaussian Naive Bayes model
from sklearn.naive_bayes import GaussianNB

print(__doc__)

# Turn down for faster convergence
train_samples = 5000
# Load data from https://www.openml.org/d/554
X, y = fetch_openml('mnist_784', version = 1, return_X_y = True)

random_state = check_random_state(0)
permutation = random_state.permutation(X.shape[0])
X = X[permutation]
y = y[permutation]
X = X.reshape((X.shape[0], -1))

# Split dataset into training set and test set
# 70% training and 30% test
Xtrain, Xtest, ytrain, ytest = train_test_split(X, y,test_size = 0.3, ran-
dom_state = 0)

scaler = StandardScaler()
Xtrain = scaler.fit_transform(Xtrain)
Xtest = scaler.transform(Xtest)

#Create a Gaussian Classifier
gnb = GaussianNB()
#Train the model using the training sets
gnb.fit(Xtrain, ytrain)
#Predict the response for test dataset
ypred = gnb.predict(Xtest)

#Evaluate the Model and Print Performance Metrics
from sklearn import metrics
print('Accuracy:', np.round(metrics.accuracy_score(ytest,ypred),4))
print('Precision:', np.round(metrics.precision_score(ytest,
          ypred,average = 'weighted'),4))
print('Recall:', np.round(metrics.recall_score(ytest,ypred,
          average = 'weighted'),4))
print('F1 Score:', np.round(metrics.f1_score(ytest,ypred,
          average = 'weighted'),4))
```

```
print('Cohen  Kappa  Score:',  np.round(metrics.cohen_kappa_score(ytest,
ypred),4))
print('Matthews  Corrcoef:',  np.round(metrics.matthews_corrcoef(ytest,
ypred),4))
print('\t\tClassification Report:\n', metrics.classification_report(ypred,
ytest))
from sklearn.metrics import confusion_matrix
print("Confusion Matrix:\n",confusion_matrix(ytest, ypred))

#Plot Confusion Matrix
from sklearn.metrics import confusion_matrix
from io import BytesIO #neded for plot
import seaborn as sns; sns.set()
import matplotlib.pyplot as plt

mat = confusion_matrix(ytest, ypred)
sns.heatmap(mat.T, square = True, annot = True, fmt = 'd', cbar = False)
plt.xlabel('true label')
plt.ylabel('predicted label');
plt.savefig("Confusion.jpg")
# Save SVG in a fake file object.
f = BytesIO()
plt.savefig(f, format = "svg")
```

## Example 3.26

The following Python code utilizes naive Bayes classifier by employing the scikit-learn library APIs. In this example we utilize the Iris dataset, which exists in sklearn.datasets. The Iris dataset is classified with naïve Bayes classifier by using 10-fold cross-validation. The classification accuracy, precision, recall, F1 score, Cohen kappa score, and Matthews correlation coefficient are calculated. Note that this example is adapted from Python–scikit-learn.

```
# ======================================================================
# Naive Bayes example with cross-validation
# ======================================================================
from sklearn.model_selection import cross_val_score
from sklearn.datasets import load_iris
#Import Gaussian Naive Bayes model
from sklearn.naive_bayes import GaussianNB
iris = load_iris()
X, y = iris.data, iris.target
```

```
#Create a Gaussian Classifier
model = GaussianNB()

CV = 10 #10-Fold Cross-Validation
#Evaluate Model Using 10-Fold Cross-Validation and Print Performance
Metrics
Acc_scores = cross_val_score(model, X, y, cv = CV)
print("Accuracy: %0.3f (+/- %0.3f)" % (Acc_scores.mean(), Acc_scores.
std() * 2))
f1_scores = cross_val_score(model, X, y, cv = CV,scoring = 'f1_macro')
print("F1 score: %0.3f (+/- %0.3f)" % (f1_scores.mean(), f1_scores.std()
* 2))
Precision_scores = cross_val_score(model, X, y,
cv = CV,scoring = 'precision_macro')
print("Precision score: %0.3f (+/- %0.3f)" % (Precision_scores.mean(),
Precision_scores.std() * 2))
Recall_scores = cross_val_score(model, X, y, cv = CV,scoring = 'recall_macro')
print("Recall score: %0.3f (+/- %0.3f)" % (Recall_scores.mean(), Recall_
scores.std() * 2))
from sklearn.metrics import cohen_kappa_score, make_scorer
kappa_scorer = make_scorer(cohen_kappa_score)
Kappa_scores = cross_val_score(model, X, y, cv = CV,scoring = kappa_scorer)
print("Kappa score: %0.3f (+/- %0.3f)" % (Kappa_scores.mean(), Kappa_
scores.std() * 2))
```

### 3.5.12 Ensemble methods

Model combinations are usually identified as *model ensembles*. They are the most effective approaches in machine learning, generally achieving better performance than the single models. But ensemble models bring an increased algorithmic cost and model complexity. There are two main motivations behind the ensemble learning: computational learning theory and statistics. A famous statistical theory says that averaging measurements can lead to a more reliable and stable estimate since we decrease the effect of random oscillations in single measurements. Therefore if we can build an ensemble model from the same training data, we might reduce the effect of random variations in single models. The main issue is how to realize diversity among these different models. The diversity is realized generally by training models on random subsets of the data, and even by building them from random subsets of the available features. Learnability of hypothesis languages is examined from the perspective of a learning model that defines what the meaning is by learnability. PAC learnability needs a hypothesis to be approximately accurate most of the time. An alternative learning model known as *weak learnability* needs a hypothesis that is learned a somehow better than chance. Even so, it is apparent that PAC-learnability is stricter than weak learnability. This was demonstrated utilizing an iterative algorithm, which repetitively creates a hypothesis targeted to correct the mistakes of the previous hypothesis by boosting. The final model combines the hypotheses learned in every iteration and thus creates an ensemble (Flach, 2012). Ensemble models have the following specifications:

- they build multiple, diverse predictive models from adapted versions of the training data by resampling or reweighting;
- they combine the predictions of these models by any means, generally by simple averaging or voting with or without weighting.

Since the idea of an ensemble method is to build a large model class from the predictions that are carefully chosen elements of it are pooled, they may achieve a better overall prediction. Breiman's random forests is an ensemble classifier based on bootstrapping, with trees being the ensemble. In other words, random forests is a "bagged" (i.e., bootstrap aggregated) version of trees. It can be seen that bagging is a very general idea. ANNs, SVMs, or any other model classifiers can be bagged. Another technique to create an ensemble model is reoptimizing sequentially and averaging the solutions. This can be achieved by boosting that utilizes a class of "weak learners" as its ensemble. A weak learner is a poor model, which still describes some crucial characteristic of the data. Hence, it is reasonable that combining over the appropriate collection of weak learners will generate a strong learner. Generally, there are two main principles producing ensemble models. First, combining models signifies a stronger model class than simply selecting one of them. Consequently, the weighted sum of predictions from a collection of models can achieve better performance than individual predictions since linear combinations of the models must produce a lower bias than any individual model. The predictions that the ensemble models are combined stay distinct since they are based on diverse assumptions, which cannot be easily merged, and they have various parameters with diverse estimates. In fact, ensemble models only enhance the model selection techniques when the models in the ensemble achieve various predictions (Clarke, Fokoue, & Zhang, 2009 Clarke, Foukoue, & Zhang, 2009). Two best-known ensemble algorithms are bagging and boosting.

### 3.5.13 Bagging

Bagging or bootstrap aggregating is an ensemble modeling algorithm trained with data subsets randomly selected from the training dataset to boost model variance. The moderate approach is to take a weighted vote or a weighted average in the case of a classification or a numerical prediction respectively. It allows you to differentiate test incidents for a specific machine learning method in order to create correct predictions. Instead of gathering independent sample datasets from the domain, bagging also deals with the original training data. Bagging is unique when resampling the original training data rather than using independent domain datasets. Different models are built in parallel from multiple samples to vote for the final model with equivalent weights. The classifier is always successful from the original training data, with considerably better predictions than the actual classifier, and never performs significantly poor. This seeks to neutralize the variance by adjusting the original training data through canceling certain instances and duplicating others. By avoiding overfitting, the classifier improves consistency and reduces bias and variance errors. Nonetheless, the biased model, which is robust in the variations in training data due to sampling, does not improve much (Witten, Frank, & Hall, 2011).

Bagging is an extremely successful ensemble learner that produces diverse models on distinct random samples of the original dataset. These samples are held uniformly with replacements that are called *bootstrap samples*. Since samples are held with replacement, the bootstrap sample will in general include duplicates, and therefore some of the original data points will be lost even if the bootstrap sample is of the same size as the original dataset. This is precisely what is needed, since differences between the bootstrap samples will produce diversity among the models in the ensemble. They can choose to aggregate the predictions of the various models by voting—the class predicted by most models wins—or by averaging, which is more fitting of the performance scores or probabilities of the base classifiers. By voting, we see that bagging generates a piecewise linear decision boundary, something unlikely with a single linear classifier. When we turn the votes from each model into estimates of probability, we see that the different boundaries of the decision divide the space of the example into segments, of which each may obtain a different score (Flach, 2012).

To construct a model, first split the dataset into training set and test set. Then get a bootstrap sample from the training data and train an indicator utilizing the sample. The previous steps should be repeated a random number of times. The models from the samples are combined by averaging the output for regression or voting in favor of classification. It consequently yields an approximation of the sampling error, likewise, indicated as the speculation error. It functions splendidly for unbalanced learning algorithms like neural systems, decision trees, and regression trees. However, it does not work properly with stable classifiers like k-nearest neighbors. The absence of understanding is the major detriment to bagging, as the strategy is utilized in the unsupervised context of group analysis (Kumari, 2012).

Bagging is an ensemble model that improves a model's performance as random forests. This approach is built on resampling to ensure that the data are described by the models on average. A successful technique is one that looks for a sufficiently large class of models that can generate a model with a small error of misclassification. But even if this is done by a method, it may be unstable. Unstable techniques are those with high variability in the selection of their model. ANN, trees, and subset selection in linear regression are unstable. Nearest-neighbors methods, on the other hand, are stable. Generally speaking, bagging can enhance the performance of unstable classifier so that it is nearly optimal (Clarke, Fokoue, & Zhang, 2009).

Bagging is particularly useful in combination with tree models, which are quite vulnerable to variations in training data. Bagging is often combined with another concept when applied to tree models. A method often referred to as subspace sampling constructs each tree from a different random subset of features. It enables even more variety in the ensemble and has the additional advantage of reducing each tree's training time. Random forests are the resulting ensemble model. The space partition of the accompanying example is basically the combination of the individual tree's partitions in the ensemble. Therefore, while the random forest partition is finer than most tree partitions, it can be mapped back to a single tree model in theory since intersection refers to the combination of the branches of two different trees. This is distinct from bagging linear classifiers, in which the ensemble has a decision boundary that a single base classifier cannot learn. One could also assume that an alternative learning algorithm for tree models is implemented by the random forest algorithm (Flach, 2012).

## Example 3.27

The following Python code utilizes bagging ensemble classifier by employing the Scikit-learn library APIs. In this example we utilize the MNIST handwritten digits dataset (for which details are explained previously). The MNIST handwritten digits dataset is divided into training and test set and then classified by using bagging ensemble classifier. The classification accuracy, precision, recall, F1 score, Cohen kappa score, and Matthews correlation coefficient are calculated. The classification report and confusion matrix are also given. Note that this example is adapted from Python–scikit-learn.

```
# ==========================================================================
# Bagging example with training and test set
# ==========================================================================
import time
import numpy as np
from sklearn.datasets import fetch_openml
# Import train_test_split function
from sklearn.model_selection import train_test_split
from sklearn.preprocessing import StandardScaler
from sklearn.utils import check_random_state
#Import Bagging ensemble model
from sklearn.ensemble import BaggingClassifier
#Import Tree model as a base classifier
from sklearn import tree

print(__doc__)

# Turn down for faster convergence
train_samples = 5000

# Load data from https://www.openml.org/d/554
X, y = fetch_openml('mnist_784', version = 1, return_X_y = True)

random_state = check_random_state(0)
permutation = random_state.permutation(X.shape[0])
X = X[permutation]
y = y[permutation]
X = X.reshape((X.shape[0], -1))

# Split dataset into training set and test set
# 70% training and 30% test
Xtrain, Xtest, ytrain, ytest = train_test_split(X, y,test_size = 0.3,
random_state = 0)
```

```
scaler = StandardScaler()
Xtrain = scaler.fit_transform(Xtrain)
Xtest = scaler.transform(Xtest)

#Create a Bagging Ensemble Classifier
" " "BaggingClassifier(base_estimator = None, n_estimators = 10, max_sam-
ples = 1.0,
max_features = 1.0, bootstrap = True, bootstrap_features = False, oob_
score = False,
warm_start = False, n_jobs = None, random_state = None, verbose = 0)" " "
bagging = BaggingClassifier(tree.DecisionTreeClassifier(),
            max_samples = 0.5, max_features = 0.5)
#Train the model using the training sets
bagging.fit(Xtrain,ytrain)
#Predict the response for test dataset
ypred = bagging.predict(Xtest)

#Evaluate the Model and Print Performance Metrics
from sklearn import metrics
print('Accuracy:', np.round(metrics.accuracy_score(ytest,ypred),4))
print('Precision:', np.round(metrics.precision_score(ytest,
            ypred,average = 'weighted'),4))
print('Recall:', np.round(metrics.recall_score(ytest,ypred,
            average = 'weighted'),4))
print('F1 Score:', np.round(metrics.f1_score(ytest,ypred,
            average = 'weighted'),4))
print('Cohen Kappa Score:', np.round(metrics.cohen_kappa_score(ytest,
ypred),4))
print('Matthews Corrcoef:', np.round(metrics.matthews_corrcoef(ytest,
ypred),4))
print('\t\tClassification Report:\n', metrics.classification_report(ypred,
ytest))
from sklearn.metrics import confusion_matrix
print("Confusion Matrix:\n",confusion_matrix(ytest, ypred))

#Plot Confusion Matrix
from sklearn.metrics import confusion_matrix
from io import BytesIO #neded for plot
import seaborn as sns; sns.set()
import matplotlib.pyplot as plt

mat = confusion_matrix(ytest, ypred)
sns.heatmap(mat.T, square = True, annot = True, fmt = 'd', cbar = False)
plt.xlabel('true label')
plt.ylabel('predicted label');
```

```
plt.savefig("Confusion.jpg")
# Save SVG in a fake file object.
f = BytesIO()
plt.savefig(f, format = "svg")
```

## Example 3.28

The following Python code utilizes bagging ensemble classifier by employing the scikit-learn library APIs. In this example we utilize the Iris dataset, which exists in sklearn.datasets. The Iris dataset is classified with bagging ensemble classifier by using 10-fold cross-validation. The classification accuracy, precision, recall, F1 score, Cohen kappa score, and Matthews correlation coefficient are calculated. Note that this example is adapted from Python–scikit-learn.

```
# ===========================================================================
# Bagging example with cross-validation
# ===========================================================================
print(__doc__)
from sklearn.model_selection import cross_val_score
from sklearn.datasets import load_iris
#Import Bagging ensemble model
from sklearn.ensemble import BaggingClassifier
#Import Tree model as a base classifier
from sklearn import tree
iris = load_iris()
X, y = iris.data, iris.target

"""BaggingClassifier(base_estimator = None,  n_estimators = 10,  max_sam-
ples = 1.0,
max_features = 1.0,  bootstrap = True,  bootstrap_features = False,  oob_
score = False,
warm_start = False, n_jobs = None, random_state = None, verbose = 0)" " "
#Create a Bagging Ensemble Classifier
model = BaggingClassifier(tree.DecisionTreeClassifier(),
        max_samples = 0.5, max_features = 0.5)

CV = 10 #10-Fold Cross Validation
#Evaluate Model Using 10-Fold Cross Validation and Print Performance
Metrics
Acc_scores = cross_val_score(model, X, y, cv = CV)
print("Accuracy: %0.3f (+/- %0.3f)" % (Acc_scores.mean(), Acc_scores.
std() * 2))
f1_scores = cross_val_score(model, X, y, cv = CV,scoring = 'f1_macro')
print("F1 score: %0.3f (+/- %0.3f)" % (f1_scores.mean(), f1_scores.std()
* 2))
```

```
Precision_scores = cross_val_score(model, X, y,
cv = CV,scoring = 'precision_macro')
print("Precision score: %0.3f (+/- %0.3f)" % (Precision_scores.mean(),
Precision_scores.std() * 2))
Recall_scores = cross_val_score(model, X, y, cv = CV,scoring = 'recall_macro')
print("Recall score: %0.3f (+/- %0.3f)" % (Recall_scores.mean(), Recall_
scores.std() * 2))
from sklearn.metrics import cohen_kappa_score, make_scorer
kappa_scorer = make_scorer(cohen_kappa_score)
Kappa_scores = cross_val_score(model, X, y, cv = CV,scoring = kappa_scorer)
print("Kappa score: %0.3f (+/- %0.3f)" % (Kappa_scores.mean(), Kappa_
scores.std() * 2))
```

### 3.5.14 Random forest

Random forest makes a practice of the decision tree as the main classifier, and the use of this ensemble learning technique is to characterize the information. The ensemble technique combines the indicators from multiple trained classifiers to classify new instances. A random forest is a type of classifier that consists of tree-organized classifiers. In those classifiers, the independent random vectors are disseminated indistinguishably. Moreover, each tree makes a unit vote for the most well-known class. A random vector is independent of the former random vectors with the same distribution, and the training test is employed to create a tree. In the case of random forests, an upper bound is determined with the purpose to acquire the generalization error as far as two parameters that are given beneath: the accurateness of the individual classifiers and the dependency between them. There are two sections for generalization of error in case of random forest. These sections are characterized as the individual classifier's strength in the forest and the correlation between them as a function of raw margin. The correlation needs to be reduced to increase the random forest's accuracy level while making sure that the strength remains intact (Goel & Abhilasha, 2017).

#### Example 3.29

The following Python code utilizes random forest classifier by employing the scikit-learn library APIs. In this example we utilize the MNIST handwritten digits dataset (for which details are explained previously). The MNIST handwritten digits dataset is divided into training and test set and then classified by using random forest classifier. The classification accuracy, precision, recall, F1 score, Cohen kappa score, and Matthews correlation coefficient are calculated. The classification report and confusion matrix are also given. Note that this example is adapted from Python–scikit-learn.

```
# ===================================================================
# Random forest example with training and testset
# ===================================================================
```

```
import time
import numpy as np
from sklearn.datasets import fetch_openml
from sklearn.model_selection import train_test_split
from sklearn.preprocessing import StandardScaler
from sklearn.utils import check_random_state
from sklearn.ensemble import RandomForestClassifier

print(__doc__)

# Turn down for faster convergence
train_samples = 5000

# Load data from https://www.openml.org/d/554
X, y = fetch_openml('mnist_784', version = 1, return_X_y = True)

random_state = check_random_state(0)
permutation = random_state.permutation(X.shape[0])
X = X[permutation]
y = y[permutation]
X = X.reshape((X.shape[0], -1))

Xtrain, Xtest, ytrain, ytest = train_test_split(
X, y, train_size = train_samples, test_size = 10000)

#Transform the data using Standard Scaler
scaler = StandardScaler()
Xtrain = scaler.fit_transform(Xtrain)
Xtest = scaler.transform(Xtest)

#In order to change to accuracy increase n_estimators
"""RandomForestClassifier(n_estimators = 'warn', criterion = 'gini', max_
depth = None,
min_samples_split = 2, min_samples_leaf = 1, min_weight_fraction_leaf = 0.0,
max_features = 'auto', max_leaf_nodes = None, min_impurity_decrease = 0.0,
min_impurity_split = None, bootstrap = True, oob_score = False, n_jobs = None,
random_state = None, verbose = 0, warm_start = False, class_weight = None)" " "
clf = RandomForestClassifier(n_estimators = 200)
#Create the Model
#Train the model with Training Dataset
clf.fit(Xtrain,ytrain)
#Test the model with Testset
ypred = clf.predict(Xtest)
```

```
#Evaluate the Model and Print Performance Metrics
from sklearn import metrics
print('Accuracy:', np.round(metrics.accuracy_score(ytest,ypred),4))
print('Precision:', np.round(metrics.precision_score(ytest,
         ypred,average = 'weighted'),4))
print('Recall:', np.round(metrics.recall_score(ytest,ypred,
         average = 'weighted'),4))
print('F1 Score:', np.round(metrics.f1_score(ytest,ypred,
average = 'weighted'),4))
print('Cohen  Kappa  Score:',  np.round(metrics.cohen_kappa_score(ytest,
ypred),4))
print('Matthews  Corrcoef:',  np.round(metrics.matthews_corrcoef(ytest,
ypred),4))
print('\t\tClassification Report:\n', metrics.classification_report(ypred,
ytest))
from sklearn.metrics import confusion_matrix
print("Confusion Matrix:\n",confusion_matrix(ytest, ypred))

#Plot Confusion Matrix
from sklearn.metrics import confusion_matrix
from io import BytesIO #neded for plot
import seaborn as sns; sns.set()
import matplotlib.pyplot as plt
mat = confusion_matrix(ytest, ypred)
sns.heatmap(mat.T, square = True, annot = True, fmt = 'd', cbar = False)
plt.xlabel('true label')
plt.ylabel('predicted label');

plt.savefig("Confusion.jpg")
# Save SVG in a fake file object.
f = BytesIO()
plt.savefig(f, format = "svg")
```

## Example 3.30

The following Python code utilizes random forest classifier by employing the scikit-learn library APIs. In this example we utilize the Iris dataset, which exists in sklearn.datasets. The Iris dataset is classified with random forest classifier by using 10-fold cross-validation. The classification accuracy, precision, recall, F1 score, Cohen kappa score, and Matthews correlation coefficient are calculated. Note that this example is adapted from Python–scikit-learn.

```
# ============================================================================
# Random forest example with cross-validation
# ============================================================================
from sklearn.ensemble import RandomForestClassifier
from sklearn.model_selection import cross_val_score
from sklearn.datasets import load_iris
iris = load_iris()
X, y = iris.data, iris.target

#In order to change to accuracy increase n_estimators
"""RandomForestClassifier(n_estimators = 'warn', criterion = 'gini', max_
depth = None,
min_samples_split = 2, min_samples_leaf = 1, min_weight_fraction_leaf = 0.0,
max_features = 'auto', max_leaf_nodes = None, min_impurity_decrease = 0.0,
min_impurity_split = None, bootstrap = True, oob_score = False, n_jobs = None,
random_state = None, verbose = 0, warm_start = False, class_weight = None)" " "
# fit model no training data
model = RandomForestClassifier(n_estimators = 200)


CV = 10 #10-Fold Cross Validation
#Evaluate Model Using 10-Fold Cross Validation and Print Performance
Metrics
Acc_scores = cross_val_score(model, X, y, cv = CV)
print("Accuracy: %0.3f (+/- %0.3f)" % (Acc_scores.mean(), Acc_scores.
std() * 2))
f1_scores = cross_val_score(model, X, y, cv = CV,scoring = 'f1_macro')
print("F1 score: %0.3f (+/- %0.3f)" % (f1_scores.mean(), f1_scores.std()
* 2))
Precision_scores = cross_val_score(model, X, y,
cv = CV,scoring = 'precision_macro')
print("Precision score: %0.3f (+/- %0.3f)" % (Precision_scores.mean(),
Precision_scores.std() * 2))
Recall_scores = cross_val_score(model, X, y,
cv = CV,scoring = 'recall_macro')
print("Recall score: %0.3f (+/- %0.3f)" % (Recall_scores.mean(), Recall_
scores.std() * 2))
from sklearn.metrics import cohen_kappa_score, make_scorer
kappa_scorer = make_scorer(cohen_kappa_score)
Kappa_scores = cross_val_score(model, X, y, cv = CV,scoring = kappa_scorer)
print("Kappa score: %0.3f (+/- %0.3f)" % (Kappa_scores.mean(), Kappa_
scores.std() * 2))
```

## Example 3.31

The following Python code is used to represent the transformation of target in regression by employing random forest regressor from the scikit-learn library. In this example we utilize the Boston house prices dataset, which exists in sklearn.datasets. This example utilizes the transformed features of the Boston house prices dataset employing ***TransformedTargetRegressor.*** TransformedTargetRegressor transforms the targets y before fitting a regression model. The predictions are mapped back to the original space via an inverse transform. It takes as an argument the regressor, which is utilized for prediction, and the transformer, which is applied to the target variable. The straight line seen in the plot demonstrates how random forest regression tries to draw a straight line, which will best minimize the residual sum of squares between the observed responses in the dataset, and the responses predicted by the random forest regressor. The correlation coefficient $R^2$, MAE, and MSE are also calculated. It can be seen from the example that the target transformation improved the performance of the random forest regression model. Note that this example is adapted from Python–scikit-learn.

```
# ===========================================================================
# Random forest regressor example with Boston house prices dataset
# ===========================================================================
# ===========================================================================
#Transforming target in regression
# ===========================================================================
import matplotlib.pyplot as plt
from sklearn.compose import TransformedTargetRegressor
from sklearn.preprocessing import QuantileTransformer
from sklearn.ensemble import RandomForestRegressor
from sklearn.model_selection import train_test_split
from sklearn.metrics import mean_squared_error, r2_score
from sklearn.metrics import mean_absolute_error
from sklearn.datasets import load_boston

# Load the Boston house prices dataset
boston = load_boston()
X = boston.data
y = boston.target
X_train, X_test, y_train, y_test = train_test_split(X, y, random_
state = 0)

# ===========================================================================
# Prediction without transformation
# ===========================================================================

# Create Regression object
regr = RandomForestRegressor(max_depth = 2, random_state = 0,
n_estimators = 100)
```

```
# Train the model using the training sets
regr.fit(X_train, y_train)
# Make predictions using the testing set
y_pred = regr.predict(X_test)

print('R^2 score without Transformation: {0:.2f}'.format(regr.score(X_
test, y_test)))
# Explained variance score: 1 is perfect prediction
print("R^2 = %0.5f" % r2_score(y_test, y_pred))
# The mean absolute error
print("MAE = %5.3f" % mean_absolute_error(y_test, y_pred))
# The mean squared error
print("MSE = %5.3f" % mean_squared_error(y_test, y_pred))

# Plot outputs
fig, ax = plt.subplots()
ax.scatter(y_test, y_pred, edgecolors = (0, 0, 0))
ax.plot([y.min(), y.max()], [y.min(), y.max()], 'k--', lw = 4)
ax.set_xlabel('Measured')
ax.set_ylabel('Predicted')
plt.title('Without Transformation')
plt.show()

# ==================================================================
# Prediction with transformation
# ==================================================================
transformer = QuantileTransformer(output_distribution = 'normal')
regressor = RandomForestRegressor(max_depth = 2, random_state = 0,
            n_estimators = 100)
regr = TransformedTargetRegressor(regressor = regressor,
            transformer = transformer)
X_train, X_test, y_train, y_test = train_test_split(X, y, random_state = 0)
regr.fit(X_train, y_train)
y_pred = regr.predict(X_test)
print('R^2 score with Transformation: {0:.2f}'.format(regr.score(X_test,
y_test)))
# Explained variance score: 1 is perfect prediction

print("R^2 = %0.5f" % r2_score(y_test, y_pred))
# The mean absolute error
print("MAE = %5.3f" % mean_absolute_error(y_test, y_pred))
# The mean squared error
```

```
print("MSE = %5.3f" % mean_squared_error(y_test, y_pred))
# Plot outputs
fig, ax = plt.subplots()
ax.scatter(y_test, y_pred, edgecolors = (0, 0, 0))
ax.plot([y.min(), y.max()], [y.min(), y.max()], 'k--', lw = 4)
ax.set_xlabel('Measured')
ax.set_ylabel('Predicted')
plt.title('With Transformation')
plt.show()
```

### 3.5.15 Boosting

Boosting is an ensemble learner model that is similar to bagging but utilizes a more complicated approach than bootstrap sampling to generate diverse training sets. The basic idea is simple and appealing. Assume that a linear classifier is trained on a dataset and we want to add another classifier to the ensemble, which works better on the misclassifications of the first classifier. A good approach is to give the misclassified instances a higher weight and to modify the classifier to take these weights into account. The basic linear classifier can estimate the class means as a weighted average (Flach, 2012).

If the learning technique is weak, it may only achieve slightly better than random estimating at forecasting the true classes. Boosting is a method that is developed to enhance the performance of certain weak learners by iteratively optimizing them on the dataset employed to achieve better performance. The iterative optimization utilizes an exponential loss function and a sequence of data-driven weights, which improves the cost of misclassifications, thus making consecutive iterations of the classifier more sensitive. Actually, the iterations form an ensemble of rules produced from a base classifier in the same way that ensemble voting by a weighted sum over the ensemble generally achieves better performance. Boosting is proposed by Schapire (Schapire, 1990) and has subsequently seen quick improvement. Boosting was initially proposed for weak learners, and the concept of weak learner is a stump. A stump can have a small error rate if it is related to a good model split, but mostly it does not, so enhancing it in one way or another is often a good idea. Similar to bagging, boosting tends to enhance the performance of unstable classifiers by decreasing their variances. There is evidence that boosting can overfit (Clarke et al., 2009).

There is some indication that neither bagging nor boosting improves much when the classifier is already pretty good (stable) with a low misclassification error. The reason is that the classifier is already almost optimal, as in LDA cases. Moreover, there is even some indication that boosting, like bagging, can degrade the performance of a classifier. This is more usual while the sample size is too small. There is a considerable inconsistency due to lack of data where the averaging technique cannot help much. Bagging and boosting are anticipated for various scenarios and are not easily comparable. For example, stumps are a weak classifier with high bias but often stable. In this case, the benefits of boosting may be inadequate since the class is limited, but bagging can achieve better performance. Larger trees might be amenable to variance reduction but might have less bias, thus they are more amenable to boosting. Finally, the approaches are diverse and encourage freewheeling applications. We can bag a boosted classifier or boost a bagged classifier. Furthermore, we can stack classifiers of diverse forms, say decision trees, ANN, SVMs, and nearest neighbors, and then boost the bagged version or take stacked ANNs and SVMs and boost the result. These kinds of options might be extremely exhausting; consequently, in order to improve ensemble methods, we need to decide carefully which classification or regression method is to be employed and how to employ it (Clarke et al., 2009).

#### 3.5.15.1 *Adaptive Boosting (AdaBoost)*

Adaptive boosting (Freund & Schapire, 1997) strategy has been proposed to expand the precision of the ensemble. The essential idea of boosting is to construct a progression of classifiers with the goal that the later classifier will concentrate more on the misclassified tuples of the last round. An ensemble of classifiers with high precision will be created since classifiers in the ensemble supplement one another. Boosting is considered to be a general strategy that is used for bringing improvement in a random learning algorithm. The model algorithm is easy to comprehend, and it does not experience overfitting. It handles both the binary classification issues just like multiclass issues are handled in the machine learning domain. AdaBoost likewise gives an expansion to the occurring regression issues. The boosting algorithm appears to be strong compared to bagging on the data with no noise. The algorithm is dependent on the datasets and is used for assembling numerous classifiers to merge them into a stronger classifier. Because of this, it is known as a successive classifiers' creation (Kumari, 2012).

To develop a classifier, we take the preparation or training set as the input. Besides that, the set of base learning algorithms are called more than once repetitively to keep up a set of weights over the preparation set. At first, all weights are set similarly,; however, in each round, the weights of inaccurately grouped examples are expanded with the goal that the frail learner is compelled to concentrate on the hard examples in the preparation data. Thirdly, this boosting can be connected by two structures, boosting by sampling and boosting by weighing. In the technique of learning by boosting, a weighted set of training can be accepted directly by the base learning algorithm. Now, with such algorithms, the entire preparation set is assigned to the base learning algorithm. Also, in boosting by sampling technique, models are drawn by displacing the preparation set with probability relative to their weights. The stopping iteration is controlled by the cross-validation technique (Kumari, 2012).

The algorithm does not require prior knowledge about the weak learner; thus it can be joined with any technique for discovering weak hypotheses. At long last, it accompanies a set of hypothetical guarantees given adequate data, and weak learner can dependably produce precise weak hypotheses. The algorithm is used on learning issues and follows two properties. The first property is that there are different hardness levels for the observed examples. The boosting algorithm will in general produce such distributions that are related to the harder examples, hence it is difficult for the weak algorithm to show efficiency in the same space. As for the second property, the algorithm cannot be changed repeatedly for different training datasets or hypotheses (Kumari, 2012).

## Example 3.32

The following Python code utilizes the AdaBoost classifier by employing the scikit-learn library APIs. In this example we utilize the MNIST handwritten digits dataset (for which details are explained previously). The MNIST handwritten digits dataset is divided into training and test set and then classified by using AdaBoost classifier. The classification accuracy, precision, recall, F1 score, Cohen kappa score, and Matthews correlation coefficient are calculated. The classification report and confusion matrix are also given. Note that this example is adapted from Python–scikit-learn.

```
# ===========================================================================
# Adaboost example with training and test set
# ===========================================================================
import time
import numpy as np
from sklearn.datasets import fetch_openml
# Import train_test_split function
from sklearn.model_selection import train_test_split
from sklearn.preprocessing import StandardScaler
from sklearn.utils import check_random_state
#Import Adaboost ensemble model
from sklearn.ensemble import AdaBoostClassifier
#Import Tree model as a base classifier
from sklearn import tree

print(__doc__)

# Turn down for faster convergence
train_samples = 5000

# Load data from https://www.openml.org/d/554
X, y = fetch_openml('mnist_784', version = 1, return_X_y = True)

random_state = check_random_state(0)
permutation = random_state.permutation(X.shape[0])
X = X[permutation]
y = y[permutation]
X = X.reshape((X.shape[0], -1))

# Split dataset into training set and test set
# 70% training and 30% test
Xtrain, Xtest, ytrain, ytest = train_test_split(X, y,test_size = 0.3, ran-
dom_state = 0)
scaler = StandardScaler()
Xtrain = scaler.fit_transform(Xtrain)
Xtest = scaler.transform(Xtest)
```

```
#Create an Adaboost Ensemble Classifier
""" AdaBoostClassifier(base_estimator = None, n_estimators = 50, learning_
rate = 1.0,
       algorithm = 'SAMME.R', random_state = None)" " "
clf = AdaBoostClassifier(tree.DecisionTreeClassifier(),n_estimators = 10, al-
gorithm = 'SAMME',learning_rate = 0.5)

#Train the model using the training sets
clf.fit(Xtrain,ytrain)
#Predict the response for test dataset
ypred = clf.predict(Xtest)

#Evaluate the Model and Print Performance Metrics
from sklearn import metrics
print('Accuracy:', np.round(metrics.accuracy_score(ytest,ypred),4))
print('Precision:', np.round(metrics.precision_score(ytest,
          ypred,average = 'weighted'),4))
print('Recall:', np.round(metrics.recall_score(ytest,ypred,
          average = 'weighted'),4))
print('F1 Score:', np.round(metrics.f1_score(ytest,ypred,
          average = 'weighted'),4))
print('Cohen Kappa Score:', np.round(metrics.cohen_kappa_score(ytest,
ypred),4))
print('Matthews Corrcoef:', np.round(metrics.matthews_corrcoef(ytest,
ypred),4))
print('\t\tClassification Report:\n', metrics.classification_report(ypred,
ytest))
from sklearn.metrics import confusion_matrix
print("Confusion Matrix:\n",confusion_matrix(ytest, ypred))

#Plot Confusion Matrix
from sklearn.metrics import confusion_matrix
from io import BytesIO #neded for plot
import seaborn as sns; sns.set()
import matplotlib.pyplot as plt

mat = confusion_matrix(ytest, ypred)
sns.heatmap(mat.T, square = True, annot = True, fmt = 'd', cbar = False)
plt.xlabel('true label')
plt.ylabel('predicted label');

plt.savefig("Confusion.jpg")
# Save SVG in a fake file object.
f = BytesIO()
plt.savefig(f, format = "svg")
```

### Example 3.33

The following Python code utilizes AdaBoost classifier by employing the scikit-learn library APIs. In this example we utilize the Iris dataset, which exists in sklearn.datasets. The Iris dataset is classified with AdaBoost classifier by using 10-fold cross-validation. The classification accuracy, precision, recall, F1 score, Cohen kappa score, and Matthews correlation coefficient are calculated. Note that this example is adapted from Python–scikit-learn.

```
# ==========================================================================
# Adaboost example with cross-validation
# ==========================================================================
print(__doc__)
from sklearn.model_selection import cross_val_score
from sklearn.datasets import load_iris
#Import Adaboost Ensemble model
from sklearn.ensemble import AdaBoostClassifier
#Import Tree model as a base classifier
from sklearn import tree
iris = load_iris()
X, y = iris.data, iris.target

#Create an Adaboost Ensemble Classifier
""" AdaBoostClassifier(base_estimator = None, n_estimators = 50, learning_
rate = 1.0,
        algorithm = 'SAMME.R', random_state = None)" " "
model = clf = AdaBoostClassifier(tree.DecisionTreeClassifier(),n_estima-
tors = 10,
        algorithm = 'SAMME',learning_rate = 0.5)
CV = 10 #10-Fold Cross Validation
#Evaluate Model Using 10-Fold Cross Validation and Print Performance
Metrics
Acc_scores = cross_val_score(model, X, y, cv = CV)
print("Accuracy: %0.3f (+/- %0.3f)" % (Acc_scores.mean(), Acc_scores.
std() * 2))
f1_scores = cross_val_score(model, X, y, cv = CV,scoring = 'f1_macro')
print("F1 score: %0.3f (+/- %0.3f)" % (f1_scores.mean(), f1_scores.std()
* 2))
Precision_scores = cross_val_score(model, X, y, cv = CV,scoring = 'preci-
sion_macro')
print("Precision score: %0.3f (+/- %0.3f)" % (Precision_scores.mean(),
Precision_scores.std() * 2))
Recall_scores = cross_val_score(model, X, y, cv = CV,scoring = 'recall_mac-
ro')
print("Recall score: %0.3f (+/- %0.3f)" % (Recall_scores.mean(), Recall_
scores.std() * 2))
```

```
from sklearn.metrics import cohen_kappa_score, make_scorer
kappa_scorer = make_scorer(cohen_kappa_score)
Kappa_scores = cross_val_score(model, X, y, cv = CV,scoring = kappa_scorer)
print("Kappa score: %0.3f (+/- %0.3f)" % (Kappa_scores.mean(), Kappa_
scores.std() * 2))
```

## Example 3.34

The following Python code is used to represent the transformation of target in regression by employing AdaBoost regressor from the scikit-learn library. In this example we utilize the Boston house prices dataset, which exists in sklearn.datasets. This example employs the transformed features of the Boston houses price dataset using ***TransformedTargetRegressor.*** TransformedTarget-Regressor transforms the targets y before fitting a regression model. The predictions are mapped back to the original space via an inverse transform. It takes as an argument the regressor, which is utilized for prediction, and the transformer, which is applied to the target variable. The straight line seen in the plot demonstrates how AdaBoost regression tries to draw a straight line, which minimizes the residual sum of squares between the observed responses in the dataset, and the responses predicted by the AdaBoost. The correlation coefficient $R^2$, MAE, and MSE are also calculated. It can be seen from the example that the target transformation improved the performance of the AdaBoost regression model. Note that this example is adapted from Python–scikit-learn.

```
# ======================================================================
# Adaboost regressor example with Boston house prices dataset
# ======================================================================
# ======================================================================
#Transforming target in regression
# ======================================================================
import matplotlib.pyplot as plt
from sklearn.compose import TransformedTargetRegressor
from sklearn.preprocessing import QuantileTransformer
from sklearn.ensemble import AdaBoostRegressor
from sklearn.model_selection import train_test_split
from sklearn.metrics import mean_squared_error, r2_score
from sklearn.metrics import mean_absolute_error
from sklearn.datasets import load_boston

# Load the Boston House prices dataset
boston = load_boston()
X = boston.data
y = boston.target
X_train, X_test, y_train, y_test = train_test_split(X, y, random_state = 0)
```

```
# ============================================================================
# Prediction without Transformation
# ============================================================================

# Create Regression object
regr = AdaBoostRegressor(random_state = 0, n_estimators = 100)
# Train the model using the training sets
regr.fit(X_train, y_train)
# Make predictions using the testing set
y_pred = regr.predict(X_test)

print('R^2 score without Transformation: {0:.2f}'.format(regr.score(X_
test, y_test)))
# Explained variance score: 1 is perfect prediction
print("R^2 = %0.5f" % r2_score(y_test, y_pred))
# The mean absolute error
print("MAE = %5.3f" % mean_absolute_error(y_test, y_pred))
# The mean squared error
print("MSE = %5.3f" % mean_squared_error(y_test, y_pred))

# Plot outputs
fig, ax = plt.subplots()
ax.scatter(y_test, y_pred, edgecolors = (0, 0, 0))
ax.plot([y.min(), y.max()], [y.min(), y.max()], 'k--', lw = 4)
ax.set_xlabel('Measured')
ax.set_ylabel('Predicted')
plt.title('Without Transformation')
plt.show()

# ============================================================================
# Prediction with transformation
# ============================================================================
transformer = QuantileTransformer(output_distribution = 'normal')
regressor = AdaBoostRegressor(random_state = 0, n_estimators = 100)
regr = TransformedTargetRegressor(regressor = regressor,
              transformer = transformer)
X_train, X_test, y_train, y_test = train_test_split(X, y, random_state = 0)
regr.fit(X_train, y_train)
y_pred = regr.predict(X_test)

print('R^2 score with Transformation: {0:.2f}'.format(regr.score(X_test,
y_test)))
# Explained variance score: 1 is perfect prediction
print("R^2 = %0.5f" % r2_score(y_test, y_pred))
```

```
# The mean absolute error
print("MAE = %5.3f" % mean_absolute_error(y_test, y_pred))
# The mean squared error
print("MSE = %5.3f" % mean_squared_error(y_test, y_pred))

# Plot outputs
fig, ax = plt.subplots()
ax.scatter(y_test, y_pred, edgecolors = (0, 0, 0))
ax.plot([y.min(), y.max()], [y.min(), y.max()], 'k--', lw = 4)
ax.set_xlabel('Measured')
ax.set_ylabel('Predicted')
plt.title('With Transformation')
plt.show()
```

#### *3.5.15.2 Gradient Boosting*

With their "bagging" procedure, Breiman (Breiman, 1996) introduced the idea of adding randomness into function estimation procedures to improve their performance. Initial implementations of AdaBoost (Freund & Schapire, 1995) also utilized random sampling, but this was considered an approximation of deterministic weighting, once the implementation of the base learner does not support observation weights, rather than as an important component. Later, Breiman (Breiman, 1999) suggested a hybrid bagging boosting procedure ("adaptive bagging") aimed for the least squares fitting of additive expansions. It replaces the base learner in regular boosting processes with the relevant bagged base learner and substitutes "out of bag" residuals for the ordinary residuals at each boosting step. Inspired by Breiman (Breiman, 1999), a minimal modification achieved gradient boosting to combine randomness as an essential part of the process. At each iteration a subsample of the training data is drawn at random (without replacement) from the full training dataset. This randomly chosen subsample is then utilized, instead of the full sample, to fit the base learner and calculate the model update for the current iteration (Friedman, 2002).

**Example 3.35**

The following Python code utilizes gradient boosting classifier by employing the scikit-learn library APIs. In this example we utilize the MNIST handwritten digits dataset (for which details were explained previously). The MNIST handwritten digits dataset is divided into training and test set and then classified by using gradient boosting classifier. The classification accuracy, precision, recall, F1 score, Cohen kappa score, and Matthews correlation coefficient are calculated. The classification report and confusion matrix are also given. Note that this example is adapted from Python–scikit-learn.

```
# ====================================================================
# Gradient boosting example with training and testset
# ====================================================================
import time
import numpy as np
from sklearn.datasets import fetch_openml
# Import train_test_split function
from sklearn.model_selection import train_test_split
from sklearn.preprocessing import StandardScaler
from sklearn.utils import check_random_state
#Import Gradient Boosting ensemble model
from sklearn.ensemble import GradientBoostingClassifier

print(__doc__)

# Turn down for faster convergence
train_samples = 5000

# Load data from https://www.openml.org/d/554
X, y = fetch_openml('mnist_784', version = 1, return_X_y = True)

random_state - check_random_statc(0)
permutation = random_state.permutation(X.shape[0])
X = X[permutation]
y = y[permutation]
X = X.reshape((X.shape[0], -1))

# Split dataset into training set and test set
# 70% training and 30% test
Xtrain, Xtest, ytrain, ytest = train_test_split(X, y,test_size = 0.3, ran-
dom_state = 0)
scaler = StandardScaler()
Xtrain = scaler.fit_transform(Xtrain)
Xtest = scaler.transform(Xtest)

#Create the Model
clf = GradientBoostingClassifier(n_estimators = 100, learning_rate = 1.0,
max_depth = 1, random_state = 0).fit(Xtrain, ytrain)
clf.score(Xtest, ytest)

#Train the model using the training sets
clf.fit(Xtrain,ytrain)
#Predict the response for test dataset
ypred = clf.predict(Xtest)
```

```
#Evaluate the Model and Print Performance Metrics
from sklearn import metrics
print('Accuracy:', np.round(metrics.accuracy_score(ytest,ypred),4))
print('Precision:', np.round(metrics.precision_score(ytest,
        ypred,average = 'weighted'),4))
print('Recall:', np.round(metrics.recall_score(ytest,ypred,
        average = 'weighted'),4))
print('F1 Score:', np.round(metrics.f1_score(ytest,ypred,
        average = 'weighted'),4))
print('Cohen  Kappa  Score:',  np.round(metrics.cohen_kappa_score(ytest,
ypred),4))
print('Matthews  Corrcoef:',  np.round(metrics.matthews_corrcoef(ytest,
ypred),4))
print('\t\tClassification Report:\n', metrics.classification_report(ypred,
ytest))
from sklearn.metrics import confusion_matrix
print("Confusion Matrix:\n",confusion_matrix(ytest, ypred))
```

## Example 3.36

The following Python code is used to represent the transformation of target in regression by employing gradient boosting regressor from the scikit-learn library. In this example we utilize the Boston house prices dataset, which exists in sklearn.datasets. This example utilizes the transformed features of the Boston house prices dataset using ***TransformedTargetRegressor.*** TransformedTarget-Regressor transforms the targets y before fitting a regression model. The predictions are mapped back to the original space via an inverse transform. It takes as an argument the regressor, which is utilized for prediction, and the transformer, which is applied to the target variable. The straight line seen in the plot demonstrates how gradient boosting regression tries to draw a straight line, which minimizes the residual sum of squares between the observed responses in the dataset, and the responses predicted by gradient boosting. The correlation coefficient $R^2$, MAE, and MSE are also calculated. It can be seen from the example that the target transformation improved the performance of the gradient boosting regression model. Note that this example is adapted from Python–scikit-learn.

```
# ========================================================================
# Gradient boosting regressor example with Boston house prices dataset
# ========================================================================
# ========================================================================
#Transforming target in regression
# ========================================================================
import matplotlib.pyplot as plt
from sklearn.compose import TransformedTargetRegressor
from sklearn.preprocessing import QuantileTransformer
from sklearn.ensemble import GradientBoostingRegressor
```

```
from sklearn.model_selection import train_test_split
from sklearn.metrics import mean_squared_error, r2_score
from sklearn.metrics import mean_absolute_error
from sklearn.datasets import load_boston
# Load the Boston House prices dataset
boston = load_boston()
X = boston.data
y = boston.target
X_train, X_test, y_train, y_test = train_test_split(X, y, random_
state = 0)

# ==========================================================================
# Prediction without transformation
# ==========================================================================

# Create linear regression object
# Fit regression model
params = {'n_estimators': 500, 'max_depth': 4, 'min_samples_split': 2,
    'learning_rate': 0.01, 'loss': 'ls'}
regr = GradientBoostingRegressor(**params)
# Train the model using the training sets
rcgr.fit(X_train, y_train)
# Make predictions using the testing set
y_pred = regr.predict(X_test)

print('R^2 score without Transformation: {0:.2f}'.format(regr.score(X_
test, y_test)))
# Explained variance score: 1 is perfect prediction
print("R^2 = %0.5f" % r2_score(y_test, y_pred))
# The mean absolute error
print("MAE = %5.3f" % mean_absolute_error(y_test, y_pred))
# The mean squared error
print("MSE = %5.3f" % mean_squared_error(y_test, y_pred))

# Plot outputs
fig, ax = plt.subplots()
ax.scatter(y_test, y_pred, edgecolors = (0, 0, 0))
ax.plot([y.min(), y.max()], [y.min(), y.max()], 'k--', lw = 4)
ax.set_xlabel('Measured')
ax.set_ylabel('Predicted')
plt.title('Without Transformation')
plt.show()
```

```
# ==========================================================================
# Prediction with transformation
# ==========================================================================
transformer = QuantileTransformer(output_distribution = 'normal')
regressor = GradientBoostingRegressor(**params)
regr = TransformedTargetRegressor(regressor = regressor,
                transformer = transformer)
X_train, X_test, y_train, y_test = train_test_split(X, y, random_state = 0)
regr.fit(X_train, y_train)
y_pred = regr.predict(X_test)

print('R^2 score with Transformation: {0:.2f}'.format(regr.score(X_test,
y_test)))
# Explained variance score: 1 is perfect prediction
print("R^2 = %0.5f" % r2_score(y_test, y_pred))
# The mean absolute error
print("MAE = %5.3f" % mean_absolute_error(y_test, y_pred))
# The mean squared error
print("MSE = %5.3f" % mean_squared_error(y_test, y_pred))

# Plot outputs
fig, ax = plt.subplots()
ax.scatter(y_test, y_pred, edgecolors = (0, 0, 0))
ax.plot([y.min(), y.max()], [y.min(), y.max()], 'k--', lw = 4)
ax.set_xlabel('Measured')
ax.set_ylabel('Predicted')
plt.title('With Transformation')
plt.show()
```

### 3.5.16 Other ensemble methods

There are numerous ensemble approaches besides bagging and boosting. The key difference is that the sense predictions of the base models are combined. The predictions of some base classifiers as features learn to produce a *metamodel*, which combines their predictions. Learning a linear metamodel is known as *stacking*. It is also feasible to combine different base models into a heterogeneous ensemble to achieve base model diversity such that base models are trained by diverse learning algorithms by employing the same training set. Hence the model ensembles are composed of a set of base models and a metamodel, which is trained to decide how base model predictions must be combined (Flach, 2012).

## Example 3.37

The following Python code utilizes Stacking metaclassifier by employing the scikit-learn library APIs. In this example, we utilize the Iris dataset, which exists in sklearn.datasets. Note that this example is adapted from Python–scikit-learn.

```
# ======================================================================
# Stacking metaclassifier example
# ======================================================================
#Before running you should install mlxtend.classifier for Staking using pip
install mlxtend
import numpy as np
import warnings
from sklearn import model_selection
from sklearn.linear_model import LogisticRegression
from sklearn.neighbors import KNeighborsClassifier
from sklearn.neural_network import MLPClassifier
from sklearn.ensemble import RandomForestClassifier
from mlxtend.classifier import StackingClassifier
from sklearn.datasets import load_iris
from sklearn.model_selection import train_test_split
from sklearn import tree

#Load Iris Dataset
iris = load_iris()
X, y = iris.data, iris.target
#Create Train and Test set
Xtrain, Xtest, ytrain, ytest = train_test_split(X, y, test_size = 0.3, ran-
dom_state = 0)

warnings.simplefilter('ignore')

#Create the Model
clf1 = KNeighborsClassifier(n_neighbors = 1)
clf2 = RandomForestClassifier(random_state = 1)
clf3 = MLPClassifier(hidden_layer_sizes = (100, ), learning_rate_
init = 0.001,
          alpha = 1, momentum = 0.9,max_iter = 1000)
DT = tree.DecisionTreeClassifier()
sclf = StackingClassifier(classifiers = [clf1, clf2, clf3],
          meta_classifier = DT)

# ======================================================================
# # Stacking example with cross-validation
# ======================================================================
print('5-fold cross validation:\n')
for clf, label in zip([clf1, clf2, clf3, sclf],
```

```
          ['KNN',
          'Random Forest',
          'Multilayer Perceptron',
          'StackingClassifier']):

scores = model_selection.cross_val_score(clf, X, y,
cv = 5, scoring = 'accuracy')
print("Accuracy: %0.3f (+/- %0.3f) [%s]"
    % (scores.mean(), scores.std(), label))
# =========================================================================
# # Stacking example with training and test set
# =========================================================================
#Train the Model with Training dataset
sclf.fit(Xtrain,ytrain)
#Test the Model with Testing dataset
ypred = sclf.predict(Xtest)

from sklearn import metrics
print('Accuracy:', np.round(metrics.accuracy_score(ytest,ypred),4))
print('Precision:', np.round(metrics.precision_score(ytest,
            ypred,average = 'weighted'),4))
print('Recall:', np.round(metrics.recall_score(ytest,ypred,
            average = 'weighted'),4))
print('F1 Score:', np.round(metrics.f1_score(ytest,ypred,
            average = 'weighted'),4))
print('Cohen  Kappa  Score:',  np.round(metrics.cohen_kappa_score(ytest,
ypred)))
print('Matthews  Corrcoef:',  np.round(metrics.matthews_corrcoef(ytest,
ypred)))
print('\t\tClassification Report:\n', metrics.classification_report(ypred,
ytest))

from sklearn.metrics import confusion_matrix
from io import BytesIO #neded for plot
import seaborn as sns; sns.set()
import matplotlib.pyplot as plt

mat = confusion_matrix(ytest, ypred)
sns.heatmap(mat.T, square = True, annot = True, fmt = 'd', cbar = False)
plt.xlabel('true label')
plt.ylabel('predicted label');

plt.savefig("Confusion.jpg")
# Save SVG in a fake file object.
f = BytesIO()
plt.savefig(f, format = "svg")
```

## Example 3.38

The following Python code utilizes voting ensemble classifier by employing the scikit-learn library APIs. In this example, we utilize the Iris dataset, which exists in sklearn.datasets. Note that this example is adapted from Python–scikit-learn.

```
# ==========================================================================
# Voting ensemble classifier example
# ==========================================================================
from sklearn import datasets
from sklearn.model_selection import cross_val_score
from sklearn.linear_model import LogisticRegression
from sklearn.naive_bayes import GaussianNB
from sklearn.ensemble import RandomForestClassifier
from sklearn.ensemble import VotingClassifier

#Load Iris Dataset
iris = load_iris()
X, y = iris.data, iris.target
#Create Train and Test set
Xtrain, Xtest, ytrain, ytest = train_test_split(X, y, test_size = 0.3, ran-
dom_state = 0)

# ==========================================================================
# Voting example with cross-validation
# ==========================================================================
#Create the Model
clf1 = KNeighborsClassifier(n_neighbors = 1)
clf2 = RandomForestClassifier(random_state = 1)
clf3 = MLPClassifier(hidden_layer_sizes = (100, ), learning_rate_
init = 0.001,
        alpha = 1, momentum = 0.9,max_iter = 1000)
eclf = VotingClassifier(estimators = [('kNN', clf1), ('RF', clf2), ('MLP',
clf3)], voting = 'hard')

print('\nPerfromance with Cross Validation')
print('5-fold cross validation:\n')
for clf, label in zip([clf1, clf2, clf3, eclf], ['kNN', 'Random Forest',
'MLP', 'Ensemble']):
scores = cross_val_score(clf, X, y, cv = 5, scoring = 'accuracy')
print("Accuracy: %0.2f (+/- %0.2f) [%s]" % (scores.mean(), scores.std(),
label))
```

```
# ===========================================================================
# Voting example with training and testset
# ===========================================================================
#Train the model using the training sets
eclf.fit(Xtrain,ytrain)
#Predict the response for test dataset
ypred = eclf.predict(Xtest)

#Evaluate the Model and Print Performance Metrics
print('\n\nPerfromance with Test Set')
from sklearn import metrics
print('Accuracy:', np.round(metrics.accuracy_score(ytest,ypred),4))
print('Precision:', np.round(metrics.precision_score(ytest,
          ypred,average = 'weighted'),4))
print('Recall:', np.round(metrics.recall_score(ytest,ypred,
          average = 'weighted'),4))
print('F1 Score:', np.round(metrics.f1_score(ytest,ypred,
          average = 'weighted'),4))
print('Cohen  Kappa  Score:',  np.round(metrics.cohen_kappa_score(ytest,
ypred),4))
print('Matthews  Corrcoef:',  np.round(metrics.matthews_corrcoef(ytest,
ypred),4))
print('\t\tClassification Report:\n', metrics.classification_report(ypred,
ytest))
from sklearn.metrics import confusion_matrix
print("Confusion Matrix:\n",confusion_matrix(ytest, ypred))
```

## Example 3.39

The following Python code is used to represent the transformation of target in regression by employing voting regressor from the scikit-learn library. In this example, we utilize the Boston house prices dataset, which exists in sklearn.datasets. The straight line seen in the plot demonstrates how voting regression tries to draw a straight line, which best minimizes the residual sum of squares between the observed responses in the dataset, and the responses predicted by regressor. The correlation coefficient $R^2$, MAE, and MSE are also calculated. It can be seen from the example that the target transformation has improved the performance of the Voting regression model. Note that this example is adapted from Python–scikit-learn.

```
# ===========================================================================
# Voting regressor example
# ===========================================================================
import matplotlib.pyplot as plt
from sklearn import datasets
```

```
from sklearn.ensemble import GradientBoostingRegressor
from sklearn.ensemble import RandomForestRegressor
from sklearn.linear_model import LinearRegression
from sklearn.ensemble import VotingRegressor
from sklearn.model_selection import train_test_split
from sklearn.metrics import mean_squared_error, r2_score
from sklearn.metrics import mean_absolute_error

# Load the Boston house prices dataset
boston = datasets.load_boston()
X = boston.data
y = boston.target
X_train, X_test, y_train, y_test = train_test_split(X, y, random_state = 0)
# Training classifiers
reg1 = GradientBoostingRegressor(random_state = 1, n_estimators = 10)
reg2 = RandomForestRegressor(random_state = 1, n_estimators = 10)
reg3 = LinearRegression()
eregr = VotingRegressor(estimators = [('gb', reg1), ('rf', reg2), ('lr',
reg3)])

# Train the model using the training sets
eregr.fit(X_train, y_train)
# Make predictions using the testing set
y_pred = eregr.predict(X_test)

print('R^2 score without Transformation: {0:.2f}'.format(eregr.score(X_
test, y_test)))
# Explained variance score: 1 is perfect prediction
print("R^2 = %0.5f" % r2_score(y_test, y_pred))
# The mean absolute error
print("MAE = %5.3f" % mean_absolute_error(y_test, y_pred))
# The mean squared error
print("MSE = %5.3f" % mean_squared_error(y_test, y_pred))

# Plot outputs
fig, ax = plt.subplots()
ax.scatter(y_test, y_pred, edgecolors = (0, 0, 0))
ax.plot([y.min(), y.max()], [y.min(), y.max()], 'k--', lw = 4)
ax.set_xlabel('Measured')
ax.set_ylabel('Predicted')
plt.title('Voting Regressor')
plt.show()
```

### 3.5.17 Deep learning

Deep learning is an enhancement to artificial neural networks (ANNs). The simple neural network is composed of an input layer, a hidden layer, and an output layer. The ANN model's parameters are the weights of every connection, which exists in the network and sometimes a bias parameter. Deep learning has recently turned out to be one of machine learning's most well-known characteristics. Deep learning has achieved exceptional accuracy and popularity in numerous fields, especially in image and audio (Sarkar et al., 2018).

If a linear model is not enough for any learning process, it is possible to describe new features that are nonlinear input functions, hence a linear model is built in the domain of those features. This requires determining the good basis functions. One way to create a new space is to use one of the extraction methods for applications such as PCA. But an MLP that extracts these features in its hidden layer is the best technique, because the first layer (feature extraction) and the second layer in which these features are incorporated to predict the output are learned together in a supervised approach. With one hidden layer, an MLP has limited ability, while with several hidden layers, an MLP may learn more complicated input functions. This is the concept behind deep neural networks, where each hidden layer combines the values in its previous layer, beginning from the networks' raw input, and learns more complicated input features. Another feature of deep networks is that successive hidden layers of more abstract descriptions are used up to the output layer in which the outputs are learned in terms of these intangible concepts. The idea is to learn feature levels of rising abstraction in deep learning with minimal human intervention (Bengio, 2009), as in several applications. The assembly that is present in the input is not recognized, so any kind of dependencies should be automatically discovered during training. A key issue with training an MLP with many hidden layers is that it is important to successively multiply the derivatives in all layers while backpropagating the error to the previous layers, and the gradient vanishes. This is also the reason why the unfolded recurrent neural networks were trained slowly. For convolutional neural networks, the condition cannot happen, as the fan-in and fan-out of hidden units are naturally negligible. A deep neural network is usually trained one layer at a time (Hinton & Salakhutdinov, 2006). The aim of each layer is to extract the relevant features from the data fed to it, and for this purpose a technique such as the autoencoder can be used. Therefore, beginning with the raw input data, an autoencoder can be trained, and the encoded representation learned from its secret layer is then used as an input to train the next autoencoder, and so on, until we reach the final layer that is trained with the labeled data in a supervised manner. They are all brought together after training all the layers one by one, and the entire network is fine-tuned with the labeled data. If there are lots of labeled data and lots of computational power, the whole deep network can be trained in a supervised manner, but the compromise is that using an unsupervised approach to initialize weights works much better than random initialization; as a result, fewer labeled data can be used to perform training more rapidly. Methods of deep learning are particularly prominent since they need less human intervention. The layers of abstraction can be considered in so many implementations that exploring such an abstract representation can be informative as well as a good description of the problem (Alpaydin, 2014; Subasi, 2019).

The deep learning area, as described earlier, is a machine learning subfield that has recently become quite prominent. The key objective is to bring machine learning technology closer to its true goal of "making intelligent machines." Deep learning is sometimes considered a fancy word for neural networks that have been rebranded. To some extent this is true, but deep learning certainly has to do with more than just simple neural networks. Deep learning–based algorithms include the use of representation learning principles in which different representations of the data are learned in different layers, which is also supported in automated feature extraction. Put another way, a deep learning approach attempts to build machine intelligence by representing data as a layered concept hierarchy in which every layer of concepts is constructed from other simpler layers. One of the core components of any deep learning algorithm is this layered architecture itself. We essentially try to learn a mapping between our data samples and our output in any simple supervised machine learning technique, and then try to predict performance for new data samples. In addition to learning mapping from inputs to outputs, representative learning tries to understand the representations in the data itself. This makes deep learning algorithms extremely powerful compared to regular techniques that require substantial expertise in areas such as feature extraction and engineering. Deep learning is also highly efficient compared to older machine learning algorithms in terms of performance as well as scalability with more and more data. There have been several notable deep learning trends and aspects we have observed over the past decade (Sarkar et al., 2018). They are summarized as follows.

- Deep learning algorithms are built on distributed representational learning, and with more data over time they start to perform better.
- Deep learning can be said to be a subfiled of neural networks; when compared to traditional neural networks, it is much more improved.
- Better software frameworks, such as TensorFlow, Theano, Caffe, MXNetet, and Keras, combined with better hardware have allowed the development of incredibly complex, multilayered deep learning models with larger sizes.
- Deep learning has multiple benefits relevant to automatic feature selection and supervised learning operations that have enabled data scientists and engineers over time to solve increasingly sophisticated problems.

The following points define most deep learning algorithms' relevant features.

- Hierarchical layered representation of concepts.
- Distributed data representational training takes place via a multilayered architecture.
- More complex and high-level features and notions are originated from simpler, low-level features.
- A "deep" neural network usually is considered to have at least more than one hidden layer besides the input and output layers. Usually it consists of a minimum of three to four hidden layers.
- Deep architectures have a multilayered structure with several nonlinear processing units for each layer. The output of each layer is the previous layer in the architecture. The input is typically the first layer, and the output is the last layer.
- It can conduct automatic extraction of features, classification, detection of anomalies, and many other tasks relevant to machine learning.

### 3.5.18 Deep neural networks

The extension of conventional artificial neural networks is deep neural networks. Compared to conventional neural networks, there are two main differences that deep neural networks have. It is shallow for conventional neural networks to have one or two hidden layers. On the other hand, there are many hidden layers in deep neural networks. For instance, a neural network of millions of neurons was used by the Google brain project. There is a wide range of models for deep neural networks, ranging from DNNs, CNNs, RNNs, and LSTMs. Recent studies have even brought us attention-based networks that focus on specific parts of a deep neural network. The larger the network and the more layers it has, the more complex the network becomes and the more resources and more time it needs to train. Deep neural networks work best with GPU-based architectures that take less time to train than classical CPUs, while recent developments have shortened training times considerably (Sarkar et al., 2018).

#### Example 3.40

The following Python code utilizes deep neural network classifier by employing the TensorFlow library. In this example we utilize the Iris dataset, which exists in sklearn.datasets. The Iris dataset is divided into training and test set and then classified by using deep neural network classifier. The classification accuracy, precision, recall, F1 score, Cohen kappa score, and Matthews correlation coefficient are calculated. The classification report and confusion matrix are also given. Note that this example is adapted from TensorFlow.org website.

```
# ==================================================================
# Deep neural network example with Iris dataset using TensorFlow
# ==================================================================
import numpy as np
from sklearn import datasets
from sklearn import metrics
from sklearn import model_selection

import tensorflow as tf

X_FEATURE = 'x' # Name of the input feature.
n_classes = 3
# Load dataset.
iris = datasets.load_iris()
Xtrain, Xtest, ytrain, ytest = model_selection.train_test_split(
    iris.data, iris.target, test_size = 0.3, random_state = 42)

# Build 3 layer DNN with 10, 20, 10 units respectively.
feature_columns = [
```

```
    tf.feature_column.numeric_column(
    X_FEATURE, shape=np.array(Xtrain).shape[1:])]
classifier=tf.estimator.DNNClassifier(
    feature_columns=feature_columns, hidden_units=[50, 150, 50], n_class-
es=n_classes)

# Train.
train_input_fn=tf.compat.v1.estimator.inputs.numpy_input_fn(
    x={X_FEATURE: Xtrain}, y=ytrain, num_epochs=None, shuffle=True)
classifier.train(input_fn=train_input_fn, steps=200)

# Predict.
test_input_fn=tf.compat.v1.estimator.inputs.numpy_input_fn(
x={X_FEATURE: Xtest}, y=ytest, num_epochs=1, shuffle=False)
predictions=classifier.predict(input_fn=test_input_fn)
ypred=np.array(list(p['class_ids'] for p in predictions))
ypred=ypred.reshape(np.array(ytest).shape)

# Score with sklearn.
score=metrics.accuracy_score(ytest, ypred)
print('Accuracy (sklearn): {0:f}'.format(score))

# Score with tensorflow.
scores=classifier.evaluate(input_fn=test_input_fn)
print('Accuracy (tensorflow): {0:f}'.format(scores['accuracy']))

#Evaluate the Model and Print Performance Metrics
from sklearn import metrics
print('Accuracy:', np.round(metrics.accuracy_score(ytest,ypred),4))
print('Precision:', np.round(metrics.precision_score(ytest,
         ypred,average='weighted'),4))
print('Recall:', np.round(metrics.recall_score(ytest,ypred,
         average='weighted'),4))
print('F1 Score:', np.round(metrics.f1_score(ytest,ypred,
         average='weighted'),4))
print('Cohen  Kappa  Score:',  np.round(metrics.cohen_kappa_score(ytest,
ypred),4))
print('Matthews  Corrcoef:',  np.round(metrics.matthews_corrcoef(ytest,
ypred),4))
print('\t\tClassification Report:\n', metrics.classification_report(ypred,
ytest))

from sklearn.metrics import confusion_matrix
from io import BytesIO #neded for plot
import seaborn as sns; sns.set()
```

```
import matplotlib.pyplot as plt
#Plot Confusion Matrix
mat = confusion_matrix(ytest, ypred)
sns.heatmap(mat.T, square = True, annot = True, fmt = 'd', cbar = False)
plt.xlabel('true label')
```

## Example 3.41

The following Python code utilizes deep neural network classifier by employing the TensorFlow library with Keras APIs. In this example we utilize the Iris dataset, which exists in sklearn.datasets. The Iris dataset is divided into training and test set and then classified by using deep neural network classifier using Keras API and TensorFlow backend. The classification accuracy is used as a performance measure. Note that this example is adapted from TensorFlow.org website.

```
# ===========================================================================
#Deep neural network example with Iris dataset using Keras API and
TensorFlow backend
# ===========================================================================
from keras.models import Sequential
from keras.layers import Dense
from sklearn import datasets

#Load Iris Dataset
iris = datasets.load_iris()
X = iris.data
y = iris.target

#Encode the Target Vector
from keras.utils import np_utils
dummy_y = np_utils.to_categorical(y)

#Create Train and Test Dataset
from sklearn.model_selection import train_test_split
Xtrain, Xtest, ytrain, ytest = train_test_split(X, y, test_size = 0.3, ran-
dom_state = 0)

# Initialize the constructor
model = Sequential()
# Add an input layer
model.add(Dense(50, activation = 'relu', input_shape = (4,)))
# Add two hidden layer
model.add(Dense(100, activation = 'sigmoid'))
```

```
model.add(Dense(50, activation = 'sigmoid'))
# Add an output layer
model.add(Dense(1, activation = 'sigmoid'))

# Compile model
model.compile(loss = 'binary_crossentropy', optimizer = 'adam', met-
rics = ['accuracy'])
# Fit model
history = model.fit(Xtrain, ytrain, validation_data = (Xtest, ytest), ep-
ochs = 500, verbose = 2)
# Evaluate the model
_, train_acc = model.evaluate(Xtrain, ytrain, verbose = 0)
_, test_acc = model.evaluate(Xtest, ytest, verbose = 0)
print('Train: %.3f, Test: %.3f' % (train_acc, test_acc))
```

### 3.5.19 Recurrent neural networks

A recurrent neural network (RNN) is a special kind of artificial neural network that permits continuing information related to past knowledge by utilizing a special kind of looped architecture. They are employed in many areas regarding data with sequences, such as predicting the next word of a sentence. These looped networks are termed recurrent because they make the same operations and computation for every element in a sequence of input data. RNNs have memory, which assist in taking information from past sequences (Sarkar et al., 2018).

RNNs were first developed in the 1980s but have recently gained attention due to a number of scientific and hardware inventions that make them computationally efficient for training. RNNs differ from feed-forward networks since they influence a particular type of neural layer, known as recurrent layers, that allows the network to maintain the state between network usage. To understand better how RNNs operate, let's examine how one functions after being properly trained. We create a new example of our model each time we want to process a new sequence. By dividing the lifetime of the network instance into discrete time steps, we can think about networks that contain recurrent layers. We feed the next element of the input into the model at each time step. Feedforward links reflect information flow from one neuron to another in which the data being moved from the current time step is the calculated neuronal activation. However, recurrent connections constitute information flow in which the data is the stored neuronal activation from the preceding time step. Therefore, neuron activations in a recurrent network reflect the network instance's accumulating state. The initial neuron activations in the recurrent layer are parameters of the model, and we define the optimal values for them just as we define the optimal values for every connection's weights during the training process. It turns out that we can actually express the instance as a feed-forward network (although irregularly structured) given a fixed lifetime (say, t time steps) of an RNN instance. By measuring the gradient dependent on the unrolled model, we can now train the RNN as well. It ensures that all the methods of backpropagation used for feedforward networks can also be applied for RNN training. We have to adjust the weights depending on the error derivatives we compute after each batch of training examples we are using. We have sets of connections in our unrolled network that are all related to the same connection in the original RNN. Nevertheless, it is not ensured that the error derivatives computed for these unrolled links will be equivalent in reality. By averaging or summing up the error derivatives over all the links that belong to the same set, we can overcome this problem. This allows us to use an error derivative that often considers all the dynamics that act on a connection's weight as we try to force the network to build an accurate output (Buduma & Locascio, 2017).

## Example 3.42

The following Python code utilizes recurrent neural network (RNN) classifier by employing the TensorFlow library with Keras APIs. In this example, we utilize the IMDB dataset, which exists in Keras. IMDB dataset has 50,000 movie reviews for text analytics or natural language processing. This dataset for binary sentiment classification includes significantly more data than previous benchmark datasets. There are 25,000 movie reviews for training and 25,000 for testing. For more dataset information, please go to http://ai.stanford.edu/~amaas/data/sentiment/. RNN employed the training and test set to train and test the model. The classification accuracy of training and test set are given separately. Note that this example is adapted from the book *Deep Learning with Python*, written by Francois Chollet (Chollet, 2018).

```
# ======================================================================
# Recurrent neural networks example with IMDB dataset
# ======================================================================
from keras.datasets import imdb
from keras.preprocessing import sequence
from keras.layers import Dense
from keras.models import Sequential
from keras.layers import Embedding, SimpleRNN

max_features = 10000 # number of words to consider as features
maxlen = 500 # cut texts after this number of words (among top max_features
most common words)
batch_size = 32

print('Loading data...')
(Xtrain, ytrain), (Xtest, ytest) = imdb.load_data(num_words = max_features)
print(len(Xtrain), 'train sequences')
print(len(Xtest), 'test sequences')

print('Pad sequences (samples x time)')
Xtrain = sequence.pad_sequences(Xtrain, maxlen = maxlen)
Xtest = sequence.pad_sequences(Xtest, maxlen = maxlen)
print('input_train shape:', Xtrain.shape)
print('input_test shape:', Xtest.shape)
```

```
#Create Model
model = Sequential()
model.add(Embedding(max_features, 32))
model.add(SimpleRNN(32))
model.add(Dense(1, activation = 'sigmoid'))

# Compile model
model.compile(optimizer = 'rmsprop',  loss = 'binary_crossentropy',  met-
rics = ['acc'])
# Fit model
history = model.fit(Xtrain, ytrain,
          epochs = 10,
          batch_size = 128,
          validation_split = 0.2)

# Evaluate the model
_, train_acc = model.evaluate(Xtrain, ytrain, verbose = 0)
_, test_acc = model.evaluate(Xtest, ytest, verbose = 0)
print('Training Accuracy: %.3f, Testing Accuracy: %.3f' % (train_acc,
test_acc))
```

### 3.5.20 Autoencoders

An autoencoder is a specific type of artificial neural network that is mainly employed for handling unsupervised machine learning tasks. Its main goal is to learn data approximations, representations, and encodings. Autoencoders can be employed for creating generative models, using dimensionality reduction, and detecting anomalies (Sarkar et al., 2018). An **autoencoder** is a sort of unsupervised neural network that is used for dimensionality reduction and feature extraction. In particular, an autoencoder is a feedforward neural network that is trained to predict the input itself. The system can minimize the reconstruction error by ensuring the hidden units capture the most appropriate features of the data. More effective descriptions can be learned by utilizing **deep autoencoders**. Unluckily training such models using back-propagation does not work well since the gradient signal becomes too small as it passes back through multiple layers, and the learning algorithm often gets stuck in poor local minima. One solution to this problem is to greedily train a series of **restricted Boltzmann machines** (**RBM**) and to employ these to initialize an autoencoder. The whole system can then be fine-tuned utilizing backprop in the usual fashion (Murphy, 2012).

### 3.5.21 Long short-term memory (LSTM) networks

RNNs are good at working on sequence-based data, however as the sequences rise, they begin to lose historical context in the sequence over time, and therefore outputs are not always expected. This is where long short-term memory networks (LSTMs) are useful. LSTMs can remember information from quite long sequence-based data and prevent problems, such as the vanishing gradient problem that usually occurs in backpropagation trained ANNs. LSTMs generally have three to four gates, including input, output, and a particular forget gate. Typically, the input gate helps or eliminates incoming stimuli and inputs to change the state of the memory cell. When needed, the output gate normally propagates the value to other neurons. The forget gate controls the self-recurrent link of the memory cell to remember and forget previous states whenever required. In particular, several LSTM cells are stacked in any deep learning network to resolve real-world problems such as sequence prediction (Sarkar et al., 2018).

The basic principle behind the development for long short-term memory (LSTM) was that the network would be built to efficiently transfer important information several timesteps into the future. There are several key components in the LSTM module. The memory cell is one of the core components of the LSTM architecture in which a tensor is defined by the bolded loop in the center of the figure. The memory cell retains crucial information it has learned over time, and the network is built over many timesteps to successfully preserve the valuable information in the memory cell. For three different phases, the LSTM model modifies the memory cell for new information at each step. First, the unit needs to identify how much of the previous memory should be kept. The basic idea of gate keep is simple. The memory state tensor from the previous step is rich in information, but some of that information may be repetitive and needs to be erased as a result. We figure out which elements are still relevant in the memory state tensor and which elements are irrelevant by trying to calculate a bit tensor (a zero and one tensor), which we are multiplying with the previous state. If a specific location in the bit tensor retains a one, this implies that the position in the memory cell is still valid and should be retained. If that specific location holds a zero instead, this indicates that the place in the memory cell is no longer relevant and should be eased. Through concatenating the input of this timestep and the output of the LSTM unit from the previous timestep, we approximate this bit tensor and add a sigmoid layer to the resultant tensor. As you may recall, a sigmoidal neuron produces a value that is either close to zero or close to one most of the time; the only exception is when the input is nearly zero. As a consequence, a good approximation of a bit tensor is the output of the sigmoidal layer, and we can use this to complete the keep gate. Once we have worked out which information is to be kept in the old state and which is to be deleted, we are ready to think about what memory state information we would like to write. This is split into two major parts. The first component is to figure out what information we would like to write to the state. This is calculated to create an intermediate tensor by the tanh layer. The second component is to work out which components we really need to include in the new state of this computed tensor and which we want to discard before writing. We do this by approximating a bit vector of zeros and ones employing the same methodology (a sigmoidal layer) that we used in the keep gate. Using our intermediate tensor, we multiply the bit vector and then add the result to construct the new state vector for the LSTM (Buduma & Locascio, 2017).

Finally, we would like the LSTM unit to provide an output at each timestep. While the state vector could be viewed explicitly as the output, the LSTM system is built to provide more versatility by generating an output tensor that is an "interpretation" or external communication of what the state vector reflects. We use an almost identical framework as the write gate: (1) the tanh layer creates an intermediate tensor from the state vector, (2) the sigmoid layer uses the current input and previous output to create a bit tensor mask, and (3) the intermediate tensor is multiplied by the bit tensor to generate the final output. So why is this better than utilizing a unit of raw RNN? The main point concerns how news spreads through the network over time as we unroll the LSTM module. The propagation of the state vector, whose relations are mainly constant over time, can be seen at the very top. As a consequence, the gradient related to the current output by an origin of several timesteps does not attenuate as significantly as in the standard RNN model. It ensures that the LSTM can learn much more easily regarding long-term relationships than our original RNN formulation. Ultimately, we want to know how simple it is with LSTM units to create arbitrary architectures. How can LSTMs be "composable?" Do we have to sacrifice the flexibility instead of a vanilla RNN to use LSTM units? Just as we can just stack RNN layers to construct more functional models with more capacity, we can stack LSTM units similarly where the second unit's input is the first unit's output, the third unit's input is the second unit's output, and so on. This ensures that we can easily replace an LSTM system anywhere we use a vanilla RNN layer. Now that we have solved the problem of vanishing gradients and acknowledge the inner workings of LSTM units, we are ready to dive into our first RNN model's implementation (Buduma & Locascio, 2017).

## Example 3.43

The following Python code utilizes LSTM classifier by employing the TensorFlow library with Keras APIs. In this example, we utilize the IMDB dataset, which exists in Keras. IMDB dataset has 50,000 movie reviews for text analytics or natural language processing. This dataset for binary sentiment classification includes significantly more data than previous benchmark datasets. There are 25,000 movie reviews for training and 25,000 for testing. For more dataset information, go to http://ai.stanford.edu/~amaas/data/sentiment/. The LSTM employed the training and test set to train and test the model. The classification accuracy of training and test set is given separately. Note that this example is adapted from the book *Deep Learning with Python*, written by Francois Chollet (Chollet, 2018).

```
# ======================================================================
# LSTM example in Keras using IMDB
# ======================================================================
from keras.datasets import imdb
from keras.preprocessing import sequence
from keras.layers import Dense
from keras.models import Sequential
from keras.layers import Embedding, LSTM

max_features = 10000 # number of words to consider as features
maxlen = 500 # cut texts after this number of words (among top max_features
most common words)
batch_size = 32
```

```
print('Loading data...')
(Xtrain, ytrain), (Xtest, ytest) = imdb.load_data(num_words = max_features)
print(len(Xtrain), 'train sequences')
print(len(Xtest), 'test sequences')

print('Pad sequences (samples x time)')
Xtrain = sequence.pad_sequences(Xtrain, maxlen = maxlen)
Xtest = sequence.pad_sequences(Xtest, maxlen = maxlen)
print('input_train shape:', Xtrain.shape)
print('input_test shape:', Xtest.shape)

#Create Model
model = Sequential()
model.add(Embedding(max_features, 32))
model.add(LSTM(32))
model.add(Dense(1, activation = 'sigmoid'))

# Compile model
model.compile(optimizer = 'rmsprop', loss = 'binary_crossentropy', met-
rics = ['acc'])
# Fit model
history = model.fit(Xtrain, ytrain,
         epochs = 2,
         batch_size = 128,
         validation_split = 0.2)

# Evaluate the model
_, train_acc = model.evaluate(Xtrain, ytrain, verbose = 0)
_, test_acc = model.evaluate(Xtest, ytest, verbose = 0)
print('Training Accuracy: %.3f, Testing Accuracy: %.3f' % (train_acc,
test_acc))
```

### 3.5.22 Convolutional neural networks

A convolutional neural network (CNN) is a modification of the artificial neural network that focuses on imitating functionality and behavior of our visual cortex. The aim of the hidden units is to learn nonlinear variations of the original inputs; this is called extraction of features or creation of features. Then these hidden features are transferred to the final Generalized Linear Model (GLM) as input. This approach is particularly useful for issues where the original input features are not individually informative. For example, each pixel in an image is not very informative; it is the pixel combination that shows us what objects exist. On the other side, the feature (word count) is informative on its own for tasks such as text classification using a bag-of-words representation, thus it is less significant to extract higher-order features.

Therefore it is not surprising that much of the research of neural networks is motivated by the recognition of visual patterns, although they were also used for certain data types, including text. The convolutional neural network is a type of MLP that is particularly well-suited for one-dimensional signals, such as speech, biomedical signals, or text, or two-dimensional signals, such as images. This is an MLP in which there are local receptive areas for the hidden units (as in the primary visual cortex) and the weights are added and shared across the image to reduce the numbers of variables. The consequence of such spatial parameter fastening is, of course, that any informative features that are "discovered" in some part of the image can be replicated elsewhere without needing to be learned individually. The resultant network shows a translation invariance, implying that patterns can be classified anywhere they appear within the input image (Murphy, 2012).

CNN is not only a deep neural network with many hidden layers but also a large network that simulates and understands stimuli as the visual cortex of the brain processes. Thus on their first encounter, even neural network specialists still find it difficult to understand this term. That is how much CNN varies from previous neural networks in theory and operation. CNN's output layer usually uses the neural network for multiclass classification. However, utilizing the original images for image recognition directly results in poor results, regardless of the method of recognition; the images should be processed to contrast the features. Otherwise, the process of recognition would have resulted in very poor results. For this purpose, different techniques have been created for extracting image features. The feature extractor was developed by specific field specialists; hence, it needed considerable cost and time while producing an inconsistent performance level. Such feature extractors are independent of machine learning. CNN uses the feature extractor in the training process instead of manually implementing it. CNN's feature extractor consists of special types of neural networks that decide the weights through the training process. The main feature and strength of CNN is that it transformed the manual feature extraction process into the automated one. CNN provides better image recognition when its neural network feature extraction becomes deeper (contains more layers), at the cost of the learning method complexities that had made CNN inefficient and neglected for some time. CNN is a neural network that extracts input image features and another neural network that classifies the image features. The input image is used by the feature extraction network. The extracted feature signals are utilized by the neural network for classification. The neural network classification then works on the basis of the image features and produces the output. The neural network for feature extraction includes convolution layer piles and sets of pooling layers. As its name implies, the convolution layer transforms the image using the process of convolution. It can be described as a series of digital filters. The layer of pooling transforms the neighboring pixels into a single pixel. The pooling layer then decreases the image dimension. As CNN's primary concern is the image; the convolution and pooling layer procedures are intuitively in a two-dimensional plane. This is one of CNN's distinctions from other neural networks (Kim, 2017).

#### 3.5.22.1 Convolution layer

New images are produced by the convolution layer called feature maps. The feature map demonstrates the original image's unique features. Contrary to the other neural network structures, the convolution layer works in a distinct way. The convolution layer does not use connection weights and a weighted sum. Rather, it includes image-converting filters. These filters are called convolution filters. The feature map is generated by the process of inputting the image through the convolution filters. Convolution is a process that is rather difficult to explain in text, as it is on the two-dimensional plane. The theory and measurement steps of convolution, however, are simple. The values in the elements of this feature map depend on whether or not the image matrix matches the convolution filter, similar to the first convolution process. The feature map generated by the convolution filter is processed by the activation function before the output is produced by the layer. The convolution layer's activation function is similar to that of the conventional neural network. Although the ReLU function is utilized in many current implementations, the sigmoid function and the tanh function are often utilized as well (Kim, 2017).

#### *3.5.22.2 Pooling layer*

The pooling layer decreases the image size as it combines adjacent pixels of an image area into a single representative value. Pooling is a popular approach that has already been used by many other image processing techniques. We must decide how to choose the pooling pixels from the image and how to set the representing value in order to implement the operations in the pooling layer. The adjacent pixels are typically chosen from the square matrix, and the combined number of pixels differs from problem to problem (Kim, 2017).

**Example 3.44**

The following Python code utilizes deep neural network classifier by using the TensorFlow library with Keras APIs. In this example we utilize the MNIST dataset, which exists in keras.datasets. The MNIST dataset contains 60,000 training and 10,000 test images. The images are classified by using convolutional neural network classifier. The classification accuracy is used as a performance measure. Note that this example is adapted from TensorFlow.org website.

```
#=======================================================================
# Convolutional neural network example
#=======================================================================
from keras import models
from keras import layers
from keras.datasets import mnist
(train_images, train_labels), (test_images, test_labels) = mnist.load_
data()

train_images = train_images.reshape((60000, 28, 28, 1))
test_images = test_images.reshape((10000, 28, 28, 1))

train_images, test_images = train_images / 255.0, test_images / 255.0

classes = [0,1,2,3,4,5,6,7,8,9]
```

```
#Built the Model
model = models.Sequential()
model.add(layers.Conv2D(32, (3, 3), activation = 'relu', input_shape = (28,
28, 1)))
model.add(layers.MaxPooling2D((2, 2)))
model.add(layers.Conv2D(64, (3, 3), activation = 'relu'))
model.add(layers.MaxPooling2D((2, 2)))
model.add(layers.Conv2D(64, (3, 3), activation = 'relu'))
model.add(layers.Flatten())
model.add(layers.Dense(64, activation = 'relu'))
model.add(layers.Dense(10, activation = 'softmax'))
model.compile(optimizer = 'adam',
        loss = 'sparse_categorical_crossentropy',
        metrics = ['accuracy'])
        #Fit the model and Test it
model.fit(x = train_images,
        y = train_labels,
        epochs = 5,
        validation_data = (test_images, test_labels))
```

## 3.6 Unsupervised learning

In supervised learning, the purpose is to map from the input to an output with correct values that are supplied by a supervisor. In unsupervised learning, there is no such supervisor and there is only input data. The goal is to discover the uniformities in the input. There is a configuration to the input space such that particular patterns appear more often than others, and we want to find out what usually happens and what does not. In statistics, this is termed *density estimation*. One approach for density estimation is *clustering*, in which the goal is to find clusters or groupings of input. In the case of a company with data of past customers, the customer data includes demographic information as well as past dealings with the company, and the company needs to find out the distribution of the profile of its customers to find out what kind of customers regularly appear. In such a case, a clustering model distributes customers similar in their attributes to the same group, providing the company with natural groupings of its customers; this is called *customer segmentation*. Once such groups are discovered, the company can choose strategies regarding services and products that are specific to different groups; this is known as *customer relationship management*. Such a grouping also allows for discovering outliers who are distinct from other customers (Alpaydin, 2014).

Numerous well-known clustering algorithms as well as *K-means* learn predictive clustering. Hence, they can learn a clustering model from training data, which can be utilized later to allocate new data to clusters. This preserves our distinction between clustering random data and learning a clustering model from training data. Nevertheless, this distinction is not especially appropriate for descriptive clustering methods. Actually, the task becomes learning an appropriate clustering model for given data. What differentiates a good clustering is that the data is divided into *coherent* clusters or groups. This accepts some way of evaluating the similarity or, as is generally more appropriate, the dissimilarity or distance of an arbitrary pair of instances. If our features are numerical, the widely used distance measure is Euclidean distance, but there are other alternatives as well. Most distance-based clustering approaches are based on the possibility of defining a "center of mass," or *exemplar*, for an arbitrary set of instances, in such a way that the exemplar minimizes some distance-related quantity over all instances in the set, called its *scatter*. A noteworthy question is how clustering techniques should be assessed. In the absence of labeled data, we cannot employ a test set in the same way that we did in classification or regression. We can utilize within-cluster scatter as a measure of the quality of a clustering (Flach, 2012).

In some situations, we do not have the freedom or flexibility of having prelabeled training; regardless, we need to extract helpful knowledge or examples from our information. In this situation, unsupervised learning techniques are incredible. These techniques are termed as unsupervised because the model or algorithm attempts to learn fundamental latent structures, relations, and patterns from given information without any assistance or supervision, such as giving information in the form of labeled outcomes or outputs. Unsupervised learning approaches can be classified as relevant to unsupervised learning in the following broad areas of machine learning tasks (Sarkar et al., 2018).

- clustering
- dimensionality reduction
- anomaly detection
- association rule-mining

Clustering techniques are machine learning approaches that attempt to find similar patterns and relations between data samples in the dataset, and then cluster these samples into different groups so that every group or cluster of data samples has some correlation based on the actual attributes or characteristics. Such approaches are fully unsupervised as they seek to cluster data by looking at data features without prior training, guidance, or knowledge of data features, relations, and associations (Sarkar et al., 2018).

There are different forms of clustering techniques, which can be categorized as follows:

- Centroid-based approaches, such as K-medoids and K-means
- Hierarchical clustering approaches, such as divisive and agglomerative
- Distribution-based clustering approaches, such as Gaussian mixture models
- Density-based techniques such as optics dbscan

## 3.6.1 K-means algorithm

In a K- means problem there is no effective solution to identifying the global minimum, and we need to utilize a heuristic algorithm. It can be seen that an iteration of K-means may never improve the scatter within the cluster, resulting in the algorithm approaching a stationary point in which no further development is possible. It is worth noting that there might be several stationary points even in the simplest data set. Generally speaking, while K-means converge in finite time to a stationary point, there can be no certainty whether the convergence point is actually the global minimum or not, no matter how far we are from it (Flach, 2012).

## Example 3.45

The following Python code utilizes k-means clustering to find the center of the clusters of breast cancer data by employing the scikit-learn library APIs. In this example we utilize the breast cancer dataset, which exists in sklearn.datasets. The cluster centers are plotted. Note that this example is adapted from scikit-learn.

```
# =====================================================================
# K-means clustering example
# =====================================================================
from sklearn import datasets
import matplotlib.pyplot as plt
import numpy as np
# #####################################################################
# Import some data to play with
Breast_Cancer = datasets.load_breast_cancer()
X = Breast_Cancer.data
y = Breast_Cancer.target

# Plot the original data points
plt.scatter(X[:, 0], X[:, 1], c = y, cmap = plt.cm.Set1,
    edgecolor = 'k')
plt.xlabel('Attribute I')
plt.ylabel('Attribute II')
plt.title('Original data Scatter')
plt.xticks(())
plt.yticks(())
#%%
from sklearn.cluster import KMeans

" " "
sklearn.cluster.KMeans(n_clusters = 2, init = 'k-means++', n_init = 10, max_
iter = 300, tol = 0.0001,
precompute_distances = 'auto', verbose = 0, random_state = None,
copy_x = True, n_jobs = None,
algorithm = 'auto')
" " "

#Find Cluster Centers
kmeans = KMeans(n_clusters = 2)
kmeans.fit(X)
y_kmeans = kmeans.predict(X)

#Plot the Cluster Centers
plt.scatter(X[:, 0], X[:, 1], c = y_kmeans, s = 50, cmap = 'viridis')
```

```
centers = kmeans.cluster_centers_
plt.scatter(centers[:, 0], centers[:, 1], c='black', s=200, alpha=0.5);
plt.xlabel('Attribute I')
plt.ylabel('Attribute II')
plt.title('Cluster Centers')
plt.xticks(())
plt.yticks(())
```

### 3.6.2 Silhouettes

How can we detect the poor quality of the clustering algorithm? Silhouettes are a useful technique. For each example that is grouped by cluster, a silhouette sorts and plots s(x). In this particular situation, in the construction of the silhouette squared Euclidean distance is utilized, but the approach can be extended to other distance metrics. It can be clearly seen that the first clustering is much stronger than the second. We can estimate the average silhouette values per cluster and over the entire dataset in addition to the graphical representation (Flach, 2012).

**Example 3.46**

The following Python code utilizes k-means clustering to find the silhouettes of synthetic data by employing the scikit-learn library APIs. In this example we utilize the generated sample data from make_blobs, which exists in the scikit-learn library. The silhouettes and cluster centers are plotted for different cases. Note that this example is taken from scikit-learn.

```
# ========================================================================
#Silhouettes example
# ========================================================================
from sklearn.datasets import make_blobs
from sklearn.cluster import KMeans
from sklearn.metrics import silhouette_samples, silhouette_score

import matplotlib.pyplot as plt
import matplotlib.cm as cm
import numpy as np

print(__doc__)

# Generating the sample data from make_blobs
# This particular setting has one distinct cluster and 3 clusters placed
close
# together.
X, y = make_blobs(n_samples = 500,
```

```
        n_features = 2,
        centers = 4,
        cluster_std = 1,
        center_box = (-10.0, 10.0),
        shuffle = True,
        random_state = 1) # For reproducibility

range_n_clusters = [2, 3, 4, 5, 6]

for n_clusters in range_n_clusters:
  # Create a subplot with 1 row and 2 columns
  fig, (ax1, ax2) = plt.subplots(1, 2)
  fig.set_size_inches(18, 7)

  # The 1st subplot is the silhouette plot
  # The silhouette coefficient can range from -1, 1 but in this example all
  # lie within [-0.1, 1]
  ax1.set_xlim([-0.1, 1])
  # The (n_clusters+1)*10 is for inserting blank space between silhouette
  # plots of individual clusters, to demarcate them clearly.
  ax1.set_ylim([0, len(X) + (n_clusters + 1) * 10])

  # Initialize the clusterer with n_clusters value and a random generator
  # seed of 10 for reproducibility.
  clusterer = KMeans(n_clusters = n_clusters, random_state = 10)
  cluster_labels = clusterer.fit_predict(X)

  # The silhouette_score gives the average value for all the samples.
  # This gives a perspective into the density and separation of the formed

  # clusters
  silhouette_avg = silhouette_score(X, cluster_labels)
  print("For n_clusters =", n_clusters,
  "The average silhouette_score is :", silhouette_avg)

  # Compute the silhouette scores for each sample
  sample_silhouette_values = silhouette_samples(X, cluster_labels)

  y_lower = 10
  for i in range(n_clusters):
  # Aggregate the silhouette scores for samples belonging to
  # cluster i, and sort them
  ith_cluster_silhouette_values = \
  sample_silhouette_values[cluster_labels == i]

  ith_cluster_silhouette_values.sort()
```

```
size_cluster_i = ith_cluster_silhouette_values.shape[0]
y_upper = y_lower + size_cluster_i

color = cm.nipy_spectral(float(i) / n_clusters)
ax1.fill_betweenx(np.arange(y_lower, y_upper),
0, ith_cluster_silhouette_values,
facecolor = color, edgecolor = color, alpha = 0.7)

# Label the silhouette plots with their cluster numbers at the middle
ax1.text(-0.05, y_lower + 0.5 * size_cluster_i, str(i))

# Compute the new y_lower for next plot
y_lower = y_upper + 10 # 10 for the 0 samples

ax1.set_title("The silhouette plot for the various clusters.")
ax1.set_xlabel("The silhouette coefficient values")
ax1.set_ylabel("Cluster label")

# The vertical line for average silhouette score of all the values
ax1.axvline(x = silhouette_avg, color = "red", linestyle = "--")

ax1.set_yticks([]) # Clear the yaxis labels / ticks
ax1.set_xticks([-0.1, 0, 0.2, 0.4, 0.6, 0.8, 1])

# 2nd Plot showing the actual clusters formed
colors = cm.nipy_spectral(cluster_labels.astype(float) / n_clusters)
ax2.scatter(X[:, 0], X[:, 1], marker = '.', s = 30, lw = 0, alpha = 0.7,
      c = colors, edgecolor = 'k')

# Labeling the clusters
centers = clusterer.cluster_centers_
# Draw white circles at cluster centers
ax2.scatter(centers[:, 0], centers[:, 1], marker = 'o',
c = "white", alpha = 1, s = 200, edgecolor = 'k')

for i, c in enumerate(centers):
ax2.scatter(c[0], c[1], marker = '$%d$' % i, alpha = 1,
s = 50, edgecolor = 'k')

ax2.set_title("The visualization of the clustered data.")
ax2.set_xlabel("Feature space for the 1st feature")
ax2.set_ylabel("Feature space for the 2nd feature")

plt.suptitle(("Silhouette analysis for KMeans clustering on sample data "
"with n_clusters = %d" % n_clusters),
fontsize = 14, fontweight = 'bold')
plt.show()
```

### 3.6.3 Anomaly detection

Anomaly detection technique is also called outlier detection, where we discover cases of abnormal events and anomalies that normally do not appear on the basis of historical data samples. Often abnormalities occur rarely, and as a result become unusual occurrences, or anomalies may not be rare in different instances, but they may arise in very short bursts over time, so they have unique patterns. Unsupervised learning techniques may be utilized to detect anomalies in such a way that they train the algorithm with normal, nonanomalous data samples on the training dataset. Once the algorithm learns the necessary data interpretations, patterns, and attribute relations in normal samples for any new fact sample, it can discover it as an anomalous or ordinary data point by using its discovered information. Anomaly-based detection techniques are highly popular in real-world situations, such as detection of security attacks or infringements, savings card fraud, fabrication anomalies, network problems, and many more (Sarkar et al., 2018).

#### Example 3.47

The following Python code presents characteristics of various anomaly detection algorithms on two-dimensional datasets by using the scikit-learn library APIs. Datasets include one or two modes to demonstrate the capability of algorithms to deal with multimodal data. For each dataset, 15% of samples are produced as random uniform noise. This percentage is the value provided to the nu parameter of the OneClassSVM and the contamination parameter of the other outlier detection algorithms. Decision boundaries among inliers and outliers are demonstrated in black, except for local outlier factor (LOF), as it has no forecast technique to be utilized with new data once it is employed for outlier detection. In this example we utilize the generated sample data from make_moons, make_blobs, which exists in the scikit-learn library. In this example sklearn.svm.OneClassSVM is sensitive to outliers and thus does not perform very well for outlier detection; sklearn.covariance.EllipticEnvelope assumes the data is Gaussian and learns an ellipse but is robust to outliers; and sklearn.ensemble.IsolationForest and sklearn.neighbors.LocalOutlierFactor seem to perform reasonably well for multimodal datasets. Note that this example is taken from scikit-learn.

```
#=========================================================================
# Anomaly detection
#=========================================================================
# Author: Alexandre Gramfort <alexandre.gramfort@inria.fr>
# Albert Thomas <albert.thomas@telecom-paristech.fr>
# License: BSD 3 clause

import time

import numpy as np
import matplotlib
import matplotlib.pyplot as plt
from sklearn import svm
```

```
from sklearn.datasets import make_moons, make_blobs
from sklearn.covariance import EllipticEnvelope
from sklearn.ensemble import IsolationForest
from sklearn.neighbors import LocalOutlierFactor

print(__doc__)

matplotlib.rcParams['contour.negative_linestyle'] = 'solid'

# Example settings
n_samples = 300
outliers_fraction = 0.15
n_outliers = int(outliers_fraction * n_samples)
n_inliers = n_samples - n_outliers

# define outlier/anomaly detection methods to be compared
anomaly_algorithms = [
  ("Robust covariance",
EllipticEnvelope(contamination = outliers_fraction)),
  ("One-Class SVM", svm.OneClassSVM(nu = outliers_fraction, kernel = "rbf",
              gamma = 0.1)),
("Isolation Forest", IsolationForest(behaviour = 'new',
              contamination = outliers_fraction,
              random_state = 42)),
  ("Local Outlier Factor", LocalOutlierFactor(
    n_neighbors = 35, contamination = outliers_fraction))]

# Define datasets
blobs_params = dict(random_state = 0, n_samples = n_inliers, n_features = 2)
datasets = [
  make_blobs(centers = [[0, 0], [0, 0]], cluster_std = 0.5,
     **blobs_params)[0],
  make_blobs(centers = [[2, 2], [-2, -2]], cluster_std = [0.5, 0.5],
     **blobs_params)[0],
  make_blobs(centers = [[2, 2], [-2, -2]], cluster_std = [1.5, .3],
     **blobs_params)[0],
  4. * (make_moons(n_samples = n_samples, noise = .05, random_state = 0)[0] -
      np.array([0.5, 0.25])),
  14. * (np.random.RandomState(42).rand(n_samples, 2) - 0.5)]
# Compare given classifiers under given settings
xx, yy = np.meshgrid(np.linspace(-7, 7, 150),
        np.linspace(-7, 7, 150))
```

```
plt.figure(figsize = (len(anomaly_algorithms) * 2 + 3, 12.5))
plt.subplots_adjust(left = .02,  right = .98,  bottom = .001,  top = .96,
wspace = .05,
        hspace = .01)

plot_num = 1
rng = np.random.RandomState(42)

for i_dataset, X in enumerate(datasets):
  # Add outliers
  X = np.concatenate([X, rng.uniform(low = -6, high = 6,
  size = (n_outliers, 2))], axis = 0)

  for name, algorithm in anomaly_algorithms:
  t0 = time.time()
  algorithm.fit(X)
  t1 = time.time()
  plt.subplot(len(datasets), len(anomaly_algorithms), plot_num)
  if i_dataset == 0:
  plt.title(name, size = 18)

  # fit the data and tag outliers
  if name == "Local Outlier Factor":
  y_pred = algorithm.fit_predict(X)
  else:
  y_pred = algorithm.fit(X).predict(X)

  # plot the levels lines and the points
  if name != "Local Outlier Factor": # LOF does not implement predict
  Z = algorithm.predict(np.c_[xx.ravel(), yy.ravel()])
  Z = Z.reshape(xx.shape)
  plt.contour(xx, yy, Z, levels = [0], linewidths = 2, colors = 'black')

  colors = np.array(['#377eb8', '#ff7f00'])
  plt.scatter(X[:, 0], X[:, 1], s = 10, color = colors[(y_pred + 1) // 2])

  plt.xlim(-7, 7)
  plt.ylim(-7, 7)
  plt.xticks(())
  plt.yticks(())
  plt.text(.99, .01, ('%.2fs' % (t1 - t0)).lstrip('0'),
  transform = plt.gca().transAxes, size = 15,
  horizontalalignment = 'right')
  plot_num += 1
plt.show()
```

### 3.6.4 Association rule-mining

Association rule-mining is usually a data mining approach used to explore and interpret large transactional datasets to identify unique patterns and rules. During transactions, these patterns define fascinating relationships and interactions between different items. Moreover, association rule-mining is often referred to as market basket study, which is utilized to analyze habits in customer purchase. Association rules help identify and forecast transactional behaviors based on information from training transactions utilizing beneficial properties. Using this approach, we can answer questions such as what items human beings tend to buy together, indicating frequent sets of goods. We can also associate or correlate products and items (Sarkar et al., 2018).

## 3.7 Reinforcement learning

The output of the machine is a sequence of acts in some implementations. In such a scenario, a single action is not important; the strategy, which is the sequence of right actions to achieve the goal, is necessary. In any intermediate state there is no such item as extraordinary intervention; an action is adequate if it is a good policy step. In such a scenario, to be able to create a policy the machine learning algorithm must be able to examine the efficacy of policies and learn from past action sequences. These methods of learning reinforcement are recognized as algorithms for reinforcement learning. A suitable analogy is game playing, where a single move alone is not very important; a series of right moves is better. A move is appropriate when this is part of a correct move for game playing. Game playing is an essential area of research for machine learning and artificial intelligence. This is because games are easy to describe and are quite challenging to play well at the same time. A game like chess has a limited number of rules, but it is very complicated because of the huge number of possible moves in each state and the large number of moves a game involves. Once we have appealing algorithms that can learn how to play games well, we can also apply them to applications that are more economically beneficial. Another field of reinforcement learning implementation is a robot navigating in an environment in search of a goal zone. The robot will move in a number of directions at any moment. After a number of trials, it must learn, from an initial state, the right sequence of acts to achieve the target state, doing so as quickly as possible and without hitting any of the obstacles (Alpaydin, 2014).

The main goal in solving a problem of machine learning is to create smart programs or intelligent agents through the learning process and to respond to changing environments. Reinforcement learning is one such machine-learning process. Learners and software program agents benefit through explicit environmental interaction with this method. This imitates the human being's learning approach. Moreover, the agent is able to learn even if the entire information or model about the environment is not accessible. An agent provides feedback as a reward or punishment for every behavior. Those conditions are mapped to actions in an environment during the learning process. Reinforcement learning algorithms optimize the incentives received in interactions with the environment at some point and establish state mapping of actions as a strategy for decision-making. The policy could be chosen immediately, or it can adapt to the environmental changes as well. Reinforcement learning differs from supervised learning, where the learning is from examples provided with the help of an expert external supervisor. It is a technique for training the approximator of a parameterized function. However, learning from interaction is not enough. It is more like learning from external instructions, so guidance arises from the situation and environment. It is often difficult to achieve examples of desired actions in interactive problems that are both accurate and representative of all the circumstances under which the agent will respond. The position one would presume is that learning is the most useful in unknown territory; an agent should be able to learn from its own experience as well as from the environment. Reinforcement learning thus incorporates the discipline of supervised learning with dynamic programming to build a machine learning framework that is very similar to the methods utilized through human learning. The tradeoff between exploration and exploitation is one of the challenges that arises in reinforcement learning and does not exist in other types of learning. To gain incentive, a reinforcement-learning machine should choose actions that are implemented previously and considered to be effective in delivering incentive. But it has to seek actions that have not been implemented before in order to explore such actions. The machine should receive the advantage of what is already learned to gain incentive, but it also must learn in order to make better choices of action in the future. The dilemma is that without failure in the mission there will be no discovery or development. The machine will pursue a range of actions and progressively choose the ones that seem to be best. To obtain a reliable estimate of its predicted reward, each behavior should be attempted in many instances on a stochastic process. Throughout supervised learning, as is usually described, the challenge of balancing development and invention does not exist. Hence, experts have a responsibility to explore invention in supervised learning. Reinforcement learning is different in numerous ways from the more extensively studied problem of supervised learning. The main difference is that input-output pair representations do not exist. Alternatively, the machine is notified with immediate reward, and the resulting condition appears after taking an action, but it is not the notification of what action must have taken in its long-term interests. It is important that the machine gains valuable experience with potential machine conditions, transitions, actions, and incentives to act effectively (Kulkarni, 2012).

## 3.8 Instance-based learning

There are various approaches to constructing machine learning models using techniques that attempt to generalize based on input data. Instance-based learning includes machine learning algorithms and techniques that use raw data points themselves to determine the effects of newer, previously unseen data samples rather than constructing a specific model on training data and then testing it. A simple example might be a K-nearest neighbors technique. The machine learning technique recognizes the interpretation of the data from the features, along with its dimensions, position of every data point, and so on. It utilizes a similarity measure such as Euclidean distance for any new data point to locate the three nearest input data points to this new data point. When a new data point is chosen, a majority of the results are simply taken for these three training factors and predict it as the response/label for this new data point. Therefore, instance-based learning works by means of seeking the input data points and using a similarity measure to predict and generalize new data points (Sarkar et al., 2018).

## 3.9 Summary

This chapter presents a select group of packages that we will use to store, analyze, and model our data on a regular basis. These libraries and frameworks can be considered the key elements of the toolbox of a data scientist. The list of packages that we cover is far from complete, but the most relevant packages are presented. We strongly suggest that you become more familiar with the packages by going through the documentation and related videos. Throughout subsequent chapters, we will continue to incorporate and clarify other important features and aspects of these frameworks. The examples in this chapter will give you an excellent grasp of understanding machine learning and solving problems in a clear and concise way, along with associated theoretical information. Often the process of learning models with various data is a reiteration of these simple steps and principles. You will learn how to use the set of tools in the coming chapters to address more complex data processing, wrangling, analysis, and visualization issues.

## References

Alpaydin, E. (2014). Introduction to machine learning. Cambridge, MA, London, England: The MIT Press.

Bengio, Y. (2009). Learning deep architectures for AI. Foundations and Trends® in Machine Learning, 2(1), 1–127.

Breiman, L., Friedman, J. H., Olshen, R. A., & Stone, C. J. (1984). Classification and regression trees. Boca Raton: Hall/CRC.

Breiman, L. (1996). Bagging predictors. Machine Learning, 24(2), 123–140.

Breiman, L. (1999). Using adaptive bagging to debias regressions. Statistics Dept., University of California, Berkeley: (Technical report 547).

Buduma, N., & Locascio, N. (2017). Fundamentals of deep learning: Designing next-generation machine intelligence algorithms. Sebastopol, CA: O'Reilly Media, Inc.

Clarke, B., Fokoue, E., & Zhang, H. H. (2009). Principles and theory for data mining and machine learning. New York, NY: Springer Science & Business Media, LLC.

Flach, P. (2012). Machine learning: The art and science of algorithms that make sense of data. Cambridge, UK: Cambridge University Press.

Chollet, F. (2018). Deep learning with Python. Shelter Island, NY: Manning Publications Co.

Freund, Y., & Schapire, R. E. (1995). *A decision-theoretic generalization of on-line learning and an application to boosting.* In P. Vitányi (Ed.), *Computational Learning Theory. EuroCOLT*. Berlin, Heidelberg: Springer Lecture Notes in Computer Science (Lecture Notes in Artificial Intelligence), vol. 904.

Freund, Y., & Schapire, R. E. (1997). A decision-theoretic generalization of on-line learning and an application to boosting. Journal of Computer and System Sciences, 55(1), 119–139.

Friedman, J. H. (2002). Stochastic gradient boosting. Computational Statistics & Data Analysis, 38(4), 367–378.

Goel, E., & Abhilasha, E. (2017). Random forest: A review. *International Journal of Advanced Research in Computer Science and Software Engineering*, *7*(1), 251–257 https://doi.org/10.23956/ijarcsse/V7I1/01113.

Han, J., Pei, J., & Kamber, M. (2011). Data mining: Concepts and techniques. San Francisco, CA: Elsevier.

Hapke, H. M., Lane, H., & Howard, C. (2019). Natural language processing in action. Shelter Island, NY: Manning Publications Co.

Hastie, T., Tibshirani, R., Friedman, J., & Franklin, J. (2005). The elements of statistical learning: Data mining, inference and prediction. The Mathematical Intelligencer, 27(2), 83–85.

Hinton, G. E., & Salakhutdinov, R. R. (2006). Reducing the dimensionality of data with neural networks. Science, 313(5786), 504–507.

Kim, P. (2017). Convolutional neural network. *MATLAB deep learning*. New York, NY: Springer Science+Business Media New York 121-147.

Kulkarni, P. (2012). *Reinforcement and systemic machine learning for decision making (Vol. 1)*. Hoboken, NJ: John Wiley & Sons Inc.

Kumari, G. T. P. (2012). A study of bagging and boosting approaches to develop meta-classifier. Engineering Science and Technology: An International Journal, *2*(5), 850–855.

Mohri, M., Rostamizadeh, A., & Talwalkar, A. (2018). Foundations of machine learning. Cambridge, MA: MIT press.

Murphy, K. P. (2012). Machine learning: A probabilistic perspective. MIT press, Cambridge, MA.

Pedregosa, F., Varoquaux, G., Gramfort, A., Michel, V., Thirion, B., Grisel, O., & Dubourg, V. (2011). Scikit-learn: Machine learning in Python. Journal of Machine Learning Research, *12*(Oct), 2825–2830.

Quinlan, J.R. (1993). Improved use of continuous attributes in C4.5. 77–90.

Quinlan, J. R. (1986). Induction of decision trees. Machine Learning, *1*(1), 81–106.

Raschka, S. (2015). Python machine learning. Birmingham, UK: Packt Publishing Ltd.

Ray, P. K., Mohanty, A., & Panigrahi, T. (2019). Power quality analysis in solar PV integrated microgrid using independent component analysis and support vector machine. *Optik*, 180, 691–698 https://doi.org/10.1016/j.ijleo.2018.11.041.

Rosenblatt, F. (1958). The perceptron: A probabilistic model for information storage and organization in the brain. Psychological Review, 65(6), 386–408.

Sanei, S. (2013). *Adaptive processing of brain signals*. United Kingdom: John Wiley & Sons.

Sarkar, D., Bali, R., & Sharma, T. (2018). *Practical machine learning with Python: A problem-solver's guide to building real-world intelligent systems*. New York, NY: Apress, Springer Science+Business Media New York.

Schapire, R. E. (1990). The strength of weak learnability. Machine Learning, 5(2), 197–227.

Subasi, A. (2019). Practical Guide for Biomedical Signals Analysis Using Machine Learning Techniques, A MATLAB Based Approach (1st Edition). United Kingdom: Academic Press.

Veit, D. (2012). 2—Neural networks and their application to textile technology. In D. Veit (Ed.), Simulation in Textile Technology (pp. 9-71). https://doi.org/10.1533/9780857097088.9.

Witten, I. H., Frank, E., & Hall, M. A. (2011). *Data mining: Practical machine learning tools and techniques*. Retrieved from https://books.google.com.sa/books?id=bDtLM8CODsQC.

Wu, X., Kumar, V., Ross Quinlan, J., Ghosh, J., Yang, Q., Motoda, H., & Steinberg, D. (2008). Top 10 algorithms in data mining. Knowledge and Information Systems, 14(1), 1–37 https://doi.org/10.1007/s10115-007-0114-2.

CHAPTER

# 4

# Classification examples for healthcare

## 4.1 Introduction

Generally the biomedical data classification process can be divided into four phases, namely (1) data acquisition and segmentation, (2) data preprocessing, (3) feature extraction/ dimension reduction, and (4) recognition and classification. As seen in Fig. 4.1, the biomedical data is recorded from the human body and then preprocessed. Data preprocessing is a technique that is utilized to transform the raw data into a useful and effective format. The data may contain noise—many irrelevant and missing parts—which should be eliminated. Then, the features are extracted from the biomedical data acquired and processed and transformed to a feature vector. The appropriate structure in the raw data is described by the feature vector. In the next step, a dimension reduction is employed to eliminate the redundant information from the feature vector, generating a reduced feature vector. In the last step, a classifier classifies the reduced feature vector (Subasi, 2019c).

## 4.2 EEG signal analysis

Electrical signals generated by the brain describe the brain function and the condition of the entire body. They offer the inspiration to use digital signal processing techniques for the electroencephalogram (EEG) obtained from the human brain. The physiological characteristics of brain activities have various issues related to the characteristics of the original sources and their real patterns. It is useful to understand the neurophysiological properties and neuronal functions of the brain in conjunction with the working principle fundamental signal generation and acquisition when dealing with these signals for recognition. EEG introduces the way of diagnosis of numerous neurological disorders and anomalies in the human body. This shows that the EEG has rich potential in using advanced signal processing methods to support the clinician in their decisions (Sanei & Chambers, 2013; Subasi, 2019c).

EEG signals are a noninvasive medical tool for analyzing several brain disorders and for better understanding of the human brain. But the variety of EEG patterns cannot be fully explained by any single mathematical or biological model. Thus understanding EEG signals essentially remains a phenomenological medical discipline (Barlow, 1993). EEGs are recordings of the electrical potentials created by the brain, usually less than 300 μV. An

**Practical Machine Learning for Data Analysis Using Python. http://dx.doi.org/10.1016/B978-0-12-821379-7.00004-7**

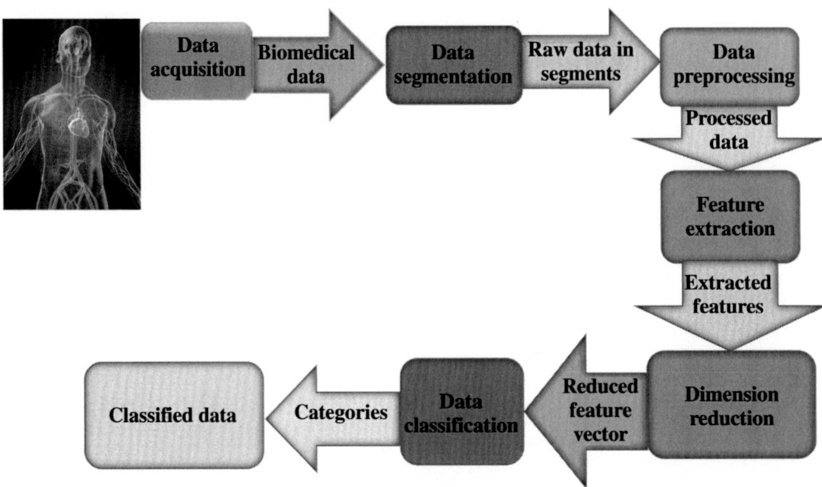


**FIGURE 4.1 A general framework for biomedical data classification.** *Source: Adapted from Subasi (2019c).*

electroencephalographer, an individual trained to qualitatively distinguish normal and abnormal EEG activity within quite long EEG records, was for several years the only person qualified for visual analysis of the EEG. Hence clinicians and researchers were left with a bunch of EEG paper records. Yet, the arrival of modern powerful computers and associated technologies opened a whole new door of possibilities for utilizing different techniques to quantify EEG signals (Bronzino, 1999).The analysis is significantly accelerated by a choice of digital signal processing techniques with distinct purposes like noise reduction and feature extraction that are not visually obtainable. EEG is an extremely effective tool for the analysis of numerous disorders like epilepsy, sleep disorders, and dementia. Furthermore, the EEG signals are important for real-time monitoring of patients with encephalopathies or the ones in comas (Sörnmo & Laguna, 2005; Subasi, 2019c). A general framework for EEG signal analysis is shown in Fig. 4.2.

## 4.2.1 Epileptic seizure prediction and detection

EEG analysis has enhanced significantly with the widespread usage of mathematical machine learning techniques. Machine learning techniques have also enabled the classification of patterns within the EEG to improve recognition, making EEG signals useful for recognition of brain disorders and key pathologies. Thus numerous studies on characteristics of EEG signals associated with neurological disorders have been conducted (Begg, Lai, & Palaniswami, 2008). Epilepsy is a neurological disorder that affects over 50 million people worldwide. It is the second most common neurological disorder after stroke. Epilepsy is a serious disorder described by temporary changes in the bioelectrical functioning of the brain. These variations produce abnormal neuronal synchronization and seizures, which affect awareness, sensation, or movement. Epileptic seizures are triggered by particularly synchronized activity of large groups of neurons. Epileptic seizures are sudden bursts of wild electrical activity in a group of neurons of the cerebral cortex. Due to the location of the

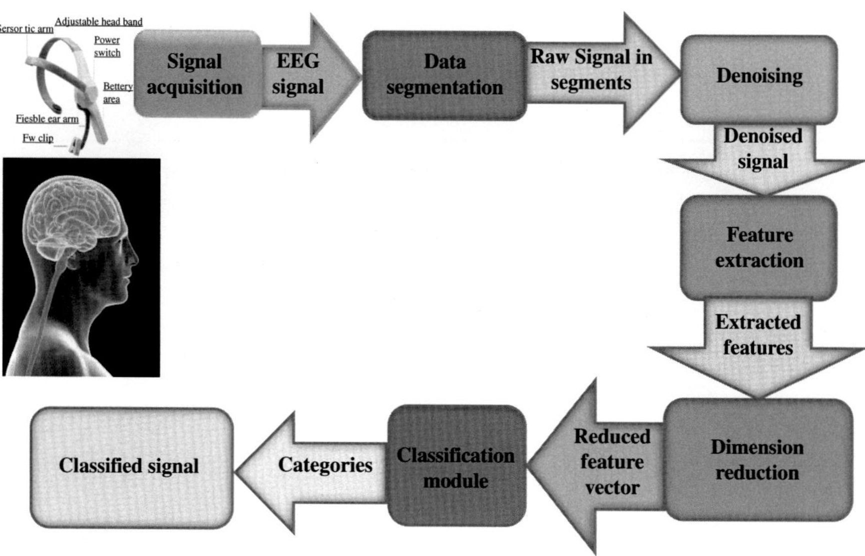


FIGURE 4.2 **A general framework for EEG signals analysis.** *Source: Adapted from Subasi (2019a).*

focus (origin) of the electrical activity of numerous brain regions, epileptic seizures may be expressed in different ways (Sörnmo & Laguna, 2005; Subasi, 2019c).

Seizure EEG signals include standard patterns that health professionals use to distinguish from normal (nonseizure) EEG signals. Hence their recognition can be utilized to respond to an upcoming or ongoing seizure. Moreover, automated recognition techniques have been assessed to reduce the amount of data and enable quicker and more accurate detection of pathological EEG waveforms that characterize epileptic seizures (Begg et al., 2008). It is generally necessary to record the EEG during long periods of time to catch an ictal EEG. In this case, the subject is often recorded on video in the hospital for a few days. Neurologists can therefore draw a parallel between EEG and visual recordings for improving their assessments. This form of recording is called a video EEG. Another form of recording can be carried out at home during at least one day and is called an ambulatory EEG. The EEG is recorded during daily activities using a small digital recording device. This is a cheaper technique than video EEG and includes both sleeping and waking phases. If the subject scratches his or her head, a noise is introduced into the EEG recording. Neurologists utilize different patterns within ictal (seizure) EEG waveforms to distinguish them from interictal (nonseizure) EEG waveforms. Any form of long-term EEG monitoring produces massive amounts of data. This data needs a lot of time to be appropriately analyzed. An efficient seizure prediction algorithm can warn a patient wearing an ambulatory recording device to consider appropriate safety precautions before the seizure occurs (Sörnmo & Laguna, 2005; Subasi, 2019c).

Recently, there have been many improvements in biomedical devices and healthcare technologies to help meet the needs of current healthcare diagnoses and treatments. Even though the innovative medical devices in healthcare centers provide fast and accurate analysis, it is necessary to continuously monitor patients with chronic diseases such as epilepsy (Chiauzzi,

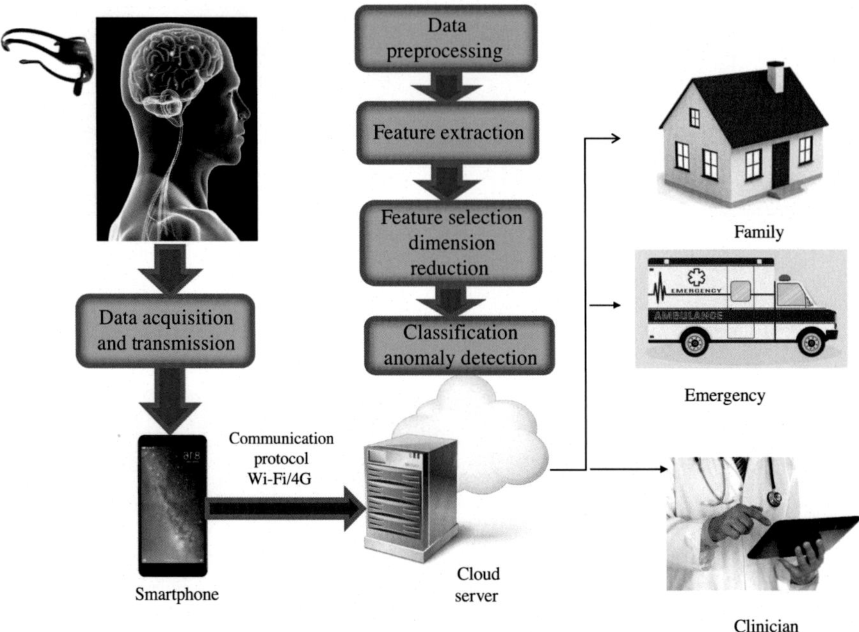


**FIGURE 4.3 A framework for cloud-based mobile epileptic patient monitoring.** *Source: Adapted from (Subasi et al. 2020a).*

Rodarte, & DasMahapatra, 2015). Fig. 4.3 shows the cloud-based mobile patient monitoring for epileptic seizure prediction. In this framework, mobile devices collect EEG signals continuously from smart headset sensors and acquiring devices to inform via internet connection emergency personnel, clinicians, and patients' families of any emergency situations (Hsieh & Hsu, 2012). In this approach, different signal processing and machine learning techniques can be used to analyze the EEG signals for epileptic seizure prediction. Epileptic seizures arise randomly and are difficult to predict (Menshawy, Benharref, & Serhani, 2015). The proper technique for predicting epileptic seizures is to monitor the patient continuously. The new trend of cloud-based, mobile patient-monitoring systems became possible due to innovative developments in smart wearable sensors, mobile sensing devices, and smartphones alongside wireless and cellular communication networks. Smart sensors can be integrated easily with a smartphone to establish a vital pillar for the development of a vital, cloud-based, mobile health-monitoring system. A smart sensor accurately collects EEG signals directly from the patient's brain and transmits the collected EEG signals to the smartphone. Then the smartphone sends the collected EEG signal to the cloud to continuously track the status of the patient. If a seizure is predicted, the application on the cloud server sends this information to the emergency department, clinician, and family of the patient (Serhani, El Menshawy, & Benharref, 2016). The epileptic seizure prediction framework shown in Fig. 4.3 is composed of (1) signal acquisition and transmission module, (2) feature extraction module, and (3) classification module. The smartphone is connected to the cloud via appropriate communication protocol (Subasi, Bandic, & Qaisar, 2020)

## Example 4.1

The following Python code is used to extract features from the EEG signals by employing discrete wavelet transform (DWT), and then it uses statistical values of DWT sub-bands. Next it classifies these data using different classifiers by employing separate training and testing datasets. The classification accuracy, precision, recall, F1 score, Cohen kappa score, and Matthews correlation coefficient are calculated. The classification report and confusion matrix are also given.

***Dataset information:*** This epilepsy dataset is a widely used EEG dataset that has five sets denoted A–E, each containing 100 single-channel EEG segments of 23.6-sec duration. Sets A and B consist of EEG recordings of five healthy volunteers utilizing a standardized electrode placement scheme. Subjects were relaxed in an awake state with eyes open (A-Z.zip) and eyes closed (B-O.zip), respectively. Sets C-N.zip, D-F.zip, and E-S.zip are taken from EEG archive of presurgical diagnosis. EEG signals are collected from subjects who had achieved complete seizure control after resection of one of the hippocampal formations, which was correctly identified as the epileptogenic zone. Set D was recorded from the epileptogenic zone, and those in set C from the hippocampal formation of the opposite hemisphere of the brain. While sets C and D contain only activity recorded during seizure-free intervals, set E only contains seizure activity. Here segments were chosen from all recordings revealing ictal activity. After 12-bit analog-to-digital conversion, the data were sampled at 173.61 Hz. Band-pass filter settings were 0.53–40 Hz (12 dB/oct.). You can download data from the following web site:

http://epileptologie-bonn.de/cms/front_content.php?idcat=193&lang=3&changelang=3

```
"""
Created on Thu May 9 12:18:30 2019
@author: asubasi
"""
# descriptive statistics
import scipy as sp
import scipy.io as sio
import pywt
import numpy as np
import scipy.stats as stats
from sklearn.metrics import classification_report
from sklearn.metrics import confusion_matrix
from sklearn import metrics
from io import BytesIO #needed for plot
import seaborn as sns; sns.set()
import matplotlib.pyplot as plt
import seaborn as sns
#Mother Wavelet db1
waveletname='db1'
level=6
#Load mat file
mat_contents = sio.loadmat('AS_BONN_ALL_EEG_DATA_1024.mat')
sorted(mat_contents.keys())
EpilepticZone_Interictal=mat_contents['EpilepticZone_Interictal']
```

```
Epileptic_Ictal=mat_contents['Epileptic_Ictal']
NonEpilepticZone_Interictal=mat_contents['NonEpilepticZone_Interictal_']
Normal_Eyes_Closed=mat_contents['Normal_Eye_Closed']
Normal_Eyes_Open=mat_contents['Normal_Eyes_Open']

Labels = [] #Empty List For Labels
Length = 1024; # Length of signal
Nofsignals=len(Normal_Eyes_Open[0]) ; #Total Number of Signal for each
class
NofClasses=3 #Number of Classes
numfeatures =48 #Number of features extracted from DWT decomposition
#Create Empty Array For Features
Extracted_Features=np.ndarray(shape=(NofClasses*Nofsignals,numfeatures),
dtype=float, order='F')
# ==========================================================================
# Define utility functions
# ==========================================================================
def print_confusion_matrix(y_test, y_pred):
  matrix = confusion_matrix(y_test, y_pred)
  plt.figure(figsize=(10, 8))
  sns.heatmap(matrix,cmap='coolwarm',linecolor='white',linewidths=1,
            annot=True,
            fmt='d')
  plt.title('Confusion Matrix')
  plt.ylabel('True Label')
  plt.xlabel('Predicted Label')
  plt.show()
def print_performance_metrics(y_test, y_pred):
  print('Accuracy:', np.round(metrics.accuracy_score(y_test, y_pred),4))
  print('Precision:', np.round(metrics.precision_score(y_test,
                    y_pred,average='weighted'),4))
  print('Recall:', np.round(metrics.recall_score(y_test, y_pred,
                         average='weighted'),4))
  print('F1 Score:', np.round(metrics.f1_score(y_test, y_pred,
                         average='weighted'),4))
  print('Cohen Kappa Score:', np.round(metrics.cohen_kappa_score(y_test,
  y_pred),4))
  print('Matthews Corrcoef:', np.round(metrics.matthews_corrcoef(y_test,
  y_pred),4))
  print('\t\tClassification Report:\n', metrics.classification_report(y_
  test, y_pred))

def print_confusion_matrix_and_save(y_test, y_pred):
  mat = confusion_matrix(y_test, y_pred)
```

```
    sns.heatmap(mat, square=True, annot=True, fmt='d', cbar=False)
    plt.title('Confusion Matrix')
    plt.ylabel('True Label')
    plt.xlabel('Predicted Label')
    plt.show()

    plt.savefig("Confusion.jpg")
    # Save SVG in a fake file object.
    f = BytesIO()
    plt.savefig(f, format="svg")

def plot_history(history):
    accuracy = history.history['accuracy']
    val_accuracy = history.history['val_accuracy']
    loss = history.history['loss']
    val_loss = history.history['val_loss']
    x = range(1, len(accuracy) + 1)

    plt.figure(figsize=(12, 5))
    plt.subplot(1, 2, 1)
    plt.plot(x, accuracy, 'b', label='Training acc')
    plt.plot(x, val_accuracy, 'r', label='Validation acc')
    plt.title('Training and validation accuracy')
    plt.legend()
    plt.subplot(1, 2, 2)
    plt.plot(x, loss, 'b', label='Training loss')
    plt.plot(x, val_loss, 'r', label='Validation loss')
    plt.title('Training and validation loss')
    plt.legend()
# ===========================================================================
# Feature extraction using the statistical values of discrete wavelet
transform
# ===========================================================================
def DWT_Feature_Extraction(signal, i, wname, level):
    coeff = pywt.wavedec(signal, wname, level=level)
    cA6,cD6,cD5,cD4, cD3, cD2, cD1=coeff
   #Mean Values of each subbands
    Extracted_Features[i,0]=sp.mean(abs(cD1[:]))
    Extracted_Features[i,1]=sp.mean(abs(cD2[:]))
    Extracted_Features[i,2]=sp.mean(abs(cD3[:]))
    Extracted_Features[i,3]=sp.mean(abs(cD4[:]))
    Extracted_Features[i,4]=sp.mean(abs(cD5[:]))
    Extracted_Features[i,5]=sp.mean(abs(cD6[:]))
    Extracted_Features[i,6]=sp.mean(abs(cA6[:]))
   #Standart Deviation of each subbands
```

```
Extracted_Features[i,7]=sp.std(cD1[:]);
Extracted_Features[i,8]=sp.std(cD2[:]);
Extracted_Features[i,9]=sp.std(cD3[:]);
Extracted_Features[i,10]=sp.std(cD4[:]);
Extracted_Features[i,11]=sp.std(cD5[:]);
Extracted_Features[i,12]=sp.std(cD6[:]);
Extracted_Features[i,13]=sp.std(cA6[:]);
#Skewness of each subbands
Extracted_Features[i,14]=stats.skew(cD1[:]);
Extracted_Features[i,15]=stats.skew(cD2[:]);
Extracted_Features[i,16]=stats.skew(cD3[:]);
Extracted_Features[i,17]=stats.skew(cD4[:]);
Extracted_Features[i,18]=stats.skew(cD5[:]);
Extracted_Features[i,19]=stats.skew(cD6[:]);
Extracted_Features[i,20]=stats.skew(cA6[:]);
#Kurtosis of each subbands
Extracted_Features[i,21]=stats.kurtosis(cD1[:]);
Extracted_Features[i,22]=stats.kurtosis(cD2[:]);
Extracted_Features[i,23]=stats.kurtosis(cD3[:]);
Extracted_Features[i,24]=stats.kurtosis(cD4[:]);
Extracted_Features[i,25]=stats.kurtosis(cD5[:]);
Extracted_Features[i,26]=stats.kurtosis(cD6[:]);
Extracted_Features[i,27]=stats.kurtosis(cA6[:]);
#Median Values of each subbands
Extracted_Features[i,28]=sp.median(cD1[:]);
Extracted_Features[i,29]=sp.median(cD2[:]);
Extracted_Features[i,30]=sp.median(cD3[:]);
Extracted_Features[i,31]=sp.median(cD4[:]);
Extracted_Features[i,32]=sp.median(cD5[:]);
Extracted_Features[i,33]=sp.median(cD6[:]);
Extracted_Features[i,34]=sp.median(cA6[:]);
#RMS Values of each subbands
Extracted_Features[i,35]=np.sqrt(np.mean(cD1[:]**2));
Extracted_Features[i,36]=np.sqrt(np.mean(cD2[:]**2));
Extracted_Features[i,37]=np.sqrt(np.mean(cD3[:]**2));
Extracted_Features[i,38]=np.sqrt(np.mean(cD4[:]**2));
Extracted_Features[i,39]=np.sqrt(np.mean(cD5[:]**2));
Extracted_Features[i,40]=np.sqrt(np.mean(cD6[:]**2));
Extracted_Features[i,41]=np.sqrt(np.mean(cA6[:]**2));
#Ratio of subbands
Extracted_Features[i,42]=sp.mean(abs(cD1[:]))/sp.mean(abs(cD2[:]))
Extracted_Features[i,43]=sp.mean(abs(cD2[:]))/sp.mean(abs(cD3[:]))
Extracted_Features[i,44]=sp.mean(abs(cD3[:]))/sp.mean(abs(cD4[:]))
Extracted_Features[i,45]=sp.mean(abs(cD4[:]))/sp.mean(abs(cD5[:]))
Extracted_Features[i,46]=sp.mean(abs(cD5[:]))/sp.mean(abs(cD6[:]))
```

```
    Extracted_Features[i,47]=sp.mean(abs(cD6[:]))/sp.mean(abs(cA6[:]))
    return Extracted_Features
#==========================================================================
# Feature extraction from normal EEG signal
#==========================================================================
for i in range(Nofsignals):
    DWT_Feature_Extraction(Normal_Eyes_Open[:,i], i, waveletname, level)
    Labels.append("NORMAL")
#==========================================================================
# Feature extraction from interictal EEG signal
#==========================================================================
for i in range(Nofsignals, 2*Nofsignals):
    DWT_Feature_Extraction(EpilepticZone_Interictal[:,i-Nofsignals],     i,
    waveletname, level)
    Labels.append("INTERICTAL")

#==========================================================================
# Feature extraction from ictal EEG signal
#==========================================================================
for i in range(2*Nofsignals, 3*Nofsignals):
    DWT_Feature_Extraction(Epileptic_Ictal[:,i-2*Nofsignals], i,  wavelet-
    name, level)
    Labels.append("ICTAL")
#%%
#==========================================================================
# Classification
#==========================================================================
X = Extracted_Features
y = Labels
# Import train_test_split function
from sklearn.model_selection import train_test_split
# Split dataset into training set and test set
# 70% training and 30% test
Xtrain, Xtest, ytrain, ytest = train_test_split(X, y,test_size=0.3, ran-
dom_state=0)
#%%
#==========================================================================
# LDA classification with training and test set
#==========================================================================
#Import LDA model
from sklearn.discriminant_analysis import LinearDiscriminantAnalysis
#Create a LDA Classifier
clf = LinearDiscriminantAnalysis(solver='lsqr', shrinkage=None)
```

```
#Train the model using the training sets
clf.fit(Xtrain,ytrain)
#Predict the response for test dataset
ypred = clf.predict(Xtest)
#Evaluate the Model and Print Performance Metrics
print_performance_metrics(ytest, ypred)

#Plot Confusion Matrix
print_confusion_matrix_and_save(ytest, ypred)

#%%
# =========================================================================
# Naive Bayes classification with training and test set
# =========================================================================
#Import Gaussian Naive Bayes model
from sklearn.naive_bayes import GaussianNB
#Create a Gaussian Classifier
gnb = GaussianNB()
#Train the model using the training sets
gnb.fit(Xtrain, ytrain)
#Predict the response for test dataset
ypred = gnb.predict(Xtest)

#Evaluate the Model and Print Performance Metrics
print_performance_metrics(ytest, ypred)

#Plot Confusion Matrix
print_confusion_matrix_and_save(ytest, ypred)

#%%
# =========================================================================
# Quadratic discriminant analysis (QDA) example
# =========================================================================
import numpy as np
from sklearn.discriminant_analysis import QuadraticDiscriminantAnalysis
from sklearn.model_selection import train_test_split
Xtrain, Xtest, ytrain, ytest = train_test_split(X, y, test_size=0.3,
random_state=1)

# Quadratic Discriminant Analysis
clf = QuadraticDiscriminantAnalysis(store_covariance=True)
clf.fit(Xtrain,ytrain)
ypred = clf.predict(Xtest)
#Evaluate the Model and Print Performance Metrics
print_performance_metrics(ytest, ypred)

#Plot Confusion Matrix
```

```
print_confusion_matrix_and_save(ytest, ypred)

#%%
from sklearn.neural_network import MLPClassifier
#Create Train and Test set
Xtrain, Xtest, ytrain, ytest = train_test_split(X, y, test_size=0.3, ran-
dom_state=0)

"""mlp=MLPClassifier(hidden_layer_sizes=(100,     ),    activation='relu',
solver='adam',
        alpha=0.0001, batch_size='auto', learning_rate='constant',
        learning_rate_init=0.001, power_t=0.5, max_iter=200,
        shuffle=True, random_state=None, tol=0.0001, verbose=False,
        warm_start=False, momentum=0.9, nesterovs_momentum=True,
        early_stopping=False, validation_fraction=0.1, beta_1=0.9,
        beta_2=0.999, epsilon=1e-08, n_iter_no_change=10)"""
#Create the Model
mlp = MLPClassifier(hidden_layer_sizes=(50, ), learning_rate_init=0.001,
        alpha=1, momentum=0.7,max_iter=1000)
#Train the Model with Training dataset
mlp.fit(Xtrain,ytrain)
#Test the Model with Testing dataset
ypred = mlp.predict(Xtest)

#Evaluate the Model and Print Performance Metrics
print_performance_metrics(ytest, ypred)

#Plot Confusion Matrix
print_confusion_matrix_and_save(ytest, ypred)

#%%
# ======================================================================
# k-NN example with training and test set
# ======================================================================
from sklearn.neighbors import KNeighborsClassifier

#Create Train and Test set
Xtrain, Xtest, ytrain, ytest = train_test_split(X, y, test_size=0.3, ran-
dom_state=0)
#Create the Model
clf = KNeighborsClassifier(n_neighbors=1)
#Train the model with Training Dataset
clf.fit(Xtrain,ytrain)
#Test the model with Testset
ypred = clf.predict(Xtest)
```

```
#Evaluate the Model and Print Performance Metrics
print_performance_metrics(ytest, ypred)

#Plot Confusion Matrix
print_confusion_matrix_and_save(ytest, ypred)

#%%
# ==========================================================================
# SVM example with training and test set
# ==========================================================================
from sklearn import svm
Xtrain, Xtest, ytrain, ytest = train_test_split(X, y, test_size=0.3, ran-
dom_state=0)

""" The parameters and kernels of SVM classifierr can be changed as follows
C = 10.0 # SVM regularization parameter
svm.SVC(kernel='linear', C=C)
svm.LinearSVC(C=C, max_iter=10000)
svm.SVC(kernel='rbf', gamma=0.7, C=C)
svm.SVC(kernel='poly', degree=3, gamma='auto', C=C)
"""
C = 10.0 # SVM regularization parameter
#Create the Model
clf =svm.SVC(kernel='poly', degree=4, gamma='auto', C=C)
#Train the model with Training Dataset
clf.fit(Xtrain,ytrain)
#Test the model with Testset
ypred = clf.predict(Xtest)

#Evaluate the Model and Print Performance Metrics
print_performance_metrics(ytest, ypred)

#Plot Confusion Matrix
print_confusion_matrix_and_save(ytest, ypred)

#%%
# ==========================================================================
# Decision tree example with training and test set
# ==========================================================================
from sklearn import tree
Xtrain, Xtest, ytrain, ytest = train_test_split(X, y, test_size=0.3, ran-
dom_state=0)
#Create the Model
clf = tree.DecisionTreeClassifier()
```

```
#Train the Model with Training dataset
clf.fit(Xtrain,ytrain)
#Test the Model with Testing dataset
ypred=clf.predict(Xtest)

#Evaluate the Model and Print Performance Metrics
print_performance_metrics(ytest, ypred)

#Plot Confusion Matrix
print_confusion_matrix_and_save(ytest, ypred)

#%%
#=========================================================================
# Extra trees classification example with training and test set
#=========================================================================
#Import Extra Trees model
from sklearn.ensemble import ExtraTreesClassifier

# Split dataset into training set and test set
# 70% training and 30% test
Xtrain, Xtest, ytrain, ytest=train_test_split(X, y,test_size=0.3, ran-
dom_state=0)

#Create the Model
clf=ExtraTreesClassifier(n_estimators=100, max_features=48)

#Train the model using the training sets
clf.fit(Xtrain,ytrain)
#Predict the response for test dataset
ypred=clf.predict(Xtest)

#Evaluate the Model and Print Performance Metrics
print_performance_metrics(ytest, ypred)

#Plot Confusion Matrix
print_confusion_matrix_and_save(ytest, ypred)

#%%
#=========================================================================
# Bagging example with training and test set
#=========================================================================
#Import Bagging ensemble model
from sklearn.ensemble import BaggingClassifier
#Import Tree model as a base classifier
```

```
from sklearn import tree

# Split dataset into training set and test set
# 70% training and 30% test
Xtrain, Xtest, ytrain, ytest = train_test_split(X, y,test_size=0.3, ran-
dom_state=0)

#Create a Bagging Ensemble Classifier
"""BaggingClassifier(base_estimator=None,    n_estimators=10,    max_sam-
ples=1.0,
max_features=1.0,    bootstrap=True,    bootstrap_features=False,    oob_
score=False,
warm_start=False, n_jobs=None, random_state=None, verbose=0)"""
bagging = BaggingClassifier(tree.DecisionTreeClassifier(),
              max_samples=0.5, max_features=0.5)
#Train the model using the training sets
bagging.fit(Xtrain,ytrain)
#Predict the response for test dataset
ypred = bagging.predict(Xtest)

#Evaluate the Model and Print Performance Metrics
print_performance_metrics(ytest, ypred)

#Plot Confusion Matrix
print_confusion_matrix_and_save(ytest, ypred)

#%%
# =======================================================================
# Random forest example with training and test set
# =======================================================================
from sklearn.ensemble import RandomForestClassifier

#In order to change to accuracy increase n_estimators
"""RandomForestClassifier(n_estimators='warn',    criterion='gini',    max_
depth=None,
min_samples_split=2, min_samples_leaf=1, min_weight_fraction_leaf=0.0,
max_features='auto', max_leaf_nodes=None, min_impurity_decrease=0.0,
min_impurity_split=None, bootstrap=True, oob_score=False, n_jobs=None,
random_state=None, verbose=0, warm_start=False, class_weight=None)"""
clf = RandomForestClassifier(n_estimators=200)
#Create the Model
#Train the model with Training Dataset
clf.fit(Xtrain,ytrain)
#Test the model with Testset
ypred = clf.predict(Xtest)
```

```
#Evaluate the Model and Print Performance Metrics
print_performance_metrics(ytest, ypred)

#Plot Confusion Matrix
print_confusion_matrix_and_save(ytest, ypred)

#%%
#=========================================================================
# AdaBoost example with training and test set
#=========================================================================
#Import AdaBoost ensemble model
from sklearn.ensemble import AdaBoostClassifier
#Import Tree model as a base classifier
from sklearn import tree

# Split dataset into training set and test set
# 70% training and 30% test
Xtrain, Xtest, ytrain, ytest = train_test_split(X, y,test_size=0.3, ran-
dom_state=0)

#Create an AdaBoost Ensemble Classifier
"""  AdaBoostClassifier(base_estimator=None,  n_estimators=50,  learning_
rate=1.0,
                algorithm='SAMME.R', random_state=None)"""
clf=AdaBoostClassifier(tree.DecisionTreeClassifier(),n_estimators=100,
algorithm='SAMME',learning_rate=0.5)

#Train the model using the training sets
clf.fit(Xtrain,ytrain)
#Predict the response for test dataset
ypred = clf.predict(Xtest)

#Evaluate the Model and Print Performance Metrics
print_performance_metrics(ytest, ypred)

#Plot Confusion Matrix
print_confusion_matrix_and_save(ytest, ypred)

#%%
#=========================================================================
# Gradient boosting example with training and test set
#=========================================================================
#Import Gradient Boosting ensemble model
from sklearn.ensemble import GradientBoostingClassifier
```

```
# Split dataset into training set and test set
# 70% training and 30% test
Xtrain, Xtest, ytrain, ytest = train_test_split(X, y,test_size=0.3, ran-
dom_state=0)

#Create the Model
clf = GradientBoostingClassifier(n_estimators=100, learning_rate=1.0,
  max_depth=1, random_state=0)

#Train the model using the training sets
clf.fit(Xtrain,ytrain)
#Predict the response for test dataset
ypred = clf.predict(Xtest)

#Evaluate the Model and Print Performance Metrics
print_performance_metrics(ytest, ypred)

#Plot Confusion Matrix
print_confusion_matrix_and_save(ytest, ypred)

#%%
# =======================================================================
# Stacking meta classifier example
# =======================================================================
#Before running you should install mlxtend.classifier for Staking using pip
install mlxtend
import numpy as np
import warnings
from sklearn import model_selection
from sklearn.linear_model import LogisticRegression
from sklearn.neighbors import KNeighborsClassifier
from sklearn.neural_network import MLPClassifier
from sklearn.ensemble import RandomForestClassifier
from mlxtend.classifier import StackingClassifier
from sklearn.model_selection import train_test_split
from sklearn import tree

#Create Train and Test set
Xtrain, Xtest, ytrain, ytest = train_test_split(X, y, test_size=0.3, ran-
dom_state=0)

warnings.simplefilter('ignore')
#Create the Model
```

```
clf1 = KNeighborsClassifier(n_neighbors=1)
clf2 = RandomForestClassifier(random_state=1)
clf3 = MLPClassifier(hidden_layer_sizes=(100, ), learning_rate_init=0.001,
        alpha=1, momentum=0.9,max_iter=1000)
DT = tree.DecisionTreeClassifier()
sclf = StackingClassifier(classifiers=[clf1, clf2, clf3],
         meta_classifier=DT)
#Evaluate the Model and Print Performance Metrics
print_performance_metrics(ytest, ypred)

#Plot Confusion Matrix
print_confusion_matrix_and_save(ytest, ypred)

#%%
# ===================================================================
# Voting example with training and test set
# ===================================================================
from sklearn import datasets
from sklearn.model_selection import cross_val_score
from sklearn.linear_model import LogisticRegression
from sklearn.naive_bayes import GaussianNB
from sklearn.ensemble import RandomForestClassifier
from sklearn.ensemble import VotingClassifier
from sklearn.model_selection import train_test_split

#Create Train and Test set
Xtrain, Xtest, ytrain, ytest = train_test_split(X, y, test_size=0.3, ran-
dom_state=0)

#Create the Models
clf1 = KNeighborsClassifier(n_neighbors=1)
clf2 = RandomForestClassifier(random_state=1)
clf3 = MLPClassifier(hidden_layer_sizes=(100, ), learning_rate_init=0.001,
        alpha=1, momentum=0.9,max_iter=1000)
eclf = VotingClassifier(estimators=[('kNN', clf1), ('RF', clf2), ('MLP',
clf3)], voting='hard')

#Train the model using the training sets
eclf.fit(Xtrain,ytrain)
#Predict the response for test dataset
ypred = eclf.predict(Xtest)

#Evaluate the Model and Print Performance Metrics
print_performance_metrics(ytest, ypred)
```

```
#Plot Confusion Matrix
print_confusion_matrix_and_save(ytest, ypred)

#%%
# =============================================================================
# Deep neural network example using Keras
# =============================================================================
from keras.models import Sequential
from keras.layers import Dense, Activation
from keras.utils.np_utils import to_categorical
from keras.utils.vis_utils import plot_model
from sklearn import preprocessing
lb = preprocessing.LabelBinarizer()
y=lb.fit_transform( Labels)
X = Extracted_Features
# Import train_test_split function
from sklearn.model_selection import train_test_split
# Split dataset into training set and test set
# 70% training and 30% test
Xtrain, Xtest, ytrain, ytest = train_test_split(X, y,test_size=0.3, ran-
dom_state=0)
InputDataDimension=numfeatures
#NofClasses
# =============================================================================
# Create a model
# =============================================================================
model = Sequential()
model.add(Dense(128,    input_dim=InputDataDimension,    init='uniform',
activation='relu'))
model.add(Dense(32, activation='relu'))
model.add(Dense(NofClasses, activation='softmax'))
#%%
# =============================================================================
# Compile the model
# =============================================================================
model.compile(loss='categorical_crossentropy',         optimizer='adam',
metrics=['accuracy'])
# =============================================================================
# Train and validate the model
# =============================================================================
history = model.fit(Xtrain, ytrain, validation_split=0.33, epochs=50,
batch_size=25,verbose=2)
#%%
```

```
#=====================================================================
# Evaluate the model
#=====================================================================
test_loss, test_acc = model.evaluate(Xtest, ytest, verbose=0)
print('\nTest accuracy:', test_acc)

#%%
#=====================================================================
# Plot the history
#=====================================================================
#Plot the Model Accuracy and Loss for Training and Validation dataset
plot_history(history)

#%%
#Test the Model with testing data
ypred_test = model.predict(Xtest,)
# Round the test predictions
max_y_pred_test = np.round(ypred_test)
#Convert binary Labels back to numbers
ypred=max_y_pred_test.argmax(axis=1)
ytest=ytest.argmax(axis=1)
#%%
#Print the Confusion Matrix
print_confusion_matrix(ytest,ypred)
#%%
#Evaluate the Model and Print Performance Metrics
print_performance_metrics(ytest,ypred)
#%%
#Print and Save the Confusion Matrix
print_confusion_matrix_and_save(ytest,ypred)
#%%
from keras.models import Sequential
from keras.layers import Dense, Activation
from keras.utils.np_utils import to_categorical
from keras.utils.vis_utils import plot_model
from sklearn import preprocessing
lb = preprocessing.LabelBinarizer()
y=lb.fit_transform( Labels)
X = Extracted_Features
# Import train_test_split function
from sklearn.model_selection import train_test_split
# Split dataset into training set and test set
 # 70% training and 30% test
Xtrain, Xtest, ytrain, ytest = train_test_split(X, y,test_size=0.3, ran-
```

```
dom_state=0)
InputDataDimension=numfeatures
# ===========================================================================
# Build a deep model using Keras
# ===========================================================================
model = Sequential()
model.add(Dense(128,    input_dim=InputDataDimension,    init='uniform',
activation='relu'))
model.add(Dense(64, activation='relu'))
model.add(Dense(32, activation='relu'))
model.add(Dense(NofClasses, activation='softmax'))
#%%
# ===========================================================================
# Compile the model
# ===========================================================================
model.compile(loss='categorical_crossentropy', optimizer='adam',
metrics=['accuracy'])
# ===========================================================================
# Train and validate the model
# ===========================================================================
history = model.fit(Xtrain, ytrain, validation_split=0.33, epochs=50,
batch_size=25,verbose=2)
#%%
# ===========================================================================
# Evaluate the model
# ===========================================================================
test_loss, test_acc = model.evaluate(Xtest, ytest, verbose=0)
print('\nTest accuracy:', test_acc)

#%%
# ===========================================================================
# Plot the history
# ===========================================================================
#Plot the model accuracy and loss for training and validation dataset
plot_history(history)

#%%
#Test the Model with testing data
ypred_test = model.predict(Xtest,)
# Round the test predictions
max_y_pred_test = np.round(ypred_test)
#Convert binary Labels back to numbers
ypred=max_y_pred_test.argmax(axis=1)
ytest=ytest.argmax(axis=1)
#%%
```

```
#Print the Confusion Matrix
print_confusion_matrix(ytest,ypred)
#%%
#Evaluate the Model and Print Performance Metrics
print_performance_metrics(ytest,ypred)
#%%
#Print and Save the Confusion Matrix
print_confusion_matrix_and_save(ytest,ypred)

#%%
"'"Adapted From Scikit Learn"'"
# =============================================================================
# ROC curves for the multiclass problem
# =============================================================================
import numpy as np
import matplotlib.pyplot as plt
from itertools import cycle
from sklearn.discriminant_analysis import LinearDiscriminantAnalysis
from sklearn import svm
from sklearn.metrics import roc_curve, auc
from sklearn.model_selection import train_test_split
from sklearn.preprocessing import label_binarize
from sklearn.multiclass import OneVsRestClassifier
from scipy import interp
X = Extracted_Features
y = Labels
# Import train_test_split function
from sklearn.model_selection import train_test_split
# Split dataset into training set and test set
# 70% training and 30% test
Xtrain, Xtest, ytrain, ytest = train_test_split(X, y,test_size=0.3, ran-
dom_state=0)
# Binarize the output
y = label_binarize(y, classes=['NORMAL','INTERICTAL','ICTAL' ])
n_classes = y.shape[1]

#%%
# shuffle and split training and test sets
random_state = np.random.RandomState(0)
X_train, X_test, y_train, y_test = train_test_split(X, y, test_size=.5,
                                                    random_state=0)

# Learn to predict each class against the other
"""classifier = OneVsRestClassifier(svm.SVC(kernel='linear',
probability=True,
```

```
                random_state=random_state))"""
classifier = OneVsRestClassifier(LinearDiscriminantAnalysis(solver='lsqr',
shrinkage=None))
y_score = classifier.fit(X_train, y_train).decision_function(X_test)

# Compute ROC curve and ROC area for each class
fpr = dict()
tpr = dict()
roc_auc = dict()
for i in range(n_classes):
  fpr[i], tpr[i], _ = roc_curve(y_test[:, i], y_score[:, i])
  roc_auc[i] = auc(fpr[i], tpr[i])

# Compute micro-average ROC curve and ROC area
fpr["micro"], tpr["micro"], _ = roc_curve(y_test.ravel(), y_score.ravel())
roc_auc["micro"] = auc(fpr["micro"], tpr["micro"])

##########################################################################
# Plot of a ROC curve for a specific class
plt.figure()
lw = 2
plt.plot(fpr[2], tpr[2], color='darkorange',
      lw=lw, label='ROC curve (area = %0.2f)' % roc_auc[2])
plt.plot([0, 1], [0, 1], color='navy', lw=lw, linestyle='--')
plt.xlim([0.0, 1.0])
plt.ylim([0.0, 1.05])
plt.xlabel('False Positive Rate')
plt.ylabel('True Positive Rate')
plt.title('Receiver operating characteristic')
plt.legend(loc="lower right")
plt.show()
##########################################################################
# Plot ROC curves for the multiclass problem

# Compute macro-average ROC curve and ROC area

# First aggregate all false positive rates
all_fpr = np.unique(np.concatenate([fpr[i] for i in range(n_classes)]))

# Then interpolate all ROC curves at this points
mean_tpr = np.zeros_like(all_fpr)
for i in range(n_classes):
    mean_tpr += interp(all_fpr, fpr[i], tpr[i])
```

```
# Finally average it and compute AUC
mean_tpr /= n_classes

fpr["macro"] = all_fpr
tpr["macro"] = mean_tpr
roc_auc["macro"] = auc(fpr["macro"], tpr["macro"])

# Plot all ROC curves
plt.figure()
plt.plot(fpr["micro"], tpr["micro"],
      label='micro-average ROC curve (area = {0:0.2f})'
          ''.format(roc_auc["micro"]),
      color='deeppink', linestyle=':', linewidth=4)

plt.plot(fpr["macro"], tpr["macro"],
      label='macro-average ROC curve (area = {0:0.2f})'
          ''.format(roc_auc["macro"]),
      color='navy', linestyle=':', linewidth=4)

colors = cycle(['aqua', 'darkorange', 'cornflowerblue'])
for i, color in zip(range(n_classes), colors):
   plt.plot(fpr[i], tpr[i], color=color, lw=lw,
        label='ROC curve of class {0} (area = {1:0.2f})'
        ''.format(i, roc_auc[i]))

plt.plot([0, 1], [0, 1], 'k--', lw=lw)
plt.xlim([0.0, 1.0])
plt.ylim([0.0, 1.05])
plt.xlabel('False Positive Rate')
plt.ylabel('True Positive Rate')
plt.title('Some extension of Receiver operating characteristic to
multi-class')
plt.legend(loc="lower right")
plt.show()
```

### 4.2.2 Emotion recognition

Emotions are a psychophysiological process triggered by the conscious and/or unconscious perceptions of a human being and are often associated with temperament, disposition, personality, mood, and motivation. Emotions play a crucial role in human communication and can be expressed either verbally, through emotional vocabulary, or by nonverbal cues such as intonation of voice, facial expressions, and gestures (Koelstra et al., 2012). More

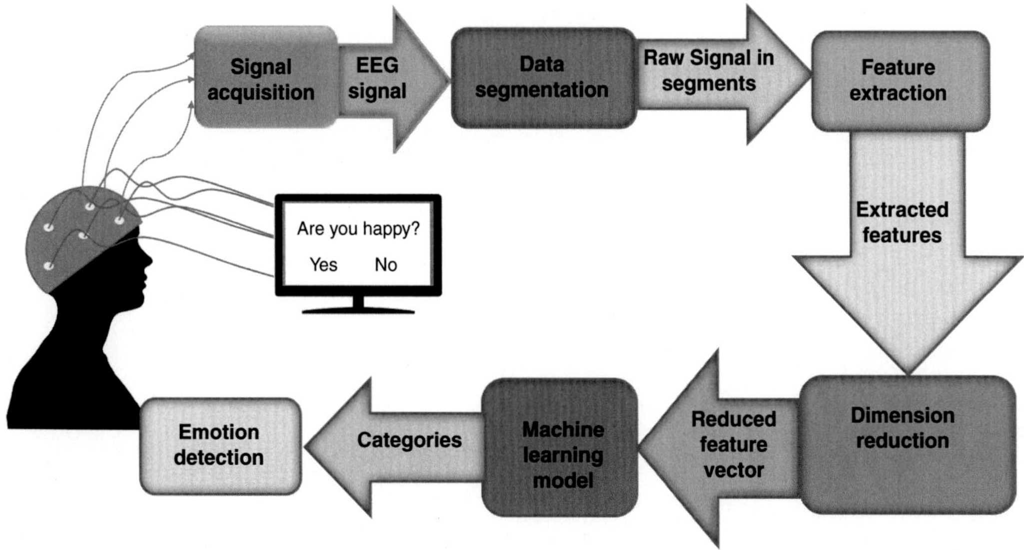


FIGURE 4.4 **A general framework for emotion recognition.**

common emotions, such as anger, happiness, surprise, fear, shame, disgust, sadness, interest, contempt, suffering, love, tension, and mirth, have been investigated by researchers in emotion understanding, control, and regulation mainly by analyzing the brain signals and images. EEG signal processing and analysis techniques have been utilized for emotion detection and recognition. Studies in engineering, computer science, neuroscience, and psychology aim to develop devices that recognize, monitor, and model emotions. In computer science, efficient evaluation is a division of the study using machine learning that deals with the design of systems and devices for processing, interpretation, and recognition of human emotions. Hence new techniques can be generated indirectly to evaluate stress, frustration, and mood through natural interactions and conversations. In addition, making computers more emotionally intelligent, particularly responding to a person's frustration in a way that lessens negative feelings, can be an essential research direction in emotion recognition and regulation. EEG helps connectivity, localization, and synchronization of the brain for different emotions to extract and process highly valuable emotion-related information. Classification and recognition of emotional EEG signals are generally complex, and sophisticated signal processing techniques are needed (Sanei, 2013; Subasi, 2019c). A general framework for emotion recognition is shown in Fig. 4.4.

## Example 4.2

The following Python code is used to extract features from EEG signals showing negative, positive, and neutral emotions using stationary wavelet transform (SWT). Next it uses statistical values of SWT sub-bands, and then classifies these data using random forest classifier by employing training and testing datasets. The classification accuracy, precision, recall, F1 score, Cohen kappa score, and Matthews correlation coefficient are calculated. The classification report and confusion matrix are also given. For this example, SEED emotion recognition data are used.

***Dataset information:*** The SEED database contains EEG signals of 15 subjects that were recorded while the subjects were watching emotional film clips. Each subject is asked to carry out the experiments in three sessions. There are 45 experiments in this dataset in total. These are the emotional film clips chosen to be used as stimuli in the experiments. The selection criteria for film clips are: (1) the length of the whole experiment should not be too long in case subjects become fatigued, (2) the videos should be understood without explanation, and (3) the videos should elicit a single desired target emotion. Different film clips (positive, neutral, and negative emotions) were chosen to receive highest match across participants. The length of each film clip is about 4 minutes. Each film clip is well-designed to produce consistent emotions and maximize the emotion itself. There are 15 trials for each experiment in total. There is a 15s hint before each clip and 10s feedback after each clip. The order of demonstration is organized in such a way that two film clips targeting the same emotion are not presented successively. For feedback, participants are asked to define their emotional responses to every film clip by responding to the questionnaire immediately after watching each clip. The EEG signals of each subject were recorded as separate files containing the name of the subjects and the date. Fifteen subjects (seven males and eight females, mean: 23.27, SD: 2.37) participated in the experiments. These files contain a preprocessed, down-sampled, and segmented version of the EEG data. The data was down-sampled to 200 Hz. A bandpass frequency filter from 0–75 Hz was used. The EEG segments associated with every movie were extracted. There are a total of 45 .mat files, one for each experiment. Every person carried out the experiment three times within a week. Every subject file includes 16 arrays; 15 arrays include preprocessed and segmented EEG data of 15 trials in one experiment. An array named LABELS contains the label of the corresponding emotional labels (−1 for negative, 0 for neutral, and +1 for positive). The EEG is acquired according to the international 10-20 system for 62 channels. The data can be downloaded from the following website:

http://bcmi.sjtu.edu.cn/~seed/index.html

```
"""
Created on Thu May 9 12:18:30 2019
@author: asubasi
"""

#=========================================================================
# Feature extraction using the statistical values of stationary wavelet
transform
#=========================================================================

import scipy.io as sio
# descriptive statistics
import scipy as sp
import pywt
import matplotlib.pyplot as plt
import numpy as np
```

```
import scipy.stats as stats
waveletname='db1'
level=6 #Decomposition Level
#Load mat file
mat_contents = sio.loadmat('EMOTIONSDAT.mat')
sorted(mat_contents.keys())
#Load each datset separately
NEGATIVE=mat_contents['NEGATIVE']
NEUTRAL=mat_contents['NEUTRAL']
POSITIVE=mat_contents['POSITIVE']

Labels = [] #Empty List For Labels
Length = 4096; # Length of signal
Nofsignal=100; #Total Number of Signal for each class
numrows =83 #Number of features extracted from Wavelet Packet
Decomposition
#Create Empty Array For Features
Extracted_Features=np.ndarray(shape=(3*Nofsignal,numrows),
dtype=float, order='F')
# ======================================================================
# Define utility functions
# ======================================================================
def SWT_Feature_Extraction(signal, i, wname, level):
  coeffs = pywt.swt(signal, wname, level=level)
  #Mean Values of each subbands
  Extracted_Features[i,0]=sp.mean(abs(coeffs[0][0]))
  Extracted_Features[i,1]=sp.mean(abs(coeffs[1][0]))
  Extracted_Features[i,2]=sp.mean(abs(coeffs[2][0]))
  Extracted_Features[i,3]=sp.mean(abs(coeffs[3][0]))
  Extracted_Features[i,4]=sp.mean(abs(coeffs[4][0]))
  Extracted_Features[i,5]=sp.mean(abs(coeffs[5][0]))
  Extracted_Features[i,6]=sp.mean(abs(coeffs[0][1]))
  Extracted_Features[i,7]=sp.mean(abs(coeffs[1][1]))
  Extracted_Features[i,8]=sp.mean(abs(coeffs[2][1]))
  Extracted_Features[i,9]=sp.mean(abs(coeffs[3][1]))
  Extracted_Features[i,10]=sp.mean(abs(coeffs[4][1]))
  Extracted_Features[i,11]=sp.mean(abs(coeffs[5][1]))
  #Standart Deviation of each subbands
  Extracted_Features[i,12]=sp.std(coeffs[0][0])
  Extracted_Features[i,13]=sp.std(coeffs[1][0])
  Extracted_Features[i,14]=sp.std(coeffs[2][0])
  Extracted_Features[i,15]=sp.std(coeffs[3][0])
  Extracted_Features[i,16]=sp.std(coeffs[4][0])
  Extracted_Features[i,17]=sp.std(coeffs[5][0])
```

```
Extracted_Features[i,18]=sp.std(coeffs[0][1])
Extracted_Features[i,19]=sp.std(coeffs[1][1])
Extracted_Features[i,20]=sp.std(coeffs[2][1])
Extracted_Features[i,21]=sp.std(coeffs[3][1])
Extracted_Features[i,22]=sp.std(coeffs[4][1])
Extracted_Features[i,23]=sp.std(coeffs[5][1])
#Median Values of each subbands
Extracted_Features[i,24]=sp.median(coeffs[0][0])
Extracted_Features[i,25]=sp.median(coeffs[1][0])
Extracted_Features[i,26]=sp.median(coeffs[2][0])
Extracted_Features[i,27]=sp.median(coeffs[3][0])
Extracted_Features[i,28]=sp.median(coeffs[4][0])
Extracted_Features[i,29]=sp.median(coeffs[5][0])
Extracted_Features[i,30]=sp.median(coeffs[0][1])
Extracted_Features[i,31]=sp.median(coeffs[1][1])
Extracted_Features[i,32]=sp.median(coeffs[2][1])
Extracted_Features[i,33]=sp.median(coeffs[3][1])
Extracted_Features[i,34]=sp.median(coeffs[4][1])
Extracted_Features[i,35]=sp.median(coeffs[5][1])
#Skewness of each subbands
Extracted_Features[i,36]=stats.skew(coeffs[0][0])
Extracted_Features[i,37]=stats.skew(coeffs[1][0])
Extracted_Features[i,38]=stats.skew(coeffs[2][0])
Extracted_Features[i,39]=stats.skew(coeffs[3][0])
Extracted_Features[i,40]=stats.skew(coeffs[4][0])
Extracted_Features[i,41]=stats.skew(coeffs[5][0])
Extracted_Features[i,42]=stats.skew(coeffs[0][1])
Extracted_Features[i,43]=stats.skew(coeffs[1][1])
Extracted_Features[i,44]=stats.skew(coeffs[2][1])
Extracted_Features[i,45]=stats.skew(coeffs[3][1])
Extracted_Features[i,46]=stats.skew(coeffs[4][1])
Extracted_Features[i,47]=stats.skew(coeffs[5][1])
#Kurtosis of each subbands
Extracted_Features[i,48]=stats.kurtosis(coeffs[0][0])
Extracted_Features[i,49]=stats.kurtosis(coeffs[1][0])
Extracted_Features[i,50]=stats.kurtosis(coeffs[2][0])
Extracted_Features[i,51]=stats.kurtosis(coeffs[3][0])
Extracted_Features[i,52]=stats.kurtosis(coeffs[4][0])
Extracted_Features[i,53]=stats.kurtosis(coeffs[5][0])
Extracted_Features[i,54]=stats.kurtosis(coeffs[0][1])
Extracted_Features[i,55]=stats.kurtosis(coeffs[1][1])
Extracted_Features[i,56]=stats.kurtosis(coeffs[2][1])
Extracted_Features[i,57]=stats.kurtosis(coeffs[3][1])
Extracted_Features[i,58]=stats.kurtosis(coeffs[4][1])
```

```
Extracted_Features[i,59]=stats.kurtosis(coeffs[5][1])
#RMS Values of each subbands
Extracted_Features[i,60]=np.sqrt(np.mean(coeffs[0][0]**2))
Extracted_Features[i,61]=np.sqrt(np.mean(coeffs[1][0]**2))
Extracted_Features[i,62]=np.sqrt(np.mean(coeffs[2][0]**2))
Extracted_Features[i,63]=np.sqrt(np.mean(coeffs[3][0]**2))
Extracted_Features[i,64]=np.sqrt(np.mean(coeffs[4][0]**2))
Extracted_Features[i,65]=np.sqrt(np.mean(coeffs[5][0]**2))
Extracted_Features[i,66]=np.sqrt(np.mean(coeffs[0][1]**2))
Extracted_Features[i,67]=np.sqrt(np.mean(coeffs[1][1]**2))
Extracted_Features[i,68]=np.sqrt(np.mean(coeffs[2][1]**2))
Extracted_Features[i,69]=np.sqrt(np.mean(coeffs[3][1]**2))
Extracted_Features[i,70]=np.sqrt(np.mean(coeffs[4][1]**2))
Extracted_Features[i,71]=np.sqrt(np.mean(coeffs[5][1]**2))
#Ratio of subbands
Extracted_Features[i,72]=sp.mean(abs(coeffs[0][0]))/sp.mean(abs (coeffs
[1][0]))
Extracted_Features[i,73]=sp.mean(abs(coeffs[1][0]))/sp.mean(abs(coeffs
[2][0]))
Extracted_Features[i,74]=sp.mean(abs(coeffs[2][0]))/sp.mean(abs (coeffs
[3][0]))
Extracted_Features[i,75]=sp.mean(abs(coeffs[3][0]))/sp.mean(abs(coeffs
[4][0]))
Extracted_Features[i,76]=sp.mean(abs(coeffs[4][0]))/sp.mean (abs(coeffs[5]
[0]))
Extracted_Features[i,77]=sp.mean(abs(coeffs[5][0]))/sp.mean(abs
(coeffs [0][1]))
Extracted_Features[i,78]=sp.mean(abs(coeffs[0][1]))/sp.mean(abs
(coeffs[1][1]))
Extracted_Features[i,79]=sp.mean(abs(coeffs[1][1]))/sp.mean(abs(coeffs
[2][1]))
Extracted_Features[i,80]=sp.mean(abs(coeffs[2][1]))/sp.mean(abs
(coeffs[3][1]))
Extracted_Features[i,81]=sp.mean(abs(coeffs[3][1]))/sp.mean(abs(coeffs
[4][1]))
Extracted_Features[i,82]=sp.mean(abs(coeffs[4][1]))/sp.mean(abs
(coeffs[5][1]))
#%%
# ===============================================================
# Feature extraction from negative emotion EEG signal
# ===============================================================
for i in range(Nofsignal):
 SWT_Feature_Extraction(NEGATIVE[i,:], i, waveletname, level)
```

```
  Labels.append("NEGATIVE")

#==========================================================================
# Feature extraction from neutral emotion EEG signal
#==========================================================================
for i in range(Nofsignal, 2*Nofsignal):
  SWT_Feature_Extraction(NEUTRAL[i-Nofsignal,:], i, waveletname, level)
  Labels.append("NEUTRAL")

#==========================================================================
# Feature extraction from positive emotion EEG signal
#==========================================================================
for i in range(2*Nofsignal, 3*Nofsignal):
  SWT_Feature_Extraction(POSITIVE[i-2*Nofsignal,:], i, waveletname, level)
  Labels.append("POSITIVE")
#%%
#==========================================================================
# Classification
#==========================================================================
X = Extracted_Features
y = Labels
# Import train_test_split function
from sklearn.model_selection import train_test_split
# Split dataset into training set and test set
# 70% training and 30% test
Xtrain, Xtest, ytrain, ytest = train_test_split(X, y,test_size=0.3, ran-
dom_state=1)

#%%
#==========================================================================
# Random forest example with training and test set
#==========================================================================
from sklearn.ensemble import RandomForestClassifier

#In order to change to accuracy increase n_estimators
"""RandomForestClassifier(n_estimators='warn',   criterion='gini',   max_
depth=None,
min_samples_split=2, min_samples_leaf=1, min_weight_fraction_leaf=0.0,
max_features='auto', max_leaf_nodes=None, min_impurity_decrease=0.0,
min_impurity_split=None, bootstrap=True, oob_score=False, n_jobs=None,
random_state=None, verbose=0, warm_start=False, class_weight=None)"""
clf = RandomForestClassifier(n_estimators=200)
#Create the Model
 #Train the model with Training Dataset
```

```
clf.fit(Xtrain,ytrain)
#Test the model with Testset
ypred = clf.predict(Xtest)

#Evaluate the Model and Print Performance Metrics
from sklearn import metrics
print('Accuracy:', np.round(metrics.accuracy_score(ytest,ypred),4))
print('Precision:', np.round(metrics.precision_score(ytest,
    ypred,average='weighted'),4))
print('Recall:', np.round(metrics.recall_score(ytest,ypred,
    average='weighted'),4))
print('F1 Score:', np.round(metrics.f1_score(ytest,ypred,
average='weighted'),4))
print('Cohen Kappa Score:', np.round(metrics.cohen_kappa_score(ytest,
ypred),4))
print('Matthews Corrcoef:', np.round(metrics.matthews_corrcoef(ytest,
ypred),4))
print('\t\tClassification Report:\n', metrics.classification_report(ypred,
ytest))

#Plot Confusion Matrix
from sklearn.metrics import confusion_matrix
print("Confusion Matrix:\n",confusion_matrix(ytest, ypred))

#%%
# ============================================================================
# Random forest example with cross-validation
# ============================================================================
from sklearn.ensemble import RandomForestClassifier
from sklearn.model_selection import cross_val_score
#In order to change to accuracy increase n_estimators
# fit model no training data
model = RandomForestClassifier(n_estimators=200)

CV=10 #10-Fold Cross Validation
#Evaluate Model Using 10-Fold Cross Validation and Print Performance
Metrics
Acc_scores = cross_val_score(model, X, y, cv=CV)
print("Accuracy: %0.3f (+/- %0.3f)" % (Acc_scores.mean(), Acc_scores.
std() * 2))
f1_scores = cross_val_score(model, X, y, cv=CV,scoring='f1_macro')
print("F1 score: %0.3f (+/- %0.3f)" % (f1_scores.mean(), f1_scores.std()
* 2))
```

```
Precision_scores = cross_val_score(model, X, y, cv=CV,scoring='precision_
macro')
print("Precision score: %0.3f (+/- %0.3f)" % (Precision_scores.mean(),
Precision_scores.std() * 2))
Recall_scores = cross_val_score(model, X, y, cv=CV,scoring='recall_macro')
print("Recall score: %0.3f (+/- %0.3f)" % (Recall_scores.mean(), Recall_
scores.std() * 2))
from sklearn.metrics import cohen_kappa_score, make_scorer
kappa_scorer = make_scorer(cohen_kappa_score)
Kappa_scores = cross_val_score(model, X, y, cv=CV,scoring=kappa_scorer)
print("Kappa score: %0.3f (+/- %0.3f)" % (Kappa_scores.mean(), Kappa_
scores.std() * 2))
```

### 4.2.3 Classification of focal and nonfocal epileptic EEG signals

The brain is divided into a number of regions that generate a synaptic electric current or local magnetic field. Localization of brain signal sources from EEGs has been an active area of research in recent years. Such source localization is essential to studying physiological, mental, pathological, and functional abnormalities of the brain, as well as various bodily disabilities, and ultimately to define the sources of abnormalities such as tumors and epilepsy. Although typically the localization of brain sources is a problematic task, there are some simple circumstances in which localization can be simplified (Sanei & Chambers, 2013; Subasi, 2019c).

The focus of epilepsy is defined by a clinical diagnosis based on the related channel, which produced abnormal signals.

Therefore, the EEG is a decisive method for epilepsy evaluation. The main issue for neurosurgery is noninvasive initial seizure discharge localization, identifying the region of the brain that contains the abnormal activity source. Although the epilepsy diagnosis depends on individual medical history, the EEG is vital for detection and diagnosis (Subasi, 2019c).

EEG signals recorded from the brain help us to understand brain functions. The aim of these records is to localize the areas of the brain where seizures begin and to assess if the patient may benefit from neurosurgical resection of these brain areas. Therefore these types of intracranial epilepsy patient recordings are challenging areas of application for analyzing the signal. This results in two different types of signals: the first type is recorded from areas of the brain where the changes of ictal EEG signal were noticed ("focal signals"), and the second type recorded from areas of the brain that were not included at the seizure's onset ("nonfocal signals"). The ictal areas may produce an interictal spike at the time of its onset, and therefore the clusters covering most spikes start at the most active zone. Localization of this zone and focus of activity in the brain determined by these spike clusters could provide evidence for exact locations of epileptogenic tissue in surgical evaluations (Subasi, 2019c).

## Example 4.3

The following Python code is used to extract features from the focal–nonfocal EEG signals using wavelet packed decomposition (WPD) and statistical values of WPD sub-bands. Next it classifies these data using various classifiers and 10-fold cross-validation. The classification accuracy, precision, recall, F1 score, Cohen kappa score, and Matthews correlation coefficient are calculated. For this example, epileptic source localization data is used.

***Dataset information:*** There are two types of files, F and N, that involve focal and nonfocal signal pairs, respectively. Each zip file contains 750 separate text files. The number in the file name is related to the index of the signal pair included in this file. Every text file includes one distinct signal pair. The x-signal is involved in the first column; the y-signal is involved in the second column. The two columns are divided by commas. All files have 10,240 rows. Succeeding rows are related to the subsequent samples. The files have no headers (Andrzejak, Schindler, & Rummel, 2012). You can download the data from the following web site:

http://ntsa.upf.edu/downloads/andrzejak-rg-schindler-k-rummel-c-2012-nonrandomness-nonlinear-dependence-and

```
"""
Created on Thu May 9 12:18:30 2019
@author: asubasi
"""
# descriptive statistics
import scipy as sp
import scipy.io as sio
import pywt
import numpy as np
import scipy.stats as stats
from sklearn.metrics import cohen_kappa_score, make_scorer
from sklearn.model_selection import cross_val_score
wname = pywt.Wavelet('db1')
level=6 #Number of decomposition level
#Load mat file
mat_contents = sio.loadmat('FOCAL_NFOCAL.mat')
sorted(mat_contents.keys())

FOCAL=mat_contents['focal_5000']
NONFOCAL=mat_contents['nfocal_5000']

Labels = [] #Empty List For Labels
NofClasses=2 #Number of Classes
Length = 4096; # Length of signal
Nofsignal=100; #Number of Signal for each Class
numfeatures =83 #Number of features extracted from Wavelet Packet
Decomposition
```

```
#Create Empty Array For Features
Extracted_Features=np.ndarray(shape=(NofClasses*Nofsignal,numfeatures),
dtype=float, order='F')
#==================================================================
# Define utility functions
#==================================================================
def kFold_Cross_Validation_Metrics(model,CV):
  Acc_scores = cross_val_score(model, X, y, cv=CV)
  print("Accuracy: %0.3f (+/- %0.3f)" % (Acc_scores.mean(), Acc_scores.
  std() * 2))
  f1_scores = cross_val_score(model, X, y, cv=CV,scoring='f1_macro')
  print("F1 score: %0.3f (+/- %0.3f)" % (f1_scores.mean(), f1_scores.std()
  * 2))
  Precision_scores = cross_val_score(model, X, y, cv=CV,scoring='precision_
  macro')
  print("Precision score: %0.3f (+/- %0.3f)" % (Precision_scores.mean(),
  Precision_scores.std() * 2))
  Recall_scores = cross_val_score(model, X, y, cv=CV,scoring='recall_macro')
  print("Recall score: %0.3f (+/- %0.3f)" % (Recall_scores.mean(), Re-
  call_scores.std() * 2))
  kappa_scorer = make_scorer(cohen_kappa_score)
  Kappa_scores = cross_val_score(model, X, y, cv=CV,scoring=kappa_scorer)
  print("Kappa score: %0.3f (+/- %0.3f)" % (Kappa_scores.mean(), Kappa_
  scores.std() * 2))
#==================================================================
# Feature extraction using the statistical values of wavelet packet
transform
#==================================================================
def WPD_Feature_Extraction(signal, i, wname, level):
  #Mean Values of each subbands
  wp= pywt.WaveletPacket(signal, wname, mode='symmetric', maxlevel=level)
  Extracted_Features[i,0]=sp.mean(abs(wp['a'].data))
  Extracted_Features[i,1]=sp.mean(abs(wp['aa'].data))
  Extracted_Features[i,2]=sp.mean(abs(wp['aaa'].data))
  Extracted_Features[i,3]=sp.mean(abs(wp['aaaa'].data))
  Extracted_Features[i,4]=sp.mean(abs(wp['aaaaa'].data))
  Extracted_Features[i,5]=sp.mean(abs(wp['aaaaaa'].data))
  Extracted_Features[i,6]=sp.mean(abs(wp['d'].data))
  Extracted_Features[i,7]=sp.mean(abs(wp['dd'].data))
  Extracted_Features[i,8]=sp.mean(abs(wp['ddd'].data))
  Extracted_Features[i,9]=sp.mean(abs(wp['dddd'].data))
  Extracted_Features[i,10]=sp.mean(abs(wp['ddddd'].data))
  Extracted_Features[i,11]=sp.mean(abs(wp['dddddd'].data))
  #Standart Deviation of each subbands
  Extracted_Features[i,12]=sp.std(wp['a'].data)
```

```
Extracted_Features[i,13]=sp.std(wp['aa'].data)
Extracted_Features[i,14]=sp.std(wp['aaa'].data)
Extracted_Features[i,15]=sp.std(wp['aaaa'].data)
Extracted_Features[i,16]=sp.std(wp['aaaaa'].data)
Extracted_Features[i,17]=sp.std(wp['aaaaaa'].data)
Extracted_Features[i,18]=sp.std(wp['d'].data)
Extracted_Features[i,19]=sp.std(wp['dd'].data)
Extracted_Features[i,20]=sp.std(wp['ddd'].data)
Extracted_Features[i,21]=sp.std(wp['dddd'].data)
Extracted_Features[i,22]=sp.std(wp['ddddd'].data)
Extracted_Features[i,23]=sp.std(wp['dddddd'].data)
#Median Values of each subbands
Extracted_Features[i,24]=sp.median(wp['a'].data)
Extracted_Features[i,25]=sp.median(wp['aa'].data)
Extracted_Features[i,26]=sp.median(wp['aaa'].data)
Extracted_Features[i,27]=sp.median(wp['aaaa'].data)
Extracted_Features[i,28]=sp.median(wp['aaaaa'].data)
Extracted_Features[i,29]=sp.median(wp['aaaaaa'].data)
Extracted_Features[i,30]=sp.median(wp['d'].data)
Extracted_Features[i,31]=sp.median(wp['dd'].data)
Extracted_Features[i,32]=sp.median(wp['ddd'].data)
Extracted_Features[i,33]=sp.median(wp['dddd'].data)
Extracted_Features[i,34]=sp.median(wp['ddddd'].data)
Extracted_Features[i,35]=sp.median(wp['dddddd'].data)
#Skewness of each subbands
Extracted_Features[i,36]=stats.skew(wp['a'].data)
Extracted_Features[i,37]=stats.skew(wp['aa'].data)
Extracted_Features[i,38]=stats.skew(wp['aaa'].data)
Extracted_Features[i,39]=stats.skew(wp['aaaa'].data)
Extracted_Features[i,40]=stats.skew(wp['aaaaa'].data)
Extracted_Features[i,41]=stats.skew(wp['aaaaaa'].data)
Extracted_Features[i,42]=stats.skew(wp['d'].data)
Extracted_Features[i,43]=stats.skew(wp['dd'].data)
Extracted_Features[i,44]=stats.skew(wp['ddd'].data)
Extracted_Features[i,45]=stats.skew(wp['dddd'].data)
Extracted_Features[i,46]=stats.skew(wp['ddddd'].data)
Extracted_Features[i,47]=stats.skew(wp['dddddd'].data)
#Kurtosis of each subbands
Extracted_Features[i,48]=stats.kurtosis(wp['a'].data)
Extracted_Features[i,49]=stats.kurtosis(wp['aa'].data)
Extracted_Features[i,50]=stats.kurtosis(wp['aaa'].data)
Extracted_Features[i,51]=stats.kurtosis(wp['aaaa'].data)
Extracted_Features[i,52]=stats.kurtosis(wp['aaaaa'].data)
Extracted_Features[i,53]=stats.kurtosis(wp['aaaaaa'].data)
```

```
Extracted_Features[i,54]=stats.kurtosis(wp['d'].data)
Extracted_Features[i,55]=stats.kurtosis(wp['dd'].data)
Extracted_Features[i,56]=stats.kurtosis(wp['ddd'].data)
Extracted_Features[i,57]=stats.kurtosis(wp['dddd'].data)
Extracted_Features[i,58]=stats.kurtosis(wp['ddddd'].data)
Extracted_Features[i,59]=stats.kurtosis(wp['dddddd'].data)
#RMS Values of each subbands
Extracted_Features[i,60]=np.sqrt(np.mean(wp['a'].data**2))
Extracted_Features[i,61]=np.sqrt(np.mean(wp['aa'].data**2))
Extracted_Features[i,62]=np.sqrt(np.mean(wp['aaa'].data**2))
Extracted_Features[i,63]=np.sqrt(np.mean(wp['aaaa'].data**2))
Extracted_Features[i,64]=np.sqrt(np.mean(wp['aaaaa'].data**2))
Extracted_Features[i,65]=np.sqrt(np.mean(wp['aaaaaa'].data**2))
Extracted_Features[i,66]=np.sqrt(np.mean(wp['d'].data**2))
Extracted_Features[i,67]=np.sqrt(np.mean(wp['dd'].data**2))
Extracted_Features[i,68]=np.sqrt(np.mean(wp['ddd'].data**2))
Extracted_Features[i,69]=np.sqrt(np.mean(wp['dddd'].data**2))
Extracted_Features[i,70]=np.sqrt(np.mean(wp['ddddd'].data**2))
Extracted_Features[i,71]=np.sqrt(np.mean(wp['dddddd'].data**2))
#Ratio of subbands
Extracted_Features[i,72]=sp.mean(abs(wp['a'].data))/sp.mean(abs(wp['aa'].
data))
Extracted_Features[i,73]=sp.mean(abs(wp['aa'].data))/sp.mean(abs(wp['aaa'].
data))
Extracted_Features[i,74]=sp.mean(abs(wp['aaa'].data))/sp.mean(abs(wp
['aaaa'].data))
Extracted_Features[i,75]=sp.mean(abs(wp['aaaa'].data))/sp.mean(abs
(wp['aaaaa'].data))
Extracted_Features[i,76]=sp.mean(abs(wp['aaaaa'].data))/sp.mean(abs(wp
['aaaaaa'].data))
Extracted_Features[i,77]=sp.mean(abs(wp['aaaaaa'].data))/sp.mean(abs
(wp['d'].data))
Extracted_Features[i,78]=sp.mean(abs(wp['d'].data))/sp.mean(abs(wp
['dd'].data))
Extracted_Features[i,79]=sp.mean(abs(wp['dd'].data))/sp.mean(abs(wp
['ddd'].data))
Extracted_Features[i,80]=sp.mean(abs(wp['ddd'].data))/sp.mean(abs
(wp['dddd'].data))
Extracted_Features[i,81]=sp.mean(abs(wp['dddd'].data))/sp.mean(abs(wp
['ddddd'].data))
Extracted_Features[i,82]=sp.mean(abs(wp['ddddd'].data))/sp.mean(abs(wp
['dddddd'].data))
```

```
# ==============================================================================
# Feature extraction from focal EEG signal
# ==============================================================================
for i in range(Nofsignal):
  WPD_Feature_Extraction(FOCAL[:,i], i, wname, level)
  Labels.append("FOCAL")
# ==============================================================================
# Feature extraction from nonfocal EEG signal
# ==============================================================================
for i in range(Nofsignal, 2*Nofsignal):
  WPD_Feature_Extraction(NONFOCAL[:,i-Nofsignal], i, wname, level)
  Labels.append("NONFOCAL")

#%%
# ==============================================================================
# Classification
# ==============================================================================
X = Extracted_Features
y = Labels
#To prevent warnings
import warnings
warnings.filterwarnings("ignore")
#%%
# ==============================================================================
# Logistic regression example with cross-validation
# ==============================================================================
from sklearn.linear_model import LogisticRegressionCV
CV=10 #10-Fold Cross Validation
#Create the Model
model = LogisticRegressionCV(cv=CV, random_state=0,
              multi_class='multinomial').fit(X, y)
#Evaluate Model Using 10-Fold Cross Validation and Print Performance
Measures
kFold_Cross_Validation_Metrics(model,CV)
#%%
# ==============================================================================
# LDA example with cross-validation
# ==============================================================================
from sklearn.discriminant_analysis import LinearDiscriminantAnalysis
# fit model no training data
#lda = LinearDiscriminantAnalysis(solver="svd", store_covariance=True)
#model = LinearDiscriminantAnalysis(solver='lsqr', shrinkage='auto')
model = LinearDiscriminantAnalysis(solver='lsqr', shrinkage=None)
CV=10 #10-Fold Cross Validation
```

```
#Evaluate Model Using 10-Fold Cross Validation
kFold_Cross_Validation_Metrics(model,CV)
#%%
# ======================================================================
# Naive Bayes example with cross-validation
# ======================================================================
#Import Gaussian Naive Bayes model
from sklearn.naive_bayes import GaussianNB
#Create a Gaussian Classifier
model = GaussianNB()
CV=10 #10-Fold Cross Validation
#Evaluate Model Using 10-Fold Cross Validation and Print Performance
Metrics
kFold_Cross_Validation_Metrics(model,CV)
#%%
# ======================================================================
# MLP example with cross-validation
# ======================================================================
from sklearn.neural_network import MLPClassifier
#Create the Model
model = MLPClassifier(hidden_layer_sizes=(60, ), learning_rate_init=0.001,
          alpha=1, momentum=0.9,max_iter=1000)
CV=10 #10-Fold Cross Validation
#Evaluate Model Using 10-Fold Cross Validation and Print Performance
Metrics
kFold_Cross_Validation_Metrics(model,CV)
#%%
from sklearn.linear_model import LogisticRegression
from elm import ELMClassifier
from random_hidden_layer import RBFRandomHiddenLayer
from random_hidden_layer import SimpleRandomHiddenLayer

nh = 75 #Number of Hidden Layer

# pass user defined transfer func
sinsq = (lambda x: np.power(np.sin(x), 2.0))
srhl_sinsq = SimpleRandomHiddenLayer(n_hidden=nh,
                       activation_func=sinsq,
                       random_state=0)

# use internal transfer funcs
srhl_tanh = SimpleRandomHiddenLayer(n_hidden=nh,
                       activation_func='tanh',
                       random_state=0)
```

```
srhl_tribas = SimpleRandomHiddenLayer(n_hidden=nh,
                         activation_func='tribas',
                         random_state=0)
srhl_hardlim = SimpleRandomHiddenLayer(n_hidden=nh,
                         activation_func='hardlim',
                         random_state=0)

# use gaussian RBF
#In order to get better accuracy decrease gamma=0.0001
srhl_rbf = RBFRandomHiddenLayer(n_hidden=nh*2, gamma=0.1, random_state=0)

log_reg = LogisticRegression()

#ELMClassifier(srhl_tanh)
#ELMClassifier(srhl_tanh, regressor=log_reg)
#ELMClassifier(srhl_sinsq)
#ELMClassifier(srhl_tribas)
#ELMClassifier(srhl_hardlim)
#ELMClassifier(srhl_rbf)
# fit model no training data
model = ELMClassifier(srhl_rbf)
CV=10 #10-Fold Cross Validation
#Evaluate Model Using 10-Fold Cross Validation and Print Performance
Metrics
kFold_Cross_Validation_Metrics(model,CV)
#%%
# =====================================================================
# k-NN example with cross-validation
# =====================================================================
from sklearn.neighbors import KNeighborsClassifier
#Create a Model
model = KNeighborsClassifier(n_neighbors=5)

CV=10 #10-Fold Cross Validation
#Evaluate Model Using 10-Fold Cross Validation and Print Performance
Metrics
kFold_Cross_Validation_Metrics(model,CV)

#%%
# =====================================================================
# SVM example with cross-validation
# =====================================================================
from sklearn import svm
```

```
""" The parameters and kernels of SVM classifierr can be changed as follows
C = 10.0 # SVM regularization parameter
svm.SVC(kernel='linear', C=C)
svm.LinearSVC(C=C, max_iter=10000)
svm.SVC(kernel='rbf', gamma=0.7, C=C)
svm.SVC(kernel='poly', degree=3, gamma='auto', C=C))
"""
C = 50.0 # SVM regularization parameter
# fit model no training data
model = svm.SVC(kernel='linear', C=C)

CV=10 #10-Fold Cross Validation
#Evaluate Model Using 10-Fold Cross Validation and Print Performance
Metrics
kFold_Cross_Validation_Metrics(model,CV)
#%%
# ==========================================================================
# Decision tree example with cross-validation
# ==========================================================================
from sklearn import tree
# fit model no training data
model = tree.DecisionTreeClassifier()

CV=10 #10-Fold Cross Validation
#Evaluate Model Using 10-Fold Cross Validation and Print Performance
Metrics
kFold_Cross_Validation_Metrics(model,CV)

#%%
# ==========================================================================
# Extra trees example with cross-validation
# ==========================================================================
#Import Extra Trees model
from sklearn.ensemble import ExtraTreesClassifier
# fit model no training data
model = ExtraTreesClassifier(n_estimators=100, max_features=83)

CV=10 #10-Fold Cross Validation
#Evaluate Model Using 10-Fold Cross Validation and Print Performance
Metrics
kFold_Cross_Validation_Metrics(model,CV)
#%%
```

```
# ======================================================================
# Bagging example with cross-validation
# ======================================================================
#Import Bagging ensemble model
from sklearn.ensemble import BaggingClassifier
#Import Tree model as a base classifier
from sklearn import tree

"""BaggingClassifier(base_estimator=None, n_estimators=10, max_sam-
ples=1.0,
max_features=1.0, bootstrap=True, bootstrap_features=False, oob_
score=False,
warm_start=False, n_jobs=None, random_state=None, verbose=0)"""
#Create a Bagging Ensemble Classifier
model = BaggingClassifier(tree.DecisionTreeClassifier(),
              max_samples=0.5, max_features=0.5)

CV=10 #10-Fold Cross Validation
#Evaluate Model Using 10-Fold Cross Validation and Print Performance
Metrics
kFold_Cross_Validation_Metrics(model,CV)
#%%
# ======================================================================
# Random forest example with cross-validation
# ======================================================================
from sklearn.ensemble import RandomForestClassifier
#In order to change to accuracy increase n_estimators
# fit model no training data
model = RandomForestClassifier(n_estimators=200)

CV=10 #10-Fold Cross Validation
#Evaluate Model Using 10-Fold Cross Validation and Print Performance
Metrics
kFold_Cross_Validation_Metrics(model,CV)

#%%
#Import Adaboost Ensemble model
from sklearn.ensemble import AdaBoostClassifier
#Import Tree model as a base classifier
from sklearn import tree
#Create an Adaboost Ensemble Classifier
"""  AdaBoostClassifier(base_estimator=None, n_estimators=50, learning_
```

```
rate=1.0,
                algorithm='SAMME.R', random_state=None)"""
model = clf=AdaBoostClassifier(tree.DecisionTreeClassifier(),
n_estimators=10,
                algorithm='SAMME',learning_rate=0.5)
CV=10 #10-Fold Cross Validation
#Evaluate Model Using 10-Fold Cross Validation and Print Performance
Metrics
kFold_Cross_Validation_Metrics(model,CV)
#%%
# ==========================================================================
# Gradient boosting example with cross-validation
# ==========================================================================
#Import Gradient Boosting ensemble model
from sklearn.ensemble import GradientBoostingClassifier
# fit model no training data
model = GradientBoostingClassifier(n_estimators=100, learning_rate=1.0,
                   max_depth=1, random_state=0)

CV=10 #10-Fold Cross Validation
#Evaluate Model Using 10-Fold Cross Validation and Print Performance
Metrics
kFold_Cross_Validation_Metrics(model,CV)
#%%
# ==========================================================================
# Voting example with cross-validation
# ==========================================================================

from sklearn.linear_model import LogisticRegression
from sklearn.naive_bayes import GaussianNB
from sklearn.neighbors import KNeighborsClassifier
from sklearn.neural_network import MLPClassifier
from sklearn.ensemble import RandomForestClassifier
from sklearn.ensemble import VotingClassifier
#Create the Model
clf1 = KNeighborsClassifier(n_neighbors=1)
clf2 = RandomForestClassifier(random_state=1)
clf3 = MLPClassifier(hidden_layer_sizes=(100, ), learning_rate_init=0.001,
         alpha=1, momentum=0.9,max_iter=1000)
eclf = VotingClassifier(estimators=[('kNN', clf1), ('RF', clf2), ('MLP',
clf3)], voting='hard')
CV=10 #10-Fold Cross Validation
```

```
#Evaluate Model Using 10-Fold Cross Validation and Print Performance
Metrics
kFold_Cross_Validation_Metrics(model,CV)

#%%
from keras.models import Sequential
from keras.layers import Dense, Activation
from keras.utils.np_utils import to_categorical
from keras.utils.vis_utils import plot_model
from keras.wrappers.scikit_learn import KerasClassifier
from sklearn import preprocessing
lb = preprocessing.LabelBinarizer()
y=lb.fit_transform(Labels)
X = Extracted_Features

#from keras.utils import to_categorical
y_binary = to_categorical(y)
#%%
# ==========================================================================
# Keras DNN example with cross-validation
# ==========================================================================
# define a Keras model
InputDataDimension=numfeatures
def my_model():
          # create model
          model = Sequential()
          model.add(Dense(128, input_dim=InputDataDimension,
          activation='relu'))
          model.add(Dense(NofClasses, activation='softmax'))
          # Compile model
          model.compile(loss='categorical_crossentropy',
          optimizer='adam', metrics=['accuracy'])
          return model

estimator = KerasClassifier(build_fn=my_model, epochs=100, batch_size=5,
verbose=1)
from sklearn.model_selection import KFold
kfold = KFold(n_splits=5, shuffle=True)
from sklearn.model_selection import cross_val_score
results = cross_val_score(estimator, X, y_binary, cv=kfold)
print("Accuracy: %.2f%% (%.2f%%)" % (results.mean()*100, results.
std()*100))
#%%
```

```
#==========================================================================
# ROC analysis for binary classification
#==========================================================================
from sklearn.discriminant_analysis import LinearDiscriminantAnalysis
from sklearn.metrics import roc_curve, auc
from sklearn.model_selection import StratifiedKFold
from scipy import interp
import matplotlib.pyplot as plt
random_state = np.random.RandomState(0)
X = Extracted_Features
y = Labels
##########################################################################
from sklearn.preprocessing import label_binarize
y = label_binarize(y, classes=['FOCAL','NONFOCAL' ])
n_classes = y.shape[1]
# Run classifier with cross-validation and plot ROC curves
cv = StratifiedKFold(n_splits=5)
classifier = LinearDiscriminantAnalysis(solver='lsqr', shrinkage=None)

tprs = []
aucs = []
mean_fpr = np.linspace(0, 1, 100)

i = 0
for train, test in cv.split(X, y):
    probas_ = classifier.fit(X[train], y[train]).predict_proba(X[test])
    # Compute ROC curve and area the curve
    fpr, tpr, thresholds = roc_curve(y[test], probas_[:, 1])
    tprs.append(interp(mean_fpr, fpr, tpr))
    tprs[-1][0] = 0.0
    roc_auc = auc(fpr, tpr)
    aucs.append(roc_auc)
    plt.plot(fpr, tpr, lw=1, alpha=0.3,
             label='ROC fold %d (AUC = %0.2f)' % (i, roc_auc))

    i += 1
plt.plot([0, 1], [0, 1], linestyle='--', lw=2, color='r',
 label='Chance', alpha=.8)

mean_tpr = np.mean(tprs, axis=0)
mean_tpr[-1] = 1.0
mean_auc = auc(mean_fpr, mean_tpr)
std_auc = np.std(aucs)
```

```
plt.plot(mean_fpr, mean_tpr, color='b',
label=r'Mean ROC (AUC = %0.2f $\pm$ %0.2f)' % (mean_auc, std_
auc),
lw=2, alpha=.8)
std_tpr = np.std(tprs, axis=0)
tprs_upper = np.minimum(mean_tpr + std_tpr, 1)
tprs_lower = np.maximum(mean_tpr - std_tpr, 0)
plt.fill_between(mean_fpr,      tprs_lower,      tprs_upper,
color='grey', alpha=.2,
 label=r'$\pm$ 1 std. dev.')
plt.xlim([-0.05, 1.05])
plt.ylim([-0.05, 1.05])
plt.xlabel('False Positive Rate')
plt.ylabel('True Positive Rate')
plt.title('Receiver operating characteristic example')
plt.legend(loc="lower right")
plt.show()
```

### 4.2.4 Migraine detection

Migraine is a continuing neurological disorder with extremely serious indicators such as pulsating pain in one or both sides of the brain, and sensitivity to the light. Notably, it is the third most widespread disorder, influencing one in every seven people. It is worth mentioning that the migraine is generally rated as the seventh most disabling disorder and the first among the neurological disorders. But migraine would often be misdiagnosed, because of its overlapping symptoms with other disorders such as tension headache, epilepsy and strokes. In the past decades, many studies have been performed aiming at the highly precise migraine identification. One specific technique from these studies has already shown promising results, which is *flash stimulation*. The foundation of this method is the analysis of the subject's neural responses, recorded with multichannel electroencephalography (EEG) under flash stimulation at different frequencies for variable amounts of seconds. One study in the literature found flash frequency at 4 Hz to be the most accurate (Akben, Subasi, & Tuncel, 2012) (Subasi, Ahmed, Aličković, & Rashik Hassan, 2019). A general framework for migraine detection is presented in Fig. 4.5.

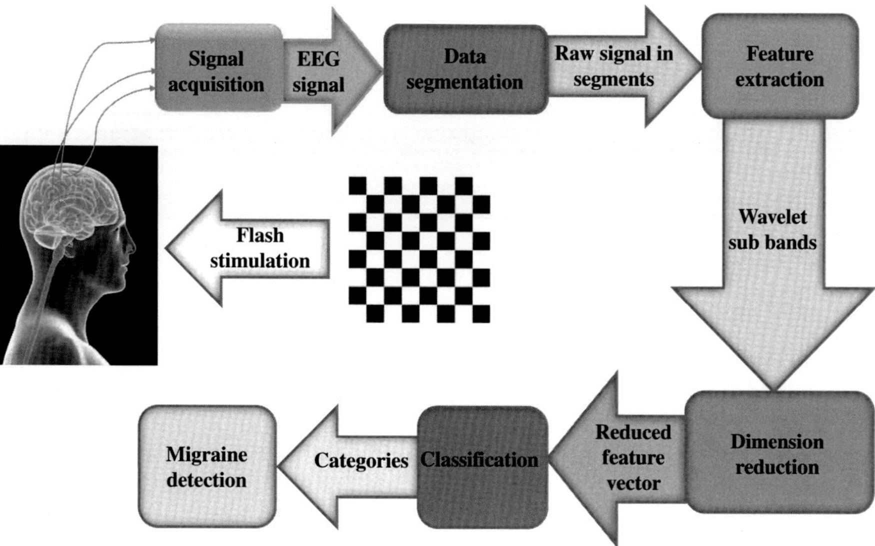


FIGURE 4.5 **A general framework for migraine detection.** *Source: Adapted from Subasi et al. (2019d).*

## Example 4.4

The following Python code is used to extract features from healthy and migraine EEG signals by employing wavelet packet decomposition (WPD). Next it uses statistical values of WPD sub-bands, and then it classifies these data using extra tree classifier with separate training and testing datasets. The classification accuracy, precision, recall, F1 score, Cohen kappa score, and Matthews correlation coefficient are calculated. The classification report and confusion matrix are also given.

***Data Set Information:*** An 18-channel (10-20 system) Nicolet One machine is used to record the data. EEG data was collected from migraineurs and healthy subjects at the Neurology Department at Kahramanmaras Sutcu Imam University. Our dataset can be described as follows:

- In all, 15 migraineurs (2 males, 13 females, without aura) of ages 20 to 34 years (mean age ± standard deviation 27 ± 4.4 years, diagnosed according to the criteria proposed by the International Headache Society, or IHS) and 15 control subjects (5 males, 10 females) of ages 19 to 35 years (mean age ± standard deviation: 26 ± 5.3 years) participated in the experiment.
- The experiment was conducted in a dimly lit room.
- None of the participants had taken any drugs before the recordings.
- All participants were in the interictal (pain-free) state while in a couchant position.
- The 10-20 EEG system was used to collect the EEG data.
- EEG signals were collected at 256 Hz sampling frequency.
- Each stimulation was 30 seconds long at the frequency of 4 Hz.

EEG frequency range from 0 to 100 Hz (Niedermeyer & da Silva, 2005). In addition, the EEG frequency bands delta (1–4 Hz), theta (4–8 Hz), alpha (8–13 Hz), beta (13–30 Hz), and gamma (30–100 Hz) are all within the 0–100 Hz range. According to Nyquist theorem, in order to capture all useful information from the EEG signals, the minimum sampling rate should be at least 200 Hz. Note that the sampling rate used in this study is 256 Hz, which is noticeably above the required 200 Hz. This dataset was used in Akben et al. (2012) and Subasi et al. (2019d), where a different analysis strategy was considered.

```
"""
Created on Thu May 9 12:18:30 2019
@author: asubasi
"""
#===========================================================================
# Feature extraction using the statistical values of wavelet packet
transform
#===========================================================================
# descriptive statistics
import scipy as sp
import scipy.io as sio
import pywt
import numpy as np
import scipy.stats as stats

wname = pywt.Wavelet('db1')
level=6 #Number of decomposition level
#Load mat file
mat_contents = sio.loadmat('Migraine.mat')
sorted(mat_contents.keys())
HEALTHY=mat_contents['Healthy']
MIGRAINE=mat_contents['Migraineur']
Labels = [] #Empty List For Labels
NofClasses=2 #Number of Classes
Length = 768; # Length of signal
Nofsignal=135; #Number of Signal for each Class
numrows =83 #Number of features extracted from Wavelet Packet
Decomposition
#Create Empty Array For Features
Extracted_Features=np.ndarray(shape=(NofClasses*Nofsignal,numrows),
dtype=float, order='F')
#===========================================================================
# Utility function for feature extraction
#===========================================================================
def WPD_Feature_Extraction(signal, i, wname, level):
#Mean Values of each subbands
```

```
wp= pywt.WaveletPacket(signal, wname, mode='symmetric', maxlevel=level)
Extracted_Features[i,0]=sp.mean(abs(wp['a'].data))
Extracted_Features[i,1]=sp.mean(abs(wp['aa'].data))
Extracted_Features[i,2]=sp.mean(abs(wp['aaa'].data))
Extracted_Features[i,3]=sp.mean(abs(wp['aaaa'].data))
Extracted_Features[i,4]=sp.mean(abs(wp['aaaaa'].data))
Extracted_Features[i,5]=sp.mean(abs(wp['aaaaaa'].data))
Extracted_Features[i,6]=sp.mean(abs(wp['d'].data))
Extracted_Features[i,7]=sp.mean(abs(wp['dd'].data))
Extracted_Features[i,8]=sp.mean(abs(wp['ddd'].data))
Extracted_Features[i,9]=sp.mean(abs(wp['dddd'].data))
Extracted_Features[i,10]=sp.mean(abs(wp['ddddd'].data))
Extracted_Features[i,11]=sp.mean(abs(wp['dddddd'].data))
#Standart Deviation of each subbands
Extracted_Features[i,12]=sp.std(wp['a'].data)
Extracted_Features[i,13]=sp.std(wp['aa'].data)
Extracted_Features[i,14]=sp.std(wp['aaa'].data)
Extracted_Features[i,15]=sp.std(wp['aaaa'].data)
Extracted_Features[i,16]=sp.std(wp['aaaaa'].data)
Extracted_Features[i,17]=sp.std(wp['aaaaaa'].data)
Extracted_Features[i,18]=sp.std(wp['d'].data)
Extracted_Features[i,19]=sp.std(wp['dd'].data)
Extracted_Features[i,20]=sp.std(wp['ddd'].data)
Extracted_Features[i,21]=sp.std(wp['dddd'].data)
Extracted_Features[i,22]=sp.std(wp['ddddd'].data)
Extracted_Features[i,23]=sp.std(wp['dddddd'].data)
#Median Values of each subbands
Extracted_Features[i,24]=sp.median(wp['a'].data)
Extracted_Features[i,25]=sp.median(wp['aa'].data)
Extracted_Features[i,26]=sp.median(wp['aaa'].data)
Extracted_Features[i,27]=sp.median(wp['aaaa'].data)
Extracted_Features[i,28]=sp.median(wp['aaaaa'].data)
Extracted_Features[i,29]=sp.median(wp['aaaaaa'].data)
Extracted_Features[i,30]=sp.median(wp['d'].data)
Extracted_Features[i,31]=sp.median(wp['dd'].data)
Extracted_Features[i,32]=sp.median(wp['ddd'].data)
Extracted_Features[i,33]=sp.median(wp['dddd'].data)
Extracted_Features[i,34]=sp.median(wp['ddddd'].data)
Extracted_Features[i,35]=sp.median(wp['dddddd'].data)
#Skewness of each subbands
Extracted_Features[i,36]=stats.skew(wp['a'].data)
Extracted_Features[i,37]=stats.skew(wp['aa'].data)
Extracted_Features[i,38]=stats.skew(wp['aaa'].data)
Extracted_Features[i,39]=stats.skew(wp['aaaa'].data)
```

```
Extracted_Features[i,40]=stats.skew(wp['aaaaa'].data)
Extracted_Features[i,41]=stats.skew(wp['aaaaaa'].data)
Extracted_Features[i,42]=stats.skew(wp['d'].data)
Extracted_Features[i,43]=stats.skew(wp['dd'].data)
Extracted_Features[i,44]=stats.skew(wp['ddd'].data)
Extracted_Features[i,45]=stats.skew(wp['dddd'].data)
Extracted_Features[i,46]=stats.skew(wp['ddddd'].data)
Extracted_Features[i,47]=stats.skew(wp['dddddd'].data)
#Kurtosis of each subbands
Extracted_Features[i,48]=stats.kurtosis(wp['a'].data)
Extracted_Features[i,49]=stats.kurtosis(wp['aa'].data)
Extracted_Features[i,50]=stats.kurtosis(wp['aaa'].data)
Extracted_Features[i,51]=stats.kurtosis(wp['aaaa'].data)
Extracted_Features[i,52]=stats.kurtosis(wp['aaaaa'].data)
Extracted_Features[i,53]=stats.kurtosis(wp['aaaaaa'].data)
Extracted_Features[i,54]=stats.kurtosis(wp['d'].data)
Extracted_Features[i,55]=stats.kurtosis(wp['dd'].data)
Extracted_Features[i,56]=stats.kurtosis(wp['ddd'].data)
Extracted_Features[i,57]=stats.kurtosis(wp['dddd'].data)
Extracted_Features[i,58]=stats.kurtosis(wp['ddddd'].data)
Extracted_Features[i,59]=stats.kurtosis(wp['dddddd'].data)
#RMS Values of each subbands
Extracted_Features[i,60]=np.sqrt(np.mean(wp['a'].data**2))
Extracted_Features[i,61]=np.sqrt(np.mean(wp['aa'].data**2))
Extracted_Features[i,62]=np.sqrt(np.mean(wp['aaa'].data**2))
Extracted_Features[i,63]=np.sqrt(np.mean(wp['aaaa'].data**2))
Extracted_Features[i,64]=np.sqrt(np.mean(wp['aaaaa'].data**2))
Extracted_Features[i,65]=np.sqrt(np.mean(wp['aaaaaa'].data**2))
Extracted_Features[i,66]=np.sqrt(np.mean(wp['d'].data**2))
Extracted_Features[i,67]=np.sqrt(np.mean(wp['dd'].data**2))
Extracted_Features[i,68]=np.sqrt(np.mean(wp['ddd'].data**2))
Extracted_Features[i,69]=np.sqrt(np.mean(wp['dddd'].data**2))
Extracted_Features[i,70]=np.sqrt(np.mean(wp['ddddd'].data**2))
Extracted_Features[i,71]=np.sqrt(np.mean(wp['dddddd'].data**2))
#Ratio of subbands
Extracted_Features[i,72]=sp.mean(abs(wp['a'].data))/sp.mean(abs(wp['aa'].
data))
Extracted_Features[i,73]=sp.mean(abs(wp['aa'].data))/sp.mean(abs
(wp['aaa'].data))
Extracted_Features[i,74]=sp.mean(abs(wp['aaa'].data))/sp.mean(abs(wp
['aaaa'].data))
Extracted_Features[i,75]=sp.mean(abs(wp['aaaa'].data))/sp.mean(abs(wp
['aaaaa'].data))
```

```
    Extracted_Features[i,76]=sp.mean(abs(wp['aaaaa'].data))/sp.mean(abs(wp
    ['aaaaaa'].data))
    Extracted_Features[i,77]=sp.mean(abs(wp['aaaaaa'].data))/sp.mean(abs
    (wp['d'].data))
    Extracted_Features[i,78]=sp.mean(abs(wp['d'].data))/sp.mean(abs(wp
    ['dd'].data))
    Extracted_Features[i,79]=sp.mean(abs(wp['dd'].data))/sp.mean(abs(wp
    ['ddd'].data))
    Extracted_Features[i,80]=sp.mean(abs(wp['ddd'].data))/sp.mean(abs
    (wp['dddd'].data))
    Extracted_Features[i,81]=sp.mean(abs(wp['dddd'].data))/sp.mean(abs(wp
    ['ddddd'].data))
    Extracted_Features[i,82]=sp.mean(abs(wp['ddddd'].data))/sp.mean(abs(wp
    ['dddddd'].data))

#%%
# =====================================================================
# Feature extraction from healthy EEG signal
# =====================================================================
for i in range(Nofsignal):
  WPD_Feature_Extraction(HEALTHY[:,i], i, wname, level)
  Labels.append("HEALTHY")
# =====================================================================
# Feature extraction from migraine EEG signal
# =====================================================================
for i in range(Nofsignal, 2*Nofsignal):
  WPD_Feature_Extraction(MIGRAINE[:,i-Nofsignal], i, wname, level)
  Labels.append("MIGRAINE")
#%%
# =====================================================================
# Classification
# =====================================================================
X = Extracted_Features
y = Labels
# Import train_test_split function
from sklearn.model_selection import train_test_split
# Split dataset into training set and test set
# 70% training and 30% test
Xtrain, Xtest, ytrain, ytest = train_test_split(X, y,test_size=0.3,
random_state=1)
#%%
# =====================================================================
# Extra trees classification example with training and test set
```

```
#=======================================================================
#Import Extra Trees model
from sklearn.ensemble import ExtraTreesClassifier
# Split dataset into training set and test set
# 70% training and 30% test
Xtrain, Xtest, ytrain, ytest = train_test_split(X, y,test_size=0.3,
random_state=0)
#Create the Model
clf = model = ExtraTreesClassifier(n_estimators=100, max_features=48)
#Train the model using the training sets
clf.fit(Xtrain,ytrain)
#Predict the response for test dataset
ypred = clf.predict(Xtest)

#Evaluate the Model and Print Performance Metrics
from sklearn import metrics
print('Accuracy:', np.round(metrics.accuracy_score(ytest,ypred),4))
print('Precision:', np.round(metrics.precision_score(ytest,
                  ypred,average='weighted'),4))
print('Recall:', np.round(metrics.recall_score(ytest,ypred,
                          average='weighted'),4))
print('F1 Score:', np.round(metrics.f1_score(ytest,ypred,
                          average='weighted'),4))
print('Cohen  Kappa  Score:',  np.round(metrics.cohen_kappa_score(ytest,
ypred),4))
print('Matthews  Corrcoef:',  np.round(metrics.matthews_corrcoef(ytest,
ypred),4))
print('\t\tClassification Report:\n', metrics.classification_report(ypred,
ytest))
#Plot Confusion Matrix
from sklearn.metrics import confusion_matrix
print("Confusion Matrix:\n",confusion_matrix(ytest, ypred))
```

## 4.3 EMG signal analysis

The main responsibility of human skeletal muscular system is to give the forces required to do several activities. This system contains two subsystems—the nervous system and the muscular system—together creating the neuromuscular system (Begg et al., 2008). The motion and arrangement of the limbs are controlled by electrical signals propagating back and forth between the muscles and the peripheral and central nervous system (Bronzino, 1999). Nerves might be understood as wires conducting electrical currents; the nerve heads (nuclei) begin in the spinal column and their long axonal bodies enlarge distant and deep, exciting single motor units in various muscles. The skeletal-muscular system consists of muscle sets attached to bones via tendons, and a motion is completed once nerve signals generate muscle contractions and relaxations, which either attract or repel the bone (Begg et al., 2008; Subasi, 2019c).

The electromyogram (EMG) signal represents the electrical state of skeletal muscles and holds data associated with the structure of the muscles to initiate a variety of body parts to activate. The EMG signal carries data associated with the controller effect of the central and peripheral nervous systems on the muscles. Naturally, the EMG signal gives an extremely useful description of the neuromuscular system since various pathological measures, regardless of appearing in the nervous system or the muscle, are visible by changes in the signal features. In recent decades, the quality of EMG signal understanding has considerably improved with the development of new signal processing techniques to understand the muscles' electrophysiology (Sörnmo & Laguna, 2005). EMG analysis is more accurate than clinical tests in defining muscle fiber types involved in abnormalities. EMG analysis can show irregular sensory-nerve phenomenon even though the patient still has normal motor-nerve conduction. Furthermore, EMG analysis may help a medical doctor diagnose conditions without the need for a muscle biopsy (Begg et al., 2008). Progresses in engineering and technology have taken electromyography beyond the conventional diagnostic procedures to consider usages in different areas such as rehabilitation, ergonomics, movement analysis, exercise physiology, and biofeedback, as well as myoelectric control of prosthesis (Sörnmo & Laguna, 2005; Subasi, 2019c).

### 4.3.1 Diagnosis of neuromuscular disorders

Neuromuscular disorders are abnormalities that initially occur in the nervous system, in the neuromuscular junctions, and in the muscle fibers. These abnormalities have different levels of severity, ranging from negligible damage of muscles to amputation caused by neuron or muscle death. In more severe illnesses like amyotrophic lateral sclerosis (ALS), death is generally assured. Premature and correct diagnosis is crucial for improved prognosis and the probability of complete rehabilitation. In most cases, clinical testing is inadequate to identify and prevent disorders from spreading because a lot of dissimilar abnormalities could result from a specific symptom. Accurate diagnosis of the disorder is, for that reason, of supreme significance so more decisive treatment can be established. Currently, electrodiagnostic studies consist of nerve conduction studies, and EMGs are utilized for the evaluation and identification of patients with neuromuscular disorders. EMG was first employed as a method of examining neuromuscular states formed on cell action capabilities throughout muscle activity. Characteristics of the EMG waveform (0.01–10 mV and 10–2000 Hz on average) can indicate the position, etiology, and kind of anatomy. As an example, EMG signal interval shows the position and network metabolic status of the muscle fiber (Emly, Gilmore, & Roy, 1992) and irregular spikes can show myopathy. On the other hand, the electrodiagnostic methods help doctors in disease diagnosis but are hardly ever helpful for confirming the diagnosis, and in complicated situations more invasive tools like muscle biopsies or more advanced imaging methods like ultrasound or MRI are essential. The interpretation of the EMG is as a rule done by trained and expert neurologists who, besides examining EMG waveforms, engage in methods pertaining to needle conduction research and muscle acoustics as well. Problems occur when there are hardly any specialists to meet the demand of patients and, as a result, it is important to develop an automated diagnostic system based on EMG readings. Relevant machine learning techniques could be used for the detection and classification of neuromuscular disorders based on EMG processing. These intelligent systems will help doctors detect anomalies in the neuromuscular system. The aim of intelligent diagnostic and artificially controlled neuromuscular systems is to preprocess the raw EMG signals and hence extract characteristic data or features. Extracted features consist of time and frequency domain data, Fourier coefficients, autoregressive coefficients, wavelet coefficients, and a wide range of quantities derived from other signal processing methods. This data can then be employed as input data for classifiers like decision trees and support vector machines to classify neuromuscular diseases. Neuromuscular disorders are typically anomalies concerning the peripheral nervous system. They can be categorized depending on the location of and reason for the disorders. Two main disorders are neuropathy and myopathy (Begg et al., 2008; Subasi, 2019c).

Neuropathy is a term that identifies disorders of nerves that cause pain and disability. The cause of neuropathic disorders is distinct, including injury, infection, diabetes, alcohol abuse, and cancer chemotherapy. Myopathy is a disorder usually associated with the skeletal muscle that is caused by injury of a muscle group or some genetic mutation. Myopathy prevents the normal functioning of affected muscles. Consequently, the patient suffering with myopathic disorders has weak muscles and, depending on the severity of the disorder, has problems performing regular tasks or finds it impossible to make any movement without utilizing the affected muscles (Begg et al., 2008; Subasi, 2019c).

The needle EMG is the typical clinical recording method utilized for diagnosis of the neuromuscular pathology. When, for instance, a patient goes to a doctor for muscle weakness, the doctor will record the needle EMG during contraction of specific muscles. This data may help identify irregular activity occurring in circumstances like muscle pain, injury to nerves in the arms and legs, pinched nerves, and muscular dystrophy. The needle EMG is also examined together with the nerve injury and can be used to determine if the injury is restored and has reverted back to normal, with complete muscle reactivity, for example, by analyzing alterations in motor unit achievement over a specific time period. The diagnostic EMG includes the examination of unexpected motor action, which can happen during muscle relaxation. In normal situations, the muscle is electrically quiet when relaxed; on the other hand, irregular spontaneous waveforms and waveform patterns can be generated that are connected with spontaneous muscular activities (Sörnmo & Laguna, 2005; Subasi, 2019c). A general framework for diagnosis of neuromuscular disorders using EMG signals is shown in Fig. 4.6.

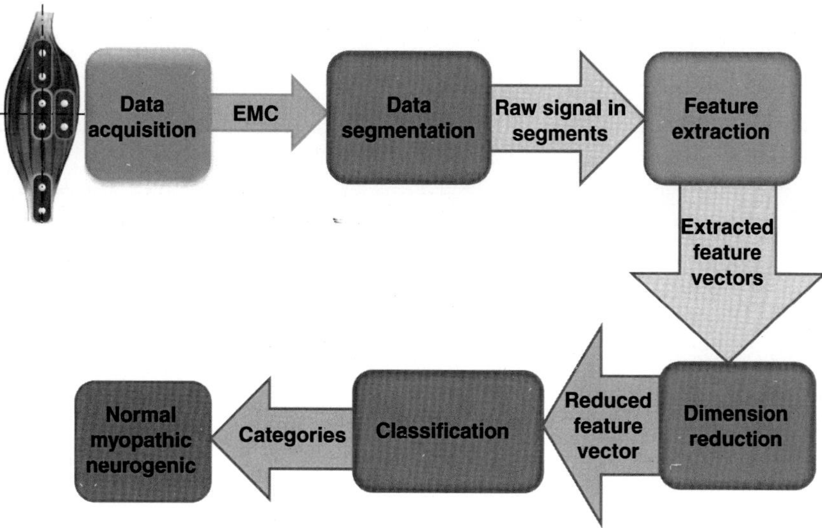


**FIGURE 4.6 A general framework for diagnosis of neuromuscular disorders using EMG signals.**

## Example 4.5

The following Python code is used to extract features from the EMG signals by employing stationary wavelet transform (SWT) and utilizing statistical values of SWT sub-bands. Then it classifies these data using SVM classifier with separate training and testing datasets. The classification accuracy, precision, recall, F1 score, Cohen kappa score, and Matthews correlation coefficient are calculated. The classification report, confusion matrix, and receiver operating characteristic (ROC) area are also given.

***Dataset information:*** EMG signals are taken from the EMGLAB website (http://www.emglab.net/). The clinical EMG signals were acquired under normal conditions for MUAP analysis. The EMG signals are recorded at low voluntary and constant level of contraction with a standard concentric needle electrode. The EMG signals were filtered between 2 Hz and 10 kHz and consist of a control group and a group of patients with ALS and myopathy. There were 10 normal subjects (4 females and 6 males) aged 21–37 years in the control group. There were 8 patients (4 females and 4 males) between 35–67 years old in the ALS group. There were 7 patients (2 females and 5 males) between 19–63 years old in the myopathy group (Nikolic, 2001). You can download the data from the following web site:
http://www.emglab.net/emglab/Signals/signals.php

```
"""
Created on Thu May 9 12:18:30 2019
```

```
@author: asubasi
"""
# ==========================================================================
# Feature extraction using the statistical values of stationary wavelet
transform
# ==========================================================================
import scipy.io as sio
# descriptive statistics
import scipy as sp
import pywt
import matplotlib.pyplot as plt
import numpy as np
import scipy.stats as stats
waveletname='db1'
level=6 #Decomposition Level
#Load mat file
mat_contents = sio.loadmat('EMGDAT.mat')
sorted(mat_contents.keys())

CONTROL=mat_contents['CON']
ALS=mat_contents['ALS']
MYOPATHIC=mat_contents['MYO']

Labels = [] #Empty List For Labels
Length = 8192; # Length of signal
Nofsignal=200; #Number of Signal
NofClasses=3; #Number of Classes
numrows =83 #Number of features extracted from Wavelet Packet
Decomposition
#Create Empty Array For Features
Extracted_Features=np.ndarray(shape=(NofClasses*Nofsignal,numrows),
dtype=float, order='F')
# ==========================================================================
# Define utility functions for feature extraction
# ==========================================================================
def SWT_Feature_Extraction(signal, i, wname, level):
   coeffs = pywt.swt(signal, wname, level=level)
   #Mean Values of each subbands
   Extracted_Features[i,0]=sp.mean(abs(coeffs[0][0]))
   Extracted_Features[i,1]=sp.mean(abs(coeffs[1][0]))
   Extracted_Features[i,2]=sp.mean(abs(coeffs[2][0]))
   Extracted_Features[i,3]=sp.mean(abs(coeffs[3][0]))
   Extracted_Features[i,4]=sp.mean(abs(coeffs[4][0]))
   Extracted_Features[i,5]=sp.mean(abs(coeffs[5][0]))
```

```
Extracted_Features[i,6]=sp.mean(abs(coeffs[0][1]))
Extracted_Features[i,7]=sp.mean(abs(coeffs[1][1]))
Extracted_Features[i,8]=sp.mean(abs(coeffs[2][1]))
Extracted_Features[i,9]=sp.mean(abs(coeffs[3][1]))
Extracted_Features[i,10]=sp.mean(abs(coeffs[4][1]))
Extracted_Features[i,11]=sp.mean(abs(coeffs[5][1]))
#Standart Deviation of each subbands
Extracted_Features[i,12]=sp.std(coeffs[0][0])
Extracted_Features[i,13]=sp.std(coeffs[1][0])
Extracted_Features[i,14]=sp.std(coeffs[2][0])
Extracted_Features[i,15]=sp.std(coeffs[3][0])
Extracted_Features[i,16]=sp.std(coeffs[4][0])
Extracted_Features[i,17]=sp.std(coeffs[5][0])
Extracted_Features[i,18]=sp.std(coeffs[0][1])
Extracted_Features[i,19]=sp.std(coeffs[1][1])
Extracted_Features[i,20]=sp.std(coeffs[2][1])
Extracted_Features[i,21]=sp.std(coeffs[3][1])
Extracted_Features[i,22]=sp.std(coeffs[4][1])
Extracted_Features[i,23]=sp.std(coeffs[5][1])
#Median Values of each subbands
Extracted_Features[i,24]=sp.median(coeffs[0][0])
Extracted_Features[i,25]=sp.median(coeffs[1][0])
Extracted_Features[i,26]=sp.median(coeffs[2][0])
Extracted_Features[i,27]=sp.median(coeffs[3][0])
Extracted_Features[i,28]=sp.median(coeffs[4][0])
Extracted_Features[i,29]=sp.median(coeffs[5][0])
Extracted_Features[i,30]=sp.median(coeffs[0][1])
Extracted_Features[i,31]=sp.median(coeffs[1][1])
Extracted_Features[i,32]=sp.median(coeffs[2][1])
Extracted_Features[i,33]=sp.median(coeffs[3][1])
Extracted_Features[i,34]=sp.median(coeffs[4][1])
Extracted_Features[i,35]=sp.median(coeffs[5][1])
#Skewness of each subbands
Extracted_Features[i,36]=stats.skew(coeffs[0][0])
Extracted_Features[i,37]=stats.skew(coeffs[1][0])
Extracted_Features[i,38]=stats.skew(coeffs[2][0])
Extracted_Features[i,39]=stats.skew(coeffs[3][0])
Extracted_Features[i,40]=stats.skew(coeffs[4][0])
Extracted_Features[i,41]=stats.skew(coeffs[5][0])
Extracted_Features[i,42]=stats.skew(coeffs[0][1])
Extracted_Features[i,43]=stats.skew(coeffs[1][1])
Extracted_Features[i,44]=stats.skew(coeffs[2][1])
Extracted_Features[i,45]=stats.skew(coeffs[3][1])
Extracted_Features[i,46]=stats.skew(coeffs[4][1])
```

```
Extracted_Features[i,47]=stats.skew(coeffs[5][1])
#Kurtosis of each subbands
Extracted_Features[i,48]=stats.kurtosis(coeffs[0][0])
Extracted_Features[i,49]=stats.kurtosis(coeffs[1][0])
Extracted_Features[i,50]=stats.kurtosis(coeffs[2][0])
Extracted_Features[i,51]=stats.kurtosis(coeffs[3][0])
Extracted_Features[i,52]=stats.kurtosis(coeffs[4][0])
Extracted_Features[i,53]=stats.kurtosis(coeffs[5][0])
Extracted_Features[i,54]=stats.kurtosis(coeffs[0][1])
Extracted_Features[i,55]=stats.kurtosis(coeffs[1][1])
Extracted_Features[i,56]=stats.kurtosis(coeffs[2][1])
Extracted_Features[i,57]=stats.kurtosis(coeffs[3][1])
Extracted_Features[i,58]=stats.kurtosis(coeffs[4][1])
Extracted_Features[i,59]=stats.kurtosis(coeffs[5][1])
#RMS Values of each subbands
Extracted_Features[i,60]=np.sqrt(np.mean(coeffs[0][0]**2))
Extracted_Features[i,61]=np.sqrt(np.mean(coeffs[1][0]**2))
Extracted_Features[i,62]=np.sqrt(np.mean(coeffs[2][0]**2))
Extracted_Features[i,63]=np.sqrt(np.mean(coeffs[3][0]**2))
Extracted_Features[i,64]=np.sqrt(np.mean(coeffs[4][0]**2))
Extracted_Features[i,65]=np.sqrt(np.mean(coeffs[5][0]**2))
Extracted_Features[i,66]=np.sqrt(np.mean(coeffs[0][1]**2))
Extracted_Features[i,67]=np.sqrt(np.mean(coeffs[1][1]**2))
Extracted_Features[i,68]=np.sqrt(np.mean(coeffs[2][1]**2))
Extracted_Features[i,69]=np.sqrt(np.mean(coeffs[3][1]**2))
Extracted_Features[i,70]=np.sqrt(np.mean(coeffs[4][1]**2))
Extracted_Features[i,71]=np.sqrt(np.mean(coeffs[5][1]**2))
#Ratio of subbands
Extracted_Features[i,72]=sp.mean(abs(coeffs[0][0]))/sp.mean(abs(coeffs[1]
[0]))
Extracted_Features[i,73]=sp.mean(abs(coeffs[1][0]))/sp.mean(abs(coeffs[2]
[0]))
Extracted_Features[i,74]=sp.mean(abs(coeffs[2][0]))/sp.mean(abs(coeffs[3]
[0]))
Extracted_Features[i,75]=sp.mean(abs(coeffs[3][0]))/sp.mean(abs(coeffs[4]
[0]))
Extracted_Features[i,76]=sp.mean(abs(coeffs[4][0]))/sp.mean(abs(coeffs[5]
[0]))
Extracted_Features[i,77]=sp.mean(abs(coeffs[5][0]))/sp.mean(abs(coeffs[0]
[1]))
Extracted_Features[i,78]=sp.mean(abs(coeffs[0][1]))/sp.mean(abs(coeffs
[1][1]))
Extracted_Features[i,79]=sp.mean(abs(coeffs[1][1]))/sp.mean(abs(coeffs
[2][1]))
```

```
    Extracted_Features[i,80]=sp.mean(abs(coeffs[2][1]))/sp.mean(abs (co-
    effs[3][1]))
    Extracted_Features[i,81]=sp.mean(abs(coeffs[3][1]))/sp.mean(abs(coeffs
    [4][1]))
    Extracted_Features[i,82]=sp.mean(abs(coeffs[4][1]))/sp.mean(abs
    (coeffs[5][1]))
#%%
# ===========================================================================
# Feature extraction from control EMG signal
# ===========================================================================
for i in range(Nofsignal):
    SWT_Feature_Extraction(CONTROL[:,i], i, waveletname, level)
    Labels.append("CONTROL")
# ===========================================================================
# Feature extraction from ALS EMG signal
# ===========================================================================
for i in range(Nofsignal, 2*Nofsignal):
    SWT_Feature_Extraction(ALS[:,i-Nofsignal], i, waveletname, level)
    Labels.append("ALS")
# ===========================================================================
# Feature extraction from myopathic EMG signal
# ===========================================================================
for i in range(2*Nofsignal, 3*Nofsignal):
    SWT_Feature_Extraction(MYOPATHIC[:,i-2*Nofsignal], i, waveletname, level)
    Labels.append("MYOPATHIC")
#%%
# ===========================================================================
# Classification
# ===========================================================================
X = Extracted_Features
y = Labels
# Import train_test_split function
from sklearn.model_selection import train_test_split
# Split dataset into training set and test set
# 70% training and 30% test
Xtrain, Xtest, ytrain, ytest = train_test_split(X, y,test_size=0.3,
random_state=1)
#%%
# ===========================================================================
# SVM example with training and test set
# ===========================================================================
from sklearn import svm
    """ The parameters and kernels of SVM classifierr can be changed as
follows
```

```
C = 10.0 # SVM regularization parameter
svm.SVC(kernel='linear', C=C)
svm.LinearSVC(C=C, max_iter=10000)
svm.SVC(kernel='rbf', gamma=0.7, C=C)
svm.SVC(kernel='poly', degree=3, gamma='auto', C=C)
"""
C = 10.0 # SVM regularization parameter
#Create the Model
clf =svm.SVC(kernel='linear', C=C)
#Train the model with Training Dataset
clf.fit(Xtrain,ytrain)
#Test the model with Testset
ypred = clf.predict(Xtest)
#Evaluate the Model and Print Performance Metrics
from sklearn import metrics
print('Accuracy:', np.round(metrics.accuracy_score(ytest,ypred),4))
print('Precision:', np.round(metrics.precision_score(ytest,
                    ypred,average='weighted'),4))
print('Recall:', np.round(metrics.recall_score(ytest,ypred,
                              average='weighted'),4))
print('F1 Score:', np.round(metrics.f1_score(ytest,ypred,
                              average='weighted'),4))
print('Cohen  Kappa  Score:',  np.round(metrics.cohen_kappa_score(ytest,
ypred),4))
print('Matthews  Corrcoef:',  np.round(metrics.matthews_corrcoef(ytest,
ypred),4))
print('\t\tClassification Report:\n', metrics.classification_report(ypred,
ytest))
#Plot Confusion Matrix
from sklearn.metrics import confusion_matrix
print("Confusion Matrix:\n",confusion_matrix(ytest, ypred))
#%%
# ==================================================================
# ROC curves for the multiclass problem
# ==================================================================
import numpy as np
import matplotlib.pyplot as plt
from itertools import cycle
from sklearn.metrics import roc_curve, auc
from sklearn.model_selection import train_test_split
from sklearn.preprocessing import label_binarize
from sklearn.multiclass import OneVsRestClassifier
from scipy import interp
```

```
# Binarize the output
y = label_binarize(y, classes=['CONTROL','ALS','MYOPATHIC' ])
n_classes = y.shape[1]
# shuffle and split training and test sets
Xtrain, Xtest, ytrain, ytest = train_test_split(X, y,test_size=0.3,
random_state=1)
# Learn to predict each class against the other
classifier = OneVsRestClassifier(svm.SVC(kernel='linear', C=C))
yscore = classifier.fit(Xtrain, ytrain).decision_function(Xtest)
# Compute ROC curve and ROC area for each class
fpr = dict()
tpr = dict()
roc_auc = dict()
for i in range(n_classes):
  fpr[i], tpr[i], _ = roc_curve(ytest[:, i], yscore[:, i])
  roc_auc[i] = auc(fpr[i], tpr[i])
# Compute micro-average ROC curve and ROC area
fpr["micro"], tpr["micro"], _ = roc_curve(ytest.ravel(), yscore.ravel())
roc_auc["micro"] = auc(fpr["micro"], tpr["micro"])
##########################################################################
# Plot of a ROC curve for a specific class
plt.figure()
lw = 2
plt.plot(fpr[2], tpr[2], color='darkorange',
      lw=lw, label='ROC curve (area = %0.2f)' % roc_auc[2])
plt.plot([0, 1], [0, 1], color='navy', lw=lw, linestyle='--')
plt.xlim([0.0, 1.0])
plt.ylim([0.0, 1.05])
plt.xlabel('False Positive Rate')
plt.ylabel('True Positive Rate')
plt.title('Receiver operating characteristic')
plt.legend(loc="lower right")
plt.show()
##########################################################################
# Plot ROC curves for the multiclass problem
# Compute macro-average ROC curve and ROC area
# First aggregate all false positive rates
all_fpr = np.unique(np.concatenate([fpr[i] for i in range(n_classes)]))
# Then interpolate all ROC curves at this points
mean_tpr = np.zeros_like(all_fpr)
for i in range(n_classes):
  mean_tpr += interp(all_fpr, fpr[i], tpr[i])
# Finally average it and compute AUC
```

```
mean_tpr /= n_classes
fpr["macro"] = all_fpr
tpr["macro"] = mean_tpr
roc_auc["macro"] = auc(fpr["macro"], tpr["macro"])
# Plot all ROC curves
plt.figure()
plt.plot(fpr["micro"], tpr["micro"],
      label='micro-average ROC curve (area = {0:0.2f})'
           ''.format(roc_auc["micro"]),
       color='deeppink', linestyle=':', linewidth=4)
plt.plot(fpr["macro"], tpr["macro"],
       label='macro-average ROC curve (area = {0:0.2f})'
           ''.format(roc_auc["macro"]),
       color='navy', linestyle=':', linewidth=4)
colors = cycle(['aqua', 'darkorange', 'cornflowerblue'])
for i, color in zip(range(n_classes), colors):
  plt.plot(fpr[i], tpr[i], color=color, lw=lw,
         label='ROC curve of class {0} (area = {1:0.2f})'
         ''.format(i, roc_auc[i]))
plt.plot([0, 1], [0, 1], 'k--', lw=lw)
plt.xlim([0.0, 1.0])
plt.ylim([0.0, 1.05])
plt.xlabel('False Positive Rate')
plt.ylabel('True Positive Rate')
plt.title('Detailed Receiver operating characteristic')
plt.legend(loc="lower right")
plt.show()
```

### 4.3.2 EMG signals in prosthesis control

Myoelectric controlled prostheses are utilized by persons with missing upper limbs and amputations. The EMG signal is recorded from the surface electrodes located on muscles and brought to the prosthesis, where its properties are analyzed and interpreted in order to activate the necessary function. Considering the category of prosthesis, the regulation data goes from simple on/off commands generated by only one muscle to complex multifunction commands generated by an assembly of muscles. The single-muscle regulator is usually based on the EMG amplitude in such a way that muscle contractions of various strengths with various amplitudes can differentiate among hand closing and opening or elbow flexion and extension. A multifunction prosthesis mixes the usage of a couple of electrodes over different muscle assemblies applying advanced signal processing techniques to increase the data amount, which is capable of being extracted relative to the active muscle state. The multifunction prosthesis achieves finer accuracy of the user's intension by analyzing transient signal patterns based on contractions, applying time, frequency, or time-frequency methods. It is crucial to understand that the development of algorithms for prosthetic control is associated with real-time control (Sörnmo & Laguna, 2005). The human hands are significant because they play a crucial role in grasping and manipulating many objects. Even the loss of a single hand affects human activity, and the prosthetic hand is a solution in equipping the armless subject. Muscle signals control hand prostheses, and control is possible after hand amputation because there are a considerable number of muscles in the arm stump to control the prosthesis (Kurzynski, Krysmann, Trajdos, & Wolczowski, 2016) (Subasi, 2019c).

Biomedical signals are the set of body signals that describe a physical variable of interest. Biomedical signals such as surface EMG (sEMG) are used to control the prostheses' movement. Upper limb prosthesis structures are mainly based on myoelectric control, characterizing EMG signals that arise during muscle contraction on the skin surface. Because most of the muscles that produce finger motion are left in the stump after hand amputation, these muscles can be utilized to control the prosthesis (Wojtczak, Amaral, Dias, Wolczowski, & Kurzynski, 2009). As the analysis of EMG signals is used generally in medical diagnostics, sports, rehabilitation, and prosthesis control, the identification of EMG signals presents considerable support for the automation of human tasks. A novel application of sEMG signal classification is the individual skeletal muscle contraction where the related EMG signals are utilized to control a machine action after classification. But the challenge is the prosthetic hand control in which the hand can achieve different movements, thus allowing for movement and even the playing of musical instruments by grasping and manipulating several objects. The loss of a hand lessens the possibility of full human function, and the loss of both hands basically reduces independence. The aim of the prosthetic hand is to relatively reestablish the function of the lost limb, especially its working functions, to be able to enact various movements and to realize different finger configurations. The muscle signals that control the prostheses are associated with healthy hand and finger movements and should be acquired noninvasively by suitable sensors positioned above the muscles on the skin. Therefore, sEMG-controlled prostheses involve a surface signal activated by the hand stump muscles and then the recognition of a category of intended prosthesis action through classification (Subasi, 2019c; Wołczowski & Zdunek, 2017;).

The hand is one of the most crucial components of human beings and is used as a basic element in the sense of feeling. The hand is employed in real-life experiences to feel surfaces and perform basic lifting functions. With a controlled muscle movement, for instance, the basic function of the arm is to grip, lift, wave, and perform other rotation motions of the arm. For amputees, the prosthesis hand is an artificial device utilized to replace a missing part. The hand prosthesis can be improved and manipulated to perform different functions of the hand. For example, the myoelectric arm utilizes a controlled muscle contraction produced from an electrical charge to transfer and strengthen the control center. In this manner, with a controlled movement, an amputee can perform normal functions of the arm like gripping, feeling, and waving among other hand-related movements (Subasi, 2019c). A general framework for prosthesis control using sEMG signals is shown in Fig. 4.7.

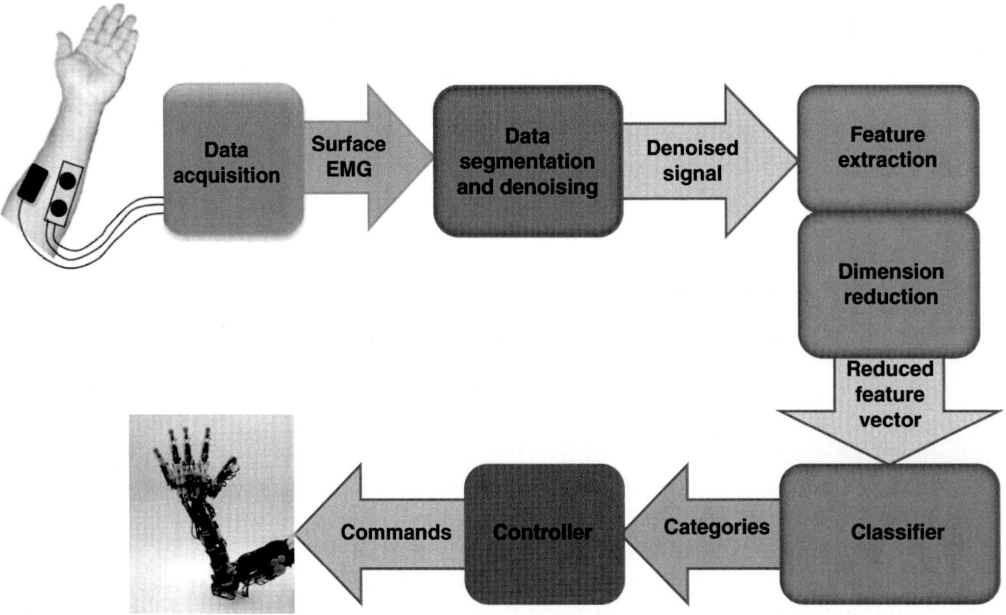


FIGURE 4.7 **A general framework for prosthesis control using sEMG signals.** *Source: Adapted from Subasi (2019b).*

## Example 4.6

The following Python code is used to extract features from sEMG signals using wavelet packed decomposition (WPD) and employs statistical values of WPD sub-bands. Then it classifies these data using multilayer perceptron classifier employing training and testing datasets. The classification accuracy, precision, recall, F1 score, Cohen kappa score, and Matthews correlation coefficient are calculated. The classification report and confusion matrix are also given. For this example, surface EMG for basic hand movements dataset will be used.

***Dataset information:*** The data were sampled at 500 Hz, band-pass filtered using a Butterworth Band Pass filter with low and high cutoff at 15 Hz and 500 Hz respectively, and a notch filter at 50 Hz to eliminate line interference artifacts. The signal was recorded from two differential EMG sensors, and the signals were conducted to a two-channel EMG system by Delsys Bagnoli Handheld EMG Systems. The experiments include freely and repeatedly grasping different items that were crucial to conducting hand movements. The force and speed were purposely left to the subject's will. There were two forearm surface EMG electrodes—flexor carpi ulnaris and extensor carpi radialis longus and brevis—detained in place by elastic bands, with the reference electrode in the middle, to collect information about muscle activation. Five healthy subjects (two males and three females) of approximately the same age (20 to 22 years old) conducted the six grasps for 30 times each. The measured time is 6 sec. There exists a mat file for each subject. The subjects were required to carry out repeatedly the following six movements that are considered daily hand grasps:

1. Spherical: for holding spherical tools
2. Tip: for holding small tools
3. Palmar: for grasping with palm facing the object
4. Lateral: for holding thin, flat objects
5. Cylindrical: for holding cylindrical tools
6. Hook: for supporting a heavy load

More information can be found in Sapsanis et al. (Sapsanis et al., 2013 Sapsanis, Georgoulas, & Tzes, 2013). You can download the data from the following web site:

https://archive.ics.uci.edu/ml/datasets/sEMG+for+Basic+Hand+movements#

```
"""
Created on Thu May 9 12:18:30 2019
@author: absubasi
"""
#=====================================================================
# Feature extraction using the statistical values of wavelet packet
transform
#=====================================================================
# descriptive statistics
import scipy as sp
import scipy.io as sio
import pywt
import numpy as np
import scipy.stats as stats

wname = pywt.Wavelet('db1')
level=6 #Number of decomposition level
#Load mat file
mat_contents = sio.loadmat('sEMG_UCI_BHM.mat')
sorted(mat_contents.keys())
CYLINDIRICAL=mat_contents['F1_cyl_ch1']
HOOK=mat_contents['F1_hook_ch1']
LATERAL=mat_contents['F1_lat_ch1']
PALMAR=mat_contents['F1_palm_ch1']
SPHERICAL=mat_contents['F1_spher_ch1']
TIP=mat_contents['F1_tip_ch1']
```

```
Labels = [ ] #Empty List For Labels
NofClasses=6 #Number of Classes
Length = 3000; # Length of signal
Nofsignal=30; #Number of Signal for each Class
numrows =83 #Number of features extracted from Wavelet Packet
Decomposition
#Create Empty Array For Features
Extracted_Features=np.ndarray(shape=(NofClasses*Nofsignal,numrows),
dtype=float, order='F')
#=====================================================================
# Feature extraction using the statistical values of wavelet packet
transform
#=====================================================================
def WPD_Feature_Extraction(signal, i, wname, level):
  #Mean Values of each subbands
  wp= pywt.WaveletPacket(signal, wname, mode='symmetric', maxlevel=level)
  Extracted_Features[i,0]=sp.mean(abs(wp['a'].data))
  Extracted_Features[i,1]=sp.mean(abs(wp['aa'].data))
  Extracted_Features[i,2]=sp.mean(abs(wp['aaa'].data))
  Extracted_Features[i,3]=sp.mean(abs(wp['aaaa'].data))
  Extracted_Features[i,4]=sp.mean(abs(wp['aaaaa'].data))
  Extracted_Features[i,5]=sp.mean(abs(wp['aaaaaa'].data))
  Extracted_Features[i,6]=sp.mean(abs(wp['d'].data))
  Extracted_Features[i,7]=sp.mean(abs(wp['dd'].data))
  Extracted_Features[i,8]=sp.mean(abs(wp['ddd'].data))
  Extracted_Features[i,9]=sp.mean(abs(wp['dddd'].data))
  Extracted_Features[i,10]=sp.mean(abs(wp['ddddd'].data))
  Extracted_Features[i,11]=sp.mean(abs(wp['dddddd'].data))
  #Standart Deviation of each subbands
  Extracted_Features[i,12]=sp.std(wp['a'].data)
  Extracted_Features[i,13]=sp.std(wp['aa'].data)
  Extracted_Features[i,14]=sp.std(wp['aaa'].data)
  Extracted_Features[i,15]=sp.std(wp['aaaa'].data)
  Extracted_Features[i,16]=sp.std(wp['aaaaa'].data)
  Extracted_Features[i,17]=sp.std(wp['aaaaaa'].data)
  Extracted_Features[i,18]=sp.std(wp['d'].data)
  Extracted_Features[i,19]=sp.std(wp['dd'].data)
  Extracted_Features[i,20]=sp.std(wp['ddd'].data)
  Extracted_Features[i,21]=sp.std(wp['dddd'].data)
  Extracted_Features[i,22]=sp.std(wp['ddddd'].data)
  Extracted_Features[i,23]=sp.std(wp['dddddd'].data)
  #Median Values of each subbands
```

```
Extracted_Features[i,24]=sp.median(wp['a'].data)
Extracted_Features[i,25]=sp.median(wp['aa'].data)
Extracted_Features[i,26]=sp.median(wp['aaa'].data)
Extracted_Features[i,27]=sp.median(wp['aaaa'].data)
Extracted_Features[i,28]=sp.median(wp['aaaaa'].data)
Extracted_Features[i,29]=sp.median(wp['aaaaaa'].data)
Extracted_Features[i,30]=sp.median(wp['d'].data)
Extracted_Features[i,31]=sp.median(wp['dd'].data)
Extracted_Features[i,32]=sp.median(wp['ddd'].data)
Extracted_Features[i,33]=sp.median(wp['dddd'].data)
Extracted_Features[i,34]=sp.median(wp['ddddd'].data)
Extracted_Features[i,35]=sp.median(wp['dddddd'].data)
#Skewness of each subbands
Extracted_Features[i,36]=stats.skew(wp['a'].data)
Extracted_Features[i,37]=stats.skew(wp['aa'].data)
Extracted_Features[i,38]=stats.skew(wp['aaa'].data)
Extracted_Features[i,39]=stats.skew(wp['aaaa'].data)
Extracted_Features[i,40]=stats.skew(wp['aaaaa'].data)
Extracted_Features[i,41]=stats.skew(wp['aaaaaa'].data)
Extracted_Features[i,42]=stats.skew(wp['d'].data)
Extracted_Features[i,43]=stats.skew(wp['dd'].data)
Extracted_Features[i,44]=stats.skew(wp['ddd'].data)
Extracted_Features[i,45]=stats.skew(wp['dddd'].data)
Extracted_Features[i,46]=stats.skew(wp['ddddd'].data)
Extracted_Features[i,47]=stats.skew(wp['dddddd'].data)
#Kurtosis of each subbands
Extracted_Features[i,48]=stats.kurtosis(wp['a'].data)
Extracted_Features[i,49]=stats.kurtosis(wp['aa'].data)
Extracted_Features[i,50]=stats.kurtosis(wp['aaa'].data)
Extracted_Features[i,51]=stats.kurtosis(wp['aaaa'].data)
Extracted_Features[i,52]=stats.kurtosis(wp['aaaaa'].data)
Extracted_Features[i,53]=stats.kurtosis(wp['aaaaaa'].data)
Extracted_Features[i,54]=stats.kurtosis(wp['d'].data)
Extracted_Features[i,55]=stats.kurtosis(wp['dd'].data)
Extracted_Features[i,56]=stats.kurtosis(wp['ddd'].data)
Extracted_Features[i,57]=stats.kurtosis(wp['dddd'].data)
Extracted_Features[i,58]=stats.kurtosis(wp['ddddd'].data)
Extracted_Features[i,59]=stats.kurtosis(wp['dddddd'].data)
#RMS Values of each subbands
Extracted_Features[i,60]=np.sqrt(np.mean(wp['a'].data**2))
Extracted_Features[i,61]=np.sqrt(np.mean(wp['aa'].data**2))
Extracted_Features[i,62]=np.sqrt(np.mean(wp['aaa'].data**2))
```

```
    Extracted_Features[i,63]=np.sqrt(np.mean(wp['aaaa'].data**2))
    Extracted_Features[i,64]=np.sqrt(np.mean(wp['aaaaa'].data**2))
    Extracted_Features[i,65]=np.sqrt(np.mean(wp['aaaaaa'].data**2))
    Extracted_Features[i,66]=np.sqrt(np.mean(wp['d'].data**2))
    Extracted_Features[i,67]=np.sqrt(np.mean(wp['dd'].data**2))
    Extracted_Features[i,68]=np.sqrt(np.mean(wp['ddd'].data**2))
    Extracted_Features[i,69]=np.sqrt(np.mean(wp['dddd'].data**2))
    Extracted_Features[i,70]=np.sqrt(np.mean(wp['ddddd'].data**2))
    Extracted_Features[i,71]=np.sqrt(np.mean(wp['dddddd'].data**2))
    #Ratio of subbands
    Extracted_Features[i,72]=sp.mean(abs(wp['a'].data))/sp.mean(abs
    (wp['aa'].data))
    Extracted_Features[i,73]=sp.mean(abs(wp['aa'].data))/sp.mean(abs(wp
    ['aaa'].data))
    Extracted_Features[i,74]=sp.mean(abs(wp['aaa'].data))/sp.mean(abs
    (wp['aaaa'].data))
    Extracted_Features[i,75]=sp.mean(abs(wp['aaaa'].data))/sp.mean(abs(wp
    ['aaaaa'].data))
    Extracted_Features[i,76]=sp.mean(abs(wp['aaaaa'].data))/sp.mean(abs
    (wp['aaaaaa'].data))
    Extracted_Features[i,77]=sp.mean(abs(wp['aaaaaa'].data))/sp.mean(abs
    (wp['d'].data))
    Extracted_Features[i,78]=sp.mean(abs(wp['d'].data))/sp.mean(abs
    (wp['dd'].data))
    Extracted_Features[i,79]=sp.mean(abs(wp['dd'].data))/sp.mean(abs(wp
    ['ddd'].data))
    Extracted_Features[i,80]=sp.mean(abs(wp['ddd'].data))/sp.mean(abs(wp
    ['dddd'].data))
    Extracted_Features[i,81]=sp.mean(abs(wp['dddd'].data))/sp.mean(abs
    (wp['ddddd'].data))
    Extracted_Features[i,82]=sp.mean(abs(wp['ddddd'].data))/sp.mean(abs(wp
    ['dddddd'].data))

#%%
# ====================================================================
# Feature extraction from cylindirical sEMG signal
# ====================================================================
for i in range(Nofsignal):
    WPD_Feature_Extraction(CYLINDIRICAL[i,:], i, wname, level)
    Labels.append("CYLINDIRICAL")
# ====================================================================
# Feature extraction from hook sEMG signal
# ====================================================================
```

```
for i in range(Nofsignal, 2*Nofsignal):
  WPD_Feature_Extraction(HOOK[i-Nofsignal,:], i, wname, level)
  Labels.append("HOOK")
#=========================================================================
# Feature extraction from lateral sEMG signal
#=========================================================================
for i in range(2*Nofsignal, 3*Nofsignal):
  WPD_Feature_Extraction(LATERAL[i-2*Nofsignal,:], i, wname, level)
  Labels.append("LATERAL")
#=========================================================================
# Feature extraction from palmar sEMG signal
#=========================================================================
for i in range(3*Nofsignal, 4*Nofsignal):
  WPD_Feature_Extraction(PALMAR[i-3*Nofsignal,:], i, wname, level)
  Labels.append("PALMAR")
#=========================================================================
# Feature extraction from spherical sEMG signal
#=========================================================================
for i in range(4*Nofsignal, 5*Nofsignal):
  WPD_Feature_Extraction(SPHERICAL[i-4*Nofsignal,:], i, wname, level)
  Labels.append("SPHERICAL")
#=========================================================================
# Feature extraction from tip sEMG signal
#=========================================================================
for i in range(5*Nofsignal, 6*Nofsignal):
  WPD_Feature_Extraction(TIP[i-5*Nofsignal,:], i, wname, level)
  Labels.append("TIP")
#%%
#=========================================================================
# Classification
#=========================================================================
from sklearn.model_selection import cross_val_score
from sklearn.metrics import cohen_kappa_score, make_scorer
X = Extracted_Features
y = Labels
#To prevent warnings
import warnings
warnings.filterwarnings("ignore")
# Import train_test_split function
from sklearn.model_selection import train_test_split
# Split dataset into training set and test set
# 70% training and 30% test
Xtrain, Xtest, ytrain, ytest = train_test_split(X, y,test_size=0.3,
random_state=1)
```

```
#%%
from sklearn.neural_network import MLPClassifier
#Create Train and Test set
Xtrain, Xtest, ytrain, ytest = train_test_split(X, y, test_size=0.3,
random_state=1)
"""mlp=MLPClassifier(hidden_layer_sizes=(100,     ),     activation='relu',
solver='adam',
         alpha=0.0001, batch_size='auto', learning_rate='constant',
         learning_rate_init=0.001, power_t=0.5, max_iter=200,
         shuffle=True, random_state=None, tol=0.0001, verbose=False,
         warm_start=False, momentum=0.9, nesterovs_momentum=True,
         early_stopping=False, validation_fraction=0.1, beta_1=0.9,
         beta_2=0.999, epsilon=1e-08, n_iter_no_change=10)"""
#Create the Model
mlp = MLPClassifier(hidden_layer_sizes=(50, ), learning_rate_init=0.001,
          alpha=1, momentum=0.7,max_iter=1000)
#Train the Model with Training dataset
mlp.fit(Xtrain,ytrain)
#Test the Model with Testing dataset
ypred = mlp.predict(Xtest)
#Evaluate the Model and Print Performance Metrics
from sklearn import metrics
print('Accuracy:', np.round(metrics.accuracy_score(ytest,ypred),4))
print('Precision:', np.round(metrics.precision_score(ytest,
                    ypred,average='weighted'),4))
print('Recall:', np.round(metrics.recall_score(ytest,ypred,
                              average='weighted'),4))
print('F1 Score:', np.round(metrics.f1_score(ytest,ypred,
                              average='weighted'),4))
print('Cohen Kappa Score:', np.round(metrics.cohen_kappa_score(ytest,
ypred),4))
print('Matthews Corrcoef:', np.round(metrics.matthews_corrcoef(ytest,
ypred),4))
print('\t\tClassification Report:\n', metrics.classification_report(ypred,
ytest))
#Plot Confusion Matrix
from sklearn.metrics import confusion_matrix
print("Confusion Matrix:\n",confusion_matrix(ytest, ypred))
```

### 4.3.3 EMG signals in rehabilitation robotics

EMG-controlled assistive devices are also used for stroke treatment in intensive therapy environments to help rehabilitation. In such cases, patients' activity goals can be achieved using the sEMG (Lum, Burgar, Shor, Majmundar, & Van der Loos, 2002; Riener, Nef, & Colombo, 2005). With recent technological improvements, active exoskeleton robots assist rehabilitation applications, human power augmentation, assistive robotics, impairment evaluation, and haptic communication in virtual and teleoperated environments. Human body commands must be understood by these robots in order to assist humans. Therefore EMG signals should be acquired and analyzed for control of the exoskeleton robot (Sasaki et al., 2005). Exoskeleton robots have two controllers working together simultaneously—the robot controller and the human muscle. Upper-limb exoskeleton robots need to be controlled differently than conventional industrial and field robots because humans operate the commands, and the control system employs these commands as part of its decision-making components. The exoskeleton accurately implements the real-life decisions of the human operator. However, there are still challenges to making decisions based on the motion-intention identifications of the robot user (Abdullah, Subasi, & Qaisar, 2017; Subasi, 2019c).

The best approach to designing an upper-limb exoskeleton robot controller is to focus on the controller input information. In modern techniques, the input consists of human biomedical signals and platform-independent control signals. Various strategies are applied in different fields of applications. The EMG signals have been successfully used as human biomedical signal inputs to some exoskeleton developments like upper-limb exoskeleton robots (Lo & Xie, 2012). For example, in Gopura et al. (2009), muscle models based on EMG control are proposed to control an upper-limb exoskeleton robot with seven degrees of freedom. The user can adapt the method. Most upper-limb-disabled people can operate it. Control methods for upper-limb exoskeleton robots using EMG are mostly of binary (on–off) nature (Lenzi et al., 2009). A good design would allow a high accuracy of the motion-intentions classification for even a physically weak person who cannot properly generate daily motions (Abdullah et al., 2017; Subasi, 2019c).

#### Example 4.7

The following Python code is used to extract features from sEMG signals related to various physical actions using WPD and employing statistical values of WPD sub-bands. Then it classifies these data using random forest classifier with separate training and testing datasets. The classification accuracy, precision, recall, F1 score, Cohen kappa score, and Matthews correlation coefficient are calculated. The classification report and confusion matrix are also given. For this example, surface EMG physical action dataset will be used.

***Dataset information:*** One female and three male subjects (age 25 to 30), who have experienced aggression in circumstances such as physical fighting, are employed in the experiment. Every subject has to implement 10 normal and 10 aggressive activities through 20 distinct experiments. The Essex robot arena was the main experimental hall in which data collection took place. The subjects' performance has been collected by the Delsys EMG apparatus, interfacing human activity with myoelectrical contractions. Based on this context, the data recording procedure included eight skin-surface electrodes located on the upper arms (biceps and triceps) and upper legs (thighs and hamstrings). The eight electrodes corresponds to each muscle channel produce eight input time series. Each time series contains ~10,000 samples (~15 actions per experimental session for each subject). You can download the data from the following web site:https://archive.ics.uci.edu/ml/datasets/EMG+Physical+Action+Data+Set

```
  """
Created on Thu May 9 12:18:30 2019
@author: absubasi
"""
#============================================================================
# Feature extraction using the statistical values of wavelet packet transform
#============================================================================
# descriptive statistics
import scipy as sp
import scipy.io as sio
import pywt
import numpy as np
import scipy.stats as stats

wname = pywt.Wavelet('db1')
level=6 #Number of decomposition level
#Load mat file
mat_contents = sio.loadmat('sEMG_UCI_PA_NOR.mat')
sorted(mat_contents.keys())
BOWING=mat_contents['Bow']
CLAPPING=mat_contents['Cla']
HANDSHAKING=mat_contents['Han']
HUGGING=mat_contents['Hug']
JUMPING=mat_contents['Jum']
RUNNING=mat_contents['Run']
SEATING=mat_contents['Sea']
STANDING=mat_contents['Sta']
WALKING=mat_contents['Wal']
WAVING=mat_contents['Wav']
Labels = [] #Empty List For Labels
NofClasses=10 #Number of Classes
Length = 512; # Length of signal
Nofsignal=72; #Number of Signal for each Class
Ch=1 #Channel To be used
numrows =83 #Number of features extracted from Wavelet Packet Decomposition
```

```
#Create Empty Array For Features
Extracted_Features=np.ndarray(shape=(NofClasses*Nofsignal,numrows),
dtype=float, order='F')
#=====================================================================
# Utility function for feature extraction using the statistical values
of WPD
#=====================================================================
def WPD_Feature_Extraction(signal, i, wname, level):
  #Mean Values of each subbands
  wp= pywt.WaveletPacket(signal, wname, mode='symmetric', maxlevel=level)
  Extracted_Features[i,0]=sp.mean(abs(wp['a'].data))
  Extracted_Features[i,1]=sp.mean(abs(wp['aa'].data))
  Extracted_Features[i,2]=sp.mean(abs(wp['aaa'].data))
  Extracted_Features[i,3]=sp.mean(abs(wp['aaaa'].data))
  Extracted_Features[i,4]=sp.mean(abs(wp['aaaaa'].data))
  Extracted_Features[i,5]=sp.mean(abs(wp['aaaaaa'].data))
  Extracted_Features[i,6]=sp.mean(abs(wp['d'].data))
  Extracted_Features[i,7]=sp.mean(abs(wp['dd'].data))
  Extracted_Features[i,8]=sp.mean(abs(wp['ddd'].data))
  Extracted_Features[i,9]=sp.mean(abs(wp['dddd'].data))
  Extracted_Features[i,10]=sp.mean(abs(wp['ddddd'].data))
  Extracted_Features[i,11]=sp.mean(abs(wp['dddddd'].data))
  #Standart Deviation of each subbands
  Extracted_Features[i,12]=sp.std(wp['a'].data)
  Extracted_Features[i,13]=sp.std(wp['aa'].data)
  Extracted_Features[i,14]=sp.std(wp['aaa'].data)
  Extracted_Features[i,15]=sp.std(wp['aaaa'].data)
  Extracted_Features[i,16]=sp.std(wp['aaaaa'].data)
  Extracted_Features[i,17]=sp.std(wp['aaaaaa'].data)
  Extracted_Features[i,18]=sp.std(wp['d'].data)
  Extracted_Features[i,19]=sp.std(wp['dd'].data)
  Extracted_Features[i,20]=sp.std(wp['ddd'].data)
  Extracted_Features[i,21]=sp.std(wp['dddd'].data)
  Extracted_Features[i,22]=sp.std(wp['ddddd'].data)
  Extracted_Features[i,23]=sp.std(wp['dddddd'].data)
  #Median Values of each subbands
  Extracted_Features[i,24]=sp.median(wp['a'].data)
  Extracted_Features[i,25]=sp.median(wp['aa'].data)
  Extracted_Features[i,26]=sp.median(wp['aaa'].data)
  Extracted_Features[i,27]=sp.median(wp['aaaa'].data)
  Extracted_Features[i,28]=sp.median(wp['aaaaa'].data)
  Extracted_Features[i,29]=sp.median(wp['aaaaaa'].data)
  Extracted_Features[i,30]=sp.median(wp['d'].data)
```

```
Extracted_Features[i,31]=sp.median(wp['dd'].data)
Extracted_Features[i,32]=sp.median(wp['ddd'].data)
Extracted_Features[i,33]=sp.median(wp['dddd'].data)
Extracted_Features[i,34]=sp.median(wp['ddddd'].data)
Extracted_Features[i,35]=sp.median(wp['dddddd'].data)
#Skewness of each subbands
Extracted_Features[i,36]=stats.skew(wp['a'].data)
Extracted_Features[i,37]=stats.skew(wp['aa'].data)
Extracted_Features[i,38]=stats.skew(wp['aaa'].data)
Extracted_Features[i,39]=stats.skew(wp['aaaa'].data)
Extracted_Features[i,40]=stats.skew(wp['aaaaa'].data)
Extracted_Features[i,41]=stats.skew(wp['aaaaaa'].data)
Extracted_Features[i,42]=stats.skew(wp['d'].data)
Extracted_Features[i,43]=stats.skew(wp['dd'].data)
Extracted_Features[i,44]=stats.skew(wp['ddd'].data)
Extracted_Features[i,45]=stats.skew(wp['dddd'].data)
Extracted_Features[i,46]=stats.skew(wp['ddddd'].data)
Extracted_Features[i,47]=stats.skew(wp['dddddd'].data)
#Kurtosis of each subbands
Extracted_Features[i,48]=stats.kurtosis(wp['a'].data)
Extracted_Features[i,49]=stats.kurtosis(wp['aa'].data)
Extracted_Features[i,50]=stats.kurtosis(wp['aaa'].data)
Extracted_Features[i,51]=stats.kurtosis(wp['aaaa'].data)
Extracted_Features[i,52]=stats.kurtosis(wp['aaaaa'].data)
Extracted_Features[i,53]=stats.kurtosis(wp['aaaaaa'].data)
Extracted_Features[i,54]=stats.kurtosis(wp['d'].data)
Extracted_Features[i,55]=stats.kurtosis(wp['dd'].data)
Extracted_Features[i,56]=stats.kurtosis(wp['ddd'].data)
Extracted_Features[i,57]=stats.kurtosis(wp['dddd'].data)
Extracted_Features[i,58]=stats.kurtosis(wp['ddddd'].data)
Extracted_Features[i,59]=stats.kurtosis(wp['dddddd'].data)
#RMS Values of each subbands
Extracted_Features[i,60]=np.sqrt(np.mean(wp['a'].data**2))
Extracted_Features[i,61]=np.sqrt(np.mean(wp['aa'].data**2))
Extracted_Features[i,62]=np.sqrt(np.mean(wp['aaa'].data**2))
Extracted_Features[i,63]=np.sqrt(np.mean(wp['aaaa'].data**2))
Extracted_Features[i,64]=np.sqrt(np.mean(wp['aaaaa'].data**2))
Extracted_Features[i,65]=np.sqrt(np.mean(wp['aaaaaa'].data**2))
Extracted_Features[i,66]=np.sqrt(np.mean(wp['d'].data**2))
Extracted_Features[i,67]=np.sqrt(np.mean(wp['dd'].data**2))
Extracted_Features[i,68]=np.sqrt(np.mean(wp['ddd'].data**2))
Extracted_Features[i,69]=np.sqrt(np.mean(wp['dddd'].data**2))
```

```
    Extracted_Features[i,70]=np.sqrt(np.mean(wp['ddddd'].data**2))
    Extracted_Features[i,71]=np.sqrt(np.mean(wp['dddddd'].data**2))
    #Ratio of subbands
    Extracted_Features[i,72]=sp.mean(abs(wp['a'].data))/sp.mean(abs
    (wp['aa'].data))
    Extracted_Features[i,73]=sp.mean(abs(wp['aa'].data))/sp.mean(abs
    (wp['aaa'].data))
    Extracted_Features[i,74]=sp.mean(abs(wp['aaa'].data))/sp.mean(abs
    (wp['aaaa'].data))
    Extracted_Features[i,75]=sp.mean(abs(wp['aaaa'].data))/sp.mean(abs(wp
    ['aaaaa'].data))
    Extracted_Features[i,76]=sp.mean(abs(wp['aaaaa'].data))/sp.mean(abs
    (wp['aaaaaa'].data))
    Extracted_Features[i,77]=sp.mean(abs(wp['aaaaaa'].data))/sp.mean(abs
    (wp['d'].data))
    Extracted_Features[i,78]=sp.mean(abs(wp['d'].data))/sp.mean(abs(wp
    ['dd'].data))
    Extracted_Features[i,79]=sp.mean(abs(wp['dd'].data))/sp.mean(abs
    (wp['ddd'].data))
    Extracted_Features[i,80]=sp.mean(abs(wp['ddd'].data))/sp.mean(abs(wp
    ['dddd'].data))
    Extracted_Features[i,81]=sp.mean(abs(wp['dddd'].data))/sp.mean(abs
    (wp['ddddd'].data))
    Extracted_Features[i,82]=sp.mean(abs(wp['ddddd'].data))/sp.mean(abs(wp
    ['dddddd'].data))
#%%
# ============================================================================
# Feature extraction from bowing sEMG signal
# ============================================================================
for i in range(Nofsignal):
  WPD_Feature_Extraction(BOWING[i,:, Ch], i, wname, level)
  Labels.append("BOWING")
# ============================================================================
# Feature extraction from clapping sEMG signal
# ============================================================================
for i in range(Nofsignal, 2*Nofsignal):
  WPD_Feature_Extraction(CLAPPING[i-Nofsignal,:, Ch], i, wname, level)
  Labels.append("CLAPPING")
# ============================================================================
# Feature extraction from handshaking sEMG signal
# ============================================================================
```

```
for i in range(2*Nofsignal, 3*Nofsignal):
  WPD_Feature_Extraction(HANDSHAKING[i-2*Nofsignal,:,Ch], i, wname, level)
  Labels.append("HANDSHAKING")
#=========================================================================
# Feature extraction from hugging sEMG signal
#=========================================================================
for i in range(3*Nofsignal, 4*Nofsignal):
  WPD_Feature_Extraction(HUGGING[i-3*Nofsignal,:, Ch], i, wname, level)
  Labels.append("HUGGING")
#=========================================================================
# Feature extraction from jumping sEMG signal
#=========================================================================
for i in range(4*Nofsignal, 5*Nofsignal):
  WPD_Feature_Extraction(JUMPING[i-4*Nofsignal,:,Ch], i, wname, level)
  Labels.append("JUMPING")
#=========================================================================
# Feature extraction from running sEMG signal
#=========================================================================
for i in range(5*Nofsignal, 6*Nofsignal):
  WPD_Feature_Extraction(RUNNING[i-5*Nofsignal,:,Ch], i, wname, level)
  Labels.append("RUNNING")
#=========================================================================
# Feature extraction from seating sEMG signal
#=========================================================================
for i in range(6*Nofsignal, 7*Nofsignal):
  WPD_Feature_Extraction(SEATING[i-6*Nofsignal,:,Ch], i, wname, level)
  Labels.append("SEATING")
#=========================================================================
# Feature extraction from standing sEMG signal
#=========================================================================
for i in range(7*Nofsignal, 8*Nofsignal):
  WPD_Feature_Extraction(STANDING[i-7*Nofsignal,:,Ch], i, wname, level)
  Labels.append("STANDING")
#=========================================================================
# Feature extraction from walking sEMG signal
#=========================================================================
for i in range(8*Nofsignal, 9*Nofsignal):
  WPD_Feature_Extraction(WALKING[i-8*Nofsignal,:,Ch], i, wname, level)
  Labels.append("WALKING")
#=========================================================================
# Feature extraction from waving sEMG signal
#=========================================================================
```

```
for i in range(9*Nofsignal, 10*Nofsignal):
  WPD_Feature_Extraction(WAVING[i-9*Nofsignal,:,Ch], i, wname, level)
  Labels.append("WAVING")
#%%
# ===========================================================================
# Classification
# ===========================================================================
from sklearn.model_selection import cross_val_score
from sklearn.metrics import cohen_kappa_score, make_scorer
X = Extracted_Features
y = Labels

#To prevent warnings
import warnings
warnings.filterwarnings("ignore")
# Import train_test_split function
from sklearn.model_selection import train_test_split
# Split dataset into training set and test set
# 70% training and 30% test
Xtrain, Xtest, ytrain, ytest = train_test_split(X, y,test_size=0.3,
random_state=1)
#%%
# ===========================================================================
# Random forest example with training and test set
# ===========================================================================
from sklearn.ensemble import RandomForestClassifier

#In order to change to accuracy increase n_estimators
"""RandomForestClassifier(n_estimators='warn',   criterion='gini',   max_
depth=None,
min_samples_split=2, min_samples_leaf=1, min_weight_fraction_leaf=0.0,
max_features='auto', max_leaf_nodes=None, min_impurity_decrease=0.0,
min_impurity_split=None, bootstrap=True, oob_score=False, n_jobs=None,
random_state=None, verbose=0, warm_start=False, class_weight=None)"""
clf = RandomForestClassifier(n_estimators=200)
#Create the Model
#Train the model with Training Dataset
clf.fit(Xtrain,ytrain)
#Test the model with Testset
ypred = clf.predict(Xtest)

#Evaluate the Model and Print Performance Metrics
from sklearn import metrics
```

```
print('Accuracy:', np.round(metrics.accuracy_score(ytest,ypred),4))
print('Precision:', np.round(metrics.precision_score(ytest,
                   ypred,average='weighted'),4))
print('Recall:', np.round(metrics.recall_score(ytest,ypred,
                             average='weighted'),4))
print('F1 Score:', np.round(metrics.f1_score(ytest,ypred,
                             average='weighted'),4))
print('Cohen Kappa Score:', np.round(metrics.cohen_kappa_score(ytest,
ypred),4))
print('Matthews Corrcoef:', np.round(metrics.matthews_corrcoef(ytest,
ypred),4))
print('\t\tClassification Report:\n', metrics.classification_report(ypred,
ytest))

#Plot Confusion Matrix
from sklearn.metrics import confusion_matrix
print("Confusion Matrix:\n",confusion_matrix(ytest, ypred))
```

## 4.4 ECG signal analysis

The electrocardiogram (ECG) is the recording of electrical activities on the body surface that originated from the heart. With the aim of tracing an ECG waveform, a differential recording among two points on the body surface is performed. Conventionally, every differential recording is called a lead. Einthoven defined three leads named by the Roman numerals I, II, and III. The voltage difference from any two sites are recorded by an ECG. The ECG signals are usually in the range of ±2 mV and need a recording bandwidth of 0.05 to 150 Hz. The 12-lead ECGs are used in limited-mode recording events such as tape-recorded ambulatory ECG (typically two leads), intensive care monitoring at the bedside (typically one or two leads), or unrestrained patients telemetered throughout regions of the hospital (one lead). The modern ECG equipment is completely integrated with an analog front end, a 12- to 16-bit analog-to-digital (A/D) converter, a computational microprocessor, and dedicated input–output (I/O) processors. These systems find a dimension matrix derived from the 12 lead signals and examine this matrix using a set of rules to attain the final set of interpretive statements. The better hospital-based system will record these changes and keep a big database of all ECGs accessible by any combination of parameters, for example, all females older than age 30 with an inferior congenital heart disease (Berbari, 2000; Subasi, 2019c).

There are many demonstrative approaches in which a specific diagnosis is made for every ECG, but there are only about five or six major classification sets for which the ECG is employed. The initial step in ECG analysis requires computation of the rate and rhythm for the atria and ventricles. This includes any conduction instability either in the connection among the different chambers or within the chambers themselves. Then feature identification, which would be connected to the presence or absence of scarring due to a myocardial infarction, would be performed. The ECG has been a principal method for evaluating chamber size or growth, but one might argue that more precise data in this area could be obtained by noninvasive imaging technologies (Berbari, 2000; Subasi, 2019c). A general framework for the ECG signals classification is shown in Fig. 4.8.

## 4.4.1 Diagnosis of heart arrhythmia

Cardiovascular disorders (CVDs) are one of the main causes of death worldwide. The design of exact and rapid techniques for automated ECG heartbeat signal classification is vital for clinical diagnosis of various CVDs (Thaler, 2017), such as an arrhythmia. Arrhythmias characterize a group of situations in which irregular electrical activities are coming from heart and are recognized by ECG beats or patterns (De Chazal, O'Dwyer, & Reilly, 2004; Pan & Tompkins, 1985). ECG is an efficient, simple, noninvasive technique for heart disease detection. Medical doctors examine several waveforms based on their characteristics (amplitude, polarity, etc.) and diagnose and treat based on this investigation (Subasi, 2019c).

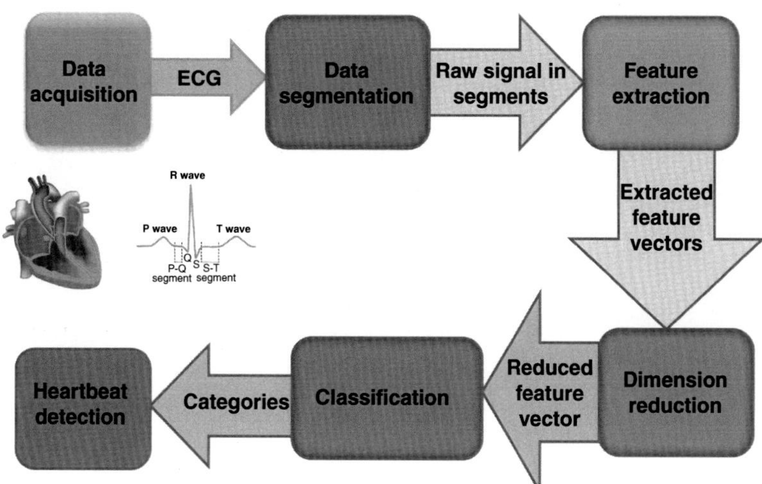


FIGURE 4.8 A general framework for ECG signal classification.

## Example 4.8

The following Python code is used to extract features from the normal atrial premature complexes (APCs), premature ventricular contractions (PCVs), left bundle branch blocks (LBBBs), and right bundle branch blocks (RBBBs) ECG signals employ stationary wavelet transform (SWT) and statistical values of SWT sub-bands. Then it classifies these data using random forest (RF) with separate training and testing datasets. The classification accuracy, precision, recall, F1 score, Cohen kappa score, and Matthews correlation coefficient are calculated. The classification report and confusion matrix are also given.

***Dataset information:*** Boston's Beth Israel Hospital and MIT have maintained a study on arrhythmia analysis and related subjects. One of the first chief achievements of this effort was the MIT-BIH Arrhythmia Database, which started distributing in 1980. The database was the first publicly accessible dataset of standard test material for the assessment of arrhythmia detectors and has been employed for this aim as well as for basic research into cardiac dynamics at more than 500 sites worldwide. The MIT-BIH Arrhythmia Database includes 48 half-hour extracts of two-channel ambulatory ECG recordings, taken from 47 subjects studied by the BIH Arrhythmia Laboratory between 1975 and 1979. Twenty-three signals were selected randomly from a set of 4000 24-hour ambulatory ECG signals recorded from a mixed population of inpatients (about 60%) and outpatients (about 40%) at Boston's Beth Israel Hospital; the remaining 25 recordings were chosen from the same set to contain less common but clinically important arrhythmias that would not be well-represented in a small random sample. The ECG signals were sampled at 360 Hz per channel with 11-bit resolution over a 10 mV range. Two or more cardiologists individually interpreted each record; disagreements were resolved to obtain computer-readable reference annotations for each beat (approximately 110,000 annotations in all) included with the database. This dataset contains many arrythmia types, including atrial premature complexes (APC), premature ventricular contractions (PVC), left bundle branch block (LBBB), and right bundle branch block (RBBB). The entire MIT-BIH Arrhythmia Database has been freely accessible since PhysioNet's inception in September 1999. You can download the data from the following website:

https://www.physionet.org/physiobank/database/mitdb/

```
"""
Created on Thu May 9 12:18:30 2019
@author: asubasi
"""
#=====================================================================
# Feature extraction using the statistical values of wavelet packet
transform
#=====================================================================
# descriptive statistics
import scipy as sp
import scipy.io as sio
import pywt
import numpy as np
import scipy.stats as stats

wname = pywt.Wavelet('db1')
```

```
level=6 #Number of decomposition level
#Load mat file
mat_contents = sio.loadmat('MITBIH_ECG.mat')
sorted(mat_contents.keys())
ECGN=mat_contents['ECGN']
ECGAPC=mat_contents['ECGAPC']
ECGPVC=mat_contents['ECGPVC']
ECGLBBB=mat_contents['ECGLBBB']
ECGRBBB=mat_contents['ECGRBBB']

Labels = [] #Empty List For Labels
NofClasses=5 #Number of Classes
Length = 320; # Length of signal
Nofsignal=300; #Number of Signal for each Class
numrows =83 #Number of features extracted from Wavelet Packet Decomposi-
tion
#Create Empty Array For Features
Extracted_Features=np.ndarray(shape=(NofClasses*Nofsignal,numrows),
dtype=float, order='F')
#=====================================================================
# Utility function for feature extraction using the statistical values
of WPD
#=====================================================================
def WPD_Feature_Extraction(signal, i, wname, level):
  #Mean Values of each subbands
  wp= pywt.WaveletPacket(signal, wname, mode='symmetric', maxlevel=level)
  Extracted_Features[i,0]=sp.mean(abs(wp['a'].data))
  Extracted_Features[i,1]=sp.mean(abs(wp['aa'].data))
  Extracted_Features[i,2]=sp.mean(abs(wp['aaa'].data))
  Extracted_Features[i,3]=sp.mean(abs(wp['aaaa'].data))
  Extracted_Features[i,4]=sp.mean(abs(wp['aaaaa'].data))
  Extracted_Features[i,5]=sp.mean(abs(wp['aaaaaa'].data))
  Extracted_Features[i,6]=sp.mean(abs(wp['d'].data))
  Extracted_Features[i,7]=sp.mean(abs(wp['dd'].data))
  Extracted_Features[i,8]=sp.mean(abs(wp['ddd'].data))
  Extracted_Features[i,9]=sp.mean(abs(wp['dddd'].data))
  Extracted_Features[i,10]=sp.mean(abs(wp['ddddd'].data))
  Extracted_Features[i,11]=sp.mean(abs(wp['dddddd'].data))
  #Standart Deviation of each subbands
  Extracted_Features[i,12]=sp.std(wp['a'].data)
  Extracted_Features[i,13]=sp.std(wp['aa'].data)
  Extracted_Features[i,14]=sp.std(wp['aaa'].data)
  Extracted_Features[i,15]=sp.std(wp['aaaa'].data)
  Extracted_Features[i,16]=sp.std(wp['aaaaa'].data)
```

```
Extracted_Features[i,17]=sp.std(wp['aaaaaa'].data)
Extracted_Features[i,18]=sp.std(wp['d'].data)
Extracted_Features[i,19]=sp.std(wp['dd'].data)
Extracted_Features[i,20]=sp.std(wp['ddd'].data)
Extracted_Features[i,21]=sp.std(wp['dddd'].data)
Extracted_Features[i,22]=sp.std(wp['ddddd'].data)
Extracted_Features[i,23]=sp.std(wp['dddddd'].data)
#Median Values of each subbands
Extracted_Features[i,24]=sp.median(wp['a'].data)
Extracted_Features[i,25]=sp.median(wp['aa'].data)
Extracted_Features[i,26]=sp.median(wp['aaa'].data)
Extracted_Features[i,27]=sp.median(wp['aaaa'].data)
Extracted_Features[i,28]=sp.median(wp['aaaaa'].data)
Extracted_Features[i,29]=sp.median(wp['aaaaaa'].data)
Extracted_Features[i,30]=sp.median(wp['d'].data)
Extracted_Features[i,31]=sp.median(wp['dd'].data)
Extracted_Features[i,32]=sp.median(wp['ddd'].data)
Extracted_Features[i,33]=sp.median(wp['dddd'].data)
Extracted_Features[i,34]=sp.median(wp['ddddd'].data)
Extracted_Features[i,35]=sp.median(wp['dddddd'].data)
#Skewness of each subbands
Extracted_Features[i,36]=stats.skew(wp['a'].data)
Extracted_Features[i,37]=stats.skew(wp['aa'].data)
Extracted_Features[i,38]=stats.skew(wp['aaa'].data)
Extracted_Features[i,39]=stats.skew(wp['aaaa'].data)
Extracted_Features[i,40]=stats.skew(wp['aaaaa'].data)
Extracted_Features[i,41]=stats.skew(wp['aaaaaa'].data)
Extracted_Features[i,42]=stats.skew(wp['d'].data)
Extracted_Features[i,43]=stats.skew(wp['dd'].data)
Extracted_Features[i,44]=stats.skew(wp['ddd'].data)
Extracted_Features[i,45]=stats.skew(wp['dddd'].data)
Extracted_Features[i,46]=stats.skew(wp['ddddd'].data)
Extracted_Features[i,47]=stats.skew(wp['dddddd'].data)
#Kurtosis of each subbands
Extracted_Features[i,48]=stats.kurtosis(wp['a'].data)
Extracted_Features[i,49]=stats.kurtosis(wp['aa'].data)
Extracted_Features[i,50]=stats.kurtosis(wp['aaa'].data)
Extracted_Features[i,51]=stats.kurtosis(wp['aaaa'].data)
Extracted_Features[i,52]=stats.kurtosis(wp['aaaaa'].data)
Extracted_Features[i,53]=stats.kurtosis(wp['aaaaaa'].data)
Extracted_Features[i,54]=stats.kurtosis(wp['d'].data)
Extracted_Features[i,55]=stats.kurtosis(wp['dd'].data)
Extracted_Features[i,56]=stats.kurtosis(wp['ddd'].data)
Extracted_Features[i,57]=stats.kurtosis(wp['dddd'].data)
```

```
    Extracted_Features[i,58]=stats.kurtosis(wp['ddddd'].data)
    Extracted_Features[i,59]=stats.kurtosis(wp['dddddd'].data)
    #RMS Values of each subbands
    Extracted_Features[i,60]=np.sqrt(np.mean(wp['a'].data**2))
    Extracted_Features[i,61]=np.sqrt(np.mean(wp['aa'].data**2))
    Extracted_Features[i,62]=np.sqrt(np.mean(wp['aaa'].data**2))
    Extracted_Features[i,63]=np.sqrt(np.mean(wp['aaaa'].data**2))
    Extracted_Features[i,64]=np.sqrt(np.mean(wp['aaaaa'].data**2))
    Extracted_Features[i,65]=np.sqrt(np.mean(wp['aaaaaa'].data**2))
    Extracted_Features[i,66]=np.sqrt(np.mean(wp['d'].data**2))
    Extracted_Features[i,67]=np.sqrt(np.mean(wp['dd'].data**2))
    Extracted_Features[i,68]=np.sqrt(np.mean(wp['ddd'].data**2))
    Extracted_Features[i,69]=np.sqrt(np.mean(wp['dddd'].data**2))
    Extracted_Features[i,70]=np.sqrt(np.mean(wp['ddddd'].data**2))
    Extracted_Features[i,71]=np.sqrt(np.mean(wp['dddddd'].data**2))
    #Ratio of subbands
    Extracted_Features[i,72]=sp.mean(abs(wp['a'].data))/sp.mean(abs(wp['aa'].
    data))
    Extracted_Features[i,73]=sp.mean(abs(wp['aa'].data))/
    sp.mean(abs(wp['aaa'].data))
    Extracted_Features[i,74]=sp.mean(abs(wp['aaa'].data))/sp.mean(abs
    (wp['aaaa'].data))
    Extracted_Features[i,75]=sp.mean(abs(wp['aaaa'].data))/sp.mean(abs(wp
    ['aaaaa'].data))
    Extracted_Features[i,76]=sp.mean(abs(wp['aaaaa'].data))/sp.mean(abs
    (wp['aaaaaa'].data))
    Extracted_Features[i,77]=sp.mean(abs(wp['aaaaaa'].data))/sp.mean(abs
    (wp['d'].data))
    Extracted_Features[i,78]=sp.mean(abs(wp['d'].data))/sp.mean(abs(wp
    ['dd'].data))
    Extracted_Features[i,79]=sp.mean(abs(wp['dd'].data))/sp.mean(abs
    (wp['ddd'].data))
    Extracted_Features[i,80]=sp.mean(abs(wp['ddd'].data))/sp.mean(abs(wp
    ['dddd'].data))
    Extracted_Features[i,81]=sp.mean(abs(wp['dddd'].data))/sp.mean(abs
    (wp['ddddd'].data))
    Extracted_Features[i,82]=sp.mean(abs(wp['ddddd'].data))/sp.mean(abs
    (wp['dddddd'].data))
#%%
# ===========================================================================
# Feature extraction from normal ECG signal
# ===========================================================================
for i in range(Nofsignal):
    WPD_Feature_Extraction(ECGN[:,i], i, wname, level)
    Labels.append("NORMAL")
```

```
#=====================================================================
# Feature extraction from APC ECG signal
#=====================================================================
for i in range(Nofsignal, 2*Nofsignal):
    WPD_Feature_Extraction(ECGAPC[:,i-Nofsignal], i, wname, level)
    Labels.append("APC")
#=====================================================================
# Feature extraction from PVC ECG signal
#=====================================================================
for i in range(2*Nofsignal, 3*Nofsignal):
    WPD_Feature_Extraction(ECGPVC[:,i-2*Nofsignal], i, wname, level)
    Labels.append("PVC")
#=====================================================================
# Feature extraction from LBBB ECG signal
#=====================================================================
for i in range(3*Nofsignal, 4*Nofsignal):
    WPD_Feature_Extraction(ECGLBBB[:,i-3*Nofsignal], i, wname, level)
    Labels.append("LBBB")
#=====================================================================
# Feature extraction from RBBB ECG signal
#=====================================================================
for i in range(4*Nofsignal, 5*Nofsignal):
    WPD_Feature_Extraction(ECGRBBB[:,i-4*Nofsignal], i, wname, level)
    Labels.append("RBBB")
#%%
#=====================================================================
# Classification using random forest
#=====================================================================
from sklearn.model_selection import cross_val_score
from sklearn.metrics import cohen_kappa_score, make_scorer
from matplotlib import pyplot as plt
#To prevent warnings
import warnings

warnings.filterwarnings("ignore")
X = Extracted_Features
y = Labels

from sklearn.model_selection import train_test_split
# Split dataset into training set and test set
# 70% training and 30% test
Xtrain, Xtest, ytrain, ytest = train_test_split(X, y,test_size=0.3, ran-
dom_state=0)

from sklearn.ensemble import RandomForestClassifier
```

```
#In order to change to accuracy increase n_estimators
"""RandomForestClassifier(n_estimators='warn',   criterion='gini',   max_
depth=None,
min_samples_split=2, min_samples_leaf=1, min_weight_fraction_leaf=0.0,
max_features='auto', max_leaf_nodes=None, min_impurity_decrease=0.0,
min_impurity_split=None, bootstrap=True, oob_score=False, n_jobs=None,
random_state=None, verbose=0, warm_start=False, class_weight=None)"""
clf = RandomForestClassifier(n_estimators=200)
clf.fit(Xtrain,ytrain)
ypred = clf.predict(Xtest)

from sklearn import metrics
print('Accuracy:', np.round(metrics.accuracy_score(ytest,ypred),4))
print('Precision:', np.round(metrics.precision_score(ytest,
                    ypred,average='weighted'),4))
print('Recall:', np.round(metrics.recall_score(ytest,ypred,
                               average='weighted'),4))
print('F1 Score:', np.round(metrics.f1_score(ytest,ypred,
                               average='weighted'),4))
print('Cohen Kappa Score:', np.round(metrics.cohen_kappa_score(ytest,
ypred)))
print('Matthews Corrcoef:', np.round(metrics.matthews_corrcoef(ytest,
ypred)))
print('\t\tClassification Report:\n', metrics.classification_report(ypred,
ytest))

from sklearn.metrics import confusion_matrix
from io import BytesIO #neded for plot
import seaborn as sns; sns.set()

mat = confusion_matrix(ytest, ypred)
sns.heatmap(mat.T, square=True, annot=True, fmt='d', cbar=False)
plt.xlabel('true label')
plt.ylabel('predicted label');

plt.savefig("Confusion.jpg")
# Save SVG in a fake file object.
f = BytesIO()
plt.savefig(f, format="svg")

#%%
"""The following PYTHON code is adapted from Scikit Learn to find the ROC
Area"""
# =====================================================================
# ROC curves for the multiclass problem
```

```
# ===================================================================
import numpy as np
import matplotlib.pyplot as plt
from itertools import cycle
from sklearn.discriminant_analysis import LinearDiscriminantAnalysis
from sklearn import svm
from sklearn.metrics import roc_curve, auc
from sklearn.model_selection import train_test_split
from sklearn.preprocessing import label_binarize
from sklearn.multiclass import OneVsRestClassifier
from scipy import interp
X = Extracted_Features
y = Labels
# Binarize the output
y = label_binarize(y, classes=['NORMAL','APC','PVC', 'LBBB','RBBB' ])
n_classes = y.shape[1]

#%%
# Import train_test_split function
from sklearn.model_selection import train_test_split
# Split dataset into training set and test set
# 70% training and 30% test
random_state = np.random.RandomState(1)
X_train, X_test, y_train, y_test = train_test_split(X, y,test_size=0.3,
random_state=0)
# Learn to predict each class against the other
"""classifier = OneVsRestClassifier(svm.SVC(kernel='linear',
probability=True,
                     random_state=random_state))"""
classifier = OneVsRestClassifier(LinearDiscriminantAnalysis(solver='lsqr',
shrinkage=None))
y_score = classifier.fit(X_train, y_train).decision_function(X_test)

# Compute ROC curve and ROC area for each class
fpr = dict()
tpr = dict()
roc_auc = dict()
for i in range(n_classes):
  fpr[i], tpr[i], _ = roc_curve(y_test[:, i], y_score[:, i])
  roc_auc[i] = auc(fpr[i], tpr[i])

# Compute micro-average ROC curve and ROC area
fpr["micro"], tpr["micro"], _ = roc_curve(y_test.ravel(), y_score.
ravel())
```

```
roc_auc["micro"] = auc(fpr["micro"], tpr["micro"])

##########################################################################
# Plot of a ROC curve for a specific class
plt.figure()
lw = 2
plt.plot(fpr[2], tpr[2], color='darkorange',
      lw=lw, label='ROC curve (area = %0.2f)' % roc_auc[2])
plt.plot([0, 1], [0, 1], color='navy', lw=lw, linestyle='--')
plt.xlim([0.0, 1.0])
plt.ylim([0.0, 1.05])
plt.xlabel('False Positive Rate')
plt.ylabel('True Positive Rate')
plt.title('Receiver operating characteristic')
plt.legend(loc="lower right")
plt.show()

##########################################################################
# Plot ROC curves for the multiclass problem
# Compute macro-average ROC curve and ROC area
# First aggregate all false positive rates
all_fpr = np.unique(np.concatenate([fpr[i] for i in range(n_classes)]))

# Then interpolate all ROC curves at this points
mean_tpr = np.zeros_like(all_fpr)
for i in range(n_classes):
  mean_tpr += interp(all_fpr, fpr[i], tpr[i])
# Finally average it and compute AUC
mean_tpr /= n_classes

fpr["macro"] = all_fpr
tpr["macro"] = mean_tpr
roc_auc["macro"] = auc(fpr["macro"], tpr["macro"])

# Plot all ROC curves
plt.figure()
plt.plot(fpr["micro"], tpr["micro"],
      label='micro-average ROC curve (area = {0:0.2f})'
          ''.format(roc_auc["micro"]),
      color='deeppink', linestyle=':', linewidth=4)

plt.plot(fpr["macro"], tpr["macro"],
      label='macro-average ROC curve (area = {0:0.2f})'
          ''.format(roc_auc["macro"]),
```

```
        color='navy', linestyle=':', linewidth=4)

colors = cycle(['aqua', 'darkorange', 'cornflowerblue'])
for i, color in zip(range(n_classes), colors):
    plt.plot(fpr[i], tpr[i], color=color, lw=lw,
         label='ROC curve of class {0} (area = {1:0.2f})'
         ''.format(i, roc_auc[i]))

plt.plot([0, 1], [0, 1], 'k--', lw=lw)
plt.xlim([0.0, 1.0])
plt.ylim([0.0, 1.05])
plt.xlabel('False Positive Rate')
plt.ylabel('True Positive Rate')
plt.title('Receiver Operating Characteristic to multi-class')
plt.legend(loc="lower right")
plt.show()
```

## 4.5 Human activity recognition

A significant amount of the elderly population endure age-related health problems. These complications, together with the apparently occurring gradual weakening in physical and cognitive capabilities of elderly people, prevent them from living alone. Recent information and communications technology (ICT) advances, along with advancements in smart sensors and smartphones, have brought about a rapid development of smart environments. Smart healthcare seems to be a promising solution to the growing aging population's challenges. To meet the needs of this growing population, smart health services are being offered. In particular, smart healthcare systems monitor and evaluate any critical health condition of the elderly in their daily activities. The smart healthcare structures not only allow the elderly to live independently, but they can also provide more sustainable healthcare services by reducing the burden of the elderly and dependent individuals on the healthcare system. Smart healthcare monitoring systems (SHMSs) have been developed as a brilliant approach for providing smart health services that suit the subjects' real needs. To resolve the different features of these structures, various solutions and approaches have been implemented. The main objective of these solutions is to provide an intelligent environment where the system monitors and analyzes subjects' health conditions and provides them with timely, intelligent health services (Mshali, Lemlouma, Moloney, & Magoni, 2018) (Subasi, Khateeb, Brahimi, & Sarirete, 2020). Fig. 4.9 shows the general framework of an SHMS.

The use of wearable devices brings medical professionals and patients together in modern healthcare systems with intelligent and automatic routine monitoring of elderly people's activity. Smart wearable sensor integration has led to the development of intelligent monitoring systems for healthcare. There is a lot of enthusiasm in this sense about the development of machine learning algorithms that play a significant role in human activity recognition (HAR). An intelligent smart healthcare monitoring system provides an automated human activity recognition by using machine learning methods to model and recognize activities of daily

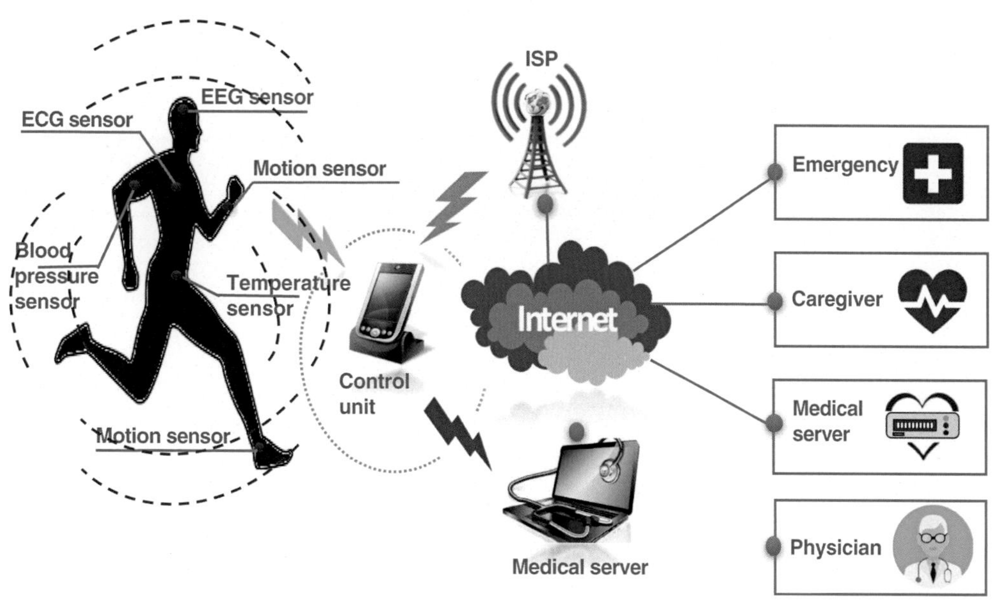


FIGURE 4.9 **The general experimental setup for smart healthcare monitoring systems (SHMS).** *Source: Adapted from Subasi et al. (2020b).*

living (ADL) accurately and effectively. Mobile phone sensors or wearable body sensors can be utilized for reliable and precise human activity recognition (Subasi et al., 2020b).

## 4.5.1 Sensor-based human activity recognition

With the advent of wireless network technologies, wearable body sensors are being increasingly introduced for intelligent daily activity monitoring in various fields, such as emergency assistance, cognitive assistance, and safety (Majumder et al., 2017; Neves, Stachyra, & Rodrigues, 2008). HAR is utilized to identify different human movements and gestures from a collection of observations on the activities of people using wearable sensors. HAR can be employed to obtain the benefits of the wearable sensors. In terms of defining complex activity, often data-driven strategies suffer from portability, extension, and perception issues, whereas knowledge-based solutions for dealing with complex temporal data are often poor (Liu, Peng, Liu, & Huang, 2015). One of the objectives of machine learning is to minimize the large quantities of data so that they simply reflect the entire data without circulation (Xu et al., 2017). With increased availability of wearable devices, the improvement of HAR tools in pervasive computing has attracted attention (Liu et al., 2015). Machine learning algorithms can process information obtained from wearable sensors. Since HAR is a very quickly growing scientific field, it has wide healthcare applications—assisted living, personal fitness assistants, home monitoring, and terrorist detection. In a smart home-healthcare system, HAR technologies could be modified to enhance and establish clinical rehabilitation processes (Hassan, Uddin, Mohamed, & Almogren, 2018). Therefore to provide preventive assistance to elderly people, caregivers could use these devices to monitor and interpret their daily living activity (Liu, Nie, Liu, &

Rosenblum, 2016). This could enable elderly people to stay in their own homes. Yet, sometimes one of the difficulties becomes to more reliably detect everyday life activities (Subasi et al., 2018).

## Example 4.9

The following Python code is used to classify sensor-based human activity recognition (HAR) data using SVM classifiers and employing separate training and testing datasets. The classification accuracy, precision, recall, F1 score, Cohen kappa score, and Matthews correlation coefficient are calculated. The classification report and confusion matrix are also given.

***Dataset information:*** The dataset is downloaded from UCI machine learning repository (UCI, 2018a). The REALDISP (REAListic sensor DISPlacement) dataset was initially collected to investigate the effects of sensor displacement in the activity recognition process in real-world settings. The dataset includes an extensive range of physical activities and sensor modalities. These settings were examined in the dataset recorded employing 9 inertial sensor units from 17 participants considering 33 fitness activities. The dataset contains simple activities that indicate movement of the entire body (e.g., walking or jumping), whereas the others focused on training individual parts. The sampling rate is 50 Hz, which is sufficient for the exercise needs. Eight of the sensors are typically located on the middle of the limb. Another one is located on the back, slightly below the scapulae (Baños et al., 2012; Banos, Toth, Damas, Pomares, & Rojas, 2014). Different sensor displacement settings are employed to evaluate the impact of the activity recognition problem complexity on the robustness of the systems.

The reduced version of the original dataset with seven activities is used in this example. To ensure a fair distribution of the various types of activities recorded for this dataset, exercises that include movement of several parts of the users' body are chosen for the seven activities.

```
"""
REALDISP Activity Recognition IDEAL Dataset
Created on Tue Jun 18 18:14:15 2019
@author: asubasi
"""
from sklearn.model_selection import train_test_split
import numpy as np
import pandas as pd

# load data
dataset = pd.read_csv("REALDISPActivityRecognitionDataset.csv")
# split data into X and Y
X = dataset.iloc[:,0:117]
y = dataset.iloc[:, 117]
class_names = dataset.iloc[:, 117]
# split data into train and test sets
Xtrain, Xtest, ytrain, ytest = train_test_split(X, y, test_size=0.3,
random_state=7)
```

```
from sklearn import svm
""" The parameters and kernels of SVM classifierr can be changed as follows
C = 10.0 # SVM regularization parameter
svm.SVC(kernel='linear', C=C)
svm.LinearSVC(C=C, max_iter=10000)
svm.SVC(kernel='rbf', gamma=0.7, C=C)
svm.SVC(kernel='poly', degree=3, gamma='auto', C=C))
"""
C = 10.0 # SVM regularization parameter
clf =svm.SVC(kernel='linear', C=C)
clf.fit(Xtrain,ytrain)
ypred = clf.predict(Xtest)

from sklearn import metrics
print('Accuracy:', np.round(metrics.accuracy_score(ytest,ypred),4))
print('Precision:', np.round(metrics.precision_score(ytest,
                    ypred,average='weighted'),4))
print('Recall:', np.round(metrics.recall_score(ytest,ypred,
                              average='weighted'),4))
print('F1 Score:', np.round(metrics.f1_score(ytest,ypred,
                              average='weighted'),4))
print('Cohen  Kappa  Score:',  np.round(metrics.cohen_kappa_score(ytest,
ypred)))
print('Matthews  Corrcoef:',  np.round(metrics.matthews_corrcoef(ytest,
ypred)))
print('\t\tClassification Report:\n', metrics.classification_report(ypred,
ytest))

from sklearn.metrics import confusion_matrix
from io import BytesIO #neded for plot
import seaborn as sns; sns.set()
import matplotlib.pyplot as plt

mat = confusion_matrix(ytest, ypred)
sns.heatmap(mat.T, square=True, annot=True, fmt='d', cbar=False)
plt.xlabel('true label')
plt.ylabel('predicted label');

plt.savefig("SVM_Confusion.jpg")
# Save SVG in a fake file object.
f = BytesIO()
plt.savefig(f, format="svg")
```

### 4.5.2 Smartphone-based recognition of human activities

Advances in information and communication technology have contributed to broader use of smartphone applications. The use of smartphone technology connects doctors and patients for real-time monitoring and healthcare management in modern healthcare applications. In addition, smartphones participating in the field healthcare have introduced smart applications such as mobile healthcare and smart healthcare monitoring systems. Mobile healthcare (m-healthcare) is a crucial feature of improvement in the forefront of this revolution. For monitoring personal health treatment and well-being, mobile devices are widely being used. Over the years, the amazing development of mobile phones has dramatically changed the behavior of people. The growth of mobile devices and smartphones with an increasing space for innovation and prospects still provides additional opportunities. Smartphones offer many advantages, such as being portable devices that do not necessarily influence the lifestyle of the user in the experiments (Boulos, Wheeler, Tavares, & Jones, 2011). A very high percentage of the world's population has access to smartphones, and the use of smartphones with internet access is increasing dramatically. HAR is another area with a wide range of possible innovations and further studies using smartphones. HAR has been shown to help detect instances of various health issues and maintain a healthy lifestyle. Recognition of human activity has become a crucial computing field due to its major effects on people in general and specifically on healthcare services. The number of elderly people who need constant care and supervision is obviously increasing. Hence, more researchers are interested in elderly cases as a field of study and development (Reyes-Ortiz, Oneto, Sama, Parra, & Anguita, 2016). Over the last few years, healthcare services have undergone considerable changes. Mobile health is the main driving force behind this revolution's front end. Mobile health (mHealth) is a mobile and IoT-supported health infrastructure that includes the use of general packet radio service (GPRS), 4G systems, global positioning system (GPS), and Bluetooth technology for mobile phones (Kay, Santos, & Takane, 2011; Subasi, Fllatah, Alzobidi, Brahimi, & Sarirete, 2019). A general framework for smartphone-based HAR is shown in Fig. 4.10.

#### Example 4.10

The following Python code is used to classify smartphone-based HAR data using the LSTM classifier employing separate training and testing datasets. The classification accuracy, precision, recall, F1 score, Cohen kappa score, and Matthews correlation coefficient are calculated. The classification report and confusion matrix are also given. This example is adapted from the https://machinelearningmastery.com/how-to-develop-rnn-models-for-human-activity-recognition-time-series-classification/.

***Dataset information:*** The dataset is downloaded from UCI repository (UCI, 2018b). The experiments were conducted with a group of 30 volunteers ages 19–48. They completed a protocol of activities consisting of six basic activities: three static postures (standing, sitting, and lying) and three dynamic activities (walking, walking downstairs, and walking upstairs). The experiment also involved postural transitions, which occurred between the static postures. These are: stand-to-sit, sit-to-stand, sit-to-lie, lie-to-sit, stand-to-lie, and lie-to-stand. All participants were carrying a smartphone (Samsung Galaxy S II) on their waist during the experiment implementation. We captured

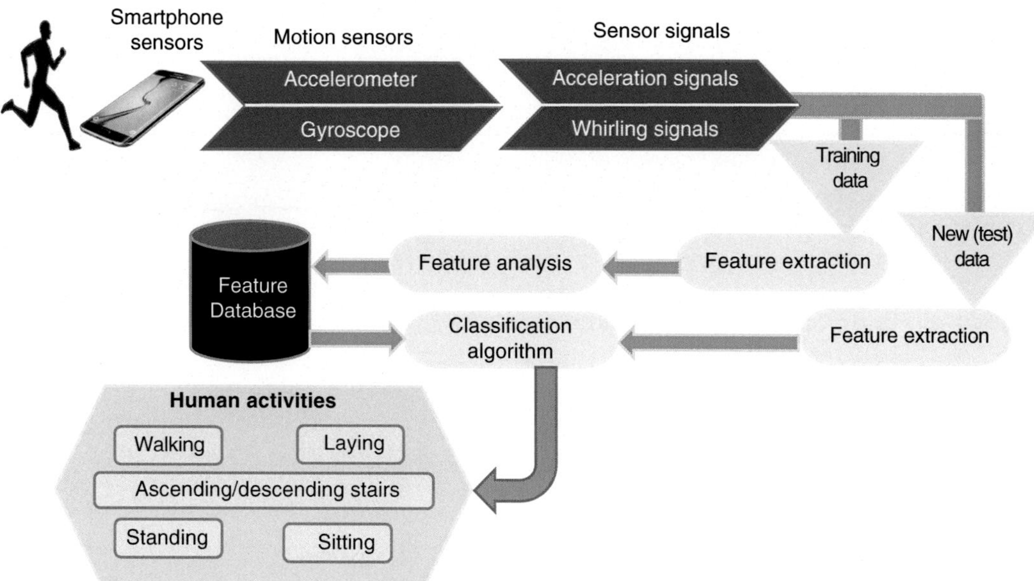


FIGURE 4.10 **A general framework for smartphone-based human activity recognition.** *Source: Adapted from Subasi et al. (2020b).*

3-axial linear acceleration and 3-axial angular velocity at a constant rate of 50 Hz utilizing the embedded accelerometer and gyroscope of the device. The experiments were recorded with video to label the data manually. The acquired dataset was randomly divided into two sets, where 70% of the volunteers were selected for generating the training data and 30% the test data.

The sensor signals (accelerometer and gyroscope) were preprocessed by utilizing noise filters and then sampled in fixed-width sliding windows of 2.56 sec and 50% overlap (128 readings/window). The sensor acceleration signal, which has gravitational and body motion components, was separated using a Butterworth low-pass filter into body acceleration and gravity. The gravitational force is assumed to have only low-frequency components, therefore a filter with 0.3 Hz cutoff frequency was applied. From each window, a vector of 561 features was taken by calculating variables from the time and frequency domain (Reyes-Ortiz et al., 2016; Subasi, et al., 2019e).

```
"""
Created on Sun Nov 24 15:50:51 2019
@author: asubasi
"""
# lstm model
from numpy import mean
from numpy import std
from numpy import dstack
from pandas import read_csv
```

```
from keras.models import Sequential
from keras.layers import Dense
from keras.layers import Flatten
from keras.layers import Dropout
from keras.layers import LSTM
from keras.utils import to_categorical
from keras import callbacks
from matplotlib import pyplot

# load a single file as a numpy array
def load_file(filepath):
            dataframe = read_csv(filepath, header=None, delim_
            whitespace=True)
            return dataframe.values

# load a list of files and return as a 3d numpy array
def load_group(filenames, prefix=''):
           loaded = list()
           for name in filenames:
                        data = load_file(prefix + name)
                        loaded.append(data)
           # stack group so that features are the 3rd dimension
           loaded = dstack(loaded)
           return loaded

# load a dataset group, such as train or test
def load_dataset_group(group, prefix=''):
           filepath = prefix + group + '/Inertial Signals/'
           # load all 9 files as a single array
           filenames = list()
           # total acceleration
           filenames += ['total_acc_x_'+group+'.txt',
           'total_acc_y_'+group+'.txt', 'total_acc_z_'+group+'.txt']
           # body acceleration
           filenames += ['body_acc_x_'+group+'.txt',
           'body_acc_y_'+group+'.txt', 'body_acc_z_'+group+'.txt']
           # body gyroscope
           filenames += ['body_gyro_x_'+group+'.txt',
           'body_gyro_y_'+group+'.txt', 'body_gyro_z_'+group+'.txt']
           # load input data
           X = load_group(filenames, filepath)
           # load class output
           y = load_file(prefix + group + '/y_'+group+'.txt')
           return X, y
```

```
# load the dataset, returns train and test X and y elements
def load_dataset(prefix="):
            # load all train
            Xtrain, ytrain = load_dataset_group('train', prefix + 'UCI HAR
            Dataset/')
            print(Xtrain.shape, ytrain.shape)
            # load all test
            Xtest, ytest = load_dataset_group('test', prefix + 'UCI HAR
            Dataset/')
            print(Xtest.shape, ytest.shape)
            # zero-offset class values
            ytrain = ytrain - 1
            ytest = ytest - 1
            # one hot encode y
            ytrain = to_categorical(ytrain)
            ytest = to_categorical(ytest)
            print(Xtrain.shape, ytrain.shape, Xtest.shape, ytest.shape)
            return Xtrain, ytrain, Xtest, ytest
# load data
Xtrain, ytrain, Xtest, ytest = load_dataset()
target_names = ['Walking',
            'Upstairs',
            'Downstairs',
            'Sitting',
            'Standing',
            'Laying' ]
#%%
# ==========================================================================
# Create an LSTM model
# ==========================================================================
verbose, epochs, batch_size = 1, 5, 64
n_timesteps,  n_features,  n_outputs = Xtrain.shape[1],  Xtrain.shape[2],
ytrain.shape[1]
model = Sequential()
model.add(LSTM(100, input_shape=(n_timesteps,n_features)))
model.add(Dropout(0.5))
model.add(Dense(100, activation='relu'))
model.add(Dense(n_outputs, activation='softmax'))
# ==========================================================================
# Compile the model
# ==========================================================================
model.compile(loss='categorical_crossentropy', optimizer='adam',
metrics=['accuracy'])
```

```
#%%
# ==========================================================================
# Enable validation to use ModelCheckpoint and EarlyStopping callbacks
# ==========================================================================
callbacks_list = [
    callbacks.ModelCheckpoint(
        filepath='best_model.{epoch:02d}-{val_loss:.2f}.h5',
        monitor='val_loss', save_best_only=True),]
# ==========================================================================
# Train the model
# ==========================================================================
history = model.fit(Xtrain,
            ytrain,epochs=epochs, batch_size=batch_size,
            callbacks=callbacks_list,
            validation_split=0.3,
            verbose=1)
#%%
# ==========================================================================
# Evaluate the model
# ==========================================================================
test_loss, test_acc = model.evaluate(Xtest, ytest, batch_size=batch_size,
verbose=verbose)
print('\nTest accuracy:', test_acc)
#%%
from matplotlib import pyplot as plt
plt.figure(figsize=(6, 4))
plt.plot(history.history['accuracy'], 'r', label='Accuracy of training
data')
plt.plot(history.history['val_accuracy'], 'b', label='Accuracy of
validation data')
plt.plot(history.history['loss'], 'r--', label='Loss of training data')
plt.plot(history.history['val_loss'], 'b--', label='Loss of validation
data')
#plt.plot(history.history['val_accuracy'], label = 'val_accuracy')
plt.title('Model Accuracy and Loss')
plt.ylabel('Accuracy and Loss')
plt.xlabel('Training Epoch')
plt.ylim(0)
plt.legend()
plt.show()
#%%
from sklearn.metrics import classification_report
import numpy as np
```

```
# Print confusion matrix for training data
y_pred_test = model.predict(Xtest,)
# Take the class with the highest probability from the train predictions
max_y_pred_test = np.round(y_pred_test)
#max_y_train = np.argmax(testy, axis=1)
#max_y_pred_train = np.argmax(y_pred_train, axis=1)
print(classification_report(ytest, max_y_pred_test))
#%%
from sklearn.metrics import confusion_matrix
import seaborn as sns
matrix = confusion_matrix(ytest.argmax(axis=1), max_y_pred_test.
argmax(axis=1))
plt.figure(figsize=(6, 4))
sns.heatmap(matrix,cmap='coolwarm',linecolor='white',linewidths=1,
         xticklabels=target_names,
         yticklabels=target_names,
         annot=True,
         fmt='d')
plt.title('Confusion Matrix')
plt.ylabel('True Label')
plt.xlabel('Predicted Label')
plt.show()
#%%
from sklearn import metrics
print('Accuracy:', np.round(metrics.accuracy_score(ytest,
max_y_pred_test),4))
print('Precision:', np.round(metrics.precision_score(ytest,
                    max_y_pred_test,average='weighted'),4))
print('Recall:', np.round(metrics.recall_score(ytest, max_y_pred_test,
                    average='weighted'),4))
print('F1 Score:', np.round(metrics.f1_score(ytest, max_y_pred_test,
                    average='weighted'),4))
print('Cohen  Kappa  Score:',  np.round(metrics.cohen_kappa_score(ytest.
argmax(axis=1), max_y_pred_test.argmax(axis=1)),4))
print('Matthews  Corrcoef:',  np.round(metrics.matthews_corrcoef(ytest.
argmax(axis=1), max_y_pred_test.argmax(axis=1)),4))

print('\t\tClassification Report:\n', metrics.classification_report(ytest,
max_y_pred_test))

#%%
from sklearn.metrics import confusion_matrix
from io import BytesIO #neded for plot
```

```
import seaborn as sns; sns.set()
import matplotlib.pyplot as plt

#Convert the binary labels back
#confusion_matrix(y_test.values.argmax(axis=1), predictions.
argmax(axis=1))
mat = confusion_matrix(ytest.argmax(axis=1), max_y_pred_test.
argmax(axis=1))
sns.heatmap(mat.T, square=True, annot=True, fmt='d', cbar=False)
plt.title('Confusion Matrix')
plt.ylabel('True Label')
plt.xlabel('Predicted Label')
plt.show()

plt.savefig("Confusion.jpg")
# Save SVG in a fake file object.
f = BytesIO()
plt.savefig(f, format="svg")
```

## 4.6 Microarray gene expression data classification for cancer detection

Cancer is one of the main causes of death all over the world. Many different cancer types have been diagnosed in a variety of tissues and organs. Because it is associated with genetic abnormalities in the cell, DNA microarrays that permit the simultaneous measurement of expression levels of genes have been utilized to describe gene-expression profiles of tumor cells. Therefore, these measurements permit the detection of anomalies in the cell (Chen, Li, & Wei, 2007). Microarray technology also permits a standardized, clinical evaluation of oncological diagnosis and prognosis. Discovering genes that typically trigger cancer will have crucial implications in understanding the biological mechanism of cancer (Rojas-Galeano, Hsieh, Agranoff, Krishna, & Fernandez-Reyes, 2008) It is crucial to find informative genes to obtain accurate results from the microarray data analysis (Xu & Zhang, 2006). Nevertheless, those studies are specific to limited cancer types, and their results have limited use because of inadequate validation in large patient age groups. Although the data retrieval process is challenging, microarray techniques have been utilized as an encouraging tool to enhance cancer diagnosis and treatment in recent decades. On the other hand, data generated from gene expression include a high level of noise and a huge number of genes relative to the number of available samples. For this reason, classification and statistical techniques with microarray data present a great challenge. Discovering genes generally regulated in cancer may have a crucial implication in understanding the common biological mechanism of cancer. Many scientists analyzed the global gene-expression profiles of different cancer types over the past years. Machine learning–based decision-making support systems help doctors and clinicians in their diagnosis and prognosis process (Vural & Subasi, 2015).

## Example 4.11

The following Python code is used to classify microarray gene expression data (Leukemia) using extra tree classifier and 10-fold cross-validation. The classification accuracy, precision, recall, F1 score, Cohen kappa score, and Matthews correlation coefficient are calculated.

***Dataset information:*** We applied the method to broadly used public microarray datasets that are acute myeloid leukemia (AML)-acute lymphoblast leukemia (ALL) and mixed-lineage leukemia (MLL) genes (http://portals.broadinstitute.org/cgi-bin/cancer/publications/pub_paper.cgi?mode=view&paper_id=63). This dataset includes measurements from leukemia patient samples taken from peripheral blood and bone marrow. ALL carrying a chromosomal translocation involving the mixed-lineage leukemia gene (MLL, ALL1, HRX) has a particularly poor prognosis. Armstrong et al. (Armstrong et al., 2002) proposed that they constitute a distinct disease, denoted as MLL, and show that the differences in gene expression are robust enough to classify leukemias correctly as MLL, ALL, or AML. Establishing that MLL is a unique entity is essential, as it mandates the examination of selectively expressed genes for urgently needed molecular targets. The measurements correspond to acute lymphoblast leukemia (ALL), acute myeloid leukemia (AML), and mixed-lineage leukemia gene (MLL), including 24, 28, and 20 samples, respectively. The samples were analyzed using Affymetrix microarrays consisting of 11,224 genes.

```
"""
Created on Tue Jun 18 18:14:15 2019
@author: asubasi
"""
import scipy.io as sio
from sklearn.model_selection import cross_val_score
from sklearn.metrics import cohen_kappa_score, make_scorer
import numpy as np
# import file into a dictionary
mat_contents = sio.loadmat('Leukemia2.mat')
sorted(mat_contents.keys())
# read in the structure
data = mat_contents['data']
# get the fields
# split data into X and y
X = data[:,1:11225]
y = data[:,0]
#%%
# =============================================================================
# Extra trees example with cross-validation
# =============================================================================
#Import Extra Trees model
from sklearn.ensemble import ExtraTreesClassifier
```

```
# fit model no training data
model = ExtraTreesClassifier(n_estimators=100, max_features=11200)

CV=10 #10-Fold Cross Validation
#Evaluate Model Using 10-Fold Cross Validation and Print Performance
Metrics
Acc_scores = cross_val_score(model, X, y, cv=CV)
print("Accuracy: %0.3f (+/- %0.3f)" % (Acc_scores.mean(), Acc_scores.
std() * 2))
f1_scores = cross_val_score(model, X, y, cv=CV,scoring='f1_macro')
print("F1 score: %0.3f (+/- %0.3f)" % (f1_scores.mean(), f1_scores.std()
* 2))
Precision_scores = cross_val_score(model, X, y, cv=CV,scoring='precision_
macro')
print("Precision score: %0.3f (+/- %0.3f)" % (Precision_scores.mean(),
Precision_scores.std() * 2))
Recall_scores = cross_val_score(model, X, y, cv=CV,scoring='recall_macro')
print("Recall score: %0.3f (+/- %0.3f)" % (Recall_scores.mean(), Recall_
scores.std() * 2))
from sklearn.metrics import cohen_kappa_score, make_scorer
kappa_scorer = make_scorer(cohen_kappa_score)
Kappa_scores = cross_val_score(model, X, y, cv=CV,scoring=kappa_scorer)
print("Kappa score: %0.3f (+/- %0.3f)" % (Kappa_scores.mean(), Kappa_
scores.std() * 2))
```

## 4.7 Breast cancer detection

Breast cancer is an incidence of malignant neoplasm within women's breast tissue. It is one of the common scourges among women. Breast cancer is one of the most dramatic causes of women's mortality around the world. With the increasing development of biomedical and computer technologies, various clinical factors related to breast cancer have been recorded. To tackle the dramatic increase of breast cancer, many researchers have considered using patient clinic records to predict breast cancer for patients. Efficient breast cancer diagnosis remains a major challenge, and early diagnosis is extremely imperative to preventing growth of the disease (Hassan, Hossain, Begg, Ramamohanarao, & Morsi, 2010).

Breast cancer is the most common cancer in females around the world, encompassing 15% of all female cancers. Despite some risk, shortening can be achieved with prevention; these approaches cannot reduce most breast cancers diagnosed in very late phases. As a result, early detection is the cornerstone of breast cancer control to improve breast cancer survival. Mammography and fine needle aspiration cytology (FNAC) are the main diagnostic methods, but these methods do not have sufficient enough diagnostic performances. There is no doubt that evaluation of data taken from patients and doctors' decisions are the most crucial elements in diagnosis. Together with mammography and FNAC, different machine learning methods can be utilized as a decision support tool in doctors' diagnosis; as a result, a better system of diagnosis can be obtained. In regard to the above-mentioned requirements, machine learning methods can be utilized to facilitate improvement of the diagnostic systems. By using machine learning–based automatic diagnostic systems, potential diagnosis mistakes from doctors can be eliminated, and medical data can be examined in detail (Aličković & Subasi, 2017).

## Example 4.12

The following Python code is used to classify the breast cancer dataset (WDBC) downloaded from UCI using Keras deep learning model with 10-fold cross-validation. The classification accuracy is calculated.

***Dataset information:*** Breast cancer is a malignant tumor arising from breast cells. Even though some risk factors (i.e., genetic risk factors, ageing, obesity, family history, not having children, and menstrual periods) increase a woman's chance of having breast cancer, it is not known yet what causes most breast cancers and how different factors initiate cells to turn cancerous. Many studies have been done to learn further, and researchers are making great progress in identifying how specific changes in DNA can cause healthy breast cells to turn cancerous (Aličković & Subasi, 2017; Jerez-Aragonés, Gómez-Ruiz, Ramos-Jiménez, Muñoz-Pérez, & Alba-Conejo, 2003; Marcano-Cedeño, Quintanilla-Domínguez, Andina, 2011).

There are two different Wisconsin breast cancer data sets in the UCI Machine Learning Repository (UCI, 2019a). The first dataset is Wisconsin breast cancer diagnostic (WBCD) dataset. This dataset includes 569 distinct instances and 32 attributes; 357 cases are benign, and 212 cases are malignant. All attributes are computed from a digitized image of a fine needle aspirate (FNA) of patients' breast tissues. All cell nuclei in breast tissues are defined by 10 real-valued features and for all these features the mean, the standard error, and the "worst" (mean of the three largest values) are computed. Hence a total of 30 attributes for all images were obtained (Aličković & Subasi, 2017).

- radius (mean of distances from center to points on the perimeter)
- texture (standard deviation of gray-scale values)
- perimeter
- area
- smoothness (local variation in radius lengths)
- compactness ($\text{perimeter}^2/\text{area} - 1.0$)
- concavity (severity of concave portions of the contour)
- concave points (number of concave portions of the contour)
- symmetry
- fractal dimension ("coastline approximation" − 1)

The second dataset is Wisconsin breast cancer original dataset and includes 699 samples taken from a breast tissue. Then, data with missing values are eliminated from the dataset; as a result, 683 cases are left. Every record in this database has nine attributes, with all values characterized by integer numbers between 1 and 10 and realized to change remarkably between benign and malignant instances. The measured nine attributes are (Aličković & Subasi, 2017; UCI, 2019a):

- clump thickness
- uniformity of cell size

- uniformity of cell shape
- marginal adhesion
- single epithelial cell size
- bare nucleoi
- bland chromatin
- normal nuclei
- mitoses

```
"""
Created on Tue Jun 18 18:14:15 2019
@author: asubasi
"""
from sklearn.model_selection import cross_val_score
from sklearn.metrics import cohen_kappa_score, make_scorer
import numpy as np
import pandas as pd
# load data
dataset = pd.read_csv("wdbc.csv")
# split data into X and Y
X = dataset.iloc[:,1:31]
y = dataset.iloc[:, 0]
class_names = dataset.iloc[:, 0]
#%%
# ===========================================================================
# Classification with Keras deep learning model with cross-validation
# ===========================================================================
from keras.models import Sequential
from keras.layers import Dense
from keras.wrappers.scikit_learn import KerasClassifier
from keras.utils import np_utils
from sklearn.model_selection import cross_val_score
from sklearn.model_selection import KFold
from sklearn.preprocessing import LabelEncoder
# encode class values as integers
encoder = LabelEncoder()
encoder.fit(y)
encoded_Y = encoder.transform(y)
# convert integers to dummy variables (i.e. one hot encoded)
dummy_y = np_utils.to_categorical(encoded_Y)
lenOfCoded=dummy_y.shape[1] # Dimension of binary coded output data
InputDataDimension=30
# define baseline model
```

```
def baseline_model():
            # create model
            model = Sequential()
            model.add(Dense(20, input_dim=InputDataDimension,
            activation='relu'))
            model.add(Dense(lenOfCoded, activation='softmax'))
            # Compile model
            model.compile(loss='categorical_crossentropy',
            optimizer='adam', metrics=['accuracy'])
            return model
estimator = KerasClassifier(build_fn=baseline_model, epochs=50, batch_
size=5, verbose=1)
kfold = KFold(n_splits=10, shuffle=True)
results = cross_val_score(estimator, X, dummy_y, cv=kfold)
print("Accuracy: %.2f%% (%.2f%%)" % (results.mean()*100, results.
std()*100))
```

## 4.8 Classification of the cardiotocogram data for anticipation of fetal risks

In a pregnancy cycle, the fetal heart rate (FHR) is one of the most significant indications regarding the fetus. Obstetricians utilize cardiotocography (CTG) to get information, which includes FHR and uterine contractions (UC), associated with the fetus. The CTG not only obtains FHR but also assists in observing the mother's contractions and other types of fetal monitoring. Generally, a proper period for antenatal CTG is after 28 weeks of pregnancy in the third trimester. This test can be used by either internal or external techniques. With internal testing, a catheter is placed in the uterus after a specific amount of expansion has taken place. In external tests, a pair of sensor nodes is attached to the mother's stomach. The CTG data generally denotes two lines. The upper line records the FHR in beats per minute. The lower line records uterine contractions. In order to find fetal risks based on CTG, machine learning techniques are an increasing trend that create decision support systems in medicine. Various studies have carried out classification of the CTG data (Sahin & Subasi, 2015). The information taken from CTG is used for early detection of a pathological state and can help the obstetrician to predict future problems and hinder a permanent impairment to the fetus. Throughout The delivery of a baby who is showing hypoxia throughout delivery can cause a temporary impairment or death. The wrong diagnosis of the FHR recordings and unsuitable treatments applied to the fetus can accomplish more than half of these deaths (Ayres-de-Campos et al., 2005; Cesarelli, Romano, & Bifulco, 2009; Gribbin & Thornton, 2006; Grivell, Alfirevic, Gyte, & Devane, 2015). While its practical, there might be some inconsistency in the success of CTG monitoring, mainly in low-risk pregnancies. If there is an incorrectly assessed fetal distress, then it may result in useless treatment, or if there is an inaccurate examination of fetal well-being, then it might not receive essential treatment (Subasi, Kadasa, & Kremic, 2019; Van Geijn, Jongsma, de Haan, & Eskes, 1980).

## Example 4.13

The following Python code is used to classify a cardiotocography dataset employing linear discriminant analysis (LDA) classifier and 10-fold cross-validation. The classification accuracy, precision, recall, F1 score, Cohen kappa score, and Matthews correlation coefficient are calculated.

***Dataset information:*** The performance of the learners utilizing the cardiotocogram (CTG) dataset downloaded from UCI (https://archive.ics.uci.edu/ml/datasets/cardiotocography) (Bache & Lichman, 2013) is evaluated. A total of 2126 fetal cardiotocograms (CTGs) were automatically processed, and the respective diagnostic features measured. The CTG data was examined by three expert obstetricians and determined normal or pathological by inspecting the status of the embryo. The CTG data has 3 classes (N = normal; S = suspect; P = pathologic) and 21 features; 13 of them are discrete and 8 are continuous. The data has the following attributes: LB, FHR baseline (beats per minute); AC, number of accelerations per second; FM, number of fetal movements per second; UC, number of uterine contractions per second; DL, number of light decelerations per second; DS, number of severe decelerations per second; DP, number of prolonged decelerations per second; ASTV, percentage of time with abnormal short-term variability; MSTV, mean value of short-term variability; ALTV, percentage of time with abnormal long-term variability; MLTV, mean value of long-term variability; width, width of FHR histogram; min, minimum of FHR histogram; max, maximum of FHR histogram; Nmax, number of histogram peaks; Nzeros, number of histogram zeros; mode, histogram mode; mean, histogram mean; median, histogram median; variance, histogram variance; tendency, histogram tendency; CLASS, FHR pattern class code (1 to 10); NSP, fetal state class code (N = normal; S = suspect; P = pathologic).

```
"""
Created on Thu May 9 12:18:30 2019
@author: absubasi
"""
from sklearn.metrics import cohen_kappa_score, make_scorer
import scipy as sp
import numpy as np
import pandas as pd
#To prevent warnings
import warnings
warnings.filterwarnings("ignore")

# load data
dataset = pd.read_csv("CTG3CLASS.csv")
# split data into X and y
X = dataset.iloc[:,0:21]
y = dataset.iloc[:, 21]
class_names = dataset.iloc[:, 21]
X=X.to_numpy() #Convert Pandas Dataframe into Numpy

#%%
```

```
#=============================================================================
# LDA classification with training and test set
#=============================================================================
# Import train_test_split function
from sklearn.model_selection import train_test_split
# Split dataset into training set and test set
# 70% training and 30% test
Xtrain, Xtest, ytrain, ytest = train_test_split(X, y,test_size=0.3, ran-
dom_state=1)
#Import LDA model
from sklearn.discriminant_analysis import LinearDiscriminantAnalysis
#Create a LDA Classifier
clf = LinearDiscriminantAnalysis(solver='lsqr', shrinkage=None)
#Train the model using the training sets
clf.fit(Xtrain,ytrain)
#Predict the response for test dataset
ypred = clf.predict(Xtest)
#Evaluate the Model and Print Performance Metrics
from sklearn import metrics
print('Accuracy:', np.round(metrics.accuracy_score(ytest,ypred),4))
print('Precision:', np.round(metrics.precision_score(ytest,
                    ypred,average='weighted'),4))
print('Recall:', np.round(metrics.recall_score(ytest,ypred,
                                 average='weighted'),4))
print('F1 Score:', np.round(metrics.f1_score(ytest,ypred,
                                 average='weighted'),4))
print('Cohen Kappa Score:', np.round(metrics.cohen_kappa_score(ytest,
ypred),4))
print('Matthews Corrcoef:', np.round(metrics.matthews_corrcoef(ytest,
ypred),4))
print('\n\t\tClassification Report:\n', metrics.classification_
report(ypred, ytest))

#Plot Confusion Matrix
from sklearn.metrics import confusion_matrix
print("Confusion Matrix:\n",confusion_matrix(ytest, ypred))

#%%
#=============================================================================
# LDA example with cross-validation
#=============================================================================
from sklearn.discriminant_analysis import LinearDiscriminantAnalysis
from sklearn.model_selection import cross_val_score
```

```
# fit model no training data
#model = LinearDiscriminantAnalysis(solver='lsqr', shrinkage='auto')
model = LinearDiscriminantAnalysis(solver='lsqr', shrinkage=None)

CV=10 #10-Fold Cross Validation
#Evaluate Model Using 10-Fold Cross Validation
Acc_scores = cross_val_score(model, X, y, cv=CV)
print("Accuracy: %0.3f (+/- %0.3f)" % (Acc_scores.mean(), Acc_scores.
std() * 2))
f1_scores = cross_val_score(model, X, y, cv=CV,scoring='f1_macro')
print("F1 score: %0.3f (+/- %0.3f)" % (f1_scores.mean(), f1_scores.std()
* 2))
Precision_scores = cross_val_score(model, X, y, cv=CV,scoring='precision_
macro')
print("Precision score: %0.3f (+/- %0.3f)" % (Precision_scores.mean(),
Precision_scores.std() * 2))
Recall_scores = cross_val_score(model, X, y, cv=CV,scoring='recall_macro')
print("Recall score: %0.3f (+/- %0.3f)" % (Recall_scores.mean(), Recall_
scores.std() * 2))
kappa_scorer = make_scorer(cohen_kappa_score)
Kappa_scores = cross_val_score(model, X, y, cv=CV,scoring=kappa_scorer)
print("Kappa score: %0.3f (+/- %0.3f)" % (Kappa_scores.mean(), Kappa_
scores.std() * 2))
```

## 4.9 Diabetes detection

Diabetes is a widespread physiological disease among humans. The term diabetic is used once a person is incapable of breaking down glucose due to lack of insulin. The human organ known as the pancreas is responsible for producing the hormone insulin, which is an essential enzyme regulates the sugar level in human blood. It generates energy to the human body using sugar; sans enough insulin, body cells cannot obtain the energy they need, thus the sugar level in the blood becomes too high and several problems can arise. Diabetes is not a curable disease; fortunately, it is treatable. In contemporary healthcare, predicting and accurately treating diseases has become of primary importance in medical prognostics disciplines. The treatment of diabetes is completely manual, normally recommended by the physician. Smith et al. (Smith, Everhart, Dickson, Knowler, Johannes, 1988) utilized the perceptron-based algorithm called ADAPtive learning routine (ADAP), which is an early neural network model, to forecast the onset of diabetes mellitus. They used the Pima Indians diabetes (PID) dataset in the experiment. This dataset is taken from the UCI machine learning repository. The dataset contains women of Pima Indian inheritance who were older than 20 years and were residents of the United States at the time of the study. The binary output variable takes either zero or one, where one indicates testing positive and zero is a testing negative for diabetes. In total

268 (34.9%) cases exist in class 1 for positive test and 500 (65.1%) cases in class 0 for negative test. There are eight clinical attributes (Ashiquzzaman et al., 2018).

## Example 4.14

The following Python code is used to classify diabetes mellitus dataset using random forest classifier. The classification accuracy, precision, recall, F1 score, Cohen kappa score, and Matthews correlation coefficient are calculated. The confusion matrix and ROC area are computed as well.

***Dataset information:*** The dataset includes 768 different instances, and all patients in the dataset are females at least 21 years old. The binary target variable takes zero or one values, while zero implies a negative test for diabetes and one indicates a positive test. There are 500 cases in class 0 and 268 cases in class 1. The population was the Pima Indian population near Phoenix, Arizona. Since 1965, Pima Indians living in the Gila River Indian community in southern Arizona have contributed in a longitudinal study of diabetes and its obstacles. This community has the world's highest reported occurrence of diabetes (50% at 35 years of age). Pima Indians have diabetes that is not related to insulin dependency, ketoacidosis, or islet-cell antibodies and is, thus, type 2 diabetes, even when it occurs in the young. Diabetic nephropathy is the prevalent form of kidney disease in this population and is similar in its clinical characteristics and conventional pathologic features to that described in other populations. It frequently results in end-stage renal disease, which develops in nearly 15 percent of diabetic Pima Indians by 20 years' duration of diabetes (Mercaldo, Nardone, & Santone, 2017). The attributes of the dataset are:

1. Number of times pregnant
2. Plasma glucose concentration at 2 hours in an oral glucose tolerance test (GTIT)
3. Diastolic blood pressure (mm Hg)
4. Triceps skin fold thickness (mm)
5. 2-hour serum insulin (μU/ml)
6. Body mass index
7. Diabetes pedigree function
8. Age (years)

```
"""
Created on Thu May 9 12:18:30 2019
@author: absubasi
"""

import scipy as sp
import numpy as np
import pandas as pd
#To prevent warnings
import warnings
warnings.filterwarnings("ignore")

# load data
from numpy import loadtxt
```

```
dataset = loadtxt('pima-indians-diabetes.csv', delimiter=",")

# split data into X and y
X = dataset[:,0:8]
y = dataset[:,8]

# Import train_test_split function
from sklearn.model_selection import train_test_split
# Split dataset into training set and test set
# 70% training and 30% test
Xtrain, Xtest, ytrain, ytest = train_test_split(X, y,test_size=0.3, ran-
dom_state=1)
#%%
# =========================================================================
# Random forest example with training and test set
# =========================================================================
from sklearn.ensemble import RandomForestClassifier

#In order to change to accuracy increase n_estimators
"""RandomForestClassifier(n_estimators='warn', criterion='gini', max_
depth=None,
min_samples_split=2, min_samples_leaf=1, min_weight_fraction_leaf=0.0,
max_features='auto', max_leaf_nodes=None, min_impurity_decrease=0.0,
min_impurity_split=None, bootstrap=True, oob_score=False, n_jobs=None,
random_state=None, verbose=0, warm_start=False, class_weight=None)"""
clf = RandomForestClassifier(n_estimators=200)
#Create the Model
#Train the model with Training Dataset
clf.fit(Xtrain,ytrain)
#Test the model with Testset
ypred = clf.predict(Xtest)

#Evaluate the Model and Print Performance Metrics
from sklearn import metrics
print('Accuracy:', np.round(metrics.accuracy_score(ytest,ypred),4))
print('Precision:', np.round(metrics.precision_score(ytest,
                    ypred,average='weighted'),4))
print('Recall:', np.round(metrics.recall_score(ytest,ypred,
                    average='weighted'),4))
print('F1 Score:', np.round(metrics.f1_score(ytest,ypred,
                    average='weighted'),4))
print('Cohen Kappa Score:', np.round(metrics.cohen_kappa_score(ytest,
ypred),4))
print('Matthews Corrcoef:', np.round(metrics.matthews_corrcoef(ytest,
ypred),4))
```

```
print('\t\tClassification Report:\n', metrics.classification_report(ypred,
ytest))

#Plot Confusion Matrix
from sklearn.metrics import confusion_matrix
print("Confusion Matrix:\n",confusion_matrix(ytest, ypred))

#%%
# ===========================================================================
# Random forest example with cross-validation
# ===========================================================================
from sklearn.ensemble import RandomForestClassifier
from sklearn.model_selection import cross_val_score
#In order to change to accuracy increase n_estimators
# fit model no training data
model = RandomForestClassifier(n_estimators=200)

CV=10 #10-Fold Cross Validation
#Evaluate Model Using 10-Fold Cross Validation and Print Performance
Metrics
Acc_scores = cross_val_score(model, X, y, cv=CV)
print("Accuracy: %0.3f (+/- %0.3f)" % (Acc_scores.mean(), Acc_scores.
std() * 2))
f1_scores = cross_val_score(model, X, y, cv=CV,scoring='f1_macro')
print("F1 score: %0.3f (+/- %0.3f)" % (f1_scores.mean(), f1_scores.std()
* 2))
Precision_scores = cross_val_score(model, X, y, cv=CV,scoring='precision_
macro')
print("Precision score: %0.3f (+/- %0.3f)" % (Precision_scores.mean(),
Precision_scores.std() * 2))
Recall_scores = cross_val_score(model, X, y, cv=CV,scoring='recall_macro')
print("Recall score: %0.3f (+/- %0.3f)" % (Recall_scores.mean(), Recall_
scores.std() * 2))
from sklearn.metrics import cohen_kappa_score, make_scorer
kappa_scorer = make_scorer(cohen_kappa_score)
Kappa_scores = cross_val_score(model, X, y, cv=10,scoring=kappa_scorer)
print("Kappa score: %0.3f (+/- %0.3f)" % (Kappa_scores.mean(), Kappa_
scores.std() * 2))

#%%
# ===========================================================================
# # Classification and ROC analysis for binary classification
# ===========================================================================
from sklearn.ensemble import RandomForestClassifier
```

```
from sklearn.metrics import roc_curve, auc
from sklearn.model_selection import StratifiedKFold
from scipy import interp
import matplotlib.pyplot as plt
random_state = np.random.RandomState(0)
########################################################################
# Run classifier with cross-validation and plot ROC curves
cv = StratifiedKFold(n_splits=5)
classifier = RandomForestClassifier(n_estimators=200)

tprs = []
aucs = []
mean_fpr = np.linspace(0, 1, 100)

i = 0
for train, test in cv.split(X, y):
  probas_ = classifier.fit(X[train], y[train]).predict_proba(X[test])
  # Compute ROC curve and area the curve
  fpr, tpr, thresholds = roc_curve(y[test], probas_[:, 1])
  tprs.append(interp(mean_fpr, fpr, tpr))
  tprs[-1][0] = 0.0
  roc_auc = auc(fpr, tpr)
  aucs.append(roc_auc)
  plt.plot(fpr, tpr, lw=1, alpha=0.3,
          label='ROC fold %d (AUC = %0.2f)' % (i, roc_auc))
  i += 1
plt.plot([0, 1], [0, 1], linestyle='--', lw=2, color='r',
         label='Chance', alpha=.8)

mean_tpr = np.mean(tprs, axis=0)
mean_tpr[-1] = 1.0
mean_auc = auc(mean_fpr, mean_tpr)
std_auc = np.std(aucs)
plt.plot(mean_fpr, mean_tpr, color='b',
        label=r'Mean ROC (AUC = %0.2f $\pm$ %0.2f)' % (mean_auc, std_auc),
        lw=2, alpha=.8)

std_tpr = np.std(tprs, axis=0)
tprs_upper = np.minimum(mean_tpr + std_tpr, 1)
tprs_lower = np.maximum(mean_tpr - std_tpr, 0)
plt.fill_between(mean_fpr, tprs_lower, tprs_upper, color='grey',
alpha=.2,
         label=r'$\pm$ 1 std. dev.')
```

```
plt.xlim([-0.05, 1.05])
plt.ylim([-0.05, 1.05])
plt.xlabel('False Positive Rate')
plt.ylabel('True Positive Rate')
plt.title('Receiver operating characteristic example')
plt.legend(loc="lower right")
plt.show()
```

## 4.10 Heart disease detection

The heart is one of the most important organs in the human body. It is the center of the circulatory system. Without proper functioning of the heart, multiple other organs would stop working. According to the American Heart Association's 2015 Heart Disease and Stroke Statistics Update, cardiovascular disease is the leading worldwide cause of death, accounting for 17.3 million deaths per year, and by 2030 it is estimated to increase to more than 23.6 million. The total number of people dying every year from cardiovascular disease is rising drastically. If heart disease is identified and diagnosed precisely at an early stage and proper subsequent treatment is provided, then considerable numbers lives can be saved, and the death rate can be reduced. Diagnosis is a complicated process in which doctors come to a conclusion based on their knowledge and the experiences they encounter with the treatment of patients suffering from similar problems and symptoms. This can lead to incorrect assumptions, as some factors are associated with various organs. The work presented in this book is intended to automate the medical diagnosis process and develop a prediction system to detect heart disease with higher accuracy by using machine learning. A number of tests are conducted on the patient for the diagnosis of a disease. With the help of machine learning techniques for predicting the disease, the number of tests can be reduced, which saves time and provides quality services at a reasonable cost (Dembla & Bhatia, 2016).

### Example 4.15

The following Python code is used to classify the Cleveland heart dataset utilizing the random forest classifier with training and testing datasets. The classification accuracy, precision, recall, F1 score, Cohen kappa score, and Matthews correlation coefficient are calculated. The classification report and confusion matrix are also given. Since the accuracy of the classifier is low, we employed two different cases with data normalization and without data normalization. By using data normalization, the performance of the classifier is improved.

***Dataset information:*** The performance of the random forest classifier is evaluated by utilizing the Cleveland heart dataset. The Cleveland heart dataset is downloaded from the UCI machine learning dataset repository (https://archive.ics.uci.edu/ml/datasets/Heart+Disease), which was provided by Detrano. The dataset comprises 303 instances and 14 attributes and is being divided into two classes of disease. The data has the following attributes: age, age in years; sex, sex (1 = male; 0 = female); cp: chest pain type (1: typical angina, 2: atypical angina, 3: nonanginal pain, 4: asymptomatic); trestbpsm resting blood pressure (in mm Hg on admission to the hospital); chol, serum cholesterol in mg/dl; fbs, fasting blood sugar > 120 mg/dl (1 = true; 0 = false); restecg, resting electrocardiographic results (0: normal, 1: having ST-T wave abnormality, 2: showing probable or definite left ventricular hypertrophy by Estes criteria); thalach: maximum heart rate achieved; exang, exercise induced angina (1 = yes, 0 = no); oldpeak, ST depression induced by exercise relative to rest; slope, the slope of the peak exercise ST segment (1: upsloping, 2: flat, 3: downsloping); ca: number of major vessels (0–3) colored by fluoroscopy; thal, 3 = normal, 6 = fixed defect, 7 = reversible defect; num, diagnosis of heart disease (angiographic disease status, 0: < 50% diameter narrowing, 1: > 50% diameter narrowing).

```
"""
Created on Tue Jun 18 18:14:15 2019
@author: asubasi
"""
import numpy as np
import pandas as pd
# load data
dataset = pd.read_csv('cleveland_heart.csv')
# split data into X and Y
X = dataset.iloc[:,0:13]
y = dataset.iloc[:, 13]
class_names = dataset.iloc[:, 13]
#%%
# =============================================================================
# Evaluation without data normalization
# =============================================================================
from sklearn.ensemble import RandomForestClassifier
from sklearn.model_selection import train_test_split
# split data into train and test sets
Xtrain, Xtest, ytrain, ytest = train_test_split(X, y, test_size=0.33, ran-
dom_state=7)
#In order to change to accuracy increase n_estimators
"""RandomForestClassifier(n_estimators='warn', criterion='gini', max_
depth=None,
min_samples_split=2, min_samples_leaf=1, min_weight_fraction_leaf=0.0,
max_features='auto', max_leaf_nodes=None, min_impurity_decrease=0.0,
min_impurity_split=None, bootstrap=True, oob_score=False, n_jobs=None,
random_state=None, verbose=0, warm_start=False, class_weight=None)"""
clf = RandomForestClassifier(n_estimators=200)
#Create the Model
#Train the model with Training Dataset
```

```
clf.fit(Xtrain,ytrain)
#Test the model with Testset
ypred = clf.predict(Xtest)
#Evaluate the Model and Print Performance Metrics
from sklearn import metrics
print('Accuracy:', np.round(metrics.accuracy_score(ytest,ypred),4))
print('Precision:', np.round(metrics.precision_score(ytest,
                    ypred,average='weighted'),4))
print('Recall:', np.round(metrics.recall_score(ytest,ypred,
                          average='weighted'),4))
print('F1 Score:', np.round(metrics.f1_score(ytest,ypred,
                          average='weighted'),4))
print('Cohen Kappa Score:', np.round(metrics.cohen_kappa_score(ytest,
ypred),4))
print('Matthews  Corrcoef:',  np.round(metrics.matthews_corrcoef(ytest,
ypred),4))
print('\t\tClassification Report:\n', metrics.classification_report(ypred,
ytest))
#Plot Confusion Matrix
from sklearn.metrics import confusion_matrix
print("Confusion Matrix:\n",confusion_matrix(ytest, ypred))
#%%
# ========================================================================
# Evaluation with data normalization
# ========================================================================
from sklearn.ensemble import RandomForestClassifier
from sklearn.model_selection import train_test_split
from sklearn import preprocessing

X_normalized = preprocessing.normalize(X, norm='l2')
# split data into train and test sets
Xtrain, Xtest, ytrain, ytest = train_test_split(X_normalized, y, test_
size=0.33, random_state=7)
#In order to change to accuracy increase n_estimators
"""RandomForestClassifier(n_estimators='warn',  criterion='gini',  max_
depth=None,
min_samples_split=2, min_samples_leaf=1, min_weight_fraction_leaf=0.0,
max_features='auto', max_leaf_nodes=None, min_impurity_decrease=0.0,
min_impurity_split=None, bootstrap=True, oob_score=False, n_jobs=None,
random_state=None, verbose=0, warm_start=False, class_weight=None)"""
clf = RandomForestClassifier(n_estimators=200)
#Create the Model
#Train the model with Training Dataset
```

```
clf.fit(Xtrain,ytrain)
#Test the model with Testset
ypred = clf.predict(Xtest)
#Evaluate the Model and Print Performance Metrics
from sklearn import metrics
print('Accuracy:', np.round(metrics.accuracy_score(ytest,ypred),4))
print('Precision:', np.round(metrics.precision_score(ytest,
                    ypred,average='weighted'),4))
print('Recall:', np.round(metrics.recall_score(ytest,ypred,
                              average='weighted'),4))
print('F1 Score:', np.round(metrics.f1_score(ytest,ypred,
                              average='weighted'),4))
print('Cohen  Kappa  Score:',  np.round(metrics.cohen_kappa_score(ytest,
ypred),4))
print('Matthews  Corrcoef:',  np.round(metrics.matthews_corrcoef(ytest,
ypred),4))
print('\t\tClassification Report:\n', metrics.classification_report(ypred,
ytest))
#Plot Confusion Matrix
from sklearn.metrics import confusion_matrix
print("Confusion Matrix:\n",confusion_matrix(ytest, ypred))
```

## 4.11 Diagnosis of chronic kidney disease (CKD)

Chronic kidney disease (CKD) is a chronic healthcare problem affecting almost 10% of the population worldwide (Cueto-Manzano et al., 2014; Pérez-Sáez et al., 2015). In real life, CKD can be found in cases related to the increased risk of hospital admission, morbidity, and death due to cardiovascular disease and the progressive loss of kidney function. Subjects diagnosed with CKD have a high risk of being affected by atherosclerosis and other types of diseases. These diseases have significant effects on their quality of life. The key consequence of the CKD finding is the kidney damage (Levin & Stevens, 2014). Numerous indications or risk factors are also related to CKD progress, so that these factors could extremely impact CKD identification. By monitoring the progressive nature of CKD, new understandings from the diagnostic computational models built on the ML concepts offer great potential to improve the diagnosis of CKD (Chen, Zhang, Zhu, Xiang, & Harrington, 2016). Numerous studies have proposed models built for diagnosis of CKD (Chen et al., 2016; Muthukumar & Krishnan, 2016; Subasi et al., 2017).

## Example 4.16

The following Python code is used to classify the chronic kidney disease (CKD) dataset (https://archive.ics.uci.edu/ml/datasets/Chronic_Kidney_Disease#) employing LDA classifier. The classification accuracy, precision, recall, F1 score, Cohen kappa score, and Matthews correlation coefficient are calculated. The confusion matrix and ROC area are computed as well.

***Dataset information:*** The CKD dataset used in this example is downloaded from the UCI machine learning repository (UCI, 2019b). The data, collected during a nearly 2-month period and donated by Soundarapandian et al., includes a total of 400 samples represented by 14 numeric and 10 nominal attributes and a class descriptor. Out of 400 samples, 250 samples belong to the CKD group, and the other 150 samples belong to the non-CKD group. Details are more discussed in Chen et al. (2016).

The attributes of the dataset are: age, age; bp, blood pressure; sg, specific gravity; al, albumin; su, sugar; rbc, red blood cells; pc, pus cell; pcc, pus cell clumps; ba, bacteria; bgr, blood glucose random; bu, blood urea; sc, serum creatinine; sod, sodium; pot, potassium; hemo, haemoglobin; pcv, packed cell volume; wc, white blood cell count; rc, red blood cell count; htn, hypertension; dm, diabetes mellitus; cad, coronary artery disease; appet, appetite; pe, pedal edema; ane, anemia; class, CKD/NOCKD.

```
"""
Created on Thu May 9 12:18:30 2019
@author: absubasi
"""
import numpy as np
import pandas as pd
from sklearn.preprocessing import LabelEncoder
#To prevent warnings
import warnings
warnings.filterwarnings("ignore")

# load data
dataset = pd.read_csv("chronic_kidney_disease.csv")
#Encode string data
for col in dataset.columns:
   if dataset[col].dtype == "object":
       encoded = LabelEncoder()
       encoded.fit(dataset[col])
       dataset[col] = encoded.transform(dataset[col])
#%%
# split data into X and y
X = dataset.iloc[:,0:24]
y = dataset.iloc[:, 24]
#%%
# Import train_test_split function
```

```
from sklearn.model_selection import train_test_split
# Split dataset into training set and test set
# 70% training and 30% test
Xtrain, Xtest, ytrain, ytest = train_test_split(X, y,test_size=0.3, ran-
dom_state=1)
#%%
# ======================================================================
# LDA example with training and test set
# ======================================================================
from sklearn.discriminant_analysis import LinearDiscriminantAnalysis
clf = LinearDiscriminantAnalysis(solver='lsqr', shrinkage=None)
#Create the Model
#Train the model with Training Dataset
clf.fit(Xtrain,ytrain)
#Test the model with Testset
ypred = clf.predict(Xtest)
#Evaluate the Model and Print Performance Metrics
from sklearn import metrics
print('Accuracy:', np.round(metrics.accuracy_score(ytest,ypred),4))
print('Precision:', np.round(metrics.precision_score(ytest,
                    ypred,average='weighted'),4))
print('Recall:', np.round(metrics.recall_score(ytest,ypred,
                              average='weighted'),4))
print('F1 Score:', np.round(metrics.f1_score(ytest,ypred,
                              average='weighted'),4))
print('Cohen Kappa Score:', np.round(metrics.cohen_kappa_score(ytest,
ypred),4))
print('Matthews  Corrcoef:',  np.round(metrics.matthews_corrcoef(ytest,
ypred),4))
print('\t\tClassification Report:\n', metrics.classification_report(ypred,
ytest))
#Plot Confusion Matrix
from sklearn.metrics import confusion_matrix
print("Confusion Matrix:\n",confusion_matrix(ytest, ypred))

from io import BytesIO #neded for plot
import seaborn as sns; sns.set()
import matplotlib.pyplot as plt

mat = confusion_matrix(ytest, ypred)
sns.heatmap(mat.T, square=True, annot=True, fmt='d', cbar=False)
```

```
plt.xlabel('true label')
plt.ylabel('predicted label');
plt.savefig("Confusion.jpg")
# Save SVG in a fake file object.
f = BytesIO()
plt.savefig(f, format="svg")

#%%
# ==========================================================================
# LDA example with cross-validation
# ==========================================================================
from sklearn.discriminant_analysis import LinearDiscriminantAnalysis
from sklearn.model_selection import cross_val_score
#In order to change to accuracy increase n_estimators
# fit model no training data
model = LinearDiscriminantAnalysis(solver='lsqr', shrinkage=None)

CV=10 #10-Fold Cross Validation
#Evaluate Model Using 10-Fold Cross Validation and Print Performance
Metrics
Acc_scores = cross_val_score(model, X, y, cv=CV)
print("Accuracy: %0.3f (+/- %0.3f)" % (Acc_scores.mean(), Acc_scores.
std() * 2))
f1_scores = cross_val_score(model, X, y, cv=CV,scoring='f1_macro')
print("F1 score: %0.3f (+/- %0.3f)" % (f1_scores.mean(), f1_scores.std()
* 2))
Precision_scores = cross_val_score(model, X, y, cv=CV,scoring='precision_
macro')
print("Precision score: %0.3f (+/- %0.3f)" % (Precision_scores.mean(),
Precision_scores.std() * 2))
Recall_scores = cross_val_score(model, X, y, cv=CV,scoring='recall_macro')
print("Recall score: %0.3f (+/- %0.3f)" % (Recall_scores.mean(), Recall_
scores.std() * 2))
from sklearn.metrics import cohen_kappa_score, make_scorer
kappa_scorer = make_scorer(cohen_kappa_score)
Kappa_scores = cross_val_score(model, X, y, cv=10,scoring=kappa_scorer)
print("Kappa score: %0.3f (+/- %0.3f)" % (Kappa_scores.mean(), Kappa_
scores.std() * 2))
```

## 4.12 Summary

Machine learning is a relatively new field and yet possibly one of computer science's most active area. Given the wide availability of digitized data and its many applications, we can assume that over the next few decades it will continue to grow at a very fast pace. Different learning issues, some resulting from the substantial increase in data size, which already involves the processing of billions of records in some applications, others related to the implementation of entirely new learning systems, are likely to present new research challenges and require new algorithmic solutions. In all cases, learning theory, algorithms, and implementations are a fascinating field of computer science and mathematics that we hope this book will explain at least to some degree (Mohri, Rostamizadeh, & Talwalkar, 2018). We defined a wide range of machine learning algorithms and techniques in the classification of the healthcare data as well as their varying implementations. The examples included at the end of each section will help the reader become more experienced with the mentioned strategies and principles, as well as the complete solutions offered separately. Some of them could also act as a point of entry for academic work and research into new questions. In the implementations, several machine learning algorithms are discussed as well as their variants, which can be used directly to extract effective solutions to real-world learning problems. Detailed descriptions and analyses of the presented algorithms will help with their implementation and adaptation to other learning scenarios.

## References

Abdullah, A.A., Subasi, A., & Qaisar, S.M. (2017). *Surface EMG Signal Classification by Using WPD and Ensemble Tree Classifiers. 62*, 475. Springer.

Akben, S. B., Subasi, A., & Tuncel, D. (2012). Analysis of repetitive flash stimulation frequencies and record periods to detect migraine using artificial neural network. Journal of Medical Systems, 36(2), 925–931.

Aličković, E., & Subasi, A. (2017). Breast cancer diagnosis using GA feature selection and Rotation Forest. Neural Computing and Applications, 28(4), 753–763.

Andrzejak, R. G., Schindler, K., & Rummel, C. (2012). Nonrandomness, nonlinear dependence, and nonstationarity of electroencephalographic recordings from epilepsy patients. Physical Review E, 86(4), 046206.

Armstrong, S. A., Staunton, J. E., Silverman, L. B., Pieters, R., den Boer, M. L., Minden, M. D., & Korsmeyer, S. J. (2002). MLL translocations specify a distinct gene expression profile that distinguishes a unique leukemia. Nature Genetics, 30(1), 41–47.

Ashiquzzaman, A., Tushar, A. K., Islam, M. R., Shon, D., Im, K., Park, J. -H., & Kim, J. (2018). Reduction of overfitting in diabetes prediction using deep learning neural network. In *IT Convergence and Security 2017*. Berlin: Springer 35 – 43.

Ayres-de-Campos, D., Costa-Santos, C., & Bernardes, J. SisPorto® Multicentre Validation Study Group. (2005). Prediction of neonatal state by computer analysis of fetal heart rate tracings: The antepartum arm of the SisPorto® multicentre validation study. *European Journal of Obstetrics & Gynecology and Reproductive Biology*, *118*(1), 52–60.

Bache, K., & Lichman, M. (2013). UCI Machine Learning Repository [http://archive. Ics. Uci. Edu/ml]. University of California, School of Information and Computer Science. Irvine, CA.

Baños, O., Damas, M., Pomares, H., Rojas, I., Tóth, M. A., & Amft, O. (2012). A benchmark dataset to evaluate sensor displacement in activity recognition. *UbiComp '12: Proceedings of the 2012 ACM Conference on Ubiquitous Computing*, 1026–1035.

Banos, O., Toth, M. A., Damas, M., Pomares, H., & Rojas, I. (2014). Dealing with the effects of sensor displacement in wearable activity recognition. Sensors, 14(6), 9995–10023.

Barlow, J. S. (1993). The electroencephalogram: Its patterns and origins. Cambridge, MA: MIT press.

Begg, R., Lai, D. T., & Palaniswami, M. (2008). Computational intelligence in biomedical engineering. Boca Raton, FL: CRC Press.

Berbari, E. J. (2000). Principles of electrocardiography. The Biomedical Engineering Handbook, 1, 1 13–11.

Boulos, M. N. K., Wheeler, S., Tavares, C., & Jones, R. (2011). How smartphones are changing the face of mobile and participatory healthcare: An overview, with example from eCAALYX. Biomedical Engineering Online, 10(1), 24.

Bronzino, J. D. (1999). Biomedical engineering handbook *(Vol. 2)*. Boca Raton, FL: CRC press.

Cesarelli, M., Romano, M., & Bifulco, P. (2009). Comparison of short term variability indexes in cardiotocographic foetal monitoring. Computers in Biology and Medicine, 39(2), 106–118.

Chen, Z., Zhang, Z., Zhu, R., Xiang, Y., & Harrington, P. B. (2016). Diagnosis of patients with chronic kidney disease by using two fuzzy classifiers. Chemometrics and Intelligent Laboratory Systems, 153, 140–145.

Chen, Z., Li, J., & Wei, L. (2007). A multiple kernel support vector machine scheme for feature selection and rule extraction from gene expression data of cancer tissue. Artificial Intelligence in Medicine, 41(2), 161–175.

Chiauzzi, E., Rodarte, C., & DasMahapatra, P. (2015). Patient-centered activity monitoring in the self-management of chronic health conditions. BMC Medicine, 13(1), 77.

Cueto-Manzano, A. M., Cortés-Sanabria, L., Martínez-Ramírez, H. R., Rojas-Campos, E., Gómez-Navarro, B., & Castillero-Manzano, M. (2014). Prevalence of chronic kidney disease in an adult population. Archives of Medical Research, 45(6), 507–513.

De Chazal, P., O'Dwyer, M., & Reilly, R. B. (2004). Automatic classification of heartbeats using ECG morphology and heartbeat interval features. IEEE Transactions on Biomedical Engineering, 51(7), 1196–1206.

Dembla, P. (2016). *Multiclass Diagnosis Model for Heart Disease using PSO based SVM*. MS Thesis, Thapar University

Emly, M., Gilmore, L. D., & Roy, S. H. (1992). Electromyography. IEEE Potentials, 11(2), 25–28.

Gopura, R.A. R. C., Kiguchi, K., & Li, Y. (2009). SUEFUL-7: A 7DOF upper-limb exoskeleton robot with muscle-model-oriented EMG-based control. 1126–1131. IEEE.

Gribbin, C., & Thornton, J. (2006). Critical evaluation of fetal assessment methods. High risk pregnancy management options. Amsterdam: Elsevier.

Grivell, R. M., Alfirevic, Z., Gyte, G. M., & Devane, D. (2015). Antenatal cardiotocography for fetal assessment. Cochrane Database of Systematic Reviews, 9.

Hassan, M. M., Uddin, M. Z., Mohamed, A., & Almogren, A. (2018). A robust human activity recognition system using smartphone sensors and deep learning. Future Generation Computer Systems, 81, 307–313.

Hassan, M. R., Hossain, M. M., Begg, R. K., Ramamohanarao, K., & Morsi, Y. (2010). Breast-cancer identification using HMM-fuzzy approach. Computers in Biology and Medicine, 40(3), 240–251.

Hsieh, J., & Hsu, M. -W. (2012). A cloud computing based 12-lead ECG telemedicine service. BMC Medical Informatics and Decision Making, 12(1), 77.

Jerez-Aragonés, J. M., Gómez-Ruiz, J. A., Ramos-Jiménez, G., Muñoz-Pérez, J., & Alba-Conejo, E. (2003). A combined neural network and decision trees model for prognosis of breast cancer relapse. Artificial Intelligence in Medicine, 27(1), 45–63.

Kay, M., Santos, J., & Takane, M. (2011). mHealth: New horizons for health through mobile technologies. World Health Organization, 64(7), 66–71.

Koelstra, S., Muhl, C., Soleymani, M., Lee, J. -S., Yazdani, A., Ebrahimi, T., & Patras, I. (2012). Deap: A database for emotion analysis; using physiological signals. IEEE Transactions on Affective Computing, 3(1), 18–31.

Kurzynski, M., Krysmann, M., Trajdos, P., & Wolczowski, A. (2016). Multiclassifier system with hybrid learning applied to the control of bioprosthetic hand. Computers in Biology and Medicine, 69, 286–297. doi: 10.1016/j.compbiomed.2015.04.023.

Lenzi, T., De Rossi, S., Vitiello, N., Chiri, A., Roccella, S., Giovacchini, F., & Carrozza, M. C. (2009). The neuro-robotics paradigm: NEURARM, NEUROExos, HANDEXOS. *2009 Annual International Conference of the IEEE Engineering in Medicine and Biology Society*, 2430–2433 Minneapolis.

Levin, A., & Stevens, P. E. (2014). Summary of KDIGO 2012 CKD Guideline: Behind the scenes, need for guidance, and a framework for moving forward. Kidney International, 85(1), 49–61.

Liu, L., Peng, Y., Liu, M., & Huang, Z. (2015). Sensor-based human activity recognition system with a multilayered model using time series shapelets. Knowledge-Based Systems, 90, 138–152.

Liu, Y., Nie, L., Liu, L., & Rosenblum, D. S. (2016). From action to activity: Sensor-based activity recognition. Neurocomputing, 181, 108–115.

Lo, H. S., & Xie, S. Q. (2012). Exoskeleton robots for upper-limb rehabilitation: State of the art and future prospects. Medical Engineering and Physics, 34(3), 261–268.

Lum, P. S., Burgar, C. G., Shor, P. C., Majmundar, M., & Van der Loos, M. (2002). Robot-assisted movement training compared with conventional therapy techniques for the rehabilitation of upper-limb motor function after stroke. Archives of Physical Medicine and Rehabilitation, 83(7), 952–959.

Majumder, S., Aghayi, E., Noferesti, M., Memarzadeh-Tehran, H., Mondal, T., Pang, Z., & Deen, M. J. (2017). Smart homes for elderly healthcare—recent advances and research challenges. Sensors, 17(11), 2496.

Marcano-Cedeño, A., Quintanilla-Domínguez, J., & Andina, D. (2011). WBCD breast cancer database classification applying artificial metaplasticity neural network. *Expert Systems with Applications*, *38*(8), 9573–9579.

Menshawy, M. E., Benharref, A., & Serhani, M. (2015). An automatic mobile-health based approach for EEG epileptic seizures detection. Expert Systems with Applications, 42(20), 7157–7174.

Mercaldo, F., Nardone, V., & Santone, A. (2017). Diabetes mellitus affected patients classification and diagnosis through machine learning techniques. Procedia Computer Science, 112, 2519–2528.

Mohri, M., Rostamizadeh, A., & Talwalkar, A. (2018). Foundations of machine learning. Cambridge MA: MIT press.

Mshali, H., Lemlouma, T., Moloney, M., & Magoni, D. (2018). A survey on health monitoring systems for health smart homes. International Journal of Industrial Ergonomics, 66, 26–56.

Muthukumar, P., & Krishnan, G. S. S. (2016). A similarity measure of intuitionistic fuzzy soft sets and its application in medical diagnosis. Applied Soft Computing, 41, 148–156.

Neves, P., Stachyra, M., & Rodrigues, J. (2008). Application of wireless sensor networks to healthcare promotion. *Journal of Communications Software and Systems*, *4*(3).

Niedermeyer, E., & da Silva, F. L. (2005). Electroencephalography: Basic principles, clinical applications and related fields. Philadelphia: Lippincott Williams & Wilkins.

Nikolic, M. (2001). Findings and firing pattern analysis in controls and patients with myopathy and amytrophic lateral sclerosis. Copenhagen: University of Copenhagen.

Pan, J., & Tompkins, W. J. (1985). A real-time QRS detection algorithm. IEEE Transactions on Biomedical Engineering, 32(3), 230–236.

Pérez-Sáez, M. J., Prieto-Alhambra, D., Barrios, C., Crespo, M., Redondo, D., Nogués, X., & Pascual, J. (2015). Increased hip fracture and mortality in chronic kidney disease individuals: The importance of competing risks. Bone, 73, 154–159.

Reyes-Ortiz, J. -L., Oneto, L., Sama, A., Parra, X., & Anguita, D. (2016). Transition-aware human activity recognition using smartphones. Neurocomputing, 171, 754–767.

Riener, R., Nef, T., & Colombo, G. (2005). Robot-aided neurorehabilitation of the upper extremities. Medical and Biological Engineering and Computing, 43(1), 2–10.

Rojas-Galeano, S., Hsieh, E., Agranoff, D., Krishna, S., & Fernandez-Reyes, D. (2008). Estimation of relevant variables on high-dimensional biological patterns using iterated weighted kernel functions. PloS One, 3(3), e1806.

Sahin, H., & Subasi, A. (2015). Classification of the cardiotocogram data for anticipation of fetal risks using machine learning techniques. Applied Soft Computing, 33, 231–238.

Sanei, S. (2013). *Adaptive processing of brain signals*. West Sussex, United Kingdom: John Wiley & Sons.

Sanei, S., & Chambers, J. A. (2013). EEG signal processing. Hoboken: John Wiley & Sons.

Sapsanis, C., Georgoulas, G., & Tzes, A. (2013). EMG based classification of basic hand movements based on time-frequency features. *21st Mediterranean Conference on Control and Automation*, 716–722.

Sasaki, D., Noritsugu, T., & Takaiwa, M. (2005). Development of active support splint driven by pneumatic soft actuator (ASSIST). *Proceedings of the 2005 IEEE International Conference on Robotics and Automation*, 520–525 Barcelona, Spain.

Serhani, M. A., El Menshawy, M., & Benharref, A. (2016). SME2EM: Smart mobile end-to-end monitoring architecture for life-long diseases. Computers in Biology and Medicine, 68, 137–154.

Smith, J. W., Everhart, J., Dickson, W., Knowler, W., & Johannes, R. (1988). Using the ADAP learning algorithm to forecast the onset of diabetes mellitus. *Proceedings of the Annual Symposium on Computer Application in Medical Care*, 261–265 American Medical Informatics Association.

Sörnmo, L., & Laguna, P. (2005). *Bioelectrical signal processing in cardiac and neurological applications (Vol. 8)*. San Diego, CA: Academic Press.

Subasi, A. (2019a). Electroencephalogram-controlled assistive devices. In K. Pal, H.-B. Kraatz, A. Khasnobish, S. Bag, I. Banerjee, & U. Kuruganti (Eds.), Bioelectronics and Medical Devices (pp. 261–284). https://doi.org/10.1016/B978-0-08-102420-1.00016-9.

Subasi, A. (2019b). Electromyogram-controlled assistive devices. *Bioelectronics and medical devices*. Amsterdam: Elsevier 285 - 311.

Subasi, A. (2019c). *Practical guide for biomedical signals analysis using machine learning techniques, a MATLAB based approach (1st ed.)*. Cambridge, MA: Academic Press.

Subasi, A., Ahmed, A., Aličković, E., & Rashik Hassan, A. (2019d). Effect of photic stimulation for migraine detection using random forest and discrete wavelet transform. Biomedical Signal Processing and Control, 49, 231–239. doi: 10.1016/j.bspc.2018.12.011.

Subasi, A., Alickovic, E., & Kevric, J. (2017). Diagnosis of chronic kidney disease by using random forest. In CMBE-BIH 2017 (pp. 589–594). Springer.

Subasi, A., Bandic, L., & Qaisar, S. M. (2020a). Cloud-based health monitoring framework using smart sensors and smartphone. *Innovation in health informatics*. Amsterdam: Elsevier 217 -L 243.

Subasi, A., Dammas, D. H., Alghamdi, R. D., Makawi, R. A., Albiety, E. A., Brahimi, T., & Sarirete, A. (2018). Sensor based human activity recognition using Adaboost ensemble classifier. *Procedia Computer Science*, *140*, 104–111. doi: 10.1016/j.procs.2018.10.298.

Subasi, A., Fllatah, A., Alzobidi, K., Brahimi, T., & Sarirete, A. (2019e). Smartphone-based human activity recognition using bagging and boosting. *Presented at the the 16th International Learning and Technology Conference* Jeddah, Saudi Arabia.

Subasi, A., Kadasa, B., & Kremic, E. (2019). Classification of the cardiotocogram data for anticipation of fetal risks using bagging ensemble classifier. *Presented at the Complex Adaptive Systems Conference*. Malvern: PA November 13.

Subasi, A., Khateeb, K., Brahimi, T., & Sarirete, A. (2020b). Human activity recognition using machine learning methods in a smart healthcare environment. *Innovation in Health Informatics*. Amsterdam: Elsevier 123 –L 144.

Thaler, M. (2017). The only EKG book you'll ever need. Philadelphia: Lippincott Williams & Wilkins.

UCI Machine Learning Repository: Breast Cancer Wisconsin (Diagnostic) Data Set. (n.d.). Retrieved November 17, 2019, from https://archive.ics.uci.edu/ml/datasets/Breast+Cancer+Wisconsin+(Diagnostic).

UCI Machine Learning Repository: Chronic_Kidney_Disease Data Set. (n.d.). Retrieved November 19, 2019, from https://archive.ics.uci.edu/ml/datasets/Chronic_Kidney_Disease#.

UCI Machine Learning Repository: REALDISP Activity Recognition Dataset Data Set. (n.d.). Retrieved June 24, 2018, from https://archive.ics.uci.edu/ml/datasets/REALDISP+Activity+Recognition+Dataset#.

UCI Machine Learning Repository: Smartphone-Based Recognition of Human Activities and Postural Transitions Data Set. (n.d.). Retrieved November 22, 2018, from https://archive.ics.uci.edu/ml/datasets/Smartphone-Based+Recognition+of+Human+Activities+and+Postural+Transitions#.

Van Geijn, H. P., Jongsma, H. W., de Haan, J., & Eskes, T. K. (1980). Analysis of heart rate and beat-to-beat variability: Interval difference index. American Journal of Obstetrics and Gynecology, 138(3), 246–252.

Vural, H., & Subasi, A. (2015). Data-mining techniques to classify microarray gene expression data using gene selection by SVD and information gain. Modeling of Artificial Intelligence, 6, 171–182.

Wojtczak, P., Amaral, T. G., Dias, O. P., Wolczowski, A., & Kurzynski, M. (2009). Hand movement recognition based on biosignal analysis. Engineering Applications of Artificial Intelligence, 22(4), 608–615.

Wołczowski, A., & Zdunek, R. (2017). Electromyography and mechanomyography signal recognition: Experimental analysis using multi-way array decomposition methods. Biocybernetics and Biomedical Engineering, 37(1), 103–113 https://doi.org/10.1016/j.bbe.2016.09.004.

Xu, X., & Zhang, A. (2006). *Boost feature subset selection: A new gene selection algorithm for microarray dataset*. Berlin: Springer 670 – 677.

Xu, Y., Shen, Z., Zhang, X., Gao, Y., Deng, S., Wang, Y., & Chang, C. (2017). Learning multi-level features for sensor-based human action recognition. Pervasive and Mobile Computing, 40, 324–338.

CHAPTER

# 5

# Other classification examples

## 5.1 Intrusion detection

One of the biggest threats to the corporate network involves attacks on its information technology (IT) infrastructure. Particularly for the companies established in a distributed manner, IT managers should extend the security outside the corporate backbone. The prospective vulnerabilities—including but not limited to Internet connections, remote and local corporate office interconnections, and links between trusted partners—should all be taken into consideration. Unfortunately the focus on security for corporate resources and internal traffic only do not help us recognize the endeavored attacks or discover the potential vulnerabilities across the company. Usually the need for intrusion detection systems (IDSs) is questioned. Why are firewalls not sufficient for security? One way to point out the difference is to classify the security threats. Do attacks arise from outside of the company network or from within? Usually firewalls act as a protecting wall between company internal networks and the outside network (Internet). Any traffic passing through is filtered according to the predefined security policies. Unfortunately all access to the Internet is not through the firewall. Some users might connect to the Internet with an unauthorized connection from their internal network. In the meantime not all threats occur outside the firewall. Actually, a great deal of security incidents and losses are traced back to insiders. Moreover, firewalls are the focus of the attackers themselves. It would be sufficient protection if you do not consider these facts. Companies with connections to public Internet domains do not have the luxury of relying on a single form of security. Therefore firewalls must be complemented with intrusion detection systems (IDSs) (Bace, 1999).

IDSs detect computer attacks and/or system misuse, and once an attack is detected they alert the appropriate people. Each IDS tool or system serves three crucial security functions—monitoring, detection, and response to any type of unauthorized activities within or outside of the company network. Any IDS program utilizes policies to identify intrusion events. Once an event is triggered, an appropriate response is delivered according to the policy. Some IDS programs can issue a warning to the systems administrator. Certain IDS programs do behave as a preventive measure and act upon a security threat. They can respond to certain attack types, like disabling an account, logging off a user, and running certain scripts. Hence the IDS program is the only practical approach designed to investigate attacks both from the inside

**Practical Machine Learning for Data Analysis Using Python. http://dx.doi.org/10.1016/B978-0-12-821379-7.00005-9**

and outside of the corporate network. Intrusions can be initiated for financial, political, or military gains or some sort of personal reason (Innella & McMillan, 2017).

An IDS is software that tracks a system's networks or operations and checks for suspicious activity and warns when unauthorized acts are observed (Tiwari, Kumar, Bharti, & Kishan, 2017). IDSs use machine learning algorithms to differentiate between normal and abnormal behaviors in a network. Machine learning has become an effective approach for minimizing the abundance of information and improving decision-making through optimizing useful knowledge by determining relationships in the data collected (Govindarajan & Chandrasekaran, 2011). Intrusion detection is a mechanism to detect events of attack that actively seek to damage the network. In order to achieve better protection and reduce damage and/or other future attempts, recording these events is crucial. Security professionals utilize sensors positioned in front of and behind firewalls and compare the results obtained by both sensors (Sahu, Mishra, Das, & Mishra, 2014). Due to the rapid growth of urbanization and the trend of Internet of Things (IoT), many security concerns and challenges have risen as well. Cyberattacks are vulnerable to sensor-based IoT devices and computers for data collection and analysis. Machine learning algorithms efficiently detect intrusions and malicious activities (Goel & Hong, 2015).

## Example 5.1

The following Python code is used to classify intrusion detection data using the decision tree classifier employing 10-fold cross-validation and separate training and test sets. The classification accuracy, precision, recall, F1 score, and entropy are calculated. The confusion matrix is also given.

***Dataset information:*** Dataset is downloaded from KDD Cup 1999 Data website (http://kdd.ics.uci.edu/databases/kddcup99/kddcup99.html). This is the dataset employed for The Third International Knowledge Discovery and Data Mining Tools competition that was conducted in conjunction with KDD-99 Fifth International Conference on Knowledge Discovery and Data Mining. The competition task was to develop a network intrusion detection system, a predictive model capable of distinguishing between "anomaly" connections, called intrusions or attacks, and normal connections. This database involves a standard set of data to be audited that contains a wide variety of intrusions simulated in a military network environment.

```
#=========================================================================
# Anomaly detection with KDD dataset using decision tree
#=========================================================================
#import the libraries
import numpy as np
import matplotlib.pyplot as plt
import pandas as pd
#Load the dataset
dataset = pd.read_csv('kddcup.data_10_percent_corrected')
dataset['normal.'] = dataset['normal.'].replace(['back.', 'buffer_
overflow.', 'ftp_write.', 'guess_passwd.', 'imap.', 'ipsweep.',
'land.', 'loadmodule.', 'multihop.', 'neptune.', 'nmap.', 'perl.',
```

```
'phf.', 'pod.', 'portsweep.', 'rootkit.', 'satan.', 'smurf.', 'spy.',
'teardrop.', 'warezclient.', 'warezmaster.'], 'attack')
x = dataset.iloc[:, :-1].values
y = dataset.iloc[:, 41].values
#%%
#encoding categorical data
from sklearn.preprocessing import LabelEncoder, OneHotEncoder
labelencoder_x_1 = LabelEncoder()
labelencoder_x_2 = LabelEncoder()
labelencoder_x_3 = LabelEncoder()
x[:, 1] = labelencoder_x_1.fit_transform(x[:, 1])
x[:, 2] = labelencoder_x_2.fit_transform(x[:, 2])
x[:, 3] = labelencoder_x_3.fit_transform(x[:, 3])
onehotencoder_1 = OneHotEncoder(categorical_features = [1])
x = onehotencoder_1.fit_transform(x).toarray()
onehotencoder_2 = OneHotEncoder(categorical_features = [4])
x = onehotencoder_2.fit_transform(x).toarray()
onehotencoder_3 = OneHotEncoder(categorical_features = [70])
x = onehotencoder_3.fit_transform(x).toarray()
labelencoder_y = LabelEncoder()
y = labelencoder_y.fit_transform(y)

#splitting the dataset into the training set and test set
from sklearn.model_selection import train_test_split
x_train, x_test, y_train, y_test = train_test_split(x, y, test_size = 0.3,
random_state = 0)

#feature scaling
from sklearn.preprocessing import StandardScaler
sc_x = StandardScaler()
x_train = sc_x.fit_transform(x_train)
x_test = sc_x.transform(x_test)

# Fitting Decision Tree to the Training set
from sklearn import tree
# fit model no training data
classifier = tree.DecisionTreeClassifier()
classifier.fit(x_train, y_train)

# Predicting the Test set results
y_pred = classifier.predict(x_test)

# Making the Confusion Matrix
from sklearn.metrics import confusion_matrix
cm = confusion_matrix(y_test, y_pred)
```

```
# Applying k-Fold Cross Validation
from sklearn.model_selection import cross_val_score
accuracies = cross_val_score(estimator = classifier, X = x_train, y = y_train,
cv = 10)

#%%
print("CV Accuracy: %0.4f (+/- %0.4f)" % (accuracies.mean(), accuracies.
std() * 2))
#the performance of the classification model
print("Test Accuracy is : %0.4f" % ((cm[0,0] + cm[1,1])/
(cm[0,0] + cm[0,1] + cm[1,0] + cm[1,1])))
recall = cm[1,1]/(cm[0,1] + cm[1,1])
print("Recall is : %0.4f" % (recall))
print("False Positive rate: %0.4f" %(cm[1,0]/(cm[0,0] + cm[1,0])))
precision = cm[1,1]/(cm[1,0] + cm[1,1])
print("Precision is: %0.4f" %(precision))
print("F-measure is: %0.4f" % (2*((precision*recall)/
(precision + recall))))
from math import log
print("Entropy is: %0.4f" % (-precision*log(precision)))
print("\nConfusion Matrix:\n", cm)
```

## 5.2 Phishing website detection

Global communication plays an important role in fast network technology development, especially in e-commerce, electronic banking, social networks, etc. These activities are now being shifted to cyberspace. Cyberspace threats focus on insecure Internet infrastructure. Consumer security is not an easy task as it contains the scam of phishing. It goes from the fall to the scam of phishing. Internet features must be taken into consideration and focus must be placed on those who are relatively experienced users (Curtis, Rajivan, Jones, & Gonzalez, 2018). Large amounts of personal information, money, and other critical data and information have been destroyed by cyberattacks. The subject of phishing attacks has been researched in recent years. This has become a popular tool for hackers generating fraudulent websites. If these websites are reviewed for further analysis, you can see they contain malicious elements, particularly when analyzing the uniform resource locators (URLs). The attacker's purpose is to use the URL to obtain as much as possible of the victim's personal information, sensitive information, financial data, passwords, usernames, and more (Gupta, Arachchilage, & Psannis, 2018). Detection of phishing attacks plays a crucial role in online banking and trading, and many users believe they are secure from such assaults. Such attacks start by sending an initial e-mail, with all applicable credentials, seeking to obtain the victim's data and information via a connection shared in the e-mail. There are few ways phishers can be detected. Two known methods are utilized to detect phishing websites. One includes verifying the URL, which involves checking if the URL is on a blacklist (Gastellier-Prevost, Granadillo, & Laurent, 2011). The other method is called the meta-heuristic approach. Using this method, several features are collected. By gathering this information by using an identification process, the URL is identified as a legitimate website or phishing website (Xiang, Hong, Rose, & Cranor, 2011). Machine learning methods are employed to search and recognize patterns and to discover connections among them (Han, Pei, & Kamber, 2011). Machine learning is important for decision-making, as decisions are based on the rules followed by the learner (Mohammad, Thabtah, & McCluskey, 2014; Subasi & Kremic, 2019; Subasi, Molah, Almkallawi, & Chaudhery, 2017).

## Example 5.2

The following Python code is used to classify phishing websites data employing random forest classifier by using separate training and test sets and 10-fold cross-validation. The classification accuracy, precision, recall, F1 score, Cohen kappa score, and Matthews correlation coefficient are calculated. The classification report and confusion matrix are also given.

***Dataset information:*** In this example, the publicly available phishing websites dataset is downloaded from the UCI machine learning repository (UCI, 2017) is used. The data is collected and donated by Mohammad et al. (Mohammad, Thabtah, & McCluskey, 2012; Mohammad et al., 2014; Mohammad, Thabtah, & McCluskey, 2015). The features that are employed in the dataset are defined in Mohammad et al. (2015). The features are: IP address, URLs with an "@" symbol, redirecting using "//" symbol, URL shortening services such as "TinyURL," long URLs to hide the suspicious elements, subdomains and multi-subdomains, adding a prefix or suffix separated by (-) to the domain, domain registration length, favicon, HTTPS (hyper text transfer protocol with secure sockets layer), usage of a nonstandard port, request URLs, the existence of "HTTPS" token in the domain part of the URL, URL of anchor, website traffic, server form handler (SFH), abnormal URLs, status bar customization, submitting information to e-mail, website forwarding, pagerank, number of links pointing to the page, disabling right-click, age of domain, IFrame redirection, usage of pop-up windows, DNS record, Google index, and statistical reports–based features (Subasi & Kremic, 2019).

```
#=========================================================================
# Phishing website example
#=========================================================================
"""
Created on Tue Jun 18 18:14:15 2019
@author: asubasi
"""
import pandas as pd
import warnings
#To prevent warnings
warnings.filterwarnings("ignore")
# load data
dataset = pd.read_csv("PhishingWebsiteDataset.csv")
#To prevent the "ValueError Input contains NaN, infinity or a value too large
for dtype('float32')"
```

```
dataset[:] = np.nan_to_num(dataset)
# split data into X and y
X = dataset.iloc[:,0:30]
y = dataset.iloc[:, 30]
class_names = dataset.iloc[:, 30]
#%%
#==========================================================================
# Random forest example with training and test set
#==========================================================================
#splitting the dataset into the training set and test set
from sklearn.model_selection import train_test_split
X_train, X_test, y_train, y_test = train_test_split(X, y, test_size = 0.3,
random_state = 0)
#%%
#feature scaling
from sklearn.preprocessing import StandardScaler
sc_X = StandardScaler()
X_train = sc_X.fit_transform(X_train)
X_test = sc_X.transform(X_test)

#%%
# Fitting Random Forest to the Training set
from sklearn.ensemble import RandomForestClassifier
#In order to change to accuracy increase n_estimators
"""RandomForestClassifier(n_estimators = 'warn', criterion = 'gini', max_
depth = None,
min_samples_split = 2, min_samples_leaf = 1, min_weight_fraction_leaf = 0.0,
max_features = 'auto', max_leaf_nodes = None, min_impurity_decrease = 0.0,
min_impurity_split = None, bootstrap = True, oob_score = False, n_
jobs = None,
random_state = None, verbose = 0, warm_start = False, class_weight = None)"""
# fit model no training data
model = RandomForestClassifier(n_estimators = 100)
model.fit(X_train, y_train)

# Predicting the Test set results
y_pred = model.predict(X_test)
#%%
from sklearn import metrics
print('Test Accuracy:', np.round(metrics.accuracy_score(y_test,y_
pred),4))
print('Precision:', np.round(metrics.precision_score(y_test,
                              y_pred,average = 'weighted'),4))
```

```
print('Recall:', np.round(metrics.recall_score(y_test,y_pred,
                                              average = 'weighted'),4))
print('F1 Score:', np.round(metrics.f1_score(y_test,y_pred,
                                              average = 'weighted'),4))
print('Cohen Kappa Score:', np.round(metrics.cohen_kappa_score(y_test,y_
pred),4))
print('Matthews Corrcoef:', np.round(metrics.matthews_corrcoef(y_test,y_
pred),4))
print('\t\tClassification Report:\n', metrics.classification_report(y_
test,y_pred))

from sklearn.metrics import confusion_matrix
print("Confusion Matrix:\n",confusion_matrix(y_test,y_pred))
#%%
from sklearn.metrics import confusion_matrix
import seaborn as sns
# Making the Confusion Matrix
cm = confusion_matrix(y_test, y_pred)
#Print the Confusion Matrix
target_names = ['Legitimite','Phishing']
plt.figure(figsize = (6, 4))
sns.heatmap(cm,cmap = 'coolwarm',linecolor = 'white',linewidths = 1,
                xticklabels = target_names,
                yticklabels = target_names,
                annot = True,
                fmt = 'd')
plt.title('Confusion Matrix')
plt.ylabel('True Label')
plt.xlabel('Predicted Label')
plt.show()
#%%
#===========================================================================
# Random forest example with cross-validation
#===========================================================================
from sklearn.ensemble import RandomForestClassifier
#In order to change to accuracy increase n_estimators
"""RandomForestClassifier(n_estimators = 'warn', criterion = 'gini', max_
depth = None,
min_samples_split = 2, min_samples_leaf = 1, min_weight_fraction_
leaf = 0.0,
max_features = 'auto', max_leaf_nodes = None, min_impurity_
decrease = 0.0,
```

```
min_impurity_split = None, bootstrap = True, oob_score = False, n_
jobs = None,
random_state = None, verbose = 0, warm_start = False, class_weight = None)"""
# fit model no training data
model = RandomForestClassifier(n_estimators = 100)

CV = 10 #10-Fold Cross Validation
#Evaluate Model Using 10-Fold Cross Validation and Print Performance
Metrics
Acc_scores = cross_val_score(model, X, y, cv = CV)
print("Accuracy: %0.3f (+/- %0.3f)" % (Acc_scores.mean(), Acc_scores.
std() * 2))
f1_scores = cross_val_score(model, X, y, cv = CV,scoring = 'f1_macro')
print("F1 score: %0.3f (+/- %0.3f)" % (f1_scores.mean(), f1_scores.std()
* 2))
Precision_scores = cross_val_score(model, X, y,
cv = CV,scoring = 'precision_macro')
print("Precision score: %0.3f (+/- %0.3f)" % (Precision_scores.mean(),
Precision_scores.std() * 2))
Recall_scores = cross_val_score(model, X, y, cv = CV,scoring = 'recall_
macro')
print("Recall score: %0.3f (+/- %0.3f)" % (Recall_scores.mean(), Recall_
scores.std() * 2))
from sklearn.metrics import cohen_kappa_score, make_scorer
kappa_scorer = make_scorer(cohen_kappa_score)
Kappa_scores = cross_val_score(model, X, y, cv = CV,scoring = kappa_scorer)
print("Kappa score: %0.3f (+/- %0.3f)" % (Kappa_scores.mean(), Kappa_
scores.std() * 2))
```

## 5.3 Spam e-mail detection

E-mail is one of the cheapest, fastest, most accurate, and most popular elements of communication. It is part of our daily lives, evolving the paths we take and changing the way we work together. E-mails are used as task managers, conversation organizers, archivers, and delivery systems for documents. The disadvantage of this achievement is that e-mails are often growing in size. Most clients organize and archive e-mails into files in order to avoid this problem and automate retrieval when appropriate. It is impossible to identify who came up with the idea that at least one person would react to an e-mail irrespective of the deal enclosed by sending advertising to many people at once. E-mail provides an effective way of delivering millions of ads without charge, and several companies are already using this tool extensively. As a consequence, millions of users' inboxes are filled with these so-called unwanted messages, often classified as "junk mail" or "spam." The ability to send spam freely creates a lot of concern in the Internet community; huge amounts of spam traffic cause delays in delivering important e-mails, and people with dial-up Internet access have to devote bandwidth to receiving junk mail. When categorizing unwanted messages, there is always the risk of removing important mail by mistake. Finally, there are a large number of spam e-mails that should not be seen by children (Subasi, Alzahrani, Aljuhani, & Aljedani, 2018).Several approaches have been provided to counter spam. There are "private" solutions, such as simple personal involvement and legal action. Some technical tools include restricting IP addresses of spammers and filtering e-mails. Yet there is still no complete and optimal way to remove spam e-mails, so the amount of junk mail continues to grow. The growing use of e-mail in previous years has resulted in the emergence and further increase of problems caused by unsolicited bulk e-mail messages. Spam e-mail filtering focuses on e-mail letter interpretation and additional information, attempting to classify spam messages. The action that is taken once spam is recognized is generally dependent on the setting in which the filter is applied. When used as a client-side filter by a single user, they are often sent to a folder containing only spam-labeled e-mails, making it easier to identify these messages (Guzella & Caminhas, 2009; Subasi et al., 2018). Spam filtering approaches are currently based on categorizing e-mails from word-automatic rules or keywords that evaluate e-mail features (Androutsopoulos, Koutsias, Chandrinos, Paliouras, & Spyropoulos, 2000).

## Example 5.3

The following Python code is used to classify the spam e-mail dataset using random forest classifier by employing separate training and test sets and 10-fold cross-validation. The classification accuracy, precision, recall, F1 score, Cohen kappa score, and Matthews correlation coefficient are calculated. The classification report and confusion matrix are also given.

***Dataset information***: E-mail dataset is downloaded from UCI machine learning data repository (Bache & Lichman, 2013). Spam e-mails came from the postmaster and individuals who had filed spam. Nonspam e-mails came from filed work and personal e-mails. These are helpful when forming a personalized spam filter. One would either have to blind such nonspam indicators or get an extensive collection of nonspam to create a general-purpose spam filter. In this database, there are 4601 messages out of which 1813 are categorized as spam. Each e-mail message is composed of 57 feature vectors.

```
#=======================================================================
# Spam e-mail filtering example
#=======================================================================
"""
Created on Tue Jun 18 18:14:15 2019
@author: asubasi
"""
from sklearn.model_selection import train_test_split
import numpy as np
import pandas as pd
```

```
# load data
dataset = pd.read_csv("SpamEmail.csv")

# split data into X and Y
X = dataset.iloc[:,0:57]
y = dataset.iloc[:, 57]
class_names = dataset.iloc[:, 57]
#%%
#==========================================================================
# Random forest example with training and test set
#==========================================================================
#splitting the dataset into the training set and test set
from sklearn.model_selection import train_test_split
X_train, X_test, y_train, y_test = train_test_split(X, y, test_
size = 0.3, random_state = 0)

#%%
#feature scaling
from sklearn.preprocessing import StandardScaler
sc_X = StandardScaler()
X_train = sc_X.fit_transform(X_train)
X_test = sc_X.transform(X_test)

#%%
# Fitting Random Forest to the Training set
from sklearn.ensemble import RandomForestClassifier
#In order to change to accuracy increase n_estimators
"""RandomForestClassifier(n_estimators = 'warn', criterion = 'gini', max_
depth = None,
min_samples_split = 2, min_samples_leaf = 1, min_weight_fraction_
leaf = 0.0,
max_features = 'auto', max_leaf_nodes = None, min_impurity_decrease = 0.0,
min_impurity_split = None, bootstrap = True, oob_score = False, n_
jobs = None,
random_state = None, verbose = 0, warm_start = False, class_
weight = None)"""
# fit model no training data
model = RandomForestClassifier(n_estimators = 100)
model.fit(X_train, y_train)

# Predicting the Test set results
y_pred = model.predict(X_test)
#%%
from sklearn import metrics
```

```
print('Test Accuracy:', np.round(metrics.accuracy_score(y_test,y_pred),4))
print('Precision:', np.round(metrics.precision_score(y_test,
                            y_pred,average = 'weighted'),4))
print('Recall:', np.round(metrics.recall_score(y_test,y_pred,
                                               average = 'weighted'),4))
print('F1 Score:', np.round(metrics.f1_score(y_test,y_pred,
                                               average = 'weighted'),4))
print('Cohen Kappa Score:', np.round(metrics.cohen_kappa_score(y_test,y_
pred),4))
print('Matthews Corrcoef:', np.round(metrics.matthews_corrcoef(y_test,y_
pred),4))
print('\t\tClassification Report:\n', metrics.classification_report(y_
test,y_pred))

from sklearn.metrics import confusion_matrix
print("Confusion Matrix:\n",confusion_matrix(y_test,y_pred))
#%%
from sklearn.metrics import confusion_matrix
import seaborn as sns
import matplotlib.pyplot as plt
# Making the Confusion Matrix
cm = confusion_matrix(y_test, y_pred)
#Print the Confusion Matrix
target_names = ['NotSPAM','SPAM' ]
plt.figure(figsize = (6, 4))
sns.heatmap(cm,cmap = 'coolwarm',linecolor = 'white',linewidths = 1,
                xticklabels = target_names,
                yticklabels = target_names,
                annot = True,
                fmt = 'd')
plt.title('Confusion Matrix')
plt.ylabel('True Label')
plt.xlabel('Predicted Label')
plt.show()
#%%
#=========================================================================
# Random forest example with cross-validation
#=========================================================================
from sklearn.ensemble import RandomForestClassifier
#In order to change to accuracy increase n_estimators
"""RandomForestClassifier(n_estimators = 'warn', criterion = 'gini', max_
depth = None,
min_samples_split = 2, min_samples_leaf = 1, min_weight_fraction_
leaf = 0.0,
```

```
max_features = 'auto', max_leaf_nodes = None, min_impurity_decrease = 0.0,
min_impurity_split = None, bootstrap = True, oob_score = False, n_
jobs = None,
random_state = None, verbose = 0, warm_start = False, class_
weight = None)"""
# fit model no training data
model = RandomForestClassifier(n_estimators = 100)

# Applying k-Fold Cross Validation
from sklearn.model_selection import cross_val_score
CV = 10 #10-Fold Cross Validation
#Evaluate Model Using 10-Fold Cross Validation and Print Performance Metrics
Acc_scores = cross_val_score(model, X, y, cv = CV)
print("Accuracy: %0.3f (+/- %0.3f)" % (Acc_scores.mean(), Acc_scores.
std() * 2))
f1_scores = cross_val_score(model, X, y, cv = CV,scoring = 'f1_macro')
print("F1 score: %0.3f (+/- %0.3f)" % (f1_scores.mean(), f1_scores.std()
* 2))
Precision_scores = cross_val_score(model, X, y, cv = CV,scoring = 'precision_
macro')
print("Precision score: %0.3f (+/- %0.3f)" % (Precision_scores.mean(),
Precision_scores.std() * 2))
Recall_scores = cross_val_score(model, X, y, cv = CV,scoring = 'recall_
macro')
print("Recall score: %0.3f (+/- %0.3f)" % (Recall_scores.mean(), Recall_
scores.std() * 2))
from sklearn.metrics import cohen_kappa_score, make_scorer
kappa_scorer = make_scorer(cohen_kappa_score)
Kappa_scores = cross_val_score(model, X, y, cv = CV,scoring = kappa_scorer)
print("Kappa score: %0.3f (+/- %0.3f)" % (Kappa_scores.mean(), Kappa_
scores.std() * 2))
```

## 5.4 Credit scoring

Credit scoring is a crucial part of banks' and other financial institutions' credit risk management systems since it eliminates risks, increases predictability, and speeds up lending decisions (Chuang & Huang, 2011; Serrano-Cinca & Gutiérrez-Nieto, 2016). Because customer credit management is critical task for financial organizations and commercial banks, they must be careful when dealing with customer loans to avoid any faulty decisions that may result in loss of opportunity or finances. In addition, incorrect customer credibility assessments can have a significant impact on the financial organization's stability. The labor-intensive customer creditworthiness evaluation is time and resource consuming. In contrast, a labor-intensive analysis is mostly reliant on the bank employee, and computer-based digital credit appraisal systems were designed and implemented to remove the "human factor" in this phase. Such a computer-based automated credit evaluation model can provide banks and financial organizations with recommendations as to whether or not a loan should be given and whether or not the loan will be returned. A number of credit models have been implemented at the moment, but there is no perfect classification among them, as some of them yield reliable outputs and some of them do not (Ala'raj & Abbod, 2016 Ala'raj & Abbod, 2016). Credit scoring by financial industries and researchers became a frequently studied field (Kumar & Ravi, 2007; Lin, Hu, & Tsai, 2012), and many models are investigated and implemented using various algorithms, such as the artificial neural network, the decision tree (Hung & Chen, 2009; Makowski, 1985), the support vector machine (Baesens et al., 2003; Huang, Chen, & Wang, 2007; Schebesch & Stecking, 2005), and case-based reasoning (Shin & Han, 2001; Wheeler & Aitken, 2000). As a result of the financial crises, the Basel Committee on Banking Supervision asked all banking and financial institutions to introduce robust credit risk analysis frameworks before giving a loan to a company or individual (Ala'raj & Abbod, 2016; Gicić & Subasi, 2019)

## Example 5.4

The following Python code is used to classify the credit scoring dataset employing XGBoost classifier by using separate training and test set and 10-fold cross-validation. The classification accuracy, precision, recall, F1 score, Cohen kappa score, and Matthews correlation coefficient are calculated. The classification report and confusion matrix are also given.

***Dataset information:*** This dataset is downloaded from UCI machine learning repository (UCI, 2019). The original dataset, provided by Prof. Hofmann, contains categorical/symbolic attributes. There are two classes (Good and Bad) and 1000 instances with 20 attributes, which are:

- status of existing checking account
- duration in month
- credit history
- purpose
- credit amount
- savings account/bonds
- present employment
- installment rate in percentage of disposable income
- personal status and sex
- other debtors/guarantors
- present residence since
- property
- age in years
- other installment plans
- housing
- number of existing credits at this bank
- job
- number of people responsible for

- telephone
- foreign worker

```
#=============================================================================
# Credit scoring example
#=============================================================================
"""
Created on Tue Jun 18 18:14:15 2019
@author: asubasi
"""

import numpy as np
import pandas as pd

# load data
dataset = pd.read_csv("german_credit.csv")
# split data into X and Y
X = dataset.iloc[:,1:20]
y = dataset.iloc[:, 0]
class_names = dataset.iloc[:,0]
#=============================================================================
# XGBoost example with training and test set
#=============================================================================
from sklearn.model_selection import train_test_split
# split data into train and test sets
Xtrain, Xtest, ytrain, ytest = train_test_split(X, y, test_size = 0.33,
random_state = 7)

from xgboost import XGBClassifier
# fit model no training data
model = XGBClassifier()
model.fit(Xtrain, ytrain)
# make predictions for test data
ypred = model.predict(Xtest)
from sklearn import metrics
print('Accuracy:', np.round(metrics.accuracy_score(ytest,ypred),4))
print('Precision:', np.round(metrics.precision_score(ytest,
                            ypred,average = 'weighted'),4))
print('Recall:', np.round(metrics.recall_score(ytest,ypred,
                                               average = 'weighted'),4))
print('F1 Score:', np.round(metrics.f1_score(ytest,ypred,
                                               average = 'weighted'),4))
print('Cohen Kappa Score:', np.round(metrics.cohen_kappa_score(ytest,
ypred),4))
```

```
print('Matthews Corrcoef:', np.round(metrics.matthews_corrcoef(ytest,
ypred),4))
print('\t\tClassification Report:\n', metrics.classification_report(ypred,
ytest))

from sklearn.metrics import confusion_matrix
from io import BytesIO #neded for plot
import seaborn as sns; sns.set()
import matplotlib.pyplot as plt

mat = confusion_matrix(ytest, ypred)
sns.heatmap(mat.T, square = True, annot = True, fmt = 'd', cbar = False)
plt.xlabel('true label')
plt.ylabel('predicted label');

plt.savefig("SVM_Confusion.jpg")
# Save SVG in a fake file object.
f = BytesIO()
plt.savefig(f, format = "svg")

#%%
#=========================================================================
# XGBoost example with cross-validation
#=========================================================================
from xgboost import XGBClassifier
# fit model no training data
model = XGBClassifier()

# Applying k-Fold Cross Validation
from sklearn.model_selection import cross_val_score
CV = 10 #10-Fold Cross Validation
#Evaluate Model Using 10-Fold Cross Validation and Print Performance Metrics
Acc_scores = cross_val_score(model, X, y, cv = CV)
print("Accuracy: %0.3f (+/- %0.3f)" % (Acc_scores.mean(), Acc_scores.
std() * 2))
f1_scores = cross_val_score(model, X, y, cv = CV,scoring = 'f1_macro')
print("F1 score: %0.3f (+/- %0.3f)" % (f1_scores.mean(), f1_scores.std()
* 2))
Precision_scores = cross_val_score(model, X, y, cv = CV,scoring = 'precision_
macro')
print("Precision score: %0.3f (+/- %0.3f)" % (Precision_scores.mean(),
Precision_scores.std() * 2))
Recall_scores = cross_val_score(model, X, y, cv = CV,scoring = 'recall_
macro')
```

```
print("Recall score: %0.3f (+/- %0.3f)" % (Recall_scores.mean(), Recall_
scores.std() * 2))
from sklearn.metrics import cohen_kappa_score, make_scorer
kappa_scorer = make_scorer(cohen_kappa_score)
Kappa_scores = cross_val_score(model, X, y, cv = CV,scoring = kappa_scorer)
print("Kappa score: %0.3f (+/- %0.3f)" % (Kappa_scores.mean(), Kappa_
scores.std() * 2))
```

## 5.5 credit card fraud detection

Global card fraud losses are calculated as $22.8 billion US in 2017 and are expected to continue growing (Jurgovsky et al., 2018). Recently, machine learning approaches began as a vital element of any detection method dealing with huge amounts of transactions (Dal Pozzolo, Caelen, Le Borgne, Waterschoot, & Bontempi, 2014). However, the current studies showed that a detection approach requires taking into account some peculiarities of the fraud phenomenon (Dal Pozzolo, Boracchi, Caelen, Alippi, & Bontempi, 2018). The development of an effective fraud detection system (FDS) thus goes beyond the implementation of some traditional off-the-shelf software libraries and needs a deep understanding of the fraud concept. It implies that it is neither instantaneous nor easy to reuse current FDSs for new settings, such as a new market or a new payment process (Lebichot, Le Borgne, He-Guelton, Oblé, & Bontempi, 2019). Perhaps one of the best test platforms for artificial intelligence algorithms is the analysis of credit card fraud. Nevertheless, this issue involves a number of relevant challenges—customer preferences expand and fraudsters adjust their tactics over time, actual transactions are far out of the range of frauds, and researchers test only a small set of transactions in a timely manner. But the vast majority of learning algorithms proposed for fraud detection are based on assumptions that hardly apply in a fraud detection system in the real world. There are two main aspects to this lack of realism: (1) the method and timing of the delivery of supervised information and (2) the metrics utilized to determine the quality of fraud detection. Credit card fraud detection is a relevant problem that draws the attention of machine learning and computational intelligence communities, where a large number of automatic solutions have been proposed (Bhattacharyya, Jha, Tharakunnel, & Westland, 2011; Dal Pozzolo et al., 2014, 2018; Jha, Guillen, & Westland, 2012; Mahmoudi & Duman, 2015; Whitrow, Hand, Juszczak, Weston, & Adams, 2009).

In a real-world FDS, the massive stream of payment requests is quickly scanned by automatic tools that determine which transactions to authorize. Classifiers are typically employed to analyze all the authorized transactions and alert the most suspicious ones. Alerts are then reviewed by qualified inspectors who notify cardholders to determine the true nature of each notified payment (either legitimate or fraudulent). In doing so, investigators receive system feedback in the form of marked transactions that can be used to train the classifier to maintain (or potentially improve) the efficiency of fraud detection over time. The vast majority of transactions cannot be verified by investigators for obvious time and cost constraints. These transactions remain unlabeled until customers discover and report frauds, or until a sufficient amount of time has elapsed such that nondisputed transactions are considered genuine

(Dal Pozzolo et al., 2018). Nowadays, enterprises and public institutions have to face a growing presence of fraud initiatives and need automatic systems to implement fraud detection (Delamaire, Abdou, & Pointon, 2009). Automatic systems are crucial as it is not often feasible or convenient for a human analyst to identify fraudulent behaviors in transaction data sets, which are frequently represented by a huge number of samples, multiple measurements, and online alerts. Detection problems are usually tackled in two distinct approaches. In the static learning approaches, a detection model is continually relearned from scratch. In the online learning approaches, the detection model is updated as soon as new data is generated. Another challenging issue in credit card fraud detection is the shortage of accessible data because of confidentiality issues, which provide little chance to the community to share real datasets and evaluate current methods (Dal Pozzolo et al., 2014).

Credit card fraud detection aims to determine if a transaction is fraudulent or not based on historical data. The assessment is extremely difficult due to changes in patterns of consumer purchases, for example, over holiday periods, and in the tactics of fraudsters themselves, particularly those they use to respond to techniques of fraud detection. Machine learning methods provide an active way of tackling issues like these (Dal Pozzolo, Caelen, & Bontempi, 2015). A traditional fraud detection system contains multiple control levels, each of which can be automatic or controlled by humans (Carcillo et al., 2018; Dal Pozzolo et al., 2018). Part of the automatic layer involves machine learning techniques, which create predictive models based on annotated transactions. In the last decade, extensive machine learning approach has led to the development of supervised, unsupervised, and semisupervised algorithms for credit card fraud detection (Carcillo et al., 2019; Sethi & Gera, 2014).

### Example 5.5

The following Python code is used to classify a credit-scoring dataset using Keras deep neural network classifier employed by using separate training and test set and 10-fold cross-validation. The classification accuracy, precision, recall, F1 score, Cohen kappa score, and Matthews correlation coefficient are calculated. The classification report and confusion matrix are also given. This example is adapted from the book *Beginning Anomaly Detection Using Python-Based Deep Learning* (Alla & Adari, 2019).

***Dataset information:*** Dataset is downloaded from Kaggle website (https://www.kaggle.com/mlg-ulb/creditcardfraud/version/3). The credit card fraud dataset was supplied by a payment service provider in Belgium. It includes the logs of a subset of transactions from the first of February 2012 to the twentieth of May 2013. The dataset was split in daily chunks and contained e-commerce fraudulent transactions. The original variables consist of the transaction amount, point of sale, currency, country of transaction, merchant type, and many others. But the original variables do not describe cardholder behavior. Combined variables are added to the original ones to describe the user behavior; for instance, the transaction amount and the card ID is utilized to calculate the average spending per week and per month of one card, the difference between the current and previous transaction, and many others. For each transaction and card, 3 months (H = 90 days) of previous transaction data to compute the aggregated variable are recorded. Hence the weekly average spending for one card is the weekly average of the last 3 months. This dataset includes both categorical and continuous variables. Chunks contain sets of daily transactions, where the average transactions per chunk (5218) are considered (Dal Pozzolo et al., 2014). This dataset contains transactions that occurred in 2 days with 492 frauds out of 284,807 transactions. It includes only numerical input variables that are the result of a PCA transformation. Due to confidentiality issues, the original features and more background information about the data is not provided. Features V1, V2, . . . V28 are the principal components achieved with PCA; the only features that have not been transformed with PCA are "Time" and "Amount." The feature "Time" contains the seconds elapsed between each transaction and the first transaction in the dataset. The feature "Amount" is the transaction amount; this feature can be used for example-dependent, cost-sensitive learning. The feature "Class" is the response variable, and it takes value 1 in case of fraud and 0 otherwise. The dataset has been collected and analyzed during a research collaboration of Worldline and the Machine Learning Group (http://mlg.ulb.ac.be) of ULB (Université Libre de Bruxelles) on big data mining and fraud detection. More details on current and past projects on related topics are available at https://www.researchgate.net/project/Fraud-detection-5 and the page of the DefeatFraud project.

```
"""
Created on Thu Dec 12 07:56:20 2019
@author: absubasi
Adapted from "Beginning Anomaly Detection Using Python-Based Deep
Learning"
"""
#=========================================================================
# Credit card fraud detection using Keras
#=========================================================================
from keras.models import Sequential
from keras.layers import Dense
from keras.wrappers.scikit_learn import KerasClassifier
from keras.utils import np_utils
from sklearn.preprocessing import LabelEncoder
import pandas as pd
import numpy as np
import matplotlib.pyplot as plt
from sklearn.metrics import classification_report
from sklearn.metrics import confusion_matrix
import seaborn as sns
from sklearn import metrics
from io import BytesIO #needed for plot
import seaborn as sns; sns.set()
#=========================================================================
# Define utility functions
#=========================================================================
def plot_model_accuracy_loss():
    plt.figure(figsize=(6, 4))
    plt.plot(history.history['accuracy'], 'r', label='Accuracy of
training data')
```

```
    plt.plot(history.history['val_accuracy'], 'b', label = 'Accuracy of
validation data')
    plt.plot(history.history['loss'], 'r--', label = 'Loss of training
data')
    plt.plot(history.history['val_loss'], 'b--', label = 'Loss of
validation data')
    plt.title('Model Accuracy and Loss')
    plt.ylabel('Accuracy and Loss')
    plt.xlabel('Training Epoch')
    plt.ylim(0)
    plt.legend()
    plt.show()

def print_confusion_matrix():
    matrix = confusion_matrix(y_test.argmax(axis = 1), max_y_pred_test.
argmax(axis = 1))
    plt.figure(figsize = (10, 8))
    sns.heatmap(matrix,cmap = 'coolwarm',linecolor = 'white',linewidths = 1,
        annot = True,
        fmt = 'd')
    plt.title('Confusion Matrix')
    plt.ylabel('True Label')
    plt.xlabel('Predicted Label')
    plt.show()

def print_performance_metrics():
    print('Accuracy:', np.round(metrics.accuracy_score(y_test, max_y_
pred_test),4))
    print('Precision:', np.round(metrics.precision_score(y_test,
                        max_y_pred_test,average = 'weighted'),4))
    print('Recall:', np.round(metrics.recall_score(y_test, max_y_pred_
test,
                                  average = 'weighted'),4))
    print('F1 Score:', np.round(metrics.f1_score(y_test, max_y_pred_
test,
                                  average = 'weighted'),4))
    print('Cohen Kappa Score:', np.round(metrics.cohen_kappa_score(y_
test.argmax(axis = 1), max_y_pred_test.argmax(axis = 1)),4))
    print('Matthews Corrcoef:', np.round(metrics.matthews_corrcoef(y_
test.argmax(axis = 1), max_y_pred_test.argmax(axis = 1)),4))
    print('\t\tClassification Report:\n', metrics.classification_report(y_
test, max_y_pred_test))
```

```
def print_confusion_matrix_and_save():
    mat = confusion_matrix(y_test.argmax(axis = 1), max_y_pred_test.
argmax(axis = 1))
    sns.heatmap(mat.T, square = True, annot = True, fmt = 'd', cbar = False)
    plt.title('Confusion Matrix')
    plt.ylabel('True Label')
    plt.xlabel('Predicted Label')
plt.show()

    plt.savefig("Confusion.jpg")
    # Save SVG in a fake file object.
    f = BytesIO()
    plt.savefig(f, format = "svg")
#%%
df = pd.read_csv("creditcard.csv", sep = ",", index_col = None)
df['Amount'] = StandardScaler().fit_transform(df['Amount'].values.
reshape(-1, 1))
df['Time'] = StandardScaler().fit_transform(df['Time'].values.reshape(-1, 1))

#%%
anomalies = df[df["Class"] == 1]
normal = df[df["Class"] == 0]
anomalies.shape, normal.shape
#%%
for f in range(0, 20):
    normal = normal.iloc[np.random.permutation(len(normal))]
data_set = pd.concat([normal[:5000], anomalies])
X = data_set.iloc[:,0:30]
y = data_set.iloc[:,30]

#%%
# encode class values as integers
encoder = LabelEncoder()
encoder.fit(y)
encoded_Y = encoder.transform(y)
# convert integers to dummy variables (i.e. one hot encoded)
dummy_y = np_utils.to_categorical(encoded_Y)
lenOfCoded = dummy_y.shape[1] # Dimension of binary coded output data
InputDataDimension = 30
#%%
#========================================================================
# Keras DNN example with cross-validation
#========================================================================
```

```
# define a Keras model
def my_model():
        # create model
        model = Sequential()
        model.add(Dense(128, input_dim = InputDataDimension,
activation = 'relu'))
# model.add(Dense(32, activation = 'relu'))
# model.add(Dense(16, activation = 'relu'))
     model.add(Dense(lenOfCoded, activation = 'softmax'))
     # Compile model
     model.compile(loss = 'categorical_crossentropy', optimizer = 'adam',
     metrics = ['accuracy'])
     return model

estimator = KerasClassifier(build_fn = my_model, epochs = 25, batch_size = 5,
verbose = 1)
kfold = KFold(n_splits = 5, shuffle = True)
results = cross_val_score(estimator, X, dummy_y, cv = kfold)
print("Accuracy: %.2f%% (%.2f%%)" % (results.mean()*100, results.
std()*100))

#%%
#===========================================================================
# Keras DNN example with training and test set
#===========================================================================
# load data
from sklearn.model_selection import train_test_split
# split data into train and test sets
X_train, X_test, y_train, y_test = train_test_split(X, y, test_size = 0.33,
random_state = 7)

# One hot encode targets
y_train = np_utils.to_categorical(y_train)
y_test = np_utils.to_categorical(y_test)
num_classes = y_test.shape[1]
InputDataDimension = 30

#%%
#===========================================================================
# Create a model
#===========================================================================
model = Sequential()
model.add(Dense(128, input_dim = InputDataDimension, init = 'uniform',
activation = 'relu'))
```

```
model.add(Dense(32, activation = 'relu'))
model.add(Dense(num_classes, activation = 'softmax'))
#%%
#===========================================================================
# Compile the model
#===========================================================================
model.compile(loss = 'categorical_crossentropy', optimizer = 'adam',
metrics = ['accuracy'])
#===========================================================================
# Train and validate the model
#===========================================================================
history = model.fit(X_train, y_train, validation_split = 0.33, epochs = 50,
batch_size = 25,verbose = 0)
#%%
#===========================================================================
# Evaluate the model
#===========================================================================
test_loss, test_acc = model.evaluate(X_test, y_test, verbose = 0)
print('\nTest accuracy:', test_acc)

#%%
#===========================================================================
# Plot the history
#===========================================================================
#Plot the Model Accuracy and Loss for Training and Validation dataset
plot_model_accuracy_loss()

#%%
#Test the Model with testing data
y_pred_test = model.predict(X_test,)
# Round the test predictions
max_y_pred_test = np.round(y_pred_test)
#%%
#Print the Confusion Matrix
print_confusion_matrix()
#%%
#Evaluate the Model and Print Performance Metrics
print_performance_metrics()
#%%
#Print and Save the Confusion Matrix
print_confusion_matrix_and_save()
#%%
# ==========================================================================
# Keras deep learning model
# ==========================================================================
```

```
# load data
from sklearn.model_selection import train_test_split
# split data into train and test sets
X_train, X_test, y_train, y_test = train_test_split(X, y, test_size = 0.33,
random_state = 7)

# One hot encode targets
y_train = np_utils.to_categorical(y_train)
y_test = np_utils.to_categorical(y_test)
num_classes = y_test.shape[1]
InputDataDimension = 30
#%%
#=========================================================================
# Build a deep model
#=========================================================================
model = Sequential()
model.add(Dense(128, input_dim = InputDataDimension, init = 'uniform',
activation = 'relu'))
model.add(Dense(64, activation = 'relu'))
model.add(Dense(32, activation = 'relu'))
model.add(Dense(num_classes, activation = 'softmax'))
#%%
#=========================================================================
# Compile the model
#=========================================================================
model.compile(loss = 'categorical_crossentropy', optimizer = 'adam',
metrics = ['accuracy'])
#=========================================================================
# Train and validate the model
#=========================================================================
history = model.fit(X_train, y_train, validation_split = 0.33, nb_epoch = 50,
batch_size = 25,verbose = 0)
#%%
#=========================================================================
# Evaluate the model
#=========================================================================
test_loss, test_acc = model.evaluate(X_test, y_test, verbose = 0)
print('\nTest accuracy:', test_acc)
#%%
#=========================================================================
# Plot the history
#=========================================================================
#Plot the Model Accuracy and Loss for Training and Validation dataset
plot_model_accuracy_loss()
```

```
#%%
#Test the Model with testing data
y_pred_test = model.predict(X_test,)
# Round the test predictions
max_y_pred_test = np.round(y_pred_test)
#%%
#Print the Confusion Matrix
print_confusion_matrix()
#%%
#Evaluate the Model and Print Performance Metrics
print_performance_metrics()
#%%
#Print and Save the Confusion Matrix
print_confusion_matrix_and_save()
```

## 5.6 Handwritten digit recognition using CNN

Handwritten digit recognition is a prevalent multiclass classification problem usually built into the software of mobile banking applications, as well as more traditional automated teller machines, to give users the ability to automatically deposit paper checks. Here each class of data consists of (images of) several handwritten versions of a single digit in the range $0 - 9$, giving a total of ten classes. Handwriting character recognition has become a common area of research because of developments in technology such as handwriting recording tools and powerful mobile computers (Elleuch, Maalej, & Kherallah, 2016). Because handwriting is highly dependent on the writer, however, it is challenging to develop a highly reliable recognition system that recognizes every handwritten character input to an application. Optical character recognition (OCR) is one of the research areas in character recognition and artificial intelligence (Pramanik & Bag, 2018). For more than 10 years, in many applications and identification algorithms, digit recognition has been efficiently investigated in the area of OCR handwriting. These include, for example, algorithms such as support vector machines (SVM), convolutional neural networks (CNN), and random forest (RF). The accuracy of the experiments however is about 95%. Since many classifiers cannot manage the original images or details properly, the extraction of features is one of the pretreatment measures aimed at reducing the data dimension and integrating the valid information (Lauer, Suen, & Bloch, 2007). Traditional feature selection is a complex and time-consuming job that cannot process the original image, whereas CNN's automated extraction method can identify features directly from the original image (Bernard, Adam, & Heutte, 2007). A CNN is a feed-forward network that extracts topological features from images. This collects features from the first layer's original image and utilizes its last layer to identify the object. Nonetheless, most classifiers such as SVM and RF cannot process raw images or data effectively, because it is a tremendous challenge to remove correct characteristics from complex patterns (Pramanik & Bag, 2018). On the other hand, CNN's automated feature extraction method will retrieve elements from the raw image directly (Bernard et al., 2007; Zhao, 2018).

A CNN is an improvement of the artificial neural network that focuses on mimicking behavior of our visual cortex. The aim of the hidden units is to learn nonlinear changes of the original inputs; this is called features extraction. Then these hidden features are transferred to the final GLM (generalized linear model) as input. This method is especially practical for the problems where the original input features are not informative independently. The CNN is a type of MLP (multilayer perceptron) that is especially well-suited for 1D signals, such as speech, biomedical signals, or text, or 2D signals such as images (Murphy, 2012).

## Example 5.6

The following Python code is used to classify MNIST handwritten digits dataset using DCNN classifier and employing separate training, validation, and testing datasets. The classification accuracy, precision, recall, F1 score, Cohen kappa score, and Matthews correlation coefficient are calculated. The classification report and confusion matrix are also given. This example is adapted from the machine learning mastery website (https://machinelearningmastery.com/handwritten-digit-recognition-using-convolutional-neural-networks-python-keras/).

***Dataset information:*** The MNIST database of handwritten digits is available from the Yann LeCun web page (http://yann.lecun.com/exdb/mnist/). It has a training set of 60,000 examples and a test set of 10,000 examples. It is a subcategory of a bigger set accessible from NIST. The digits are size-normalized and centered in a fixed-size image. It is a decent database for researchers who want to try machine learning techniques on real-world data while spending minimal efforts on preprocessing and formatting. The original black and white (bilevel) images from NIST are size-normalized to fit in a 20-by-20 pixel box while conserving the aspect ratio. The resultant images include gray levels as a result of the anti-aliasing method utilized by the normalization algorithm. The images were centered in a 28-by-28 image by calculating the center of mass of the pixels and translating the image to position this point at the center of the 28-by-28 field. The digit images in the MNIST set were initially chosen by Chris Burges and Corinna Cortes utilizing bounding-box normalization and centering. Yann LeCun improved the dataset by positioning according to center of mass within in a larger window.

```
"""
Created on Wed Oct 9 15:54:40 2019
@author: absubasi
https://machinelearningmastery.com/handwritten-digit-recognition-using-
convolutional-neural-networks-python-keras/
"""
#======================================================================
# MNIST handwritten digit recognition
#======================================================================
from keras.datasets import mnist
from keras.models import Sequential
from keras.layers import Dense
from keras.layers import Dropout
from keras.layers import Flatten
```

```
from keras.layers.convolutional import Conv2D
from keras.layers.convolutional import MaxPooling2D
from keras.layers import BatchNormalization
from keras.utils import np_utils
import matplotlib.pyplot as plt
import matplotlib.pyplot as plt
from sklearn.metrics import classification_report
from sklearn.metrics import confusion_matrix
import seaborn as sns
import numpy as np
from sklearn import metrics
from io import BytesIO #needed for plot
import seaborn as sns; sns.set()

#=======================================================================
# Define utility functions
#=======================================================================
def plot_model_accuracy_loss():
    plt.figure(figsize=(6, 4))
    plt.plot(history.history['accuracy'], 'r', label='Accuracy of
training data')
    plt.plot(history.history['val_accuracy'], 'b', label='Accuracy of
validation data')
    plt.plot(history.history['loss'], 'r--', label='Loss of training
data')
    plt.plot(history.history['val_loss'], 'b--', label='Loss of
validation data')
    plt.title('Model Accuracy and Loss')
    plt.ylabel('Accuracy and Loss')
    plt.xlabel('Training Epoch')
    plt.ylim(0)
    plt.legend()
    plt.show()

def print_confusion_matrix():
    matrix=confusion_matrix(y_test.argmax(axis=1), max_y_pred_test.
argmax(axis=1))
    plt.figure(figsize=(10, 8))
    sns.heatmap(matrix,cmap='coolwarm',linecolor='white',linewidths=1,
                annot=True,
                fmt='d')
    plt.title('Confusion Matrix')
    plt.ylabel('True Label')
```

```
    plt.xlabel('Predicted Label')
    plt.show()

def print_performance_metrics():
      print('Accuracy:', np.round(metrics.accuracy_score(y_test, max_y_
pred_test),4))
    print('Precision:', np.round(metrics.precision_score(y_test,
                                        max_y_pred_test,average='weighted'),4))
      print('Recall:', np.round(metrics.recall_score(y_test, max_y_pred_
test,
                                              average='weighted'),4))
    print('F1 Score:', np.round(metrics.f1_score(y_test, max_y_pred_test,
                                              average='weighted'),4))
print('Cohen Kappa Score:', np.round(metrics.cohen_kappa_score(y_test.
argmax(axis=1), max_y_pred_test.argmax(axis=1)),4))
print('Matthews Corrcoef:', np.round(metrics.matthews_corrcoef(y_test.
argmax(axis=1), max_y_pred_test.argmax(axis=1)),4))
print('\t\tClassification Report:\n', metrics.classification_report(y_test,
max_y_pred_test))

def print_confusion_matrix_and_save():
    mat=confusion_matrix(y_test.argmax(axis=1), max_y_pred_test.
argmax(axis=1))
    sns.heatmap(mat.T, square=True, annot=True, fmt='d',
cbar=False)
    plt.title('Confusion Matrix')
    plt.ylabel('True Label')
    plt.xlabel('Predicted Label')
    plt.show()

    plt.savefig("Confusion.jpg")
    # Save SVG in a fake file object.
    f=BytesIO()
    plt.savefig(f, format="svg")

#%%
#===========================================================================
# Multilayer perceptrons model
#===========================================================================
# load data
(X_train, y_train), (X_test, y_test)=mnist.load_data()
# Flatten 28*28 images to a 784 vector for each image
num_pixels=X_train.shape[1] * X_train.shape[2]
```

```
X_train = X_train.reshape((X_train.shape[0], num_pixels)).
astype('float32')
X_test = X_test.reshape((X_test.shape[0], num_pixels)).astype('float32')
# Normalize inputs from 0-255 to 0-1
X_train = X_train / 255
X_test = X_test / 255
# One hot encode targets
y_train = np_utils.to_categorical(y_train)
y_test = np_utils.to_categorical(y_test)
num_classes = y_test.shape[1]
#=========================================================================
# Build a Keras model
#=========================================================================
model = Sequential()
model.add(Dense(num_pixels, input_dim = num_pixels,
    kernel_initializer = 'normal', activation = 'relu'))
model.add(Dense(num_classes, kernel_initializer = 'normal',
activation = 'softmax'))
#=========================================================================
# Compile the model
#=========================================================================
model.compile(loss = 'categorical_crossentropy', optimizer = 'adam',
metrics = ['accuracy'])
#=========================================================================
# Train and validate the model
#=========================================================================
history = model.fit(X_train, y_train, validation_split = 0.3, epochs = 10,
batch_size = 200, verbose = 2)
#%%
#=========================================================================
# Evaluate the model
#=========================================================================
test_loss, test_acc = model.evaluate(X_test, y_test, verbose = 0)
print('\nTest accuracy:', test_acc)
#%%
#=========================================================================
# Plot the history
#=========================================================================
#Plot the Model Accuracy and Loss for Training and Validation dataset
plot_model_accuracy_loss()

#%%
#Test the Model with testing data
y_pred_test = model.predict(X_test,)
```

```
# Round the test predictions
max_y_pred_test = np.round(y_pred_test)
#Print the Confusion Matrix
print_confusion_matrix()
#%%
#Evaluate the Model and Print Performance Metrics
print_performance_metrics()
#%%
#Print and Save the Confusion Matrix
print_confusion_matrix_and_save()
#%%
#=========================================================================
# 1 Convolutional neural network for MNIST digit recognition
#=========================================================================
# load data
(X_train, y_train), (X_test, y_test) = mnist.load_data()
# reshape to be [samples][width][height][channels]
X_train = X_train.reshape((X_train.shape[0], 28, 28, 1)).
astype('float32')
X_test = X_test.reshape((X_test.shape[0], 28, 28, 1)).astype('float32')
# normalize inputs from 0-255 to 0-1
X_train = X_train/255
X_test = X_test/255
# one hot encode outputs
y_train = np_utils.to_categorical(y_train)
y_test = np_utils.to_categorical(y_test)
num_classes = y_test.shape[1]
#%%
#=========================================================================
# Build a model
#=========================================================================
model = Sequential()
model.add(Conv2D(32, (5, 5), input_shape = (28, 28, 1),
activation = 'relu'))
model.add(MaxPooling2D())
model.add(Dropout(0.2))
model.add(Flatten())
model.add(Dense(128, activation = 'relu'))
model.add(Dense(num_classes, activation = 'softmax'))
#=========================================================================
# Compile model
#=========================================================================
model.compile(loss = 'categorical_crossentropy', optimizer = 'adam',
metrics = ['accuracy'])
```

```
#==========================================================================
# Train the model
#==========================================================================
history = model.fit(X_train, y_train, validation_split = 0.3, epochs = 10,
batch_size = 200, verbose = 2)
#%%
#==========================================================================
# Evaluate the model
#==========================================================================
test_loss, test_acc = model.evaluate(X_test, y_test, verbose = 0)
print('\nTest accuracy:', test_acc)

#%%
#Plot the Model Accuracy and Loss for Training and Validation dataset
plot_model_accuracy_loss()
#%%
#Test the Model with testing data
y_pred_test = model.predict(X_test,)
# Round the test predictions
max_y_pred_test = np.round(y_pred_test)
#Print the Confusion Matrix
print_confusion_matrix()

#%%
#Evaluate the Model and Print Performance Metrics
print_performance_metrics()
#%%
#Print and Save the Confusion Matrix
print_confusion_matrix_and_save()

#%%
#==========================================================================
# 3 Convolutional neural network for MNIST digit recognition
#==========================================================================
# load data
(X_train, y_train), (X_test, y_test) = mnist.load_data()
# reshape to be [samples][width][height][channels]
X_train = X_train.reshape((X_train.shape[0], 28, 28, 1)).
astype('float32')
X_test = X_test.reshape((X_test.shape[0], 28, 28, 1)).astype('float32')
# normalize inputs from 0-255 to 0-1
X_train = X_train / 255
X_test = X_test / 255
# one hot encode outputs
y_train = np_utils.to_categorical(y_train)
```

```
y_test = np_utils.to_categorical(y_test)
num_classes = y_test.shape[1]
#%%
#=========================================================================
# Build model
#=========================================================================
model = Sequential()
model.add(Conv2D(32, (5, 5), input_shape = (28, 28, 1),
activation = 'relu'))
model.add(MaxPooling2D())
model.add(Conv2D(64, (3, 3), activation = 'relu'))
model.add(MaxPooling2D((2, 2)))
model.add(Conv2D(64, (3, 3), activation = 'relu'))
model.add(Flatten())
model.add(Dense(64, activation = 'relu'))
model.add(Dense(num_classes, activation = 'softmax'))
#=========================================================================
# Compile model
#=========================================================================
model.compile(loss = 'categorical_crossentropy', optimizer = 'adam',
metrics = ['accuracy'])
#=========================================================================
# Train the model
#=========================================================================
history = model.fit(X_train, y_train, validation_split = 0.3, epochs = 10,
batch_size = 200, verbose = 2)
#%%
#=========================================================================
# Evaluate the model
#=========================================================================
test_loss, test_acc = model.evaluate(X_test, y_test, verbose = 0)
print('\nTest accuracy:', test_acc)
#%%
#Plot the Model Accuracy and Loss for Training and Validation dataset
plot_model_accuracy_loss()
#%%
#Test the Model with testing data
y_pred_test = model.predict(X_test,)
# Round the test predictions
max_y_pred_test = np.round(y_pred_test)
#Print the Confusion Matrix
print_confusion_matrix()
#%%
#Evaluate the Model and Print Performance Metrics
```

```
print_performance_metrics()
#%%
#Print and Save the Confusion Matrix
print_confusion_matrix_and_save()
#%%
#==========================================================================
# 4 Convolutional neural network for MNIST digit recognition
#==========================================================================
# load data
(X_train, y_train), (X_test, y_test) = mnist.load_data()
# reshape to be [samples][width][height][channels]
X_train = X_train.reshape((X_train.shape[0], 28, 28, 1)).
astype('float32')
X_test = X_test.reshape((X_test.shape[0], 28, 28, 1)).astype('float32')
# normalize inputs from 0-255 to 0-1
X_train = X_train / 255
X_test = X_test / 255
# one hot encode outputs
y_train = np_utils.to_categorical(y_train)
y_test = np_utils.to_categorical(y_test)
num_classes = y_test.shape[1]
#%%
#==========================================================================
# Build model
#==========================================================================
model = Sequential()
model.add(Conv2D(32, (5, 5), input_shape = (28, 28, 1),
activation = 'relu'))
model.add(BatchNormalization())
model.add(Conv2D(32, kernel_size = (3, 3), activation = 'relu'))
model.add(BatchNormalization())
model.add(MaxPooling2D((2, 2)))
model.add(Dropout(0.25))
model.add(Conv2D(64, (3, 3), activation = 'relu'))
model.add(BatchNormalization())
model.add(Dropout(0.25))
model.add(Conv2D(128, kernel_size = (3, 3), activation = 'relu'))
model.add(BatchNormalization())
model.add(MaxPooling2D(pool_size = (2, 2)))
model.add(Dropout(0.25))
model.add(Flatten())
model.add(Dense(512, activation = 'relu'))
model.add(BatchNormalization())
model.add(Dropout(0.5))
```

```
model.add(Dense(128, activation='relu'))
model.add(BatchNormalization())
model.add(Dropout(0.5))
model.add(Dense(num_classes, activation='softmax'))
#=============================================================================
# Compile model
#=============================================================================
model.compile(loss='categorical_crossentropy', optimizer='adam',
metrics=['accuracy'])
#=============================================================================
# Train the model
#=============================================================================
history=model.fit(X_train, y_train, validation_split=0.3, epochs=10,
batch_size=200, verbose=2)
#=============================================================================
#%%
#=============================================================================
# Evaluate the model
#=============================================================================
test_loss, test_acc=model.evaluate(X_test, y_test, verbose=0)
print('\nTest accuracy:', test_acc)
#%%
#Plot the Model Accuracy and Loss for Training and Validation dataset
plot_model_accuracy_loss()
#%%
#Test the Model with testing data
y_pred_test=model.predict(X_test,)
# Round the test predictions
max_y_pred_test=np.round(y_pred_test)
#Print the Confusion Matrix
print_confusion_matrix()
#%%
#Evaluate the Model and Print Performance Metrics
print_performance_metrics()
#%%
#Print and Save the Confusion Matrix
print_confusion_matrix_and_save()
```

## 5.7 Fashion-MNIST image classification with CNN

A CNN is not only a deep neural network with many hidden layers but also a large network that simulates and understands stimuli as the visual cortex of the brain processes. CNN's output layer typically uses the neural network for multiclass classification. CNN uses the feature extractor in the training process instead of manually implementing it. CNN's feature extractor consists of special types of neural networks that decide the weights through the training process. CNN provides better image recognition when its neural network feature extraction becomes deeper (contains more layers), at the cost of the learning method complexities that had made CNN inefficient and neglected for some time. CNN is a neural network that extracts input image features and another neural network classifies the image features. The input image is used by the feature extraction network. The extracted feature signals are utilized by the neural network for classification. The neural network classification then works on the basis of the image features and produces the output. The neural network for feature extraction includes convolution layer piles and sets of pooling layers. As its name implies, the convolution layer transforms the image using the process of the convolution. It can be described as a series of digital filters. The layer of pooling transforms the neighboring pixels into a single pixel. The pooling layer then decreases the image dimension. As CNN's primary concern is the image, the convolution and pooling layers' procedures are intuitively in a two-dimensional plane. This is one of CNN's distinctions with other neural networks (Kim, 2017).

Recently, Zalando research issued a new image dataset that is similar to the well-known MNIST handwritten digits database. This dataset is designed for machine learning classification tasks and includes 60,000 training and 10,000 test gray scale images composed of 28-by-28 pixels. Every training and test case is related to one of ten labels (0–9). Zalando's new dataset is mainly the same as the original handwritten digits data. But instead of having images of the digits 0–9, Zalando's data involves images with 10 different fashion products. Hence the dataset is named fashion-MNIST dataset and can be downloaded from GitHub (https://github.com/zalandoresearch/fashion-mnist) and Kaggle website (https://www.kaggle.com/zalando-research/fashionmnist) or from Keras directly (Zhang, 2019).

## Example 5.7

The following Python code is used to classify fashion-MNIST image dataset using deep CNN classifier and employing separate training, validation, and testing datasets. The classification accuracy, precision, recall, F1 score, Cohen kappa score, and Matthews correlation coefficient are calculated. The classification report and confusion matrix are also given. This example is adapted from the TensorFlow web page (https://www.tensorflow.org/tutorials/keras/classification).

***Dataset information:*** Fashion-MNIST is a dataset of Zalando's article images—composed of a training set of 60,000 examples and a test set of 10,000 examples. Every sample is a 28-by-28 grayscale image, related to a label from 10 classes. Zalando intends fashion-MNIST to serve as a direct drop-in replacement for the original MNIST dataset for benchmarking machine learning algorithms. It has the same image size and structure of training and testing splits. Each training and test sample is assigned to one of the following labels:

- t-shirt/top
- trouser
- pullover
- dress

- coat
- sandal
- shirt
- sneaker
- bag
- ankle boot

Actually, the fashion-MNIST data is envisioned to be a direct drop-in replacement for the old MNIST handwritten digits data, because there were many problems with the handwritten digits. For instance, many digits can be correctly distinguished by simply looking at a few pixels. Even with linear classifiers high classification accuracy can be achieved. The fashion-MNIST data promises to be more diverse so that machine learning algorithms can learn more advanced features to separate the individual classes reliably. In this example several CNN-based deep learning models will be created to assess performances on fashion-MNIST dataset. The models will be built employing the Keras framework. The original training data (60,000 images) divided into 80% training (48,000 images) and 20% validation (12,000 images) to optimize the classifier while retaining the test data (10,000 images) to finally assess the accuracy of the model on the unseen data. This helps to prevent overfitting on the training data and determine whether the learning rate should be lowered and train for more epochs if validation accuracy is higher than training accuracy or stop overtraining if training accuracy shifts higher than the validation (Zhang, 2019).

```
#========================================================================
# Classify FASHION-MNIST images of clothing with CNN
#========================================================================
"""
Created on Tue Dec 3 15:34:19 2019
@author: absubasi
"""
# TensorFlow and tf.keras
import tensorflow as tf
from tensorflow import keras
from keras.models import Sequential
from keras.layers import Dense
from keras.layers import Dropout
from keras.layers import Flatten
from keras.layers.convolutional import Conv2D
from keras.layers.convolutional import MaxPooling2D
from keras.layers import BatchNormalization
# Helper libraries
import numpy as np
import matplotlib.pyplot as plt
from sklearn.metrics import confusion_matrix
import seaborn as sns
from sklearn import metrics
```

```
from io import BytesIO #needed for plot
import seaborn as sns; sns.set()
#=================================================================
# Define utility functions
#=================================================================
def plot_model_accuracy_loss():
    plt.figure(figsize = (6, 4))
    plt.plot(history.history['accuracy'], 'r', label = 'Accuracy of 
training data')
    plt.plot(history.history['val_accuracy'], 'b', label = 'Accuracy of 
validation data')
    plt.plot(history.history['loss'], 'r--', label = 'Loss of training 
data')
    plt.plot(history.history['val_loss'], 'b--', label = 'Loss of 
validation data')
    plt.title('Model Accuracy and Loss')
    plt.ylabel('Accuracy and Loss')
    plt.xlabel('Training Epoch')
    plt.ylim(0)
    plt.legend()
    plt.show()

def print_confusion_matrix(y_test,y_pred):
# matrix = confusion_matrix(y_test.argmax(axis = 1), max_y_pred_test.
argmax(axis = 1))
    matrix = confusion_matrix(y_test, y_pred)
    plt.figure(figsize = (10, 8))
    sns.heatmap(matrix,cmap = 'coolwarm',linecolor = 'white',
linewidths = 1,
                annot = True,
                fmt = 'd')
    plt.title('Confusion Matrix')
    plt.ylabel('True Label')
    plt.xlabel('Predicted Label')
    plt.show()

def print_performance_metrics(y_test,y_pred):
    print('Accuracy:', np.round(metrics.accuracy_score(y_test, y_
pred),4))
    print('Precision:', np.round(metrics.precision_score(y_test, y_
pred,
                                              average = 'weighted'),4))
    print('Recall:', np.round(metrics.recall_score(y_test, y_pred,
                                              average = 'weighted'),4))
```

```
    print('F1 Score:', np.round(metrics.f1_score(y_test, y_pred,
                                                average = 'weighted'),4))
    print('Cohen Kappa Score:', np.round(metrics.cohen_kappa_score(y_test,
y_pred),4))
    print('Matthews Corrcoef:', np.round(metrics.matthews_corrcoef(y_test,
y_pred),4))
    print('\t\tClassification Report:\n', metrics.classification_report(y_
test, y_pred))

def print_confusion_matrix_and_save(y_test, y_pred):
    mat = confusion_matrix(y_test, y_pred)
    sns.heatmap(mat.T, square = True, annot = True, fmt = 'd', cbar = False)
    plt.title('Confusion Matrix')
    plt.ylabel('True Label')
    plt.xlabel('Predicted Label')
    plt.show()

    plt.savefig("Confusion.jpg")
    # Save SVG in a fake file object.
    f = BytesIO()
    plt.savefig(f, format = "svg")
#%%
#from keras.datasets import mnist
fashion_mnist = keras.datasets.fashion_mnist
(X_train, y_train), (X_test, y_test) = fashion_mnist.load_data()

class_names = ['T-shirt/top', 'Trouser', 'Pullover', 'Dress', 'Coat',
               'Sandal', 'Shirt', 'Sneaker', 'Bag', 'Ankle boot']
#%%
# Each image's dimension is 28 x 28
img_rows, img_cols = 28, 28
input_shape = (img_rows, img_cols, 1)

# Prepare the training images
X_train = X_train.reshape(X_train.shape[0], img_rows, img_cols, 1)
X_train = X_train.astype('float32')
# Prepare the test images
X_test = X_test.reshape(X_test.shape[0], img_rows, img_cols, 1)
X_test = X_test.astype('float32')
"""
Scale these values to a range of 0 to 1 before feeding them to the neural
network model.
To do so, divide the values by 255.
```

```
It's important that the training set and the testing set be preprocessed in
the same way:"""
X_train = X_train / 255.0
X_test = X_test / 255.0
#%%
#=========================================================================
# Build the model with 1 CNN
#=========================================================================
num_classes = 10
model = Sequential()
model.add(Conv2D(32, (3, 3), activation = 'relu', input_shape = input_
shape))
model.add(MaxPooling2D(pool_size = (2, 2)))
model.add(Dropout(0.2))
model.add(Flatten())
model.add(Dense(128, activation = 'relu'))
model.add(Dense(num_classes, activation = 'softmax'))
#%%
#=========================================================================
# Compile the model for numerical labels
#=========================================================================
model.compile(optimizer = 'adam',
              loss = 'sparse_categorical_crossentropy',
              metrics = ['accuracy'])
#%%
#=========================================================================
# Train and validate the model
#=========================================================================
history = model.fit(X_train, y_train, validation_split = 0.3, epochs = 10,
batch_size = 200, verbose = 2)
#%%
#=========================================================================
# Evaluate the model
#=========================================================================
test_loss, test_acc = model.evaluate(X_test, y_test, verbose = 0)
print(" Test Accuracy is : %0.4f" % test_acc)
#%%
#Plot the Model Accuracy and Loss for Training and Validation dataset
plot_model_accuracy_loss()
#%%
#Test the Model with testing data
y_pred_test = model.predict(X_test,)
# Round the test predictions
max_y_pred_test = np.round(y_pred_test)
```

```
#Convert binary labels into categorical
y_pred =max_y_pred_test.argmax(axis = 1)
#Print the Confusion Matrix
print_confusion_matrix(y_test, y_pred)
#%%
#Evaluate the Model and Print Performance Metrics
print_performance_metrics(y_test, y_pred)
#%%
#Print and Save the Confusion Matrix
print_confusion_matrix_and_save(y_test, y_pred)
#%%
#=========================================================================
# Build the model with 3 CNN
#=========================================================================
num_classes = 10
model = Sequential()
model.add(Conv2D(32, (3, 3), activation = 'relu', input_shape = input_
shape))
model.add(MaxPooling2D((2, 2)))
model.add(Conv2D(64, (3, 3), activation = 'relu'))
model.add(MaxPooling2D((2, 2)))
model.add(Conv2D(64, (3, 3), activation = 'relu'))
model.add(Flatten())
model.add(Dense(64, activation = 'relu'))
model.add(Dense(num_classes, activation = 'softmax'))
#%%
#=========================================================================
# Compile the model for numerical labels
#=========================================================================
model.compile(optimizer = 'adam',
              loss = 'sparse_categorical_crossentropy',
              metrics = ['accuracy'])
#%%
#=========================================================================
# Train and validate the model
#=========================================================================
history = model.fit(X_train, y_train, validation_split = 0.3, epochs = 10,
batch_size = 200, verbose = 2)
#%%
#=========================================================================
# Evaluate the model
#=========================================================================
test_loss, test_acc = model.evaluate(X_test, y_test, verbose = 0)
print("Test Accuracy is : %0.4f" % test_acc)
```

```
#%%
#Plot the Model Accuracy and Loss for Training and Validation dataset
plot_model_accuracy_loss()
#%%
#Test the Model with testing data
y_pred_test = model.predict(X_test,)
# Round the test predictions
max_y_pred_test = np.round(y_pred_test)
#Convert binary labels into categorical
y_pred =max_y_pred_test.argmax(axis = 1)
#Print the Confusion Matrix
print_confusion_matrix(y_test, y_pred)
#%%
#Evaluate the Model and Print Performance Metrics
print_performance_metrics(y_test, y_pred)
#%%
#Print and Save the Confusion Matrix
print_confusion_matrix_and_save(y_test, y_pred)
#%%
#=======================================================================
# Build the model with 4 CNN
#=======================================================================
num_classes = 10
model = Sequential()
model.add(Conv2D(32, (3, 3), activation = 'relu', input_shape = input_
shape))
model.add(BatchNormalization())

model.add(Conv2D(32, kernel_size = (3, 3), activation = 'relu'))
model.add(BatchNormalization())
model.add(MaxPooling2D((2, 2)))
model.add(Dropout(0.25))

model.add(Conv2D(64, (3, 3), activation = 'relu'))
model.add(BatchNormalization())
model.add(Dropout(0.25))
model.add(Conv2D(128, kernel_size = (3, 3), activation = 'relu'))
model.add(BatchNormalization())
model.add(MaxPooling2D(pool_size = (2, 2)))
model.add(Dropout(0.25))
model.add(Flatten())
```

```
model.add(Dense(512, activation = 'relu'))
model.add(BatchNormalization())
model.add(Dropout(0.5))

model.add(Dense(128, activation = 'relu'))
model.add(BatchNormalization())
model.add(Dropout(0.5))
model.add(Dense(num_classes, activation = 'softmax'))
#%%
#==========================================================================
# Compile the model for numerical labels
#==========================================================================
model.compile(optimizer = 'adam',
              loss = 'sparse_categorical_crossentropy',
              metrics = ['accuracy'])
#%%
#==========================================================================
# Train and validate the model
#==========================================================================
history = model.fit(X_train, y_train, validation_split = 0.3, epochs = 10,
batch_size = 200, verbose = 2)
#%%
#==========================================================================
# Evaluate the model
#==========================================================================
test_loss, test_acc = model.evaluate(X_test, y_test, verbose = 0)
print("Test Accuracy is : %0.4f" % test_acc)
#%%
#Plot the Model Accuracy and Loss for Training and Validation dataset
plot_model_accuracy_loss()
#%%
#Test the Model with testing data
y_pred_test = model.predict(X_test,)
# Round the test predictions
max_y_pred_test = np.round(y_pred_test)
#Convert binary labels into categorical
y_pred =max_y_pred_test.argmax(axis = 1)
#Print the Confusion Matrix
print_confusion_matrix(y_test, y_pred)
#%%
#Evaluate the Model and Print Performance Metrics
print_performance_metrics(y_test, y_pred)
#%%
#Print and Save the Confusion Matrix
print_confusion_matrix_and_save(y_test, y_pred)
```

## 5.8 CIFAR image classification using CNN

At the moment, machine learning is driven by extensively experimental work based on progress in a few main tasks. But the impressive accuracy numbers of the best performing models are questionable, as these models have been selected for several years now using the same test sets. The reliability of CIFAR-10 classifiers can be assessed by creating a new test set of really unknown objects to understand the danger of overfitting. While it is found that the new test set is as close as possible to the original data distribution, for a wide range of deep learning models, a large fall in accuracy of 4% to 10% is realized. Newer models with higher performance, however, show a smaller drop and better overall performance, implying that this drop is not likely due to overfitting based on adaptivity. Machine learning has become a highly revolutionary field over the past decade (Recht, Roelofs, Schmidt, Shankar, 2018). Recently, in many computer vision problems, the CNN has accomplished better success. CNN exhibits many properties with the brain's visual system, partly inspired by neuroscience. A significant difference is that CNN is usually a feed-forward architecture, although recurrent connections are common in the visual system (Liang & Hu, 2015). The majority of published papers, motivated by a rise in research into deep learning, have adopted a model where the main justification for a new learning methodology is its improved performance on a few key benchmarks. Simultaneously, there is little clarification as to why a new method is a successful improvement over previous research. Rather, our sense of progress depends largely on a small number of standard benchmarks like CIFAR-10, ImageNet, or MuJoCo (Recht et al., 2018).

### Example 5.8

The following Python code is used to classify phishing websites dataset using DCNN classifier employing 10-fold cross-validation, as well as separate training and testing datasets. The classification accuracy, precision, recall, F1 score, Cohen kappa score, and Matthews correlation coefficient are calculated. The classification report and confusion matrix are also given. This example is adapted from Tensorflow web page (https://www.tensorflow.org/tutorials/images/cnn).

***Dataset information:*** The CIFAR-10 and CIFAR-100 are labeled subsets of the 80 million tiny images dataset. They were collected by Alex Krizhevsky, Vinod Nair, and Geoffrey Hinton. The CIFAR-10 dataset includes 60,000 32-by-32 color images in 10 classes, with 6,000 images per class. There are 50,000 training images and 10,000 test images. The dataset is split into five training batches and one test batch, each with 10,000 images. The test batch contains exactly 1,000 randomly selected images from each class. The training batches contain the remaining images in random order, but some training batches may include more images from one class than another. The CIFAR-10 dataset can be downloaded from the CIFAR website (https://www.cs.toronto.edu/~kriz/cifar.html) or from Keras directly. The classes of the dataset are:

- airplane
- automobile
- bird
- cat

- deer
- dog
- frog
- horse
- ship
- truck

```
"""
Created on Tue Dec 3 15:45:50 2019
@author: absubasi
Convolutional Neural Network (CNN)
https://www.tensorflow.org/tutorials/images/cnn
"""
#=============================================================================
# Classification of CIFAR images using CNN
#=============================================================================
import tensorflow as tf
from keras.models import Sequential
from keras.layers import Dense
from keras.layers import Dropout
from keras.layers import Flatten
from keras.layers.convolutional import Conv2D
from keras.layers.convolutional import MaxPooling2D
from keras.layers import BatchNormalization
from keras.utils import np_utils
from tensorflow.keras import datasets, layers, models
import matplotlib.pyplot as plt
import numpy as np
from sklearn.metrics import confusion_matrix
from sklearn import metrics
from io import BytesIO #needed for plot
import seaborn as sns; sns.set()
#=============================================================================
# Define utility functions
#=============================================================================
def plot_model_accuracy_loss():
    plt.figure(figsize=(6, 4))
    plt.plot(history.history['accuracy'], 'r', label='Accuracy of 
training data')
    plt.plot(history.history['val_accuracy'], 'b', label='Accuracy of 
validation data')
    plt.plot(history.history['loss'], 'r--', label='Loss of training 
data')
```

```
    plt.plot(history.history['val_loss'], 'b--', label='Loss of 
validation data')
    plt.title('Model Accuracy and Loss')
    plt.ylabel('Accuracy and Loss')
    plt.xlabel('Training Epoch')
    plt.ylim(0)
    plt.legend()
    plt.show()

def print_confusion_matrix():
    matrix = confusion_matrix(y_test, y_pred)
    plt.figure(figsize=(10, 8))
    sns.heatmap(matrix,cmap='coolwarm',linecolor='white',linewidths=1,
                annot=True,
                fmt='d')
    plt.title('Confusion Matrix')
    plt.ylabel('True Label')
    plt.xlabel('Predicted Label')
    plt.show()

def print_performance_metrics():
    print('Accuracy:', np.round(metrics.accuracy_score(y_test, y_
pred),4))
    print('Precision:', np.round(metrics.precision_score(y_test,
                            y_pred,average='weighted'),4))
    print('Recall:', np.round(metrics.recall_score(y_test, y_pred,
                            average='weighted'),4))
    print('F1 Score:', np.round(metrics.f1_score(y_test, y_pred,
                            average='weighted'),4))
   print('Cohen Kappa Score:', np.round(metrics.cohen_kappa_score(y_test, 
y_pred),4))
   print('Matthews Corrcoef:', np.round(metrics.matthews_corrcoef(y_test, 
y_pred),4))
     print('\t\tClassification Report:\n', metrics.classification_report(y_
test, y_pred))

def print_confusion_matrix_and_save():
    mat = confusion_matrix(y_test, y_pred)
    sns.heatmap(mat.T, square=True, annot=True, fmt='d', cbar=False)
    plt.title('Confusion Matrix')
    plt.ylabel('True Label')
    plt.xlabel('Predicted Label')
    plt.show()

    plt.savefig("Confusion.jpg")
```

```
    # Save SVG in a fake file object.
    f = BytesIO()
    plt.savefig(f, format = "svg")
#%%
# load data
(X_train, y_train), (X_test, y_test) = datasets.cifar10.load_data()
# Normalize pixel values to be between 0 and 1
X_train, X_test = X_train / 255.0, X_test / 255.0
#%%
class_names = ['airplane', 'automobile', 'bird', 'cat', 'deer',
               'dog', 'frog', 'horse', 'ship', 'truck']
plt.figure(figsize = (10,10))
for i in range(25):
    plt.subplot(5,5,i + 1)
    plt.xticks([])
    plt.yticks([])
    plt.grid(False)
    plt.imshow(X_train[i], cmap = plt.cm.binary)
    # The CIFAR labels happen to be arrays,
    # which is why you need the extra index
    plt.xlabel(class_names[y_train[i][0]])
plt.show()
#%%
#========================================================================
# 1 Convolutional neural network for CIFAR image classification
#========================================================================
# load data
(X_train, y_train), (X_test, y_test) = datasets.cifar10.load_data()
# Normalize pixel values to be between 0 and 1
X_train, X_test = X_train / 255.0, X_test / 255.0
# Each image's dimension is 32 x 32
img_rows, img_cols = 32, 32
input_shape = (img_rows, img_cols, 3)
#%%
#========================================================================
# Build model
#========================================================================
num_classes = 10
model = Sequential()
model.add(Conv2D(32, (3, 3), activation = 'relu', input_shape = input_
shape))
model.add(MaxPooling2D())
model.add(Dropout(0.2))
```

```
model.add(Flatten())
model.add(Dense(128, activation = 'relu'))
model.add(Dense(num_classes, activation = 'softmax'))
#%%
#=====================================================================
# Compile the model for numerical labels
#=====================================================================
model.compile(optimizer = 'adam',
    loss = 'sparse_categorical_crossentropy',
    metrics = ['accuracy'])
#%%
#=====================================================================
# Compile the model for binary labels
#=====================================================================
#model.compile(loss = 'categorical_crossentropy', optimizer = 'adam',
metrics = ['accuracy'])
#%%
#=====================================================================
# Train and validate the model
#=====================================================================
history = model.fit(X_train, y_train, validation_split = 0.3, epochs = 10,
batch_size = 200, verbose = 2)
#%%
#=====================================================================
# Evaluate the model
#=====================================================================
test_loss, test_acc = model.evaluate(X_test, y_test, verbose = 0)
print("Test Accuracy is : %0.4f" % test_acc)
#%%
#Plot the Model Accuracy and Loss for Training and Validation dataset
plot_model_accuracy_loss()
#%%
#Test the Model with testing data
y_pred_test = model.predict(X_test,)
# Round the test predictions
max_y_pred_test = np.round(y_pred_test)
#Print the Confusion Matrix
print_confusion_matrix()
#%%
#Evaluate the Model and Print Performance Metrics
print_performance_metrics()
#%%
#Print and Save the Confusion Matrix
print_confusion_matrix_and_save()
```

```
#%%
#=========================================================================
# 3 Convolutional neural network for CIFAR image classification
#=========================================================================
# load data
(X_train, y_train), (X_test, y_test) = datasets.cifar10.load_data()
# Normalize pixel values to be between 0 and 1
X_train, X_test = X_train / 255.0, X_test / 255.0
# Each image's dimension is 32 x 32
img_rows, img_cols = 32, 32
input_shape = (img_rows, img_cols, 3)
#%%
#=========================================================================
# Build model
#=========================================================================
num_classes = 10
model = Sequential()
model.add(Conv2D(32, (3, 3), activation = 'relu', input_shape = input_
shape))
model.add(MaxPooling2D((2, 2)))
model.add(Conv2D(64, (3, 3), activation = 'relu'))
model.add(MaxPooling2D((2, 2)))
model.add(Conv2D(64, (3, 3), activation = 'relu'))
model.add(Flatten())
model.add(Dense(64, activation = 'relu'))
model.add(Dense(num_classes, activation = 'softmax'))
#%%
#=========================================================================
# Compile the model for numerical labels
#=========================================================================
model.compile(optimizer = 'adam',
              loss = 'sparse_categorical_crossentropy',
              metrics = ['accuracy'])
#%%
#=========================================================================
# Compile the model for binary labels
#=========================================================================
#model.compile(loss = 'categorical_crossentropy', optimizer = 'adam',
metrics = ['accuracy'])
#%%
#=========================================================================
# Train and validate the model
#=========================================================================
```

```
history = model.fit(X_train, y_train, validation_split = 0.3, epochs = 10,
batch_size = 200, verbose = 2)
#%%
#=========================================================================
# Evaluate the model
#=========================================================================
test_loss, test_acc = model.evaluate(X_test, y_test, verbose = 0)
print("Test Accuracy is : %0.4f" % test_acc)
#%%
#Plot the Model Accuracy and Loss for Training and Validation dataset
plot_model_accuracy_loss()
#%%
#Test the Model with testing data
y_pred_test = model.predict(X_test,)
# Round the test predictions
max_y_pred_test = np.round(y_pred_test)
#Print the Confusion Matrix
print_confusion_matrix()
#%%
#Evaluate the Model and Print Performance Metrics
print_performance_metrics()
#%%
#Print and Save the Confusion Matrix
print_confusion_matrix_and_save()
#%%
#=========================================================================
# 4 Convolutional neural network for CIFAR image classification
#=========================================================================
# load data
(X_train, y_train), (X_test, y_test) = datasets.cifar10.load_data()
# Normalize pixel values to be between 0 and 1
X_train, X_test = X_train / 255.0, X_test / 255.0
#=========================================================================
# Build model
#=========================================================================
num_classes = 10
model = Sequential()
model.add(Conv2D(32, (3, 3), activation = 'relu', input_shape = (32, 32, 3)))
model.add(BatchNormalization())
model.add(Conv2D(32, kernel_size = (3, 3), activation = 'relu'))
model.add(BatchNormalization())
model.add(MaxPooling2D((2, 2)))
model.add(Dropout(0.25))
```

```
model.add(Conv2D(64, (3, 3), activation = 'relu'))
model.add(BatchNormalization())
model.add(Dropout(0.25))
model.add(Conv2D(128, kernel_size = (3, 3), activation = 'relu'))
model.add(BatchNormalization())
model.add(MaxPooling2D(pool_size = (2, 2)))
model.add(Dropout(0.25))
model.add(Flatten())
model.add(Dense(512, activation = 'relu'))
model.add(BatchNormalization())
model.add(Dropout(0.5))
model.add(Dense(128, activation = 'relu'))
model.add(BatchNormalization())
model.add(Dropout(0.5))
model.add(Dense(num_classes, activation = 'softmax'))
#%%
#========================================================================
# Compile the model for numerical labels
#========================================================================
model.compile(optimizer = 'adam',
              loss = 'sparse_categorical_crossentropy',
              metrics = ['accuracy'])
#%%
#========================================================================
# Compile the model for binary labels
#========================================================================
#model.compile(loss = 'categorical_crossentropy', optimizer = 'adam',
metrics = ['accuracy'])
#%%
#========================================================================
# Train and validate the model
#========================================================================
history = model.fit(X_train, y_train, validation_split = 0.3, epochs = 10,
batch_size = 200, verbose = 2)
#%%
#========================================================================
# Evaluate the model
#========================================================================
test_loss, test_acc = model.evaluate(X_test, y_test, verbose = 0)
print("Test Accuracy is : %0.4f" % test_acc)
#%%
#Plot the Model Accuracy and Loss for Training and Validation dataset
plot_model_accuracy_loss()
#%%
```

```
#Test the Model with testing data
y_pred_test = model.predict(X_test,)
# Round the test predictions
max_y_pred_test = np.round(y_pred_test)
#Convert binary labels back to Numerical
y_pred = max_y_pred_test.argmax(axis = 1)
#Print the Confusion Matrix
print_confusion_matrix()
#%%
#Evaluate the Model and Print Performance Metrics
print_performance_metrics()
#%%
#Print and Save the Confusion Matrix
print_confusion_matrix_and_save()
```

## 5.9 Text classification

The role of automated text classification is to classify documents into predetermined categories, typically applying machine learning algorithms. Generally speaking, organizing and using the huge amounts of information, which exist in unstructured text format, is one of the most important techniques. Classification of text is a widely studied field of language processing and text mining study. A document is represented in traditional text classification as a bag of words in which the words terms are cut from their finer context, that is, their location in a sentence or in a document. Only the wider document context is utilized in the vector space with some type of term frequency information. Hence, semantics of words, which can be derived in a sentence from the finer sense of the word's location and its relationships with neighboring words, are generally ignored. Nonetheless, meaning of words semantic relations between words and documents are essential as methods, which capture semantics, generally achieve better performance in classification (Altinel & Ganiz, 2018).

Due to the wide range of sources that generate enormous amounts of data, such as social networks, blogs/forums, websites, e-mails, and digital libraries that publish research papers, text mining studies have become increasingly important in recent years. With new technological advances, such as speech-to-text engines and digital assistants or smart personal assistants, the growth of electronic textual information will no doubt keep increasing. A fundamental problem is the automatic processing, organization, and handling of this textual data. Text mining has several important applications such as classification, filtering of documents, summarization, and sentiment analysis/opinion classification. Machine learning and natural language processing (NLP) techniques work together to detect and automatically classify patterns from different types of documents (Altinel & Ganiz, 2018; Sebastiani, 2005).

Semantic word relationships are considered in semantic text classification methods to generally measure the similarities between documents. The semantic approach focuses on word meaning and hidden linguistic relations between words and therefore between documents (Altinel & Ganiz, 2018). Advantages of classification of semantic text over conventional classification of text are described as:

- Finding implicit or explicit relationships between the words.
- Extracting and using latent word–document relationships.
- Ability of generating representative keywords for the existing classes.
- Semantic text understanding that increases classification performance.
- Ability to manage synonymy and polysemy compared to traditional algorithms for text classification, as they use semantic relationships between words.

Different semantic-based techniques have been proposed to combine semantic relations between words in text classification. These techniques can be categorized into five types, namely, domain knowledge–based (ontology-based) methods, corpus-based methods, deep learning–based methods, word/character-enhanced methods, and linguistic-enriched methods (Altinel & Ganiz, 2018).

- Domain knowledge–based (language-dependent) methods: Domain knowledge–based systems use ontology or thesaurus to classify concepts in documents. Examples of knowledge bases are dictionaries, thesauri, and encyclopedic resources. Common knowledge bases are WordNet, Wiktionary, and Wikipedia. Among them, WordNet is by far the most utilized knowledge base.
- Corpus-based (language-independent) methods: In these schemes, some mathematical calculations are performed to identify latent similarities in the learning corpus between words (Zhang, Gentile, & Ciravegna, 2012). One of the well-known, corpus-based algorithms is latent semantics analysis (LSA) (Deerwester, Dumais, Furnas, Landauer, & Harshman, 1990).
- Deep learning–based methods: Recently deep learning has gained more attention in semantic text analysis.
- Word/character sequence–enhanced methods: Word/character sequence–boosted approaches treat words or characters as string sequences that are extracted from documents by conventional string-matching methods.
- Linguistic-enriched methods: These methods employ lexical and syntactic rules for extracting the noun phrases, entities, and terminologies from a document to create a representation of the document (Altinel & Ganiz, 2018).

## Example 5.9

The following Python code is used to classify a text dataset using different classifiers employing 10-fold cross-validation and also separate training and testing datasets. The classification accuracy, precision, recall, F1 score, Cohen kappa score, and Matthews correlation coefficient are calculated. The classification report and confusion matrix are also given. This example is adapted from the Kaggle web page (https://www.kaggle.com/sanikamal/text-classification-with-python-and-keras).

***Dataset information:*** In the experiments, three real world datasets are utilized. Amazon dataset includes scores and reviews for products sold on amazon.com in the cell phones and accessories category and is part of the dataset collected by McAuley and Leskovec (McAuley & Leskovec, 2013). Scores are on an integer scale from 1 to 5. Scores 4 and 5 are considered positive, and scores 1 and 2 are considered negative. IMDb is a movie review sentiment dataset (https://www.kaggle.com/lakshmi25npathi/imdb-dataset-of-50k-movie-reviews) initially created by Maas et al. (Maas et al., 2011) as a benchmark for sentiment analysis. This dataset includes a total of 100,000 movie reviews posted on imdb.com. There are 50,000 unlabeled reviews, and the remaining 50,000 are split into a set of 25,000 reviews for training and 25,000 reviews for testing. Each of the labeled reviews has a binary sentiment label, either positive or negative. Yelp is a dataset from the Yelp dataset challenge (https://www.yelp.com/dataset/challenge) that contains the restaurant reviews. Scores are on an integer scale from 1 to 5. Scores 4 and 5 are considered positive, and 1 and 2 are considered negative (Kotzias, Denil, De Freitas, & Smyth, 2015).

```
#=========================================================================
# Text classification example
#=========================================================================
"""
Created on Thu Dec 12 12:02:11 2019
@author: absubasi
Text Classification With Python and Keras
"""
import pandas as pd # data processing, CSV file I/O (e.g. pd.read_csv)
import matplotlib.pyplot as plt
plt.style.use('ggplot')
#importing the libraries
import numpy as np
from sklearn.feature_extraction.text import CountVectorizer
from sklearn.model_selection import train_test_split
from sklearn.linear_model import LogisticRegression
from sklearn.preprocessing import LabelEncoder
from sklearn.preprocessing import OneHotEncoder
from sklearn.model_selection import RandomizedSearchCV
from keras.models import Sequential
from keras import layers
from keras.preprocessing.text import Tokenizer
from keras.preprocessing.sequence import pad_sequences
from keras.wrappers.scikit_learn import KerasClassifier
from sklearn.model_selection import cross_val_score
from sklearn import metrics
from sklearn.metrics import confusion_matrix
import seaborn as sns
import matplotlib.pyplot as plt
from io import BytesIO #needed for plot
import seaborn as sns; sns.set()
```

```
#===========================================================================
# Define utility functions
#===========================================================================
def kFold_Cross_Validation_Metrics(model,CV):
    Acc_scores = cross_val_score(model, X, y, cv = CV)
    print("Accuracy: %0.3f (+/- %0.3f)" % (Acc_scores.mean(), Acc_
scores.std() * 2))
    f1_scores = cross_val_score(model, X, y, cv = CV,scoring = 'f1_
macro')
    print("F1 score: %0.3f (+/- %0.3f)" % (f1_scores.mean(), f1_scores.
std() * 2))
    Precision_scores = cross_val_score(model, X, y, cv = CV,scoring =
'precision_macro')
    print("Precision score: %0.3f (+/- %0.3f)" % (Precision_scores.
mean(), Precision_scores.std() * 2))
    Recall_scores = cross_val_score(model, X, y, cv = CV,scoring = 'recall_
macro')
    print("Recall score: %0.3f (+/- %0.3f)" % (Recall_scores.mean(),
Recall_scores.std() * 2))
    from sklearn.metrics import cohen_kappa_score, make_scorer
    kappa_scorer = make_scorer(cohen_kappa_score)
    Kappa_scores = cross_val_score(model, X, y, cv = CV,scoring = kappa_
scorer)
    print("Kappa score: %0.3f (+/- %0.3f)" % (Kappa_scores.mean(),
Kappa_scores.std() * 2))

def Performance_Metrics(model,y_test,y_pred):
    print('Test Accuracy:', np.round(metrics.accuracy_score(y_test,y_
pred),4))
    print('Precision:', np.round(metrics.precision_score(y_test,
                                y_pred,average = 'weighted'),4))
    print('Recall:', np.round(metrics.recall_score(y_test,y_pred,
                                               average = 'weighted'),4))
    print('F1 Score:', np.round(metrics.f1_score(y_test,y_pred,
                                               average = 'weighted'),4))
    print('Cohen Kappa Score:', np.round(metrics.cohen_kappa_score(y_
test,y_pred),4))
    print('Matthews Corrcoef:', np.round(metrics.matthews_corrcoef(y_
test,y_pred),4))
    print('\t\tClassification Report:\n', metrics.classification_report(y_
test,y_pred))
    print("Confusion Matrix:\n",confusion_matrix(y_test,y_pred))
```

```
def print_confusion_matrix(y_test, y_pred, target_names):
    matrix = confusion_matrix(y_test, y_pred)
    plt.figure(figsize = (10, 8))
    sns.heatmap(matrix,cmap = 'coolwarm',linecolor = 'white',linewidths = 1,
                xticklabels = target_names,
                yticklabels = target_names,
                annot = True,
                fmt = 'd')
    plt.title('Confusion Matrix')
    plt.ylabel('True Label')
    plt.xlabel('Predicted Label')
    plt.show()

def print_confusion_matrix_and_save(y_test, y_pred):
    #Print the Confusion Matrix
    matrix = confusion_matrix(y_test, y_pred)
    plt.figure(figsize = (6, 4))
    sns.heatmap(matrix, square = True, annot = True, fmt = 'd', cbar =
False)
    plt.title('Confusion Matrix')
    plt.ylabel('True Label')
    plt.xlabel('Predicted Label')
    plt.show()
    #Save The Confusion Matrix
    plt.savefig("Confusion.jpg")
    # Save SVG in a fake file object.
    f = BytesIO()
    plt.savefig(f, format = "svg")

def print_metrics(X_test, y_test):
    score = classifier.score(X_test, y_test)
    print('Accuracy for {} data: {:.4f}'.format(source, score))
    # Predicting the Test set results
    y_pred = classifier.predict(X_test)
    precision = np.round(metrics.precision_score(y_test,
                        y_pred,average = 'weighted'),4)
    print('Precision for {} data: {:.4f}'.format(source, precision))
    recall = np.round(metrics.recall_score(y_test,y_pred,
                                          average = 'weighted'),4)
    print('Recall for {} data: {:.4f}'.format(source, recall))
    f1score = np.round(metrics.f1_score(y_test,y_pred,
                                          average = 'weighted'),4)
    print('F1 Score for {} data: {:.4f}'.format(source, f1score))
```

```
    kappa = np.round(metrics.cohen_kappa_score(y_test,y_pred),4)
    print('Cohen Kappa Score for {} data: {:.4f}'.format(source, kappa))
    matthews = np.round(metrics.matthews_corrcoef(y_test,y_pred),4)
    print('Matthews Corrcoef: for {} data: {:.4f}'.format(source, mat-
thews))
     print('\t\tClassification Report:\n', metrics.classification_report(y_
test,y_pred))

def plot_history(history):
    accuracy = history.history['accuracy']
    val_accuracy = history.history['val_accuracy']
    loss = history.history['loss']
    val_loss = history.history['val_loss']
    x = range(1, len(accuracy) + 1)

    plt.figure(figsize = (12, 5))
    plt.subplot(1, 2, 1)
    plt.plot(x, accuracy, 'b', label = 'Training acc')
    plt.plot(x, val_accuracy, 'r', label = 'Validation acc')
    plt.title('Training and validation accuracy')
    plt.legend()
    plt.subplot(1, 2, 2)
    plt.plot(x, loss, 'b', label = 'Training loss')
    plt.plot(x, val_loss, 'r', label = 'Validation loss')
    plt.title('Training and validation loss')
    plt.legend()

def plot_model_accuracy_loss():
    plt.figure(figsize = (6, 4))
    plt.plot(history.history['accuracy'], 'r', label = 'Accuracy of
training data')
    plt.plot(history.history['val_accuracy'], 'b', label = 'Accuracy of
validation data')
    plt.plot(history.history['loss'], 'r--', label = 'Loss of training
data')
    plt.plot(history.history['val_loss'], 'b--', label = 'Loss of
validation data')
    plt.title('Model Accuracy and Loss')
    plt.ylabel('Accuracy and Loss')
    plt.xlabel('Training Epoch')
    plt.ylim(0)
    plt.legend()
    plt.show()
```

```
#%%
#=========================================================================
# Load and prepare data
#=========================================================================

filepath_dict = {'yelp': 'yelp_labelled.txt',
                 'amazon': 'amazon_cells_labelled.txt',
                 'imdb': 'imdb_labelled.txt'}
df_list = []
for source, filepath in filepath_dict.items():
    df = pd.read_csv(filepath, names = ['sentence', 'label'], sep = '\t')
    df['source'] = source # Add another column filled with the source
name
    df_list.append(df)
#%%
df = pd.concat(df_list)
df.iloc[0]
#%%
df_yelp = df[df['source'] == 'yelp']
sentences = df_yelp['sentence'].values
y = df_yelp['label'].values

sentences_train, sentences_test, y_train, y_test = train_test_
split(sentences, y, test_size = 0.33, random_state = 1000)
vectorizer = CountVectorizer()
vectorizer.fit(sentences_train)
X = vectorizer.transform(sentences)
X_train = vectorizer.transform(sentences_train)
X_test = vectorizer.transform(sentences_test)
#%%
#=========================================================================
# XGBoost example with cross-validation
#=========================================================================
from xgboost import XGBClassifier
# Create a Model
model = XGBClassifier()
#Evaluate Model Using 10-Fold Cross Validation and Print Performance
Metrics
CV = 10 #10-Fold Cross Validation
kFold_Cross_Validation_Metrics(model,CV)
#%%
#=========================================================================
# XGBoost example with training and testing set
#=========================================================================
```

```
model.fit(X_train, y_train)
# Predicting the Test set results
y_pred = model.predict(X_test)
target_names = ['NO','YES' ]
#Print the Confusion Matrix
print_confusion_matrix(y_test, y_pred, target_names)
# Print The Performance Metrics
Performance_Metrics(model,y_test,y_pred)
#Print and Save the Confusion Matrix
print_confusion_matrix_and_save(y_test, y_pred)
#%%
from xgboost import XGBClassifier
for source in df['source'].unique():
    df_source = df[df['source'] == source]
    sentences = df_source['sentence'].values
    y = df_source['label'].values
    sentences_train, sentences_test, y_train, y_test = train_test_split(
    sentences, y, test_size = 0.25, random_state = 1000)
    vectorizer = CountVectorizer()
    vectorizer.fit(sentences_train)
    X_train = vectorizer.transform(sentences_train)
    X_test = vectorizer.transform(sentences_test)
    classifier =XGBClassifier()
    classifier.fit(X_train, y_train)
    score = classifier.score(X_test, y_test)
    print('Accuracy for {} data: {:.4f}'.format(source, score))
    print_metrics(X_test, y_test)
#%%
from sklearn.neural_network import MLPClassifier
"""mlp = MLPClassifier(hidden_layer_sizes = (100,), activation = 'relu',
solver = 'adam',
              alpha = 0.0001, batch_size = 'auto', learning_rate =
              'constant',
              learning_rate_init = 0.001, power_t = 0.5, max_iter = 200,
              shuffle = True, random_state = None, tol = 0.0001, verbose =
              False,
              warm_start = False, momentum = 0.9, nesterovs_momentum =
              True,
              early_stopping = False, validation_fraction = 0.1, beta_1
              = 0.9,
              beta_2 = 0.999, epsilon = 1e-08, n_iter_no_change = 10)"""
for source in df['source'].unique():
    df_source = df[df['source'] == source]
    sentences = df_source['sentence'].values
    y = df_source['label'].values
```

```
    sentences_train, sentences_test, y_train, y_test = train_test_split(
            sentences, y, test_size = 0.25, random_state = 1000)
    vectorizer = CountVectorizer()
    vectorizer.fit(sentences_train)
    X_train = vectorizer.transform(sentences_train)
    X_test = vectorizer.transform(sentences_test)
    classifier =MLPClassifier(hidden_layer_sizes = (50,25), learning_rate_
init = 0.001,
                        alpha = 1, momentum = 0.9,max_iter = 1000)
    classifier.fit(X_train, y_train)
    print_metrics(X_test, y_test)
#%%
from sklearn.neighbors import KNeighborsClassifier
for source in df['source'].unique():
    df_source = df[df['source'] == source]
    sentences = df_source['sentence'].values
    y = df_source['label'].values
    sentences_train, sentences_test, y_train, y_test = train_test_split(
            sentences, y, test_size = 0.25, random_state = 1000)
    vectorizer = CountVectorizer()
    vectorizer.fit(sentences_train)
    X_train = vectorizer.transform(sentences_train)
    X_test = vectorizer.transform(sentences_test)
    classifier =KNeighborsClassifier(n_neighbors = 5)
    classifier.fit(X_train, y_train)
    print_metrics(X_test, y_test)
#%%
from sklearn import svm
""" The parameters and kernels of SVM classifier can be changed as
follows
C = 10.0 # SVM regularization parameter
svm.SVC(kernel = 'linear', C = C)
svm.LinearSVC(C = C, max_iter = 10000)
svm.SVC(kernel = 'rbf', gamma = 0.7, C = C)
svm.SVC(kernel = 'poly', degree = 3, gamma = 'auto', C = C))
"""
C = 100.0 # SVM regularization parameter
for source in df['source'].unique():
    df_source = df[df['source'] == source]
    sentences = df_source['sentence'].values
    y = df_source['label'].values
    sentences_train, sentences_test, y_train, y_test = train_test_split(
        sentences, y, test_size = 0.25, random_state = 1000)
    vectorizer = CountVectorizer()
```

```
    vectorizer.fit(sentences_train)
    X_train = vectorizer.transform(sentences_train)
    X_test = vectorizer.transform(sentences_test)
    classifier =svm.LinearSVC(C = C, max_iter = 10000)
    classifier.fit(X_train, y_train)
    print_metrics(X_test, y_test)
#%%
from sklearn import metrics
# Fitting Random Forest to the Training set
from sklearn.ensemble import RandomForestClassifier
#In order to change to accuracy increase n_estimators
"""RandomForestClassifier(n_estimators = 'warn', criterion = 'gini', max_
depth = None,
min_samples_split = 2, min_samples_leaf = 1, min_weight_fraction_leaf = 0.0,
max_features = 'auto', max_leaf_nodes = None, min_impurity_decrease = 0.0,
min_impurity_split = None, bootstrap = True, oob_score = False, n_jobs =
None,
random_state = None, verbose = 0, warm_start = False, class_weight =
None)"""
for source in df['source'].unique():
    df_source = df[df['source'] == source]
    sentences = df_source['sentence'].values
    y = df_source['label'].values
    sentences_train, sentences_test, y_train, y_test = train_test_split(
    sentences, y, test_size = 0.25, random_state = 1000)
    vectorizer = CountVectorizer()
    vectorizer.fit(sentences_train)
    X_train = vectorizer.transform(sentences_train)
    X_test = vectorizer.transform(sentences_test)
    classifier =RandomForestClassifier(n_estimators = 100)
    classifier.fit(X_train, y_train)
    print_metrics(X_test, y_test)
#%%
#=====================================================================
# Use Keras deep models
#=====================================================================
from sklearn.metrics import confusion_matrix
from sklearn import metrics
from io import BytesIO #needed for plot
import seaborn as sns; sns.set()
import matplotlib.pyplot as plt
import numpy as np
import seaborn as sns
```

```
#==============================================================================
# Create a Keras model
#==============================================================================
input_dim = X_train.shape[1] # Number of features

model = Sequential()
model.add(layers.Dense(100, input_dim = input_dim, activation = 'relu'))
model.add(layers.Dense(50, activation = 'relu'))
model.add(layers.Dense(1, activation = 'sigmoid'))
#%%
#==============================================================================
# Compile the model
#==============================================================================
model.compile(loss = 'binary_crossentropy',
              optimizer = 'adam',
              metrics = ['accuracy'])
#==============================================================================
# Train and validate the model
#==============================================================================
history = model.fit(X_train, y_train,
                    epochs = 20,
                    verbose = True,
                    validation_split = 0.33,
                    batch_size = 10)
#%%
#==============================================================================
# Evaluate the model
#==============================================================================
loss, accuracy = model.evaluate(X_train, y_train, verbose = False)
print("Training Accuracy: {:.4f}".format(accuracy))
loss, accuracy = model.evaluate(X_test, y_test, verbose = False)
print("Testing Accuracy: {:.4f}".format(accuracy))
#%%
#==============================================================================
# Plot the history
#==============================================================================
#Plot the Model Accuracy and Loss for Training and Validation dataset
plot_history(history)
plot_model_accuracy_loss()
#%%
#Test the Model with testing data
y_pred_test = model.predict(X_test,)
# Round the test predictions
y_pred = np.round(y_pred_test)
#%%
```

```
target_names = ['NO','YES' ]
#Print the Confusion Matrix
print_confusion_matrix(y_test, y_pred, target_names)
# Print The Perfromance Metrics
Performance_Metrics(model,y_test,y_pred)
#Print and Save the Confusion Matrix
print_confusion_matrix_and_save(y_test, y_pred)

#%%
tokenizer = Tokenizer(num_words = 5000)
tokenizer.fit_on_texts(sentences_train)

X_train = tokenizer.texts_to_sequences(sentences_train)
X_test = tokenizer.texts_to_sequences(sentences_test)

vocab_size = len(tokenizer.word_index) + 1 # Adding 1 because of reserved
0 index
print(sentences_train[2])
print(X_train[2])

#%%
for word in ['the', 'all','fan']:
    print('{}: {}'.format(word, tokenizer.word_index[word]))

#%%
maxlen = 100

X_train = pad_sequences(X_train, padding = 'post', maxlen = maxlen)
X_test = pad_sequences(X_test, padding = 'post', maxlen = maxlen)

print(X_train[0, :])

#%%
embedding_dim = 50
#==========================================================================
# Create a deep Keras model with embedding
#==========================================================================
model = Sequential()
model.add(layers.Embedding(input_dim = vocab_size,
                           output_dim = embedding_dim,
                           input_length = maxlen))
model.add(layers.Flatten())
#model.add(layers.Dense(300, activation = 'relu'))
model.add(layers.Dense(100, activation = 'relu'))
model.add(layers.Dense(50, activation = 'relu'))
```

```
model.add(layers.Dense(1, activation = 'sigmoid'))
#%%
#=========================================================================
# Compile the model
#=========================================================================
model.compile(loss = 'binary_crossentropy',
              optimizer = 'adam',
              metrics = ['accuracy'])
#=========================================================================
# Train and validate the model
#=========================================================================
#history = model.fit(X_train, y_train, validation_split = 0.33, nb_epoch
= 50, batch_size = 25,verbose = 0)
history = model.fit(X_train, y_train,
                    epochs = 20,
                    verbose = True,
                    validation_split = 0.33,
                    batch_size = 10)
loss, accuracy = model.evaluate(X_train, y_train, verbose = False)
print("Training Accuracy: {:.4f}".format(accuracy))
loss, accuracy = model.evaluate(X_test, y_test, verbose = False)
print("Testing Accuracy: {:.4f}".format(accuracy))
#%%
#=========================================================================
# Plot the history
#=========================================================================
#Plot the Model Accuracy and Loss for Training and Validation dataset
plot_history(history)
plot_model_accuracy_loss()
#%%
#Test the Model with testing data
y_pred_test = model.predict(X_test,)
# Round the test predictions
y_pred = np.round(y_pred_test)
#%%
#Test the Model with testing data
y_pred_test = model.predict(X_test,)
# Round the test predictions
y_pred = np.round(y_pred_test)
#%%
target_names = ['NO','YES' ]
#Print the Confusion Matrix
print_confusion_matrix(y_test, y_pred, target_names)
# Print The Perfromance Metrics
```

```
Performance_Metrics(model,y_test,y_pred)
#Print and Save the Confusion Matrix
print_confusion_matrix_and_save(y_test, y_pred)
#%%
embedding_dim = 50
#=========================================================================
# Create a deep Keras model with embedding and pooling
#=========================================================================
model = Sequential()
model.add(layers.Embedding(input_dim = vocab_size,
                           output_dim = embedding_dim,
                           input_length = maxlen))
model.add(layers.GlobalMaxPool1D())
model.add(layers.Dense(10, activation = 'relu'))
model.add(layers.Dense(1, activation = 'sigmoid'))
model.compile(optimizer = 'adam',
              loss = 'binary_crossentropy',
              metrics = ['accuracy'])
model.summary()
#%%
history = model.fit(X_train, y_train,
                    epochs = 20,
                    verbose = True,
#                    validation_data = (X_test, y_test),
                    validation_split = 0.33,
                    batch_size = 10)
loss, accuracy = model.evaluate(X_train, y_train, verbose = 1)
print("Training Accuracy: {:.4f}".format(accuracy))
loss, accuracy = model.evaluate(X_test, y_test, verbose = 1)
print("Testing Accuracy: {:.4f}".format(accuracy))
#%%
#=========================================================================
# Plot the history
#=========================================================================
#Plot the Model Accuracy and Loss for Training and Validation dataset
plot_history(history)
plot_model_accuracy_loss()
#%%
#Test the Model with testing data
y_pred_test = model.predict(X_test,)
# Round the test predictions
y_pred = np.round(y_pred_test)
#%%
```

```
target_names=['NO','YES' ]
#Print the Confusion Matrix
print_confusion_matrix(y_test, y_pred, target_names)
# Print The Perfromance Metrics
Performance_Metrics(model,y_test,y_pred)
#Print and Save the Confusion Matrix
print_confusion_matrix_and_save(y_test, y_pred)
#%%
embedding_dim=100
#=====================================================================
# Use Keras convolutional neural networks (CNN) model with word
embedding
#=====================================================================
model=Sequential()
model.add(layers.Embedding(vocab_size, embedding_dim, input_length=
maxlen))
model.add(layers.Conv1D(128, 5, activation='relu'))
#model.add(layers.Conv1D(64, 5, activation='relu'))
model.add(layers.GlobalMaxPooling1D())
model.add(layers.Dense(32, activation='relu'))
#model.add(layers.Dense(32, activation='relu'))
model.add(layers.Dense(1, activation='sigmoid'))
model.compile(optimizer='adam',
              loss='binary_crossentropy',
              metrics=['accuracy'])
model.summary()
#%%
history=model.fit(X_train, y_train,
                    epochs=20,verbose=True,
#                    validation_data=(X_test, y_test),
                    validation_split=0.33,batch_size=20)
loss, accuracy=model.evaluate(X_train, y_train, verbose=1)
print("Training Accuracy: {:.4f}".format(accuracy))
loss, accuracy=model.evaluate(X_test, y_test, verbose=1)
print("Testing Accuracy: {:.4f}".format(accuracy))

#%%
#=====================================================================
# Plot the history
#=====================================================================
#Plot the Model Accuracy and Loss for Training and Validation dataset
plot_history(history)
plot_model_accuracy_loss()
#%%
```

```
#Test the Model with testing data
y_pred_test = model.predict(X_test,)
# Round the test predictions
y_pred = np.round(y_pred_test)
#%%
target_names = ['NO','YES' ]
#Print the Confusion Matrix
print_confusion_matrix(y_test, y_pred, target_names)
# Print The Perfromance Metrics
Performance_Metrics(model,y_test,y_pred)
#Print and Save the Confusion Matrix
print_confusion_matrix_and_save(y_test, y_pred)
```

## 5.10 Summary

Machine learning has begun to be employed in our daily lives. The amount of data that grows day by day will be the key skill for researchers working in a data-driven industry. Data instances in machine learning include the number of features. Classification is one of the crucial tasks of machine learning and is utilized to position an unknown piece of data in a known group. In order to train or build a classifier, the training data set is utilized. It can greatly improve the quality of life by building an intelligent computer similar to the reliability of a human expert. If a piece of software is created to support the decision of the doctor, it will be easier to treat patients. Better weather forecasts will lead to less water shortages and increased food supply (Harrington, 2012). In the classification of various data as well as their different implementations, a wide range of machine learning algorithms and techniques are identified in this chapter. Presented separately at the end of each section, such examples include the complete solutions, which will help the reader become more familiar with machine learning techniques and principles. Some of them may also act as an entry point for academic work and research into new questions. Numerous machine learning algorithms are discussed and implemented, as well as their variants, which can be utilized directly to achieve efficient solutions to real world learning problems. Detailed explanations and assessments of the presented algorithms can help with their implementation and adaptation to other learning scenarios.

## References

Ala'raj, M., & Abbod, M. F. (2016). A new hybrid ensemble credit scoring model based on classifiers consensus system approach. *Expert Systems with Applications*, *64*, 36–55 https://doi.org/10.1016/j.eswa.2016.07.017.

Alla, S., & Adari, S. K. (2019). In *Beginning anomaly detection using Python-based deep learning* (1st ed.). New York: Apress, Springer.

Altinel, B., & Ganiz, M. C. (2018). Semantic text classification: A survey of past and recent advances. *Information Processing & Management*, *54*(6), 1129–1153.

Androutsopoulos, I., Koutsias, J., Chandrinos, K.V., Paliouras, G., & Spyropoulos, C.D. (2000). An evaluation of naive Bayesian anti-spam filtering, Proceedings of the 11th European Conference on Machine Learning, Barcelona

Bace, R. (1999). An introduction to intrusion detection and assessment for system and network security management, ICSA Intrusion Detection Systems Consortium Technical Report

Bache, K., & Lichman, M. (2013). UCI Machine Learning Repository [http://archive.Ics.Uci.Edu/ml]. University of California, School of Information and Computer Science. Irvine, CA.

Baesens, B., Van Gestel, T., Viaene, S., Stepanova, M., Suykens, J., & Vanthienen, J. (2003). Benchmarking state-of-the-art classification algorithms for credit scoring. *Journal of the Operational Research Society*, *54*(6), 627–635.

Bernard, S., Adam, S., & Heutte, L. (2007). In *Using random forests for handwritten digit recognition* (pp. 1043–1047). Parana: Ninth International Conference on Document Analysis and Recognition (ICDAR 2007).

Bhattacharyya, S., Jha, S., Tharakunnel, K., & Westland, J. C. (2011). Data mining for credit card fraud: A comparative study. *On Quantitative Methods for Detection of Financial Fraud*, *50*(3), 602–613 https://doi.org/10.1016/j.dss.2010.08.008.

Carcillo, F., Dal Pozzolo, A., Le Borgne, Y. -A., Caelen, O., Mazzer, Y., & Bontempi, G. (2018). Scarff: A scalable framework for streaming credit card fraud detection with spark. *Information Fusion*, *41*, 182–194.

Carcillo, F., Le Borgne, Y. -A., Caelen, O., Kessaci, Y., Oblé, F., & Bontempi, G. (2019). Combining unsupervised and supervised learning in credit card fraud detection. *Information Sciences*.

Chuang, C., & Huang, S. (2011). A hybrid neural network approach for credit scoring. *Expert Systems*, *28*(2), 185–196.

Curtis, S. R., Rajivan, P., Jones, D. N., & Gonzalez, C. (2018). Phishing attempts among the dark triad: Patterns of attack and vulnerability. *Computers in Human Behavior*, *87*, 174–182.

Dal Pozzolo, A., Boracchi, G., Caelen, O., Alippi, C., & Bontempi, G. (2018). Credit card fraud detection: A realistic modeling and a novel learning strategy. *IEEE Transactions on Neural Networks and Learning Systems*, *29*(8), 3784–3797.

Dal Pozzolo, A., Caelen, O., & Bontempi, G. (2015). In *When is undersampling effective in unbalanced classification tasks?* (pp. 200–215). Berlin: Springer.

Dal Pozzolo, A., Caelen, O., Le Borgne, Y. -A., Waterschoot, S., & Bontempi, G. (2014). Learned lessons in credit card fraud detection from a practitioner perspective. *Expert Systems with Applications*, *41*(10), 4915–4928.

Deerwester, S., Dumais, S. T., Furnas, G. W., Landauer, T. K., & Harshman, R. (1990). Indexing by latent semantic analysis. *Journal of the American Society for Information Science*, *41*(6), 391–407.

Delamaire, L., Abdou, H., & Pointon, J. (2009). Credit card fraud and detection techniques: A review. *Banks and Bank Systems*, *4*(2), 57–68.

Elleuch, M., Maalej, R., & Kherallah, M. (2016). A new design based-SVM of the CNN classifier architecture with dropout for offline Arabic handwritten recognition. *Procedia Computer Science*, *80*, 1712–1723.

Gastellier-Prevost, S., Granadillo, G. G., & Laurent, M. (2011). In *Decisive heuristics to differentiate legitimate from phishing sites* (pp. 1–9). La Rochelle, France: 2011 Conference on Network and Information Systems Security.

Gicic´, A., & Subasi, A. (2019). Credit scoring for a microcredit data set using the synthetic minority oversampling technique and ensemble classifiers. *Expert Systems*, *36*(2), e12363.

Goel, S., & Hong, Y. (2015). Security Challenges in Smart Grid Implementation. In Smart Grid Security (pp. 1–39). Springer.

Govindarajan, M., & Chandrasekaran, R. (2011). Intrusion detection using neural based hybrid classification methods. *Computer Networks*, *55*(8), 1662–1671.

Gupta, B. B., Arachchilage, N. A., & Psannis, K. E. (2018). Defending against phishing attacks: Taxonomy of methods, current issues and future directions. *Telecommunication Systems*, *67*(2), 247–267.

Guzella, T. S., & Caminhas, W. M. (2009). A review of machine learning approaches to spam filtering. *Expert Systems with Applications*, *36*(7), 10206–10222.

Han, J., Pei, J., & Kamber, M. (2011). *Data mining: Concepts and techniques*. Amsterdam: Elsevier.

Harrington, P. (2012). *Machine learning in action*. Shelter Island, NY: Manning Publications Co.

Huang, C. -L., Chen, M. -C., & Wang, C. -J. (2007). Credit scoring with a data mining approach based on support vector machines. *Expert Systems with Applications*, *33*(4), 847–856.

Hung, C., & Chen, J. -H. (2009). A selective ensemble based on expected probabilities for bankruptcy prediction. *Expert Systems with Applications*, *36*(3), 5297–5303.

Innella, P., & McMillan, O. (2017, February 17). An Introduction to IDS Symantec Connect. Retrieved February 17, 2017, from https://www.symantec.com/connect/articles/introduction-ids.

Jha, S., Guillen, M., & Westland, J. C. (2012). Employing transaction aggregation strategy to detect credit card fraud. *Expert Systems with Applications*, *39*(16), 12650–12657.

Jurgovsky, J., Granitzer, M., Ziegler, K., Calabretto, S., Portier, P. -E., He-Guelton, L., & Caelen, O. (2018). Sequence classification for credit-card fraud detection. *Expert Systems with Applications*, *100*, 234–245.

Kim, P. (2017). Convolutional neural network. In MATLAB deep learning (pp. 121–147). Springer.

Kotzias, D., Denil, M., De Freitas, N., & Smyth, P. (2015). In *From group to individual labels using deep features* (pp. 597–606). New York: ACM.

Kumar, P. R., & Ravi, V. (2007). Bankruptcy prediction in banks and firms via statistical and intelligent techniques–A review. *European Journal of Operational Research*, *180*(1), 1–28.

Lauer, F., Suen, C. Y., & Bloch, G. (2007). A trainable feature extractor for handwritten digit recognition. *Pattern Recognition*, *40*(6), 1816–1824.

Lebichot, B., Le Borgne, Y. -A., He-Guelton, L., Oblé, F., & Bontempi, G. (2019). In *Deep-learning domain adaptation techniques for credit cards fraud detection* (pp. 78–88). Berlin: Springer.

Liang, M., & Hu, X. (2015). In *Recurrent convolutional neural network for object recognition* (pp. 3367–3375). Boston: 2015 IEEE Conference on Computer Vision and Pattern Recognition (CVPR).

Lin, W., Hu, Y., & Tsai, C. (2012). Machine learning in financial crisis prediction. *IEEE Transactions on Systems, Man, and Cybernetics, Part C (Applications and Reviews)*, *42*(4), 421–436.

Maas, A. L., Daly, R. E., Pham, P. T., Huang, D., Ng, A. Y., & Potts, C. (2011). In *Learning word vectors for sentiment analysis* (pp. 142–150). Portland, OR: Proceedings of the 49th Annual Meeting of the Association for Computational Linguistics: Human Language Technologies.

Mahmoudi, N., & Duman, E. (2015). Detecting credit card fraud by modified Fisher discriminant analysis. *Expert Systems with Applications*, *42*(5), 2510–2516.

Makowski, P. (1985). Credit scoring branches out. *Credit World*, *75*(1), 30–37.

McAuley, J., & Leskovec, J. (2013). In *Hidden factors and hidden topics: Understanding rating dimensions with review text* (pp. 165–172). New York: ACM.

Mohammad, R. M., Thabtah, F., & McCluskey, L. (2012). In *An assessment of features related to phishing websites using an automated technique* (pp. 492–497). London: 2012 International Conference for Internet Technology and Secured Transactions.

Mohammad, R. M., Thabtah, F., & McCluskey, L. (2014). Intelligent rule-based phishing websites classification. *IET Information Security*, *8*(3), 153–160.

Mohammad, R.M., Thabtah, F., & McCluskey, L. (2015). Phishing websites features. Unpublished. Available via: http://eprints.hud.ac.uk/id/eprint/24330/6/MohammadPhishing14July2015.pdf.

Murphy, K. P. (2012). *Machine learning: A probabilistic perspective*. Cambridge, MA: MIT press.

Pramanik, R., & Bag, S. (2018). Shape decomposition-based handwritten compound character recognition for Bangla OCR. *Journal of Visual Communication and Image Representation*, *50*, 123–134.

Recht, B., Roelofs, R., Schmidt, L., & Shankar, V. (2018). Do CIFAR-10 classifiers generalize to CIFAR-10? ArXiv Preprint ArXiv:1806.00451.

Sahu, M., Mishra, B. K., Das, S. K., & Mishra, A. (2014). Intrusion detection system using data mining. *I-Manager's Journal on Computer Science*, *2*(1), 19.

Schebesch, K. B., & Stecking, R. (2005). Support vector machines for classifying and describing credit applicants: Detecting typical and critical regions. *Journal of the Operational Research Society*, *56*(9), 1082–1088.

Sebastiani, F. (2005). Text categorization. In Encyclopedia of Database Technologies and Applications (pp. 683–687). IGI Global.

Serrano-Cinca, C., & Gutiérrez-Nieto, B. (2016). The use of profit scoring as an alternative to credit scoring systems in peer-to-peer (P2P) lending. *Decision Support Systems*, *89*, 113–122.

Sethi, N., & Gera, A. (2014). A revived survey of various credit card fraud detection techniques. *International Journal of Computer Science and Mobile Computing*, *3*(4), 780–791.

Shin, K., & Han, I. (2001). A case-based approach using inductive indexing for corporate bond rating. *Decision Support Systems*, *32*(1), 41–52.

Subasi, A., Alzahrani, S., Aljuhani, A., & Aljedani, M. (2018). In *Comparison of decision tree algorithms for spam e-mail filtering* (pp. 1–5). Riyadh, Saudi Arabia: 2018 1st International Conference on Computer Applications & Information Security (ICCAIS).

Subasi, A., & Kremic, E. (November 13, 2019). In *Comparison of Adaboost with multiboosting for phishing website detection*Malvern, PA: Presented at the Complex Adaptive Systems Conference.

Subasi, A., Molah, E., Almkallawi, F., & Chaudhery, T. J. (2017). In *Intelligent phishing website detection using random forest classifier* (pp. 1–5). Ras Al Khaimah, UAE: 2017 International Conference on Electrical and Computing Technologies and Applications (ICECTA).

Tiwari, M., Kumar, R., Bharti, A., & Kishan, J. (2017). Intrusion detection system. *International Journal of Technical Research and Applications*, *5*, 2320–8163.

UCI Machine Learning Repository: Phishing Websites Data Set. (n.d.). Retrieved January 29, 2017, from https://archive.ics.uci.edu/ml/datasets/Phishing+Websites#.

UCI Machine Learning Repository: Statlog (German Credit Data) Data Set. (n.d.). Retrieved November 29, 2019, from https://archive.ics.uci.edu/ml/datasets/Statlog+(German+Credit+Data).

Wheeler, R., & Aitken, S. (2000). Multiple algorithms for fraud detection. *Knowledge-Based Systems*, *13*(2–3), 93–99.

Whitrow, C., Hand, D. J., Juszczak, P., Weston, D., & Adams, N. M. (2009). Transaction aggregation as a strategy for credit card fraud detection. *Data Mining and Knowledge Discovery*, *18*(1), 30–55.

Xiang, G., Hong, J., Rose, C. P., & Cranor, L. (2011). Cantina+: A feature-rich machine learning framework for detecting phishing web sites. *ACM Transactions on Information and System Security (TISSEC)*, *14*(2), 21.

Zhang, Y. (2019). Evaluation of CNN Models with Fashion MNIST Data (Iowa State University). Retrieved from https://lib.dr.iastate.edu/creativecomponents/364.

Zhang, Z., Gentile, A., & Ciravegna, F. (2012). *Recent advances in methods of lexical semantic relatedness*. Cabridge, UK: Cambridge University.

Zhao, K. (2018). Handwritten Digit Recognition and Classification Using Machine Learning. M. Sc. in Computing (Data Analytics),Technological University Dublin.

CHAPTER

# 6

# Regression examples

## 6.1 Introduction

The label space was a discrete set of classes in all the tasks considered for classification. In this chapter we will take into consideration the case of a real-valued target variable. A *function estimator*, also known as a *regressor*, is a mapping $\hat{f}: X \rightarrow R$. The regression learning problem is to learn a function estimator from examples $(x_i, f(x_i))$. For instance, we would like to learn an estimator for the Dow Jones index or the FTSE 100 based on chosen economic indicators. While this may seem to be a natural and innocent generalization of discrete classification, it is not without its drawbacks. For one thing, we switched to one with infinite resolution from a relatively low-resolution target variable. Trying to match this accuracy in the function estimator will almost certainly lead to overfitting. Moreover, some of the target values in the examples are more likely because of the variations, which the model cannot capture. Hence it is quite logical to assume that the examples are noisy and that the estimator is supposed to capture only the general trend or function shape (Flach, 2012).

Regression is a process in which the difference between models of grouping and grading comes into play. The grouping model theory involves separating the instance space into segments and learning a local model in each segment as simply as possible. For example, the local model is a majority classifier in decision trees. In the same way, we might estimate a constant value in each leaf to obtain a regression tree. This would result in a piecewise constant curve in a univariate problem. Such a grouping model is capable of exactly matching the given points, just as a sufficiently high-degree polynomial, and the same caveat applies to overfitting. A rule of thumb is that the number of parameters estimated from the data must be slightly lower than the number of data points in order to prevent overfitting (Flach, 2012).

We saw that models of classification can be assessed by applying a loss function to the margins, penalizing negative margins (misclassifications) and rewarding positive margins (correct classification). Regression models are assessed by using a loss function to the *residuals* $f(x)-\hat{f}(x)$. Unlike classification loss function, a regression loss function would usually be symmetrical around 0, even though it is possible that there are different weights for positive and negative residuals. The ordinary choice here is to take the squared residual as the loss function. This has the benefit of statistical consistency and the presumption that the observed function values are the true values contaminated with additive; normally distributed noise can also be justified. When we underestimate the number of parameters in the model, we

**Practical Machine Learning for Data Analysis Using Python. http://dx.doi.org/10.1016/B978-0-12-821379-7.00006-0**

cannot reduce the loss to zero, irrespective of how much training data we have. On the other hand, the model will be more dependent on the training sample with a larger number of parameters, so small variations in the training sample will lead to a significantly different model. This is the so-called *bias–variance dilemma*: a low complexity model suffers less from variability because of the random variations in the training data, but it might lead to a systematic bias. On the contrary, a high-complexity model eliminates such bias but can suffer nonsystematic errors because of the variance (Flach, 2012).

## 6.2 Stock market price index return forecasting

The efficient market hypothesis claims that current stock values at that moment reflect all available information on the market; however, on the basis of that information, the public cannot make successful trades. Others assume that the markets are ineffective, partly because of the psychological factors of the different market participants together with the market's inability to respond instantaneously to newly released information. Therefore financial variables such as stock prices, stock market index values, and financial derivative prices are considered predictable. This allows one to obtain a return above the market average by analyzing information provided to the general public with findings that are better than random (Zhong & Enke, 2017).

Stock price prediction is crucial in the financial world. In the world of big data, accurate and reliable stock market forecasts are becoming increasingly important. When trying to make precise forecasts, there are too many factors that go into the stock market fluctuations. Machine learning is particularly helpful in this way, as it has the ability to use large amounts of data and learn from errors. One of the most interesting issues in the financial world is the estimation of market index movement of prices. In particular, the statistical method does not provide an automatic solution, as it involves variations and changes to reach regularity and stationarity in the target value at each step. More efficient methods are required to mitigate the limitations of traditional statistical approaches in order to follow the market's dynamic and nonstationary character. Financial professionals have come up with several different ways of making sound trading decisions, such as machine learning techniques (Şenyurt & Subaşı, 2015).

Stock markets are influenced by several extremely correlated factors. These factors include: (1) economic variables, such as exchange rates, commodity prices, interest rates, monetary growth rates, and general economic conditions; (2) industry specific variables, such as growth rates of industrial production and consumer prices; (3) company specific variables, such as changes in company's policies, income statements, and dividend yields; (4) psychological variables of investors, such as investors' expectations and institutional investors' choices; and (5) political variables, such as the occurrence and release of important political events. Each one of these factors interacts in a very complex manner. Moreover, the stock market is naturally a nonlinear, dynamic, nonparametric, nonstationary, noisy, and chaotic system. However investors are hoping to make substantial profit because of the potential market inefficiencies by developing trading strategies based on increasingly accurate forecasts of financial variables. Hence analyzing the movements of the stock market is challenging and attractive for investors and researchers. For example, financial time series forecasting may be classified as either univariate or multivariate analysis of the input variables. For univariate analysis, only the financial time series itself is considered as the input, whereas in multivariate analysis the input variables may be a lagged time series or another form of information, such as a technical indicator, fundamental indicator, or intermarket indicator. Therefore statistical and machine learning techniques have been utilized to analyze the stock markets (Zhong & Enke, 2017).

In today's smart finance world, the market price forecasting profession and the associated decision-supporting framework plays a crucial role. Scientists have been conducting detailed research for a long time to understand the underlying stock market mechanism and to forecast the outcome of the market price accurately. Because money business is all about earning high financial profits, each player on the market is pursuing some intelligent computational model, which can consistently pick winners and write off losers. Daily market values are a sequence of numbers storing data over time that computational models need to process. While the use of artificial intelligence (AI) in finance is not novel, problem-solving has been the biggest boost ever in AI—including new ideas and methods to develop better techniques, such as deep learning that focuses on issues rather than equations. Numerous studies have presented the effectiveness of artificial intelligence techniques over traditional models such as ARMA, ARIMA, and linear regression in forecasting problems, which show better prediction performance of artificial intelligence–based schemes (Şenyurt & Subaşı, 2015) Table 6.1

**TABLE 6.1** Technical indicators for stock market (Şenyurt & Subaşı, 2015)

| Name of indicator | Formula |
|---|---|
| *Accumulation/distribution oscillator | $\frac{((Close-Low)-(High-Close))}{(High-Low)} \times Period's\ Volume$ |
| *Chaikin oscillator | *(3 day EMA of ADL)-(10 day EMA of ADL)* |
| *Money flow multiplier* | $\frac{((Close-Low)-(High-Close))}{(High-Low)}$ |
| *Money flow volume* | *money flow multiplier × volume for the period* |
| *ADL* | *previous ADL +current period's money flow volume* |
| *Moving average convergence divergence | *MACD line* = (12 *day EMA*-26 *day EMA*) |
| | *(MACD) Signal line* = 9 day EMA of MACD line |
| *Stochastic oscillator | $\%K = 100 \times \left[\frac{(C-L14)}{(H14-L14)}\right]$<br>C = *the most recent closing price*<br>L14 = *the low of the 14 previous trading sessions*<br>H14 = *the highest price traded during the same 14 day period*<br>%D = 3- *period moving average of %K* |

*(Continued)*

**TABLE 6.1** Technical indicators for stock market (Şenyurt & Subaşı, 2015) (*Cont.*)

| Name of indicator | Formula |
|---|---|
| *Acceleration | *difference between two momentums separated by some numbers of periods* |
| *Momentum | $\left[\left(\frac{close(J)}{close(J-N)}\right)\times 100\right]$<br>J = *current interval*<br>N = *the gap between the intervals that are being compared* |
| *Chaikin volatility | $\left[\left(\frac{(EMA(High-Low)-EMA(High-Low\ 10\ days\ ago))}{EMA(High-Low\ 10\ days\ ago)}\right)\times 100\right]$ |
| *Fast stochastics | |
| Fast %K | $\left[\frac{(Close-Low)}{(High-Low)}\right]\times 100$ |
| Fast %D | *simple moving average of Fast % K (3 periods)* |
| *Stochastic slow | |
| Slow %K | *equal to Fast % D (3 period moving average of Fast* |
| Slow %D | a moving average of slow % K (3 periods) |
| *William's %R | $\left[\frac{(Highest\ high-Close)}{(Highest\ high-Lowest\ low)}\right]\times 100$ |
| *Negative volume index (NVI) | $\left[\frac{(Close[today]-Close[yesterday])}{(Close[yesterday])}\right]\times NVI[yesterday]$ |
| *Positive volume index (PVI) | $\left[\frac{(Close[today]-Close[yesterday])}{(Close[yesterday])}\right]\times PVI[yesterday]$ |
| *Relative strength index (RSI) | $100-\left[\frac{100}{1+RS^*}\right],\ RS^*=\frac{average\ of\ x\ days'up\ closes}{average\ of\ x\ days'down\ closes}$ |
| *Accumulation/distribution line (ADL) | *previous ADL +current period's money flow volume* |
| *Money flow multiplier* | $\frac{((Close-Low)-(High-Close))}{(High-Low)}$ |
| *Money flow volume* | money flow multiplies × volume for the period |
| *Bollinger band | |
| *Middle band* | *20 day simple moving average (SMA)* |

**TABLE 6.1** Technical indicators for stock market (Şenyurt & Subaşı, 2015) (*Cont.*)

| Name of indicator | Formula |
|---|---|
| *Upper band* | 20 *day* SMA + (20 *day standard deviantionor price* × 2) |
| *Lower band* | 20 *day SMA* – (20 *days tandard deviationor price* × 2) |
| *Highest high | *generates a vector of highest high values for the past 14 period* |
| *Lowest low | *generates a vector of lowest low values for the past 14 periods* |
| *Median price | *MP = (High + Low)/2* |
| *On-balance volume | *If close for the period is higher than the previous close OBV = OBV [previous period]+ Volume [current period]*<br>*If close for the period is lower than the previous close OBV = OBV [previous period]+ Volume [current period]*<br>*If close for the period is equal to the previous close OBV = OBV [previous period]* |
| *Price rate of change | *(Closing price(today) – Closing price(n periods ago)) / Closing price(n periods ago)* |
| *Price-volume trend | |
| *Closing price percentage change* | *(Closing price(today) – Closing price(n periods ago)) / Closing price(n periods ago)* |
| *Price-volume trend* | *Percentage change* Volume(today) + PVT(yesterday)* |
| *Typical price | *(High + Low + Close)/3* |
| *Volume rate of change | *(Volume(today)-Volume(n periods ago)) /Volume(n periods ago)*100* |
| *Weighted close | *((Close*2) +High +Low)/4* |
| *William's accumulation/ distribution | |
| *True range high (TRH)* | *Yesterday's close or today's high, whichever is greater* |
| *True range low (TRL)* | *Yesterday's close or today's low, whichever is less* |
| *Today's A/D* | *Today's close – TRL (If today's close is greater than yesterday's close)*<br>*Today's close-TRH (If today's close is less than yesterday's close)*<br>*0 (If today's close is equal to yesterday's close)* |
| *Williams's A/D | *Today's A/D + Yesterday's Williams's A/D* |

## Example 6.1

The following Python code is used to forecast stock market price index return employing different classifiers with separate training and testing datasets. Statistical quality measures, including mean-absolute error (MAE), mean squared error (MSE), and correlation coefficient (R), are calculated. Scatter plot, real, and predicted values are also plotted.

***Dataset information:*** NASDAQ, DOWJONES, S&P, RUSSEL, and NYSE composite indexes represent different stock markets worldwide. Datasets can be downloaded from Yahoo finance website using the following command:

```
yahoo_data = pdr.data.get_data_yahoo('^IXIC', start_date, stop_date)
"""
```

```
Created on Fri Dec 13 14:00:48 2019
@author: subasi
This example uses regression model to predict stock prices
For this example, Technical Indicators are also calculated on stock data.
Some part of this example is taken from
https://www.kaggle.com/kratisaxena/stock-market-technical-indicators-
visualization
Please refer the above kernel for visualization part." " "
#=====================================================================
# Stock market analysis
#=====================================================================
#%%
# Import Modules
import pandas as pd
import numpy as np
from datetime import datetime
import statsmodels.api as sm
import copy
import matplotlib.pyplot as plt
from IPython.display import Image
from matplotlib.pylab import rcParams
from statsmodels.tsa.stattools import adfuller
from statsmodels.tsa.stattools import acf, pacf
from sklearn.linear_model import LinearRegression
from statsmodels.tsa.arima_model import ARMA, ARIMA
from sklearn.metrics import explained_variance_score
from numpy import array
from pandas import read_csv
from sklearn.metrics import mean_squared_error, r2_score
from sklearn.metrics import mean_absolute_error
import matplotlib.pyplot as plt
#You should install mpl_finance module before using
#pip install mpl_finance
from mpl_finance import candlestick_ohlc #parse_yahoo_historical_ochl
rcParams['figure.figsize'] = 15, 5
#You should install pandas_datareader module before using
#!pip install pandas_datareader
import pandas_datareader as pdr
#=====================================================================
# Define utility functions
#=====================================================================
def plot_model_loss(history):
  plt.figure(figsize = (6, 4))
  plt.plot(history.history['loss'], 'r--', label = 'Loss of training
  data')
```

```
  plt.plot(history.history['val_loss'], 'b--', label='Loss of
  validation data')
  plt.title('Model Error')
  plt.ylabel('Loss')
  plt.xlabel('Training Epoch')
  plt.ylim(0)
  plt.legend()
  plt.show()

def print_performance_metrics(ytest, ypred):
# The mean absolute error
print("MAE = %5.3f" % mean_absolute_error(ytest, ypred))
# Explained variance score: 1 is perfect prediction
print("R^2 = %0.5f" % r2_score(ytest, ypred))
# The mean squared error
print("MSE = %5.3f" % mean_squared_error(ytest, ypred))

def plot_scatter(ytest, ypred):
fig, ax = plt.subplots()
ax.scatter(ytest, ypred, edgecolors = (0, 0, 0))
ax.text(10, ytest.max()-10, r'$R^2$ = %.2f, MAE = %.2f' % (
  r2_score(ytest, ypred), mean_absolute_error(ytest, ypred)))
ax.plot([ytest.min(), ytest.max()], [ytest.min(), ytest.max()], 'k--',
lw = 4)
ax.set_xlabel('Measured')
ax.set_ylabel('Predicted')
plt.show()

def plot_real_predicted(ytest, ypred):
  plt.plot(ytest[1:200], color = 'red', label = 'Real data')
  plt.plot(ypred[1:200], color = 'blue', label = 'Predicted data')
  plt.title('Prediction')
  plt.legend()
  plt.show()
#=====================================================================
# Download data from Yahoo Finance and save it as a csv file
#=====================================================================
start_date = pd.to_datetime('2009-12-01')
mid_date = pd.to_datetime('2014-12-01')
stop_date = pd.to_datetime('2019-12-01')

#NASDAQ
yahoo_data = pdr.data.get_data_yahoo('^IXIC', start_date, stop_date)
```

```
yahoo_data.to_csv('NASDAQ.csv')
#DOW JONES
yahoo_data = pdr.data.get_data_yahoo('^DJI', start_date, stop_date)
yahoo_data.to_csv('DOWJONES.csv')
#S&P 500 (^GSPC)
yahoo_data = pdr.data.get_data_yahoo('^GSPC', start_date, stop_date)
yahoo_data.to_csv('S&P.csv')
#Russell 2000 (^RUT)
yahoo_data = pdr.data.get_data_yahoo('^RUT', start_date, stop_date)
yahoo_data.to_csv('RUSSEL.csv')
#NYSE
yahoo_data = pdr.data.get_data_yahoo('^NYA', start_date, stop_date)
yahoo_data.to_csv('NYSE.csv')
#==========================================================================
# Add various technical indicators in the data frame
#==========================================================================
""There are four types of technical indicators. Let us take 4 sets
of indicators and test which performs better in prediction of stock
markets. These 4 sets of technical indicators are:
RSI, Volume (plain), Bollinger Bands, Aroon, Price Volume Trend,
acceleration bands
Stochastic, Chaikin Money Flow, Parabolic SAR, Rate of Change, Volume
weighted average Price, momentum
Commodity Channel Index, On Balance Volume, Keltner Channels, Triple
Exponential Moving Average, Normalized Averager True Range, directional
movement indicators
MACD, Money flowindex, Ichimoku, William %R, Volume MINMAX, adaptive
moving average""
# Create copy of data to add columns of different sets of technical
indicators
dff = pd.read_csv("DOWJONES.csv")
techind = copy.deepcopy(dff)
#%%
#==========================================================================
# Calculate the relative strength index (RSI)
#==========================================================================
# Relative Strength Index
# Avg(PriceUp)/(Avg(PriceUP) + Avg(PriceDown)*100
# Where: PriceUp(t) = 1*(Price(t)-Price(t-1)){Price(t)- Price(t-1) > 0};
# PriceDown(t) = -1*(Price(t)-Price(t-1)){Price(t)- Price(t-1) < 0};
 def rsi(values):
   up = values[values > 0].mean()
   down = -1*values[values < 0].mean()
   return 100 * up / (up + down)
```

```
# Add Momentum_1D column for all 15 stocks.
# Momentum_1D = P(t) - P(t-1)
techind['Momentum_1D'] = (techind['Close']-techind['Close'].shift(1)).
fillna(0)
techind['RSI_14D'] = techind['Momentum_1D'].rolling(center = False,
window = 14).apply(rsi).fillna(0)
#=========================================================================
# Calculate the volume (plain)
#=========================================================================
techind['Volume_plain'] = techind['Volume'].fillna(0)
#=========================================================================
# Calculate the Bollinger bands
#=========================================================================
def bbands(price, length = 30, numsd = 2):
  " " " returns average, upper band, and lower band" " "
  #ave = pd.stats.moments.rolling_mean(price,length)
  ave = price.rolling(window = length, center = False).mean()
  #sd = pd.stats.moments.rolling_std(price,length)
  sd = price.rolling(window = length, center = False).std()
  upband = ave + (sd*numsd)
  dnband = ave - (sd*numsd)
  return np.round(ave,3), np.round(upband,3), np.round(dnband,3)
techind['BB_Middle_Band'], techind['BB_Upper_Band'], techind['BB_Lower_
Band'] = bbands(techind['Close'], length = 20, numsd = 1)
techind['BB_Middle_Band'] = techind['BB_Middle_Band'].fillna(0)
techind['BB_Upper_Band'] = techind['BB_Upper_Band'].fillna(0)
techind['BB_Lower_Band'] = techind['BB_Lower_Band'].fillna(0)
#=========================================================================
# Calculate the Aroon oscillator
#=========================================================================
def aroon(df, tf = 25):
   aroonup = []
   aroondown = []
   x = tf
   while x< len(df['Date']):
   aroon_up = ((df['High'][x-tf:x].tolist().index(max(df['High']
   [x-tf:x])))/float(tf))*100
   aroon_down = ((df['Low'][x-tf:x].tolist().index(min(df['Low']
   [x-tf:x])))/float(tf))*100
   aroonup.append(aroon_up)
   aroondown.append(aroon_down)
   x + = 1
   return aroonup, aroondown
```

```
listofzeros = [0] * 25
up, down = aroon(techind)
aroon_list = [x - y for x, y in zip(up,down)]
if len(aroon_list) = =0:
  aroon_list = [0] * techind.shape[0]
  techind['Aroon_Oscillator'] = aroon_list
 else:
  techind['Aroon_Oscillator'] = listofzeros + aroon_list
#=========================================================================
# Calculate the price volume trend
#=========================================================================
#PVT = [((CurrentClose - PreviousClose) / PreviousClose) x
Volume] + PreviousPVT
techind["PVT"] = (techind['Momentum_1D']/ techind['Close'].
shift(1))*techind['Volume']
techind["PVT"] = techind["PVT"]-techind["PVT"].shift(1)
techind["PVT"] = techind["PVT"].fillna(0)
#=========================================================================
# Calculate the acceleration bands
#=========================================================================
def abands(df):
  #df['AB_Middle_Band'] = pd.rolling_mean(df['Close'], 20)
  df['AB_Middle_Band'] = df['Close'].rolling(window = 20, center = False).
  mean()
  # High * ( 1+4 * (High - Low) / (High + Low))
  df['aupband'] = df['High'] * (1 + 4 * (df['High']-df['Low'])/
  (df['High'] + df['Low']))
  df['AB_Upper_Band'] = df['aupband'].rolling(window = 20, center = False).
  mean()
  # Low *(1 - 4 * (High - Low)/ (High + Low))
  df['adownband'] = df['Low'] * (1 - 4 * (df['High']-df['Low'])/
  (df['High'] + df['Low']))
  df['AB_Lower_Band'] = df['adownband'].rolling(window = 20,
  center = False).mean()
abands(techind)
techind = techind.fillna(0)
#=========================================================================
# Drop unwanted columns
#=========================================================================
columns2Drop = ['Momentum_1D', 'aupband', 'adownband']
techind = techind.drop(labels = columns2Drop, axis = 1)
```

```
#==========================================================================
# Calculate the stochastic oscillator (%K and %D)
#==========================================================================
def STOK(df, n):
    df['STOK'] = ((df['Close'] - df['Low'].rolling(window=n,
    center=False).mean()) / (df['High'].rolling(window=n,
    center=False).max() - df['Low'].rolling(window=n, center=False).
    min())) * 100
    df['STOD'] = df['STOK'].rolling(window=3, center=False).mean()

STOK(techind, 4)
techind = techind.fillna(0)
#==========================================================================
# Calculate the Chaikin money flow
#==========================================================================
def CMFlow(df, tf):
    CHMF = []
    MFMs = []
    MFVs = []
    x = tf

while x < len(df['Date']):
    PeriodVolume = 0
    volRange = df['Volume'][x-tf:x]
    for eachVol in volRange:
    PeriodVolume+=eachVol

    MFM = ((df['Close'][x] - df['Low'][x]) - (df['High'][x] - df['Close']
    [x])) / (df['High'][x] - df['Low'][x])
    MFV = MFM*PeriodVolume

    MFMs.append(MFM)
    MFVs.append(MFV)
    x += 1

y = tf
while y < len(MFVs):
PeriodVolume = 0
volRange = df['Volume'][x-tf:x]
for eachVol in volRange:
PeriodVolume+=eachVol
consider = MFVs[y-tf:y]
```

```
   tfsMFV = 0

   for eachMFV in consider:
   tfsMFV+=eachMFV

   tfsCMF = tfsMFV/PeriodVolume
   CHMF.append(tfsCMF)
   y + = 1
   return CHMF
listofzeros = [0] * 40
CHMF = CMFlow(techind, 20)
if len(CHMF) = =0:
   CHMF = [0] * techind.shape[0]
   techind['Chaikin_MF'] = CHMF
 else:
   techind['Chaikin_MF'] = listofzeros + CHMF
#==========================================================================
# Calculate the parabolic SAR
#==========================================================================
def psar(df, iaf = 0.02, maxaf = 0.2):
   length = len(df)
   dates = (df['Date'])
   high = (df['High'])
   low = (df['Low'])
   close = (df['Close'])
   psar = df['Close'][0:len(df['Close'])]
   psarbull = [None] * length
   psarbear = [None] * length
   bull = True
   af = iaf
   ep = df['Low'][0]
   hp = df['High'][0]
   lp = df['Low'][0]
   for i in range(2,length):
   if bull:
   psar[i] = psar[i - 1] + af * (hp - psar[i - 1])
   else:
   psar[i] = psar[i - 1] + af * (lp - psar[i - 1])
   reverse = False
   if bull:
   if df['Low'][i] < psar[i]:
   bull = False
   reverse = True
   psar[i] = hp
```

```
lp = df['Low'][i]
af = iaf
else:
if df['High'][i] > psar[i]:
bull = True
reverse = True
psar[i] = lp
hp = df['High'][i]
af = iaf
if not reverse:
if bull:
if df['High'][i] > hp:
hp = df['High'][i]
af = min(af + iaf, maxaf)
if df['Low'][i - 1] < psar[i]:
psar[i] = df['Low'][i - 1]
if df['Low'][i - 2] < psar[i]:
psar[i] = df['Low'][i - 2]
else:
if df['Low'][i] < lp:
lp = df['Low'][i]
af = min(af + iaf, maxaf)
if df['High'][i - 1] > psar[i]:
psar[i] = df['High'][i - 1]
if df['High'][i - 2] > psar[i]:
psar[i] = df['High'][i - 2]
if bull:
psarbull[i] = psar[i]
else:
psarbear[i] = psar[i]
#return {"dates":dates, "high":high, "low":low, "close":close,
"psar":psar, "psarbear":psarbear, "psarbull":psarbull}
#return psar, psarbear, psarbull
df['psar'] = psar
#df['psarbear'] = psarbear
#df['psarbull'] = psarbull
psar(techind)
#================================================================
# Calculate the price rate of change
#================================================================
# ROC = [(Close - Close n periods ago) / (Close n periods ago)] * 100
techind['ROC'] = ((techind['Close'] - techind['Close'].shift(12))/
(techind['Close'].shift(12)))*100
```

```
techind = techind.fillna(0)
#=====================================================================
# Calculate the volume weighted average price
#=====================================================================
techind['VWAP'] = np.cumsum(techind['Volume'] * (techind['High'] + techind
['Low'])/2) / np.cumsum(techind['Volume'])
techind = techind.fillna(0)
techind.tail()
#=====================================================================
# Calculate the momentum
#=====================================================================
techind['Momentum'] = techind['Close'] - techind['Close'].shift(4)
techind = techind.fillna(0)
techind.tail()
#=====================================================================
# Calculate the commodity channel index
#=====================================================================
def CCI(df, n, constant):
  TP = (df['High'] + df['Low'] + df['Close']) / 3
  CCI = pd.Series((TP - TP.rolling(window = n, center = False).mean())
  / (constant * TP.rolling(window = n, center = False).std())) #,
  name = 'CCI_' + str(n))
  return CCI
techind['CCI'] = CCI(techind, 20, 0.015)
techind = techind.fillna(0)
#=====================================================================
# Calculate on balance volume
#=====================================================================
" " "If the closing price is above the prior close price then: Current
OBV = Previous OBV + Current Volume
If the closing price is below the prior close price then: Current
OBV = Previous OBV - Current Volume
If the closing prices equals the prior close price then: Current
OBV = Previous OBV (no change)" " "
new = (techind['Volume'] * (~techind['Close'].diff().le(0) * 2 -1)).cum-
sum()
techind['OBV'] = new
#%%
#=====================================================================
# Calcualte the Keltner channels
#=====================================================================
def KELCH(df, n):
  KelChM = pd.Series(((df['High'] + df['Low'] + df['Close']) /
  3).rolling(window=n, center = False).mean(), name = 'KelChM_' + str(n))
```

```
    KelChU = pd.Series(((4 * df['High'] - 2 * df['Low'] + df['Close']) /
    3).rolling(window=n, center = False).mean(), name = 'KelChU_' + str(n))
    KelChD = pd.Series(((-2 * df['High'] + 4 * df['Low'] + df['Close']) /
    3).rolling(window=n, center = False).mean(), name = 'KelChD_' + str(n))
    return KelChM, KelChD, KelChU
KelchM, KelchD, KelchU = KELCH(techind, 14)
techind['Kelch_Upper'] = KelchU
techind['Kelch_Middle'] = KelchM
techind['Kelch_Down'] = KelchD
techind = techind.fillna(0)
#======================================================================
# Calculate the triple exponential moving average
#======================================================================
" " "Triple Exponential MA Formula:
T-EMA = (3EMA - 3EMA(EMA)) + EMA(EMA(EMA))
Where:
EMA = EMA(1) + α* (Close - EMA(1))
α = 2 / (N + 1)
N = The smoothing period." " "
techind['EMA'] = techind['Close'].ewm(span = 3,min_periods = 0,ad-
just = True,ignore_na = False).mean()
techind = techind.fillna(0)
techind['TEMA'] = (3 * techind['EMA'] - 3 * techind['EMA'] *
techind['EMA']) + (techind['EMA']*techind['EMA']*techind['EMA'])
#======================================================================
# Calculation of normalized average true range¶
#======================================================================
" " "True Range = Highest of (High - low, abs(High - previous close),
abs(low - previous close))
Average True Range = 14 day MA of True Range
Normalized Average True Range = ATR / Close * 100" " "
techind['HL'] = techind['High'] - techind['Low']
techind['absHC'] = abs(techind['High'] - techind['Close'].shift(1))
techind['absLC'] = abs(techind['Low'] - techind['Close'].shift(1))
techind['TR'] = techind[['HL','absHC','absLC']].max(axis = 1)
techind['ATR'] = techind['TR'].rolling(window = 14).mean()
techind['NATR'] = (techind['ATR'] / techind['Close']) *100
techind = techind.fillna(0)
#======================================================================
# Calculate the average directional movement index (ADX)
#======================================================================
" " "Calculating the DMI can actually be broken down into two parts.
First, calculating the+DI and -DI, and second, calculating the ADX.
```

```
To calculate the+DI and -DI you need to find the+DM and -DM (Directional
Movement).+DM and -DM are calculated using the High, Low, and Close for
each period. You can then calculate the following:
Current High - Previous High = UpMove Previous Low - Current
Low = DownMove
If UpMove > DownMove and UpMove > 0, then+DM = UpMove, else+DM = 0 If
DownMove > Upmove and Downmove > 0, then -DM = DownMove, else -DM = 0
Once you have the current+DM and -DM calculated, the+DM and -DM lines
can be calculated and plotted based on the number of user defined
periods.
+DI = 100 times Exponential Moving Average of (+DM / Average True Range)
-DI = 100 times Exponential Moving Average of (-DM / Average True Range)
Now that - + DX and -DX have been calculated, the last step is
calculating the ADX.
ADX = 100 times the Exponential Moving Average of the Absolute Value of
(+DI - -DI) / (+DI + -DI)" " "
def DMI(df, period):
  df['UpMove'] = df['High'] - df['High'].shift(1)
  df['DownMove'] = df['Low'].shift(1) - df['Low']
  df['Zero'] = 0

  df['PlusDM'] = np.where((df['UpMove'] > df['DownMove']) &
  (df['UpMove'] > df['Zero']), df['UpMove'], 0)
  df['MinusDM'] = np.where((df['UpMove'] < df['DownMove']) &
  (df['DownMove'] > df['Zero']), df['DownMove'], 0)

  df['plusDI'] = 100 * (df['PlusDM']/df['ATR']).ewm(span = period,min_
  periods = 0,adjust = True,ignore_na = False).mean()
  df['minusDI'] = 100 * (df['MinusDM']/df['ATR']).ewm(span = period,min_
  periods = 0,adjust = True,ignore_na = False).mean()

  df['ADX'] = 100 * (abs((df['plusDI'] - df['minusDI'])/
  (df['plusDI'] + df['minusDI']))).ewm(span = period,min_
  periods = 0,adjust = True,ignore_na = False).mean()
DMI(techind, 14)
techind = techind.fillna(0)
#=================================================================
# Drop unwanted columns
#=================================================================
columns2Drop = ['UpMove', 'DownMove', 'ATR', 'PlusDM', 'MinusDM', 'Zero',
'EMA', 'HL', 'absHC', 'absLC', 'TR']
techind = techind.drop(labels = columns2Drop, axis = 1)
#=================================================================
# Calculate the MACD
#=================================================================
```

```
#MACD: (12-day EMA - 26-day EMA)
techind['26_ema']=techind['Close'].ewm(span=26,min_periods=0,ad-
just=True,ignore_na=False).mean()
techind['12_ema']=techind['Close'].ewm(span=12,min_periods=0,ad-
just=True,ignore_na=False).mean()
techind['MACD']=techind['12_ema'] - techind['26_ema']
techind=techind.fillna(0)
#=======================================================================
# Calculate the money flow index
#=======================================================================
" " "Typical Price=(High+Low+Close)/3
Raw Money Flow=Typical Price x Volume
The money flow is divided into positive and negative money flow.
Positive money flow is calculated by adding the money flow of all the days
where the typical price is higher than the previous day's typical price.
Negative money flow is calculated by adding the money flow of all the days
where the typical price is lower than the previous day's typical price.
If typical price is unchanged then that day is discarded.
Money Flow Ratio=(14-period Positive Money Flow)/(14-period Negative
Money Flow)
Money Flow Index=100 - 100/(1+Money Flow Ratio)" " "
def MFI(df):
   # typical price
   df['tp']=(df['High']+df['Low']+df['Close'])/3
   #raw money flow
   df['rmf']=df['tp'] * df['Volume']
   # positive and negative money flow
   df['pmf']=np.where(df['tp']>df['tp'].shift(1), df['tp'], 0)
   df['nmf']=np.where(df['tp']<df['tp'].shift(1), df['tp'], 0)
   # money flow ratio
   df['mfr']=df['pmf'].rolling(window=14,center=False).sum()/
   df['nmf'].rolling(window=14,center=False).sum()
   df['Money_Flow_Index']=100 - 100 / (1+df['mfr'])
MFI(techind)
techind=techind.fillna(0)
#=======================================================================
# Calculate the Ichimoku cloud
#=======================================================================
" " "Turning Line=( Highest High+Lowest Low ) / 2, for the past 9 days
Standard Line=( Highest High+Lowest Low ) / 2, for the past 26 days
Leading Span 1=( Standard Line+Turning Line ) / 2, plotted 26 days
ahead of today
Leading Span 2=( Highest High+Lowest Low ) / 2, for the past 52 days,
plotted 26 days ahead of today
```

```
Cloud = Shaded Area between Span 1 and Span 2" " "
def ichimoku(df):
  # Turning Line
  period9_high = df['High'].rolling(window = 9,center = False).max()
  period9_low = df['Low'].rolling(window = 9,center = False).min()
  df['turning_line'] = (period9_high + period9_low) / 2

  # Standard Line
  period26_high = df['High'].rolling(window = 26,center = False).max()
  period26_low = df['Low'].rolling(window = 26,center = False).min()
  df['standard_line'] = (period26_high + period26_low) / 2

  # Leading Span 1
  df['ichimoku_span1'] = ((df['turning_line'] + df['standard_line']) /
  2).shift(26)

  # Leading Span 2
  period52_high = df['High'].rolling(window = 52,center = False).max()
  period52_low = df['Low'].rolling(window = 52,center = False).min()
  df['ichimoku_span2'] = ((period52_high + period52_low) / 2).shift(26)

  # The most current closing price plotted 22 time periods behind
  (optional)
  df['chikou_span'] = df['Close'].shift(-22) # 22 according to
  investopedia
ichimoku(techind)
techind = techind.fillna(0)
#==================================================================
# Calculate the William %R
#==================================================================
" " "%R = -100 * ( ( Highest High - Close) / ( Highest High - Lowest Low
) )" " "
def WillR(df):
  highest_high = df['High'].rolling(window = 14,center = False).max()
  lowest_low = df['Low'].rolling(window = 14,center = False).min()
  df['WillR'] = (-100) * ((highest_high - df['Close']) / (highest_high -
  lowest_low))
WillR(techind)
techind = techind.fillna(0)
#==================================================================
# Calculate the MINMAX
#==================================================================
def MINMAX(df):
  df['MIN_Volume'] = df['Volume'].rolling(window = 14,center = False).min()
  df['MAX_Volume'] = df['Volume'].rolling(window = 14,center = False).max()
```

```
MINMAX(techind)
techind = techind.fillna(0)
#==========================================================================
# Calculate the adaptive moving average
#==========================================================================
def KAMA(price, n = 10, pow1 = 2, pow2 = 30):
    " " " kama indicator " " "
    " " " accepts pandas dataframe of prices " " "
    absDiffx = abs(price - price.shift(1) )
    ER_num = abs( price - price.shift(n) )
    ER_den = absDiffx.rolling(window = n,center = False).sum()
    ER = ER_num / ER_den
    sc = ( ER*(2.0/(pow1 + 1)-2.0/(pow2 + 1.0)) + 2/(pow2 + 1.0) ) ** 2.0
    answer = np.zeros(sc.size)
    N = len(answer)
    first_value = True

    for i in range(N):
    if sc[i] !=sc[i]:
    answer[i] = np.nan
    else:
    if first_value:
    answer[i] = price[i]
    first_value = False
    else:
    answer[i] = answer[i-1] + sc[i] * (price[i] - answer[i-1])
    return answer
techind['KAMA'] = KAMA(techind['Close'])
techind = techind.fillna(0)
#==========================================================================
# Drop unwanted columns
#==========================================================================
columns2Drop = ['26_ema', '12_ema','tp','rmf','pmf','nmf','mfr']
techind = techind.drop(labels = columns2Drop, axis = 1)

techind.index = techind['Date']
techind = techind.drop(labels = ['Date'], axis = 1)
#save Save dataset as a file
techind.to_csv('TechIndout.csv')
#%%
# = =======================================================
# Regression model
# = =======================================================
# importing necessary libraries
```

```
import numpy as np
import matplotlib
import matplotlib.pyplot as plt
from distutils.version import LooseVersion
from sklearn.model_selection import train_test_split
from sklearn.metrics import median_absolute_error, r2_score
from sklearn.metrics import mean_absolute_error, mean_squared_error

# Create the dataset
a = np.array(techind)
#Skip first 50 rows as they contain zeros
X = a[50:2400,8:43 ]
#y = a[50:2400,4 ]
y = a[51:2401,4 ] #To forecast one day ahead
X_train, X_test, y_train, y_test = train_test_split(X, y, random_
state = 1)
###########################################################################
#%%
from sklearn.datasets import make_regression
from sklearn.model_selection import train_test_split
from sklearn.compose import TransformedTargetRegressor
from sklearn.metrics import median_absolute_error, r2_score
from sklearn.ensemble.forest import RandomForestRegressor
from sklearn.preprocessing import QuantileTransformer, quantile_transform
#=========================================================================
# Create random forest regressor model
#=========================================================================
regr = RandomForestRegressor(n_estimators = 100)
#=========================================================================
# Train the model
#=========================================================================
regr.fit(X_train, y_train)
#=========================================================================
# Predict unseen data with the model
#=========================================================================
y_pred = regr.predict(X_test)
#=========================================================================
# Evaluate the model and print performance metrics
#=========================================================================
print_performance_metrics(y_test,y_pred)
#%%
#=========================================================================
# Plot scatter
#=========================================================================
plot_scatter(y_test,y_pred)
```

```
#%%
#=========================================================================
# Plot real and predicted outputs
#=========================================================================
plot_real_predicted(y_test,y_pred)
#%%
#=========================================================================
# Create linear regression model
#=========================================================================
from sklearn import linear_model
# Create linear regression object
regr = linear_model.LinearRegression()
# Train the model using the training sets
regr.fit(X_train, y_train)
# Make predictions using the testing set
y_pred = regr.predict(X_test)
#=========================================================================
# Evaluate the model and print performance metrics
#=========================================================================
print_performance_metrics(y_test,y_pred)
#%%
#=========================================================================
# Plot scatter
#=========================================================================
plot_scatter(y_test,y_pred)
#%%
#=========================================================================
# Plot real and predicted outputs
#=========================================================================
plot_real_predicted(y_test,y_pred)
#%%
#=========================================================================
# Create MLP regressor model
#=========================================================================
from sklearn.neural_network import MLPClassifier
# Create MLP regressor object
" " "mlp = MLPClassifier(hidden_layer_sizes = (100, ), activation = 'relu',
solver = 'adam',
   alpha = 0.0001, batch_size = 'auto', learning_rate = 'constant',
   learning_rate_init = 0.001, power_t = 0.5, max_iter = 200,
   shuffle = True, random_state = None, tol = 0.0001, verbose = False,
   warm_start = False, momentum = 0.9, nesterovs_momentum = True,
   early_stopping = False, validation_fraction = 0.1, beta_1 = 0.9,
   beta_2 = 0.999, epsilon = 1e-08, n_iter_no_change = 10)" " "
mlp = MLPClassifier(hidden_layer_sizes = (100, ), learning_rate_init = 0.001,
   alpha = 1, momentum = 0.9,max_iter = 1000)
```

```
# Train the model using the training sets
regr.fit(X_train, y_train)
# Make predictions using the testing set
y_pred = regr.predict(X_test)
#=========================================================================
# Evaluate the model and print performance metrics
#=========================================================================
print_performance_metrics(y_test,y_pred)
#%%
#=========================================================================
# Plot scatter
#=========================================================================
plot_scatter(y_test,y_pred)
#%%
#=========================================================================
# Plot real and predicted outputs
#=========================================================================
plot_real_predicted(y_test,y_pred)
#%%
#=========================================================================
# Create k-NN regressor model
#=========================================================================
from sklearn.neighbors import KNeighborsRegressor
# Create a Regression object
print("Training Regressor...")
regr = KNeighborsRegressor(n_neighbors = 2)
# Train the model using the training sets
regr.fit(X_train, y_train)
# Make predictions using the testing set
y_pred = regr.predict(X_test)
#=========================================================================
# Evaluate the model and print performance metrics
#=========================================================================
print_performance_metrics(y_test,y_pred)
#%%
#=========================================================================
# Plot scatter
#=========================================================================
plot_scatter(y_test,y_pred)
#%%
#=========================================================================
# Plot real and predicted outputs
#=========================================================================
```

```
plot_real_predicted(y_test,y_pred)
#%%
#=============================================================================
# Create SVR regressor model
#=============================================================================
from sklearn.svm import SVR
# Create a Regression object
print("Training Regressor...")
regr = SVR(gamma = 'scale', C = 200.0, epsilon = 0.2)
# Train the model using the training sets
regr.fit(X_train, y_train)
# Make predictions using the testing set
y_pred = regr.predict(X_test)
#=============================================================================
# Evaluate the model and print performance metrics
#=============================================================================
print_performance_metrics(y_test,y_pred)
#%%
#=============================================================================
# Plot scatter
#=============================================================================
plot_scatter(y_test,y_pred)
#%%
#=============================================================================
# Plot real and predicted outputs
#=============================================================================
plot_real_predicted(y_test,y_pred)
```

## 6.3 Inflation forecasting

Inflation, which is the percentage change in the average price level, is one of the most important indicators of economic activity. It has an impact on households, investors, governments, and policymakers' decisions. High rates of inflation deteriorate levels of economic growth, decrease real wages, and increase cost of production. Similarly, a low inflationary environment is considered to be a negative economic indicator associated with lower demand levels in the economy. It is therefore crucial to forecast inflation in different time horizons. The machine learning models are used for inflation forecasting and for the forecasting of other macroeconomic variables as well (Ülke, Sahin, & Subasi, 2018).

## Example 6.2

The following Python code is used for inflation forecasting employing different classifiers with separate training and testing datasets. The statistical quality measures, including mean-absolute error (MAE), mean squared error (MSE), and correlation coefficient (R), are calculated. Scatter plot, real, and predicted values are also plotted.

***Dataset information:*** In order to forecast inflation, four measures of the monthly price index can be used. These are the consumer price index (CPI) for all items, the CPI excluding food and energy (core-CPI), the personal consumption expenditure deflator (PCE), and the PCE excluding food and energy (Core-PCE). Considering the models as predictors of inflation, six economic activities—namely the civilian unemployment rate (UNEM), the index of industrial production (IP), real personal consumption expenditure (INC), employees on nonfarm payrolls (WORK), housing starts (HS), and the term spread (SPREAD), defined as the yield on the 5-year treasury bond minus the 3-month treasury bill—can be considered. These data were collected from the Federal Reserve Bank of Saint Louis database, FRED, spanning from January 1984 until December 2014. Furthermore, the stationarity conditions, regime change, volatility (noise), and distribution of series are crucial points for forecasting. For inflation forecasting, CPI, core-CPI, PCI, and core-CPI can be considered separately (Ülke et al., 2018).

```
" " "
Created on Tue May 21 19:39:42 2019
@author: asubasi" " "
#=======================================================================
# Inflation forecasting
#=======================================================================
# importing necessary libraries
import numpy as np
import pandas as pd
import matplotlib.pyplot as plt
from sklearn.model_selection import train_test_split
from sklearn.metrics import mean_absolute_error,mean_squared_error,
r2_score

# Load Inflation data set
Dataset = pd.read_csv("Inflation.csv")
# Create the dataset
rng = np.random.RandomState(1)
a = np.array(Dataset)
X = a[0:370,5:10 ]
y = a[0:370,10 ]
X_train, X_test, y_train, y_test = train_test_split(X, y, test_size = 0.3,
random_state = 1)
#%%
# Create a regression model
from sklearn.ensemble.forest import RandomForestRegressor
regr = RandomForestRegressor(n_estimators = 100)
```

```
# Train the model using the training sets
regr.fit(X_train, y_train)
# Make predictions using the testing set
y_pred = regr.predict(X_test)
#=======================================================================
# Evaluate the model and print performance metrics
#=======================================================================
# The mean absolute error
print("MAE = %5.3f" % mean_absolute_error(y_test, y_pred))
# Explained variance score: 1 is perfect prediction
print("R^2 = %0.5f" % r2_score(y_test, y_pred))
# The mean squared error
print("MSE = %5.3f" % mean_squared_error(y_test, y_pred))
#%%
#=======================================================================
# Plot scatter
#=======================================================================
fig, ax = plt.subplots()
ax.scatter(y_test, y_pred, edgecolors = (0, 0, 0))
ax.text(-10, 15, r'$R^2$ = %.2f, MAE = %.2f' % (
    r2_score(y_test, y_pred), mean_absolute_error(y_test, y_pred)))
ax.plot([y_test.min(), y_test.max()], [y_test.min(), y_test.max()], 'k--
', lw = 4)
ax.set_xlabel('Measured')
ax.set_ylabel('Predicted')
#ax.set_xlim([0, 10])
#ax.set_ylim([0, 10])
plt.show()
#%%
#=======================================================================
# Plot real and predicted outputs
#=======================================================================
plt.plot(y_test[1:200], color = 'red', label = 'Real data')
plt.plot(y_pred[1:200], color = 'blue', label = 'Predicted data')
plt.title('Prediction')
plt.legend()
plt.show()
```

## 6.4 Electrical load forecasting

Load is a major and crucial information for facilities and traders in power generation, particularly in production planning, day-to-day operations, unit commitment, and economic dispatch. Load forecasting is carried out at different intervals based on requirements: long-term load forecasting includes one to several years for plant and infrastructure investment decisions; mid-term load forecasting includes a few days to several months for maintenance scheduling and forward contract negotiation; short-term load forecasting (STLF) includes 1 hour to a few days for real-time generation control and energy transaction planning (Bozkurt, Biricik, & Tayşi, 2017). Short-term, mid-term, and long-term planning or forecasting is a common concept found in the literature in the sense of the time horizon of planning or forecasting. Short-term planning is typically an hourly, regular, or weekly power system operational planning, and one of the most crucial aspects during this phase is reliable and precise electricity demand forecasting. On the electricity market, reliable short-term forecasts are necessary since they could impact the price of electricity that is provided to consumers. On the other hand, mid-term power system operational planning is usually prepared on a time horizon of one or more months, while long-term planning is usually prepared on an annual basis. Long-term electricity demand forecasting is usually presented for several years and is an input in the process of building new generating unit planning (Sikiric, Avdakovic, & Subasi, 2013).

Smart grids are designed to create integrated and efficient energy supply networks that enhance the reliability and quality of power supply, as well as network security, energy efficiency, and demand management aspects. Modern power distribution structures are enabled by advanced monitoring infrastructures, which generate a huge amount of data, enabling fine grain analysis and enhanced forecasting performance. The forecasting of electrical loads is a particularly crucial task in the energy field, because it helps with decision-making, the promotion of optimal pricing strategies, the easy integration of renewables, and the reduction of maintenance costs. Management and successful operations in critical infrastructure like smart grids take significant advantage of accurate power demand forecasting that remains a challenging task due to its nonlinear nature. Recently, deep learning has appeared to achieve impressive performance in a wide range of tasks, from the classification of images to machine translation. Applications of deep learning models to the problem of electrical load forecasting are gaining interest among researchers as well as the industry. This example utilizes a real-world dataset for electric load forecasting using the deep learning model with short-term forecast (hourly). In particular, we concentrate on recurrent neural networks, sequence-to-sequence models, and temporal convolutional neural networks along with architectural variants known in the signal processing community and the load-forecasting community (Gasparin, Lukovic, & Alippi, 2019).

Well-known supply-demand balance laws are also applicable in energy markets: prices increase during the hours of higher demand and reduce during the hours of lower demand such as evenings, weekends, and holidays. In a huge power plant, demand is developed hourly and output cannot be started or stopped instantly; thus, development planning is mostly carried out on a daily basis. STLF therefore plays a key role in the management of operations in the electricity markets. Electrical load is a typical time series, because it involves consecutive hourly measurements. An important part of the time series analysis is forecasting, which focuses on predicting future events based on time series (Bozkurt et al., 2017). Because deregulation of the distribution of electricity and the broad use of renewables have a major impact on regular market prices, STLF is of fundamental importance for efficient power supply (Gasparin et al., 2019). Engineers try to identify key factors influencing electricity consumption during forecasting, such as GDP growth, demographic and climate change, consumer standards and preferences, etc. Air temperature is one of the most important factors in short-term and mid-term forecasting. Ambient temperature, human social behavior, and other variables also provide crucial information during the forecasting process so that forecast outcomes can be much more reliable (Sikiric et al., 2013).

## Example 6.3

The following Python code is used for electrical load forecasting employing the LSTM model with separate training and testing datasets. The statistical quality measures, including mean-absolute error (MAE), mean squared error (MSE), and correlation coefficient (R), are calculated. Scatter plot, real, and predicted values are also drawn. This example is adapted from machinelearningmastery (https://machinelearningmastery.com/how-to-develop-lstm-models-for-time-series-forecasting/)

***Dataset information:*** One of the most complex types of time series for forecasting is short-term load data. Such data are considered nonlinear, with a lot of intraseasonality that makes it even more difficult to solve the problem. This data is chosen to utilize the deep learning models, because short-term load forecasting is a complex forecasting problem. Thus the hourly load data of the power supply company of the city of Johor in Malaysia produced in 2009 and 2010 were utilized to implement deep learning Keras models for load forecasting. Temperature time series was combined with hourly load data to enhance the performance of the model (Sadaei, e Silva, de, Guimarães, & Lee, 2019). The dataset can be downloaded from the Mendeley website (https://data.mendeley.com/datasets/f4fcrh4tn9/1).

```
"""
Created on Thu Oct 10 11:07:13 2019
@author: asubasi
"""
#=======================================================================
# Load forecasting with univariate LSTM
#=======================================================================
from numpy import array
from keras.models import Sequential
from keras.layers import LSTM
from keras.layers import Dense
from pandas import read_csv
from sklearn.metrics import mean_squared_error, r2_score
from sklearn.metrics import mean_absolute_error
import matplotlib.pyplot as plt
#=======================================================================
# Define utility functions
#=======================================================================
def plot_model_loss(history):
plt.figure(figsize = (6, 4))
plt.plot(history.history['loss'], 'r--', label = 'Loss of training data')
plt.plot(history.history['val_loss'], 'b--', label = 'Loss of validation
data')
plt.title('Model Error')
plt.ylabel('Loss')
plt.xlabel('Training Epoch')
```

```
    plt.ylim(0)
    plt.legend()
    plt.show()

def plot_real_predicted(ytest, ypred):
    plt.plot(ytest[1:200], color = 'red', label = 'Real data')
    plt.plot(ypred[1:200], color = 'blue', label = 'Predicted data')
    plt.title('Prediction')
    plt.legend()
    plt.show()

def print_performance_metrics(ytest, ypred):
    # The mean absolute error
    print("MAE = %5.3f" % mean_absolute_error(ytest, ypred))
    # Explained variance score: 1 is perfect prediction
    print("R^2 = %0.5f" % r2_score(ytest, ypred))
    # The mean squared error
    print("MSE = %5.3f" % mean_squared_error(ytest, ypred))

def plot_scatter(ytest, ypred):
    fig, ax = plt.subplots()
    ax.scatter(ytest, ypred, edgecolors = (0, 0, 0))
    ax.text(10, ytest.max()-10, r'$R^2$ = %.2f, MAE = %.2f' % (
    r2_score(ytest, ypred), mean_absolute_error(ytest, ypred)))
    ax.plot([ytest.min(), ytest.max()], [ytest.min(), ytest.max()], 'k--',
    lw = 4)
    ax.set_xlabel('Measured')
    ax.set_ylabel('Predicted')
    plt.show()

# split a univariate sequence into samples
def split_sequence(sequence, n_steps):
X, y = list(), list()
for i in range(len(sequence)):
# find the end of this pattern
end_ix = i + n_steps
# check if we are beyond the sequence
if end_ix > len(sequence)-1:
break
# gather input and output parts of the pattern
seq_x, seq_y = sequence[i:end_ix], sequence[end_ix]
X.append(seq_x)
y.append(seq_y)
return array(X), array(y)
```

```
#============================================================================
# Prepare dataset
#============================================================================
# Load all data
dataset = read_csv('malaysia_all_data_for_paper.csv')
# define input sequence
raw_seq = dataset.values[:,2]
# choose a number of time steps
X_train=dataset.values[0:10000,2]
X_test = dataset.values[10000:17000,2]
n_steps = 5
# Split data into training and testing samples
Xtrain, ytrain = split_sequence(X_train, n_steps)
Xtest, ytest = split_sequence(X_test, n_steps)
#%%
n_features = 1
Xtrain = Xtrain.reshape((Xtrain.shape[0], Xtrain.shape[1], n_features))
#============================================================================
# Build and compile the model
#============================================================================
model = Sequential()
model.add(LSTM(50, activation = 'relu', input_shape = (n_steps,
n_features)))
model.add(Dense(1))
model.compile(optimizer = 'adam', loss = 'mse')
#============================================================================
# Train the model
#============================================================================
#model.fit(Xtrain, ytrain, epochs = 50, verbose = 1)
history = model.fit(Xtrain, ytrain, validation_split = 0.3,
       epochs = 50, batch_size = 20, verbose = 2)
#============================================================================
# Plot the model loss for training and validation dataset
#============================================================================
plot_model_loss(history)
#%%
#============================================================================
# Predict unseen data with the model
#============================================================================
Xtest = Xtest.reshape((Xtest.shape[0], Xtest.shape[1], n_features))
ypred = model.predict(Xtest, verbose = 2)
#============================================================================
# Evaluate the model and print performance metrics
#============================================================================
```

```
print_performance_metrics(ytest, ypred)
#%%
#=====================================================================
# Plot scatter
#=====================================================================
plot_scatter(ytest, ypred)
#%%
#=====================================================================
# Plot real and predicted outputs
#===================================
```

## Example 6.4

The following Python code is used for electrical load forecasting employing the convolutional neural network model with separate training and testing datasets. The statistical quality measures including mean-absolute error (MAE), mean squared error (MSE), and correlation coefficient (R) are calculated. Scatter plot, real, and predicted values are also drawn. This example is adapted from machinelearningmastery (https://machinelearningmastery.com/how-to-develop-convolutional-neural-network-models-for-time-series-forecasting/).

***Dataset information:*** One of the most complex types of time series for forecasting is short-term load data. Such data are considered nonlinear, with a lot of intraseasonality that makes it even more difficult to solve this problem. This data is chosen to utilize the deep learning models since short-term load forecasting is a complex forecasting problem. Thus the hourly load data of the power supply company of the city of Johor in Malaysia produced in 2009 and 2010 were utilized to implement deep learning Keras models for load forecasting. Temperature time series was combined with hourly load data to enhance the performance of the model (Sadaei et al., 2019) The dataset can be downloaded from the Mendeley website (https://data.mendeley.com/datasets/f4fcrh4tn9/1).

```
" " "
Created on Mon Oct 14 10:32:03 2019
@author: asubasi " " "
#=====================================================================
# Load forecasting with convolutional neural network model
#=====================================================================
from numpy import array
from keras.models import Sequential
from keras.layers import Dense
from keras.layers import Flatten
from keras.layers.convolutional import Conv1D
from keras.layers.convolutional import MaxPooling1D
from pandas import read_csv
from sklearn.metrics import mean_squared_error, r2_score
from sklearn.metrics import mean_absolute_error
```

```
import matplotlib.pyplot as plt
#==========================================================================
# Define utility functions
#==========================================================================
def plot_model_loss(history):
  plt.figure(figsize = (6, 4))
  plt.plot(history.history['loss'], 'r--', label = 'Loss of training
  data')
  plt.plot(history.history['val_loss'], 'b--', label = 'Loss of
  validation data')
  plt.title('Model Error')
  plt.ylabel('Loss')
  plt.xlabel('Training Epoch')
  plt.ylim(0)
  plt.legend()
  plt.show()

def plot_real_predicted(ytest, ypred):
  plt.plot(ytest[1:200], color = 'red', label = 'Real data')
  plt.plot(ypred[1:200], color = 'blue', label = 'Predicted data')
  plt.title('Prediction')
  plt.legend()
  plt.show()

def print_performance_metrics(ytest, ypred):
  # The mean absolute error
  print("MAE = %5.3f" % mean_absolute_error(ytest, ypred))
  # Explained variance score: 1 is perfect prediction
  print("R^2 = %0.5f" % r2_score(ytest, ypred))
  # The mean squared error
  print("MSE = %5.3f" % mean_squared_error(ytest, ypred))

def plot_scatter(ytest, ypred):
  fig, ax = plt.subplots()
  ax.scatter(ytest, ypred, edgecolors = (0, 0, 0))
  ax.text(10, ytest.max()-10, r'$R^2$ = %.2f, MAE = %.2f' % (
  r2_score(ytest, ypred), mean_absolute_error(ytest, ypred)))
  ax.plot([ytest.min(), ytest.max()], [ytest.min(), ytest.max()], 'k--',
  lw = 4)
  ax.set_xlabel('Measured')
  ax.set_ylabel('Predicted')
  plt.show()

# split a univariate sequence into samples
```

```
def split_sequence(sequence, n_steps):
X, y = list(), list()
for i in range(len(sequence)):
# find the end of this pattern
end_ix = i + n_steps
# check if we are beyond the sequence
if end_ix > len(sequence)-1:
break
# gather input and output parts of the pattern
seq_x, seq_y = sequence[i:end_ix], sequence[end_ix]
X.append(seq_x)
y.append(seq_y)
return array(X), array(y)
#%%
#======================================================================
# Univariate convolutional neural network models for load forecasting
#======================================================================
# load all data
dataset = read_csv('malaysia_all_data_for_paper.csv')

X_train=dataset.values[0:10000,2]
X_test = dataset.values[10000:17000,2]

# split a univariate sequence into samples
def split_sequence(sequence, n_steps):
X, y = list(), list()
for i in range(len(sequence)):
# find the end of this pattern
end_ix = i + n_steps
# check if we are beyond the sequence
if end_ix > len(sequence)-1:
break
# gather input and output parts of the pattern
seq_x, seq_y = sequence[i:end_ix], sequence[end_ix]
X.append(seq_x)
y.append(seq_y)
return array(X), array(y)
n_steps = 5
# split into samples
Xtrain, ytrain = split_sequence(X_train, n_steps)
Xtest, ytest = split_sequence(X_test, n_steps)
# reshape from [samples, timesteps] into [samples, timesteps, features]
n_features = 1
```

```
Xtrain = Xtrain.reshape((Xtrain.shape[0], Xtrain.shape[1], n_features))
#%%
#=============================================================================
# Build and compile the model
#=============================================================================
model = Sequential()
model.add(Conv1D(filters = 64, kernel_size = 2, activation = 'relu', input_
shape = (n_steps, n_features)))
model.add(MaxPooling1D(pool_size = 2))
model.add(Flatten())
model.add(Dense(50, activation = 'relu'))
model.add(Dense(1))
model.compile(optimizer = 'adam', loss = 'mse')
#=============================================================================
# Train the model
#=============================================================================
history = model.fit(Xtrain, ytrain, validation_split = 0.3,
        epochs = 50, batch_size = 20, verbose = 2)
#=============================================================================
# Plot the model loss for training and validation dataset
#=============================================================================
plot_model_loss(history)
#%%
#=============================================================================
# Predict unseen data with the model
#=============================================================================
Xtest = Xtest.reshape((Xtest.shape[0], n_steps, n_features))
ypred = model.predict(Xtest, verbose = 0)
#=============================================================================
# Evaluate the model and print performance metrics
#=============================================================================
print_performance_metrics(ytest, ypred)
#%%
#=============================================================================
# Plot scatter
#=============================================================================
plot_scatter(ytest, ypred)
#%%
#=============================================================================
# Plot real and predicted outputs
#=============================================================================
plot_real_predicted(ytest, ypred)
```

## 6.5 Wind speed forecasting

Governments, regulators, and energy companies currently use a broad range of tools to promote the implementation of various renewable energy technologies, including incentives for projects, funds, cash, and tax credits. Recently rapid growth was seen in realizing the advantages of wind power as a key role in reducing emissions and oil dependence, diversifying energy supplies, and providing low-cost electricity. Many countries developed policies that support the exploration of renewable energy technology, in particular, solar and wind energy. Wind velocity and nonlinear fluctuations are the main components of aerodynamic load prediction and wind turbine efficiency. Determining the characteristics of wind speed is critical for measuring the power generated, the loads and stress on rotor blades, and the fatigue of structural components. Unlike conventional power plants, the electricity produced by wind turbines mainly depends on weather conditions, in particular, the magnitude of the wind speed (Shen, Zhou, Li, Fu, & Lie, 2018). A wind turbine's capacity is proportional to the cube of the wind speed. Therefore it is highly recommended to predict the wind speed distribution accurately so that the power generated by the wind turbine can be collected efficiently, especially when we know that wind speed is fluctuating. Investigating the generation of wind energy at a given location involves an intensive study of the distribution of wind in terms of availability, direction, hourly distribution, variation, and frequency. The wind speed forecast could be very short term (up to 30 minutes), short term (30 min to 6 hours), medium term (6 hours to 24 hours), and long term (up to 7 days) (Okumus & Dinler, 2016). Over recent years, numerous techniques have been used to measure wind speed. Such techniques are based on (1) physical modeling, where a significant amount of data is derived from the weather forecast; (2) statistical modeling using data input and output to find patterns; and (3) hybrid modeling using a mixture of data (Lei, Shiyan, Chuanwen, Hongling, & Yan, 2009). Physical modeling involves an unnecessary computational power in addition to poor performance. Statistical modeling uses the study of time series, and the application of machine learning tries to find relations between present and future (Sideratos & Hatziargyriou, 2007). Hence a common approach to predict wind speed is by using artificial intelligence and machine learning tools, where a large number of historical input data is employed as training to learn the relationship and dependence of the input/output data.

### Example 6.5

The following Python code is used for wind speed forecasting employing convolutional neural network (CNN) with separate training and testing datasets. The statistical quality measures, including mean-absolute error (MAE), mean squared error (MSE), and correlation coefficient (R), are calculated. Scatter plot, real, and predicted values are also drawn. This example is adapted from machinelearningmastery (https://machinelearningmastery.com/how-to-develop-convolutional-neural-network-models-for-time-series-forecasting/).

***Dataset information:*** Investigating wind energy production from wind turbine machines in each location requires a rigorous study of wind distribution in terms of its availability, direction, hourly distribution, diurnal variation, and frequency. Data used in this example have been collected from the King Abdullah City for Atomic and Renewable Energy K.A.CARE (https://rratlas.kacare.gov.sa) as part of the Renewable Resource Monitoring and Mapping (RRMM) program. Hourly data provided, from May 2013 to July 2016, include different attributes such as air temperature, wind direction and speed, global horizontal irradiance (GHI), relative humidity, and barometric pressure. A rotating shadow-band radiometer is utilized for the measurement of diffuse horizontal irradiance (DHI), direct normal irradiance (DNI), and global horizontal irradiance (GHI). An air temperature probe is employed to measure air temperature, and a barometer and relative humidity probe are employed to measure the pressure and the relative humidity respectively. Finally, an anemometer and wind vane are employed to measure the wind speed and wind direction respectively.

```
"""
Created on Mon Oct 14 10:32:03 2019
@author: absubasi
"""
#=======================================================================
# Wind speed forecasting
#=======================================================================
from numpy import array
from keras.models import Sequential
from keras.layers import Dense
from keras.layers import Flatten
from keras.layers.convolutional import Conv1D
from keras.layers.convolutional import MaxPooling1D
from pandas import read_csv
from sklearn.metrics import mean_squared_error, r2_score
from sklearn.metrics import mean_absolute_error
import matplotlib.pyplot as plt
#=======================================================================
# Define utility functions
#=======================================================================
def plot_model_loss(history):
  plt.figure(figsize = (6, 4))
  plt.plot(history.history['loss'], 'r--', label = 'Loss of training
  data')
  plt.plot(history.history['val_loss'], 'b--', label = 'Loss of
  validation data')
  plt.title('Model Error')
  plt.ylabel('Loss')
  plt.xlabel('Training Epoch')
  plt.ylim(0)
  plt.legend()
  plt.show()
```

```
def plot_real_predicted(ytest, ypred):
  plt.plot(ytest[1:200], color = 'red', label = 'Real data')
  plt.plot(ypred[1:200], color = 'blue', label = 'Predicted data')
  plt.title('Prediction')
  plt.legend()
  plt.show()

 def print_performance_metrics(ytest, ypred):
  # The mean absolute error
  print("MAE = %5.3f" % mean_absolute_error(ytest, ypred))
  # Explained variance score: 1 is perfect prediction
  print("R^2 = %0.5f" % r2_score(ytest, ypred))
  # The mean squared error
  print("MSE = %5.3f" % mean_squared_error(ytest, ypred))

 def plot_scatter(ytest, ypred):
  fig, ax = plt.subplots()
  ax.scatter(ytest, ypred, edgecolors = (0, 0, 0))
  ax.text(10, ytest.max()-10, r'$R^2$ = %.2f, MAE = %.2f' % (
  r2_score(ytest, ypred), mean_absolute_error(ytest, ypred)))
  ax.plot([ytest.min(), ytest.max()], [ytest.min(), ytest.max()], 'k--',
  lw = 4)
  ax.set_xlabel('Measured')
  ax.set_ylabel('Predicted')
  plt.show()
#%%#==================================================================
# Convolutional neural network models for wind forecasting
#===================================================================
from numpy import array
from keras.models import Sequential
from keras.layers import Dense
from keras.layers import Flatten
from keras.layers.convolutional import Conv1D
from keras.layers.convolutional import MaxPooling1D
from pandas import read_csv
# load all data
dataset = read_csv('Wind.csv')

Xtrain=dataset.values[0:17000,0:12]
ytrain=dataset.values[1:17001,12] #Forecast One hour ahead
Xtest = dataset.values[17000:27000,0:12]
ytest = dataset.values[17001:27001,12] #Forecast One hour ahead
# reshape from [samples, timesteps] into [samples, timesteps, features]
n_features = 1
```

```
Xtrain = Xtrain.reshape((Xtrain.shape[0], Xtrain.shape[1], n_features))
Xtest = Xtest.reshape((Xtest.shape[0], Xtrain.shape[1], n_features))
#%%
#===========================================================================
# Build and compile the model
#===========================================================================
model = Sequential()
model.add(Conv1D(filters = 128, kernel_size = 2, activation = 'relu', input_
shape = (Xtrain.shape[1], n_features)))
model.add(MaxPooling1D(pool_size = 2))
model.add(Flatten())
model.add(Dense(64, activation = 'relu'))
model.add(Dense(1))
model.compile(optimizer = 'adam', loss = 'mse')
#===========================================================================
# Train the model
#===========================================================================
#history = model.fit(Xtrain, ytrain, epochs = 100, verbose = 1)
history = model.fit(Xtrain, ytrain, validation_split = 0.3, epochs = 50,
batch_size = 20, verbose = 2)
#===========================================================================
# Plot the model loss for training and validation dataset
#===========================================================================
plot_model_loss(history)
#%%
#===========================================================================
# Predict unseen data with the model
#===========================================================================
ypred = model.predict(Xtest, verbose = 0)
#===========================================================================
# Evaluate the model and print performance metrics
#===========================================================================
print_performance_metrics(ytest, ypred)
#%%
#===========================================================================
# Plot scatter
#===========================================================================
plot_scatter(ytest, ypred)
#%%
#===========================================================================
# Plot real and predicted outputs
#===========================================================================
plot_real_predicted(ytest, ypred)
#%%
```

```
#=========================================================================
# Multivariate CNN model for wind speed forecasting
#=========================================================================
# multivariate cnn example
from numpy import array
from numpy import hstack
from keras.models import Sequential
from keras.layers import Dense
from keras.layers import Flatten
from keras.layers.convolutional import Conv1D
from keras.layers.convolutional import MaxPooling1D
from pandas import read_csv
# load all data
dataset = read_csv('Wind.csv')

Xtrain=dataset.values[0:17000,0:12]
ytrain=dataset.values[1:17001,12] #Forecast One hour ahead
Xtest = dataset.values[17000:27000,0:12]
ytest = dataset.values[17001:27001,12] #Forecast One hour ahead
n_steps = 12
# reshape from [samples, timesteps] into [samples, timesteps, features]
n_features = 1
Xtrain = Xtrain.reshape((Xtrain.shape[0], Xtrain.shape[1], n_features))
Xtest = Xtest.reshape((Xtest.shape[0], Xtrain.shape[1], n_features))
#%%
#=========================================================================
# Build and compile the model
#=========================================================================
model = Sequential()
model.add(Conv1D(filters = 128, kernel_size = 2, activation = 'relu',
    input_shape = (n_steps, n_features)))
model.add(MaxPooling1D(pool_size = 2))
model.add(Flatten())
model.add(Dense(64, activation = 'relu'))
model.add(Dense(1))
model.compile(optimizer = 'adam', loss = 'mse')
#=========================================================================
# Train the model
#=========================================================================
#history = model.fit(Xtrain, ytrain, epochs = 100, verbose = 1)
history = model.fit(Xtrain, ytrain, validation_split = 0.3, epochs = 50,
batch_size = 20, verbose = 2)
#=========================================================================
# Plot the model loss for training and validation dataset
#=========================================================================
```

```
plot_model_loss(history)
#%%
#=========================================================================
# Predict unseen data with the model
#=========================================================================
Xtest = Xtest.reshape((Xtest.shape[0], n_steps, n_features))
ypred = model.predict(Xtest, verbose = 0)
#=========================================================================
# Evaluate the model and print performance metrics
#=========================================================================
print_performance_metrics(ytest, ypred)
#%%
#=========================================================================
# Plot scatter
#=========================================================================
plot_scatter(ytest, ypred)
#%%
#=========================================================================
# Plot real and predicted outputs
#=========================================================================
plot_real_predicted(ytest, ypred)
```

## 6.6 Tourism demand forecasting

In general, the demand for tourism has shown steady growth. Nevertheless, due to the uncertainty of determining factors and external measures, this sector has undergone multiple fluctuations. Scientists, policymakers, and practitioners have paid serious attention to the cycles of tourism growth and demand ripple as they try to predict future tourist flows. The demand for tourism is determined by tourist arrivals, tourism expenses, or length of stay. Such statistics are correlated with multiple types of variability, such as the seasonality of the regions of origin and destination, the business cycles associated with exchange rates and levels of income, or various environmental impacts related to climate change or special events. Tourism is expanding from developed countries to newly industrialized countries with the rapid expansion of international tourism due to social, cultural, political, and technological changes. This growth will result in a mix of costs and benefits, as more countries/regions of tourist destinations compete for scarce resources. Accurate forecasts are therefore crucial for destinations in which decision-makers are trying to capitalize on the tourism industry trends and/or balance their local ecological and social carrying capacities. In these cases, international tourism demand forecasters have tried to take into account the overall conditions of the markets, destinations, and even neighboring or competing countries/regions that may impact their tourist flows (Song, Li, & Cao, 2018; Song, Qiu, & Park, 2019).

Time series models forecast the tourism demand based on historical trends. Such models try to identify patterns, slopes, and cycles between time series data by utilizing measurement sequences produced over successive periods. Unlike random sampling approaches, the time series forecasting models are based on successive values reflecting consecutive measurements taken at regularly spaced intervals such as monthly, quarterly, or annually. The time series models produce predictions of future values for the upcoming time series once a trend is formed (Song et al., 2019).

Vacant hotel rooms, unpurchased tickets for events, and unused food items reflect unnecessary costs and unrealized sales, a combination that presents a potential threat to financial stability. In short, many tourism and hospitality goods cannot be preserved for future demand, making it vital to forecast the need for accurate tourism demand. Precise tourism demand forecasts therefore provide important support for political, tactical, and operational decisions. Governments, for instance, need specific tourism criteria for informed decision-making on problems such as capacity building and accommodation site planning. Organizations need predictions to make tactical decisions relevant to brochures on tourism promotion, and tourism and hospitality professionals need accurate predictions for organizational decisions such as staffing and scheduling. Accurate tourism demand forecasting is therefore an important component that produces critical information for decision-making relevant to tourism. Many tourism demand forecasting studies fall within the well-established category of quantitative approach that builds the model from training data on past tourist arrival volumes and specific tourism need predictive factors. The ability to choose all potentially good relations in a dataset will therefore allow greater flexibility in creating more accurate predictive models. Time series, econometric, and artificial intelligence models offer excellent forecasting efficiency, breaking the function engineering barrier based on the destination market's domain knowledge (Law, Li, Fong, & Han, 2019).

For both public and private actors, demand forecasting in the tourism sector is of great economic importance. Since we have no ability to store most tourism products, demand forecasting accuracy plays an important role for the tourism industry in improving its decision-making, productivity in management, competitiveness, and sustainable economic growth. Classical statistical methods are the most commonly used models for forecasting of time series analysis. Such models have the limitation of being linear models. For most real-life problems, the relationship between the variables is not linear and the use of linear models for such problems is not effective. Conventional statistical methods such as multiple linear regressions are suitable for data showing specific patterns such as trend, seasonality, and cyclicality (Cankurt & Subasi, 2016). Recent advances in artificial intelligence, especially in deep learning, have offered ways to circumvent the above barriers and allow for more accurate tourism demand forecasting (Pouyanfar et al., 2019). Deep network architectures extend artificial neural network models with more than two nonlinear layers of computation and have been shown to be efficient for different applications. Their success is usually attributed to their built-in engineering ability that motivates us to breach these two barriers in the field of machine learning simultaneously. In terms of contextual information for the study of time series, deep network architectures also have some advantages in robust and hierarchical nonlinear relationships. Recurrent neural network (RNN), long short-term memory (LSTM), and attention mechanism in particular are capable of handling and learning long-term dependencies. Such resources make deep learning an alternative solution for tourism demand forecasting (Law et al., 2019).

## Example 6.6

The following Python code is used for tourism demand forecasting employing different regression models with separate training and testing datasets. The statistical quality measures, including mean-absolute error (MAE), mean squared error (MSE), and correlation coefficient (R), are calculated. Scatter plot, real, and predicted values are also plotted. Target transformation is also used to see the effect of target transformation. As you can see from the examples, target transformation is effective for some regressor models but not effective for others.

***Dataset information:*** In this example, tourism demand forecasting data for Turkey is utilized. Since tourism is the world's largest industry and Turkey is one of the biggest players on the tourism market, every work on tourism is producing great economic value and making major contributions to the tourism sector. In addition to modern and well-tourism infrastructure, price stability, and high-quality tourism services, Turkey has exciting potential with long and rich heritage challenges in culture and history, beautiful nature, four-season climate, and hospitable people in Europe and the Mediterranean. In this example, the number of tourists with monthly frequency is selected as a metric to measure the tourism demand in Turkey between 1992 and 2010 from the top 24 ranked tourism clients of Turkey. The number of ministry licensed hotel beds in Turkey, consumer price indexes (CPI), and exchange rates of tourism clients of Turkey were included in the models as environmental and economic time series that might affect foreign tourism demand in Turkey.

The input variables are the list of wholesale prices index, US dollar selling, 1 ounce gold London selling price USD, hotel bed capacity of Turkey, CPI of leading clients of Turkey (namely Austria, Belgium, Canada, Denmark, France, Germany, Greece, Italy, Netherlands, Norway, Poland, Spain, Sweden, Switzerland, Turkey, United Kingdom, United States, Russian Federation), number of the tourists coming from the leading clients of Turkey (namely Germany, Russia, France, Iran, Bulgaria, Georgia, Greece, Ukraine, Azerbaijan, Austria, Belgium, Denmark, Holland, England, Spain, Sweden, Switzerland, Italy, Norway, Poland, Romania, USA, Iraq, Syria), exchange rate of the leading countries of Turkey (Canadian dollar, Danish crone, Norwegian crone, Polish zloty, Swedish crone, Swiss franc, Turkish lira, British pound, Russian ruble), year, month, season, and number of the former tourists. Monthly time series data were collected from the Ministry of the Tourism of the Republic of Turkey (www.turizm.gov.tr), State Institute of Statistics of Turkey (www.die.gov.tr), Databank of the Central Bank of the Republic of Turkey (http://evds.tcmb.gov.tr), TÜRSAB (www.tursab.org.tr), and World Bank databank (http://databank.worldbank.org) (Cankurt & Subasi, 2016).

```
"""
Created on Fri Aug 2 01:23:04 2019
@author: asubasi
"""
#=======================================================================
# Tourism demand forecasting example
#=======================================================================
import matplotlib.pyplot as plt
import numpy as np
```

```
from sklearn.metrics import mean_squared_error, r2_score
from sklearn.metrics import mean_absolute_error
from sklearn.model_selection import train_test_split
#=====================================================================
# Define utility functions
#=====================================================================
def print_performance_metrics(ytest, ypred):
  # The mean absolute error
  print("MAE = %5.3f" % mean_absolute_error(ytest, ypred))
  # Explained variance score: 1 is perfect prediction
  print("R^2 = %0.5f" % r2_score(ytest, ypred))
  # The mean squared error
  print("MSE = %5.3f" % mean_squared_error(ytest, ypred))

def plot_scatter(ytest, ypred):
  fig, ax = plt.subplots()
  ax.scatter(ytest, ypred, edgecolors = (0, 0, 0))
  ax.text(ypred.max()-4.5, ytest.max()-0.1, r'$R^2$ = %.2f, MAE = %.2f' % (
  r2_score(ytest, ypred), mean_absolute_error(ytest, ypred)))
  ax.plot([ytest.min(), ytest.max()], [ytest.min(), ytest.max()], 'k--',
  lw = 4)
  ax.set_xlabel('Measured')
  ax.set_ylabel('Predicted')
  plt.show()

def plot_real_predicted(ytest, ypred):
  plt.plot(ytest[1:200], color = 'red', label = 'Real data')
  plt.plot(ypred[1:200], color = 'blue', label = 'Predicted data')
  plt.title('Prediction')
  plt.legend()
  plt.show()
# = ===================================================================
# Load the tourism dataset
# = ===================================================================
import pandas as pd
dataset = pd.read_csv('TurkeyVisitors.csv')
AllData = dataset.iloc[:, :].values
X = AllData[:,1:60]
y = AllData[:,60]
Xtrain, Xtest, ytrain, ytest = train_test_split(X, y, test_size = 0.33,
random_state = 0)
#%%
```

```
#=====================================================================
# Linear regression example
#=====================================================================
import matplotlib.pyplot as plt
from sklearn import linear_model
#=====================================================================
# Forecasting without target transformation
#=====================================================================
# Create linear regression object
regr = linear_model.LinearRegression()
# Train the model using the training sets
regr.fit(Xtrain, ytrain)
# Make predictions using the testing set
ypred = regr.predict(Xtest)
#=====================================================================
# Evaluate the model and print performance metrics
#=====================================================================
print_performance_metrics(ytest, ypred)
#%%
#=====================================================================
# Plot scatter
#=====================================================================
plot_scatter(ytest, ypred)
#%%
#=====================================================================
# Plot real and predicted outputs
#=====================================================================
plot_real_predicted(ytest, ypred)
#%%
#=====================================================================
# Forecasting with target transformation
#=====================================================================
from sklearn.preprocessing import QuantileTransformer
from sklearn.compose import TransformedTargetRegressor
transformer = QuantileTransformer(output_distribution = 'normal')
# Create linear regression object
regr = linear_model.LinearRegression()
regr = TransformedTargetRegressor(regressor = regr,
    transformer = transformer)
X_train, X_test, y_train, y_test = train_test_split(X, y, test_
size = 0.33, random_state = 0)
regr.fit(X_train, y_train)
y_pred = regr.predict(X_test)
```

```
#=============================================================================
# Evaluate the model and print performance metrics
#=============================================================================
print_performance_metrics(y_test,y_pred)
#%%
#=============================================================================
# Plot scatter
#=============================================================================
plot_scatter(y_test, y_pred)
#%%
#=============================================================================
# Plot real and predicted outputs
#=============================================================================
plot_real_predicted(y_test, y_pred)
#%%
from sklearn.neural_network import MLPRegressor
#=============================================================================
# ANN regression example
#=============================================================================
#=============================================================================
# Forecasting without target transformation
#=============================================================================
# Create MLP regression object
print("Training MLPRegressor...")
regr = MLPRegressor(activation = 'logistic')
# Train the model using the training sets
regr.fit(Xtrain, ytrain)
# Make predictions using the testing set
ypred = regr.predict(Xtest)
#=============================================================================
# Evaluate the model and print performance metrics
#=============================================================================
print_performance_metrics(ytest, ypred)
#%%
#=============================================================================
# Plot scatter
#=============================================================================
plot_scatter(ytest, ypred)
#%%
#=============================================================================
# Plot real and predicted outputs
#=============================================================================
plot_real_predicted(ytest, ypred)
#%%
```

```
#==========================================================================
# Forecasting with target transformation
#==========================================================================
from sklearn.preprocessing import QuantileTransformer
from sklearn.compose import TransformedTargetRegressor
transformer = QuantileTransformer(output_distribution = 'normal')
# Create MLP regression object
print("Training MLPRegressor...")
regr = MLPRegressor(activation = 'logistic')
regr = TransformedTargetRegressor(regressor = regr,
    transformer = transformer)
regr.fit(X_train, y_train)
y_pred = regr.predict(X_test)
#==========================================================================
# Evaluate the model and print performance metrics
#==========================================================================
print_performance_metrics(y_test,y_pred)
#%%
#==========================================================================
# Plot scatter
#==========================================================================
plot_scatter(y_test, y_pred)
#%%
#==========================================================================
# Plot real and predicted outputs
#==========================================================================
plot_real_predicted(y_test, y_pred)
#%%
#==========================================================================
# k-NN regression example
#==========================================================================
from sklearn.neighbors import KNeighborsRegressor
#==========================================================================
# Forecasting without target transformation
#==========================================================================
# Create a Regression object
print("Training Regressor...")
regr = KNeighborsRegressor(n_neighbors = 2)
# Train the model using the training sets
regr.fit(Xtrain, ytrain)
# Make predictions using the testing set
ypred = regr.predict(Xtest)
```

```
#==============================================================
# Evaluate the model and print performance metrics
#==============================================================
print_performance_metrics(ytest, ypred)
#%%
#==============================================================
# Plot scatter
#==============================================================
plot_scatter(ytest, ypred)
#%%
#==============================================================
# Plot real and predicted outputs
#==============================================================
plot_real_predicted(ytest, ypred)

#%%
#==============================================================
# Forecasting with target transformation
#==============================================================
from sklearn.preprocessing import QuantileTransformer
from sklearn.compose import TransformedTargetRegressor
transformer = QuantileTransformer(output_distribution = 'normal')
# Create a Regression object
print("Training Regressor...")
regr = KNeighborsRegressor(n_neighbors = 2)
regr = TransformedTargetRegressor(regressor = regr,
    transformer = transformer)
regr.fit(X_train, y_train)
y_pred = regr.predict(X_test)
#==============================================================
# Evaluate the model and print performance metrics
#==============================================================
print_performance_metrics(y_test,y_pred)
#%%
#==============================================================
# Plot scatter
#==============================================================
plot_scatter(y_test, y_pred)
#%%
#==============================================================
# Plot real and predicted outputs
#==============================================================
plot_real_predicted(y_test, y_pred)
```

```
#%%
#=====================================================================
# Random forest regressor example
#=====================================================================
from sklearn.ensemble.forest import RandomForestRegressor
#=====================================================================
# Forecasting without target transformation
#=====================================================================
# Create Random Forest Regressor Model
regr = RandomForestRegressor(n_estimators = 100)
# Train the model using the training sets
regr.fit(Xtrain, ytrain)
# Make predictions using the testing set
ypred = regr.predict(Xtest)
#=====================================================================
# Evaluate the model and print performance metrics
#=====================================================================
print_performance_metrics(ytest, ypred)
#%%
#=====================================================================
# Plot scatter
#=====================================================================
plot_scatter(ytest, ypred)
#%%
#=====================================================================
# Plot real and predicted outputs
#=====================================================================
plot_real_predicted(ytest, ypred)
#%%
#=====================================================================
# Forecasting with target transformation
#=====================================================================
from sklearn.compose import TransformedTargetRegressor
from sklearn.preprocessing import QuantileTransformer
transformer = QuantileTransformer(output_distribution = 'normal')
regr = RandomForestRegressor(n_estimators = 100)
regr = TransformedTargetRegressor(regressor = regr,
    transformer = transformer)
regr.fit(X_train, y_train)
y_pred = regr.predict(X_test)
#=====================================================================
# Evaluate the model and print performance metrics
#=====================================================================
```

```
print_performance_metrics(y_test,y_pred)
#%%
#==========================================================================
# Plot scatter
#==========================================================================
plot_scatter(y_test, y_pred)
#%%
#==========================================================================
# Plot real and predicted outputs
#==========================================================================
plot_real_predicted(y_test, y_pred)
#%%
#==========================================================================
# SVR regression example
#==========================================================================
from sklearn.svm import SVR
#==========================================================================
# Forecasting without target transformation
#==========================================================================
#Create Regression object
regr = SVR(gamma = 'scale', C = 200.0, epsilon = 0.2)
# Train the model using the training sets
# Train the model using the training sets
regr.fit(Xtrain, ytrain)
# Make predictions using the testing set
ypred = regr.predict(Xtest)
#==========================================================================
# Evaluate the model and print performance metrics
#==========================================================================
print_performance_metrics(ytest, ypred)
#%%
#==========================================================================
# Plot scatter
#==========================================================================
plot_scatter(ytest, ypred)
#%%
#==========================================================================
# Plot real and predicted outputs
#==========================================================================
plot_real_predicted(ytest, ypred)
#%%
```

```
#==========================================================================
# Forecasting with target transformation
#==========================================================================
from sklearn.compose import TransformedTargetRegressor
from sklearn.preprocessing import QuantileTransformer
transformer = QuantileTransformer(output_distribution = 'normal')
regr = TransformedTargetRegressor(regressor = regr,
    transformer = transformer)
regr.fit(X_train, y_train)
y_pred = regr.predict(X_test)
#==========================================================================
# Evaluate the model and print performance metrics
#==========================================================================
print_performance_metrics(y_test,y_pred)
#%%
#==========================================================================
# Plot scatter
#==========================================================================
plot_scatter(y_test,y_pred)
#%%
#==========================================================================
# Plot real and predicted outputs
#==========================================================================
plot_real_predicted(y_test,y_pred)

#%%
#==========================================================================
# Gradient boosting regression example
#==========================================================================
from sklearn.ensemble import GradientBoostingRegressor
#==========================================================================
# Create a regressor model
#==========================================================================
regr = GradientBoostingRegressor(n_estimators = 100, learning_rate = 0.1,
  max_depth = 1, random_state = 0, loss = 'ls').fit(X_train, y_train)
#==========================================================================
# Forecasting without target transformation
#==========================================================================
# Train the model using the training sets
regr.fit(Xtrain, ytrain)
# Make predictions using the testing set
ypred = regr.predict(Xtest)
```

```
#==============================================================================
# Evaluate the model and print performance metrics
#==============================================================================
print_performance_metrics(ytest, ypred)
#%%
#==============================================================================
# Plot scatter
#==============================================================================
plot_scatter(ytest, ypred)
#%%
#==============================================================================
# Plot real and predicted outputs
#==============================================================================
plot_real_predicted(ytest, ypred)
#%%
#==============================================================================
# Forecasting with target transformation
#==============================================================================
from sklearn.compose import TransformedTargetRegressor
from sklearn.preprocessing import QuantileTransformer
transformer = QuantileTransformer(output_distribution = 'normal')
regr = GradientBoostingRegressor(n_estimators = 100, learning_rate = 0.1,
  max_depth = 1, random_state = 0, loss = 'ls').fit(X_train, y_train)
regr = TransformedTargetRegressor(regressor = regr,
    transformer = transformer)
X_train, X_test, y_train, y_test = train_test_split(X, y, random_
state = 0)
regr.fit(X_train, y_train)
y_pred = regr.predict(X_test)
#==============================================================================
# Evaluate the model and print performance metrics
#==============================================================================
print_performance_metrics(y_test,y_pred)
#%%
#==============================================================================
# Plot scatter
#==============================================================================
plot_scatter(y_test,y_pred)
#%%
#==============================================================================
# Plot real and predicted outputs
#==============================================================================
plot_real_predicted(y_test,y_pred)
```

## 6.7 House prices prediction

Growth of secondary mortgage markets has required the use of increasingly sophisticated analytical, econometric, and machine learning approaches for pricing mortgage credit risks. For mortgage pricing and underwriting, as well as for more general housing market research, house price forecasting is needed. Since it is difficult to collect timely and consistent regional economic data, univariate time series methods can be preferred over structural housing market models, especially for short-term forecasts. Time series models are frequently utilized and have become popular in many applications for financial modeling. The role of asymmetries and nonlinearities relevant to changing underlying economic conditions has become increasingly popular in recent years. Intuitively, the regime-switching paradigm is very relevant to an application for real estate, as real estate markets have traditionally been susceptible to booms and bust. The basic intuition underlying this model is that housing markets behave differently in different economic conditions, resulting in distinct shifts in the characteristics of home price indices in the time series. For instance, shocks on the housing market may be more permanent during a recession, or home price volatility may increase, while the opposite may occur during a boom. Because of regional economies and demographic variations, the defining characteristics of the various regimes are likely to vary depending on the geographic area (Crawford & Fratantoni, 2003). There are significant differences across the United States in real income growth rates and levels. In addition, this heterogeneity should be expressed in real house prices. The impacts of specific shocks on whether observed house prices, such as increases in interest rates and oil prices, or nonobserved effects, such as technological change, could also vary across areas (Holly, Pesaran, & Yamagata, 2010).

Over recent years, the trends of residential house prices in the euro area have shown significant volatility. The growth rate of house prices in the euro area grew steadily through the middle of this decade, only to drop sharply in recent years. The rise and subsequent fall in inflation of house prices shows a time-varying difference between real house prices and their fundamental determinants of supply and demand. These recent developments seem to be consistent with a long-term trend characterized by transient fluctuations in house prices from a wide-ranging, long-term evolution of normal demand for housing and supply fundamentals. Combined with a lower volatility of demand-determinants, such as income and a slower supply response, many metrics widely used to calculate the equilibrium value of house prices signaled a varying degree of over- or under-value of house prices vis-à-vis certain fundamentals. As a consequence, good house price forecasting models such as machine learning techniques are needed. In particular, this approach is utilized to receive impulse response functions to selected shocks—a shock of temporary housing demand along with permanent financing costs, shocks of economical technology and housing technology—as well as a decomposition variance and permanent-transitory contribution based on this shock interpretation. The machine learning approach reveals not only that the model has superior forecasting efficiency for naive time series models but also that the cointegrating relationship can help to predict recent developments in house prices with greater accuracy than models without such a long-term balance condition (Gattini & Hiebert, 2010).

## Example 6.7

The following Python code is used to forecast California house prices employing different regression models with separate training and testing datasets. The statistical quality measures, including mean-absolute error (MAE), mean squared error (MSE), and correlation coefficient (R), are calculated. Scatter plot, real, and predicted values are also plotted.

***Dataset information:*** The data was collected from the variables employing all the block groups in California from the 1990 census. The data includes 20,640 observations on 9 characteristics, which are shown below (Pace & Barry, 1997).

| | |
|---|---|
| Longitude | A measure of how far west a house is; a higher value is farther west |
| Latitude | A measure of how far north a house is; a higher value is farther north |
| HousingMedianAge | Median age of a house within a block; a lower number is a newer building |
| TotalRooms | Total number of rooms within a block |
| TotalBedrooms | Total number of bedrooms within a block |
| Population | Total number of people residing within a block |
| Households | Total number of households, a group of people residing within a home unit, within a block |
| MedianIncome | Median income for households within a block of houses (measured in tens of thousands of U.S. dollars) |
| MedianHouseValue | Median house value for households within a block (measured in U.S. dollars) |

```
#=========================================================================
# House prices prediction using California housing data set
#=========================================================================
import matplotlib.pyplot as plt
import numpy as np
from sklearn.neighbors import KNeighborsRegressor
from sklearn.datasets.california_housing import fetch_california_housing
from sklearn.metrics import mean_squared_error, r2_score
from sklearn.metrics import mean_absolute_error
from sklearn.model_selection import train_test_split
from sklearn.metrics import mean_squared_error, r2_score
from sklearn.metrics import mean_absolute_error
import matplotlib.pyplot as plt
#=========================================================================
# Define utility functions
#=========================================================================
def print_performance_metrics(ytest, ypred):
   # The mean absolute error
   print("MAE = %5.3f" % mean_absolute_error(ytest, ypred))
   # Explained variance score: 1 is perfect prediction
   print("R^2 = %0.5f" % r2_score(ytest, ypred))
   # The mean squared error
   print("MSE = %5.3f" % mean_squared_error(ytest, ypred))
```

```
def plot_scatter(ytest, ypred):
   fig, ax = plt.subplots()
   ax.scatter(ytest, ypred, edgecolors = (0, 0, 0))
   ax.text(ypred.max()-4.5, ytest.max()-0.1, r'$R^2$ = %.2f, MAE = %.2f' % (
         r2_score(ytest, ypred), mean_absolute_error(ytest, ypred)))
   ax.plot([ytest.min(), ytest.max()], [ytest.min(), ytest.max()], 'k--',
   lw = 4)
   ax.set_xlabel('Measured')
   ax.set_ylabel('Predicted')
   plt.show()

def plot_real_predicted(ytest, ypred):
   plt.plot(ytest[1:200], color = 'red', label = 'Real data')
   plt.plot(ypred[1:200], color = 'blue', label = 'Predicted data')
   plt.title('Prediction')
   plt.legend()
   plt.show()
# =======================================================================
# Load the California housing dataset
# = =====================================================================
cal_housing = fetch_california_housing()
X, y = cal_housing.data, cal_housing.target
names = cal_housing.feature_names
Xtrain, Xtest, ytrain, ytest = train_test_split(X, y, test_size = 0.3,
random_state = 0)

#%%
#=======================================================================
# Linear regression example
#=======================================================================
import matplotlib.pyplot as plt
from sklearn import linear_model
# Create linear regression object
regr = linear_model.LinearRegression()
# Train the model using the training sets
regr.fit(Xtrain, ytrain)
# Make predictions using the testing set
ypred = regr.predict(Xtest)
#=======================================================================
# Evaluate the model and print performance metrics
#=======================================================================
print_performance_metrics(ytest, ypred)
#%%
```

```
#=========================================================================
# Plot scatter
#=========================================================================
plot_scatter(ytest, ypred)
#%%
#=========================================================================
# Plot real and predicted outputs
#=========================================================================
plot_real_predicted(ytest, ypred)
#%%
from sklearn.neural_network import MLPRegressor
#=========================================================================
# ANN regression example
#=========================================================================
# Create MLP regression object
print("Training MLPRegressor...")
regr = MLPRegressor(activation = 'logistic')
# Train the model using the training sets
regr.fit(Xtrain, ytrain)
# Make predictions using the testing set
ypred = regr.predict(Xtest)
#=========================================================================
# Evaluate the model and print performance metrics
#=========================================================================
print_performance_metrics(ytest, ypred)
#%%
#=========================================================================
# Plot scatter
#=========================================================================
plot_scatter(ytest, ypred)
#%%
#=========================================================================
# Plot real and predicted outputs
#=========================================================================
plot_real_predicted(ytest, ypred)

#%%
#=========================================================================
# k-NN regression example
#=========================================================================
from sklearn.neighbors import KNeighborsRegressor
# Create a Regression object
print("Training Regressor...")
regr = KNeighborsRegressor(n_neighbors = 2)
```

```
# Train the model using the training sets
regr.fit(Xtrain, ytrain)
# Make predictions using the testing set
ypred = regr.predict(Xtest)
#========================================================================
# Evaluate the model and print performance metrics
#========================================================================
print_performance_metrics(ytest, ypred)
#%%
#========================================================================
# Plot scatter
#========================================================================
plot_scatter(ytest, ypred)
#%%
#========================================================================
# Plot real and predicted outputs
#========================================================================
plot_real_predicted(ytest, ypred)

#%%
#========================================================================
# Random forest regressor example
#========================================================================
from sklearn.ensemble.forest import RandomForestRegressor
# Create Random Forest Regressor Model
regr = RandomForestRegressor(n_estimators = 100)
# Train the model using the training sets
regr.fit(Xtrain, ytrain)
# Make predictions using the testing set
ypred = regr.predict(Xtest)
#========================================================================
# Evaluate the model and print performance metrics
#========================================================================
print_performance_metrics(ytest, ypred)
#%%
#========================================================================
# Plot scatter
#========================================================================
plot_scatter(ytest, ypred)
#%%
#========================================================================
# Plot real and predicted outputs
#========================================================================
```

```
plot_real_predicted(ytest, ypred)
#%%
#==============================================================================
# SVR regression example
#==============================================================================
from sklearn.svm import SVR
#Create Regression object
regr = SVR(gamma = 'scale', C = 50.0, epsilon = 0.2)
# Train the model using the training sets
regr.fit(Xtrain, ytrain)
# Make predictions using the testing set
ypred = regr.predict(Xtest)
#==============================================================================
# Evaluate the model and print performance metrics
#==============================================================================
print_performance_metrics(ytest, ypred)
#%%
#==============================================================================
# Plot scatter
#==============================================================================
plot_scatter(ytest, ypred)
#%%
#==============================================================================
# Plot real and predicted outputs
#==============================================================================
plot_real_predicted(ytest, ypred)
#%%
#==============================================================================
# Gradient boosting regressor example
#==============================================================================
from sklearn.ensemble import GradientBoostingRegressor
#==============================================================================
# Create a regressor model
#==============================================================================
regr = GradientBoostingRegressor(n_estimators = 100, learning_rate = 0.1,
  max_depth = 1, random_state = 0, loss = 'ls')
# Train the model using the training sets
regr.fit(Xtrain, ytrain)
# Make predictions using the testing set
ypred = regr.predict(Xtest)
#==============================================================================
# Evaluate the model and print performance metrics
#==============================================================================
```

```
print_performance_metrics(ytest, ypred)
#%%
#=======================================================================
# Plot scatter
#=======================================================================
plot_scatter(ytest, ypred)
#%%
#=======================================================================
# Plot real and predicted outputs
#=======================================================================
plot_real_predicted(ytest, ypred)

#%%
#=======================================================================
# AdaBoost regressor example
#=======================================================================
from sklearn.ensemble import AdaBoostRegressor
#=======================================================================
# Create a regressor model
#=======================================================================
regr = AdaBoostRegressor(random_state = 0, n_estimators = 100)
# Train the model using the training sets
regr.fit(Xtrain, ytrain)
# Train the model using the training sets
regr.fit(Xtrain, ytrain)
# Make predictions using the testing set
ypred = regr.predict(Xtest)
#=======================================================================
# Evaluate the model and print performance metrics
#=======================================================================
print_performance_metrics(ytest, ypred)
#%%
#=======================================================================
# Plot scatter
#=======================================================================
plot_scatter(ytest, ypred)
#%%
#=======================================================================
# Plot real and predicted outputs
#=======================================================================
plot_real_predicted(ytest, ypred)
```

### Example 6.8

The following Python code is used to forecast Boston house prices employing different regression models with separate training and testing datasets. The statistical quality measures, including mean-absolute error (MAE), mean squared error (MSE), and correlation coefficient (R), are calculated. Scatter plot, real, and predicted values are also plotted. Target transformation is also used to see the effect of target transformation. As you can see from the examples, target transformation is effective for some regressor models but not effective for others.

***Dataset information:*** This dataset includes information collected by the U.S. Census Service regarding housing in the area of Boston, Mass. It was taken from the StatLib archive (http://lib.stat.cmu.edu/datasets/boston) and has been utilized broadly throughout literature to test benchmark algorithms. The dataset contains only 506 cases. The data was originally published by Harrison and Rubinfeld (Harrison & Rubinfeld, 1978). There are 14 attributes in each case of the dataset. They are:

1. CRIM—per capita crime rate by town
2. ZN—proportion of residential land zoned for lots over 25,000 sq ft
3. INDUS—proportion of nonretail business acres per town
4. CHAS—Charles river dummy variable (1 if tract bounds river; 0 otherwise)
5. NOX—nitric oxides concentration (parts per 10 million)
6. RM—average number of rooms per dwelling
7. AGE—proportion of owner-occupied units built prior to 1940
8. DIS—weighted distances to five Boston employment centers
9. RAD—index of accessibility to radial highways
10. TAX—full-value property-tax rate per $10,000
11. PTRATIO—pupil–teacher ratio by town
12. B—1000(Bk - 0.63)^2 where Bk is the proportion of blacks by town
13. LSTAT—% lower status of the population
14. MEDV—median value of owner-occupied homes in $1000s

```
"""
Created on Fri Aug 2 01:23:04 2019
@author: asubasi
"""
#=======================================================================
# House prices prediction example with Boston house prices dataset
#=======================================================================
import matplotlib.pyplot as plt
import numpy as np
from sklearn.metrics import mean_squared_error, r2_score
from sklearn.metrics import mean_absolute_error
from sklearn.model_selection import train_test_split
#=======================================================================
# Define utility functions
#=======================================================================
```

```
def print_performance_metrics(ytest, ypred):
  # The mean absolute error
  print("MAE = %5.3f" % mean_absolute_error(ytest, ypred))
  # Explained variance score: 1 is perfect prediction
  print("R^2 = %0.5f" % r2_score(ytest, ypred))
  # The mean squared error
  print("MSE = %5.3f" % mean_squared_error(ytest, ypred))

def plot_scatter(ytest, ypred):
  fig, ax = plt.subplots()
  ax.scatter(ytest, ypred, edgecolors = (0, 0, 0))
  ax.text(ypred.max()-4.5, ytest.max()-0.1, r'$R^2$ = %.2f, MAE = %.2f' % (
  r2_score(ytest, ypred), mean_absolute_error(ytest, ypred)))
  ax.plot([ytest.min(), ytest.max()], [ytest.min(), ytest.max()], 'k--',
  lw = 4)
  ax.set_xlabel('Measured')
  ax.set_ylabel('Predicted')
  plt.show()

def plot_real_predicted(ytest, ypred):
  plt.plot(ytest[1:200], color = 'red', label = 'Real data')
  plt.plot(ypred[1:200], color = 'blue', label = 'Predicted data')
  plt.title('Prediction')
  plt.legend()
  plt.show()
# = =============================================================
# Load the Boston house prices dataset
# = =============================================================
from sklearn.datasets import load_boston
boston = load_boston()
X = boston.data
y = boston.target
Xtrain, Xtest, ytrain, ytest = train_test_split(X, y, test_size = 0.33,
random_state = 0)
#%%
#===============================================================
# Linear regression example
#===============================================================
import matplotlib.pyplot as plt
from sklearn import linear_model
#===============================================================
# Forecasting without target transformation
#===============================================================
# Create linear regression object
regr = linear_model.LinearRegression()
```

```
# Train the model using the training sets
regr.fit(Xtrain, ytrain)
# Make predictions using the testing set
ypred = regr.predict(Xtest)
#=======================================================================
# Evaluate the model and print performance metrics
#=======================================================================
print_performance_metrics(ytest, ypred)
#%%
#=======================================================================
# Plot scatter
#=======================================================================
plot_scatter(ytest, ypred)
#%%
#=======================================================================
# Plot real and predicted outputs
#=======================================================================
plot_real_predicted(ytest, ypred)
#%%
#=======================================================================
# Forecasting with target transformation
#=======================================================================
from sklearn.preprocessing import QuantileTransformer
from sklearn.compose import TransformedTargetRegressor
transformer = QuantileTransformer(output_distribution = 'normal')
# Create linear regression object
regr = linear_model.LinearRegression()
regr = TransformedTargetRegressor(regressor = regr,
    transformer = transformer)
X_train, X_test, y_train, y_test = train_test_split(X, y, test_
size = 0.33, random_state = 0)
regr.fit(X_train, y_train)
y_pred = regr.predict(X_test)
#=======================================================================
# Evaluate the model and print performance metrics
#=======================================================================
print_performance_metrics(y_test,y_pred)
#%%
#=======================================================================
# Plot scatter
#=======================================================================
plot_scatter(y_test, y_pred)
#%%
#=======================================================================
```

```
# Plot real and predicted outputs
#=======================================================================
plot_real_predicted(y_test, y_pred)

#%%
#=======================================================================
# ANN regression example
#=======================================================================
from sklearn.neural_network import MLPRegressor
#=======================================================================
# Forecasting without target transformation
#=======================================================================
# Create MLP regression object
print("Training MLPRegressor...")
regr = MLPRegressor(activation = 'logistic')
# Train the model using the training sets
regr.fit(Xtrain, ytrain)
# Make predictions using the testing set
ypred = regr.predict(Xtest)
#=======================================================================
# Evaluate the model and print performance metrics
#=======================================================================
print_performance_metrics(ytest, ypred)
#%%
#=======================================================================
# Plot scatter
#=======================================================================
plot_scatter(ytest, ypred)
#%%
#=======================================================================
# Plot real and predicted outputs
#=======================================================================
plot_real_predicted(ytest, ypred)

#%%
#=======================================================================
# Forecasting with target transformation
#=======================================================================
from sklearn.preprocessing import QuantileTransformer
from sklearn.compose import TransformedTargetRegressor
transformer = QuantileTransformer(output_distribution = 'normal')
# Create MLP regression object
print("Training MLPRegressor...")
regr = MLPRegressor(activation = 'logistic')
```

```
regr = TransformedTargetRegressor(regressor = regr,
    transformer = transformer)
regr.fit(X_train, y_train)
y_pred = regr.predict(X_test)
#==========================================================================
# Evaluate the model and print performance metrics
#==========================================================================
print_performance_metrics(y_test,y_pred)
#%%
#==========================================================================
# Plot scatter
#==========================================================================
plot_scatter(y_test, y_pred)
#%%
#==========================================================================
# Plot real and predicted outputs
#==========================================================================
plot_real_predicted(y_test, y_pred)
#%%
#==========================================================================
# k-NN regression example
#==========================================================================
from sklearn.neighbors import KNeighborsRegressor
#==========================================================================
# Forecasting without target transformation
#==========================================================================
# Create a Regression object
print("Training Regressor...")
regr = KNeighborsRegressor(n_neighbors = 2)
# Train the model using the training sets
regr.fit(Xtrain, ytrain)
# Make predictions using the testing set
ypred = regr.predict(Xtest)
#==========================================================================
# Evaluate the model and print performance metrics
#==========================================================================
print_performance_metrics(ytest, ypred)
#%%
#==========================================================================
# Plot scatter
#==========================================================================
plot_scatter(ytest, ypred)
#%%
#==========================================================================
# Plot real and predicted outputs
```

```
#=========================================================================
plot_real_predicted(ytest, ypred)

#%%
#=========================================================================
# Forecasting with target transformation
#=========================================================================
from sklearn.preprocessing import QuantileTransformer
from sklearn.compose import TransformedTargetRegressor
transformer = QuantileTransformer(output_distribution = 'normal')
# Create a Regression object
print("Training Regressor...")
regr = KNeighborsRegressor(n_neighbors = 2)
regr = TransformedTargetRegressor(regressor = regr,
    transformer = transformer)
regr.fit(X_train, y_train)
y_pred = regr.predict(X_test)
#=========================================================================
# Evaluate the model and print performance metrics
#=========================================================================
print_performance_metrics(y_test,y_pred)
#%%
#=========================================================================
# Plot scatter
#=========================================================================
plot_scatter(y_test, y_pred)
#%%
#=========================================================================
# Plot real and predicted outputs
#=========================================================================
plot_real_predicted(y_test, y_pred)
#%%
#=========================================================================
# Random forest regressor example
#=========================================================================
from sklearn.ensemble.forest import RandomForestRegressor
#=========================================================================
# Forecasting without target transformation
#=========================================================================
# Create random forest regressor model
regr = RandomForestRegressor(n_estimators = 100)
 # Train the model using the training sets
 regr.fit(Xtrain, ytrain)
 # Make predictions using the testing set
```

```
ypred = regr.predict(Xtest)
#==========================================================================
# Evaluate the model and print performance metrics
#==========================================================================
print_performance_metrics(ytest, ypred)
#%%
#==========================================================================
# Plot scatter
#==========================================================================
plot_scatter(ytest, ypred)
#%%
#==========================================================================
# Plot real and predicted outputs
#==========================================================================
plot_real_predicted(ytest, ypred)
#%%
#==========================================================================
# Forecasting with target transformation
#==========================================================================
from sklearn.compose import TransformedTargetRegressor
from sklearn.preprocessing import QuantileTransformer
transformer = QuantileTransformer(output_distribution = 'normal')
regr = RandomForestRegressor(n_estimators = 100)
regr = TransformedTargetRegressor(regressor = regr,
    transformer = transformer)
regr.fit(X_train, y_train)
y_pred = regr.predict(X_test)
#==========================================================================
# Evaluate the model and print performance metrics
#==========================================================================
print_performance_metrics(y_test,y_pred)
#%%
#==========================================================================
# Plot scatter
#==========================================================================
plot_scatter(y_test, y_pred)
#%%
#==========================================================================
# Plot real and predicted outputs
#==========================================================================
plot_real_predicted(y_test, y_pred)
#%%
#==========================================================================
# SVR regression example
#==========================================================================
```

```
from sklearn.svm import SVR
#=====================================================================
# Forecasting without target transformation
#=====================================================================
#Create Regression object
regr = SVR(gamma = 'scale', C = 200.0, epsilon = 0.2)
# Train the model using the training sets
# Train the model using the training sets
regr.fit(Xtrain, ytrain)
# Make predictions using the testing set
ypred = regr.predict(Xtest)
#=====================================================================
# Evaluate the model and print performance metrics
#=====================================================================
print_performance_metrics(ytest, ypred)
#%%
#=====================================================================
# Plot scatter
#=====================================================================
plot_scatter(ytest, ypred)
#%%
#=====================================================================
# Plot real and predicted outputs
#=====================================================================
plot_real_predicted(ytest, ypred)
#%%
#=====================================================================
# Forecasting with target transformation
#=====================================================================
from sklearn.compose import TransformedTargetRegressor
from sklearn.preprocessing import QuantileTransformer
transformer = QuantileTransformer(output_distribution = 'normal')
regr = TransformedTargetRegressor(regressor = regr,
    transformer = transformer)
regr.fit(X_train, y_train)
y_pred = regr.predict(X_test)
#=====================================================================
# Evaluate the model and print performance metrics
#=====================================================================
print_performance_metrics(y_test,y_pred)
#%%
#=====================================================================
# Plot scatter
#=====================================================================
plot_scatter(y_test,y_pred)
```

```
#%%
#==============================================================================
# Plot real and predicted outputs
#==============================================================================
plot_real_predicted(y_test,y_pred)

#%%
#==============================================================================
# Gradient boosting regression example
#==============================================================================
from sklearn.ensemble import GradientBoostingRegressor
#==============================================================================
# Create a regressor model
#==============================================================================
regr = GradientBoostingRegressor(n_estimators = 100, learning_rate = 0.1,
  max_depth = 1, random_state = 0, loss = 'ls').fit(X_train, y_train)
#==============================================================================
# Forecasting without target transformation
#==============================================================================
# Train the model using the training sets
regr.fit(Xtrain, ytrain)
# Make predictions using the testing set
ypred = regr.predict(Xtest)
#==============================================================================
# Evaluate the model and print performance metrics
#==============================================================================
print_performance_metrics(ytest, ypred)
#%%
#==============================================================================
# Plot scatter
#==============================================================================
plot_scatter(ytest, ypred)
#%%
#==============================================================================
# Plot real and predicted outputs
#==============================================================================
plot_real_predicted(ytest, ypred)
#%%
#==============================================================================
# Forecasting with target transformation
#==============================================================================
from sklearn.compose import TransformedTargetRegressor
from sklearn.preprocessing import QuantileTransformer
transformer = QuantileTransformer(output_distribution = 'normal')
```

```
regr = GradientBoostingRegressor(n_estimators = 100, learning_rate = 0.1,
  max_depth = 1, random_state = 0, loss = 'ls').fit(X_train, y_train)
regr = TransformedTargetRegressor(regressor = regr,
    transformer = transformer)
X_train, X_test, y_train, y_test = train_test_split(X, y, random_state = 0)
regr.fit(X_train, y_train)
y_pred = regr.predict(X_test)
#==========================================================================
# Evaluate the model and print performance metrics
#==========================================================================
print_performance_metrics(y_test,y_pred)
#%%
#==========================================================================
# Plot scatter
#==========================================================================
plot_scatter(y_test,y_pred)
#%%
#==========================================================================
# Plot real and predicted outputs
#==========================================================================
plot_real_predicted(y_test,y_pred)
```

## 6.8 Bike usage prediction

With more people living in cities, a growing population has led to increased emissions of pollution, noise, congestion, and greenhouse gases. The use of bike-sharing systems (BSSs) is one possible approach to addressing these problems. In many cities, BSSs are an important part of urban mobility and are sustainable and environmentally friendly. When urban density and its associated problems increase, there is likely to be more BSSs in the future due to relatively low capital and operating costs, ease of installation, pedal support for people who are physically unable to pedal long distances or on difficult terrain, and better tracking of bikes (Ashqar et al., 2017; DeMaio, 2009). Bike-sharing systems for promoting green transport and a healthy lifestyle have been deployed in many cities. One of the key factors for optimizing the utility of such systems is to place bike stations at places that best meet the demand for the trips of riders. Generally, urban planners depend on dedicated surveys to understand the demand for local bike trips, which is expensive in terms of time and work, especially when they need to compare several locations. In recent years, more and more cities have launched initiatives for bike sharing to encourage environmental sustainability and promote a healthy lifestyle (Pucher, Dill, & Handy, 2010). These systems for bike sharing allow people to pick up and drop off public bikes at self-service stations for short trips within a community. Given the large investment in infrastructure needed to support a bike-sharing scheme, such as arranging parking facilities and making the roads more bike friendly, maximizing the value of shared bikes is important for urban planners. One of the key factors for encouraging citizen involvement in a bike-sharing system is to place bike stations at locations that best meet potential users' trip demands (Chen et al., 2015; García-Palomares, Gutiérrez, & Latorre, 2012).

Machine learning tools help to build a precise model of prediction that estimates demand for bike trips between pairs of locations. The machine learning models can therefore be employed to predict even if one or both of these locations currently do not have bike stations in place and can be used as a planning tool when determining how to extend the bike-sharing network of a community. By providing predictions of the demand for trips between each origin–destination pair, machine learning approach provides not only an estimation of how much incoming and outgoing demand will be realized if a new bike station is installed, but also where the incoming/outgoing demand will originate and end, predicting the impact on the existing network of this new station (Divya, Somya, & Peter, 2015).

## Example 6.9

The following Python code is used to forecast bike usage employing random forest regressor with separate training and testing datasets. The statistical quality measures, including mean-absolute error (MAE), mean squared error (MSE), and correlation coefficient (R), are calculated. Scatter plot, real, and predicted values are also plotted.

***Dataset information:*** The bike-sharing data is utilized by Fanaee-T and Gama (Fanaee-T & Gama, 2014). It can be downloaded from UCI machine learning repository (https://archive.ics.uci.edu/ml/datasets/bike+sharing+dataset). The dataset contains two separate sets of information: hour.csv and day.csv. Both hour.csv and day.csv have the following fields, except hr, which is not available in day.csv.

- instant: record index
- dteday: date
- season: season (1:winter, 2:spring, 3:summer, 4:fall)
- yr: year (0: 2011, 1:2012)
- mnth: month ( 1 to 12)
- hr: hour (0 to 23)
- holiday: weather day is holiday or not (extracted from [Web Link])
- weekday: day of the week
- workingday: if day is neither weekend nor holiday is 1, otherwise is 0.
- weathersit:
- 1: Clear, few clouds, partly cloudy
- 2: Mist + cloudy, mist + broken clouds, mist + few clouds, mist
- 3: Light snow, light rain + thunderstorm + scattered clouds, light rain + scattered clouds
- 4: Heavy rain + ice pellets + thunderstorm + mist, snow + fog
- temp: normalized temperature in Celsius; the values are derived via (t-t_min)/(t_max-t_min), t_min = -8, t_max = +39 (only in hourly scale)
- atemp: normalized feeling temperature in Celsius; the values are derived via (t-t_min)/(t_max-t_min), t_min = -16, t_max = +50 (only in hourly scale)
- hum: normalized humidity; the values are divided to 100 (max)

- windspeed: normalized wind speed; the values are divided to 67 (max)
- casual: count of casual users
- registered: count of registered users
- cnt: count of total rental bikes including both casual and registered

```
" " "
Created on Fri Aug 2 01:23:04 2019
@author: asubasi
" " "
#=======================================================================
# Bike-sharing example
#=======================================================================
import pandas as pd
import numpy as np
import matplotlib.pyplot as plt
import zipfile
import requests, io, os
import warnings
from sklearn.model_selection import train_test_split
from sklearn.ensemble import RandomForestRegressor
from sklearn.metrics import mean_squared_error, r2_score, mean_absolute_
error
from scipy import stats
#=======================================================================
# Define utility functions
#=======================================================================
def print_performance_metrics(ytest, ypred):
  # The mean absolute error
  print("MAE = %5.3f" % mean_absolute_error(ytest, ypred))
  # Explained variance score: 1 is perfect prediction
  print("R^2 = %0.5f" % r2_score(ytest, ypred))
  # The mean squared error
  print("MSE = %5.3f" % mean_squared_error(ytest, ypred))

def plot_scatter(ytest, ypred):
  fig, ax = plt.subplots()
  ax.scatter(ytest, ypred, edgecolors = (0, 0, 0))
  ax.text(ypred.max()-4.5, ytest.max()-0.1, r'$R^2$ = %.2f, MAE = %.2f' % (
  r2_score(ytest, ypred), mean_absolute_error(ytest, ypred)))
  ax.plot([ytest.min(), ytest.max()], [ytest.min(), ytest.max()], 'k--',
  lw = 4)
  ax.set_xlabel('Measured')
  ax.set_ylabel('Predicted')
  plt.show()
```

```
def plot_real_predicted(ytest, ypred):
  plt.plot(ytest[1:200], color = 'red', label = 'Real data')
  plt.plot(ypred[1:200], color = 'blue', label = 'Predicted data')
  plt.title('Prediction')
  plt.legend()
  plt.show()

#Unzip downloaded data
def unzip_from_UCI(UCI_url, dest = ''):
  #Downloads and unpacks datasets from UCI in zip format
  response = requests.get(UCI_url)
  compressed_file = io.BytesIO(response.content)
  z = zipfile.ZipFile(compressed_file)
  print ('Extracting in %s' % os.getcwd() + '\\' + dest)
  for name in z.namelist():
  if '.csv' in name:
  print ('\tunzipping %s' %name)
  z.extract(name, path = os.getcwd() + '\\' + dest)
  # data cleaning i.e. removing outliers
  def remove_outliers(data, type):
    print("Shape of {} Data frame before removing Outliers: {}".
    format(type, data.shape))
    no_outliers = data[(np.abs(stats.zscore(data)) < 3).all(axis = 1)]
    print("Shape of {} Data frame before removing Outliers: {}".
    format(type, no_outliers.shape))
    return no_outliers

  #%%
  #Ignore Warnings
  warnings.filterwarnings("ignore")
  #Download data from UCI website
  UCI_url = 'https://archive.ics.uci.edu/ml/machine-learning-databas-
  es/00275/Bike-Sharing-Dataset.zip'
  unzip_from_UCI(UCI_url, dest = 'bikesharing')

  #Read and drop missing values if any
  hourly_data = pd.read_csv("bikesharing/hour.csv", na_values = '?').
  dropna()
  daily_data = pd.read_csv("bikesharing/day.csv", na_values = '?').drop-
  na()
  #%%
  #change date to int
  list_dh = []
  for i in hourly_data['dteday']:
    list1 = i.split('-')
```

```
  list_dh.append(int(list1[2]))
dfh = pd.DataFrame(list_dh, columns = ['dteday'])
hourly_data[['dteday']] = dfh[['dteday']]

list_dd = []
for i in daily_data['dteday']:
  list2 = i.split('-')
  list_dd.append(int(list2[2]))
dfd = pd.DataFrame(list_dd, columns = ['dteday'])
daily_data[['dteday']] = dfd[['dteday']]

no_outliers = remove_outliers(hourly_data,'Hourly')
y_hour = no_outliers.cnt
x_hour = no_outliers.drop(['cnt','instant','registered','casual'],ax
is = 1)

no_outliers = remove_outliers(daily_data,'Daily')
y_day = no_outliers.cnt
x_day = no_outliers.drop(['cnt','instant','registered','casual'],ax
is = 1)

#%%
# choosing alpha as 0.8 where coefficients of holiday, atemp and
windspeed are becoming zero.
x_hour = x_hour.drop(['holiday','atemp','windspeed'],axis = 1)

# choosing alpha as 0.3 where coefficients of holiday is becoming zero.
x_day = x_day.drop(['holiday','dteday','mnth'],axis = 1)

#Splitting data
X_hour_train, X_hour_test, Y_hour_train, Y_hour_test = train_test_
split(x_hour, y_hour, test_size = 0.3, random_state = 5)
X_day_train, X_day_test, Y_day_train, Y_day_test = train_test_split(x_
day, y_day, test_size = 0.3, random_state = 5)

#Random Forest Regressor
rgr = RandomForestRegressor(n_estimators = 200, n_jobs = -1, min_
samples_split = 4)
print('\nRandom Forest')

#%%
#General Model training and Testing for Hourly Data
print("\n\t Hour Dataset")
rgr.fit(X_hour_train, Y_hour_train)
predictions = rgr.predict(X_hour_test)
```

```
print_performance_metrics(Y_hour_test, predictions)
# Plot outputs
plot_scatter(Y_hour_test, predictions)
plot_real_predicted(np.array(Y_hour_test), predictions)
#%%
#General Model training and Testing for Daily Data
print("\n\t Day Dataset")
rgr.fit(X_day_train, Y_day_train)
predictions = rgr.predict(X_day_test)
print_performance_metrics(Y_day_test, predictions)
# Plot outputs
plot_scatter(Y_day_test, predictions)
plot_real_predicted(np.array(Y_day_test), predictions)
```

## 6.9 Summary

In this chapter we present many examples related to the regression learning problem, which involves forecasting or predicting correct, real-evaluated labels as closely as possible using data. Since regression is a common task with different applications in machine learning, this particular chapter is dedicated to explaining and studying it. Regression is a process in which you determine the difference between models of grouping and grading. The grouping model theory involves dividing the instance space into segments and learning a local model in each segment as simply as possible. In previous chapters the learning tasks focused primarily on classification problems. In this chapter different machine learning algorithms and deep learning methods for regression, including both finite and infinite sets of hypotheses, are presented. The application of these algorithms to different fields is discussed in detail. These fields are stock market price index return forecasting, inflation forecasting, electrical load forecasting, wind speed forecasting, tourism demand forecasting, house prices prediction, and bike usage prediction.

## References


Ashqar, H. I., Elhenawy, M., Almannaa, M. H., Ghanem, A., Rakha, H. A., & House, L. (2017). In *Modeling bike availability in a bike-sharing system using machine learning* (pp. 374–378). IEEE.

Bozkurt, Ö. Ö., Biricik, G., & Tayşi, Z. C. (2017). Artificial neural network and SARIMA based models for power load forecasting in Turkish electricity market. PloS One, 12(4), e0175915.

Cankurt, S., & Subasi, A. (2016). Tourism demand modelling and forecasting using data mining techniques in multivariate time series: A case study in Turkey. Turkish Journal of Electrical Engineering & Computer Sciences, 24(5), 3388–3404.

Chen, L., Zhang, D., Pan, G., Ma, X., Yang, D., Kushlev, K., & Li, S. (2015). In *Bike sharing station placement leveraging heterogeneous urban open data* (pp. 571–575). ACM.

Crawford, G. W., & Fratantoni, M. C. (2003). Assessing the forecasting performance of regime-switching, ARIMA and GARCH models of house prices. Real Estate Economics, 31(2), 223–243.

DeMaio, P. (2009). Bike-sharing: History, impacts, models of provision, and future. Journal of Public Transportation, 12(4), 3.

Divya, S., Somya, S., & Peter, I. (2015). Predicting bike usage for New York City's bike sharing system. Association for the Advancement of Artificial Intelligence, 110–114.

Fanaee-T, H., & Gama, J. (2014). Event labeling combining ensemble detectors and background knowledge. Progress in Artificial Intelligence, 2(2-3), 113–127.

Flach, P. (2012). Machine learning: The art and science of algorithms that make sense of data. Cambridge, UK: Cambridge University Press.

García-Palomares, J. C., Gutiérrez, J., & Latorre, M. (2012). Optimizing the location of stations in bike-sharing programs: A GIS approach. Applied Geography, 35(1-2), 235–246.

Gasparin, A., Lukovic, S., & Alippi, C. (2019). Deep learning for time series forecasting: The electric load case. *ArXiv Preprint ArXiv:1907.09207*.

Gattini, L., & Hiebert, P. (2010). Forecasting and assessing Euro area house prices through the lens of key fundamentals.

Harrison, D., Jr., & Rubinfeld, D. L. (1978). Hedonic housing prices and the demand for clean air. Journal of Environmental Economics and Management, 5(1), 81–102.

Holly, S., Pesaran, M. H., & Yamagata, T. (2010). A spatio-temporal model of house prices in the USA. Journal of Econometrics, 158(1), 160–173.

Law, R., Li, G., Fong, D. K. C., & Han, X. (2019). Tourism demand forecasting: A deep learning approach. Annals of Tourism Research, 75, 410–423.

Lei, M., Shiyan, L., Chuanwen, J., Hongling, L., & Yan, Z. (2009). A review on the forecasting of wind speed and generated power. Renewable and Sustainable Energy Reviews, 13(4), 915–920.

Okumus, I., & Dinler, A. (2016). Current status of wind energy forecasting and a hybrid method for hourly predictions. Energy Conversion and Management, 123, 362–371.

Pace, R. K., & Barry, R. (1997). Sparse spatial autoregressions. Statistics & Probability Letters, 33(3), 291–297.

Pouyanfar, S., Sadiq, S., Yan, Y., Tian, H., Tao, Y., Reyes, M. P., & Iyengar, S. (2019). A survey on deep learning: Algorithms, techniques, and applications. ACM Computing Surveys (CSUR), 51(5), 92.

Pucher, J., Dill, J., & Handy, S. (2010). Infrastructure, programs, and policies to increase bicycling: An international review. Preventive Medicine, 50, S106–S125.

Sadaei, H. J., e Silva, P. C., de, L., Guimarães, F. G., & Lee, M. H. (2019). Short-term load forecasting by using a combined method of convolutional neural networks and fuzzy time series. Energy, *175*, 365–377.

Şenyurt, G., & Subaşı, A. (2015). Effects of technical market indicators on stock market index direction forecasting. Modeling of Artificial Intelligence, 6(2), 137–149.

Shen, X., Zhou, C., Li, G., Fu, X., & Lie, T. (2018). Overview of wind parameters sensing methods and framework of a novel MCSPV recombination sensing method for wind turbines. Energies, 11(7), 1747.

Sideratos, G., & Hatziargyriou, N. D. (2007). An advanced statistical method for wind power forecasting. IEEE Transactions on Power Systems, 22(1), 258–265.

Sikiric, G., Avdakovic, S., & Subasi, A. (2013). Comparison of machine learning methods for electricity demand forecasting in Bosnia and Herzegovina. Southeast Europe Journal of Soft Computing, 2(2).

Song, H., Li, G., & Cao, Z. (2018). Tourism and economic globalization: An emerging research agenda. Journal of Travel Research, 57(8), 999–1011.

Song, H., Qiu, R. T., & Park, J. (2019). A review of research on tourism demand forecasting. Annals of Tourism Research, 75, 338–362.

Ülke, V., Sahin, A., & Subasi, A. (2018). A comparison of time series and machine learning models for inflation forecasting: Empirical evidence from the USA. Neural Computing and Applications, 30(5), 1519–1527.

Zhong, X., & Enke, D. (2017). A comprehensive cluster and classification mining procedure for daily stock market return forecasting. Neurocomputing, 267, 152–168.

CHAPTER

# 7

# Clustering examples

## 7.1 Introduction

Clustering is one of the most commonly used experimental data analysis methods. Throughout all disciplines, from social sciences to biology to computer science, by defining meaningful categories among data points people try to obtain an initial sense of their results. For instance, retailers cluster customers, on the basis of their customer profiles, for the purpose of targeted marketing; computational biologists cluster genes on the basis of similarities in their expression in diverse researches; and astronomers cluster stars on the basis of their distinct closeness. The first question to be answered is, of course, what is clustering? Clustering is the process of intuitively grouping a collection of objects in such a way that identical objects end up in the same category and divide dissimilar objects into different groups. This definition is obviously rather imprecise and perhaps vague. Yet, it is not easy to find a more accurate definition. There are several reasons for this. One fundamental problem is that in many cases the two objectives stated in the previous statement contradict one another. Mathematically speaking, similarity (or proximity) is not a transitive relationship, whereas cluster sharing is a relationship of equivalence, and particularly a transitive relationship. More specifically, there can be a long series of objects, $x_1, \ldots, x_m$, where each $x_i$ is very similar to its two neighbors, $x_{i-1}$ and $x_{i+1}$, but $x_1$ and $x_m$ are very dissimilar. If we want to make sure that two elements share the same cluster if they are identical, then we have to place all the sequence elements in the same cluster. In that case, however, we end up sharing a cluster with dissimilar elements ($x_1$ and $x_m$) by violating the second criterion. A clustering algorithm, which highlights not separating nearby points, clusters this input by dividing it horizontally on both lines. On the other hand, a clustering approach, which stresses that distant points do not share the same cluster, clusters the same input by dividing it vertically (Shalev-Shwartz & Ben-David, 2014).

Another fundamental problem for clustering is the lack of "ground truth," which is a common problem with unsupervised learning. We've been dealing primarily with supervised learning in the book so far (e.g., the issue of learning a classifier from labeled data on training). The purpose of supervised learning is simple—we want to train a classifier to predict as accurately as possible the labels of future examples. In addition, by estimating the empirical loss, a supervised learner can estimate the success or risk of the hypotheses utilizing the labeled training data. Clustering, on the other hand, is an unsupervised learning problem;

**Practical Machine Learning for Data Analysis Using Python. http://dx.doi.org/10.1016/B978-0-12-821379-7.00007-2**

namely, we are not trying to predict any labels. Rather we want some practical way to organize the data. Hence there is no straightforward clustering performance assessment method. In addition, it is not clear what the "correct" clustering for that data is or how to assess a proposed clustering, even on the basis of full knowledge of the underlying data distribution (Shalev-Shwartz & Ben-David, 2014).

## 7.2 Clustering

Clustering is a mechanism in which related objects are bunched together. There are two types of inputs we can use. In similarity-based clustering, the input to the algorithm is a matrix of dissimilarity or distance matrix D. The input to the algorithm in feature-based clustering is a matrix or design matrix X feature matrix of N x D. Similarity-based clustering has the advantage of allowing domain-specific similarity or kernel functions to be conveniently included. The benefit of feature-based clustering is that it applies to "raw" data, which is potentially noisy. Besides the two input types, there are two potential output types: **flat clustering**, also called **partition clustering**, where we divide the objects into disjoint sets, and **hierarchical clustering**, where a nested partition tree is formed (Murphy, 2012).

A matrix of dissimilarity D is a matrix in which $d_{i,i} = 0$ and $d_{i,j} \geq 0$ is a "distance" measure between i and j. In the strict sense, subjectively determined dissimilarities are seldom distances, as the inequality of the triangle, $d_{i,j} \leq d_{i,k} + d_{j,k}$, does not often hold. Some algorithms claim that D is a true matrix of distance, but others do not. If we have a similarity matrix S, by applying any monotonically decreasing function, for example, $D = \max(S) - S$, we can convert it to a dissimilarity matrix. The most common way of describing object dissimilarity is in terms of their attributes' dissimilarity. The square (Euclidean) distance, city block distance, correlation coefficient, and hamming distance are some common attribute dissimilarity functions (Murphy, 2012).

For the k-means clustering algorithm in which k initial points are selected to represent the initial cluster centers, all data points are allocated to the closest one, the mean value of the points in each cluster is calculated to form its current cluster core, and replication continues until there are no cluster changes. This procedure only works when you know the number of clusters beforehand, and this section begins by describing what you can do if not. First, we look at strategies for "agglomeration" to construct a hierarchical clustering structure—that is, beginning with individual instances and merging them successively into clusters. So, we look at a system that incrementally works; that is, any new instance is processed as it occurs. Finally, we are investigating a statistical method of clustering based on a mixture model with various distributions of probability, one for each cluster. It does not separate instances into disjoint clusters, as does k-means, but rather assigns instances probabilistically to classes (Witten, Frank, Hall, & Pal, 2016).

Clustering is one of human beings' most rudimentary mental practices, used to accommodate the enormous amount of information we obtain each day. It would be difficult to handle each piece of information as a single entity. Therefore, human beings appear to categorize things into clusters (i.e., objects, individuals, events). The specific attributes of the entities it comprises are then characterized by each cluster. We must presume, as in the case of supervised learning, that all patterns are defined in terms of features that form one-dimensional feature vectors. The basic steps to be taken by an expert to establish a clustering function are as follows:

- ***Feature selection*:** Features should be chosen properly in order to encode as much information as possible about the value function. Once again, a major goal is parsimony and thus minimal duplication of knowledge among the features. As in the supervised classification, preprocessing of features may be needed in subsequent stages before they are used.
- ***Proximity measure*:** This measure defines how the two feature vectors are similar or dissimilar. It is necessary to ensure that all selected characteristics contribute equally to the proximity measure calculation and there are no features that dominate others. This should be taken care of during preprocessing.
- ***Clustering criterion*:** This criterion relies on the definition given to the term by the expert on the basis of the form of clusters of the dataset. The criterion of clustering can be expressed through a cost function or some other rules.
- ***Clustering algorithms*:** This phase refers to the selection of a particular algorithmic scheme that unravels the clustering structure of the data set, having adopted a proximity measure and a clustering criterion.
- ***Validation of the results*:** Once the results have been obtained from the clustering algorithm, we will check their correctness. Usually this is done using suitable measures.
- ***Interpretation of the results*:** In many cases, to draw the correct conclusions, the application expert should combine the clustering findings with other experimental evidence and interpretation.

A phase known as the clustering tendency should be involved in a number of cases. It includes various tests determining whether or not there is a clustering pattern in the data available. For instance, the dataset may be entirely random in nature, so it would be pointless to try to unravel clusters. Different feature choices, proximity measures, clustering criteria, and clustering algorithms might result in completely different clustering results (Theodoridis, Pikrakis, Koutroumbas, & Cavouras, 2010).

### 7.2.1 Evaluating the output of clustering methods

The most difficult and frustrating aspect of cluster analysis is the validation of clustering structures. Without a strong effort to do so, cluster analysis would remain a black art accessible only to those true believers with great experience and confidence. Clustering is an unsupervised learning technique, so it is difficult to assess the output quality of any given technique. If we use probabilistic models, we can always evaluate a test set's likelihood, but this has two drawbacks: firstly, it does not evaluate any clustering found by the model directly, and secondly, it does not apply to nonprobabilistic methods. And now we are discussing certain non-probability-based success indicators. Conceptually, the aim of clustering is to assign similar points to the same cluster and to ensure that dissimilar points are present in different clusters. Such quantities can be measured in several forms. Such internal requirements can, however, be of limited benefit. An alternative is to use any external data type to validate the system. For instance, if we have labels for each object then we can compare the clustering with the labels using different metrics like silhouette (Murphy, 2012).

### 7.2.2 Applications of cluster analysis

In a number of applications, clustering is a major tool. The application areas in which clustering is useful can be summarized as follows (Theodoridis et al., 2010):

- *Data reduction:* The amount of data available, N, is often very high in several instances, and as a result, its processing becomes very challenging. In order to organize the data into a number of "important" clusters and treat each cluster as a single entity, cluster analysis can be utilized. For instance, a representative for each cluster is specified in data transmission. Instead of transmitting the data samples, we then transmit a code number that corresponds to the cluster representative where each specific sample is located. Hence the data compression is accomplished.
- *Hypothesis generation*: In this case, we apply cluster analysis to a dataset to conclude some hypotheses regarding the nature of the data. To propose hypotheses, clustering is used here as a tool. It is then important to test these hypotheses using other datasets.
- *Hypothesis testing*: Cluster analysis is used to test the validity of a given hypothesis in this sense.
- *Prediction based on groups*: In this case, the cluster analysis is applied to the existing dataset and the subsequent clusters are identified based on the characteristics of the patterns through which they are formed. In the sequel, if we are given an ambiguous pattern, we can evaluate the cluster to which it is more likely to belong and define it on the basis of the respective cluster category.

### 7.2.3 Number of possible clustering

Different proximity metrics give a different description of similar and dissimilar terms related to the types of clusters that must be identified by our clustering process. As it is mentioned, various combinations of a proximity measure and a clustering scheme can result in different outcomes to be interpreted by the expert. The best way to designate the feature vectors $x_i$, $i = 1, \ldots, N$, of a set $X$ to clusters would be to describe all possible partitions and to choose the most sensible one according to a previously chosen criterion. But even for moderate values of N, this is not possible (Theodoridis et al., 2010).

### 7.2.4 Types of clustering algorithms

Clustering algorithms can be seen as schemes that provide sensitive clustering by considering only a small portion of the set that comprises all possible X partitions. The outcome depends on the algorithm and criteria used. A clustering algorithm is therefore a learning process that attempts to identify the specific features of the clusters that underlie the dataset. It is possible to divide clustering algorithms into the following major categories:

- ***Sequential algorithms:*** Such algorithms create a single cluster. They are quite straightforward and fast. In most of them, all the feature vectors are given to the algorithm once or a few times. Normally the final result depends on the order the vectors are given to the algorithm. Depending on the distance metric used, these techniques tend to generate compact, hyperspherically, or hyperellipsoidally shaped clusters.

- ***Hierarchical clustering algorithms:*** Such methods will also be categorized into two groups.
  - *Agglomerative algorithms:* Such algorithms in each stage generate a clustering sequence of decreasing number of clusters. The clustering generated by merging two clusters into one at each stage results from the previous one. Single and full connection algorithms are the key representatives of the agglomerative algorithms. Such algorithms are ideal for the recovery of big clusters and compact clusters.
  - *Divisive algorithms:* These algorithms work in the opposite direction; that is, at each stage they generate a clustering sequence of m. The clustering is created by dividing a single cluster into two results from the previous one at each stage.
- ***Clustering algorithms based on cost function optimization:*** This group includes algorithms in which a cost function, J, quantifies as "sensitive" to determine a clustering. The number of m clusters is usually kept unchanged. Most of these algorithms use differential calculus principles when attempting to optimize J. They end when a local optimum of J is decided. Also, algorithms of this category are called iterative function optimization techniques. The following subcategories are included in this category:
  - *Hard or crisp clustering algorithms* are when a vector belongs to a particular cluster exclusively. The assignment of the vectors to individual clusters is done optimally on the basis of the accepted criterion of optimality. The Isodata or Lloyd algorithm is the most popular algorithm in this group.
  - *Probabilistic clustering algorithms* are a special type of hard clustering algorithms that adopt Bayesian classification arguments and each vector x is assigned to the cluster $C_i$ for which $P(C_i \mid x)$ (i.e., the a posteriori probability) is maximum. Such probabilities are calculated through an optimization process that is properly defined.
  - *Fuzzy clustering algorithms* are when a vector belongs up to a certain degree to a particular cluster.
  - *Possibilistic clustering algorithms* are when we test the probability of a vector x being a part of a cluster $C_i$.
  - *Boundary detection algorithms* are when, instead of identifying the clusters themselves by the feature vectors, they iteratively update the boundaries of the regions where clusters are located. Although these algorithms evolve from a theory of cost function optimization, they are different from the algorithms described previously (Theodoridis et al., 2010).

Apart from these clustering algorithms, branch and bound clustering algorithms, genetic clustering algorithms, stochastic relaxation methods, valley-seeking clustering algorithms, competitive learning algorithms, morphological transformation technique–based algorithms, density-based algorithms, subspace clustering algorithms, and kernel-based methods are also types of clustering algorithms (Theodoridis et al., 2010).

## 7.3 The k-means clustering algorithm

K-means clustering begins with the description of a cost function over a parameterized set of possible clustering, and the objective of the clustering algorithm is to find a minimum cost partitioning (clustering). The clustering function is turned into an optimization problem under this model. The objective function is a function ranging from pairs of an input, (X, d), and a suggested clustering solution $C = (C_1, \ldots, C_k)$ to positive real numbers. The target of a clustering algorithm is described as finding, for a given input (X, d), a clustering C so that G((X, d),C) is minimized, given such an objective function that is denoted by G. To achieve this goal, a suitable search algorithm must be utilized. K-means clustering is therefore a specific common approximation algorithm rather than the cost function or the corresponding exact solution to the minimization problem. Most common objective functions include as a parameter the number of clusters, k. In practice, it is often up to the clustering algorithm user to choose the parameter k that is best suited to the clustering problem. Some of the most common objective functions are defined in the following. The k-means objective function is one of the most common objectives in clustering. The objective function k-means measures the square distance from each point in X to its cluster's centroid. For instance, in digital communication tasks, where X members can be interpreted as a set of signals to be transmitted, the k-means objective function is important. In practical clustering applications, the k-means objective function is quite common. But it turns out that it is always computationally infeasible to find the optimal solution for k-means. Instead, a simple iterative algorithm is often used, so the term k-means clustering in many cases refers to the outcome of this algorithm rather than the clustering that minimizes the objective cost of k-means (Shalev-Shwartz & Ben-David, 2014).

## Example 7.1

The following Python code utilizes k-means clustering to find the center of the clusters of breast cancer data by using the scikit-learn library APIs. In this example, the breast cancer dataset that exists in sklearn.datasets is utilized. Scatter plot is presented to show the effectiveness of the algorithm. The cluster centers are plotted in as scatter plot. Note that this example is adapted from scikit-learn.

```
# ======================================================================
# K-means clustering example
# ======================================================================
from sklearn import datasets
import matplotlib.pyplot as plt
import numpy as np
from sklearn.cluster import KMeans
#%%
# ######################################################################
# Import some data to play with
Breast_Cancer = datasets.load_breast_cancer()
X = Breast_Cancer.data
y = Breast_Cancer.target

# Plot the original data points
plt.scatter(X[:, 0], X[:, 1], c = y, cmap = plt.cm.Set1,
        edgecolor = 'k')
plt.xlabel('Attribute I')
plt.ylabel('Attribute II')
```

```
plt.title('Original data Scatter')
plt.xticks(())
plt.yticks(())
#%%
" " "

sklearn.cluster.KMeans(n_clusters = 8, init = 'k-means + +', n_
init = 10, max_iter = 300, tol = 0.0001,
precompute_distances = 'auto', verbose = 0, random_state = None,
copy_x = True, n_jobs = None,
algorithm = 'auto')
" " "
#Find Cluster Centers
kmeans = KMeans(n_clusters = 2)
kmeans.fit(X)
y_kmeans = kmeans.predict(X)

#Plot the Cluster Centers
plt.scatter(X[:, 0], X[:, 1], c = y_kmeans, s = 50, cmap = 'viridis')
centers = kmeans.cluster_centers_
plt.scatter(centers[:, 0], centers[:, 1], c = 'black', s = 200,
alpha = 0.5);
plt.xlabel('Attribute I')
plt.ylabel('Attribute II')
plt.title('Cluster Centers')
plt.xticks(())
plt.yticks(())
```

## 7.4 The k-medoids clustering algorithm

Each cluster is represented by the mean of its vectors in the k-means algorithm, but the cluster is represented by a vector selected among the elements of X in the k-medoids methods, and we will refer to it as the medoid. In addition to their medoid, each cluster includes all vectors in X that (1) are not employed as medoids in other clusters and (2) are closer to their medoid than those representing the other clusters. There are two benefits over the k-means algorithm to represent clusters using medoids. First, it can be utilized for datasets originating from either continuous or discrete domains, while k-means is only suitable for continuous domains since the mean of a subset of data vectors is not essentially a point lying in the domain for a discrete domain context. Second, k-medoids algorithms appear to be less sensitive than k-means algorithms to outliers. It should be remembered, however, that a cluster's mean has a strong geometric and statistical meaning that is not necessarily true with medoids. Moreover, the algorithms for the calculation of the best set of medoids needs more computational power compared to the k-means algorithm. PAM (partitioning around medoids), CLARA (clustering large applications), and CLARANS (clustering large applications based on randomized search) are the well-known k-medoids algorithms. Remember that the last two algorithms are inspired from the PAM but are more effective than PAM in handling large datasets (Theodoridis et al., 2010).

## Example 7.2

The following Python code utilizes k-medoids clustering to find the center of the clusters of synthetic data and Mall_Customers data (https://www.kaggle.com/akram24/mall-customers) by using the KMedoids clustering function. Scatter plot is presented to show the effectiveness of the algorithm. The cluster centers are plotted in as scatter plot.

```
# ======================================================================
# K-medoids clustering example
# ======================================================================
from k_medoids import KMedoids
import numpy as np
import matplotlib.pyplot as plt
#Define a distance utility function
def example_distance_func(data1, data2):
   "'example distance function"'
   return np.sqrt(np.sum((data1 - data2)**2))
#%%
# K-Medoids Clustering using synthetic data with 3 clusters
from sklearn.datasets import make_blobs
# ######################################################################
# Generate sample data
np.random.seed(0)
batch_size = 45
centers = [[1, 1], [-1, -1], [1, -1]]
n_clusters = len(centers)
X, labels_true = make_blobs(n_samples = 300, centers = centers, cluster_
std = 0.7)

model = KMedoids(n_clusters = n_clusters, dist_func = example_distance_
func)
model.fit(X, plotit = True, verbose = True)
plt.show()
#%%
# K-Medoids clustering using Mall_Customers data
import pandas as pd
#loading the dataset
# Importing the Mall_Customers dataset by pandas
dataset = pd.read_csv('Mall_Customers.csv')
X = dataset.iloc[:, [2,3,4]].values
```

```
model = KMedoids(n_clusters = 5, dist_func = example_distance_func)
model.fit(X, plotit = True, verbose = True)
plt.show()
```

## 7.5 Hierarchical clustering

Hierarchical clustering algorithms have different philosophies. In particular, they generate a hierarchy of clustering instead of producing a single clustering. In the social sciences and biological taxonomy, this sort of algorithm is usually found. Hierarchical clustering algorithms build a hierarchy of nested clustering. More precisely, these algorithms include N steps, as many as the number of data vectors. A new clustering on the basis of the clustering generated at the previous step t-1 is obtained at each step t (Theodoridis et al., 2010). Two main approaches exist in hierarchical clustering: bottom-up, or agglomerative, clustering and top-down, or divisive, clustering. These methods take a matrix of dissimilarity between the objects as their input. At each step, the most similar groups are combined in the bottom-up method. Groups are divided in the top-down approach using different criteria. Remember that both agglomerative and divisive clustering are merely heuristics that do not optimize any well-defined objective function. Therefore, in any formal sense, it is difficult to assess the quality of the clustering they create. In fact, they will always generate a clustering of the input data, even if the data does not have any structure (e.g., random noise) (Murphy, 2012).

### 7.5.1 Agglomerative clustering algorithm

Agglomerative clustering begins with N groups, each containing initially one entity, and then the two most similar groups merge at each stage until there is a single group containing all the data. A typical heuristic for large N is to run k-means first and then apply hierarchical clustering to the cluster centers estimated. A binary tree called a dendrogram will represent the merging process. The initial groups (objects) are on the leaves (at the bottom of the figure), and we join them in the tree each time when two groups are merged. The height of the divisions is the dissimilarity between the groups being joined. The tree root (which is at the top) is a category with all the data. We produce a clustering of a given size if we cut the tree at any given height. In addition, there are three variants of agglomerative clustering, depending on how we define the dissimilarity between object categories (Murphy, 2012).

Alternatively, we can assume that if two vectors at level t of the hierarchy come together in a single cluster, they will remain in the same cluster for all subsequent clusters. This is another way to view the nesting property. A nesting property drawback is that there is no way to recover from a "poor" clustering, which might have arisen at an earlier hierarchy level. A threshold dendrogram, or simply a dendrogram, is an efficient way of describing the sequence of clusters generated by an agglomerative algorithm. Each phase of the general agglomerative scheme (GAS) is related to a dendrogram stage. Cutting the dendrogram may result in a clustering at a specific level. A dendrogram of proximity is a dendrogram that takes into account the proximity level in which two clusters are first merged. Once a measure of dissimilarity (similarity) is employed, the proximity dendrogram is termed a dissimilarity

(similarity) dendrogram. This method can be utilized at any stage as an indicator of natural or forced cluster formation. Similarly, a suitable level for cutting the dendrogram related to the resulting hierarchy must be calculated (Theodoridis et al., 2010).

## Example 7.3

The following Python code utilizes agglomerative clustering to cluster the customers as Careful, Standard, Target, Careless, and Sensible using Mall_Customers data (https://www.kaggle.com/akram24/mall-customers) and standard scikit-learn library APIs. Customers' dendrogram is plotted against the Euclidean distance. In addition, the clusters are plotted in a scatter plot to show five different customer groups. Note that this example is adapted from the web page (https://www.kdnuggets.com/2019/09/hierarchical-clustering.html).

```
# =====================================================================
# Agglomerative clustering example
# =====================================================================
import numpy as np
import matplotlib.pyplot as plt
import pandas as pd
dataset = pd.read_csv('Mall_Customers.csv')
#%%
" " "Out of all the features, CustomerID and Genre are irrelevant fields
and can be dropped and create a matrix of independent variables by select
only Age and Annual Income." " "
X = dataset.iloc[:, [3, 4]].values
import scipy.cluster.hierarchy as sch
dendrogrm = sch.dendrogram(sch.linkage(X, method = 'ward'))
plt.title('Dendrogram')
plt.xlabel('Customers')
plt.ylabel('Euclidean distance')
plt.show()

#%%
from sklearn.cluster import AgglomerativeClustering
hc = AgglomerativeClustering(n_clusters = 5, affinity = 'euclidean',
linkage = 'ward')
y_hc = hc.fit_predict(X)
# Visualising the clusters
plt.scatter(X[y_hc == 0, 0], X[y_hc == 0, 1], s = 50, c = 'red', label =
'Careful')
plt.scatter(X[y_hc == 1, 0], X[y_hc == 1, 1], s = 50, c = 'blue', label =
'Standard')
plt.scatter(X[y_hc == 2, 0], X[y_hc == 2, 1], s = 50, c = 'green', label =
'Target')
plt.scatter(X[y_hc == 3, 0], X[y_hc == 3, 1], s = 50, c = 'cyan', label
= 'Careless')
```

```
plt.scatter(X[y_hc == 4, 0], X[y_hc == 4, 1], s = 50, c = 'magenta',
label = 'Sensible')
plt.title('Clusters of customers')
plt.xlabel('Annual Income (k$)')
plt.ylabel('Spending Score (1-100)')
plt.legend()
plt.show()
```

## Example 7.4

The following Python code utilizes agglomerative clustering to group the customers using Mall_Customers data (https://www.kaggle.com/akram24/mall-customers) and standard scikit-learn library APIs. Scatter plot is presented to show the effectiveness of the algorithm. In this example, we present the effect of imposing a connectivity graph to capture local structure in the customer data. It is possible to see two implications of implementing a connectivity. First, clustering is much quicker with a connectivity matrix. Second, a single, average, and complete linkage is unstable when using a connectivity matrix and tends to create a few clusters that grow very fast. Nonetheless, average and complete linkage tackle this filtration behavior by including all the distances between two clusters when combining them (while only the shortest distance among clusters is considered to exaggerate the behavior). The connectivity graph removes this process for average and total connection, making it look like the more fragile single connection. Having a very small number of neighbors in the graph introduces a geometry similar to that of a single connection that is well-known for having this instability of percolation. This is presented in this example. Note that this example is adapted from scikit-learn.

```
# Authors: Gael Varoquaux, Nelle Varoquaux
# License: BSD 3 clause
import time
import matplotlib.pyplot as plt
import numpy as np

from sklearn.cluster import AgglomerativeClustering
from sklearn.neighbors import kneighbors_graph
import pandas as pd
#2 Importing the Mall_Customers dataset by pandas
dataset = pd.read_csv('Mall_Customers.csv')
X = dataset.iloc[:, [3,4]].values

# Create a graph capturing local connectivity. Larger number of neighbors
# will give more homogeneous clusters to the cost of computation
# time. A very large number of neighbors gives more evenly distributed
```

```
# cluster sizes, but may not impose the local manifold structure of
# the data
knn_graph = kneighbors_graph(X, 30, include_self = False)

for connectivity in (None, knn_graph):
      for n_clusters in (4, 5, 6):
      plt.figure(figsize = (10, 4))
      for index, linkage in enumerate(('average',
      'complete',
      'ward',
      'single')):
      plt.subplot(1, 4, index + 1)
      model = AgglomerativeClustering(linkage = linkage,
      connectivity = connectivity,
      n_clusters = n_clusters)
      t0 = time.time()
      model.fit(X)
      elapsed_time = time.time() - t0
      plt.scatter(X[:, 0], X[:, 1], c = model.labels_,
      cmap = plt.cm.nipy_spectral)
      plt.title('linkage = %s\n(time %.2fs)' % (linkage, elapsed_time),
      fontdict = dict(verticalalignment = 'top'))
      plt.axis('equal')
      plt.axis('off')
      plt.subplots_adjust(bottom = 0, top = .89, wspace = 0,
      left = 0, right = 1)
      plt.suptitle('n_cluster = %i, connectivity = %r' %
      (n_clusters, connectivity is not None), size = 17)
plt.show()
```

### 7.5.2 Divisive clustering algorithm

The divisive algorithms adopt the counter-strategy of agglomerative schemes. There is a single set in the first cluster, X. We are looking for the best possible partitioning of X into two clusters in the first step. The straightforward approach is to consider all possible X partitions in two sets and, according to a predetermined criterion, to choose the maximum. This process is then extended to each of the two sets created in the preceding stage iteratively. The final clustering includes a number of N clusters, each with a single X vector. Various choices of g give rise to various algorithms. One can easily observe that even for moderate values of N, this divisive scheme is computationally very demanding. Compared with the agglomerative system, this is its main drawback. Therefore some further computational simplifications are needed if these schemes are to be of any practical use. One option is to make choices and not to look for all possible cluster partitions. This can be accomplished by ruling out several partitions under a preset criterion as not reasonable. The cluster division is based on all the features (coordinates) of the feature vectors in the previous algorithm. These type of algorithms are also known as polythetic algorithms. On the other hand, there are divisive algorithms at each stage that achieve a cluster division based on a single feature. These are the algorithms known as monothetic (Theodoridis et al., 2010).

Divisive clustering begins with all the data in a single cluster and then, in a top-down manner, splits each cluster into two daughter clusters. Since there are $2^{N-1}-1$ ways to divide a group of $N$ items into two groups, it is hard to compute the optimal split, hence several heuristics are utilized. One approach is to pick the largest diameter cluster and divide it into two using the k-means or k-medoids algorithm with K = 2. This is known as the **bisecting k-means** algorithm (Steinbach, Karypis, & Kumar, 2000). We can repeat this until we have any number of clusters desired. This can be utilized as an alternative to standard k-means, but a hierarchical clustering is also induced. Another strategy is to construct from the dissimilarity graph a minimum spanning tree and then make new clusters by breaking the connection related to the largest dissimilarity. Divisive clustering is less common than clustering in agglomerations, but it has two benefits. First, it can be quicker because it only takes O(N) time if we break for a constant number of levels. Secondly, the splitting decisions are made in view of all the results, while the bottom-up methods make myopic merge decisions (Murphy, 2012).

## Example 7.5

The following Python code utilizes divisive clustering to plot a dendrogram of amino acid sequence of human genes. In this example, amino acid sequence of human genes is utilized. The dendrogram plot presents the effectiveness of the algorithm. Note that this example is adapted from github (https://github.com/ronak-07/Divisive-Hierarchical-Clustering). A phylogenetic tree or evolutionary tree is a branching diagram or "tree" displaying the implied evolutionary relations between different biological species based upon similarities and differences in their physical or genetic characteristics. The goal of this example is to build the phylogenetic tree based on DNA/protein sequences of species given in the dataset employing divisive (top-down) hierarchical clustering.

```
# ======================================================================
# Divisive clustering
# ======================================================================
import numpy as np
import scipy
import matplotlib.pyplot as plt
from scipy.cluster import hierarchy
global g
import time
# ======================================================================
# Define utility functions
# ======================================================================
def subtract(indices,splinter):
```

```
l3 = [x for x in indices if x not in splinter]
return l3

def divisive(a,indices,splinter,sub):
if(len(indices) = =1):
return
avg = []
flag = 0
for i in indices:
if(i not in splinter):
sum = 0
for j in indices:
if(j not in splinter):
sum = sum + a[i][j]
if((len(indices)-len(splinter)-1) = =0):
avg.append(sum)
else:
avg.append(sum/(len(indices)-len(splinter)-1))
if(splinter):
k = 0
for i in sub:
total = 0
for j in splinter:
total = total + a[i][j]
avg[k] = avg[k] - (total/(len(splinter)))
k + = 1
positive = []
for i in range(0,len(avg)):
if(avg[i] > 0):
positive.append(avg[i])
flag = 1
if(flag = =1):
splinter.append(sub[avg.index(max(positive))])
sub.remove(sub[avg.index(max(positive))])
divisive(a,indices,splinter,sub)
else:
splinter.append(indices[avg.index(max(avg))])
sub[:] = subtract(indices,splinter)
divisive(a,indices,splinter,sub)

def original_subset(indices):
sp = np.zeros(shape = (len(indices),len(indices)))
for i in range(0,len(indices)):
```

```
for j in range(0,len(indices)):
sp[i][j] = a[indices[i]][indices[j]]
return sp

def original_max(x):
new = original_subset(x)
return new.max()

def diameter(l):
return original_max(l)

def recursive(a,indices,u,v,clusters,g):
clus_s.append(len(indices))
d.append(diameter(indices))
parents[g] = indices
g- = 1
divisive(a,indices,u,v)
clusters.append(u)
clusters.append(v)
new = []
for i in range(len(clusters)):
new.append(clusters[i])
final.append(new)
x = []
y = []
store_list = []
max = -1
f = 0
for list in clusters:
if(diameter(list) > max):
if(len(list)! = 1):
f = 1
max = diameter(list)
store_list = (list)
if(f = =0):
return
else:
clusters.remove(store_list)
recursive(a,store_list,x,y,clusters,g)

def augmented_dendrogram(*args, **kwargs):
data = scipy.cluster.hierarchy.dendrogram(*args, **kwargs)
if not kwargs.get('no_plot', False):
```

```
for i, d in zip(data['icoord'], data['dcoord']):
x = 0.5 * sum(i[1:3])
y = d[1]
plt.plot(x, y, 'ro')
plt.annotate("%.3g" % y, (x, y), xytext = (0,12),textcoords = 'offset
points',va = 'top', ha = 'center')
return data

# ========================================================================
# Main program
# ========================================================================
a = np.load('distance_matrix.npy')
size = len(a)
g = (size-1)*2
parents = {}
final = []
clusters = []
indices = []
clus_s = []
d = []
Z = np.zeros(shape = (size-1,4))
p = []
q = []
ans = []
for i in range(0,len(a)):
indices.append(i)

for i in range(0,size):
list = []
list.append(i)
parents[i] = list

start = time.time()
recursive(a,indices,p,q,clusters,g)
print("Clustering done\t" + str(time.time()-start))
for i in range(0,len(d)):
Z[size-i-2][2] = d[i]
Z[size-i-2][3] = clus_s[i]

for i in range(len(final)-1,0,-1):
for j in range(0,len(final[i-1])):
if final[i-1][j] not in final[i]:

ans.append(final[i-1][j])
ans.append(indices)
```

```
for i in range(0,len(ans)):
if(len(ans[i]) < = 2):
Z[i][0] = ans[i][0]
Z[i][1] = ans[i][1]
else:
s = 0
add = []
common = []
for j in range(len(ans)-1,-1,-1):
if(set(ans[j]) < set(ans[i])):
common = ans[j]
break;
x = (subtract(ans[i],common))
for key in parents.keys():
if(parents[key] = =common):
Z[i][0] = key
break;
for key in parents.keys():
if(set(parents[key]) = =set(x)):
Z[i][1] = key
s = 1
break;
if(s = =0):
print(Z[i][0],Z[i][1],x)
names = [i for i in range(0,size)]
#%%
# ==============================================================================
# Plot dendrogram of divisive clustering
# ==============================================================================
plt.figure(figsize = (15, 15))
plt.title('Hierarchical Clustering Dendrogram (Divisive)')
plt.xlabel('Sequence No.')
plt.ylabel('Distance')
augmented_dendrogram(Z,labels = names,show_leaf_
counts = True,p = 25,truncate_mode = 'lastp')
plt.show()
```

## 7.6 The fuzzy c-means clustering algorithm

One of the challenges related to the probabilistic algorithms is the presence of the pdfs, for which a suitable model must be assumed. However, when the clusters are not compact but shell-shaped, it is not easy to handle instances. Fuzzy clustering algorithms are a family of clustering algorithms that release themselves from such constraints. Over the past three decades, these methods have been the focus of intensive research. The main point differentiating the two methods is that a vector belongs to more than one cluster simultaneously in the fuzzy schemes, whereas each vector belongs exclusively to one cluster in the probabilistic schemes. The number of clusters and their shape is presumed to be known a priori. The cluster shape is defined by the set of parameters adopted. The majority of the well-known fuzzy clustering algorithms are developed by minimizing a cost function (Theodoridis et al., 2010).

The extensively studied and implemented fuzzy c-means (FCM) clustering algorithm requires a priori knowledge of the number of clusters. If FCM anticipates a desired number of clusters, and if it is possible to guess the positions for each cluster center, then the rules of output strongly depend on the selection of initial values. The FCM algorithm generates an appropriate cluster pattern to minimize by iteration an objective function that is based on cluster locations. It is also possible to automatically determine the number and initial position of cluster centers through search techniques available in the mountain clustering process. By measuring a search measure called the mountain function at each grid point, this approach considers each distinct grid point as a possible cluster core. It is a subtractive method of clustering with enhanced computational effort, where data points are viewed as candidates for cluster centers rather than grid points. The estimate is strictly proportional to the number of data points and irrespective of the dimension of the problem by applying this approach. In this process, a high-potential data point that is a function of distance measurement is known as a cluster center, and data points close to new cluster centers are penalized to monitor the emergence of new cluster centers. Occasionally, a gradual membership of both clusters can be considered to be the points between cluster centers. This is compensated, of course, by distorting the meanings of "low" and "high." The fuzzified c-means algorithm enables each data point to belong to a cluster to a degree defined by a membership grade, thereby allowing each point to belong to several clusters. The fuzzy c-means algorithm partitions a set of K data points identified as m-dimensional vectors into c fuzzy clusters and finds a cluster center in each cluster to minimize an objective function. Fuzzy c-means is different from hard c-means, mostly as it uses fuzzy partitioning, where a point can belong to numerous clusters with membership degrees. The membership matrix M is allowed to have elements in the range [0, 1] to satisfy the fuzzy partitioning. Nonetheless, to maintain the properties of the M matrix, the total membership of all clusters of a point must always be equal to unity (Sumathi & Paneerselvam, 2010).

## Example 7.6

The following Python code utilizes fuzzy c-means clustering algorithm to find the center of the clusters of Iris dataset. In this example, the Iris dataset that exists in sklearn.datasets is utilized. Scatter plot is presented to show the effectiveness of the algorithm. The cluster centers are plotted in as scatter plot. Note that this example is adapted from the web page (https://github.com/omadson/fuzzy-c-means). In order to call you should use "pip install fuzzy-c-means" or download the library from the web page (https://pypi.org/project/fuzzy-c-means/).

```
# ============================================================
# Fuzzy c-means clustering example
# ============================================================
```

```
#pip install fuzzy-c-means
from fcmeans import FCM
from sklearn.datasets import make_blobs
from matplotlib import pyplot as plt
from seaborn import scatterplot as scatter
import numpy as np
import pandas as pd
from sklearn import datasets
from sklearn.datasets import load_iris
iris = load_iris()
X = iris['data']
y = iris['target']
# Plot the original data points
plt.scatter(X[y == 0, 0], X[y == 0, 1], s = 80, c = 'orange',
label = 'Iris-setosa')
plt.scatter(X[y == 1, 0], X[y == 1, 1], s = 80, c = 'yellow',
label = 'Iris-versicolour')
plt.scatter(X[y == 2, 0], X[y == 2, 1], s = 80, c = 'green',
label = 'Iris-virginica')
plt.xlabel('Sepal length')
plt.ylabel('Sepal width')
plt.title('Original data points')
plt.legend()
#%%
# fit the fuzzy-c-means
fcm = FCM(n_clusters = 3)
fcm.fit(X)
# outputs
fcm_centers = fcm.centers
fcm_labels = fcm.u.argmax(axis = 1)
# plot result
f, axes = plt.subplots(1, 2, figsize = (11,5))
scatter(X[:,0], X[:,1], ax = axes[0])
scatter(X[:,0], X[:,1], ax = axes[1], hue = fcm_labels)
scatter(fcm_centers[:,0], fcm_centers[:,1],
ax = axes[1],marker = "s",s = 200)
plt.show()
```

## 7.7 Density-based clustering algorithms

Clusters are known in this sense as one-dimensional space regions that are "dense" in points of X. Many density-based algorithms do not place any restrictions on the form of the resulting clusters. Therefore, these algorithms are capable of recovering arbitrarily shaped clusters. We can also manage the outliers effectively. In addition, these algorithms' time complexity is less, making them able to process large datasets. DBSCAN, DBCLASD, DENCLUE, and OPTICS are the popular density-based algorithms. While these algorithms share the same basic philosophy, they differ in the quantification of the density (Theodoridis et al., 2010).

## 7.7.1 The DBSCAN algorithm

The "density" as defined in DBSCAN (density-based spatial clustering of applications with noise) is calculated around a point x as the number of points in X falling within a certain region in the one-dimensional space around x. The algorithm's results are strongly influenced by the choice of both ε and q. Different parameter values can generate completely different results. Such parameters should be selected to allow the algorithm to detect the least "dense" cluster. In practice, to determine their "best" combination for the dataset at hand, one must test with different values for both ε and q. The DBSCAN is not suitable for cases where the clusters in X have large density differences and are not suitable for high-dimensional results. The OPTICS (ordering points to identify the clustering structure) algorithm is an extension of DBSCAN that overcomes the need to carefully pick the parameters ε and q. It produces a density-based cluster ordering, which describes the intrinsic hierarchical cluster structure of the dataset in an understandable manner. Experiments show that OPTICS's computational complexity is approximately 1.6 of the computational complexity needed by DBSCAN. On the other hand, in practice, for different values of ε and q, one has to run DBSCAN more than once (Theodoridis et al., 2010).

### Example 7.7

The following Python code utilizes DBSCAN clustering algorithm to find the clusters by using the scikit-learn library APIs. In this example, the synthetic data is utilized. Scatter plot is presented to show the effectiveness of the algorithm. Different measures are also calculated. Note that this example is adapted from scikit-learn.

```
# ======================================================================
# DBSCAN clustering
# ======================================================================
import numpy as np
from sklearn.cluster import DBSCAN
from sklearn import metrics
from sklearn.datasets import make_blobs
from sklearn.preprocessing import StandardScaler

# ######################################################################
# Generate sample data
centers = [[1, 1], [-1, -1], [1, -1]]
X, labels_true = make_blobs(n_samples = 750, centers = centers, cluster_
std = 0.4,
        random_state = 0)
X = StandardScaler().fit_transform(X)
```

```
# #########################################################################
# Compute DBSCAN
db = DBSCAN(eps = 0.3, min_samples = 10).fit(X)
core_samples_mask = np.zeros_like(db.labels_, dtype = bool)
core_samples_mask[db.core_sample_indices_] = True
labels = db.labels_

# Number of clusters in labels, ignoring noise if present.
n_clusters_ = len(set(labels)) - (1 if -1 in labels else 0)
n_noise_ = list(labels).count(-1)

print('Estimated number of clusters: %d' % n_clusters_)
print('Estimated number of noise points: %d' % n_noise_)
print("Homogeneity: %0.3f" % metrics.homogeneity_score(labels_true,
labels))
print("Completeness: %0.3f" % metrics.completeness_score(labels_true,
labels))
print("V-measure: %0.3f" % metrics.v_measure_score(labels_true, labels))
print("Adjusted Rand Index: %0.3f"
      % metrics.adjusted_rand_score(labels_true, labels))
print("Adjusted Mutual Information: %0.3f"
      % metrics.adjusted_mutual_info_score(labels_true, labels))
print("Silhouette Coefficient: %0.3f"
      % metrics.silhouette_score(X, labels))
#%%
# #########################################################################
# Plot result
import matplotlib.pyplot as plt

# Black removed and is used for noise instead.
unique_labels = set(labels)
colors = [plt.cm.Spectral(each)
       for each in np.linspace(0, 1, len(unique_labels))]
for k, col in zip(unique_labels, colors):
if k == -1:
          # Black used for noise.
         col = [0, 0, 0, 1]

class_member_mask = (labels == k)

xy = X[class_member_mask & core_samples_mask]
plt.plot(xy[:, 0], xy[:, 1], 'o', markerfacecolor = tuple(col),
markeredgecolor = 'k', markersize = 14)
xy = X[class_member_mask & ~core_samples_mask]
```

```
plt.plot(xy[:, 0], xy[:, 1], 'o', markerfacecolor = tuple(col),
markeredgecolor = 'k', markersize = 6)
plt.title('Estimated number of clusters: %d' % n_clusters_)
plt.show()
```

### 7.7.2 OPTICS clustering algorithms

It is possible to extend the DBSCAN algorithm so that many distance parameters are processed simultaneously, that is, the density-based clusters are built simultaneously with respect to different densities. Nonetheless, we would need to follow a specific order in which objects are processed while extending a cluster to achieve a consistent result. We always have to pick an object that can be reached by density with respect to the lowest $\varepsilon$ value to ensure that clusters are finished first with respect to higher density (i.e., smaller $\varepsilon$ values). In theory, the OPTICS algorithm operates as such an extended DBSCAN algorithm for an infinite number of distance parameters that are less than a "generating distance" $\varepsilon$. The only difference is that we do not allocate memberships to the unit. Rather we store the order in which the objects are processed and the information that an extended DBSCAN algorithm would use to assign memberships to the cluster. OPTICS algorithm generates a database order, additionally storing the core distance for each object and an appropriate reachability-distance. We will see that this knowledge is sufficient to remove all clustering based on density in relation to any distance $\varepsilon'$ that is smaller than the distance $\varepsilon$ produced from this order. The runtime of the OPTICS algorithm is almost the same as the runtime for DBSCAN due to its conceptual equivalence to the DBSCAN algorithm. It just turned out that OPTICS's run-time was almost always 1.6 times DBSCAN's run-time. That an abstraction is possible only indicates that the cluster ordering of a dataset actually contains the information about that dataset's intrinsic clustering structure (Ankerst, Breunig, Kriegel, & Sander, 1999).

**Example 7.8**

The following Python code utilizes OPTICS clustering algorithm to find the clusters by using the scikit-learn library APIs. This example employs synthetic data, which is generated so that the clusters have different densities. The class sklearn.cluster.OPTICS is first utilized with its Xi cluster detection method and then we set specific thresholds on the reachability that is related to class sklearn.cluster.DBSCAN. We can see that the different clusters of OPTICS's Xi method can be recovered with different choices of thresholds in DBSCAN. Reachability plot and scatter plot are presented to show the effectiveness of the algorithm. Note that this example is adapted from scikit-learn.

```
# ======================================================================
# Optics clustering example
# ======================================================================
# Authors: Shane Grigsby <refuge@rocktalus.com>
# Adrin Jalali <adrin.jalali@gmail.com>
# License: BSD 3 clause
from sklearn.cluster import OPTICS, cluster_optics_dbscan
```

```
import matplotlib.gridspec as gridspec
import matplotlib.pyplot as plt
import numpy as np
import pandas as pd
# Generate synthetic sample data
np.random.seed(0)
n_points_per_cluster = 250
C1 = [-5, -2] + .8 * np.random.randn(n_points_per_cluster, 2)
C2 = [4, -1] + .1 * np.random.randn(n_points_per_cluster, 2)
C3 = [1, -2] + .2 * np.random.randn(n_points_per_cluster, 2)
C4 = [-2, 3] + .3 * np.random.randn(n_points_per_cluster, 2)
C5 = [3, -2] + 1.6 * np.random.randn(n_points_per_cluster, 2)
C6 = [5, 6] + 2 * np.random.randn(n_points_per_cluster, 2)
X = np.vstack((C1, C2, C3, C4, C5, C6))
#Use OPTICS for Clustering
clust = OPTICS(min_samples = 50, xi = .05, min_cluster_size = .05)

# Run the fit
clust.fit(X)

labels_050 = cluster_optics_dbscan(reachability = clust.reachability_,
      core_distances = clust.core_distances_,
      ordering = clust.ordering_, eps = 0.5)
labels_200 = cluster_optics_dbscan(reachability = clust.reachability_,
      core_distances = clust.core_distances_,
      ordering = clust.ordering_, eps = 2)

space = np.arange(len(X))
reachability = clust.reachability_[clust.ordering_]
labels = clust.labels_[clust.ordering_]

plt.figure(figsize = (15, 10))
G = gridspec.GridSpec(2, 3)
ax1 = plt.subplot(G[0, :])
ax2 = plt.subplot(G[1, 0])
ax3 = plt.subplot(G[1, 1])
ax4 = plt.subplot(G[1, 2])

# ========================================================================
# Reachability plot
# ========================================================================
colors = ['g.', 'r.', 'b.', 'y.', 'c.']
for klass, color in zip(range(0, 5), colors):
Xk = space[labels == klass]
```

```
Rk = reachability[labels == klass]
ax1.plot(Xk, Rk, color, alpha = 0.3)
ax1.plot(space[labels == -1], reachability[labels == -1], 'k.', alpha = 0.3)
ax1.plot(space, np.full_like(space, 2., dtype = float), 'k-', alpha = 0.5)
ax1.plot(space, np.full_like(space, 0.5, dtype = float), 'k-.', alpha = 0.5)
ax1.set_ylabel('Reachability (epsilon distance)')
ax1.set_title('Reachability Plot')

# ======================================================================
# Plot OPTICS clustering results
# ======================================================================
colors = ['g.', 'r.', 'b.', 'y.', 'm.']
for klass, color in zip(range(0, 5), colors):
Xk = X[clust.labels_ == klass]
ax2.plot(Xk[:, 0], Xk[:, 1], color, alpha = 0.3)
ax2.plot(X[clust.labels_ == -1, 0], X[clust.labels_ == -1, 1], 'k + ',
alpha = 0.1)
ax2.set_title('Automatic Clustering\nOPTICS')

# ======================================================================
# Plot DBSCAN at 0.5 clustering results
# ======================================================================
colors = ['r', 'greenyellow', 'olive', 'g', 'b', 'c']
for klass, color in zip(range(0, 6), colors):
Xk = X[labels_050 == klass]
ax3.plot(Xk[:, 0], Xk[:, 1], color, alpha = 0.3, marker = '.')
ax3.plot(X[labels_050 == -1, 0], X[labels_050 == -1, 1], 'k + ',
alpha = 0.1)
ax3.set_title('Clustering at 0.5 epsilon cut\nDBSCAN')

# ======================================================================
# Plot DBSCAN at 2. clustering results
# ======================================================================
colors = ['r.', 'm.', 'y.', 'c.']
for klass, color in zip(range(0, 4), colors):
Xk = X[labels_200 == klass]
ax4.plot(Xk[:, 0], Xk[:, 1], color, alpha = 0.3)
ax4.plot(X[labels_200 == -1, 0], X[labels_200 == -1, 1], 'k + ',
alpha = 0.1)
ax4.set_title('Clustering at 2.0 epsilon cut\nDBSCAN')

plt.tight_layout()
plt.show()
```

## 7.8 The expectation of maximization for Gaussian mixture model clustering

The problem is that we do not know either of the following: the distribution from which each training instance came or the five parameters of the mixture model. We are therefore adopting and iterating the technique used for the k-means clustering algorithm. Beginning with initial assumptions for the five parameters, we utilize them to measure each instance's cluster probabilities, we utilize these probabilities to reestimate the parameters, and then we repeat them. This is called the EM algorithm to maximize expectations. The first step—calculating the probabilities of the cluster, which are the "expected" class values—is "expectation"; the second step, calculating the distribution parameters, is "maximizing" the probability of the distributions given the available data (Witten et al., 2016).

Now that we saw the Gaussian mixture model for two distributions, let us consider how to apply it to conditions that are more concrete. It is quite straightforward to adjust the algorithm from two-class problems to multiclass problems as long as the number k of normal distributions is given in advance. The model can easily be extended to multiple attributes from a single numeric attribute per instance as long as it is assumed that attributes are independent. The probabilities are multiplied for each attribute to obtain the joint probability for the instance. The independence assumption no longer holds when the dataset is understood to contain correlated attributes in advance. Instead, a normal bivariate distribution can model two attributes together, each having its own mean value, but the two standard deviations are replaced by a "covariance matrix" with four numeric parameters. Standard statistical techniques are available to estimate instance class probabilities and to estimate the mean and covariance matrix, provided the instances and their class probabilities. A multivariate distribution can accommodate multiple correlated attributes. The number of parameters increases with the square of the number of jointly varying attributes. Expectation—calculating the cluster to which each instance belongs, provided the parameters of the distribution—is just like evaluating an unknown instance's class. Maximization—estimating the parameters from the classified instances—is just like evaluating the probabilities of the attribute-value from the training instances, with the minor distinction being allocated probabilistically rather than categorically to classes in the EM algorithm instances (Witten et al., 2016).

### Example 7.9

The following Python code utilizes Gaussian mixture models (GMM) clustering algorithm to find the clusters by using the scikit-learn library APIs. This example employs Iris dataset. Although GMM are generally employed for clustering, we can compare the found clusters with the actual classes from the dataset. Predicted labels are plotted on both training and held-out test data using a variety of GMM covariance types on the Iris dataset. GMMs with spherical, diagonal, full, and tied covariance matrices are compared in increasing order of performance. Although it is expected the full covariance will achieve the best performance in general, it is prone to overfitting on small datasets and does not generalize well to held-out test data. On the plots, training data is shown as dots, while test data is shown as crosses. Although the Iris dataset is four-dimensional, just the first two dimensions are shown here. Note that this example is adapted from scikit-learn.

```
# =======================================================================
# GMM clustering
# =======================================================================
# Author: Ron Weiss <ronweiss@gmail.com > , Gael Varoquaux
# Modified by Thierry Guillemot <thierry.guillemot.work@gmail.com>
# License: BSD 3 clause

import matplotlib as mpl
import matplotlib.pyplot as plt

import numpy as np

from sklearn import datasets
from sklearn.mixture import GaussianMixture
from sklearn.model_selection import StratifiedKFold

colors = ['navy', 'red', 'green']

def make_ellipses(gmm, ax):
        for n, color in enumerate(colors):
        if gmm.covariance_type == 'full':
        covariances = gmm.covariances_[n][:2, :2]
        elif gmm.covariance_type == 'tied':
        covariances = gmm.covariances_[:2, :2]
        elif gmm.covariance_type == 'diag':
        covariances = np.diag(gmm.covariances_[n][:2])
        elif gmm.covariance_type == 'spherical':
        covariances = np.eye(gmm.means_.shape[1]) * gmm.covariances_[n]
        v, w = np.linalg.eigh(covariances)
        u = w[0] / np.linalg.norm(w[0])
        angle = np.arctan2(u[1], u[0])
        angle = 180 * angle / np.pi # convert to degrees
        v = 2. * np.sqrt(2.) * np.sqrt(v)
        ell = mpl.patches.Ellipse(gmm.means_[n, :2], v[0], v[1],
        180 + angle, color = color)
        ell.set_clip_box(ax.bbox)
        ell.set_alpha(0.5)
        ax.add_artist(ell)
        ax.set_aspect('equal', 'datalim')

iris = datasets.load_iris()
# Break up the dataset into non-overlapping training (75%) and testing
# (25%) sets.
skf = StratifiedKFold(n_splits = 4)
```

```
# Only take the first fold.
train_index, test_index = next(iter(skf.split(iris.data, iris.target)))

X_train = iris.data[train_index]
y_train = iris.target[train_index]
X_test = iris.data[test_index]
y_test = iris.target[test_index]

n_classes = len(np.unique(y_train))

# Try GMMs using different types of covariances.
estimators = {cov_type: GaussianMixture(n_components = n_classes,
         covariance_type = cov_type, max_iter = 20, random_state = 0)
         for cov_type in ['spherical', 'diag', 'tied', 'full']}
n_estimators = len(estimators)

plt.figure(figsize = (3 * n_estimators // 2, 6))
plt.subplots_adjust(bottom = .01, top = 0.95, hspace = .15,
wspace = .05,
left = .01, right = .99)
for index, (name, estimator) in enumerate(estimators.items()):
        # Since we have class labels for the training data, we can
        # initialize the GMM parameters in a supervised manner.
        estimator.means_init = np.array([X_train[y_train ==
        i].mean(axis = 0)
        for i in range(n_classes)])

        # Train the other parameters using the EM algorithm.
        estimator.fit(X_train)

        h = plt.subplot(2, n_estimators // 2, index + 1)
        make_ellipses(estimator, h)

        for n, color in enumerate(colors):
        data = iris.data[iris.target == n]
        plt.scatter(data[:, 0], data[:, 1], s = 0.8, color = color,
        label = iris.target_names[n])
        # Plot the test data with crosses
        for n, color in enumerate(colors):
        data = X_test[y_test == n]
        plt.scatter(data[:, 0], data[:, 1], marker = 'x', color = color)
        y_train_pred = estimator.predict(X_train)
```

```
        train_accuracy = np.mean(y_train_pred.ravel() == y_train.ravel()) * 100
        plt.text(0.05, 0.9, 'Train accuracy: %.1f' % train_accuracy,
        transform = h.transAxes)
        y_test_pred = estimator.predict(X_test)
        test_accuracy = np.mean(y_test_pred.ravel() == y_test.ravel()) * 100
        plt.text(0.05, 0.8, 'Test accuracy: %.1f' % test_accuracy,
         transform = h.transAxes)
        plt.xticks(())
        plt.yticks(())
        plt.title(name)
plt.legend(scatterpoints = 1, loc = 'lower right', prop = dict(size = 12))
plt.show()
```

## 7.9 Bayesian clustering

There's a problem, though, in GMM—overfitting. If we are not sure which attributes depend on each other, why not be on the safe side and decide that all the attributes are covariant? The reason is that the more parameters there are, the greater the probability of overfitting the resulting structure to the training data, and covariance significantly increases the number of parameters. Throughout machine learning, the problem of overfitting arises, and probabilistic clustering is no exception. There are two ways it can occur: by defining too many clusters and by specifying too many parameters for distributions. The extreme case of too many clusters happens when there is one for each data point—then it is clear that the training data will be overfitted. In addition, when any of the normal distributions becomes so small that the cluster is based on just one data point, problems will arise in the GMM with EM model. Implementations also usually insist that there are at least two different data values in clusters. The problem of overfitting occurs when there are too many parameters. If you are not sure which attributes are covariant, you may try out different possibilities and select the one that maximizes the overall data likelihood due to the clustering that is found. However, the more parameters, the greater the average likelihood of results—not necessarily due to better clustering but due to overfitting—would appear. The more parameters to play with, the simpler it is to find a seemingly good clustering. It would be good to penalize the model for introducing new parameters. Recently, complete Bayesian hierarchical clustering techniques have been developed that generate a distribution of probability over possible hierarchical structures representing a dataset as output. One of the main ways to do this is to follow a Bayesian approach where each parameter has a prior distribution of probability. Therefore whenever a new parameter is added, it is important to integrate its prior probability into the overall probability figure. Since this includes multiplying the total likelihood by a number less than 1 (the previous likelihood), it will penalize the addition of new parameters automatically. The updated criteria will have to yield a gain that outweighs the cost in order to enhance the overall probability. AutoClass is an exhaustive Bayesian clustering strategy that utilizes all parameters of the finite-mixing model with prior distributions. It enables both numeric and nominal attributes and uses the EM algorithm to estimate the probability distribution parameters in order to best fit the data. Since there is no guarantee that the EM algorithm will converge to the optimum global, the process will be repeated for several different initial value sets. AutoClass considers various cluster numbers and can consider the various covariance quantities and different types of underlying distribution of probability for numeric attributes (Witten et al., 2016).

### Example 7.10

The following Python code compares two Gaussian mixture model (GMM) clustering algorithms. It plots the confidence ellipsoids of a mixture of two Gaussians generated by expectation maximization ("GaussianMixture") and variational inference ("BayesianGaussianMixture" with a Dirichlet process prior). This example employs synthetic data, which is generated so that the clusters have different densities. Both models have access to five components with which to fit the data. Note that the expectation maximization model needs to employ all five components; on the other hand, the variational inference model efficiently only employs as many as are required for a good fit. It can be also seen that the expectation maximization model divides some components randomly since it is trying to fit too numerous components, but the Dirichlet process model adjusts the number of states automatically. Note that this example is adapted from scikit-learn.

```
=============================================
Comparison of Gaussian mixture models with EM and Bayesian
=============================================
import itertools
import numpy as np
from scipy import linalg
import matplotlib.pyplot as plt
import matplotlib as mpl
from sklearn import mixture

color_iter = itertools.cycle(['navy', 'c', 'cornflowerblue', 'gold',
'    darkorange'])

def plot_results(X, Y_, means, covariances, index, title):
    splot = plt.subplot(2, 1, 1 + index)
    for i, (mean, covar, color) in enumerate(zip(
    means, covariances, color_iter)):
    v, w = linalg.eigh(covar)
    v = 2. * np.sqrt(2.) * np.sqrt(v)
    u = w[0] / linalg.norm(w[0])
    # as the DP will not use every component it has access to
    # unless it needs it, we shouldn't plot the redundant
    # components.
    if not np.any(Y_ == i):
    continue
```

```
    plt.scatter(X[Y_ == i, 0], X[Y_ == i, 1], .8, color = color)

    # Plot an ellipse to show the Gaussian component
    angle = np.arctan(u[1] / u[0])
    angle = 180. * angle / np.pi # convert to degrees
    ell = mpl.patches.Ellipse(mean, v[0], v[1], 180. + angle,
    color = color)
    ell.set_clip_box(splot.bbox)
    ell.set_alpha(0.5)
    splot.add_artist(ell)

    plt.xlim(-9., 5.)
    plt.ylim(-3., 6.)
    plt.xticks(())
    plt.yticks(())
    plt.title(title)

# Number of samples per component
n_samples = 500

# Generate random sample, two components
np.random.seed(0)
C = np.array([[0., -0.1], [1.7, .4]])
X = np.r_[np.dot(np.random.randn(n_samples, 2), C),
        .7 * np.random.randn(n_samples, 2) + np.array([-6, 3])]
# Fit a Gaussian mixture with EM using five components
gmm = mixture.GaussianMixture(n_components = 5, covariance_
type = 'full').fit(X)
plot_results(X, gmm.predict(X), gmm.means_, gmm.covariances_, 0,
        'Gaussian Mixture')

# Fit a Dirichlet process Gaussian mixture using five components
dpgmm = mixture.BayesianGaussianMixture(n_components = 5,
        covariance_type = 'full').fit(X)
plot_results(X, dpgmm.predict(X), dpgmm.means_, dpgmm.covariances_, 1,
        'Bayesian Gaussian Mixture with a Dirichlet process prior')
plt.show()
```

## 7.10 Silhouette analysis

How can we detect the poor quality of the clustering algorithm? Silhouette is a useful technique. For each example that is grouped by cluster, a silhouette sorts and plots s(x). In this particular situation, in the construction of the silhouette, squared Euclidean distance is utilized, but the approach can be extended to other distance metrics. It can be clearly seen that the first clustering is much stronger than the second. We can estimate the average silhouette values per cluster and over the entire data set in addition to the graphical representation (Flach, 2012). Silhouette analysis can be utilized to examine the amount of separation between the clusters. The silhouette plot shows how close each point in a cluster is to points in the neighboring clusters and thus provides a way to visually determine parameters such as the number of clusters. This measure has a range of [-1, 1]. Silhouette coefficients close to + 1 imply that the sample is far from neighboring clusters. A value of 0 means that the sample is on or very close to the decision boundary between two neighboring clusters, and negative values suggest that the samples may have been allocated to the wrong cluster.

## Example 7.11

The following Python code utilizes k-means clustering to find the silhouettes of marketing data by using the scikit-learn library APIs. This example employs marketing data to see the silhouettes and cluster centers. The silhouettes and cluster centers are plotted for different cases. Note that this example is taken from scikit-learn.

In this example the silhouette analysis is utilized to select an optimal value for "n_clusters." The silhouette plot shows that the "n_clusters" value of 2, 3, and 6 are a bad pick for the given data due to the presence of clusters with below average silhouette scores and also due to wide fluctuations in the size of the silhouette plots. Silhouette analysis is more ambivalent in deciding between 4 and 5. Also from the thickness of the silhouette plot the cluster size can be visualized. The silhouette plot for cluster 0 when "n_clusters" is equal to 2 is bigger in size due to the grouping of the 3 subclusters into one big cluster. Nevertheless, when the "n_clusters" are equal to 4 or 5, all the plots are more or less of similar thickness and hence are of similar sizes as can be confirmed from the labeled scatter plot on the right.

```
==========================================================================
Selecting the number of clusters with silhouette analysis on k-means
clustering
==========================================================================
from sklearn.cluster import KMeans
from sklearn.metrics import silhouette_samples, silhouette_score
import matplotlib.pyplot as plt
import matplotlib.cm as cm
import numpy as np
import pandas as pd
# Import the Mall Customers dataset by pandas
dataset = pd.read_csv('Mall_Customers.csv')
X = dataset.iloc[:, [3,4]].values
range_n_clusters = [2, 3, 4, 5, 6]
for n_clusters in range_n_clusters:
       # Create a subplot with 1 row and 2 columns
       fig, (ax1, ax2) = plt.subplots(1, 2)
       fig.set_size_inches(18, 7)
```

```
# The 1st subplot is the silhouette plot
# The silhouette coefficient can range from -1, 1 but in this example
all
# lie within [-0.1, 1]
ax1.set_xlim([-0.1, 1])
# The (n_clusters + 1)*10 is for inserting blank space between silhou-
ette
# plots of individual clusters, to demarcate them clearly.
ax1.set_ylim([0, len(X) + (n_clusters + 1) * 10])

# Initialize the clusterer with n_clusters value and a random gen-
erator
# seed of 10 for reproducibility.
clusterer = KMeans(n_clusters = n_clusters, random_state = 10)
cluster_labels = clusterer.fit_predict(X)

# The silhouette_score gives the average value for all the sam-
ples.
# This gives a perspective into the density and separation of the
formed
# clusters
silhouette_avg = silhouette_score(X, cluster_labels)
print("For n_clusters =", n_clusters,
"The average silhouette_score is :", silhouette_avg)

# Compute the silhouette scores for each sample
sample_silhouette_values = silhouette_samples(X, cluster_labels)
y_lower = 10
for i in range(n_clusters):
# Aggregate the silhouette scores for samples belonging to
# cluster i, and sort them
ith_cluster_silhouette_values = \
sample_silhouette_values[cluster_labels == i]
ith_cluster_silhouette_values.sort()
size_cluster_i = ith_cluster_silhouette_values.shape[0]
y_upper = y_lower + size_cluster_i
color = cm.nipy_spectral(float(i) / n_clusters)
ax1.fill_betweenx(np.arange(y_lower, y_upper),
0, ith_cluster_silhouette_values,
facecolor = color, edgecolor = color, alpha = 0.7)

# Label the silhouette plots with their cluster numbers at the middle
ax1.text(-0.05, y_lower + 0.5 * size_cluster_i, str(i))
# Compute the new y_lower for next plot
y_lower = y_upper + 10 # 10 for the 0 samples
```

```
        ax1.set_title("The silhouette plot for the various clusters.")
        ax1.set_xlabel("The silhouette coefficient values")
        ax1.set_ylabel("Cluster label")

        # The vertical line for average silhouette score of all the values
        ax1.axvline(x = silhouette_avg, color = "red", linestyle = "--")

        ax1.set_yticks([]) # Clear the yaxis labels / ticks
        ax1.set_xticks([-0.1, 0, 0.2, 0.4, 0.6, 0.8, 1])

        # 2nd Plot showing the actual clusters formed
        colors = cm.nipy_spectral(cluster_labels.astype(float) / n_clus-
        ters)
        ax2.scatter(X[:, 0], X[:, 1], marker = '.', s = 30, lw = 0, al-
        pha = 0.7,
        c = colors, edgecolor = 'k')
        # Labeling the clusters
        centers = clusterer.cluster_centers_
        # Draw white circles at cluster centers
        ax2.scatter(centers[:, 0], centers[:, 1], marker = 'o',
        c = "white", alpha = 1, s = 200, edgecolor = 'k')
        for i, c in enumerate(centers):
        ax2.scatter(c[0], c[1], marker = '$%d$' % i, alpha = 1,
        s = 50, edgecolor = 'k')

        ax2.set_title("The visualization of the clustered data.")
        ax2.set_xlabel("Feature space for the 1st feature")
        ax2.set_ylabel("Feature space for the 2nd feature")

         plt.suptitle(("Silhouette analysis for KMeans clustering on
        sample
          data "
        "with n_clusters = %d" % n_clusters),
        fontsize = 14, fontweight = 'bold')
plt.show()
```

## 7.11 Image segmentation with clustering

Images are known as one of the most significant ways of transmitting information. A crucial aspect of machine learning is to understand images and extract the information from them so that the knowledge can be used for certain tasks. The use of images for robotic navigation would be an example. Other applications such as extracting malignant tissues from body scans and so on are an integral part of medical diagnosis. One of the first steps toward recognizing images is to segment them and find various objects in them. Features such as the histogram plots and the transformation of the frequency domain can be used to do this (Tatiraju & Mehta, 2008).

In image recognition and computer vision, image segmentation is an important preprocessing procedure. Image segmentation corresponds to the decomposition of an image with the same attributes in a number of nonoverlapping relevant areas. Image segmentation is a crucial technique in digital image processing, and segmentation accuracy directly affects follow-up tasks' effectiveness. The current segmentation techniques have achieved many successes to varying degrees, considering their complexity and difficulty, but research on this dimension still faces many problems. Clustering analysis algorithm splits the datasets according to a certain standard into different groups, so it has a broad implementation in the segmentation of images. Image segmentation as one of the main digital image processing techniques, coupled with relevant professional skills, is commonly used for machine vision, facial recognition, fingerprint recognition, traffic control systems, satellite image tracking objects (roads, woods, etc.), pedestrian detection, medical imaging, and many other areas and is worth exploring in-depth (Zheng, Lei, Yao, Gong, & Yin, 2018).

Since the image segmentation plays a crucial role in many applications for image processing, several algorithms for image segmentation have been developed in the last decades. But these algorithms are continuously being pursued, as image segmentation is a challenging problem that requires a good solution for the subsequent image-processing steps. Clustering algorithm was not originally developed exclusively for image processing; the computer vision community adopted it for image segmentation. For example, the k-means algorithm needs a priori knowledge of the number of clusters (k) to be grouped into. Every pixel of the image is allocated to the cluster whose centroid is nearest to the pixel repeatedly and iteratively. Based on the pixels allocated to that cluster, the centroid of each cluster is decided. Both the choice of pixel membership in the clusters and the computation of the centroids are based on calculating distances. The Euclidean distance is most commonly utilized since it is simple to calculate. The problem is that using Euclidean distance will lead to errors in the final segmentation of the image (Gaura, Sojka, & Krumnikl, 2011).

### Example 7.12

The following Python code is utilized for segmenting the images of Greek coins in regions by using the scikit-learn library APIs. In this example the coins dataset, which exists in skimage.data, is utilized. This example utilizes "spectral_clustering" on a graph created from voxel-to-voxel difference on an image to divide this image into multiple, partly homogeneous regions. This process (spectral clustering on an image) is an effective approximate solution for finding normalized graph cuts. There are two options to assign labels:

- "K-means" spectral clustering will cluster samples in the embedding space employing a k-means algorithm.
- "Discrete" will iteratively search for the closest partition space to the embedding space.

Note that this example is adapted from scikit-learn.

```
# ============================================================================
# Image segmentation with clustering
# ============================================================================
# Author: Gael Varoquaux <gael.varoquaux@normalesup.org > , Brian Cheung
# License: BSD 3 clause
import time
import numpy as np
from distutils.version import LooseVersion
from scipy.ndimage.filters import gaussian_filter
import matplotlib.pyplot as plt
import skimage
from skimage.data import coins
from skimage.transform import rescale
from sklearn.feature_extraction import image
from sklearn.cluster import spectral_clustering

# these were introduced in skimage-0.14
if LooseVersion(skimage.__version__) >= '0.14':
        rescale_params = {'anti_aliasing': False, 'multichannel': False}
else:
        rescale_params = {}
# load the coins as a numpy array
orig_coins = coins()

# Resize it to 20% of the original size to speed up the processing
# Applying a Gaussian filter for smoothing prior to down-scaling
# reduces aliasing artifacts.
smoothened_coins = gaussian_filter(orig_coins, sigma = 2)
rescaled_coins = rescale(smoothened_coins, 0.2, mode = "reflect",
        **rescale_params)

# Convert the image into a graph with the value of the gradient on the
# edges.
graph = image.img_to_graph(rescaled_coins)

# Take a decreasing function of the gradient: an exponential
# The smaller beta is, the more independent the segmentation is of the
# actual image. For beta = 1, the segmentation is close to a voronoi
beta = 10
eps = 1e-6
graph.data = np.exp(-beta * graph.data / graph.data.std()) + eps

# Apply spectral clustering (this step goes much faster if you have
pyamg
```

```
# installed)
N_REGIONS = 25

##########################################################################
# Visualize the resulting regions

for assign_labels in ('kmeans', 'discretize'):
      t0 = time.time()
      labels = spectral_clustering(graph, n_clusters = N_REGIONS,
      assign_labels = assign_labels, random_state = 42)
      t1 = time.time()
      labels = labels.reshape(rescaled_coins.shape)

      plt.figure(figsize = (5, 5))
      plt.imshow(rescaled_coins, cmap = plt.cm.gray)
      for l in range(N_REGIONS):
      plt.contour(labels == l,
       colors = [plt.cm.nipy_spectral(l / float(N_REGIONS))])
      plt.xticks(())
      plt.yticks(())
      title = 'Spectral clustering: %s, %.2fs' % (assign_labels, (t1 - t0))
      print(title)
      plt.title(title)
plt.show()
```

## 7.12 Feature extraction with clustering

K-means clustering reduces the data dimension by finding appropriate representatives or *centroids* for clusters, or groups, of data points. All elements of every cluster are then characterized by their cluster's corresponding centroid. Thus the problem of clustering is partitioning data into clusters with similar characteristics, and with k-means this characteristic especially has geometric closeness in the feature space. When this is represented clearly, it can be employed to create a learning problem for an accurate recovery of cluster centroids, dropping the impractical notion. If we denote the centroid of the $k$th cluster by $\mathbf{c}_k$ and the set of indices of the subset of those $P$ data points by $S_k$, and $\mathbf{x}_1 \ldots \mathbf{x}_P$, belongs to this cluster, then the points in the $k$th cluster must lie close to its centroid for all $k = 1 \ldots K$. These necessary relations can be represented more appropriately by first stacking the centroids column-wise into the *centroid matrix.*

$$C = c_1\, c_2 \cdot c_K \tag{7.1}$$

Then designating by $\mathbf{e}k$ the $k$th standard basis vector (that is a $K \times 1$ vector with a 1 in the $k$th slot and zeros elsewhere), we may represent $\mathbf{C}_{ek} = \mathbf{c}k$, and hence the relations in Eq. (7.1) can be represented for each $k$ as

$$C_{ek} \approx x_p \text{ for all } p \in S_k \tag{7.2}$$

Next, to write these equations even more appropriately we stack the data column-wise into the *data matrix* $\mathbf{X} = \mathbf{x}_1, \mathbf{x}_2 \cdots \mathbf{x}_P$ and produce a $K \times P$ *assignment matrix* $\mathbf{W}$. The $p$th column of this matrix, represented as $\mathbf{w}p$, is the standard basis vector related to the cluster to which the $p$th point belongs, that is, $\mathbf{w}p = \mathbf{e}k$ if $p \in Sk$. With this $\mathbf{w}p$ notation we can represent each equation in Eq. (7.2) as $\mathbf{Cw}p \approx \mathbf{x}p$ for all $p \in Sk$, or using matrix notation all $K$ such relations simultaneously as

$$CW \approx X. \tag{7.3}$$

We can forget the assumption that we know the locations of cluster centroids and have knowledge of which points are assigned to them—that is, the accurate depiction of the centroid matrix $\mathbf{C}$ and assignment matrix $\mathbf{W}$. We want to *learn* the correct values for these two matrices. In particular, we know that the ideal $\mathbf{C}$ and $\mathbf{W}$ fulfill the compact relationships depicted in Eq. (7.3), that is, that $\mathbf{CW} \approx \mathbf{X}$ or in other words that $\mathbf{CW} - \mathbf{X}2F$ is small, while $\mathbf{W}$ **is** composed of appropriately selected standard basis vectors associated with the data points to their respective centroids. Note that the aim is nonconvex, and since we cannot minimize over both $\mathbf{C}$ and $\mathbf{W}$ at the same time, it is solved via *alternating minimization*, that is, by alternately minimizing the objective function over one of the variables ($\mathbf{C}$ or $\mathbf{W}$) while keeping the other variable fixed (Watt, Borhani, & Katsaggelos, 2016).

### Example 7.13

The following Python code presents the usage of k-means and GMM clustering algorithms as a feature extractor. We will utilize the Iris dataset, which includes three types (class) of Iris flowers (Setosa, Versicolour, and Virginica) with four attributes: sepal length, sepal width, petal length, and petal width. In this example we utilize the sklearn.cluster.KMeans and sklearn.mixture.Gaussian-Mixture to extract the features of the Iris dataset. In scikit-learn, k-means and GMM are implemented as a cluster object that are sklearn.cluster.KMeans and sklearn.mixture.GaussianMixture and are employed to extract the features. Note that this example is adapted from Python–scikit-learn.

```
# ===============================================================
# Feature extraction with k-means and GMM clustering
# ===============================================================
"""
Created on Mon Dec 23 11:35:28 2019
@author: absubasi
"""
from sklearn import metrics
from sklearn.metrics import confusion_matrix
import seaborn as sns
```

```
import matplotlib.pyplot as plt
from io import BytesIO #needed for plot
# ===================================================================
# Define utility functions
# ===================================================================
def print_confusion_matrix_and_save(y_test, y_pred):
#Print the Confusion Matrix
matrix = confusion_matrix(y_test, y_pred)
plt.figure(figsize = (6, 4))
sns.heatmap(matrix, square = True, annot = True, fmt = 'd',
cbar = False)
plt.title('Confusion Matrix')
plt.ylabel('True Label')
plt.xlabel('Predicted Label')
plt.show()
#Save The Confusion Matrix
plt.savefig("Confusion.jpg")
# Save SVG in a fake file object.
f = BytesIO()
plt.savefig(f, format = "svg")

def Performance_Metrics(y_test,y_pred):
print('Test Accuracy:', np.round(metrics.accuracy_score(y_test,y_
pred),4))
print('Precision:', np.round(metrics.precision_score(y_test,
y_pred,average = 'weighted'),4))
print('Recall:', np.round(metrics.recall_score(y_test,y_pred,
average = 'weighted'),4))
print('F1 Score:', np.round(metrics.f1_score(y_test,y_pred,
average = 'weighted'),4))
print('Cohen Kappa Score:', np.round(metrics.cohen_kappa_score(y_
test,y_pred),4))
print('Matthews Corrcoef:', np.round(metrics.matthews_corrcoef(y_
test,y_ pred),4))
print('\t\tClassification Report:\n', metrics.classification_report(y_
test,y_pred))
print("Confusion Matrix:\n",confusion_matrix(y_test,y_pred))

# ===================================================================
# Random forest classifier with k-means for feature extraction
# ===================================================================
#load Data
from sklearn.datasets import load_iris
import numpy as np
```

```
iris = load_iris()
X = iris['data']
y = iris['target']
#Extract Features
from sklearn.cluster import KMeans
kmeans = KMeans(n_clusters = 6).fit(X)
distances = np.column_stack([np.sum((X - center)**2, axis = 1)**0.5 for
center in kmeans.cluster_centers_])

from sklearn.model_selection import train_test_split
from sklearn.ensemble import RandomForestClassifier
# Split dataset into training set and test set
# 70% training and 30% test
Xtrain, Xtest, ytrain, ytest = train_test_split(distances, y,test_
size = 0.3, random_state = 0)
#In order to change to accuracy increase n_estimators
#Classify Data
" " "RandomForestClassifier(n_estimators = 'warn', criterion = 'gini',
max_depth = None,
min_samples_split = 2, min_samples_leaf = 1, min_weight_fraction_
leaf = 0.0,
max_features = 'auto', max_leaf_nodes = None, min_impurity_
decrease = 0.0,
min_impurity_split = None, bootstrap = True, oob_score = False, n_
jobs = None,
random_state = None, verbose = 0, warm_start = False, class_
weight = None)" " "
clf = RandomForestClassifier(n_estimators = 200)
#Create the Model
#Train the model with Training Dataset
clf.fit(Xtrain,ytrain)
#Test the model with Testset
ypred = clf.predict(Xtest)

#Evaluate the Model and Print Performance Metrics
Performance_Metrics(ytest,ypred)
print_confusion_matrix_and_save(ytest, ypred)
#%%
# ======================================================================
# Random forest classifier with GMM for feature extraction
# ======================================================================
#load Data
from sklearn.datasets import load_iris
import numpy as np
```

```
iris = load_iris()
X = iris['data']
y = iris['target']
#Extract Features
from sklearn.mixture import GaussianMixture
gmm = GaussianMixture(n_components = 8).fit(X)
proba = gmm.predict_proba(X)

from sklearn.model_selection import train_test_split
from sklearn.ensemble import RandomForestClassifier
# Split dataset into training set and test set
# 70% training and 30% test
Xtrain, Xtest, ytrain, ytest = train_test_split(proba, y,test_
size = 0.3, random_state = 0)
#In order to change to accuracy increase n_estimators
" " "RandomForestClassifier(n_estimators = 'warn', criterion = 'gini',
max_depth = None,
min_samples_split = 2, min_samples_leaf = 1, min_weight_fraction_
leaf = 0.0,
max_features = 'auto', max_leaf_nodes = None, min_impurity_
decrease = 0.0,
min_impurity_split = None, bootstrap = True, oob_score = False, n_
jobs = None,
random_state = None, verbose = 0, warm_start = False, class_
weight = None)" " "
clf = RandomForestClassifier(n_estimators = 200)
#Create the Model
#Train the model with Training Dataset
clf.fit(Xtrain,ytrain)
#Test the model with Testset
ypred = clf.predict(Xtest)

#Evaluate the Model and Print Performance Metrics
Performance_Metrics(ytest,ypred)
print_confusion_matrix_and_save(ytest, ypred)
#%%
# ======================================================================
# k-NN classifier with k-means for feature extraction
# ======================================================================
#load Data
from sklearn.datasets import load_iris
import numpy as np
iris = load_iris()
X = iris['data']
```

```
y = iris['target']
#Extract Features
from sklearn.cluster import KMeans
kmeans = KMeans(n_clusters = 6).fit(X)
distances = np.column_stack([np.sum((X - center)**2, axis = 1)**0.5 for
center in kmeans.cluster_centers_])

from sklearn.model_selection import train_test_split
# Split dataset into training set and test set
# 70% training and 30% test
Xtrain, Xtest, ytrain, ytest = train_test_split(distances, y,test_
size = 0.3, random_state = 0)
from sklearn.neighbors import KNeighborsClassifier
clf = KNeighborsClassifier(n_neighbors = 1)
#Create the Model
#Train the model with Training Dataset
clf.fit(Xtrain,ytrain)
#Test the model with Testset
ypred = clf.predict(Xtest)

#Evaluate the Model and Print Performance Metrics
Performance_Metrics(ytest,ypred)
print_confusion_matrix_and_save(ytest, ypred)

#%%
# ======================================================================
# k-NN classifier with GMM for feature extraction
# ======================================================================
#load Data
from sklearn.datasets import load_iris
import numpy as np
iris = load_iris()
X = iris['data']
y = iris['target']
#Extract Features
from sklearn.mixture import GaussianMixture
gmm = GaussianMixture(n_components = 4).fit(X)
proba = gmm.predict_proba(X)

from sklearn.model_selection import train_test_split
# Split dataset into training set and test set
# 70% training and 30% test
Xtrain, Xtest, ytrain, ytest = train_test_split(proba, y,test_
size = 0.3, random_state = 0)
```

```
from sklearn.neighbors import KNeighborsClassifier
clf = KNeighborsClassifier(n_neighbors = 1)
#Create the Model
#Train the model with Training Dataset
clf.fit(Xtrain,ytrain)
#Test the model with Testset
ypred = clf.predict(Xtest)

#Evaluate the Model and Print Performance Metrics
Performance_Metrics(ytest,ypred)
print_confusion_matrix_and_save(ytest, ypred)

#%%
# ======================================================================
# MLP classifier with k-means for feature extraction
# ======================================================================
#load Data
from sklearn.datasets import load_iris
import numpy as np
iris = load_iris()
X = iris['data']
y = iris['target']
#Extract Features
from sklearn.cluster import KMeans
kmeans = KMeans(n_clusters = 6).fit(X)
distances = np.column_stack([np.sum((X - center)**2, axis = 1)**0.5 for
center in kmeans.cluster_centers_])

from sklearn.model_selection import train_test_split
# Split dataset into training set and test set
# 70% training and 30% test
Xtrain, Xtest, ytrain, ytest = train_test_split(distances, y,test_
size = 0.3, random_state = 0)
from sklearn.neural_network import MLPClassifier
clf = MLPClassifier(hidden_layer_sizes = (100, ), learning_rate_
init = 0.001,
alpha = 1, momentum = 0.9,max_iter = 1000)
#Create the Model
#Train the model with Training Dataset
clf.fit(Xtrain,ytrain)
#Test the model with Testset
ypred = clf.predict(Xtest)
#Evaluate the Model and Print Performance Metrics
Performance_Metrics(ytest,ypred)
```

```
print_confusion_matrix_and_save(ytest, ypred)
#%%
# ==========================================================================
# MLP classifier with GMM for feature extraction
# ==========================================================================
#load Data
from sklearn.datasets import load_iris
import numpy as np
iris = load_iris()
X = iris['data']
y = iris['target']
#Extract Features
from sklearn.mixture import GaussianMixture
gmm = GaussianMixture(n_components = 8).fit(X)
proba = gmm.predict_proba(X)

from sklearn.model_selection import train_test_split
# Split dataset into training set and test set
# 70% training and 30% test
Xtrain, Xtest, ytrain, ytest = train_test_split(proba, y,test_
size = 0.3, random_state = 0)
from sklearn.neural_network import MLPClassifier
clf = MLPClassifier(hidden_layer_sizes = (100, ), learning_rate_
init = 0.001,
alpha = 1, momentum = 0.9,max_iter = 1000)
#Create the Model
#Train the model with Training Dataset
clf.fit(Xtrain,ytrain)
#Test the model with Testset
ypred = clf.predict(Xtest)

#Evaluate the Model and Print Performance Metrics
Performance_Metrics(ytest,ypred)
print_confusion_matrix_and_save(ytest, ypred)
```

## 7.13 Clustering for classification

How can unlabeled data be utilized for classification? The idea is to employ naïve Bayes to utilize the EM iterative clustering algorithm to learn classes from a small, labeled dataset and then extend it to a large, unlabeled dataset. Hence in the first step, use the labeled data to train a classifier. In the second step, apply it to the unlabeled data for class probabilities labeling (the "expectation" step). In the third step, use all data labels to train a new classifier (the "maximization" step). In the last step, iterate until convergence. The EM method ensures that parameters of the model are found that have equal or greater likelihood for each iteration. The key question that can only be answered empirically is whether these calculations of higher probability parameters can improve the performance of classification. This could work well intuitively. Those are used by the EM method to generalize the learned model in order to use data that do not appear in the labeled dataset. EM generalizes the model iteratively to classify data correctly. This could work with any algorithm for classification and iterative clustering. But it's essentially a bootstrapping technique, and you need to be careful to make sure the feedback loop is positive. It seems better to use probabilities rather than hard decisions since it helps the process converge slowly instead of jumping to incorrect conclusions. Together with the standard probabilistic EM technique, naïve Bayes is a particularly suitable alternative since both share the same basic assumption: independence between attributes or, more specifically, conditional independence between class attributes. However, in this way, coupling naïve Bayes and EM works well in the classification of documents. Employing less than one-third of the labeled training instances as well as five times as many unlabeled ones, it can achieve the performance of a traditional learner in a particular classification task. If labeled instances are costly but unlabeled ones are essentially free, this is a good tradeoff. With a small number of labeled documents, by adding other unlabeled documents, classification accuracy can be dramatically improved (Witten et al., 2016).

Two methodological refinements have been shown to enhance the performance. The first is inspired by experimental evidence showing that the inclusion of unlabeled data will decrease rather than improve the performance when there are many labeled data. Inherently, hand-labeled data must be less noisy than automatically labeled data. The remedy is to add a weighting parameter, which decreases the contribution of the unlabeled data. By maximizing the weighted probability of labeled and unlabeled instances, this can be integrated into EM's maximization stage. The second improvement is to allow multiple clusters for each class. The EM clustering algorithm assumes that a mixture of various probability distributions, one per cluster, produces the data randomly. Initially, each labeled document is assigned randomly to each of its components in a probabilistic fashion with several clusters per class. The EM algorithm's maximization step remains as it was before, but the expectation step is adjusted not only to probabilistically label each example with the classes but to assign it to the components within the class (Witten et al., 2016).

### Example 7.14

The following Python code utilizes k-means clustering for classification of handwritten digits by using the scikit-learn library APIs. In this example, the handwritten digits dataset that exists in sklearn.datasets is utilized. The classification accuracy, precision, recall, F1 score, Cohen kappa score, and Matthews correlation coefficient are calculated. The classification report and confusion matrix are also given. Note that this example is adapted from scikit-learn.

```
# =============================================================
# Clustering as a classifier
# =============================================================
```

```
#k-means on digits
import seaborn as sns
import matplotlib.pyplot as plt
from io import BytesIO #needed for plot
from sklearn.metrics import confusion_matrix
from sklearn import metrics
import numpy as np
# ==========================================================================
# Define utility functions
# ==========================================================================
def print_confusion_matrix_and_save(y_test, y_pred):
#Print the Confusion Matrix
matrix = confusion_matrix(y_test, y_pred)
plt.figure(figsize = (6, 4))
sns.heatmap(matrix, square = True, annot = True, fmt = 'd',
cbar = False)
plt.title('Confusion Matrix')
plt.ylabel('True Label')
plt.xlabel('Predicted Label')
plt.show()
#Save The Confusion Matrix
plt.savefig("Confusion.jpg")
# Save SVG in a fake file object.
f = BytesIO()
plt.savefig(f, format = "svg")

def Performance_Metrics(y_test,y_pred):
print('Test Accuracy:', np.round(metrics.accuracy_score(y_test,y_
pred),4))
print('Precision:', np.round(metrics.precision_score(y_test,
y_pred,average = 'weighted'),4))
print('Recall:', np.round(metrics.recall_score(y_test,y_pred,
 average = 'weighted'),4))
print('F1 Score:', np.round(metrics.f1_score(y_test,y_pred,
 average = 'weighted'),4))
print('Cohen Kappa Score:', np.round(metrics.cohen_kappa_score(y_
test,y_pred),4))
print('Matthews Corrcoef:', np.round(metrics.matthews_corrcoef(y_
test,y_pred),4))
print('\t\tClassification Report:\n', metrics.classification_report(y_
test,y_pred))
print("Confusion Matrix:\n",confusion_matrix(y_test,y_pred))
```

```
# ========================================================================
from sklearn.cluster import KMeans
from sklearn.datasets import load_digits
digits = load_digits()
digits.data.shape

kmeans = KMeans(n_clusters = 10, random_state = 0)
clusters = kmeans.fit_predict(digits.data)
kmeans.cluster_centers_.shape

fig, ax = plt.subplots(2, 5, figsize = (8, 3))
centers = kmeans.cluster_centers_.reshape(10, 8, 8)
for axi, center in zip(ax.flat, centers):
axi.set(xticks = [], yticks = [])
axi.imshow(center, interpolation = 'nearest', cmap = plt.cm.binary)

#%%
from scipy.stats import mode
labels = np.zeros_like(clusters)
for i in range(10):
mask = (clusters == i)
labels[mask] = mode(digits.target[mask])[0]

# Evaluate and Print the Performance Metrics
Performance_Metrics(digits.target, labels)
#Print and Save Confusion Matrix
print_confusion_matrix_and_save(digits.target, labels)

#%%
from sklearn.manifold import TSNE

# Project the data: this step will take several seconds
tsne = TSNE(n_components = 2, init = 'random', random_state = 0)
digits_proj = tsne.fit_transform(digits.data)

# Compute the clusters
kmeans = KMeans(n_clusters = 10, random_state = 0)
clusters = kmeans.fit_predict(digits_proj)

# Permute the labels
labels = np.zeros_like(clusters)
for i in range(10):
mask = (clusters == i)
labels[mask] = mode(digits.target[mask])[0]
```

```
# Evaluate and Print the Perfromance Metrics
Performance_Metrics(digits.target, labels)
#Print and Save Confusion Matrix
print_confusion_matrix_and_save(digits.target, labels)
```

## 7.14 Summary

In this chapter we present many examples related to clustering problems, which contain unsupervised learning techniques. Since clustering is a popular task with different applications in machine learning, this particular chapter is dedicated to explaining and studying it. Clustering is the process of automatically grouping a collection of objects in such a way that identical objects end up in the same category and divide dissimilar objects in different groups. For instance, retailers cluster customers, on the basis of their customer profiles, for the purpose of targeted marketing; computational biologists cluster genes on the basis of similarities in their expression in diverse researches; and astronomers cluster stars on the basis of their distinct closeness. In the previous chapters the learning tasks focused primarily on supervised learning problems. In this chapter we present several unsupervised machine learning algorithms for clustering. Besides the utilization of clustering in grouping unlabeled data, they can be used for image segmentation, feature extraction, and classification as well. We discussed in detail the application of these algorithms in different fields.

## References


Ankerst, M., Breunig, M. M., Kriegel, H. -P., & Sander, J. (1999). OPTICS: ordering points to identify the clustering structure. *ACM, 28*, 49–60.

Flach, P. (2012). *Machine learning: The art and science of algorithms that make sense of data*. Cambridge, United Kingdom: Cambridge University Press.

Gaura, J., Sojka, E., & Krumnikl, M. (2011). *Image segmentation based on k-means clustering and energy-transfer proximity*. Berlin: Springer 567–577.

Murphy, K. P. (2012). *Machine learning: A probabilistic perspective*. Cambridge, MA: MIT press.

Shalev-Shwartz, S., & Ben-David, S. (2014). *Understanding machine learning: From theory to algorithms*. Cambridge, United Kingdom: Cambridge University Press.

Steinbach, M., Karypis, G., & Kumar, V. (2000). A comparison of document clustering techniques. *KDD Workshop on Text Mining, 400*, 525–526 Boston.

Sumathi, S., & Paneerselvam, S. (2010). *Computational intelligence paradigms: Theory & applications using MATLAB*. Boca Raton, FL: CRC Press.

Tatiraju, S., & Mehta, A. (2008). Image Segmentation using k-means clustering, EM and Normalized Cuts. *Department of EECS, 1*, 1–7.

Theodoridis, S., Pikrakis, A., Koutroumbas, K., & Cavouras, D. (2010). *Introduction to pattern recognition: A matlab approach*. Cambridge, MA: Academic Press.

Watt, J., Borhani, R., & Katsaggelos, A. K. (2016). *Machine learning refined: Foundations, algorithms, and applications*. Cambridge, United Kingdom: Cambridge University Press.

Witten, I. H., Frank, E., Hall, M. A., & Pal, C. J. (2016). *Data Mining: Practical machine learning tools and techniques*. Burlington, MA: Morgan Kaufmann.

Zheng, X., Lei, Q., Yao, R., Gong, Y., & Yin, Q. (2018). Image segmentation based on adaptive K-means algorithm. *EURASIP Journal on Image and Video Processing, 1*, 68.

# Index

Note: Page numbers followed by "f " indicate figures, "t" indicate tables.

Printed in the United States
By Bookmasters